NOSTRADAMUS

THE TRUTH

FIVE CENTURIES OF PROPHECIES

VALIDATED

THE LONG AWAITED EXPLANATION OF THIS
REMARKABLE MAN'S PREDICTIONS
CAN NOW BE
TOLD

DAVID L ROPER

oRVID
EDITIONS

First Published 2009 by
Orvid Editions

ISBN
978-0-9543873-1-0

Typeset by Acumen

A catalogue record for this book is available
from the British Library

Neither the author nor the publisher assumes responsibility for the content or accuracy of third-party websites, nor the continuation of material
at the aforementioned websites, which were deemed to be competent at
the time of access.

www.orvid.co.uk

CONTENTS

DEDICATION

AUTHOR

David Roper's ancestry can be traced on one side to a 19th century titled estate in northeast France. He was educated in England, where he received an honours degree in Philosophy, Mathematics and a postgraduate qualification in Education. His interest in *Time* broadened as an undergraduate during his study of relativity under the guidance of Jocelyn Bell Burnell. After graduating he began making an in-depth study of prophecy, for which his work on Nostradamus, together with its implications for the sciences became a major interest.

ACKNOWLEDGEMENTS

A volume such as this could not have been written had it not been for books I have consulted. I therefore gratefully acknowledge the work of Charles A Ward whose Oracles of Nostradamus was based upon earlier editions by Daniel Defoe, Anatole Le Pelletier, Eugène Bareste, Balthazar Guynaud and Theophilus de Garancières. I also acknowledge ideas presented in the works of James Laver, Stewart Robb, K Chodkiewicz, Erika Cheetham, Edgar Leoni, Geoffrey Ashe, and David Ovason. And I am particularly indebted to Greg Lindahl for reproducing Cotgrave's 1611 English/French Dictionary, and making it freely available on the Internet. Credit is also due to A.-J. Greimas for his highly prized dictionary of ancient French: a valuable source for anyone hoping to understand the language of Les Prophéties.

I would also like to thank Janet Tyson whose company, Ecce Nova Editions was in the midst of publishing this book when misfortune intervened. Nevertheless, it is through Janet's generosity in donating the illustrations planned for each of the chapters that they can now be included. Credit for the artwork is due to Nicola Robinson, with whom I had many pleasant discussions in deciding what best suited each chapter.

INTRODUCTION

Nostradamus The Truth: Five Centuries of Prophecies Validated is a title that may strike many readers as unlikely to be correct. Surely, it will be said, Nostradamus's prophecies have been disproved. Did he not date some of his predictions, and these failed to materialise? What better reason can there be than failure, to retire this man to a footnote in history?

And, of course, these views cannot be denied, they are part of the modern age, which embraces scientific methods, and ascribes all events to material causes and the natural laws that govern them. Prophecy, were it to exist, would contradict scientific investigation. The scientific method is founded upon cause and effect, with cause necessarily preceding effect. Prophecy would deny this by allowing the existence of an effect before its cause has had time to bring it about.

This raises a much vexed question – what is time? Scientists employ it in many formulae but cannot explain it. Isaac Newton believed that time was universal; which is to say, the same moment exists universally and coevally across space. Albert Einstein's theory of relativity led him to accept that past, present, and future, are coexistent. Today, theoretical physicists talk about event horizons where, according to their calculations, time stands still – eternity captured in a moment. Surprisingly, Nostradamus held a similar view.

If we attempt to put Einstein's view of time into perspective, it is similar to traversing a landscape across which, where we have come from, and where we have yet to go, coexist with our present position. In that same landscape, nothing moves; everything is motionless, everything remains immutable, except the changing scene experienced by the percipient. This is not a new idea. In the fifth century BC, the philosopher Parmenides, the first thinker to argue philosophically from a purely logical basis, arrived at the same conclusion. Motion and change are impossible, he said; they are illusions. His follower, Zeno of Elea, then proposed the paradox of the *Arrow* as proof. If time consists of a finite number of instants, then at any one of these instants an arrow cannot move; for if it did move, then that instant would be divisible, and by definition not an instant. Alternatively, if time is composed of infinitely many instants between any two points, then still the arrow cannot move. This is because a gap will always exist between point A, where the arrow is located, and point B, where the arrow must travel if it is to move. There is no *next* point to which it can move; apart from which, it would take infinite time to cross infinite points. But if nothing moves at any one moment, then nothing ever moves. Motion is an illusion.

The discovery of differential calculus is thought by some to have overcome Zeno's paradox, since it is used to calculate acceleration at a single instant of time. But then Zeno would have replied that everything that occurs in the world is part of the same illusion, which includes motion and therefore acceleration. He would also, presumably, have correctly pointed out that calculus achieves its success by imposing limits to a sum of infinite points. To actually count those points would still take infinite time; calculus simply imposes a least number to the count.

In the seventeenth century, the philosopher René Descartes had a different idea. He deduced that for the world to exist as it is, then it must undergo a re-creative process at every instant. Clearly, if the past and future do not coexist with the present, then the past is destroyed as every new instant is born. Even so, this does not dispense with Zeno's cunning argument, for were this world of perpetual instants to exist in reality; there is still nothing that could move during each of these instants; it would be the instants moving. Modern-day quantum theorists, too, are faced by the same counter argument.

This all too brief look at some of the great minds that have tried to explain time brings us back to the subject of Nostradamus. For if past, present and future do coexist, unified for all eternity, then true prophecy is not impossible, at least, theoretically. We shall later see how Nostradamus explains this in terms of his own prevision.

I have referred to his prescient ability deliberately, for unlike sceptics who retain their own agenda, I am now unable to doubt Nostradamus's ability to record future events. Indeed, research into the plethora of examples he produced to prove this precognitive ability, when matched against the history that fulfilled these predictions, leave no easy access for honest refutation. A valid objection would have to discover that the original verse was a forgery written after the event; or that the translation had misappropriated words, so as to make the prediction fit with what later occurred; or that the history, said to fulfil a prophecy, never happened. In none of these cases is this possible, since the care and attention required to render these objections invalid has been scrupulously maintained.

Contrary to the dissent that has previously attended prophecies made by Nostradamus, the errors it is claimed his oracles contain are actually errors on the part of his detractors. That is to say, mistakes abound in the translation of his verses. And the scholarly subtleties that have been woven into his verses to obscure the truth of what they predict – a necessity if free will is to be protected – have been entirely overlooked. To add to this, a superficial and incomplete understanding of the history of the events, which he predicted would happen, has often led to a rush to expose him as inept, or worse still, a charlatan.

This book is intended to set the record straight. Literal translations from French to English, complete with explanations for the more difficult words, accompany fully referenced, historical records that identify the events he predicted. Everything is explained in a manner that can be independently checked.

What becomes remarkable from this exercise is that Nostradamus appears never once to have put a foot wrong. In almost two hundred quatrains to date, covering most major events, directly or indirectly affecting his native France, everything he wrote has come true. From the time of the first volume's publication in 1555, up until the present day, everything he said would happen, within this timeframe, has now happened. Even the dates he gave, supposedly proved incorrect by the non-occurrence of what he predicted, can now be shown to be entirely accurate. The alleged fault lying instead with the complainant's failure to reach the level of intelligence at which these prophecies were written.

The implication of Nostradamus's gift of prophecy is profound, and it affects every living person. The reason for this is straightforward. No one can consistently say what will happen in the future if the future is non-existent. One can only describe in recognizable detail what will later occur, if what will later occur already exists, even though it exists in the future. But if it exists in the future, then the future must be linked to preceding events; and these, by repeated regression, linked to other preceding events. What are called past and future, then become terms relative to a nominated present; and together these combine to form an eternal timescape. Time, to paraphrase Einstein, is the impression that is experienced when we travel at the speed of light through this eternal and immutable timescape.

Given that Einstein's concept of time is correct, and Nostradamus has provided verifiable evidence through the total accuracy of his prophecies to confirm that Einstein was correct, then everything that ever was and will be, presently exists and will forevermore do so. But these past and future states must then, together, form a block universe that is both static and unchanging. Moreover, since there is nowhere in this, our temporal universe that future states of the universe can be supposed to exist, they must exist in the mind of their Creator, as indeed was averred by the seer. Hence prophecy leads to a proof of God.

On the flip side, a block universe also implies predestination, and a subsequent loss of choice. To counter this, advances made in quantum mechanics, wherein particles are subject to probability waves, have recently persuaded some physicists that determinism can be avoided; notwithstanding Zeno's paradox, which yet remains an obstacle to be overcome.

This conflict between relativity theory and quantum mechanics has enthused scientists to attempt a grand united theory, which if successful would unite the two theories together. It is also suggested it could help to solve the dichotomy between free will and determinism. For this reason, the controversy surrounding free will is revisited and discussed at greater length in the Afterword. Before then, we shall look at the life of Nostradamus, and what he had to say about prophecy and the special ability he possessed to record future events.

It is the provision and compilation of evidence that gives this book its subtitle: complete with a timeline of historical events, mostly centred upon France. At the same time, a strict adherence to the actual words of each prophecy, in their original form, is shown to accompany the historical records that confirm all that he foretold.

Lest it be suggested that the predictions made by Nostradamus have been 'forced' into known historical records, then this accusation can be immediately rebutted. It has only been by the most scrupulous research that the accuracy of these predictions can now be established. In achieving that end, it has more often than not been the case that the history confirming a prediction only came to light because a prophecy pointed towards its existence: not the other way round.

The other bone of contention concerns the translation of these oracles from French into English. Might it not be suggested that since the verses have been written in French, then it resides with the French to better understand them? This, too, is erroneous. While it is true, the verses are almost entirely in French – very often old French – and sometimes interspersed with Latin, and less often: Greek, Italian, and Spanish, the French scholar is in the same position as any other national; there are also two quatrains, one requiring knowledge of German, and the other, Russian. At the same time a number of verses are found to contain anagrams, paragrams, the use of syncope, and other similar, scholarly devices: all of which have been used by others in the past for literary purposes, including asyntactic lines (the disordering of syntax) and asyndeton (the omission of articles and pronouns for the sake of economy). It is because of the many contrivances to defeat prior knowledge of what has been predicted that Nostradamus has deservedly acquired the reputation for obscurity, but undeservedly the name of charlatan. For his oracles are masterpieces in the art of epexegesis. As such, sceptics have never extended their intellectual ability to resolve his wordplay, believing instead that time spent this way would be wasted.

Nevertheless, it is still to be expected that inept debunkers will protest that it is possible to translate these quatrains in more than one way, thereby allowing alternative commentaries to be composed. Particular attention has been paid to this objection but no evidence has been found of even one instance occurring where this applies.

It is, however, certainly true that if one selects certain phrases from a quatrain while ignoring others these may be open to more than one interpretation. To guard against this, each quatrain must be shown to present a chain in which each link is represented by a word, phrase or sentence taken from the quatrain under inspection. There can be no weak or missing links. Each link must also be connected to an independently written historical reference, which is open to verification. Only when every word, phrase or sentence in a given quatrain satisfies these requirements is one able to say with confidence that Nostradamus predicted this event, and that no other incident in history exactly complies with the details he gave.

It is this that has been repeatedly demonstrated throughout the chapters that now follow: along a timeline that runs from 1557 to 2009. Those unable to rid their minds of the pernicious belief that Nostradamus was a charlatan, and his prophecies all bogus, are therefore challenged to apply the same procedure given above to the sixains, allegedly by Nostradamus but which are in fact counterfeit; they were published one year short of forty after his death. Since the 58 sixains are false prophecies and quite meaningless in terms of future events, any attempt to give them a prophetic appearance by using the rigorous procedure required for acceptance, must fail. Such failures can then be compared with the continual successes derived from the genuine article, *Les Prophéties*.

1

INTRODUCING

MICHEL DE NOSTREDAME

MICHEL DE NOSTREDAME (Nostradamus was the Latinised form of his name *à la mode* among scholars of his time) was born on Thursday 14 December 1503 (24 December according to the Gregorian calendar in use today) in southern France inside the little town of St-Rémy-de-Provence. Little is known about his childhood, but it is clear that his parents were in comfortable circumstances, and his education was well provided for. He was sent first to Avignon, reportedly to study the Humanities, and it was from there that he later applied to study medicine at Montpellier University. However, plague of the utmost severity appears to have interfered with the commencement of his studies, and the university closed in his eighteenth year; it was not until he was twenty-six that he returned to apply for readmission.

It was during this interim period that he travelled exten-
sively, obtaining knowledge of medical herbs and their application to the maladies of his time. Narbonne, Toulouse, and Bordeaux were among the towns he visited, where from the age of
twenty-two, working as a pharmacist, he began applying his
knowledge for the relief of the sick and needy.

He was an avid reader, especially the books of Latin and
Greek authors; he also acquired a familiarity with the languages
of Spain and Italy. Amongst his other accomplishments were the
philosophy and mathematics of his day, which included Copernicus. But even more importantly for his subsequent fame, he
became acquainted with Iamblicus' *De Mysteriis Ægyptiorum*: a
work published in Latin in 1497, and one that he most surely
used when working on *Les Prophéties*. For, there is contained
within this book certain practices that he refers to within the first
two quatrains of his opening set of one hundred verses. These
refer to the mystical preparations practiced by the prophetess of
Branchos at Didyma, and which Nostradamus confessed to having repeated (See Appendix).

Precisely when Nostradamus obtained his license to practice
medicine is now unknown. A contemporary of his Jean-Aimé de
Chavigny, author of an early biographical sketch, states merely
that he *'retook, and passed his Doctorate'*. The claim that he 'retook' the
qualifications required to become a medical practitioner in all
probability refers to an existing entry in the University's records
dated 3 October 1529. This shows that Nostradamus's name had
been struck from the Medical School's *Liber Scholasticorum* register. An explanatory note clarifies the position by stating that this
action was taken because he had been a pharmacist, and had
spoken badly of doctors. But on 23 October 1529, Nostradamus
was reinstated. The Medical School's register of enrolments confirms this with a declaration in his own handwriting, still extant,
in which he now swears, *"to observe the statutes, rights and privileges,
present and future."* To this, he has added: *"I have paid the registration fee
and choose Antoine Romier as patron."* It appears that he had been reprimanded for his outspokenness, and been made to declare his
conformity with the discipline of the medical college in his own
hand. It may, of course, be added that when Charles IX's royal

progress through France reached Salon de Crau, where Nostradamus lived, he was recognized by the Court as a medical doctor, and appointed '*Physician-in-Ordinary*' to the King.

After leaving Montpellier, he journeyed to Agen and for some years settled there as an associate of the scholar, soldier and physician, Jules-César Scaliger. Scaliger shared Nostradamus's interest in *Time,* for it was he who first proposed that long periods of time should be counted in 'Julian Days', thus avoiding the irregularities that occur when counting in months and years. But the friendship between the two men eventually withered, and they parted. It was during this period in Nostradamus's life, and when he was already into his early thirties that he married '*une fort honorable demoiselle*'. Nothing is known for certain about his wife, or even her name, although it has been suggested she was Henriette d'Encausse; nor do we know the names of the son and daughter she bore, except that all three suddenly died, presumably of the plague, but smallpox cannot be discounted.

Nostradamus responded to this personal tragedy by returning to Provence and an unsettled life of travel. While in Marseilles he was invited by the *Parlement de Provence* to take up the position of doctor in Aix, where he stayed for three years.

In 1546, plague broke out, and the city voted him a salary to stay. The reports made by Seigneur de Launay in his book, *Le Théâtre du Monde,* was said to have been provided by Nostradamus. It was while in Aix that he recorded the modesty of the women in the city, for they began sewing themselves into their winding sheets once the plague had taken hold, so that they would not be exposed naked after death.

From Aix, he journeyed to Salon de Crau, which lies midway between Avignon and Marseilles. And it was there on Friday 11 November 1547 that he remarried. His new wife was Anne Ponsarde, the young widow of Jean Beaulme, a patient whom he is said to have attended before the man's death.

Marriage did not detain him in Salon, for he left there to embark upon a journey that took him across the French border to Italy and to many of its towns and cities: amongst the more notable were Milan, Venice, Genoa, and Savona. It would seem that the purpose of his visit was to meet up with men of learning and acquire what new knowledge he could, for this was the time of the Renaissance. This rebirth of the Humanities *"originated in Italy, where scholarship was stimulated by classical manuscripts, foundation of libraries and academies."* It was into the midst of this new order of humanism and individuality that Nostradamus arrived, and from where he would later return to his wife in Salon, armed with the means to write his masterpiece, *Les Prophéties*.

From this, it may be assumed that while in Italy, with access to the manuscript treasures of the ancient world, he rediscovered the methods of the two ancient Oracles at Didyma and Delphi, and how to adapt these to his own natural ability. This could explain his act of vandalism, which has been much criticised, but which he stoutly defended. *"I had at my disposal many volumes which had been hidden for a great many centuries. But dreading what use might be made of them, after reading them I consigned them to the flames."* His justification for burning these books was to prevent them falling into the hands of his son. *"[M]y son, I beg that you will never want to employ your understanding on such dreams and vanities as dry up the body, and put the soul in perdition and cause trouble to the weak senses. I caution you especially against the vanity of the more than execrable magic, condemned of yore by the Holy Scriptures and the Canons of the Church."* From this, it can be seen that Nostradamus distanced himself, and his gift, from that of *'execrable magic'*.

There is uncertainty as to how long Nostradamus remained in Italy, but by 1552 he was again living in Salon with his new wife, possibly still in her twenties or early thirties, for she would later give birth to six children over the forthcoming twelve years; the eldest, Madeleine, born in 1551 or 1552.

A document still extant refers to *'Monsur le Docteur Nostradamus'* owning a house in the Farreiroux district *"facing the windmill of Estienne Lassale and the house belonging to Juanette Texier's heirs."* This house, a four-story tenement, has been identified and restored. It is presently the town's Nostradamus Museum.

It was in this dwelling, in the uppermost room of the house, that the seer began to experiment with his rediscovery of the ancient means of foretelling the future once used by the priesthood at Didyma and Delphi. The success of these attempts can be found in the content of his book of prophecies, which have enjoyed an almost continuous publication for the past four and a half centuries, and which have been printed in every major language of the western world.

By the spring of 1555, the first volume of his predictions had been completed, and was then on sale. By this time, Nostradamus was already well-known for his astrological predictions and as the author of almanacs: an advantage that greatly helped in making known his book of prophecies.

We are told that Nostradamus was a little undersized but of robust build and vigorous in spirit. His forehead was broad and open, beneath which were grey eyes and a straight even nose; his expression was one of kindliness.

Although a taciturn man, and given to bouts of silent thought, yet, as the occasion demanded and in agreeable company, he was said to be an excellent conversationalist. Amongst his many attributes was an excellent retentive memory, a penetrating insight into a wide range of problems, and an enviable ability to quickly comprehend whatsoever he wished. Although sometimes irascible, he nevertheless possessed a lively wit, and was generally of a cheerful disposition. His sense of humour, however, had a tendency towards bitterness; this trait becomes apparent when studying his prophecies.

He held steadfast to the Catholic faith, believing it to be a path to salvation. In pursuit of his religion, he practiced prayer, fasting, and a participation in charitable work. When angry, he was liable to be severe. However, both patience and kindness were ascribed to him, as were his love and recommendation of free speech. Several times his tongue seems to have been responsible for causing him trouble. On one occasion, while observing a statue of the Virgin Mother being cast, his vocal lack of appreciation at the result was reported to the Church authorities, and a case was prepared against him by the Inquisition. Wisely, it seems, he chose absence as the better part of valour.

Unlike the typical stereotype of a charlatan that he is often described to have been, Nostradamus took an active interest in community affairs. Adam de Craponne, a brilliant military engineer, formerly employed by the Duke of Guise, returned to his home in Salon with the idea of constructing a canal from the river Durance. His intention was to irrigate the arid land outside the town. Nostradamus donated a generous portion of his own money to help this development proceed.

The recognition of his community spirit and great learning was readily acknowledged when he was chosen to compose a welcoming address for the arrival of Princess Marguerite, Duchess of Savoy (King Henri II's sister on her journey through Provence in the winter of 1559). The Duchess prolonged her stay at Salon in order to converse more closely with the seer. This is readily understandable, since Nostradamus's prediction that Henri II, her brother, would be killed in a martial field had just occurred, and had been the talk of Paris.

On another occasion, the seer was asked by the local authorities to compose Latin inscriptions for the new water fountains that were being installed in Salon, for it was principally as a scholar and medical doctor that he achieved local renown.

Plague became an inescapable feature of life in Europe at that time, and was to remain so thereafter. Nostradamus was reportedly involved in several attempts at combating the frequent outbreaks of this fatal disease; and that he tended many of the sick and dying at the peril of becoming infected himself, must speak very highly of his character and personal fortitude.

Every age experiences a transition between old certainties and new ideas, although these take different forms and concern different walks of life. The age in which Nostradamus lived saw a continuation of the exploration begun in the previous century, with new voyages being undertaken to the Americas, Africa, and Asia. It was also at this time that Magellan set out to circumnavigate the world.

Religion was also part of the transition then taking place, as society started to come to terms with an expanding world. Luther nailed his thesis to the church door in Wittenberg and began the Reformation. Copernicus proposed the idea that it was the Earth that revolved around the Sun, and not the Sun around the Earth, as was then universally accepted. This not only defied common sense, it also commenced decades of acrimonious debate within both church and university. The printed word had also begun its spread across Western Europe, and this allowed Tyndale's translation of the New Testament to be printed and circulated abroad, permitting ordinary men and women to read for themselves the scripture they had only previously heard from the pulpit.

It was with the arrival of the printing press that Nostradamus's literary aspirations began to emerge. A treatise on Cosmetics (1552) was followed by one on Conserves (1555). Another on Contagious Infirmities (1559) preceded an essay concerning Remedies against the Plague and other pestilent fevers. These were soon to be accompanied by a regular output of almanacs in which he sought to provide astrological guidance for the year ahead. But it was his intended one thousand quatrains, 942 of which were published between 1555 and 1558 that subsequently became his *Magnum Opus*. In this, he detailed, albeit with much in cryptic language, the immediate future of France, and subsequently the world at large: his prophetic knowledge apparently only coming to a halt when the year 3797 was reached.

As we shall later discover, the termination of his prophecies is not without religious significance. It may therefore surprise his Christian detractors to learn that his commitment to this religion extended to using his gift for discovering the dates of Jesus' Birth and Crucifixion. If he is to be believed, his ability to correctly date events in the future was on a par with that of dating incidents in the past.

It is, however, Nostradamus's self-confessed visionary experiences that separate him from the astrologers of his day. Unlike his other publications, he at first retained these experiences, solely for his own satisfaction. In the letter to his son, he admits to this. *"For a long time I have been making predictions, far in advance of events that have since come to pass . . . However, because of the harm both to the present and much of the future, I remained silent, and avoided putting them into writing."*

There also seems to have been an air of religious observance in his hesitation to publish, for he quotes from *Matthew* vii, 6, which warns the faithful not to cast pearls before swine, lest these treasures become trampled underfoot: wise words, indeed, if the venom some have poured out against his person and his predictions are anything to judge by.

In terms of his religious observance, there can be no doubt that Nostradamus accepted his visions of the future originated

7

from God. In his epistle to Henri II he confided: – *"I readily admit that all proceeds from God, and render to Him thanks, honour and immortal praise."* In his preface to the first part of Les Prophéties (later referred to as the *Centuries*) he had made a similar confession: – *the perfect knowledge of events cannot be acquired without divine inspiration, since all prophetic inspiration derives its prime motivating force from God.* Towards the end of his narrative, he enlarged upon this.

> *All is predicted by divine inspiration, and by means of the angelic spirit with which the one prophesying is inspired, rendering him anointed with prophecies, illuminating him, moving him before his fantasy through diverse, nocturnal apparitions. With astronomic calculations certifying the prophecy.*

If taken at his word, Nostradamus is confessing to a form of mediation between the Deity and himself. This, he says, is conducted by an 'angelic spirit', which illuminates his 'nocturnal apparitions' of the future. Moreover, these futuristic visions are correlated to specific times that have been calculated according to the position of the planets in the zodiac. It is as if Nostradamus has constructed an astronomical clock, correlated to the calendar; then, having done so, he meditates upon specific planetary arrangements so that he may receive a mental picture of some major event, or events, occurring during that arrangement, associated, as it is, to a calendar date. He then accounts for his success by explaining that a mediating spirit, a *divus* or a divine intelligence, generates this foreknowledge within him, based upon information that has been obtained from the fount of all knowledge, God. He certainly admitted to something of this nature when he disclosed: *"With divine and supernatural inspiration, integrated with astronomical computations, one can name places and periods of time accurately. . . . By this means, past, present and future become one eternity."* Nor does he seem to entertain the least doubt concerning this claim; and neither does he question his ability to be made aware of the future. As he explains: *"I cannot fail, err or be deceived, though I am the greatest sinner."* At a later point, he added: *"If I had wanted to date each quatrain, I could have done so, but this would not have been agreeable to those interpreting them."*

Athough this claim is contentious, Nostradamus validates it by referring to God as the source of his prophecy; *"the perfect knowledge of events cannot be acquired without divine inspiration, since all prophetic inspiration receives its prime motivating force from God the Creator."* Never once did he claim the same for astrology, nor for his published almanacs, which appear to have contained the *Présages* that were later republished as an additional feature to *Les Prophéties*

The *Sixains,* which carry his name as author, were published many years after his death, and show no evidence of being prophetic; very likely, they are the frauds of another person who believed, as professional sceptic James Randi has suggested, that if words are loosely but cunningly spun together, they can be made to appear prophetic. However, when Randi's conjecture is examined and put to the test using the *Sixains,* his rashly judged assumption turns out to be complete nonsense.

In the hundredth quatrain of *Century VI*, Nostradamus invoked against such ignoramuses and more especially astrologers who attempted to link *Les Prophéties* with their practices:

> *They who read these verses, assess maturely,*
> *The profane, the vulgar and the ignorant touch not.*
> *All astrologers, simpletons, and barbarians are at a great distance.*
> *Whoever acts differently, he is rightly accursed.*

The seer's reverence for the divine nature of his prophetic legacy to the world has been clearly, and categorically, reserved for the one thousand quatrains that he intended to publish as a result of his nocturnal meditations.

Questions surrounding Nostradamus's position as a prophet may nevertheless be raised. For example, did he understand all that he was shown prophetically? The priestess at Didyma did not. Her utterances were written down, versified, and then interpreted by priests attending the ceremony. In a similar plight was the biblical prophet Daniel. His visions of the future were, to him, incomprehensible, and he was compelled to ask for angelic guidance that he might understand their meaning. (*Daniel* 7:16).

In the case of Nostradamus, we have two open letters: one to his fourteen-month-old son César, the other to King Henri II, the year before his death, and which, respectively, preface the two volumes that make up his major work. In these, Nostradamus appears to warn in prose what the quatrains contain in verse. Unfortunately, attempts to relate all that he says in these letters to specific quatrains have met with only occasional success. One is therefore left with the suspicion that he was not in full possession of the understanding required to know what was contained within his completed oracles.

This need not be surprising. In order to illustrate the same point, Geoffrey Ashe, (*The Book of Prophecy*, p.204) recounts Sir Arthur Conan Doyle's short story, *The Silver Mirror*, in order to provide a possible reason for Nostradamus being unaware of the full meaning contained within his visions.

The Silver Mirror concerns the story of an accountant working long hours into the night on a fraud case. In the same room is an antique, silver-framed mirror. In moments of extreme weariness the accountant catches glimpses of a woman reflected in the glass. At first, it is only her face masked with horror that appears; then it is a full length view, showing her seated in a chair and attired in a black velvet dress; later still, he sees a small man with a pointed beard, crouching by her side and clutching at her dress, his face etched with terror. On a subsequent occasion, the mirror brings into full view a group of men who prise the bearded man away from the woman and stab him to death.

Eventually, after a period of incessant hard work, the accountant is overcome with exhaustion, and forced to convalesce in a nursing home. Whilst there, he relates his strange experience with the mirror to a doctor. The mirror is examined, and discovered to have once belonged to Mary Queen of Scots. The doctor then realises that what the accountant saw was a visual recording of the Queen's secretary, Rizzio, being murdered. Somehow, the mirror had retained the emotional energy discharged at the time of the murder, and this had been picked up by the weary accountant as a replay of the murder scene. The accountant, knowing nothing of Scotland's past, was therefore in a similar position to Nostradamus when viewing a scene from the future. Neither one has possession of the requisite knowledge to understand the underlying story behind what they see taking place. Instead, it requires someone in possession of that knowledge to explain the event.

It must therefore remain an open question as to whether or not Nostradamus was ever in receipt of that special knowledge or was he no better placed than the Pythia at Delphi, or the priestess at Didyma. And, of course, the further his foresight ventured into the future, the stranger the world would appear to him. And, even if he had an all-knowing guide to help him understand his visions, the sheer amount of detailed information covering more than twenty-two centuries of future political intrigue, scientific inventions and natural disasters would, arguably, be too overwhelming for the mind of a fifteenth-century scholar to assimilate, irrespective of his intelligence.

One is therefore forced to consider the very real likelihood that Nostradamus was largely ignorant of what lay at the source of his prescient verses. In the first of his quatrains, he may have actually confirmed this, for he revealed that what he had witnessed during his nocturnal vigils was *'not believed vain'*.

Consequently, despite the apparent lack of his having received any accompanying explanation for the dramas unfolding within his visions, if indeed that is the truth, he nevertheless remained totally convinced of their accuracy, and of their divine origin. Quite possibly, he thought himself sufficiently competent to explain to Henri II what he had seen and heard. He was certainly up to the task when he predicted: *"the Christian Church will be persecuted more fiercely than ever it was in Africa, and this will last up to the year 1792, which they will believe to mark a renewal of time."*

The de-Christianising of France began with the sequestering of Church lands in 1790, combined with legislation demoting priests to the rank of civil servants. Crimes against religious orders and their members thereafter increased rapidly, eventually reaching a peak on 2 September 1792 with the September Massacres. Priests, nuns, and novices were rounded up, imprisoned, and murdered in a frenzy of judicial killing that lasted several days. That same month, the Revolutionary Calendar was introduced across France, which marked a renewal of the way time was to be recorded. The new Calendar officially commenced on 22 September 1792, thus commemorating the beginning of the French Republic in Year One, and the end of the monarchy.

Nostradamus's first volume of oracles went on sale during the first week of May 1555. Before going to print, he had asked for, and received, the necessary authority for its publication from Hugh de Puy, the King's Councillor and Lieutenant of Lyons; the book's front cover proudly displays *'With Privilege'*, to indicate

11

this, together with details of the license to publish, which can be seen on the book's second page.

On Sunday 14 July that year, Nostradamus set out for Paris, having been summoned by the King: although unbeknown to him, contrary voices had been advising Henri II against inviting the seer. A surviving entry in a diary kept by Jean Guérard of Lyons records Nostradamus's stay at his house during the last week of July 1555. *"At this same time there passed through the city an astrologer called Michel de Nostre Dame. . . . He was on his way to the Court of the King to which he had been summoned."*

It also appears from Guérard's further record that Nostradamus feared he would be beheaded before the 25 August, and was anticipating great danger to himself. This suggests that he had cast his own horoscope before embarking upon the journey, and it boded ill. It also suggests that the infallible source of his recently published prophecies was not subject to his command, but that he received his divinations of the future at the discretion of his *divus*.

Nostradamus arrived in the French capital on 15 August, and reported his arrival to the Constable, Anne de Montmorency. His interview with the King and Queen quickly followed and this would have taken place at the Saint Germaine-de-Laye Palace in the northern part of the city. At the conclusion of the meeting, King Henri ordered that Nostradamus be lodged in the palace of Cardinal de Bourbon, Archbishop of Sens, which was situated beside the river Seine.

Inside the safety of the palace, Nostradamus's astuteness seems to have come to the fore, because for the next *'ten or twelve days'* he was confined to his room, suffering a very sudden and exceedingly painful attack of gout, thus taking him safely past the danger period around 25 August. After 'recovering', he appears to have met with the Queen again, presumably to deliver horoscopes for her children. It was then that matters took a dramatic turn. After returning from the Palace that evening, he was visited by a *'Grand Lady'* from the Court who stayed late and spoke to him of private matters. The next morning she returned to warn him that plans were afoot for the Justice Department to detain him for questioning. In some haste, Nostradamus bade farewell to Paris, having had no time to settle a loan of *'two Rose nobles and two crowns'* received from Jean Morel d'Embrun, a well-known benefactor of writers and a disciple of Erasmus.

The seer's safe arrival back in Provence during September was noticeable on two accounts: firstly, it heralded a string of personal attacks against him, and secondly, he began preparing for the publication of the second part of his intended one thousand oracular quatrains. The volume of 1555 had contained the first 353 verses, for which two first editions of this book still exist, one in Vienna, the other in Albi. The remainder of the verses was published in 1558 at Lyon but, to date, no first editions have been found, although Pierre Leffen of Leyden owned a copy, which he used for his edition of 1650. One therefore either has to rely upon copies made from this lost edition, or from the complete set, published two years after Nostradamus's death, which was edited, although not always reliably, by one of his acolytes, Jean Aimé de Chavigny. In both the copy of the 1558 edition, and the complete set of prophecies printed in 1568, the seventh set of an intended one hundred quatrains is incomplete.

No explanation has been given, and although Nostradamus lived for another eight years, he never made good the omitted verses. This suggests that he had not kept a copy of his manuscript. But in 1589 Pierre Ménier of Paris published a copy of the Centuries that included Nos. 73; 80; 82 and 83. His source is unknown: as is that of another publisher of the Centuries, Claude Garcin of Marseilles. In 1643 he produced an edition of the prophecies that contained two more of the missing verses, Nos. 43 and 44. The mystery surrounding Century VII remains.

During the period following publication of his second set of prophecies, a poem by the great French poet, Pierre de Ronsard (1524-85) appeared, praising Nostradamus, for whom, he says: *"[He] has for many a year predicted the great part of our destiny. I would not have believed him, had not Heaven, which assigns good and evil to mankind, been his inspiration."*

A spate of spiteful attacks then followed as if to quench the fire of his growing fame. His former friend, Scaliger, referred to him as a *'vile driveller'*, and asked *'Credulous France'* who is the dumber, *"this evil buffoon, or you who spend too much time fawning on his impostures?"*

Another critic was the astrologer Laurens Videl who accused Nostradamus of being *"so ignorant that it is impossible to find anyone to whom you are second in ignorance."* Worse followed: this time from the poisonous verse of someone calling himself Hercules le François: a pseudonym believed to be that of Guillaume Farel, who served Calvin.

> *This sorcerer who deceives the world*
> *Under the pretext of good faith*
> *Remember to protest*
> *That if his cackling was to take hold*
> *The laws [of nature] would all be changed*
> *And he would invent us another God.*

There was even a verbal assault from one of the foremost political figures in France, Michael de l'Hôpital, who held a senior governmental position equivalent to first minister. *"Nostradamus conjures up ambiguous prophecies . . . what madness! . . . This seeing into the future does not come from God. For it is forbidden for mortals to know in advance the events that are to come."*

Nostradamus survived these critical attacks, but in 1560-61 he was forced to take evasive action, when gangs of Cabans ran riot through the streets of Salon for several months, threatening all who came under suspicion of being heretics. It was during this killing spree that his wife's cousin, Etienne Hozier, who had been chief witness at their wedding, was murdered.

Once, while visiting Marseilles, Nostradamus was arrested in a round-up of Huguenot suspects. The charge against him was that of spreading inflammatory literature. He was taken for questioning to the castle at Marignane outside the city walls, but released soon afterwards. The seer's response to this aggravation was to lease a house in Avignon for the safekeeping of his family. But after the death of the Caban leader, the danger subsided. And once the authorities had restored order, Nostradamus was able to resume life in Salon.

In 1561, Nostradamus still had five years of his allotted time on earth remaining. It was also the year that marked the birth of Diane, his wife's sixth and final child. His fame as a prophet had now spread to other countries: as we know from foreign ambassadors who reported the latest news in the French court back to their superiors. The deaths of King Henri II (10 July 1559), and his eldest son and successor, King Francis II (5 December 1560), were described by the ambassadors from Spain and Venice as having been recognized at court, from the predictions made by Nostradamus. In England, Sir William Cecil (later Lord Burghley and Queen Elizabeth's principal minister of State) saw the French seer as an instrument of subversive propaganda. Elizabeth's astrologer John Dee, unable to match Nostradamus's prophecies, behaved like the fox in Aesop's fable who, after failing to reach the grapes, went away declaring them sour.

On 24 January 1564 the Queen-mother Catherine de' Medici left Paris with her thirteen-year-old son King Charles IX, to embark on a tour of France that would last two years. The royal party reached Salon de Crau in October of that year. The Queen's intention was to once again consult with Nostradamus, which she did inside the seer's house.

It was during this visit that the now aging physician sought permission to examine Henri of Navarre, the King's second cousin, who was then ten years old and living at Court with his cousins, the Valois children. Nostradamus wanted to see the boy in the flesh so that he could inspect the moles on the prince's skin. Satisfied by what he saw, Nostradamus remarked to the greatly astonished Master of the Household, that if he should live a long life, he would see this boy one day become King of Navarre and France.

> *It was scarcely to be expected, however, that he would one day succeed to the throne of France, since Catherine de Médicis had already borne three sons to the reigning king, Henry II, and would soon bear him a fourth.*
> (Encyclopaedia Britannica)

Moreover, the young prince was a Huguenot, and Catholic France would never accept a Protestant as king. This prophecy therefore runs contrary to the accusation that Nostradamus's successes were merely the result of obvious guesses.

It is also absurd to suppose that the moles had any predictive power. It is far more probable that Nostradamus had seen moles on a future king of France during one of his nocturnal *séances*. Since they did not belong to any of the sons of Henri II, he sought to discover if they belonged to their cousin, Henri of Navarre.

In the spread of years following the death of Nostradamus, the four immediate successors to the throne, and each a son of Henri II, all died without producing an heir. This left Henri of Navarre, with his kingdom in the southwest of France and northwest of Spain, to become King Henri IV. In fact, it fulfilled the prophecy made to the Master of the Household several decades earlier, which against all the odds had finally come to pass.

The royal party continued its progress *en route* for Arles. It was from there that a messenger was sent back to Salon for Nostradamus to join them. During the consultations that followed, the seer was raised to the office of Physician-in-Ordinary and Councillor to the King of France. Royal recognition for his medical work, and an appreciation for his forward thinking had now been added to his growing reputation, but it came late in life. Eighteen months later, on the morning of Tuesday 2 July 1566 (12 July N.S.), he was discovered dead in his study. The coldness of his body suggested that he had died late during the previous night. An almanac that he had written for this year included an entry for 1 July. It read: *'A Strange Migration'*; this has been seen by many as a prediction of his own death.

If Chavigny, who seems to have acted as Nostradamus's amanuensis, can be believed, then there is reason to consider it being true. Chavigny, who took up residence in Salon to be close to Nostradamus, recorded in his *Brief Discourse on the Life of M. Michel Nostradamus* that the seer –

> . . . *truly knew the time of his death to the day, even to the hour, I can attest as a fact, I recall clearly that at the end of June of the said year [1566] he wrote in his own hand in the 'Ephemerides of Jean Stadius' these Latin words "Hic prope mors est." That is to say "my death draws near." And the day before he exchanged this life for the next, I having assisted him for a very considerable time, and very late taking leave of him until morning, he said these words to me: "You will not see me alive at sunrise."*

According to his personal wish, he was buried in the Church of the Cordelias, then part of a Franciscan Friary. His wife provided a fitting memorial tablet attesting to:

> *Michel de Nostredame, unique among all humanity in being judged worthy, whose near divine pen described the future happenings of the whole world as influenced by the stars.*

16

Nostradamus had been taught the study of astrology by his maternal grandfather, (or great grandfather as others have maintained) before going to Avignon to study the Humanities, and, as is often the case, the lessons he learned while young stayed with him throughout his life.

In bringing to a close this introduction to Nostradamus, it is fitting that it should end with a quotation in his own words. This predicts not only his enduring fame, but also the immortality of the human soul.

> *"In life I am immortal, and in death even more so:*
> *After my death my name will live on throughout the world."*

2

THE LAST OF THE VALOIS

Nostradamus published the first part of his intended one thousand oracles in the spring of 1555. It is therefore natural to assume their content will refer to events after that date.

In 1555 Henri II was King of France, and his wife, Catherine de' Medici, the mother of their seven surviving children: three daughters and four sons. The Valois dynasty looked set to continue into the distant future. But France was also at war, embroiled in the Habsburg-Valois conflict, which had rumbled on since 1494, when Charles VIII, having been invited by the Duke of Milan, invaded Italy to back his claim to Naples. In fact, both cities Naples and Milan were later given to the sons of Henri II by Pope Paul IV in December 1555.

Nostradamus begins his prophecies with a reference to the loss of Naples and Milan at a time when France was about to lose its war with Spain. The deciding battle was fought at Saint-Quentin on 10 August 1557, when Spain successfully invaded

Picardy from the Netherlands. A French counter-attack took place at Gravelines (1558), but this resulted in further French losses. At the same time, Francis 2nd Duke of Guise was in Naples, attempting to secure the city for France, but news of his country's defeat brought him hurriedly back before he could complete the conquest.

C.IV: 34

Le grand mené captif d'eftrange terre,
D'or enchainé au roy CHYREN offert,
Qui dans Aufonne, Millan perdra la guerre,
Et tout fon oft mis à feu & à fer.

The great man led captive of a foreign land,
Enchained by gold, offered to the king, HENRY,
Which, with Naples, Milan, he will lose the war,
And all his troops put to fire and weapon.

mené, (O.Fr.) conduire, to lead; Chyren, (Latin anagram): Henryc/us, also Chyr[o]n, (Latin) tutor of heroes; Ausonne, (Ausonia, prehistoric part of southern Italy in which the Kingdom of Naples later became situated); ost, (O.Fr.) troops; fer, (O.Fr.) arme.

THE GREAT MAN LED CAPTIVE OF A FOREIGN LAND

The Battle of Saint-Quentin was fought by Henri II's favourite, Anne de Montmorency Constable of France. *"[O]n 10 August 1557 battle was joined, and the Constable suffered a catastrophic defeat."* Spain's victory was not only the cause of devastating French losses; it also resulted in the capture of Anne de Montmorency, **THE GREAT MAN** of France. He was taken prisoner by Emmanuel-Philibert, the Duke of Savoy, and **LED** across the French border to Ghent, where he was held hostage: – **CAPTIVE OF A FOREIGN LAND**.[1]

HE WILL LOSE THE WAR AND ALL HIS TROOPS PUT TO FIRE AND WEAPON

With the French army defeated and **ALL HIS TROOPS PUT TO FIRE AND WEAPON**,[2] Henri realised the **WAR WAS NOW LOST**,[3] and he would have to submit to the proposals contained in the peace treaty offered by Spain.

ENCHAINED BY GOLD, OFFERED TO KING HENRI

In the negotiations that followed, Savoy **OFFERED** to return Montmorency **TO THE KING** in exchange for a huge ransom in *gold*, which **HENRI** could not immediately afford to pay. The Constable was therefore, figuratively speaking, **ENCHAINED BY GOLD**.[4]

Henri was eventually able to accept Savoy's ransom offer, but payment had to be delayed for a year until instalments could be

19

agreed. The Grand Master of France was finally released in December 1558. And in the following year, the treaty of Cateau-Cambrésis was signed (April 1559).

Having LOST THE WAR, Henri was compelled to cede the cities of NAPLES and MILAN to Spain. Four years earlier, in December 1555, these two cities had been given to Henri's two sons by Pope Paul IV: *Naples* had gone to Charles (later Charles IX), and *Milan* to Edouard (later Henri III).

The next quatrain is a split prophecy which, in part, pursues the theme of the peace treaty agreed between France and Spain. It also introduces by name two of the key players, the dukes of Guise and Alba. However, because both names are given, the timescale for fulfilling the prophecy has been extended and the dates inverted. This prevented the early discovery of its meaning, and preserved the free will of those fulfilling the prophecy.

C.VII: 29

Le grand duc d'Albe ſe viendra rebeller,
A ſes grans peres fera le tradiment:
Le grand de Guiſe le viendra debeller:
Captif mené & dreſſé monument.

The great Duke of Alba will himself come to rebel,
To his grandfathers he will make the betrayal:
The great man of Guise will agree it, ending the war,
Captive (Méré) led, and a remembrance directed.

grans, (Sp) grands; tradiment, (Latinism) trad/o, to betray; debeller, (Latinism) debell/o, to end a war; viendra, (O.Fr.) conviendra; mené, (paragram) – Mé[r]é; also to lead away; dresser, (O.Fr.) to direct, instruct; monument, (O.Fr.) remembrance of.

The treaty of Cateau-Cambrésis, negotiated between France, Spain, and England, with different interests dividing the three parties, was signed on separate days in April 1559. It finally ended France's sixty year dream of conquest in Italy, for which much blood and treasure had been spent. Henri II directed the Cardinal of Lorraine, THE GREAT MAN OF GUISE, TO AGREE IT. The Cardinal being at that time:[1] *"one of the foremost members of the powerful Roman Catholic house of Guise and perhaps the most influential Frenchman during the middle years of the 16th century. He was intelligent, avaricious, and cautious."* He was also the King's chief negotiator for ENDING THE WAR with Spain.[2]

20

Cardinal Lorraine was the son of François of Lorraine, the 2nd Duke of Guise. This outstanding general in his time served four French kings – Francis 1, Henri II, Francis II, and Charles IX. It was in February 1563 that he laid siege to Orleans: the first military action in a conflict that was to lead to France's internal wars of Religion.

The House of Guise was staunchly Catholic, and the 2nd Duke was intent upon opposing the Huguenots led by Louis, Prince of Condé. But, on the 18th February, Jean Poltrot de Méré, a young Huguenot sympathiser, concealed himself behind some bushes and shot the Duke from behind. Guise died six days later.

CAPTIVE MÉRÉ LED

Nostradamus's choice of words can sometimes appear erratic, but when this occurs it may betray a hidden meaning. In the present oracle it is the word *mené* that attracts attention. It certainly means *led*, but leaves the future to explain in what way it is to be understood. In the present case, by employing the word as seen, the seer has supplied exactly the right word to construct a paragram; that is, *"A play on words by alteration of a letter or letters. Quite often a facetious and low form of humour."* [3] Thus, *mené* can be changed to Mé[r]é. MÉRÉ was the man LED [4] INTO CAPTIVITY, and thereafter to his execution for the crime of having killed the duc de Guise.

This type of word play is typical of Nostradamus's strategy and his inclination towards black humour. Changing one letter in an anagram was also allowed in France, as confirmed by the *Dictionnaire de Trévoux* under *'Anagramme'*. But when Nostradamus uses this strategy, he treats the word as a paragram before scrambling the letters to form an anagram. Such anagrams, however, are always perfect; that is to say, the anagram and the paragram from which it was derived are meaningfully connected. We shall come across these paragram–anagrams later, where for brevity they will be termed 'paranagrams'.

AND A REMEMBRANCE DIRECTED

On the day after Méré's execution, the funeral of the Duke of Guise took place. [5] In REMEMBRANCE OF the great man's service to France, the state DIRECTED that a funeral of almost royal proportions be conducted.

. . . the cortège, composed of twenty-two town criers ringing bells, important citizens carrying burning torches, and representatives of the Church and nobility all processed through Paris. A large troop of armed militiamen accompanied them. Thousands of mourners lined the streets.[6]

From the death of Guise, we now direct attention to the first two lines of the oracle. This concerns Fernando Alvarez de Toledo, Duke of Alba.

THE GREAT DUKE OF ALBA

"After the Peace of Cateau-Cambrésis (1559), Alba became one of Philip II's two leading ministers."[7] He had been born into a wealthy Spanish family, which enjoyed a long tradition of having served the kings of Castile. In his own time, he achieved notoriety for the ruthless manner in which he put down rebellions, chiefly by executing their leaders; particularly gruesome was his setting up of the 'Council of Blood', which resulted in 1,105 executions or deportations. It was also *"In the last phase of the Franco-Spanish War in Italy, [that] he out manoeuvred the Duke of Guise and forced Pope Paul IV to come to terms with Spain (1557)."*[8]

WILL, HIMSELF, COME TO REBEL: HE WILL MAKE THE BETRAYAL TO HIS GRANDFATHERS

The fighting between France and Spain had brought these two great men, Alba and Guise, together at the close of the war. But it was several years later, in 1572, while serving in the Netherlands that Alba reached an impasse and was unable to make further military progress. His *"failure and the intrigues of the Gómez party at court induced Philip to recall him (1573)."*[9] It was the first step towards the Duke, HIMSELF, COMING TO REBEL,[10] but IT WOULD BE A BETRAYAL TO HIS GRANDFATHERS' unblemished record of service to Spain that suffered most.[11] This came about because Alba's son wished to marry. Philip sensed a threat to his position through the proposed union, and forbade it. But the Duke and his son rebelled against the order, and *"Alba was placed under house arrest on his estates after his son had married against the king's wishes."*[12]

This prophecy was unusual in that it openly named two contemporaries of Nostradamus, Alba and Guise. Because of this openness a timescale for its fulfilment was constructed to extend beyond any sustained interest that these names may have invoked at the time. The seer has therefore laid his cards on the table right at the beginning. He has no intention of providing an easy-to-follow timetable of events, especially when he has named names. Neither is it his intention to predict a future that will allow it to be altered by someone, because of what he has written. To prevent this happening, the dates on which the events became fulfilled were not only wide apart; they were also presented to the reader in reverse order. This is the exception that proves the rule. The vast majority of Nostradamus's predictions, as will soon be demonstrated, become fulfilled in date order. It is only when the seer has given exceptional clues to identify what is to come about that he scrambles the order in which the predicted events will occur.

The next prophecy is quite different in that it relates to events that occurred within little more than a week. Its fulfilment also caused a local riot in Paris, when it was realised that Nostradamus had predicted the death of the King. An effigy of the seer was made, and then set on fire to vent the frustration of the mob at not getting their hands on the man himself.

C.I: 35

Le lyon ieune, le vieux furmontera,
En champ bellique par fingulier duelle,
Dans caige d'or les yeux luy creuera:
Deux claffes vne, puis mourir, mort cruelle.

The young lion will overcome the aged one,
In a martial field, by single combat,
Inside a cage of gold, his eyes punctured,
Two ranks one, then dying, cruel death.

The Cateau-Cambrésis treaty contained a clause announcing two marriages. King Philip of Spain was to wed the thirteen-year-old French Princess, Elizabeth de Valois, and the Duke of Savoy consented to a marriage with Henri II's thirty-six year-old sister, Princess Marguerite. To celebrate these two weddings, Henri seized the opportunity of holding a week of festivities, including a tournament in which he intended to participate.

IN A MARTIAL FIELD BY SINGLE COMBAT, INSIDE A CAGE OF GOLD, HIS EYES PUNCTURED

On Friday 30 June 1559, **IN A MARTIAL FIELD, BY SINGLE COMBAT,**[1] Henri II fulfilled the prophecy made by Nostradamus. The King rode three challenges. Two were against the dukes of Nemours and Guise; the third was against the Comte de Montgomery. The first two jousts went in the King's favour, but on the third run he was almost unseated by the young lieutenant, causing the King to demand a re-match. His decision proved fatal. The two combatants met midfield, but on impact, Montgomery's lance shattered and the King was thrown to the ground. He lay there unconscious with a long splinter jutting from his tilting helm. After removing the headpiece more splinters were discovered. The longest had penetrated his forehead just above the right eye and pierced the left one. HIS EYES had been PUNCTURED.[2] Five further splinters were eventually removed. Spectators at the tournament, who later recalled the event, noted *"that the tilting helm strangely resembled a cage, and that the king's visor was actually gilded."*[3]

THE YOUNG LION WILL OVERCOME THE AGED ONE

It is also appropriate that Nostradamus should have called the victor: *the young lion*, for Montgomery, was A YOUNG serving officer in the Scottish Guards: a regiment for which Scotland's heraldic beast is the red LION. Equally notable is the reference to Henri II as THE AGED ONE. This has connotations with the King's leonine character, and dates back to the time when he first became King. The people of Lyons had recognized his leonine character, both as a monarch and a hunter. To mark this feature, the dignitaries of the city honoured his arrival to their city by presenting him with a magnificent mechanical LION, emblazoned with the heraldic arms of his wife, Catherine de' Medici.

TWO RANKS ONE

After his accident, Henri was carried from the tournament field *"to the near-by Hôtel des Tournelles, and here lay in a state of virtual; unconsciousness for nine days."* [4] On 8 July, the King rallied, and was sufficiently lucid to order that his sister's wedding now proceed. At the stroke of midnight in the nearby church of St Paul, TWO RANKS in the hierarchy of French nobility became ONE, as a Princess and a Duke united in marriage.[5]

Past commentators have tended to apply this phrase, through contorted translation, to the wounds suffered by Henri II. But the prophecies are *continuous*; Nostradamus has moved on to the next event just before the King's death. The royal weddings had, of course been the reason for the tournament.

THEN, on the morning of July 10th, Henri's state of health began to deteriorate, and it was evident he was on the point of dying.[6] Both hands and feet had become grossly swollen from the infection that had set in from the wounds to his head and eye, and he was clearly in dreadful pain. His passing proved to be a particularly **CRUEL DEATH**.[7]

As an interesting aside to this prophecy, the Queen's daughter Princess Marguerite de Valois, related that on the night before the third day of these celebrations, her mother had a premonitory dream in which she saw her husband, the King, lying injured with blood covering his face. Next morning she begged Henri not to enter the lists that day, but to his peril, he refused to listen.

Should any doubt exist concerning Nostradamus's prescient knowledge of Henri II's blindness in one eye, it may possibly be lessened by the next prophecy. This specifically refers to the year when someone with a single eye rules France. Since a splinter had pierced Henri II's left eye, leaving him blind in that eye, attention must have been attracted to this prophecy at the time. To obscure his foreknowledge from premature detection, the seer has therefore reverted to his former strategy of writing a split prophecy: with each part separated by thirteen years; yet, despite this, the prophecy remains united with regard to its subject matter.

C.III: 55

En l'an qu'un oeil en France regnera,
La court fera à un bien fafcheux trouble:
Le grand de Bloys fon ami tuera:
Le regne mis en mal & doute double.

In the year that one eye shall reign in France,
The court will be in a most troublesome dispute:
The great man of Blois will kill his friend:
The kingdom put in difficulty and double doubt.

There is subtlety in the first line. It specifically focuses upon **THE YEAR THAT** a person with **ONE EYE** shall have power over the country: but this is not to say that this person will also reign for the whole of that year. It was Henri II, with his sight reduced to one eye,

25

who REIGNED IN FRANCE from the time of his accident on 30 June, until his death on 10 July.[1] This ten-day period therefore identifies THE YEAR as 1559. It also places us in a position to recognize the trouble brewing at court, which began shortly before the King's accident, and continued for some time after his death.

THE COURT WILL BE IN A MOST TROUBLESOME DISPUTE

A most troublesome dispute did, indeed, break out on 10 June 1559, three weeks before the King's fatal accident.[2] It occurred at the quarterly meeting of the judiciary, when Henri II and Cardinal Lorraine arrived to witness proceedings. It was there that they heard a young magistrate, Anne du Bourg, openly criticizing the sentencing to death of several members of the Paris *Parlement* because of their Calvinistic – that is, heretical – beliefs. Why, he asked those assembled, should these people be condemned to death for their personally held belief in Christ, when adulterers and murderers often escaped punishment?

Henri II immediately recognized himself as a serial adulterer, and the target of this oratory. His response was to order the arrest of du Bourg and several other councillors who had expressed sympathy with this opinion. However, before any action could be taken against those arrested, the King lay dead, having suffered a fatal accident on the tournament field.

The death of Henri II did not save du Bourg. Under the influence of the powerful Guise family, fifteen-year-old Francis II was persuaded to pursue his father's policies against the Huguenots. This decision caused widespread dissent, thus furthering THIS MOST TROUBLESOME DISPUTE AT COURT.

In September and again in November, legislation was passed, which decreed the burning of all houses used for Huguenot meetings, and the death penalty for anyone failing to reveal the location of these dwellings. One month after these edicts were passed, Anne du Bourg was, himself, publicly burnt at the stake (23 December 1559). Afterwards, his death sent shudders amongst those at Court to see such a highborn figure dealt with so harshly.

Thirteen years elapsed before the second half of this prophecy became fulfilled. And, as before, it involved the King sanctioning the death of a nobleman holding Protestant sympathies.

Charles IX, identified as *the great man of Blois* on account of his residence at Blois, was soon to fulfil Nostradamus's prophecy.

THE GREAT MAN OF BLOIS WILL KILL HIS FRIEND

In the year 1570, Gaspard de Coligny, despite being leader of the Huguenots, had become a close friend and confidante of the twenty-year-old King Charles IX. So close was their friendship that Charles even called Coligny *'Mon Père'*. But on St Bartholomew's Eve, after having been harangued by the Queen-mother, **THE GREAT MAN OF BLOIS AGREED TO KILL HIS FRIEND.** [3] *"Kill them all, so that not one will be left to reproach me for it."* [4] He is said to have exclaimed.

The first murder was organized by the young duc de Guise, who had believed Poltrot de Méré's confession implicating Coligny in the assassination of his father, even though it was extracted under torture. And it was Guise's murder of Coligny that triggered the slaughter of many thousands in Paris, in what became known as the St Bartholomew's Day Massacre. The carnage then spilled out to other major towns across France, so that the killing went on for several days.

THE KINGDOM PUT IN DIFFICULTY

After the Massacre had run its course, and with **THE KINGDOM PUT IN DIFFICULTY** as a consequence of this religious pogrom, Catherine's role as Queen-mother steadily declined, as did the influence of the King. Ordinary Protestants now had reason to *doubt* their personal safety, and were unwilling to give Charles IX their allegiance.

AND DOUBLE DOUBT

Suspicion also spread through the country concerning the role played by the King's mother. And, in both France and the Courts of pro-Catholic Europe, *doubt* was cast upon Catherine de' Medici's professed innocence in the massacre. In other words, there was now **DOUBLE DOUBT** [5] concerning the roles played by the King and the Queen-mother.

We now turn to the thirteen-year period between the two halves of this prophecy, when another prediction found its way into the history books. Documentary evidence, still extant, confirms that the court was aware of its fulfilment at the time. A letter sent to Spain by Philip's ambassador to France, included a report concerning Nostradamus's latest prediction. The subject of the court's interest was Francis II, a youth of sixteen and former Dauphin, who had succeeded to the throne following the death of his father Henri II in 1559. However, to date, no book containing Century X, published prior to that by Rigaud in 1568 has been discovered. Nevertheless, Nostradamus's surviving letter to Henri II, in which he refers to an edition dated 27 June 1558, must be the book to which the Court was referring, for it includes the prophecy which had captured the Court's attention.

C.X: 39

Premier fils vefue malheureux mariage,
Sans nuls enfans deux Ifles en difcord,
Auant dixhuict incompetant eage,
De l'autre pres plus bas fera l'accord.

The first son, widow, unfortunate marriage,
Without children, two Isles in discord,
Before eighteen, an inept period,
Of the near other, he will lessen the accord.

vefue (veufe), (O.Fr.) veuve; eage, (O.Fr.) âge; plus bas fera, = he will make much lower; i.e., lessen.

THE FIRST SON, WIDOW

THE FIRST SON of France,[1] up until the death of Henri II, had been the dauphin, François. After his father's fatal accident, and not yet sixteen, he became King Francis II. His wife, Mary Stuart, whom he had married in April 1558, was history's tragic queen, popularly known as Mary Queen of Scots. She became a WIDOW upon the death of her young husband in December 1560.[2]

UNFORTUNATE MARRIAGE, WITHOUT CHILDREN

The MARRIAGE was, indeed, UNFORTUNATE in that Francis was ill conditioned for matrimony. Sickly from childhood, and a sullen youth, it was said that he had still to reach puberty, even into his seventeenth year, and this may be the reason why the oracle emphasizes the couple being WITHOUT CHILDREN.[3]

TWO ISLES IN DISCORD

In November 1558, Elizabeth I succeeded to the English throne, but only amidst controversy. Some wanted a Catholic queen, and Mary Stuart was the popular choice to fulfil that role. In fact, Mary Queen of Scotland actually proclaimed herself 'Queen of England', thus potentially uniting both the major parts of the

British Isles. But in 1559, the nobles in Scotland rose up in revolt against the English, and the TWO kingdoms in the British ISLES were therefore IN DISCORD. [4]

From 1560 onwards, as a result of this disagreement between England and Scotland, John Knox was able to establish a Calvinist regime north of the border, thereby further adding to the religious divisions of the time.

BEFORE EIGHTEEN

Meanwhile, in France, the death of Francis II meant that Mary's role as Queen of that nation was of short duration. The young King died on 5 December 1560, just three days BEFORE Mary's **18**th birthday. And, with Francis having reigned for a little *less than eighteen* months, the emphasis given by the prediction to BEFORE EIGHTEEN, [5] becomes doubly appropriate.

INEPT PERIOD

The years immediately following Henri II's fatal accident in 1559 proved to be an INEPT PERIOD for France.[6] First in line for the throne had been Francis II, a sickly boy of fifteen, who was easy prey for the powerful and influential Guise family. His ten-year-old brother, Charles IX, quickly followed him; being fatherless, young and without political judgement he, too, was easily influenced by the power-hungry factions surrounding him.

OF THE NEAR OTHER HE WILL LESSEN THE ACCORD

The youthful inexperience of these boy-kings allowed the noble families of France to vie for power in the political vacuum caused by the lack of a strong leadership. Consequently, when Charles IX, THE NEAR OTHER, succeeded to the reign under the regency of his mother, Catherine de' Medici, [7] powerful opposing forces were on hand, ready to go to war for control of the weakened throne. Within two years of Charles's succession, France was in the grip of its Wars of Religion, thus fulfilling Nostradamus's prophecy that Charles IX, being THE NEAR OTHER, HE WILL LESSEN THE ACCORD.

The civil wars that had so badly *lessened the accord* in France were a series of conflicts differing in their degrees of violence and involvement. The 1st War ran from April 1562 to March 1563; the 2nd War from September 1567 to March 1568; the 3rd

War from August 1568 to August 1570; the 4th War from December 1572 to June 1573. Charles IX died in May 1574, a broken man not yet twenty-four years of age.[8]

Because of Charles IX's minority at the time of his succession, Catherine de' Medici was given the office of Queen-regent. Her first act in this capacity was to get the *conseil* to elect the 1st Prince of Condé Louis de Bourbon to political office. It was a strategic move designed to neutralize the influence of François de Lorraine, 2nd duc de Guise. His power and influence in the country had grown enormously during the reign of Francis II, and he saw himself as the rightful regent of a country that was ruled by a child and its mother.

Condé was of a similar mind. At the time of his appointment to office, he had been languishing in prison awaiting execution for having organized a *coup* against the young duc de Guise and his brother. Condé's intention had been to release the hold Guise had over the boy-King, Francis II (the Amboise conspiracy, 16/17 March 1560). With two such ambitious men as Guise and Condé, each seeking an opportunity to exercise control over the country, conflict between them was inevitable.

C.III: 41

Boffeu fera efleu par le confeil,
Plus hideux monftre en terre n'aperceu.
Le coup volant prelat creuera l'oeil,
Le traiftre au roy pour fidele receu.

A hunchback will be elected by the conseil,
A more hideous monster on earth was not perceived.
The flying blow will pierce the chief, the eye,
The traitor to the King received as for a faithful friend.

confeil, (O.Fr.) avis; prelat, (O.Fr.) chef en général.

A HUNCHBACK: A MORE HIDEOUS MONSTER ON EARTH WAS NOT PERCEIVED

Louis de Bourbon, Prince of Condé was **A HUNCHBACK;**[1] he was also leader of the Huguenot party. Yet, despite his affiliation to the Protestant religion, Condé continued to live a licentious lifestyle, which he coupled with political ambition.[2] Nostradamus clearly disliked this deformed, duplicitous man, as is evident from this prophecy. It was also a sentiment shared by Condé's Calvinist supporters, for they subsequently denounced their leader as one who had sold his principles in return for political privileges.

"Calvin condemned Condé as a 'wretch who, in his vanity, had betrayed his God'."[3]

It was, however, precisely these character traits that the Queen-mother required to combat the Duke of Guise's political ambitions. Consequently, after Catherine had first pardoned the Prince for his treason against Francis II, her deceased son, she arranged for Condé to be ELECTED BY THE CONSEIL privé to a place on the King's Council. After taking office, the Queen-mother granted him the governorship of Picardy.[4]

It was in this new role that Condé took an active part in the Wars of Religion, but never for reasons of conscience. Instead, it was because he believed himself to be the rightful regent of France during Charles IX's minority. And it was with this goal in mind that he took up arms in the Second War of Religion. But while fighting at Jarna, in the Third War of Religion – a conflict, which proved to be the bloodiest of them all – Condé was captured. The King's brother, the duc d'Anjou, had joined the battlefield that day and, to his credit, won a splendid victory against the Huguenot army. Now, with Condé a prisoner-of-war, d'Anjou decided the opportunity had arrived to rid himself of this detestable man who was also the leader of the protestant Huguenots: hence, Nostradamus's use of *'prelat'*. D'Anjou therefore confided to his chief guard, Montesquioi, that Condé should not survive captivity. On 13 March 1569, while crossing the River Charente, Montesquioi fired his pistol at Condé's head, and THE FLYING BLOW[5] PIERCED THE CHIEF'S head, killing him instantly.[6]

> N.B. On two other occasions Nostradamus has used the phrase, 'piercing the eye' when referring to someone who has been shot through the head. Later, as these oracles progress, this expression will be seen to apply to the assassination of the Marshal d'Ancre and the shooting of Mussolini, both men having been shot through the head.

The oracle's final line turns to Condé's successor as head of the Huguenots, Gaspard de Châtillon, Comte de Coligny. This was a man who, for nearly ten years, had fought against the armies of Charles IX; that is to say, he was A TRAITOR TO THE KING.[7] But in 1571, in pursuit of peace and an end to religious warfare, Charles IX and the Queen-mother invited Coligny to return to Court.

RECEIVED AS A FAITHFUL FRIEND

The Protestant leader accepted the invitation, and lost little time in winning the affection of the fatherless monarch. The King, as mentioned before, RECEIVED Coligny AS A FAITHFUL FRIEND, even to the extent of calling him *"Mon Père."*[8]

The return of Coligny to court is of special interest because not only does he appear again in the next quatrain, but Condé's name and the manner of his death have very cleverly been inserted into the same oracle. The medical term for drilling a hole into a person's skull is *trepan*; the same word occurs in the French language. Hence: 'Condé trepan' means 'Condé trepanned'. The French word 'contrebandé', meaning 'outside the law', can be split into, con-treban-dé. By treating it as a paranagram, we obtain, firstly: Con–*trepan*–dé and secondly: Condé trepan. One can see from this example how Nostradamus employs very subtle methods to conceal the names of great men in seemingly innocent word formations.

C.VI: 75

Le grand Pilot par Roy ſera mandé,
Laiſſer la claſſe pour plus haut lieu attaindre:
Sept ans après ſera contrebandé,
Barbare armée viendra Veniſe craindre.

The great Pilot will be sent for by the King,
Leaving the army in order to attain a higher position:
Seven years later he will be contraband (Condé trepanned)
The foreign army will appear, Venice fearing.

Classe, (L) classis = political class, army, fleet; haut, (O.Fr.) élevé; contrebandé, (paranagram) Condé trepan; barbare, (Greek), foreign tongue.

THE GREAT PILOT

Gaspard de Coligny became Admiral of France in 1552; hence, THE GREAT PILOT.[1] Although the title of admiral appears nautical, in France it can also refer to a commander on land. It was while languishing in captivity for two years, following his capture at the battle of St Quentin that Coligny decided to convert to the Protestant faith. It was a decision that would play a major part in his life, and to what happened later.

In March 1562, as a result of the massacre of Protestants at Vassy, and the occupation of Paris by Guise for the Catholics, the Admiral left Court to join Louis de Bourbon 1st Prince of Condé at Meaux, and together the pair took the city of Orleans. It was this conquest that began the first of the civil wars, which continued in France until the end of the century.

WILL BE SENT FOR BY THE KING

By the end of the 1560s, Coligny had risen to become head of the political wing of the Huguenot party and Commander–in-Chief of its army. Such was the power and influence he now wielded, particularly across the south and west of France that it became impossible for Charles IX to ignore him. After much conferring between Charles and the Huguenot leader, he was SENT FOR BY THE KING.

LEAVING THE ARMY IN ORDER TO ATTAIN A HIGHER POSITION

"On 12 September 1571 Gaspard de Coligny arrived to join the Court at Blois . . . armed with a promise of safe conduct signed by the King, Anjou and Catherine."[2] His return to Court began with an ambitious campaign to re-unite France by allying the country with William I of Orange and Queen Elizabeth I of England, against the might of Spain in the Netherlands. These high-minded ideas meant that by LEAVING THE Huguenot-Politiques and the Protestant ARMY for service to the Crown, he had ATTAINED A HIGHER POSITION as councillor, and advocate to the King.[3]

Nostradamus now switches subjects without warning. He does this on a number of occasions, because it is an excellent method for throwing the determined investigator off the scent. Like the Delphic Oracle, Nostradamus is deliberately ambiguous when the solution to his foresight appears capable of becoming known before the predicted event has been fulfilled. This is seen by disbelievers as a fault with prophecy. Quite the reverse is true. It is because prophecy *is* a reality, the source of which exists outside of time and space, as will be argued in the Afterword, that free will has to be protected from 'outside' interference. For this reason, genuine prophets can rarely foretell their own future, lest they attempt to change it.

If prophecies were used to influence freewill so that it could alter these future events: then these future events could not have

33

existed in the first place, since they were not real parts of the future. If future events did not exist, then they could not be foreseen by a prophet. Sceptics, materialists, atheists, all base their disbelief in the paranormal on the sole existence of a three-dimensional world with its fleeting moments of time. Prophecy implies a block universe, where all states of time are coeval. Nostradamus affirmed this in his introductory letter to the *Centuries* four hundred years before Hermann Minkowski arrived at the same conclusion, closely followed by Albert Einstein. Time dilation, resulting from experimental evidence based upon the theory of Special Relativity is presently forcing the same concept upon a reluctant body of scientists. Their reluctance to accept this is because it undermines cause and effect: both being necessarily coeval within a block universe. All scientific theories based upon a three-dimensional world in which time passes, moment by moment, therefore become *theories from perception*. The greater truth depends upon an understanding that the familiar three-dimensional world in which all creatures live and move and have their being is derived from a block universe. Evolutionists and cosmologists particularly take note! The Big Bang may well mark the beginning of the three-dimensional universe, but not a block universe (see the Afterword).

SEVEN YEARS LATER HE WILL BE CONTRABAND – CONDÉ TREPANNED

The change of subject mentioned above refers to the Prince of Condé. He, too, left Court in 1562. But SEVEN YEARS LATER CONDÉ WAS TREPANNED. Alternatively, HE WAS CONTRABAND; that is to say, Condé was denied the law: having been killed by a shot to the head in 1569.[4] As a prince of the blood, it was his legal right to stand trial before his peers, but his murder denied him that right.

THE FOREIGN ARMY WILL APPEAR: VENICE FEARING

In the final line of this quatrain, Nostradamus provides further evidence of his timing ability. In the spring of 1570, one year after Condé's assassination, a FOREIGN ARMY APPEARED in the Mediterranean. This was a Turkish fleet, composed of three squadrons.[5] To disguise their intention, the ships crisscrossed the Aegean Sea before heading for the southern coast of Cyprus, where they landed an occupation force. Up until that time, Cyprus had belonged to *Venice*. But with VENICE FEARING the loss of its island would encourage further attacks, the city joined forces with the union recently established between Pope Pius V and Spain.[6] Together the new trio formed a Holy League that was determined to resist Turkey from gaining further territory.

This oracle began in 1562, at a time when Charles IX was still a minor, and his mother, regent of France. We now move to 1564, and pick up the train of events that began with the young King's two-year progress across his kingdom. The tour was politically important because it gave Catherine de' Medici an opportunity to pursue French interests in Navarre and Spain. As part of her itinerary, she had arranged two meetings, one with her son-in-law, Philip II of Spain – it will be recalled he had married her daughter Elizabeth, as part of the treaty of Cateau-Cambrésis – the other was with Jeanne d'Albret, Queen of Navarre, whose son would one day become King Henri IV. But, as Nostradamus predicted, things would not go well with the Queen-mother's plan.

C.II: 88

Le circuit du grand faict ruineux,
Le nom feptiefme du cinquiefme fera:
D'vn tiers plus grand l'eftrange belliqueux,
Mouton, Lutece, Aix ne garantira.

The round trip of the great one made ruinous,
The seventh title will result from the fifth:
Of a third, more great; the foreigner war-like,
Ram, Paris, Aix will not furnish a guarantee.

circuit, (O.Fr.) voyage circulaire; nom, (O.Fr.) titre; Lutece, (Latinism) Lutetia = Latin name for Paris; garantira, (O.Fr.) fournir une garantie.

THE ROUND TRIP OF THE GREAT ONE

The grand tour, or **ROUND TRIP OF** France, arranged by the Queen-mother Catherine de' Medici for her thirteen-year-old son King Charles IX, **THE GREAT ONE**, left Paris on 24 January 1564.[1] It would continue until 1 May 1566. The idea was to present the young King to the people, and encourage their allegiance to the monarchy. This seemed especially necessary at the time, because of the bloodletting that had occurred during the recent civil war (April 1562–March 1563).

MADE RUINOUS

While on tour, it was Catherine's intention to visit her daughter

Elizabeth, and her son-in-law Philip II. But her real aim was to propose two marriages. The first of these involved a union between her son Edouard (later Henri III) and Philip's sister Juana. The other marriage was to be between her daughter Marguerite and the King's son Don Carlos. But to Catherine's intense annoyance, Philip refused even to meet with her. Instead, he sent his emissary, the Duke of Alba, who dismissed both marriages out of hand.

Worse was to follow. Alba urged the Queen to renounce the peace treaty made with the Huguenots, the *Edict of Amboise*. This was a peace settlement, made on 2 March 1560, which pardoned all past crimes of religion in France on condition that the accused abjure their heresy. Spain did not approve. Alba strongly believed that religious dissidents had to be terrorized, and this was best achieved by executing their leaders.

Catherine therefore left Bayonne having gained nothing. On the contrary, she had aroused suspicions amongst the Huguenots, and placed in serious jeopardy the one fragile chance she had of bringing a lasting peace to France. Further disappointment awaited her at Navarre.

Catherine arrived in this southern kingdom, which divided France from Spain in the southwest, with the intention of forming a friendship with its Queen, Jeanne d'Albret, a stalwart defender of the Huguenot cause. But their coming together only caused further friction, and the unresolved enmity between these two Queens was to become yet another factor in the Wars of Religion that were to bedevil France for the next thirty years. In short, the Queen-mother's two major initiatives had not merely failed; they had, in fact, proved RUINOUS to any future prospect of peace.[2] Indeed, it was because of Alba, *"at Bayonne [and his] conversations with Catherine de Medici which led to the 2nd of the French Wars of Religion."*[3]

THE SEVENTH TITLE WILL RESULT FROM THE FIFTH

The second and third lines of this quatrain deviate from the King's tour, in order to predict the future of the Queen-mother's other children. Thus, *the seventh* child born to Catherine de' Medici and Henri II was Hercule (18. 3. 1555) duc d'Alençon. *The fifth* child was Edouard-Alexandre (b. 20 .9. 1551) duc d'Anjou.

When Charles IX died in 1574, the crown passed to his brother Edouard who chose to be known as Henri III. This released THE ducal TITLE d'Anjou, and it passed down the male line to his brother Hercule, *the seventh* child. Consequently, THE TITLE of THE SEVENTH child had RESULTED FROM that of THE FIFTH, [4] as Nostradamus foretold would happen.

THE THIRD MORE GREAT

Princess Claude was THE THIRD of Catherine's children, and she married another THIRD, Charles III of Lorraine. During the reign of Charles IX, his youngest brother Alençon had been promised the position of Lieutenant-General of France: the title had been surrendered by Edouard in December 1573, when he left France to become King of Poland. But Charles feared that Alençon might misuse the military power that went with this title, and perhaps seize the throne himself. The King therefore retracted his promise, and instead gave the position of Lieutenant-General to his brother-in-law, Charles III, *'the Great Duke of Lorraine'*, who therefore became even MORE GREAT. [5]

THE FOREIGNER WARLIKE

The other son-in-law of the Queen-mother was Philip II of Spain, THE FOREIGNER in the family. He had married Catherine's eldest daughter Elizabeth on 22 June 1559. Mother and daughter did not meet again until at Bayonne, during Charles IX's progress across France. The year after this meeting, Philip adopted a WAR-LIKE mood, and proposed to Catherine that he march 20,000 Spanish militia through eastern France, *en route* for Flanders. [6] The Queen-mother was appalled, believing it *'would set fire to the kingdom'*, and she declined. Philip was therefore forced to send the Duke of Alba at the head of 10,000 men through *'Savoy, Milan and Lorraine'*, in order to reach the Netherlands. Whilst there, Alba, acting on behalf of his King; that is, Catherine's son-in-law, executed or deported 1,105 of the 12,302 he brought to trial.

The reign of Charles IX is noted for two catastrophic events. The first of these was the outbreak of the French Wars of Religion, which began in April 1562; the second was his personal involvement in the Paris massacres, which started ten years later on the Eve of St Bartholomew's Day. Nostradamus alludes to both, as we shall now see, through the apt and judicious use of a single word apiece.

RAM

The first word, **RAM**, is another name for the constellation of Aries. Attention is therefore directed to the four weeks between March 21 and April 19. For it was between these dates that the Wars of Religion began (2 April 1562).[7] These conflicts were, in fact, a series of: *"petty and inconclusive civil wars between great noble connections fighting for the control of the crown."*[8] There would be nine wars in all, and they would occupy France until 1598.

PARIS

Charles's second great tragedy was the part he played in the massacres that began on the Eve of St. Bartholomew's Day. The killing spree broke out in **PARIS** on the night of 24 August 1572, and quickly spread across France.[9] Three thousand people perished in the capital alone, and another ten thousand in towns across France. *Paris* would not experience such bloodshed again until the French Revolution, two centuries later.

AIX WILL NOT FURNISH A GUARANTEE

The Edict of Amboise (2 March 1560), which had been the cause of contention between Alba and the Queen-regent in Bayonne, met with new opposition in the south of France. The parliament at **AIX**-en-Provence condemned it as unacceptable to them. In support of their opposition, the members made a defiant stand against the treaty by **REFUSING** outright **TO FURNISH A GUARANTEE** of pardon to anyone who had committed a crime of religion.[10] Retribution for this defiance towards the Crown was swift. On 23 October 1564, while still on his grand tour of France, the King suspended the *parlement* at Aix, and replaced it with a special commission of Parisian *parlementaires*.

Charles IX's progress through France is also of special note to those interested in the life of Nostradamus. Among the royal guests who visited the seer at Salon-de-Crau in October 1564, was Henri de Bourbon Prince of Navarre and Béarn. This ten-year-old was the second cousin to King Charles IX. Catherine de' Medici, with three young sons of her own, one of whom was already King of France, and with the Valois line of succession seemingly secure, requested Nostradamus to predict this young prince's future.

"The master of Henri's household was therefore amazed when Nostradamus visited him secretly, begging to see the young Prince. Afterwards the old seer told him: 'if you live, you will have for a master a King of France and Navarre'."[11]

The young man for whom Nostradamus made this prediction later grew to manhood and became Henri IV, one of France's greatest kings.

Nostradamus did not only predict for French rulers. He was also curious about the future of the papacy. Therefore, whenever a reigning pope was foreseen to be politically involved with France, Nostradamus forecast the occasion with a prophecy. In this respect, Catholics will be aware that the election of each new pope is considered to be a gift from God. Interestingly, therefore, Nostradamus's source of foreknowledge appears no less accurate when predicting the outcome of a papal election, than it has shown to be concerning the French monarchy. If Catholic thinking is correct when it teaches upon matters concerning the divine intervention of the Holy Spirit during the election of a pope, then the papacy will have no difficulty in accepting the prophecies of Nostradamus, nor the source of his inspiration. For, surely, they will readily agree it is only God who could conceivably achieve the total accuracy that is repeatedly demonstrated in these prophetic pronouncements.

C.X: 91

Clergé Romain l'an mil fix cens & neuf,
Au chef de l'an feras election
D'vn gris & noir de la Compagne yffu,
Qui onc ne feut fi maling.

Clergy, the Roman year 1609,
At the head of the year you will make an election
Of one grey and black, issued from the Compagne,
Who, at one time, was never so malicious

Compagne, (paragram) Compagn[i], and / or C[a]mpagne = the fields. Note that the first line is asyntactic to protect free will.

The oracle begins by appearing to state unambiguously that there will be a papal election in the year 1609, and the new pope will be recognized by the colours grey and black, also by his rural upbringing. This is a naïve approach. Nostradamus seldom, if indeed ever, predicts so openly. As he remarked in his letter to Henri II: *"Oh most Serene King . . . such secrets should not be bared except in enigmatic sentences having, however, only one sense and meaning, and nothing ambiguous or amphibological inserted."* One can therefore look in vain at what happened inside the Vatican during the year 1609. There was no election that year. In fact, one had to wait twelve years, until 9 February 1621, before a new pope was elected. Clearly, one must dig below the shallow ground of naivety if this prophecy is to be understood. Yet, at the same time, the solution must be available to independent scholarship, and not be reliant upon the personal imagination and bias of the interpreter, for which he or she always remains the sole authority.

CLERGY! THE ROMAN YEAR 1609

Look again at the word 'Roman'. It begs attachment to the noun, 'Clergy'. But the possibility cannot be discounted that it is also there to draw attention to the year 1609, adjacent to it. If that were the case, then Nostradamus would be referring to the Roman calendar inaugurated by Julius Caesar in March 45 BC. And, if we test this hypothesis, the year 1609 – commencing at the starting point of 45 BC – becomes 1564 AD [1] (there was no year zero). Suddenly the prophecy becomes alive with potential.

The year 1564 proved to be of outstanding importance in the Catholic Church. Between 13 December 1545 and 4 December 1563, the Council of Trent had been busy re-defining Christian doctrine, and exploring new ways of ridding the Church from the abuses that had accumulated in the past. The *Clergy* was also intent upon answering many serious points in theology. These were the ones raised by Protestants, particularly those by Luther and Calvin. On 26 January 1564 (**THE ROMAN YEAR 1609**), Pius IV was finally able to announce in public the decrees arrived at by the Council of Trent.[2] These were to provide the clergy with a framework of *'doctrinal clarity and ecclesiastical discipline'*, which would last for many centuries to come. Six months later, on 30 June 1564, Pius IV published *Benedictus Deus*, which confirmed the doctrine in formal terms.

1609, according to the Roman style of dating was a milestone that marked the theological deliberations of the Roman Catholic

Church. Nostradamus's is therefore correct when he draws the attention of the CLERGY to THE ROMAN YEAR 1609.

The next line in the prophecy continues to focus attention upon what was happening in Rome. It also provides a valuable lesson to those willing to study these prophecies seriously. They are not – as should be obvious from the foregoing oracles – focussed upon a single event on a single day. Instead, they are, as Nostradamus himself said: *perpetual.* They continue over a period of time, highlighting events that occur along the world's timeless corridor. It is, in fact, rather like walking along a passageway and viewing video clips of the most momentous events in history. Imagine a person from the past walking along this corridor. That person would see the same pictures, but for him or her, these would be scenes of future events. Such, then, we may now conjecture, were the many experiences of Nostradamus, whose visions appeared as if through a burning mirror.

AT THE HEAD OF THE YEAR, YOU WILL MAKE AN ELECTION

Pius IV died in December of the following year. After nine days of mourning, the cardinals met in conclave to choose his successor. AT THE HEAD OF THE YEAR (7 January) THEY MADE AN ELECTION. Their choice was Michele Ghislieri (Michel Gislier in French: 'gh' is not an opening combination in the Gallic tongue) who became Pius V. His election came as a complete surprise, although not to Nostradamus, for once again he has left clues to identify the successful candidate.

OF ONE GREY AND BLACK, BROUGHT FORTH FROM THE FIELDS

First of all there is the timing of the election, *at the head of the year*. No pope, either before or since, has ever been elected earlier than 7 January, the first week of the year. Secondly, it immediately followed the declaration of the Council of Trent, dated *1609, Roman* style, which is predicted in the first line of the oracle. Thirdly, Nostradamus refers to the elected pope as being *of grey and black*. The Pope's surname Gislier allows a paranagram to be formed: *viz.* Gisl( )er. This is an anagram of '*Grisle*', an old French word for GREY. Fourthly, BLACK refers to this particular Pope's entry into a religious order. At the age of fourteen, he changed his name from Antonio to Michele and became a Dominican. Dominicans are known as '*Black Friars*', [3] the sobriquet is derived

41

from the *black* mantle and *black* scapula that they wear. Fifthly, Ghislieri was born into humble circumstances. Before he entered the Dominican Order, he worked i*n the fields 'as a shepherd'.* [4] And it was **FROM THE FIELDS** that he was **BROUGHT FORTH** to a new life in the Church.

BROUGHT FORTH FROM THE COMPAGNI

The word 'Compagne', with its capital letter also suggests that a name or proper noun is to be understood. But for Pope Pius V, this does not apply. Moreover, the word is unusual in that it allows two paragrams to be formed. The first, 'C(a)mpagne', followed by 'yssu' allows the translation: 'brought forth from the fields', and this was true of Michele Ghislieri.

However, the second paragram, 'Compagni', followed by 'yssu' allows the translation: **BROUGHT FORTH FROM THE COMPAGNI**, which means born of the Compagni family. This immediately becomes prophetic, and even more so when it is read in conjunction with the final line of Nostradamus's oracle. The reason for this is because the successor to Pius V was *issued* or *brought forth* from the *'Bon-compagni'* family. Ugo Bon-compagni became Pope Gregory XIII on 14 May 1572. [5]

AT ONE TIME WAS NEVER SO MALICIOUS

One does not have to look far into the history of this pontiff's reign to discover that he **AT ONE TIME WAS NEVER SO MALICIOUS:** [6] *"Gregory XIII had publicly rejoiced at the St Bartholomew's day massacre of Huguenots on 24 August 1572 by attending a service of thanksgiving at the French church of San Luigi in Rome."* He also ordered that a medal be struck to commemorate the many thousands of Huguenots who had been butchered in the streets. Historians have rightly denounced his response, describing the murders that took place in France as *"one of the bloodiest massacres in European history."* Pope Gregory's **ONE-TIME, MALICIOUS** act in fulfilment of this prophecy is therefore rather obvious.

There is, however, a deeper level of prophecy in this quatrain. It commenced with a date from the calendar introduced by Julius Caesar, hence the Julian calendar. It ended with a prophecy of Pope Gregory XIII. It was this Pope who revised the Julian calendar, and by doing so, gave his papal name to what is now called the Gregorian calendar; it is this that is in use across the world today.

The quatrain also marks the first in a trilogy of dated oracles. Each one has, at first sight, been allocated to the first decade of the seventeenth-century. However, each of these three dates can only be correctly understood when assigned to a particular calendar. For, as in the case above, it was Nostradamus's confessed desire to obscure his predictions, lest he influence the natural course of future events. Three times, we shall see him state the year in which his prediction would be fulfilled, and three times he qualifies his announcement with an added word that provides a clue to the calendar he used.

It is also of some note that unlike other quatrains, Nostradamus made no attempt to set this particular verse to rhyme. Observe how the final line ends abruptly after only seven syllables. One possibility is that Nostradamus never edited this oracle. It is a suggestion that also finds support in the haphazard way it is presented. Each subject seems to fuse in with the one that follows, and this has caused past commentators to give up at ever understanding it, preferring instead to write it off as a failure. Yet, factually, everything is correct, although this only becomes apparent when clear separations are shown between the several subjects contained in its construction. A possibility also exists that these four lines represent a unique example of an oracle in its original form, or perhaps, Nostradamus's evening vigil was interrupted before the verse was completed.

A noted contemporary of Nostradamus was Mary Queen of Scots. For a short time she was also Queen of France (1559-60), having married Francis II in 1558. Mary has already appeared in C.X: 39 (see above) as the widow of the French King, and in the context of *two Isles in discord*. After the death of her husband, Mary Stuart returned to her native Scotland. Five years later, in July 1565, she remarried, this time to Henri Stuart Lord Darnley. But the marriage was not successful, and Mary's love interest was soon responding to the advances of James Hepburn, 4th Earl of Bothwell. His marriage to Lady Jane Gordon had ended in divorce after just one year, due to his adultery with a serving maid. Tragedy was certain to follow.

C.VIII: 23

Lettres trouvées de la Royne les coffres,
Point de fubfcrit fans aucun nom d'autheur,
Par la police feront cachez les offres,
Qu'on ne fçaura qui fera l'amateur.

Letters of the Queen found [in] the coffers,
Place of signature without any name of author,
The proposals will be hidden by the administration,
That one will not know who will be the lover.

fubfcrit, (Latinism) subscript/us; police, (O.Fr.) administration publique; offres, (O.Fr.) propositions, proposals; amateur, (Latinism) amator.

LETTERS OF THE QUEEN FOUND IN THE COFFERS

On the night of 9 February 1567, the body of Lord Darnley was found strangled in the grounds of Kirk o' Field, and his house destroyed by an explosion. Presumably the destruction of the house was a failed attempt at concealing the murder. The Scottish nobility was incensed by the crime, and immediately ordered the arrest of Bothwell's servants. Among those detained was George Dalgleish. While undergoing torture, he confessed to his investigators that he knew where incriminating evidence might be found. This, he said, was inside a house in Potterow. After a thorough search of the premises, a small **COFFER** was **FOUND;** inside was **ANOTHER COFFER** – a gilded casket – containing **LETTERS OF THE QUEEN.** [1]

PLACE OF SIGNATURE WITHOUT ANY NAME OF AUTHOR

The contents of these letters were to prove disappointing, for there was **NO SIGNATURE TO IDENTIFY THE AUTHOR,** nor was the name of the writer evident. Furthermore, not only did they lack any date, but the letters had neither a proper beginning nor a proper ending. [2]

THE PROPOSALS WILL BE HIDDEN BY THE ADMINISTRATION

Three weeks after Darnley's murder, the Earl of Bothwell was arrested for the crime and put on trial. He was also charged with a string of other offences relating to the content of the Casket Letters. Yet, remarkably, none of the letters were ever produced as evidence. In fact, **THE PROPOSALS** in the letters, and their very existence remained **HIDDEN BY THE ADMINISTRATORS** for a full eighteen months after their discovery. [3] Interestingly, when going to his execution, John Hay confided that the murder of Darnley was committed by Scottish nobles, who then tried to frame Bothwell and Mary for the crime. In which case, the letters would likely be forgeries, since at least one of the documents implicated the pair.

ONE WILL NOT KNOW WHO WILL BE THE LOVER

Mary, of course, completely denied all knowledge of the letters. It was therefore thought unnecessary to show them to her, and the case against the Queen was not pursued. In the event, only copies of the letters now survive. And so, who wrote them, and WHO THE LOVER WAS, CONTINUES TO REMAIN UNKNOWN, even to the present day.[4]

Mary's close relationship with Bothwell and the murder of his rival in love, her legitimate husband, turned the Scottish nobility against her. In 1567, under pressure, she was forced to abdicate. And in an attempt to separate her from further political influence, she was confined behind castle walls on the island of Lochleven. But ten months later an escape was planned. On 2 May 1568, with the help of devoted friends, Mary Stuart was smuggled out of her castle prison and taken across the water to where a waiting army had gathered. The plan was to restore her to the Scottish throne as quickly as possible.

C.I: 86

La grande royne quand fe verra vaincu,
Fera exces de mafculin courraige:
Sus cheual fluue paffera toute nue,
Suite par fer: à foy fera oultrage.

The great queen, when she shall see herself vanquished,
Will make excess of masculine courage:
On a horse, she will cross a river, as it were, naked:
Retinue in iron: to herself she will do injury.

fluve, (Latinism) fluv/us; toute, (O.Fr.) as it were.

THE GREAT QUEEN,

Eleven days after her escape from Lochleven, THE GREAT QUEEN Mary Stuart arrived at Langside, south of Glasgow, ready to wage battle for the recovery of her throne.

WHEN SHE SHALL SEE HERSELF VANQUISHED, WILL MAKE EXCESS OF MASCULINE COURAGE

On a hillside overlooking the battlefield, she was able to watch the fighting as her forces engaged the earl of Moray's army. But it was soon apparent that her side was losing, and she was about to SEE HERSELF VANQUISHED. It was then, WITH AN EXCESS OF MASCULINE

COURAGE that she mounted a charger and would have – *"like another Zenobia ridden into the battle, to encourage her troops to advance."* In words written by her servant to Catherine de' Medici: *"she would have led them to the charge in person."* [1] But upon arriving amongst her men, she found them in a quarrelsome mood, more interested in fighting each other than engaging the enemy.

ON HORSEBACK, SHE WILL CROSS A RIVER

Realizing that all was now lost, Mary quit the field of battle and headed south. Her flight ON HORSEBACK took her to Dumfries and ACROSS THE RIVER Dee,[2] *"where her escort destroyed the ancient wooden bridge to avoid pursuit."* Finally, she arrived on the shoreline of the Solway Firth. On 16 May, she crossed by boat into England, believing that her cousin, Queen Elizabeth, would give her sanctuary. She was to be disappointed.

AS IT WERE, NAKED

Up until her arrival in England, everything had been rushed; first, the secretive dash across water from Lochleven, then the hurried preparation for battle at Langside, and finally her subsequent flight into England; it was because of this haste that Mary had been forced to travel entirely without clothes of her own; AS IT WERE, NAKED, (Nostradamus clearly had his tongue in his cheek when he wrote this). Everything, including the disguise she wore when escaping from Lochleven down to her undergarments were borrowed: [3] *"a hurried escape from danger, in disguise, had left her with nothing in the way of a change of clothes."*

RETINUE IN IRON

The boat carrying Mary into England landed at Workington in Cumberland. Upon coming ashore, she was taken to nearby Carlisle Castle. From that time onwards, Mary was kept constantly under armed guard; this was to become her RETINUE IN IRON for the remainder of her life.[4]

After vainly appealing to Elizabeth for aid, she was removed to the castle at Bolton, and from there, she was taken to the medieval fortress of Tutbury. Her next place of confinement was the moated manor of Chartley Hall; finally, she was sent to Fotheringay, where she remained until her execution.

TO HERSELF, SHE WILL DO INJURY

After enduring seventeen years of captivity, Mary's final act was to **DO INJURY TO HERSELF.** A Catholic admirer had been plotting to free her, and at the same time assassinate Elizabeth. Coded letters passed between the former Scots Queen and her would-be rescuer. But, unbeknown to them their messages were being intercepted. The code she used was broken, and the secrets passing between her and her correspondent were read. The letters, all in her handwriting, clearly confirmed her complicity in the plot, and she was tried for treason and beheaded on 8 February 1587.[5]

Attention now shifts to France, and the Wars of Religion. These conflicts would continue, sporadically until the end of the century. The first war began with the capture of Orleans on 2 April 1562, when Louis, Prince of Condé took the city for the Huguenots, and Poltrot de Méré assassinated the Duke of Guise outside its walls.

The death of Condé has already been predicted, but Nostradamus has something more to impart concerning the death of the prince. And he now adds details to the events surrounding his capture. These were of special interest at the time, because they were not only humiliating but also illegal; recall that Condé was *'contraband'*: – outside the law.

C.III: 66

Le grand Baillif d'Orleans mis à mort,
Sera par vn de fang vindicatif:
De mort merite ne mourra, ne par fort,
Des pieds & mains mal le faifoit captif.

*The great Governor of Orleans put to death,
It shall be by one of vindictive blood:
He will not die from a worthy death, nor by vote,
By feet and hands, spitefully having bound him captive.*

Baillif, (O.Fr.) Gouverneur; fort, (O.Fr.) suffrage; mal, (O.Fr.) méchant; faifoit, (O.Fr.) faisser = to truss up.

THE GREAT GOVERNOR OF ORLEANS PUT TO DEATH

Through the good fortune of having captured the city at the outbreak of the First War of Religion, **THE GREAT** man, Louis, Prince of Condé, Head of the Huguenots, was able to declare himself **GOVERNOR OF ORLEANS.**[1] Three years later, he cemented his union with the city by marrying Françoise d'Orléans. But in 1569, he was **PUT TO DEATH.** It is this last event that occupies the predictive element of the quatrain.

47

HAVING SPITEFULLY BOUND HIM CAPTIVE BY HAND AND FOOT

It was during the 3rd War of Religion, while attempting to give support to Coligny's army at Jarnac in Poitou, that Condé was unhorsed and TAKEN CAPTIVE. Although having broken a leg from his fall, the Prince was nevertheless BOUND HAND AND FOOT and SPITEFULLY thrown head first over the back of a donkey.[2] In this ignominious position, suffering acute pain, he was led from the battlefield as a figure of ridicule.

HE WILL NOT DIE FROM A WORTHY DEATH, NOR BY VOTE

The capture of Condé was a huge triumph for the King's Catholic forces. What happened next was entirely illegal. A Prince of the royal bloodline had the right of nobility. This required that he be tried by *Parlement*, and if found guilty, a sentence could then be passed after a *vote* had been taken and agreed upon by his fellow peers. In Condé's case, this right was deliberately denied him. Instead, HE DIED AN UNWORTHY DEATH,[3] WITHOUT the VOTE[4] to which he was entitled; his life ending by a single gunshot to the head while held in captivity.

IT SHALL BE BY ONE OF VINDICTIVE BLOOD

The duc d'Anjou was known for his spiteful frame of mind. It was a trait he had inherited from his mother, Catherine de' Medici whose reputation for *vindictiveness* was well-known.[5] Nostradamus knew of her record, and had several times met her personally. Consequently, when he predicted the man who would order Condé's murder, it was not directly of d'Anjou that he spoke, but the VINDICTIVE BLOOD which he inherited from his mother.

This oracle has an interesting if inconsequential background. Commentators in the past have accepted the modern French meaning for *bailiff* and discovered that there was a local mayor of Orleans named Jérôme Groslot, who had apparently opened the gates to Condé in 1562. Since this was beneficial to the Calvinists, no action was taken against him until after Condé's death in 1569. In November that year, Groslot was arrested and condemned for his betrayal of the city, but being poorly guarded, he is said to have freed himself. The confusion between Groslot and Condé occurs because of the change in meaning to the word *bailiff*. Originally, a bailiff was the representative of the king, as Condé was in 1562, having recently been appointed to the King's Council by the Queen-regent in 1561 (see C.III: 41). It is therefore of some importance to note that much of what Nostradamus predicted was written in ancient French: this quatrain being an example.

Nostradamus's predictions are wide reaching, and not confined to events on land. One of the greatest sea battles of all time was fought just two years after Condé's assassination. The conflict occurred because Turkey had invaded Cyprus (see C.VI: 75). The island formerly belonged to Venice, and its loss was seen as a possible prelude to further invasions taking place. The triple alliance between Pope Pius V, Spain, and Venice responded to Turkish aggression by agreeing to combine their armies and form a Holy League (25 May 1571). This was to be their means of defending the territories they held against future attacks by the infidel.

C.IX: 42

De Barcellone, de Gennes & Venise,
De la Secille peste Monet vnis,
Contrare Barbare classe prendront la vise,
Barbar, poulse bien loing iusqu'à Thunis.

From Barcelona, from Genoa & Venice,
From Sicily, Juan moulds, unites,
Against a foreign fleet they will take strength,
Foreign tongues driven far away, even at Tunis.

Peste, (O.Fr. pester) pétrir; vise, (Latinism) vis; Monet, (Latinism) Moneta: Surname of Juno, (paranagram) Jun[a] = Juan, also, Moner/es: (Latin) = vessels with a single bank of oars; i.e., galleys; Barbare, (Greek.) foreign tongue.

FROM BARCELONA, FROM GENOA AND VENICE

In preparation for the battle to come, ships from VENICE AND GENOA,[1] many of which were galleys similar to the full size replica on display at the Maritime Museum in BARCELONA [2] (from where the Spanish fleet set sail), reached Messina on 24 August 1571. Of the fleet numbering 206 galleys, Spain contributed 80, and Venice 109. These were accompanied by a further 6 Venetian galleasses carrying substantial armoury.

FROM SICILY JUAN MOULDS, UNITES

With two hundred ships gathered together, the armada departed FROM SICILY bound for Corfu.[3] It arrived there on 15 September.

The Holy League's coalition forces had been placed in the hands of Don **JUAN** of Austria,[4] the half-brother of Philip II. Under his command, the quarrelsome admirals with their different opinions were **MOULDED** into a **UNITED** fighting force ready for battle.[5]

AGAINST THE FOREIGN FLEET THEY WILL TAKE STRENGTH

From Corfu, the ships of the Holy League advanced **AGAINST THE FOREIGN FLEET** that lay in the Gulf of Petros, near Lepanto (Návpaktos). In the naval battle that followed, **THE STRENGTH** of the allied force proved too great for the Turkish navy.[6] After a battle lasting five hours, Ali Pasha had lost 50 ships sunk and another 137 captured. Of his fighting force, 20,000 had been killed, wounded or captured, and 10,000 of his Christian galley slaves were set free. The victory of the alliance finally brought to an end the myth of Ottoman invincibility. The battle also made a great impact on European morale, because after the Ottomans had been overcome, they were unable to operate in the Mediterranean for many years afterwards.[7]

EVEN AT TUNIS

The Turkish loss of Tunis occurred two years after Lepanto. Don Juan having been fired by success became anxious to engage in further campaigns. But Philip was wary of his half-brother's motives, and allowed him only one further operation. This was to be an assault against the Turkish held city of **TUNIS**, which Don Juan conquered in 1573.[8]

The Massacre of St. Bartholomew's Day has been referred to above, both with reference to Pope Gregory XIII, who struck a medal to commemorate it, and to King Charles IX, who initiated it. But the massacre was not the King's original intention. It came about because Charles IX had been browbeaten into agreeing the murder of his former friend and companion, Gaspard de Coligny. His mother Catherine de' Medici had spent hour after hour remonstrating with her young son, forcing him to believe that the Huguenot leader was a conspirator and a threat to his throne. In fact, the truth was that the Queen-mother had been behind a bungled attempt on Coligny's life, and she was fearful that an enquiry would reveal her part in the plot. She needed Coligny dead to protect herself. But when word got out that the

King had given his consent to the killing of the Huguenot leader, mob rule took over.

C.IV: 47

Le noir farouche quand aura effayé,
Sa main fanguine par feu, fer, arcs tendus:
Treftout le peuple fera tant effraie:
Voyr les plus grans par col & pieds pendus.

The king black, savage, when he will have tried
His bloody hand, with fire, iron, and stretched bows:
Absolutely all of the people will be so afraid:
Witnessing the greatest ones hung by neck and feet.

Le noir (O.Fr.) black colour, also noir, (paranagram) roi[n]; Treftout, emphasis upon tout; col, (O.Fr.) cou.

THE KING BLACK, SAVAGE

The colour *black* was formerly used in art to signify *'evil, falsehood, error'*. [1] Nostradamus uses the same word in C.IX: 20, when describing Louis XVI's infamous flight to Varennes. But it was Charles IX, two hundred and twenty years earlier, who was first described as BLACK. This was because the KING gave permission for the assassination of Coligny: a man who till then had been his faithful friend. The murder ignited anti-Protestant passions in Paris to so great a degree that there was no containing the violence that flowed from it.[2] Even the King took an active part. The killing thereafter quickly spread to other towns and cities. By the time it had subsided, many thousands were dead.

WHEN HE WILL HAVE TRIED HIS BLOODY HAND WITH FIRE

In Paris, the murders happened *"under the eye of the king, himself, who enjoyed the sacrifice, and with a fowling-piece, from the windows of the palace, diverted himself with killing the few stragglers, who were attempting to make their escape."*[3]

IRON AND STRETCHED BOWS

Those coming under the eye of the *savage king* were the frightened people who had entered the palace courtyard while trying to escape their would-be killers on the streets outside. But upon entering the square they were confronted by the IRON AND STRETCHED BOWS of *"the King's archers, who pushed the terrified men and women on to the halberds of the Swiss guards, who impaled their unarmed quarry with grim efficiency."*[4]

51

ABSOLUTELY ALL OF THE PEOPLE WILL BE SO AFRAID

This orgy of burning and killing lasted for three days, terrifying the people as the numbers of dead rapidly increased. Three thousand people were murdered in Paris, alone, and another ten thousand in the provinces, most notably Bordeaux, Toulouse, Rouen, Lyons, Troyes, and Orleans.[5]

WITNESSING THE GREATEST ONES HUNG BY NECK AND FEET

Coligny, the warlord, the statesman, the Huguenot chief, and King Charles's councillor was the first to die. Whilst laying in bed at the Hôtel de Béthisy, recovering from the wound inflicted during the Queen-mother's bungled attempt at plotting his assassination, a partisan of the duc de Guise named Besme, broke into the room, and stabbed him. He was then disembowelled and thrown from the upstairs window of the Hôtel. The mob in wait below dragged the still breathing man away and HUNG HIM BY THE NECK from a gibbet. But, being discontented with what they had done, they took him down and cut off his head: this was later dispatched to Pope Gregory XIII as a Catholic trophy. Coligny's decapitated body was then tossed into the Seine, but then quickly recovered so that it could again be hung from the gibbet at Montfaucon. However, since the torso was headless, the body had to be HUNG BY ITS FEET.[6]

Catherine de' Medici's spitefulness, vindictiveness, her conspiracies, and the suspicions she aroused over the deaths (some say unnatural deaths) of her two sons, Francis and Charles – deaths that benefited her political ambitions by giving her two regencies – was much in evidence in the case of Gabriel, Comte de Montgomery.

It had been this knight's terrible misfortune to be the accidental cause of Henri II's death during a tournament joust that had been arranged to celebrate the double wedding of his sister, and daughter (C.I: 35). Whilst lucid, the King had commanded that no reprisals should be taken against his victor. Nevertheless, Montgomery wisely left Paris. His first call was to the family estate in Normandy, but even there he felt unsafe and soon after departed for England. Many years later, excited by the Protestant cause in the French Wars of Religion, he judged it safe to return and play his part in what was happening.

The choice proved fatal. While defending the castle at Domfront, he was betrayed and taken prisoner. When Catherine de' Medici received news of his capture her vindictive nature cried out for vengeance. In Montgomery she saw the living cause of the disasters that had plagued France since the death of her husband. Ignoring her deceased husband's plea for clemency in this matter, she at once began planning the Count's trial with a view to his execution.

C.III: 30

Celuy qu'en luite & fer au fait bellique,
Aura porté plus grand que lui le pris:
De nuit au lit fix lui feront la pique
Nud fans harnois fubit fera furpris.

The one that in contest and weapon at the martial act,
Will have taken the prize greater than he:
By night in bed, six will take the grudge to him,
Naked, without armour, swiftly he will be surprised.

luite = lutte; fer, (O.Fr.) arme; pique, (O.Fr.) quarrel, grudge; subit, (O.Fr.) swift, quick, hasty.

THE ONE THAT IN CONTEST AND WEAPON AT THE MARTIAL ACT

This verse begins with a recognizable description of Count Montgomery's victory over Henri II in the summer of 1559. The event took place IN a CONTEST held to celebrate two marriages: that of the King's daughter Elizabeth, and the other of his sister Marguerite. It was AT THE MARTIAL ACT of jousting; involving two iron clad combatants charging on horseback at each other with shield and lance that Montgomery's WEAPON shattered on impact, fatally wounding the King.

WILL HAVE TAKEN THE PRIZE GREATER THAN HE

Montgomery therefore becomes THE ONE who WILL HAVE TAKEN THE PRIZE for defeating his opponent, King Henri II: a man GREATER THAN HE.[1] After the accident, Montgomery left France to spend fifteen years in voluntary exile in England. At the end of that time, he judged it safe to return to his homeland. His intention was to join the Protestant cause in the French Wars of Religion, and he began with several early victories. But it was while defending the medieval fortress at Domfront with its walls several metres thick, that he found himself outnumbered.

15,000 Royalist (and more significantly Catholic) troops laid siege to 110 Protestant rebels holding the fortress of Domfront. The rebel leader Count Gabriel de Montgomery withstood the assault until treacherously captured in the early hours of May 26th.[2]

SWIFTLY SURPRISED: NAKED WITHOUT ARMOUR

His betrayal came at night, when one of his men secretly opened the fortress gates to the enemy. A small number of the Maréchal's men entered the castle, and quietly mounting the stairs SWIFTLY SURPRISED Montgomery while asleep, thus finding him NAKED WITHOUT ARMOUR. − *"Unarmed, Montgomery was captured in his bedchamber after a traitor had opened the gates during the night to the Royalist troops."*[3]

BY NIGHT SIX WILL TAKE THE GRUDGE TO HIM

SIX was the number of men thought sufficient to accomplish the kidnapping of a single person [Frieda, p.329]. However, given the cryptic nature of these oracles, and their propensity to contain double meanings, it is not impossible that *six* also refers to the month of June, when Catherine de' Medici quite literally TOOK HER GRUDGE TO HIM.

News of Montgomery's capture reached Catherine de' Medici three days later at Vincennes, where she was administering to her dying son, Charles IX. With some satisfaction at reviving THE GRUDGE she bore Montgomery, the Queen-mother gave the King the news. *"Madame, all human affairs no longer mean anything to me,"* he replied. But they meant everything to Catherine: for having obtained from Charles his signature, authorising her to assume the regency after his death, she lost no time in seeking revenge for her dead husband.

Montgomery had to be punished . . . Filled with hatred for the man who had 'killed' her husband, it became her obsession that he should be brought to justice for his 'regicide'.[4]

After Montgomery's capture, he was transferred to Caen and from there to the Conciergerie in Paris, where he was encased horizontally in an iron cage to await trial. On 3rd June, three days after the death of Charles IX, the Paris *Parlement* ratified Catherine's new powers as regent. Three weeks later, armed with the executive power that went with her position as ruler of France, she ordered Montgomery's trial to commence. On 27 June 1574, he *"was decapitated and écartelé (quartered)."*[5]

An alternative account of the siege at Domfront also exists. This alleges that Montgomery surrendered the castle in exchange for his life and the lives of his men. This is more believable if applied to an agreement made between the Catholic Commander, Maréchal Matignon, and the man who betrayed Montgomery. Nostradamus has foretold which of these two accounts is correct.

C.VI: 11

Des fept rameaulx à trois feront reduictz,
Les plus aifnés feront fuprins par mort:
Fratricider les deux feront feduictz,
Les coniurés en dormant feront mort.

From seven branches they will be reduced to three,
The most senior will be surprised by death:
The two will be seduced to fratricide,
The oath-takers in Dormans (napping) will be dead.

conjurés, (Latinism) coniur/o: (military), to take and oath; dormant, (paragram) sleeping, also Dorman[s].

FROM SEVEN BRANCHES THEY WILL BE REDUCED TO THREE

During the reign of Henri II and Catherine de' Medici, the Queen gave birth to ten children of which *seven* survived into adulthood: the age of majority at that time being fourteen. But by 1575, the year after Charles IX's death, the Queen-mother's *seven* children; that is, **THE SEVEN BRANCHES**, had been **REDUCED** by death **TO THREE**.[1]

THE MOST SENIOR WILL BE SURPRISED BY DEATH

In 1575, the *three* surviving children were King Henri III (b. 1551), Marguerite, (b. 1553), and Hercule, (b. 1555). The order in which Henri III's four eldest siblings died is as follows: Francis II, b.1544, d.1560; Elisabeth, b.1545, d.1568; Charles IX, b.1550, d.1574; Claude, b.1547, d.1575.[2] The mathematical probability of specifying that it will be **THE** four **MOST SENIOR TO BE SURPRISED BY DEATH** is one chance in thirty-five. In other words, had Nostradamus been using guesswork, he had thirty-four opportunities of being wrong, and only one chance of making the right choice.

THE TWO WILL BE SEDUCED TO FRATRICIDE

In September 1575, just months after the death of their sister Claude, **THE TWO** surviving brothers became **FRATRICIDAL**. Henri III had decided upon a policy of keeping his two remaining siblings apart, so that he could exercise better control over their political aspirations. In particular, he was suspicious of the confidences shared between his brother, his sister, and her husband Henri of Navarre. In an attempt to divide them, he first spread the false tale of a love affair involving Marguerite and a courtier. Next, he engaged the services of the beautiful Charlotte, Baroness de Sauve. She was instructed to SEDUCE THE TWO men, Navarre and Alençon, and to set them against each other in the single pursuit of her sexual favours.

Eventually, because of the tensions produced by this love triangle, Alençon secretly left Court, *raging against his brother*. His destination was Dreux, where he joined Henri III's enemies, the *Huguenot-Politiques*. Furious, at Alençon's treachery, the King, too, became FRATRICIDAL. He put together a squadron of loyal officers, ordering them to bring back his brother *"dead or alive."* [3]

At the time when repercussions to these intrigues were taking place, an armed force of German Reiters led by Guillaume de Thoré, entered France. This fighting force of trained militia belonged to the cavalry of John Casimir, son of the Palatine Elector in Bavaria; they were mercenaries: men who had sworn to serve their military commander.

THE OATH-TAKERS IN DORMANS, SLEEPING, WILL BE DEAD

In the month following Alençon's escape from Paris, Thoré's German Reiters invaded northern France in an attempt to advance the Protestant cause. AT DORMANS (10 October 1575) they were met by Henri duc de Guise at the head of a Catholic army. THE OATH-TAKERS; that is, mercenaries, were ill prepared for the encounter – caught SLEEPING – and Guise imposed a heavy defeat on them, leaving many of their number DEAD. [4]

Politically, because the King had threatened the life of his brother, the duc d'Alençon, the whole of France was placed in a state of unease. It was therefore left to the Queen-mother to restore order.

C.III: 39

Les fept en trois feront mis en concord
Pour fubiuguer des alpes & Apennines:
Mais la tempefte & Ligure couade,
Les profligent en fubites ruines.

The seven into three will be placed in harmony,
For the subduing of the Alps and Apennines:
But the violent combat and League, dastardly,
Destroying them in sudden ruin.

tempeſte, (O.Fr.) combat violent; Ligure, (epenthesis) Ligue; couade, (O.Fr.) dastardly, cowardly; profligent, (Latinism) proflig/o.

As a result of the growing disunity between her three children, Catherine de' Medici set about accomplishing a peaceful reunion by bringing her two sons together for a meeting. The result of this diplomacy was the treaty known as the *'Peace of Monsieur'*. But, it was achieved only at the expense of compromises. Thus, as is often the case, by helping one side in the debate, it aggravated the other.

THE SEVEN INTO THREE

As we have already seen, by 1575, **THE SEVEN** surviving children of Henri II and Catherine de' Medici had been reduced by death **TO THREE:**[1] Henri III, King of France, his younger brother Hercule-François, Duke of Alençon and Marguerite, Queen of Navarre: also called Margot.

Alençon not only hated his brother Henri, but had even plotted to take the crown for himself. Henri, in turn, detested his sister Margot. This dysfunctional situation worsened in 1576 when Margot's husband Henri of Navarre, escaped from the close supervision imposed upon him at Court. As a result, Margot was arrested as an accomplice. For some time afterwards she feared the King would take advantage of her captivity, and have her murdered.

WILL BE PLACED IN HARMONY

It was to heal these family wounds that their mother stepped in with a remedy. The state was disintegrating fast. If the nation and the Valois dynasty were to be saved, then the King must act; he must make peace with his brother. On 6 May 1576, an agreement between the two brothers was reached, and the *Peace of Beaulieu*, also known as the *Peace of Monsieur*, was signed. Six months later, the two brothers met at a country manor called Ollainville, where they: *"kissed and embraced each other"*, agreeing to put aside their differences.[2]

In June of the following year, to complete this contrived HARMONY BETWEEN THE Queen-mother's THREE surviving children; Margot agreed to join her two brothers at Chenonceau for a banquet that had been arranged by their mother to celebrate Alençon's military success at La Charité-sur-Loire. We shall read more of this victory further down.

FOR THE SUBDUING

In 1576, the year that coincided with the reconciliation of the two brothers and their sister, an attempt, based upon their renewed unity, was made TO SUBDUE animosity between the two immovable rocks of western religion – Calvinism and Catholicism. This relied for its success upon the treaty Henri III and his brother d'Alençon had signed up to. Included within it were sixty-three articles that gave Huguenots an assurance of virtual parity with the Catholics. The treaty also condemned the St. Bartholomew's Day Massacre as a criminal act. [3]

OF THE ALPS AND APENNINES

Note, particularly, the two mountain ranges referred to in this oracle; each one is an allegorical references to the rock-hard locations that were the centres of Calvinist and Catholic operations. For instance, THE Savoy ALPS overlook Geneva [4] where John Calvin had established his base for the Huguenot revolt against Rome, and which eventually led to France's thirty-six years of intermittent religious warfare. THE APENNINES stretch through central Italy, and include the Umbrian-Marchigian range from where the river Tiber flows into Rome, the heart of the Catholic religion. [5]

The attempt at brokering a peaceful solution between these two rock-hard religious factions failed. The Catholics saw it as being too favourable to the Huguenots, and in 1576, they made known their displeasure by forming the Holy Catholic League. Its intention was to draw members of the Roman Church together under the leadership of the powerful duc de Guise. He was to act as a rallying point for the recruitment of men, arms, and money in an effort to encourage allegiance to the Catholic Church in France. In fact, it acted as a trigger for the Sixth War of Religion (March – December 1577). [6]

On 2 May, in the midst of this war, the Huguenot town of Charité-sur-Loire became the scene of **VIOLENT COMBAT** when it was overrun by the Dukes of Nevers and Anjou. (After the reconciliation between Henri III and his brother, Alençon was given the ducal title Anjou: see C.II: 88). It was for the conquest of this town that the Queen-mother threw a banquet at Chenonceau, when Marguerite attended to complete the unity between the Queen-mother's three surviving children (see above).

With Charité-sur-Loire in the League's hands, Anjou demanded that all Huguenots should be executed. But Guise intervened to prevent the intended massacre. Anjou therefore turned his attention to another Protestant town, Issoire in the Auvergne.

On 12 June, Issoire was forced to surrender to Anjou's Catholic army, now part of **THE LEAGUE**. Again, Anjou demanded the deaths of all Huguenots. But there was no one now to deny him his bloodlust, and while **DESTROYING THEM** he reduced the town to **SUDDEN RUIN**. In all, some three thousand citizens were murdered.[7]

This proved to be a particularly **DASTARDLY** act on Anjou's part, because his victims shared the same religious beliefs that only a few months previously he had accepted as his own. For after fleeing the Court, he had joined the Huguenots at Dreux to support their religion.

Some commentators believe Nostradamus dabbled in magic: that he outwardly embraced the Christian Church, while secretly practising occultism. If so, then he was doubly rewarded, because in the next oracle he visits the past in order to provide the exact date on which Jesus Christ was crucified.

C.VI: 54

Au poinct du iour au fecond chant du coq,
Ceulx de Tunes, de Fez, & de Bugie:
Par les Arabes captif le Roy Maroq,
L'an mil fix cens & fept, de Liturgie.

*At daybreak, at the second crowing of the cock,
Those of Tunis, of Fez, and of Bougie:
By reason of the Arabs, the King captive, Morocco,
The year 1607, from Liturgy.*

AT DAYBREAK AT THE SECOND CROWING OF THE COCK

The opening line of this quatrain is taken straight from the Bible (*Mark* 14:30 & 14:72). It concerns the prediction made by Jesus to the Apostle Peter on the night of his betrayal and arrest; in other words, the eve of Christ's crucifixion. We shall see its importance to this oracle below.

The three towns mentioned in the quatrain are all in North Africa, each one being situated in a different country; that is, Tunisia, Morocco and Algeria: (Bougie is the former name of Bejaïa). At the time this prediction was fulfilled, Murad III was Sultan of Turkey and he controlled all three towns.[1]

In 1578 the deposed Moroccan Caliph al-Mutawakkil, joined forces with King Sebastian of Portugal in a bid to conquer the whole of Morocco. Portugal already held the northern half of the country, having first taken Ceuta, opposite Gibraltar in 1415. King Sebastian was therefore already *King of Morocco*, and he believed it to be his divine mission in life to conquer the whole of that country and convert its population to Christianity.

THOSE OF TUNIS, OF FEZ AND OF BOUGIE

Opposition to the invasion came from an *Arab* section and from Caliph Abd al-Malik, who was supported by Murad III of Turkey: in other words those of **TUNIS, FEZ, AND BOUGIE** who were under the rule of Murad III. It was also Abd al-Malik who had deposed al-Mutawakkil, King Sebastian's ally.

BY REASON OF THE ARABS, THE KING A CAPTIVE IN MOROCCO

The reference to an *Arab* involvement is historically correct. Between 1525 and 1554, the Sa'dids had established their rule over Morocco by taking control of the southern part of the country. The Sa'dids were of *Arab* origin, and claimed to be sharifs; that is, descendants of the prophet, Muhammad.[2] As Moslems, they were therefore opposed to becoming Christian converts.

Together, the forces of Abd al-Malik and his Sa'did Moroccans met the alliance of King Sebastian and al-Mutawakkil at Ksar el-Kebir on 4 August 1578. In the ensuing conflict, known as the Battle of the Three Kings, the Portuguese, although numbering 20,000 armed men, were heavily defeated **BY THE ARABS** and their North African allies. Forced to retreat, the army of Sebastian reached only as far as the Wadi al-Makhazin, which it found in full flow. Trapped between the water and the Sa'dids of Abd al-Malik, Sebastian and al-Mutawakkil had no choice but to surrender. **THE KING** was now a **CAPTIVE IN MOROCCO**, but what happened next is undocumented. It is known only that the bodies of both King Sebastian and al-Mutawakkil were later discovered drowned in the Wadi.[3]

THE YEAR 1607, FROM LITURGY

Nostradamus has predicted this event for 1607. But, again, as before, in C.X: 91, the year is not to be taken at face value; the clue to its meaning occurs in the word, *Liturgy*: a reference to the Last Supper, which took place on the evening Jesus predicted that before the crowing of the cock at daybreak, Peter would deny knowing him. And it is to this that Nostradamus makes a reference in the opening line of this quatrain. Therefore, to understand the calculation required for dating this prophecy, it is necessary to count the years that passed between the Last Supper and 1607. But since the year of Christ's crucifixion remains unknown, it is necessary to count backwards, using the date Nostradamus has given, and the date when this prediction was fulfilled. Consequently, 1607 minus 1578 equals 29. This must then be the year in which Jesus was crucified. Or, in other words: **THE YEAR 1607**, counting from the time of Christ's Crucifixion; that is **FROM LITURGY**, leaves a difference of 1578: the year when this prophecy involving King Sebastian of Morocco became fulfilled.

In fact, the date of Christ's crucifixion, according to the Jewish calendar, would have been the 13th of Nissan, 3789: equivalent to Friday 13th of April 29 AD. This was the day before Passover, which commenced at sundown on the 14th of Nissan. Jesus would therefore have been thirty-three years of age at the time of his death. This calculation coincides with the gospel of *St John* (19:31-36), which states that the crucifixion took place on Preparation Day (i.e., preparation for celebrating the Passover).[4]

Readers interested in biblical prophecy may wish to know that the coming of the Messiah had exercised the minds of the prophets long before the birth of Jesus. *Psalm 22* verses 1-18, foretell in detail the very same sufferings experienced by Jesus on the cross. It is therefore difficult to suppose that history will repeat itself, and bring the Psalmist's prophecy to a second ful-filment for the satisfaction of those awaiting a later Messiah.

As to whether or not one accepts 29 AD as the true date of Je-sus' death on the cross rather depends upon the confidence one has in Nostradamus's ability to predict the future, and to cor-rectly date what he foresaw. What remains certain is that Nostradamus has deliberately inserted this prophecy into his selection of oracles to foretell a somewhat inconsequential event in Portuguese history. There seems to be no reason for this other than his need to find an event for 1578, so as to arrive at 1607.

Why is 1607 so important? It is because Nostradamus uses this same year in order to date the birth of Jesus Christ. He achieves this by once again supplying a suitable word as a clue. In this way, 1607 is made to be a complementary date; on one occasion it is used to count the number of years from the Cruci-fixion: on the second occasion it is used to reckon the number of years from the birth of Jesus. The ingenuity required to achieve these two important dates in the Christian calendar from a single year, based upon the prediction of events long after the death of the man who made them, surpasses the remarkable, and is left for the reader to ponder over. It is also noteworthy that both prophecies dated 1607 also refer to events centred upon the Christian religion. For the Crucifixion, it is King Sebastian's at-tempt to convert Morocco to Christianity; for the Birth, it is the Christian fight against Copernican's revolutionary system of or-biting planets, as we shall discover in Chapter 3.

The next oracle appears designed to shed further light upon Nostradamus's self-confessed ability to date events correctly. From 1562 up until 1598, France was embroiled in its Wars of Religion. Exactly half way between these two dates is the year 1580, and the seer specifically refers to this year, adding some-what cryptically, the words, *plus and minus*. This would seem to indicate that the same number of years should be added to 1580 as are subtracted from it. Since the Wars began in 1562, and the quatrain specifically refers to 1580, thus producing a difference of 18 years, the implication is that a further 18 years must be added to 1580 in order to arrive at the date when the Wars would finally end. Factually, this is historically correct. The Wars of Religion which began in 1562 ended in 1598; which is to say: IN THE YEAR **1580** MINUS AND PLUS 18.

To those who can only refer this to yet another coincidence, Nostradamus adds two more dates. The second part to this split quatrain refers to the year **1703**. During that year, he predicted five political changes would take place, which they did.

For some reason, it seems he was not content with this prophecy, and in a footnote first published c.1700, and reproduced by Anatole le Pelletier in 1867, Nostradamus provided an alternative prediction. This proved to be a warning of extreme weather conditions in France for the winter of **1708-9** – the season that came to be known in France as the *'Great Winter'*.

C.VI: 2

En l'an cinq cens octante plus & moins,
On attendra le fiecle bien eftrange:
En l'an fept cens, & trois cieux en tefmoings
Que plufieurs regnes vn à cinq feront change.

The alternative ending

En l'an fept cens et neuf cieux feront tefmoings,
Que pour de l'or en bled non fans peine il change.

In the year '580 plus and minus,
One will notice the most peculiar period:
In the year '703, the heavens as witness,
When several realms, one to five, will change.

In the year '709, the skies shall be proof,
When not without grief, he exchanges abroad its corn for gold.

attendra, (Latinism) atten/do; regne, (O.Fr.) royaume; pour, (O.Fr.) dehors

IN THE YEAR **1580** PLUS AND MINUS

1580 was not only the year when France reached the halfway point in its Wars of Religion; hence, PLUS AND MINUS that year, it also marked the occurrence of *'the Lovers' War'*. In April, the Huguenots of Montauban launched an offensive, which they claimed was prompted by an affair between Henri of Navarre's wife, Marguerite, and the vicomte de Turenne.[1] The conflict began after some offensive remarks were made by Henri III about his sister Marguerite, and it continued for more than seven months. Although relatively minor, the skirmishes were classified as the 7th War of Religion. It was finally brought to a close on 26 November with the Peace of Fleix.

France's Wars of Religion were fought intermittently for 38 years, and marked A MOST PECULIAR PERIOD in the history of France.

> *Town was divided against town, village against village, family against family. Armed affrays and assassinations were committed out of religious fanaticism, others in pursuit of private vengeance, others, as in all times when the hideous taint of espionage infects the body politic out of a sense of terror.*[2]

The next date in the oracle can now be considered. In this, we are told that FIVE REALMS WILL CHANGE IN THE YEAR 1703; these changes can now be verified as follows:

[1] On 18 May 1703, following eleven days of fighting, John Churchill 1st Duke of Marlborough finally took Bonn, defeating Louis XIV's ally, the Archbishop of Cologne, and depriving him of his territorial rule along the Rhine.[3]

[2] In the same year, Portugal detached itself from French rule by the aid of the Treaties of Methuen. The first treaty was signed in May 1703, and guaranteed the country's new alliance with Archduke Charles, second son of Emperor Leopold of Austria; the second, was signed in December, and was a trade agreement. This new alliance gave Portugal a new ruler, Sebastien Pombal, who became the country's virtual dictator protected by Joseph I.[4]

[3] 1703 was also the year that brought change to the country ruled by Victor Amadeus II. He had ruled Savoy from the age of nine under the regency of his French mother. He later married Louis XIV's niece, Anna d'Orléans. At the beginning of the War of the Spanish Succession he allied himself with the interests of France, but in 1703 the position changed and he took sides with France's enemies, the Habsburgs. Louis XIV responded to this change by invading Savoy and depriving him of its rule.[5]

[4] The fourth change occurred in Turkey. In 1703, Mehmed IV died and his son, Ahmed III became the country's new Sultan. Ahmed fostered good relations with France and adopted the lifestyle of Louis XIV as his role model. As a consequence, he built several palaces on a grand scale and gave frequent parties in the fashion set by the Court at Versailles.[6]

[5] The fifth and final change to occur in 1703 took place at Kartli in Georgia on the Black Sea coast. Turkey had overrun the whole region as far back as 1578, but fifty years later, the occupying force was Persia. In **1703**, Vakhtang VI became regent of the district and, subsequently, King of Kartli. In fact, his reign was the most outstanding amongst all others. For among his achievements were those of lawgiver and scholar. He also introduced printing into the country and set up a commission of academics to compile and edit the history of Georgia.[7]

IN 1709, THE SKIES SHALL BE PROOF,

The footnote or afterthought, which Nostradamus applied to this oracle, predicted the harshness of **THE GREAT WINTER OF 1709**.[8] It eventually took so fierce a hold on the country that it forced the authorities to take action.

WHEN NOT WITHOUT GRIEF

The terrible winter of 1709 brought GRIEF to many; both cold and hunger killed thousands of people as famine spread across the land. Bonfires had to be lit in the town squares to alleviate suffering, and the rivers Loire and Rhine froze over to form a bridge of ice. This caused consternation amongst villagers dwelling along the banks, for the people feared it would invite invasion. And in the cemeteries, the dead lay unburied because the frozen ground had become too solid for digging.

HE EXCHANGES ABROAD ITS CORN FOR GOLD

On 19 April, the *Paris Parlement* ordered every city and every parish to accept responsibility for the poor in their area. It also directed that a proportion of every person's income (approximately 3%) be paid monthly to either the *Bureau de Bienfaisance* or the *Comité de Charité* to compensate for the damaged harvest. Even *the King, Louis XIV*, was not exempted from this tax, and HE had to pay *'4,220 livres'* from his own purse. The total revenue was then EXCHANGED FOR CORN from ABROAD, most notably from Dalmatia and North Africa.[9]

After providing these dated prophecies, Nostradamus resumes the course of France's future history with further evidence of his prescient powers by naming two of the country's leading families. In the 1580s, the Houses of Lorraine and

Vendôme each believed themselves to be the legitimate successor to the French throne, should the last of the Valois kings die childless as seemed probable. Nostradamus therefore outlined some of the major events that were to take place involving these two Houses shortly before Henri III's death.

C.X: 18

Le ranc Lorrain fera place à Vendofme,
Le hault mys bas, & le bas mys en hault,
Le filz d'Hamon fera efleu dans Rome
Et les deux grands feront mys en deffault

The resentful Lorraine will give place to Vendôme,
The high placed low, and the low placed on high,
The son of Haman will be raised up inside Rome,
And the two great ones will be placed in default.

ranc, (O.Fr. & apocope - rancor) ressentiment; efleu, (O.Fr.) eslever = to raise in rank or dignity; Hamon, (biblical name) Haman.

After Charles IX died in 1574 without producing a legitimate heir, his younger brother Edouard changed his name to Henri before succeeding to the throne. This line of inexperienced youths, which began with Francis II, was the principal reason why Henri of Lorraine, 3rd Duke of Guise, Prince of Joinville, and his brother Louis, Cardinal of Lorraine, were able to exercise so much power in the affairs of France. So effective were they politically that ultimately they came to be seen as the virtual rulers of the country; indeed, it was even said at the time that together with Henri III, France was ruled by three kings.

THE RESENTFUL LORRAINE WILL GIVE PLACE TO VENDÔME

The oracle, however, predicts *resentment* within the House of Lorraine. This came about when Guise and his brother were both murdered by order of the King: an action that was intended to remove the two obstacles to his total sovereignty. It was these deaths that compelled the House of **LORRAINE TO GIVE FIRST PLACE TO VENDÔME**: a rival dynastic family headed by the duc de *Vendôme*.

France had desperately needed to find a suitable successor to Henri III who, though married since 1575, was without an heir and unlikely to produce one. The duc de Guise and his brother had always seen themselves as eventual successors, but their assassination removed this option, and this explains the House of **LORRAINE'S** deep **RESENTMENT** at the murders: a resentment that was to have fatal consequences for the King.

THE HIGH PLACED LOW AND THE LOW PLACED ON HIGH

Up until their deaths in December 1588, Henri duc de Guise and Cardinal Lorraine had been at the very peak of political power. Both men had risen to so **HIGH** a degree that they were already seen as the real power in France. But at a conference held in Henri III's château at Blois, both men were **PLACED LOW** – quite literally placed low – by the assassin's knife. This left the way open for Vendôme, the lesser of the two claimants, to be **PLACED ON HIGH** as France's future king.[1]

The Duke of **VENDÔME** was already King of Navarre and a second cousin of Henri III: he was therefore a legitimate successor to the throne. But he was also a Protestant, and because of this his original nomination by Henri had been overturned by the powerful Guise faction, backed by the equally influential Holy Catholic League. However, after the deaths of Guise and his brother, the opportunity presented itself for Vendôme to renew his challenge for the crown.

Three times Vendôme's claim to succeed Henri III was made, only to be rejected. Wilting under pressure from the Catholics, Henri III was forced to retract the promise he made to Vendôme that he would declare him his successor. This rejection was also reinforced by Pope Sixtus V, who excommunicated Vendôme in 1585 for heresy, thus ensuring that Catholics in France would never accept a Huguenot for their king. Previously, in December 1584, the Pope had ratified the secret treaty of Joinville made between the Holy Catholic League and Philip II of Spain. This contained a clause agreeing that Cardinal Bourbon would succeed Henri III as King Charles X of France.

Behind this political manoeuvring was a hidden agenda. The Wars of Religion had turned Catholic France into a divided nation. Large parts of the country had come under Protestant administration. Essentially, a heretic state was operating inside a Catholic state, and it was conducting its affairs according to the tenets of its religion.[2] A very similar situation had occurred many years before in Susa, where the *'Book of Esther'* recounts what happened in that city, and how King Xerxes restored order.

His solution was to elect a man named *Haman* into office, with the understanding that he would purge the kingdom of its heretics.

THE SON OF HAMAN WILL BE RAISED UP INSIDE ROME

When Sixtus V ratified the treaty of Joinville, and acknowledged Cardinal Bourbon as the future king of France, **A SON OF HAMAN WAS RAISED UP INSIDE ROME.** Charles X was to be the new *Haman,* and with the assistance of the Holy Catholic League, he would purge France of its Huguenot heretics.[3]

THE TWO GREAT ONES PLACED IN DEFAULT

Things did not go according to plan. In December 1588, both Henri duc de Guise and his brother Cardinal Lorraine were summoned to a meeting of the Estates-General at the Château de Blois; whereupon, on the 23rd and 24th of the month **THE TWO GREAT ONES** were assassinated. Consequently, their non-attendance at the assembly **PLACED** them **IN DEFAULT.**[4] This bitter comment represents a further example of Nostradamus's dark humour. Further instances will be remarked upon as the oracles unfold.

The assassination of the two most powerful men in France by order of the King was a world-shaking event. Only the passing of four centuries has paled its impact. Nostradamus was seemingly aware of the shock it would cause at the time, and his oracles seize upon both murders as a subject worthy of further examination. But first we must look at what led to these murders.

C.III: 50

La republique de la grande cité.
A grand rigeur ne voudra confentir:
Roy fortir hors par trompete cité,
L'efchele au mur, la cité repentir.

The republic of the great city,
With great strictness will not be willing to consent:
The King departing outside by reason of trumpet city,
The ladder at the wall, the city regretting.

THE REPUBLIC OF THE GREAT CITY

Although it is a familiar fact that France was made a republic during the French Revolution, it is less well known that Paris effectively, and alone, transformed itself into a *republic* during the French Wars of Religion; hence, **THE REPUBLIC OF THE GREAT CITY.** It is also to be noted that all references to the 'great city', when made without qualification, are intended to be understood as referring to the great city of Paris.

The transition to a republic began in 1584 with the formation of the Holy Catholic League, led by the duc de Guise and governed by a Committee of Sixteen. The League saw itself as the last bastion of the true faith in a kingdom whose ruler was not only too lenient, but who had also nominated a Protestant, Henri of Navarre Duke of Vendôme, to succeed him. *Better A Republic Than A Huguenot King* was the defiant cry that thrilled the hearts of the Paris League.[1]

WITH GREAT STRICTNESS WILL NOT BE WILLING TO CONSENT

Faced with the choice of who should succeed Henri III, the Committee of Sixteen were **NOT WILLING TO CONSENT** to the King's nomination of a Protestant king to rule France. Instead, **WITH GREAT STRICTNESS**, they insisted that Henri sign the Treaty of Nemours (7 July 1585). According to its terms, Cardinal Charles de Bourbon would take the French crown as Charles X, if Henri remained childless. As an additional safeguard, they insisted that Vendôme and all Protestants must be deprived of the right to hold public office.[2]

THE KING DEPARTING OUTSIDE

On 9 May 1588, the conflict between the King's authority and the Leaguers came to a head. In defiance of Henri III's orders, the duc de Guise entered Paris at the head of an armed escort. The King, fearing that a *coup* had been planned, responded by bringing his own troops into the city. In what became known as the Day of the Barricades, Paris rose up and rebelled against the King, forcing him to seek shelter behind the palace walls. Finally, four days later, and in fear for his life, **THE KING** took to horse **DEPARTING OUTSIDE** the city for the safety of Chartres.[3]

BY REASON OF TRUMPET CITY

Six months earlier, the King had sent Anne de Joyeuse duc d'Arques and a favourite of the Paris Leaguers to his death, alongside 300 noblemen killed at the hands of Henri of Navarre's Huguenots. On 12 September 1587, Henri III had joined his army stationed along the river Loire. His aim was to defeat a troop of 8,000 German *reiters* before they could join up with Navarre's army in the Midi. At the same time, he ordered Joyeuse to confront Navarre's army approaching from the south. Joyeuse's army met the opposing force on the plains of Bordeaux (battle of Coutras, 20 October 1587). In a two-hour long battle, the guns of the Protestant army wreaked havoc among Joyeuse's infantry. When the fighting was over, both the duc d'Arques and his brother Claude were found amongst three hundred noblemen who had lost their lives. By contrast, the King failed to intercept the German insurgents. Instead, it was the League's leader, Guise, who met and defeated them at Auneau.

In Paris, the League blamed the King for the defeat at Coutras and the loss of so many noblemen. The *Seize* insisted that Henri should have met Navarre himself, instead of sending Joyeuse to his death.[4] It was therefore **BY REASON OF** the military disaster on the plains of Bordeaux, some seventeen or eighteen miles outside **TRUMPET CITY** – Bordeaux is so named because of its Château-Trompette, (Trumpet Castle), which until its destruction in the 17th century, guarded the city's entrance – that the King's already weakened authority diminished still further. Six months later in May, fearing for his life, the King fled Paris having lost all authority to govern there.

With Henri III absent, Paris operated as a republic, and the gates were barred against the King's return. Henri was therefore compelled to lay siege to the city in his attempt to starve the League leaders into submission and regain authority. But, on 1 August 1589 he was assassinated, and it was left to his successor, Henri of Navarre, to prove himself by continuing the struggle.

LADDER AT THE WALL

At nightfall, with Paris in the midst of suffering the privations of a second siege, which began in May 1590, Henri IV made an effort to enter the capital by placing a **LADDER AT THE WALL**.[5] *"During the night of 10th September 1590, Henri IV attempted to take Paris by scaling the walls near the papal gate, between Porte Saint-Jacques and the Porte Saint-Marcel."*[6] But a disturbance in the night air attracted the attention of four guards. Together with a librarian and a lawyer, and armed only with pickaxe handles, the six men beat off the attempt.[7]

As the siege inside Paris continued, hunger increasingly occupied the minds of its people. *"Donkeys began to disappear, then – as would happen in 1870 – cats and dogs, and even rats."* [8] There were also reports of *"little children disguised as meat . . . [and] experiments in milling bones out of the graveyards for flour."* [9] With **THE CITY REGRETTING** having to suffer *"the most crippling siege in the history of any major European city since that of Constantinople by the Turks,"* [10] help at last arrived from Spain. The Duke of Parma succeeded in floating food supplies down the river Seine, while also forcing Henri to withdraw. By then, the privations through hunger and disease had cost the lives of between 40,000 and 50,000 citizens (Horne, 2002 p.81).

The Day of the Barricades (May 1588) proved to be a pivotal point in French history, and it set in motion a chain reaction. Firstly, it caused Henri III to flee the city in fear for his life. Secondly, it placed the duc de Guise in the position of a surrogate king with total control over the capital city. Thirdly, it inflamed the mind of the humiliated King, causing him to seek revenge: a revenge that would lead to the murders of the two Guise brothers. Fourthly, their deaths invoked the hatred of the deceased's family, who began plotting Henri III's assassination. When this chain of events had run its course, a new dynasty would occupy the line of succession to the throne – the Bourbons.

C.IX: 96

Dans cité entrer exercit defniée,
Duc entrera par perfuafion,
Aux foibles portes clam armée amenée,
Mettront feu, mort, effufion de fang.

Inside the city, troops entering, spurned,
The Duke will enter by persuasion,
At the feeble gates, acclaim, troops prevailed upon,
They will employ fire, death, effusion of blood.

Defniée, (O.Fr.) repousser; exercit, (Latinism) exercit/us; clam, (Latinism) clam/or; amenée, (O.Fr.) pousser; foibles, (O.Fr.) feeble.

INSIDE THE CITY, TROOPS ENTERING SPURNED

On 11 May 1588, at the request of Henri III, Swiss **TROOPS** began **ENTERING THE CITY** of Paris, accompanied by soldiers drawn from the royal army,[1] but they were quickly **SPURNED** by the Parisians: their arrival only serving to inflame an already aggravated populace.[2] For centuries Paris had jealously guarded its ancient right to defend itself. But Henri had been advised a *coup* was about to be sprung, and he placed his own protection before the preferences of the Parisians.

> *The citizens were outraged when they saw the soldiers being deployed around the city . . . During the night the citizens erected barricades of huge barrels filled with rocks and stones to block the streets.*[3]

The erection of these temporary barriers served as *gates*:[4] their strength lying not in their *feeble* structure but in the resolution of the volunteers guarding them.

THE DUKE WILL ENTER BY PERSUASION

The King's anxiety at the threat of a *coup* began when he learned that the Duke of Guise had been invited by the League's Committee of Sixteen to enter Paris with an armed escort. Henri responded by ordering Guise to stay away. But if the Duke had any reservations concerning these conflicting instructions, they were removed by Catherine de' Medici; she sent an envoy to Guise, convincing him that he must come to Paris. This decided the matter, and **THE DUKE ENTERED BY PERSUASION.**[5]

The underlying reason for this invitation appears to have been Catherine de' Medici's desire to become regent of France once more, and seeing Guise as the strong man who would do her bidding.

AT THE FEEBLE GATES, ACCLAMATION

With the barricades in place, only those considered friendly to the League were allowed to pass through. Catherine de' Medici was one permitted to bypass the barriers on her way to Mass at the Saint-Chapelle. Another **AT THE FEEBLE GATES** was the Duke of Guise, who received the **ACCLAMATION:** *"'Vive Guise! ' 'To Rheims, we must bring Monsieur to Rheims!' "*[6] This was a clear indication that the citizens of Paris were already viewing Guise as the next king of France, as Rheims was the traditional city for the coronation of its monarchs. In fact, he was offered the crown but declined it.

TROOPS PREVAILED UPON; FIRE, DEATH, EFFUSION OF BLOOD

The **MEN AT ARMS** loyal to Henri III, who confronted the bourgeois members of the League and the students from the Sorbonne manning the barricades, received a very different reception.

They were **PREVAILED UPON** *"with stones and a few troops [were] . . . killed by snipers."*[7] The number of troops killed was given as sixty. Later that day, after a number of incidents involving **FIRE, DEATH, AND THE EFFUSION OF BLOOD**, Guise sent a letter to the Governor of Orleans, in which he wrote: – *"I have defeated the Swiss, cut to pieces part of the guards of the King and I am holding the Louvre so closely invested that I shall give a good account of those within it."*[8]

To Guise's future peril, the King was one of those trapped inside the Louvre, and he was incandescent with rage at his enforced confinement, bent upon revenge.

The prediction of Henri III's enforced confinement inside the palace continues in the next verse. It begins by focusing on the thoughts and intentions going through his mind, as he fretted under siege conditions inside the Louvre Palace. The outcome of these deliberations forms the remaining part of the quatrain.

C.III: 51

Paris coniure vn grand meurtre commetre,
Bloys le fera fortir en plain effect:
Ceux d'Orleans vouldront leur chef remettre,
Angiers, Troye, Langres, leur feront vn meſſait

Paris adjures a great man to commit murder,
Blois will cause him to leave flat, in fact:
Those of Orleans will want their chief restored,
Angers, Troyes, Langres, will do a wrong to themselves.

coniure, (O.Fr.) adjure; en effect = in fact; plain, (O.Fr.) flat; mesfait, (O.Fr.) faire du tort à.

PARIS ADJURES A GREAT MAN TO COMMIT MURDER

In **PARIS**, the barricades were in place and Guise appeared triumphant. *"The King, meanwhile, fell into a murderous rage that Guise had disobeyed his command and come to Paris."* He sought advice from Villequier, d'Ornano, and Cheverny: three men who were with him at the time. Alphonse, Comte d'Ornano, suggested that an attempt be made to assassinate Guise. *"If your majesty will issue the command, I will bring you the head of the duc de Guise, or secure his person."* (Freer, 1858). Three others then joined the party: the Comte de Guiche, Bellièvre and the abbé d'Elbène, who brought fresh news that the Queen-mother wanted to arrange a meeting between her son and the duc de Guise. Henri paused irresolute; the abbé d'Elbène and Ornano, detecting the fierce impulse which actuated the king's mind, approached, and boldly advised his majesty to receive the duke in that very cabinet, and cause him to be assassinated on the spot as just retribution for his rebellion and disobedience. The abbé d'Elbêne confirmed the advice with a Latin aphorism. *"Percutiam pastorem et dispergentur oves."* [Kill the shepherd and disperse the sheep]. *"The counsel seemed pleasing to the king, who thereupon fell into a fit of musing."* A plan for Guise's murder was then put together.[1]

Lognac and his five Gascons took up their positions, while Henri angrily dealt with the remonstrations and prayers of his ministers. Although they seemed to make some impression upon him, he declared that Guise would not live to confront him again, but that he would cause him to be shot, and his head severed from his body, and placed on a pike in front of the Louvre before the expiration of another hour. Henri then gave Lognac the signal, upon the hearing of which, he was to rush into the queen's chamber and do just execution on the rebel.

But the Queen-mother appeared at that moment, and divined from her son's manner that some dreadful catastrophe was about to take place. Skilfully, she talked the Duke out of the room and out of immediate danger.

BLOIS WILL CAUSE HIM TO LEAVE FLAT, IN FACT

Having failed to rid himself of his enemy, the King sought a new opportunity. In December 1588, the duc de Guise arrived at the Château de **BLOIS**, the residence of Henri III, to attend a meeting of the Estates-General. On the morning of December 23rd, Guise was summoned for a private audience with the King. As he entered the chamber adjoining the royal bedroom, a group of the King's bodyguard, led by Lognac and his Gascons, fell upon the Duke, and stabbed him to death.[2] Guise's lifeless body was then carried from the castle and incinerated; his ashes were dispersed in the adjacent river Loire. There are, however, conflicting stories of the manner by which the body of Guise was disposed.

THOSE OF ORLEANS WILL WANT THEIR CHIEF RESTORED

When the citizens of **ORLEANS** heard what had taken place at *Blois*, and who was to replace Guise as the head of their city, they seized the gates. And in their anger, a deputation of eight citizens was forthwith elected to proceed to *Blois* to urge the king to remove Entragues, who the city refused to accept as governor.

They **WANTED THEIR CHIEF** from the family of Guise **RESTORED**, and it was with this wish that they prayed the now captive prince of Joinville, who had become the new duc de Guise, might be invested in that office.[3]

Orleans was not the only city to be affected during this time of upheaval and uncertainties. Each of the towns referred to in the prophecy contained people responsible for **DOING THEMSELVES A MISDEED**.[4] In **ANGERS**, the Huguenots were among the first to suffer when the Duke of Montpensier, Guise's brother-in-law, decided to rid the city of Protestants by decapitating all those in captivity.

At **TROYES**, in April 1590, about two thousand citizens repelled a Royalist assault. This led to over one hundred deaths, and was followed by an assault on the Royalist prisoners held inside the city's prison. Thirty-seven inmates were subsequently killed when the jailer, Pierre Gourdault opened the prison gates to allow a mob, led by town councillor Laurent Dautruy, to enter.

LANGRES was a city that initially came under the authority of the League. But its Bishop was afterwards forced to appear before the King, and suffer admonishment for his many activities against the people under his authority, and without first having heard their representations. Consequently, Henri III annulled all the decrees sanctioned by the Bishop, and commanded that he now return to *Langres*, *"and live in peace with your flock."* Vassy or Wassy situated in the Haute-Marne, a diocese of *Langres*, had been a major cause of the French Wars of Religion: when on 1 March 1562, the duc de Guise, travelling with an armed escort, espied a company of Huguenots worshipping inside a barn. *"The duke's men broke into the barn and a slaughter ensued."* When news reached Paris, Condé left to raise forces and take Orleans; this began the French Wars of Religion.[5]

In an atmosphere of civil unrest, brought about by the enormity of the crime committed by Henri III against the Duke of Guise and Cardinal Lorraine, repercussions from the murdered brothers' family were to be expected. Also to be considered was the effect this would have upon the citizens of Orleans, concerning the question of a successor to the Duke of Guise as head of the League. These matters, pressing at the time, are subjects that appear in the next oracle.

C.I: 85

Par la refponfe de dame, roy troublé,
Ambaffadeurs mefpriferont leur vie:
Le grand fes freres contrefera doublé,
Par deux mourront, ire, haine, enuie.

Through the response of the woman, the King troubled,
Envoys will make light of their life:
The great man will act contrary to his brothers, twice greater,
Through anger, hatred, envy, two will die.

Ambaffadeurs, (figurative) envoys, messengers; mefpriferont, (O.Fr. mespriser) neglect, make light of; contrefera, (O.Fr.) agir d'une manière contraire à; doublé, (O.Fr.) twice as big; as great again; of as much worth again.

THROUGH THE RESPONSE OF THE WOMAN, THE KING TROUBLED

In Paris, Madame de Montpensier, sister of the murdered duc de Guise and Cardinal Lorraine, and known as the *'Fury of the League'*, was inconsolable.

When informed of the assassination of her brother, her ungovernable passion nearly destroyed her life. Her face for a few minutes became suffused. Then she lay motionless and livid. After an interval her cries of despair, horror and rage resounded through . . . the vast hotel. She tore her hair, and in words of appalling purport cursed the tyrant . . . The duchess then vehemently harangued the Seize [the sixteen council members]. She exhorted them to rise and avenge the cruel perfidy of the king, to whom she applied epithets the most degrading and ignominious. Raising her hands aloft, the duchess then vowed that henceforth her own life should be devoted to revenge.[1]

It was THROUGH THE vehement RESPONSE OF THE WOMAN that the KING now had good reason to be TROUBLED. For within a short while of making her outburst, Madame de Montpensier had engaged the services of Jacques Clément: a man of unstable mind whom she began to groom as a future regicide.

Elsewhere, as a response to the brutal murders that had taken place inside the Château de Blois, the city of Orleans erupted in protest. To further inflame their already raised tempers, the citizens next learned that the detested M. d'Entragues had been chosen to govern them in place of the young duc de Guise. Believing that the King's mind could yet be changed, a delegation was dispatched to Blois to petition Henri into accepting the

Prince de Joinville (the palace at Joinville was the stately home of the Guise family) as their preferred choice. But when they arrived at Blois they were met by Henri III,[2] with *"harsh words. 'I command you to receive and obey M. d'Entragues as your governor,' said the King. 'If you do it not willingly, I will soon compel your obedience.'"*

ENVOYS WILL MAKE LIGHT OF THEIR LIFE

Now that Guise and the Cardinal had been removed from the scene, Henri was in no mood to listen to those still influenced by the deceased. In fact, by coming to Blois to make their objections heard, **THE ENVOYS HAD NEGLECTED, OR MADE LIGHT OF THEIR LIVES**. This became clear when the King dispatched the Maréchal d'Aumont to Orleans at the head of his Swiss troops, accompanied by a further detachment of his *gardes du corps*, intent upon seeing that dissent would be ruthlessly punished.

THE GREAT MAN WILL ACT CONTRARY TO HIS BROTHERS, TWICE GREATER

Charles duc de Mayenne was the third Guise brother. On 12 February 1589, the *Seize* appointed him Lieutenant General of the kingdom. But to the League's dismay.

> *He possessed no gifts of eloquence like his deceased brother, nor had he that gracious and affable address and princely bearing which conduced so greatly to the duke's popularity; he was, on the contrary, dry, phlegmatic, and practical. . . . before declaring himself the mortal foe of his sovereign, Mayenne desired to ascertain whether that course would be most conducive to his interests.[3]*

In the event, Mayenne, although he had now become the **GREAT MAN** of France in his role as Lieutenant General of the kingdom, lost twice on the battlefield to his rival, Henri of Navarre. And, **ACTING CONTRARY TO HIS** two power-hungry **BROTHERS**: they having been **TWICE GREATER** than he, he lost little time in resigning his office and abandoning all further ambition to become France's next Catholic King.

THROUGH ANGER, HATRED, ENVY, TWO WILL DIE

The final line to this oracle looks back in time to the murders of Henri of Lorraine, 3rd Duke of Guise, and the Cardinal of Lorraine: **TWO** who **WILL DIE** at Blois according to the earlier prophecy. The reason for their murder has been summed up nicely in the words of Nostradamus. Firstly, there was **ANGER** in the heart of the King, primarily at the Duke's overriding ambition to be the next Lieutenant General of the realm, and perhaps later dethrone him in favour of the Queen-mother's renewed regency. Secondly, Henri harboured **HATRED** against Guise for the way in which he and his brother had used the League to usurp the power of the monarchy, even to the extent of forcing him to flee Paris in fear for his life. And thirdly, there was **ENVY** at the enormous support and adulation that Guise attracted around him, and which the King had been taught to accept as being the prerogative of his own royal person.[4]

Before he became King, Henri III had himself been Lieutenant General of France, and had taken command of the royal army for the duration of the Third War of Religion (1568-70). This was one of the bloodiest conflicts in the entire series of hostilities. Nostradamus now dwells upon the fatalistic aspects of Henri's death, drawing attention to the circumstances where opportunities for this were at their greatest. Yet when the King's death did occur, it was quite unexpected. Remarkably, also, is the detailed description Nostradamus gives of the mental anguish suffered by the King's assassin, even though this was a man born in 1567, one year after Nostradamus's death.

C.I: 97

Ce que fer flamme n'a fceu paracheuer,
La doulce langue au confeil viendra faire:
Par repos, fonge, le Roy fera refuer,
Plus l'ennemi en feu, fang militaire.

That which iron, flame, have not sanction to accomplish,
The Clement tongue will arrive to do at the deliberation:
Through sleep, dreaming, the King will cause [him] to be delirious,
More the enemy from accepting destiny: military blood.

fceu, (sceau); paracheuer, (O.Fr.) accomplish; doulce, (O.Fr. abbrev.) douceur = clemencie, also clément, synonym for doux (Cassell's French English Dictionary); confeil, (O.Fr.) délibération; refuer, (O.Fr.) délirer; feu, (O.Fr.) qui a accepté son destin also qui a une bonne ou mauvaise destinée.

THAT WHICH IRON, FLAME, HAVE NOT SANCTION TO ACCOMPLISH

Many times on the battlefield, before becoming King of France, Henri III could very easily have met with an early death. He had led the fight against Condé at Jarnac (13 March 1569), and at the battle of Moncontour in Poitou (3 October 1569) he was nearly killed when he was unhorsed, only being rescued by the prompt action of his bodyguard. Henri also emerged unscathed along the approach roads to La Rochelle: a dangerously hostile area for Catholics, because of its location close to the Huguenot stronghold. After taking Niort, Henri had laid siege to Saint-Jean d'Angély, and was repulsed three times before the town fell.[1] But according to Nostradamus: IRON AND FLAME WOULD NOT HAVE SANCTION TO ACCOMPLISH Henri's death in battle. That event would be left to the action of an assassin.

THE CLEMENT TONGUE WILL ARRIVE TO DO AT THE DELIBERATION
Twenty-two-year-old Jacques *Clément* was an ex-soldier from the village of Serbonnes, outside Sens, who abandoned military life to become a Dominican friar. It was then that he was taken in by Madame Montpensier, who began appealing to the visions he reputedly had: seeing them as a means of exacting her revenge against the King.

In July 1589 Clément left Paris for St. Cloud, carrying an important document that he wished to bring to the King's notice in person. Upon arriving at the palace, a meeting was arranged for August 1st, so that CLÉMENT could pass the document over to Henri for his deliberation.[2]

In a letter written to his wife Louise of Lorraine, the King explained what happened next.

> *'After presenting me with letters from the said president, the said monk, pretending that he had some secret communication to make, I desired the said Bellegarde and my attorney-general to retire a little. This wicked wretch then gave me a stab with a knife, thinking to kill me.'*[3]

Henri had initially been persuaded that the injury was not life threatening when he dictated the letter, but shortly afterwards, his condition worsened. In fact, the knife had penetrated his intestines, causing internal bleeding. The wound proved fatal. *"At four o'clock on the morning of Tuesday, August 2nd, Henri III. ceased to exist."* And with the King's last dying breath, the Valois dynasty expired.

THROUGH SLEEP, DREAMING, THE KING WILL CAUSE HIM TO BE DELIRIOUS
The Duchess of Montpensier, sister of the murdered duc de Guise and Cardinal Lorraine had wanted Henri III dead. She was a Catholic zealot of the most extreme kind, and had seen in Clément a possible tool for her aim. She had therefore given him her hospitality and nurtured in him a desire to kill the King.[4]

"To merit the favour of his sibyl, therefore, the young monk assiduously dreamed his dreams, denounced the tyrant Henri de Valois, and advocated his assassination." But the magnitude of the enterprise, and the praise and favour of those urging him on eventually took effect.

> *The brain of Clement appears to have given way under the terrible excitements to which he was subjected. Mysterious voices whispered in his ears at night when alone in his cell, adjuring him to avenge the oppressed people. He was assured that, as soon as the decisive blow had been struck, angels would bear him away from the scene of his crime; and that his body, invisible to mortal eyes, would be miraculously borne back to his convent.[5]*

MORE THE ENEMY FROM ACCEPTING DESTINY

The Duchess of Montpensier deliberately played upon Clément's dreams and his delirium at the thought of killing the King.

> *[She] appealed to his visions in proof that he was destined to accomplish some great achievement . . . Clement at length applied to his superiors, and asked them whether 'he might kill the king?' They replied by falling at his feet transported at the contemplation, as they declared, of the holy and chosen instrument of Divine vengeance.[6]*

It is plain to see from this that Clément was **MORE THE ENEMY FROM ACCEPTING HIS DESTINY**, urged upon him by those inciting him to do the deed, than from an act of his own devising.

MILITARY BLOOD

One month after the King's assassination, and with the succession still disputed, **MILITARY BLOOD** was spilt at Arques (21 September 1589), and then again at Ivry (14 March 1590).[7] A fresh outbreak of civil war had begun in which Henri of Navarre, Duke of Vendôme, sought recognition from the people as the legitimate successor to Henri III. Ranged against him were the forces of the Catholic League led by Charles, Duke of Mayenne. Both battles, fought at Arques and Ivry, ended with a victory for Navarre thus strengthening his claim to the throne.

Although the House of Valois ended with Henri III's death, it is appropriate that this chapter should conclude with the fate of the woman who did most to bring it about; that is, Catherine de' Medici. Some biographers excuse her, explaining that the loss of her husband at a time when her sons were under age placed an enormously unfair burden upon her, both in her role as a mother and as the regent of a religiously divided country. The fact is that she gloried in the prospect of power. She was an astute politician, and believed she alone had the ability to save France.

With this certainty came the early realisation that her first son had not the requisite qualities of kingship, and were he out of the way, France would be the better for her government. As to whether the death of Francis II was as natural as reported at the time is not beyond suspicion. The Queen-mother was, with good reason, reputedly a student of poisons, and Hamlet's father, the King of Denmark, died of a similar affliction to that of the French King, occasioned by poison dripped into his ear. (*Hamlet* was written by Edward de Vere 17th Earl of Oxford, according to extant statements made by Ben Jonson, Thomas Thorpe and Henry Chettle, although his plays and poems only became known through his allonym William Shakespeare. As a nobleman in the Court of Elizabeth I, Oxford was well versed in matters close to the French monarchy. He had also been received at Court by Henri III in Paris, and had communicated with Henri IV whose wife, Marguerite, he wrote into *Love's Labour's Lost*.)[1]

The domination Catherine asserted over her second son Charles IX, for whom she was first regent and then the power behind the throne, led to the Massacre of St. Bartholomew's Day, and soon afterwards the sudden death of the King. Foul play by the Queen-mother has never been ruled out there either. Certainly, she benefited from her son's death, for she obtained his dying signature, which gave her the regency of France until her favourite son, Henri III, returned from Poland to take the Crown. She then had the temerity to claim that the regency had been forced upon her.

Possibly, she saw herself in the role of a future policy advisor. But when Henri's kingship reached its lowest point, just prior to the Day of the Barricades, she was not against conspiring with her son's bitter enemy, the duc de Guise; presumably with the notion that together with Guise, she might regain power once more.

Nostradamus was never in doubt as to the character of Catherine de' Medici. He had met the woman personally, and on more than one occasion had cast horoscopes for her family. In the following oracle he expresses very clearly what he thought of her.

C.I: 10

Serpens tranfmis dans la caige de fer
Ou les enfans feptains du roy font pris:
Les vieux & peres fortiront bas de l'enfer,
Ains mourir voir de fon fruict mort & crys.

A serpent transferred inside the metal cage,
Where the seven children of the king are taken:
The old men & fathers will emerge from the bottom of hell,
At this time perishing, seeing her offspring dead: howls as well.

Serpens, (Latin) serpent; fer, (O.Fr.) métal; ains (O.Fr. auçon) today; mort, (O.Fr.) fatal

A SERPENT

"Catherine de' Medici was well versed in the arts of Machiavelli – and of poison." Her cabinet of toxic substances inside her closet at the Château de Blois has been preserved. There was also her 'Flying Squad': a bevy of court beauties, which she took with her to soften-up visiting dignitaries and make them more favourable to her policies. Small wonder, therefore, that Catherine's youngest son called her *'Madame la Serpente'* [2] But there was another reason for calling her a *serpent*. Some years after the death of her husband, she chose to employ a supplementary coat of arms, which consisted of a SERPENT biting its tail in the form of a circle.

TRANSFERRED INSIDE THE METAL CAGE

Catherine de' Medici died of pleurisy at 1.30 pm on 5 January 1589. After her death, the body was sent for embalming, but the operation was bungled through a lack of the relevant herbs. Without these, the body began to putrefy. Because of this, the corpse was TRANSFERRED to a lead-lined coffin. The oracle derisorily calls it A METAL CAGE, and this was interred in an unmarked grave at the church of Saint-Sauveur. Paris steadfastly refused to accept the dead queen's body, believing her complicit in Guise's murder, and so for the next twenty-one years it lay buried at Blois.[3] Eventually, in 1610, Anne de France, the illegitimate daughter of Catherine's husband, arranged for the body to be re-interred at Saint-Denis. And, her body was TRANSFERRED INSIDE THE METAL CAGE to the Valois rotunda.

Catherine de' Medici 'had already made elaborate plans for her last resting place alongside her husband, and **THE SEVEN CHILDREN OF THE KING**. They were to be interred inside a specially constructed circular chapel at the north end of the transept in the abbey at Saint-Denis.[4] Construction began in 1563 but was never completed. Despite this, sufficient work was carried out for the initial burials to take place. Inevitably, the passage of years took its toll, and the building fell into a state of decay. In 1719 it was demolished, and the bodies were removed to another tomb inside the basilica.[5]

As a practising Catholic, Nostradamus would have been aware of Jesus Christ's vision of hell, which is recorded in the New Testament as a place where evildoers go after their earthly death to wail and gnash their teeth, through having surrendered themselves to the gratifications offered by the world. The seer's words in the third line of this oracle may therefore be taken as a judgment made by the forefathers of the last of the Valois kings from their place in the abyss.

The oracle concludes by summarizing the failure and finality of the House of Valois, which ruled France for 261 years (1328 – 1589). The four sons of Henri II and Catherine de' Medici died without heir or honour. Francis II, an almost perpetual invalid, showed no interest in governing France and reigned only one year. Charles IX's part in that *'carnival of butchery'* known as the Massacre of St. Bartholomew's Eve, will be forever remembered in the annals of infamy. Henri III's reign is likewise acknowledged for the blood of the Huguenots he spilled during the Wars of Religion; for his political ineptness and his loss of power when confronted by the Duke of Guise; for the fratricidal hatred of his brother; and for the assassination of the Guise brothers. One historian's epitaph for Henri III says pointedly: *"The worst ruler of the worst dynasty that has ever governed."* The fourth son, Alençon, never became king. This did not stop him from presiding over the murder of 3,000 citizens in the town of Issoire, or for organizing the *'French Fury'* in Antwerp, for which, afterwards, he was branded a common criminal.[6] All four sons, however, had one thing in common—their mother: *'Madame la Serpente'*.

This mention of hell is easily written-off as a religious myth: just a colourful way of describing the end of the Valois dynasty. Nonetheless, it does bear a similarity to one of several visions experienced by three children at Fatima in Portugal. It was on 13 July 1917 that Lucia, Francisco and Jacinta, surrounded by a crowd numbering approximately 5,000 that they again saw, in a vision, Mary the mother of Jesus. They later described what they were shown, and what she told them.

> *We could see a vast sea of fire. Plunged in the flames were demons and lost souls, as if they were red-hot coals, transparent and black or bronze-coloured, in human form, which floated about in the conflagration, borne by the flames which issued from them, with clouds of smoke falling on all sides as sparks fall in a great conflagration without weight or equilibrium, amid shrieks and groans of sorrow and despair that horrified us and caused us to tremble with fear. The devils could be distinguished by horrible and loathsome forms of animals, frightful and unknown, but transparent like black coals that have turned red-hot.[7]*

The apparition of Mary then told the children: *"You saw Hell where the souls of poor sinners go."*

Of course, western culture, based as it is upon scientific materialism, technology and finance has long since distanced itself from beliefs of this kind. But, then, it has also moved away from God, prophecy, and the survival after death of the conscious self. Yet, given that prophetic knowledge is a reality, then it can be argued that God and the immortality of the soul are reasonable conclusions to draw. This chapter and those that now follow support this thesis. In the final part of this book, the Afterword, different strands from several sources will be drawn together to weave a cord that will either break under discussion, or bind together these opposing sides in what may eventually prove to be an unbreakable embrace.

3

THE FIRST BOURBONS

The death of Henri III brought to an end the House of Valois as the bloodline of the French royal family. It was replaced by the House of Bourbon. *The House of Bourbon is an important European royal house, a branch of the Capetian dynasty. Bourbon kings first ruled Navarre and France in the 16th century.*

Henri IV, first of the Bourbon kings of France, began his reign with great promise. But, before he could begin, he first had to obtain the acceptance of the people who were to be his subjects. These were mainly Catholics, and they wanted a king who shared their faith. Arch-protestant though he was, Henri resolved the problem by the simple expedient of converting to Catholicism: whereafter, the gates of Paris opened to welcome their new King. The Pope was therefore able to lift the excommunication placed upon him, and it is with Sixtus V that this chapter begins: the death of this Pope having been aggravated by the many heated arguments he held with Spain's envoy concerning Rome's acceptance of Henri IV.

C.X: 12

Efleu en Pape, d'efleu fera mocqué,
Subit foudain efmeu prompt & timide,
Par trop bon doulx à mourir prouocqué,
Crainte eftainte la nuit de fa mort guide.

Elected as Pope, by the elected he will be mocked,
Sudden, unexpected emotion at hand, likewise timidity
Through too much good-natured meekness: to die provoked,
The night of his death leads to complete apprehension.

Subit, (Latinism) unexpected; efmeu, (O.Fr.) émotion; prompt, (Latinism) promptu; doulx, (O.Fr.) sweet, gentle, meek, pleasing; eftainte, (O.Fr. estain) complet.

Amongst the numerous stories that circulated after the death of Nostradamus was one that told of the seer's chance encounter with Felice Peretti. An apocryphal story relates that while travelling through Italy, the seer encountered a party of Franciscans: whereupon, seized by a sudden impulse, he bent down on one knee before a young member of the party. Being curious, one of the friars asked the passing doctor why he had done this. Nostradamus is said to have replied that it was out of respect for his Holiness. The friar who received this reverent acknowledgement was to become Sixtus V: a pope who was elected into office almost twenty years after the seer's death. Whether this story is true or false is of little consequence when compared with the documented prediction Nostradamus did make for this pontiff.

ELECTED AS POPE

Sixtus V was elected to office on 24 April 1585.[1] Three years later the Pope was shown an edited adaptation of the Vulgate Bible. What he read caused him such disappointment that he decided to produce an edition of his own. At first sight it appeared to be an enormous undertaking. Nevertheless, despite the obvious difficulties, after just eighteen months he succeeded in preparing for publication an edition of his own, and by the beginning of May 1590, the Bible was ready for sale. A papal Bull accompanied its launch, *Aeternus Ille*. This declared the new Bible to be – *"true, lawful, authentic and unquestioned in all public and private discussions, readings, preachings and explanations."* Anyone contravening the Bull would be excommunicated.

SUDDEN, UNEXPECTED EMOTION IN EVIDENCE AND TIMIDITY

In the middle of April, just two weeks prior to the Bible's public distribution, the first priority copies were delivered to the cardinals *elected* to office. It was then THAT A SUDDEN UNEXPECTED EMOTION took hold of those receiving these advanced copies. Unbelievable as it may seem, Pope Sixtus V's Bible was *"so full of blunders that it had to be withdrawn after his death."* Working from the *Louvain* text, Sixtus had felt free to add sentences for clarification, to translate difficult words according to personal whim, and to change the references that had previously been put together by Robert Stephanus in 1555: replacing them with those of his own. Even some titles to the Psalms were altered, and an entire verse here and there omitted. But fear of excommunication caused the clergy to remain silent. As the Spanish ambassador pointed out in a letter addressed to Philip II: it is through their TIMIDITY that the cardinals have preferred to stay silent, *"for fear Sixtus might give them a taste of his sharp tongue."*

BY THE ELECTED HE WILL BE MOCKED

After the Pope's Bible had been dissected BY THOSE ELECTED to the government of the papacy, they were distraught, and their disdain for Sixtus' lack of care could only be MOCKED in subdued, shocked tones as each new error was discussed. Understandably, the book was hastily withdrawn as soon as it was safe do so.[2]

TOO MUCH GOOD-NATURED MEEKNESS

The cardinals had realised all too well the damaging effects these errors would have for the papacy once they became public knowledge. But what added to the turmoil was the fact that the Pope had threatened to excommunicate all those disagreeing with his translation.[3] While Sixtus V lived, this GOOD-NATURED MEEKNESS on the part of the clergy prevented any one of them from confronting *'the iron pope'* with his errors.[4]

TO DIE PROVOKED

Sixtus V died on 27 August 1590, after suffering successive attacks of malaria. His DEATH, however, was almost certainly PROVOKED by an ongoing dispute over Henri IV's right of succession to the French throne. Spain's ambassador repeatedly demanded that the Pope continue to acknowledge the excommunication placed upon Henri in 1585, which had excluded him from becoming the recognized King of France. But Sixtus resisted this demand, and in the final weeks of the Pope's illness there were so many *'acrimonious confrontations'* between these two men that it must have hastened his demise.[5]

THE NIGHT OF HIS DEATH

On **THE NIGHT OF HIS DEATH,** Rome suffered a storm, so fierce; it was later thought Sixtus had caused the elements to give expression to his departing soul. Next day, when the news of his decease reached the public ear, the storm of the night before found a new expression in the minds of those who had been his subjects. They now felt free to come out onto the streets in protest against his reign. A riotous mob soon gathered together, and as emotions rose, a destructive mood developed amongst them.

LEADS TO COMPLETE APPREHENSION

Citizens in the centre of Rome became gripped by **COMPLETE APPRE-HENSION** at what was beginning to take place amongst certain groups of the population. Rioters had banded together and marched on the Capitol where a statue of Sixtus V stood. The monument was immediately set upon, and swiftly pulled to the ground where it was reduced to rubble. This actually helped dissipate the anger of the crowd, which had been bent upon venting its resentment against this greatly despised figure. And from then onwards the disruption in the city started to fade for want of a new target upon which to direct their ill-feeling.[6]

Nostradamus now turns to the reign of Henri IV. Unlike his predecessor, who wore pearl necklaces and matching earrings, this Henri was a man of rustic charm, and immensely popular with the people. *"He cared for the common people of France and wished to see them prosperous and happy."* But before becoming king, he had to establish himself in the eyes of the League and the Committee of Sixteen. These were the men who controlled Paris with a ruthlessness that would not be seen again inside the capital until Robespierre's Committee of Public Safety appeared two centuries later. Henri desperately needed to win support from the *Seize*, for without it he would not be recognized by the people as the country's legitimate king.

An interregnum is rare in French history. Questions of succession are usually determined well in advance. The crown is therefore passed, either from one brother to another or from father to son, or to grandson, or even to great grandson, without too much ado. A problem only occurs when the monarch dies without brother or issue. Since the first publication of these quatrains, an interregnum has occurred only once in France. Nostradamus therefore had only one chance of getting his prediction correct, and he did so with panache, naming the successor to the throne, as well as describing in some detail the other contenders.

C.IX: 50

MENDOSUS toft viendra à fon hault regne,
Mettant arriere vn peu le Norlaris,
Le Rouge blefme, le mafle à l'interregne,
Le ieune crainte & frayeur Barbaris.

(Vendôme) the faulty one will soon come to his high reign,
Putting behind a little the Northland (Lorraine):
The Red One, pale; the male at the interregnum,
The young man, apprehension, and the foreign tongue, dread.

Mendosus, (Latin & paranagram) the faulty one, & Vendosm[e]; Norlaris, (paranagram, & portmanteau) Lorrain[e], & Nor' + laris (O.Fr.) north land; Barbaris, (Gk.) Βαρβαρος: foreign tongue. Cross-references: Mendosus, C.IX: 45; Norlaris, C.VIII: 60.

Henri IV, King of Navarre and France, inherited the duchy of *Vendôme* from his father, and in 1598, he presented it to his illegitimate son Caesar, born 1594. *"Henry de Bourbon-Navarre was the son of Antoine de Bourbon, Duke de Vendôme, and Jeanne d'Albret, queen of Navarre from 1555."*

VENDÔME, THE FAULTY ONE, WILL TO COME TO HIS HIGH REIGN

Henri was also **THE FAULTY ONE** in the eyes of Catholic France. The fault lay in the fact that he was a Huguenot: a person who protested against papal authority. But after the League had suffered several military defeats at the hands of *Vendôme*, it was compelled to concede his claim to the crown. Hence, **VENDÔME** was able **TO COME TO HIS HIGH REIGN** as Nostradamus had predicted many years before at Salon, when the King was still a pre-pubescent boy. Nevertheless, concessions were required. In order to obtain the League's full approval, the King had to agree to convert to Catholicism. This was achieved on 25 July 1593 in the abbey of St

Denis. Afterwards, Henri was said to have declared – *"Paris is worth a Mass."*[1]

PUTTING BEHIND THE NORTHLAND, LORRAINE

Before *Vendôme* rose to power, the House of *Lorraine* had seen itself as first in line to provide the next king of France. But, as we have seen, this ambition was abruptly cut short by the duc de Guise's assassination in December 1588: by which time he had already acquired the title, *'King of Paris.'* The loss of Guise as the principal contender, combined with defeats on the battlefield at the hands of *Vendôme*, PUT the House of LORRAINE'S aspirations further BEHIND in what was really a vain attempt at finding a suitable successor.[2]

THE RED ONE PALE

Chief amongst the contenders at the time was Cardinal de Bourbon, a prince of the blood, and already seen by Catholics as the future Charles X. His merit lay in the fact that the Pope had already agreed to his appointment. He is described by Nostradamus as THE RED ONE because the cardinal's robes are that colour. But Charles was also PALE, because he was very ill and had not long to live. Henri III had imprisoned him at Chinon at the time he ordered the duke of Guise to be cut down, and the Cardinal was never released. He died in 1590 at the age of sixty-seven.[3]

THE MALE AT THE INTERREGNUM

In their search to replace Charles X, the League chose Mayenne. He was from the House of Lorraine, and brother of the two murdered men. But his military losses in two major battles at Arques and Ivry, combined with the internal bickering in the League, weakened his claim. Nostradamus refers to him as THE MALE, which implies competition from a female contender. *"Mayenne curbed the extremists who sought to put the Spanish Infanta Isabella on the French throne; in 1593 he summoned a meeting of the States General in Paris, which upheld the principles of the Salic law of succession against Isabella's claim."*[4] Mayenne eventually yielded to *Vendôme's* right of succession in September 1595.

THE YOUNG MAN, APPREHENSION

Charles of Lorraine 4th duc de Guise was aged seventeen when his father was murdered. His arrest quickly followed and he was *"transferred to the Château of Tours, in which he was imprisoned for three years, escaping in 1591."*[5] After arriving inside the capital city, which the League still held: *"He was welcomed with enthusiasm by the Paris mob, which hoped he would wed the Infanta of Spain and, with the help of Philip II, secure for himself the throne of France."*[6] But Mayenne strongly opposed this plan: believing that it would open the door to Spain's ambitions. **THE YOUNG MAN** shared this **APPREHENSION** and withdrew his support for the arrangement.[7]

AND THE FOREIGN TONGUE, DREAD

Nevertheless, Spain continued to remain a contender for the throne. Philip II had married Elizabeth, eldest daughter of Henri II and Catherine de' Medici, in 1560 as part of the Cateau-Cambrésis treaty. Their child, the Infanta Isabella Clara Eugenia, was therefore proposed as Queen of France. But Spain was still France's ancient enemy, and the Salic law forbidding female succession to the throne also prevailed. Antagonistic as the Leaguers were to the accession of *Vendôme*, **A FOREIGN TONGUE** filled them with even greater **DREAD**: believing, as they did, that it was Spain's intention to secure France as a satellite nation.[8]

In the end, it was Henri IV's conversion to the Catholic faith in July 1593 that enabled the excommunication placed upon him in September 1585, by Pope Sixtus V, to be removed.

Upon his acceptance as the nation's legitimate king, Henri IV set about the enormous task before him of uniting the country and restoring to it the territory it had been forced to cede during the civil war. Some of the key features of this endeavour are predicted in the next oracle.

C.IX: 45

Ne fera foul iamais de demander,
Grand MENDOSVS obtiendra fon empire,
Loin de la cour fera contremander,
Piedmont, Picard. Paris Tyrron le pire.

*He will never ever be heartily sick of demanding,
Great VENDÔME will obtain his sovereignty:
Far from court he will begin countermanding,
Piedmont, Picardy, Paris, Etruria the worst.*

MENDOSVS (Latin) the faulty one, also (paranagram) VENDOSM[E]; Picard. (abbreviation) Picard[ie]; Tyrron, (Latinism) Tyrrhen/ia. Cross-references: MENDOSVS, C.IX: 50; Vendôsme, C.X: 18.

GREAT VENDÔME WILL OBTAIN HIS SOVEREIGNTY

GREAT VENDÔME, *the faulty one*, has previously been identified as the Duke of VENDÔME and King of Navarre, who succeeded to the French throne as Henri IV following the murder of Henri III in 1589. But it was not until 27 February 1594, at Chartres, that Henri IV was crowned King of France. Even then, he was able to OBTAIN HIS SOVEREIGNTY only by renouncing his *one great fault:* he was, in the eyes of Catholics, a Protestant heretic, and to win their acceptance he had to publicly convert to the Roman religion.[1]

HE WILL NEVER EVER BE HEARTILY SICK OF DEMANDING

Henri IV lost little time in establishing his authority, and his efforts were subsequently rewarded by the title, GREAT. Under his sovereignty anarchy was reduced, agriculture promoted, commerce encouraged, peace restored, public works accomplished, marshlands reclaimed, roads improved, revenue increased, and the national debt decreased.[2] *"Consulting daily with his Conseil des Affaires,- a strong inner ring of ministers,- he issued oral as often as written orders, and insisted on being obeyed."*[3] In short: HE WILL NEVER BE HEARTILY SICK OF DEMANDING.

FAR FROM COURT HE WILL BEGIN COUNTERMANDING: PIEDMONT

Militarily, Henri IV soon BEGAN COUNTERMANDING the territorial losses to the kingdom that had occurred during the French Wars of Religion. In 1588, during the War of the 3 Henris, Charles Emmanuel I Duke of Savoy had captured the French held fortress of Saluzzo in PIEDMONT. This had once been France's gateway to Italy. In 1600, Henri IV responded by invading Savoy, and forcing the Duke to return the fortress.[4]

PICARDY

Five years earlier, (January 1595), Henri had declared war on Spain, but Spanish forces responded by marching south from the Netherlands and occupying Doullens and Cambrai in *Picardy*. Two years later, in March 1597 the region's historic capital Amiens was also taken. Another ten months were to pass before Henri successfully regrouped and retook Amiens, driving the enemy out of PICARDY, and bringing Spain to the negotiating table. Peace was eventually restored in 1598 with the *'treaty of Vervins'.*[5]

It is, perhaps, curious to see **PARIS** described **FAR FROM COURT**. But at the time of Henri III's death, the Catholic League controlled the capital city, and its members refused to acknowledge *Vendôme* as the country's lawful king. Henri IV and his Court were therefore barred from Paris.[6] But after his coronation at Chartres the King began preparations to conquer the city. In the event, this proved unnecessary. The governor Charles de Crossé-Brissac and the mayor secretly arranged for two gates to be opened.[7] Henri was therefore able to enter **PARIS** unopposed on 22 March 1594.

ETRURIA THE WORST

Etruria was the ancient region of northwest Italy that once covered Tuscany and part of Umbria. Through expansion, the Etruscans occupied much of the central-northern part of the country. In 1610 Henri IV signed the *'treaty of Brussolo'* with the Duke of Savoy. Together they intended to march into northern Italy – old *Etruria* – and liberate the duchy of Milan from its Spanish master. Henri was about to embark upon this undertaking when a religious fanatic stabbed him to death.[8] In this context **ETRURIA** marked **THE WORST** enterprise of his campaigns, because it signalled the end of his reign.

Spain's military response to Henri IV's declaration of war in 1595 included a fleet of ships sent by Philip II across the Mediterranean to harass the southern coast of France. The oracle below concerns events that followed this enterprise.

C.III: 88

De Barcelonne par mer ſi grand armee,
Toute Marſeille de frayeur tremblera:
Iſles faiſies de mer aide fermée,
Ton traditeur en terre nagera.

From Barcelona so great an army by sea,
All Marseilles will tremble with fear,
Islands seized, from the sea aid shut off,
Your traitor will swim on land.

FROM BARCELONA, SO GREAT AN ARMY BY SEA

Following Henri IV's declaration of war on Spain in 1595, Philip II responded by attacking Picardy in northern France. At the same time his forces swept north from Milan to reinforce the Duke of Lorraine in Brittany. While **AT SEA**, a flotilla of twelve ships, together with A GREAT ARMY FROM BARCELONA, arrived at the strategic port of Marseilles in a bid to assist the League. The naval commander Charles Doria had been ordered to establish a blockade and prevent aid or supplies reaching the city from the seaward side.

MARSEILLES WILL TREMBLE WITH FEAR

The people of MARSEILLES were therefore placed in considerable FEAR at the prospect of the ensuing conflict, and the accompanying loss of trade. Spain, on the other hand, expected a less hostile reception. *"During the wars of religion, Marseilles took part against the Protestants, and long refused to acknowledge Henri IV."*

ISLANDS SEIZED, AID SHUT OFF FROM THE SEA

Importantly, Marseilles possesses two offshore islands; Ratonneau and Pomègues, The latter, with its historic château later became widely known through Dumas' *The Count of Monte Cristo* (1845). A hundred miles or so to the east are the Lérins, four islands off the coast of Cannes. A former commentator of this oracle, Balthazar Guynaud (1693), claimed that Doria had also captured these: St. Marguerite (where the 'Man in the Iron Mask' was imprisoned) and St. Honnorat being the two largest. It was, however, Ratonneau and Pomègues that were the obvious strategic targets, for by SEIZING THE ISLANDS, AID for the beleaguered city of Marseilles was effectively SHUT OFF FROM THE SEA.

YOUR TRAITOR WILL SWIM ON LAND

Inside Marseilles, Charles de Casau, a councillor motivated by a desire to make peace, offered to provide help for the Spanish invader. But on 17 February 1596 another citizen, Pierre Libertat, learned of Casau's betrayal and in the highly charged atmosphere of foreign occupation, Libertat ran the city's betrayer through with his sword. Nostradamus's tendency towards dark humour, usually reserved for the last line of his oracles, takes over at this point by informing Marseilles: YOUR TRAITOR WILL SWIM ON LAND. It was reported that de Casau's bloodstained body was dragged through the *'muddy channels of the streets'* of Marseilles as a dire warning of the fate awaiting other defectors.

Both this quatrain and its interpretation have been the subject of a number of past commentaries. Charles A. Ward (1891) gave his source for the story as Anatole le Pelletier (1867). He quoted

Theophilus de Garencières (1672) and Balthazar Guynaud (1693, 1709) as having supplied the names and dates. This being so, the episode seems to have been more of a local affair than a national one. A detailed local history of Marseilles is required to furnish the appropriate references. The interest to Nostradamus would appear to reside in the fact that he had once practised medicine in that city, and was later arrested there, accused of spreading inflammatory literature amongst the population.

Prophecies that follow the future march of history must necessarily span a number of years to keep pace. The next oracle is one that appears to do this by using words appropriate to the time that each predicted event took place. It concerns the assassination of Henri IV (*le Grand*), and emphasises the immediate appointment of his wife as regent. Coming as it does after the lengthy interregnum that preceded Henri's succession, the speed of Marie de' Médicis' appointment becomes an important feature of this oracle. Also, this prophecy is interesting from another viewpoint, for it represents a further example of Nostradamus using the paragram as a basis for an anagram. In this instance, the strategy is employed to introduce the surname of Luynes: the man whose *coup* brought an end to the regency of Henri IV's widow.

C.IX: 36

Vn grand Roy prins entre les mains d'vn loyne,
Non loing de Pafque confufion coup cultre:
Perpet. captifs temps que fouldre en la hufne,
Lors que trois freres fe blefferont, & murtre

A great King taken between the hands of a young man,
Not far from Easter, confusion, a knife blow:
Continuation, captives, time when a thunderbolt at the top (Luynes),
At the time three brothers will take offence to themselves, and murder.

loyne, (O.Fr.) Jeune; cultre, (Latinism) culter; Perpet. (Medieval Latin, abbrev.) Perpet/uatio; la hufne, (paranagram) l' [y]usne = Luynes.

A GREAT KING

Both Henri III and Henri IV were victims of the assassin's knife, but only the latter was known as **A GREAT KING**.[1] *"Henry IV died a victim of the fanaticism he wanted to eradicate. . . . Too often misunderstood during his lifetime, his tragic end seemed finally to have opened the eyes of his people. They soon bestowed on him the appellation Henry the Great."*[2]

95

Henri IV's life was TAKEN BETWEEN THE HANDS OF A YOUNG MAN named François Ravaillac. He had formerly been a schoolmaster in Touvre near Angoulême.[3] At the time of the crime, he was aged about thirty-one, and had recently become incensed at the King's *'traffic with heretic'*.

The assassination took place on Friday 14 May 1610, NOT FAR FROM EASTER (33 days in fact: 2 days before Rogation Sunday). During this year Easter Sunday fell on 11 April.[4] The Christian festival of Easter was held over many weeks, and it was inside the church where the King's body was laid out that *"the flowers left over from the Easter celebrations were just beginning to fade."*

The murder occurred while the King was travelling by coach along the Rue de la Ferronnerie in Paris. A runaway pig had caused a hold-up in the flow of traffic, and the King's carriage was brought to a halt just long enough for the assassin to act. It was by sheer coincidence that Ravaillac was standing nearby. He climbed onto the wheel, leaned through the window, and THRUST A KNIFE into the King's chest.[5]

So sudden was the murder that for a few seconds there was total CONFUSION.[6] Henri's companions remained rooted to their seats, unable to comprehend what had just happened: even the assassin seemed frozen to the wheel. Unlike Jacques Clément, who had been slain on the spot and thrown from the window after knifing Henri III, Ravaillac was captured, put to torture, and subsequently executed in a most gruesome fashion.

The succession to the throne by the King's elder son followed within hours. Arrangements for the CONTINUATION of the monarchy had been made necessary by the long, drawn-out interregnum that occurred after Henri III's death; this had proved to be a bloody and acrimonious affair.[7] To overcome any repetition of a similar occurrence, the King had made prior arrangements for the Queen to become regent during the minority of their son if the need arose. This also insured the efficient pursuance of any policies that were then being negotiated. Consequently, just one day after the death of her husband, a tearful Marie de' Médicis, was pronounced regent to Louis XIII by the *Paris Parlement*.

CAPTIVES, TIME WHEN A THUNDERBOLT AT THE TOP, LUYNES

The Queen-mother continued her regency until 1614, when the King was judged to be of age. Nevertheless, for a further three years after that, she continued to govern through her minister, the Marshal d'Ancre. Then came **A THUNDERBOLT AT THE TOP**, bringing with it a sudden and dramatic change. Louis XIII had decided to sweep aside his mother's administration and take control of the country himself. Acting **AT A TIME WHEN** France's ministers were **ALL BEHIND BARS**; [8] that is, **CAPTIVES**, Charles d'Albert, seized the opportunity to strike **AT THE VERY TOP**. Proceeding with the full authority of the King, d'Ancre was murdered, and the Queen-mother exiled. For his reward, d'Albert was made duc de **LUYNES**, Governor of Picardy, Constable of France and Keeper of the Seals. In effect he became France's new ruler. [9]

It was during this period that a new figure emerged on the political landscape – Armand Jean du Plessis, Bishop of Luçon, the future Cardinal Richelieu. Luynes and his spies watched this particular bishop and his family members with growing concern: especially Luçon's interest in the activity surrounding the Queen-mother, who was under house arrest inside the Château de Blois.

THEN THREE BROTHERS WILL TAKE OFFENCE TO THEMSELVES

On 7 April 1618, fearing that a *coup* was about to be sprung against him, Luynes persuaded Louis XIII to issue a royal directive exiling Richelieu and his associates. The King obliged, and **THREE BROTHERS**, Richelieu, Henri, and their brother-in-law, Pontcourlay, **HAVING BROUGHT OFFENCE TO THEMSELVES**, were sent to Avignon, where their actions would no longer pose a threat to Luynes. [10]

AND MURDER

By the following year, Richelieu had not only contrived his release from exile, he had also managed to manipulate his brother Henri into the position of Governor at the Castle of Angers. The appointment proved a death sentence. The former governor, the Marquis de Thémines, took umbrage at this act of nepotism and deliberately provoked a quarrel with his successor. A fight broke out between the two men, and Henri Marquis de Richelieu was **MURDERED** in a street fight.[11]

In the aftermath of Henri IV's assassination, the reign of France had been placed in the hands of his widow, Marie de' Médicis, mother to the boy King, Louis XIII. Her time in power was not a happy one. The Princes of the Blood resented her position as regent, and continually undermined her authority. To counter their influence she sought assistance from Concino Concini, the husband of a Florentine friend, whom she made Marshal d'Ancre. But he abused his power by growing rich at the country's expense.

C.VI: 63

La dame feule au regne demeuree,
L'vnic eftaint premier au lict d'honneur:
Sept ans fera de douleur exploree,
Puis longue vie au regne par grand heur.

The woman alone in the continued reign,
The unique one (Luçon) entirely foremost at the lit de justice,
Seven years she will be explored by sorrow,
Then a long life in the reign through great happenstance.

unic/us, (Latinism) unique, also paranagram, L'vn(o)c = Luçon; eftaint, (O.Fr.) tout entier; lict d'honneur = lit de justice.

THE WOMAN ALONE IN THE CONTINUED REIGN

THE WOMAN can only be Marie de' Médicis, the widow of Henri IV, who immediately became Regent upon the death of her husband; that is, *"in accordance with his wishes, the boy King and the Parlement of Paris pronounced her Regent in a lit de justice."*[1] The Queen-mother's appointment was intended to **CONTINUE THE REIGN** in as smooth a manner as possible, in contrast to the lengthy interregnum that had preceded her husband's succession.[2] But, with no man by her side, and faced with hostility and revolt from the Princes of the Blood who coveted her appointment as regent, she was forced to rule the country **ALONE**.[3]

LUÇON, THE UNIQUE ONE

It was during her term as regent that Marie made a significant appointment. She engaged the Bishop of **LUÇON** as France's Secretary of State (25 November 1616).[4] This politically astute prelate would later become **UNIQUE** as Cardinal Richelieu, Louis XIII's principal advisor in all matters politic.

It is noteworthy that Nostradamus has written *L'vnic*. Elsewhere, as in C.VIII: 7 and again in C.VIII: 32, the word is spelt conventionally, 'unique'. Why has he deviated in this one instance? It is because *L'vnic* forms a particularly appropriate paranagram, L'vn[o]c, for Luçon. The letter 'u' and 'v' are equivalent in Latin, and 'unic' is the Latin stem for unic/us.

FOREMOST AT THE LIT DE JUSTICE

From the very outset of his political career, *Luçon* achieved a position of considerable responsibility. His first position as one of the Queen-mother's chief ministers placed him FOREMOST AT THE King's LIT DE JUSTICE. The *lit* was a traditional seat of government where the King and his ministers met to discuss impending issues. It consisted of a pile of cushions on which the monarch traditionally reclined.[5]

SEVEN YEARS SHE WILL BE EXPLORED BY SORROW

On 24 April 1617, Marie de' Médicis' role as the effective head of state came to an abrupt end with the assassination of her chief minister Concini. *"God help me!" cried the Queen-mother; "I have reigned for seven years; now the only crown to which I can look forward will be a heavenly one."*[6] For SEVEN YEARS, Marie de' Médicis had retained control of the government of France, although often IN A STATE OF SORROW. Her period in office had begun with the tears she shed in 1610, following the assassination of her husband, and her natural anxiety as to how she would cope as regent. Her office ended in 1617, as tearfully as it had begun, with the murders of her two Florentine companions, Concini and his wife Leonora Galigai. Their deaths coincided with her own exile to Blois, watched over by Louis XIII, as she wept profusely during her departure.[7]

THEN A LONG LIFE IN THE REIGN

During her seven years in power, the Queen-mother had had to contend with the aspirations of the Princes of the Blood, which several times escalated into open revolt; the defiant attitude of the Huguenots, who seized every opportunity to take action against her authority; and the increasing antipathy of her son, the King:[8] a hostility that would eventually lead to open warfare between the two. Yet, despite the many trials and tribulations she endured, although it must be said the attraction of political power was the cause of many of her problems, she survived into her seventieth year. This was deemed to be A LONG LIFE in the age she lived, where average life expectancy fell short of fifty. Her death came on 3 July 1642, IN THE REIGN of her son, whose own demise followed ten months later on 14 May 1643.

THROUGH HUGE HAPPENSTANCE

Her longevity was, of course, due to the HUGE HAPPENSTANCE of possessing an enduring maternal relationship with the King, even though it was greatly scarred. Without that relationship, she would undoubtedly have ended her days, prematurely, on the executioner's block. For despite her involvement in several plots against her son, committed on the behalf of her second son Gaston, Louis XIII could never bring himself to order the execution of his own mother. Instead, he settled for exiling her: at first to Blois, and then to Compiègne, from where she later fled to Flanders. Her final days were spent in the Spanish Netherlands in the company of Gaston, both of whom were still plotting to overthrow the King.[9]

We now turn to the third of the prophecies in the trilogy of seventeenth-century dated oracles. As mentioned in Chapter 2, each has its own source for arriving at the intended date, and this has been cleverly devised to accord with a clue provided by the seer. For a second time, Nostradamus names the year as 1607: the same year as that given in C.VI: 54.

The reason for linking events to this year is because both the birth year and the date of Jesus Christ's death can be derived from it. In other words, by using 1607 as a starting point, Nostradamus has dated the two most important events in the Christian calendar.

C.VIII: 71

Croiſtra le nombre ſi grand des aſtronomes,
Chaſſez, bannis & livres cenſurez,
L'an mil ſix cens & ſept par ſacre glomes,
Que nul aux ſacres ne ſeront aſſeurez.

The number of astronomers will grow so great,
Pursued, banned and books censured,
The year 1607 by sacred clue,
When none at the sacraments will be certain.

glomes, (Latinism) glom/us = a clue; affeurez, (O.Fr.) être certain.

N.B. The double negative: 'nul . . . ne' is intended as emphasis.

Interest in astronomy was revitalised by Copernicus follow-ing the publication of his theory that the Earth revolved around the Sun (*De revolutionibus orbium coelestium,* 1543). This interest received a further boost when Kepler published *Mysterium cosmographicum* in 1596: a book concerned with the structure of the heavens. Kepler's ideas were to prove a forerunner to the dis-covery of his 'first law' (1605) that the planets travel in ellipses. His major work, *Astronomia Nova,* which introduced his second law that the radius between a planet and the sun sweeps out equal areas in equal time was published four years later in 1609.

THE NUMBER OF ASTRONOMERS WILL GROW SO GREAT

The inevitable effect of these theories was that THE NUMBER OF AS-TRONOMERS GREW GREATLY, and it brought to the forefront Galileo, whose telescopic observations of the night sky were to change mankind's view of the universe forever.[1]

Official opposition to Galileo's ideas first began to emerge in the spring of 1612, when the Archbishop decided that his talk concerning the motion of the Earth was so blasphemous that it could be denounced from the pulpit. The following year, Galileo was compelled to issue a public letter in defence of his work and his person. But by 1616, he had become such a nuisance to the Church, that he was even excluded from making contact with the papacy's official astronomers.

PURSUED, BANNED AND BOOKS CENSURED

On 5 March 1616, the Congregation of the Index took action and suspended Copernicus' book, which had been the first to pro-mote the idea that the earth orbited the sun, declaring the idea to be contrary to Holy Scripture. Another book was similarly cited; that of Fr. Paolo Antonio Foscarini, who had attempted to recon-cile the Bible with Copernicus. His book was condemned out-right. Catholics were prohibited from reading it, and an order was made for the book to be destroyed. The hapless printer from

Naples was then arrested and Fr. Foscarini died very suddenly, and very unexpectedly: some say under suspicious circumstances. Galileo's book: *A Dialogue Concerning the Two Chief World Systems, Ptolemaic & Copernican,* would remain on the Index of Forbidden Books (*Librorum Prohibitorum*) until 1835.[2]

> *Galileo's increasingly overt Copernicanism began to cause trouble for him. . . . the tide in Rome was turning against the Copernican theory, and in 1615, when the cleric Paolo Antonio Foscarini (c. 1565-1616) published a book arguing that the Copernican theory did not conflict with scripture, Inquisition consultants examined the question and pronounced the Copernican theory heretical. Foscarini's book was banned, as were some more technical and non-theological works, such as Johannes Kepler's Epitome of Copernican Astronomy. Copernicus's own 1543 book, De revolutionibus orbium coelestium libri vi ('Six Books Concerning the Revolutions of the Heavenly Orbs'), was suspended until corrected . . . An improperly prepared document placed in the Inquisition files at this time states that Galileo was admonished 'not to hold, teach, or defend' the Copernican theory 'in any way whatever, either orally or in writing'.[3]*

THE YEAR 1607 BY SACRED CLUE

Although THE YEAR 1607 is clearly referred to by Nostradamus, this number can only be understood as a recognisable date when it is calculated *by sacred clue*. Since the oracle is about the stars and the controversy that erupted in the Church because of the observations that were being made at the time, a link connecting astronomy with scripture appears to have been intended. The obvious solution to the SACRED CLUE is therefore the Star of Bethlehem, which, it is said, appeared at the time of Jesus' birth.

Mankind's present system for numbering the years begins, supposedly, at the time of Jesus' birth, 1 AD or the Common Era, as it is now defined. But this is recognised to be an incorrect calculation made by the 6th century monk Dionysius Exiguus in 523. He counted back to the reign of Augustus, but forgot that the Emperor had reigned for four years under the name of Octavian. He also omitted to consider that there is no year zero, although zero has a place in the number line.

These errors aside, according to the Gospel of Saint Matthew, the birth of Jesus occurred when the Star of Bethlehem shone in the eastern sky. It is therefore possible that the oracle's date of *1607 by sacred clue* is intended for 1612. The additional five years are accounted for by those omitted by Dionysius. 1612 also ties in with the year when Galileo's discoveries were first denounced from the pulpit. In short, had Dionysius Exiguus calculated correctly, Year One would have begun in what is now 5 BCE, whereas the year we call 1607, the date given by Nostradamus, would then be 1612.

According to this calculation, Nostradamus has predicted the date when hostilities against astronomers would begin, with Galileo the first in line, starting in 1612. Moreover, 5 BCE fits precisely with Herod's death one year later in 4 BCE. For this date allows the baby Jesus to be taken to Egypt to avoid Herod's murderous command, which, as King of Judaea, he directed against infants and the new born in that region.

At a time when the Bible and Christianity were being subjected to doubt through a succession of discoveries that were deemed to be in conflict with Holy Scripture, Nostradamus has produced a prophecy that dates this particular period. And it has been achieved by counting the number of years that were to pass from the time of Jesus' birth up until the time of Galileo. But where does the Star of Bethlehem fit into this picture? By consulting the astronomical records for 5 BCE, as others have done in the past, it is possible to discover there was a brief appearance of a new star that rose in the east and shone for ten weeks. *"Ancient Chinese astronomers recorded this as an unusually bright star that appeared in the eastern sky for 70 days."* [4]

This star, which some have thought to be a supernova, appeared during late February, the whole of March and early April, and was located in the constellation of Aquila, just below Altair. By computer simulation it would have appeared to observers in Jerusalem as though it were suspended above Bethlehem. Some, however, have interpreted the Chinese record to mean a comet, or hairy star. But astronomers of that day had no experience of a supernova, and any sudden appearance of an unusual celestial body would most likely be recorded as a comet.

The Star of Bethlehem as *the sacred clue* fits well with events seen in the night sky, and increases further still when added to the fact that one year earlier, in the constellation of Aries, Jupiter was occluded by the Moon (20 March 6 BCE). In astrology Aries governs Judea. The occlusion of Jupiter in Aries would therefore be interpreted as auguring the death of the Judean king. (Herod died two years later, in 4 BC). It was presumably the combination of these astronomical events, when interpreted astrologically by the Magi that motivated them to seek further information by visiting the capital of Judea. It was there they learned of the biblical prophecy: *'a king of the Jews was to be born in Bethlehem'.*[5]

WHEN NONE AT THE SACRAMENTS WILL BE CERTAIN

The fears nursed by the Church, which first surfaced in 1612 and continued thereafter, were to reflect the dismay felt at man's unique position in the universe coming under threat. Aristotle's teaching had earlier been brought into line with Catholic theology, but this was now being overturned. And the Bible, the Word of God, seemed in danger of becoming superseded by the discoveries made in astronomy. Poetry, plays and literature during the first half of the seventeenth century were written reflecting the *'confusion and dismay'*, of the people: WHEN NONE AT THE SACRAMENTS WILL any longer BE CERTAIN, concerning the Church and its teaching.[6]

We shall now leave the misfortunes of astronomers and the plight of the Church in order to focus on the trouble that beset France at this time: in particular, the fate of Marie de' Medici's friends, Leonora Galigai and her husband Concino Concini. It may be recalled that the Marshal was murdered during Luynes *coup d'état*: an act that was also instrumental in removing the Queen-mother from power. Once again, Nostradamus plays with words, and in doing so provides two more names that just happen to be the correct ones for what subsequently occurred.

C.VII: 1

L'ARC du threfor par Achilles deceu,
Aux procreés fceu la quadrangulaire:
Au faict Royal le comment fera fceu,
Corps veu pendu au veu du populaire.

Ancre (The Moneybox) of the treasury beguiled by Achille,
The quadrangular (place) known to the made ones:
At the Royal deed, the why and wherefore shall be understood,
Body seen hung to the view of the rabble.

L'ARC, (Latin: arc/a, & paranagram); [n]e Arc = Ancre; deceu, (O.Fr. decevoir) beguile, gull, disappoint; procréer (O.Fr.) to make; sceu, (O.Fr.) known, understood, perceived.

Capital letters usually indicate the existence of a hidden name, and this is no exception. The Marshal *d'ANCRE* was Marie de' Médicis' chief adviser and husband of her close friend and foster sister, Leonora Galigai. But the couple were hugely unpopular with the French people. During Concini's term in office, which gave him overall control OF THE TREASURY, he amassed a vast fortune.[1] By 1616, he reckoned his personal wealth – his MONEYBOX – to be in excess of seven million livres.

> *[The Concinis] ambition and greed knew no bounds. They used public money to buy estates, offices and honors for themselves and their relatives. They took bribes from those who wanted government favors, and they got a large revenue by selling pardons to rich criminals. The money, which Henry IV had accumulated, was wasted by them, and by Marie, in gifts, pensions, and salaries.*[2]

Concini's misappropriation of the treasury *'was first complained of . . . by Achille d'Harlay'*, Comte de Beaumont, a man of honourable reputation. As premier President of the Paris *Parlement*, his name has been used by Nostradamus as a synecdoche for the French parliament as a whole.[3] Outwardly loyal to the administration; it was left to the members serving under him to *"attack the Florentine, Concini, as they were later to attack Mazarin whom he resembled."*[4] BEGUILED BY the outwardly respectful attitude of ACHILLE, Concini failed to exercise caution as the net closed around him. The many favours and especially the continuing confidence of the Queen-mother had led the Marshal to believe his position was secure. But the King had cause to detest the arrogance of this man.

Charles d'Albert, the royal falconer and himself a favourite of Louis XIII, was quick to take advantage of the deterioration in Concini's relationship with the King. He realised that a *coup* would not only please Louis, but it would also help promote his own political ambitions. Acting under the King's authority, Baron Vitry, the captain of the royal bodyguard, was approached with a plan for removing *d'Ancre*.

On the morning of 24 April 1617, the Marshal crossed the Pont Neuf accompanied by his retinue and entered *the quadrangle* heading for *'the great door facing on to Saint-Germain l'Auxerrois'*. It was to be for the last time. Unbeknown to him, a warrant for his arrest had been made out. Vitry approached *d'Ancre* with the words: *"The King has commanded me to seize your person."* As the Marshal turned, three shots were heard from the guards accompanying Vitry, and Concini fell to the ground dead.[5]

News of what had just taken place in THE QUADRANGLE was quickly made KNOWN TO Concini's wife, the Marquise d'Ancre. Both she and her husband had, quite literally, been *made* by the Queen-mother through title and by wealth – *'risen from a humble rank to arrogant enjoyment of riches and nobility'* – hence, they were THE MADE ONES. Upon hearing of her husband's murder, the marchioness retreated to her apartment where she was arrested while attempting to conceal her jewellery inside a mattress.[6] After being put on trial and found guilty of witchcraft, she was beheaded at the Place de la Grève (8 July 1617). *"What a lot of people to see a poor woman die,"* were her final words. Her body was then publicly burnt.

THE WHY AND WHEREFORE AT THE ROYAL DEED UNDERSTOOD

The facts relating to the King's involvement in the murder of Concini – THE WHY AND WHEREFORE AT THE ROYAL DEED – were soon UNDERSTOOD by the people, but public opinion supported his action.

> *[T]he King had organized the assassination of the Queen-mother's minister, Concini . . . Louis had now reached the point when he was determined to rid himself of the Maréchal. Few were in his secret. 'You are to confer with De Luynes,' were the king's commands to Vitry, the captain of the body-guard, 'and do as he tells you.'* [7]

BODY HUNG TO THE VIEW OF THE RABBLE

After Concini's murder, the body was secretly taken to the church of St. Germain l'Auxerrois. Following the briefest of ceremonies, it was interred inside a cavity that had been specially prepared beneath the church organ. The site was then plastered over so that it might pass unnoticed. But the crowd went in search of the body next day, and the hiding place was revealed.[8] The angry mob ripped open the concealed cavity, and after cutting down bell ropes from the church tower to harness the body, it was dragged through the streets to the gallows that Concini had only recently erected on the Pont Neuf. There, the BODY was HUNG upside down TO THE VIEW OF THE RABBLE.[9]

106

The political and domestic upheaval that occurred when Concini was assassinated by order of the King arose from the fractured relationship between Louis XIII and his mother. This had developed during the years of her regency when the Queen-mother had elevated Concini to a position of such wealth, power and influence that it vied even with that of the King. This distorted Concini's political vision, and the disrespect he showed Louis XIII, even while in his presence, was to eventually prove his undoing.

C.VII: 11

L'enfant Royal contemnera la mere,
Oeil, piedz bleffes, rude, innobeiffant:
Nouuelle à dame eftrange & bien amere
Seront tués des fiens plus de cinq cens.

The Royal child will despise his mother.
Eye, feet injured, boorish, not dutiful unto:
News for the foreign woman, and very bitter,
More than five hundred of her own will be killed.

des siens, (O.Fr.) of his or her faction, side, party, followers.

THE ROYAL CHILD WILL DESPISE HIS MOTHER

This oracle is a good example of Nostradamus's ability to mean what he says without explicitly saying what he means. To members of Louis XIII's Court, the opening line of the oracle would have instantly brought recognition. **THE ROYAL CHILD DID DESPISE HIS MOTHER**, not least because *"the mother of Louis XIII seems throughout to have sought the subjection of her son, and to have maintained him in a state of pupilage most detrimental to his career, either as man or monarch."*[1]

Louis had succeeded to the throne after the assassination of his father Henri IV. But because he was only eight-years of age at the time, it was left to his mother, Marie de' Medicis, to administer the affairs of France. Her role as regent officially ended when the King reached maturity (October 1614), but, *"It was hinted . . . that the favourite combined with Marie de Médicis to keep Louis from any participation in affairs."*[2] Unsurprisingly, therefore, as the King grew older his resentment increased; he was also especially sensitive to any lack of deference to his position as head of state, as Concini would soon discover to his peril.

The focus of the oracle now shifts from Louis XIII onto Concini, the Marshal of France, who had become a major cause of the

King's disaffection with his mother. Nostradamus's abrupt strategy of shifting attention from one person to another without any reference of change is a feature of these oracles, and he uses it to frustrate the expectation that one line of prophetic verse will continue uninterrupted to the next. In the present case, this stratagem has proved necessary, because the opening line was, at the time, clearly capable of identifying *the Royal child* as Louis XIII. He had become known at Court for *despising his mother*. It is therefore by switching identities that would-be interpreters are thrown off course. Only after the event, are they in a position to realise how very cunningly they have been outwitted by the deviousness of the seer; his intention, as always, being to protect the free-will of those concerned.

EYE, THE FEET INJURED

The assassination of Concini was carried out on 24 April 1617 when Concini was stopped outside the *Palais de Louvre* and shot through the head.[3] As previously remarked when discussing the murder of Condé (C.III: 41), Nostradamus always refers to the **EYE** when predicting a victim's death by a shot to the head. In the seer's view, it is as if the shot has opened up an extra socket in the skull. This convention will be encountered again when commenting upon the death of Mussolini, where 'eye' is expressed in the plural to account for the several shots to the head that killed *Il Duce*.

After Concini's murder, his body was stripped: *"one of the clogs, worn to protect the shoes, was dragged off the foot, and no time was lost by the underlings in rifling the dead."*[4] This meant that when a harness was made for the body to be dragged through the streets, the corpse was barefoot, causing **THE FEET** to appear **INJURED**.

BOORISH, NOT DUTIFUL UNTO

The King's decision to rid himself of Concini may have been cemented one November day in 1616, inside the great gallery of the Louvre. The King was idly standing near one of the windows overlooking the Seine when Concini appeared. Without even once acknowledging Louis' presence; that is, **NOT BEING DUTIFUL TO** his King, the Marshal went over to another window *"and received obeisance from a hundred persons who had accompanied him and who doffed their headgear in his honour."*[5] Concini's **BOORISH** attitude seems to have been the final act that persuaded an increasingly seething King to have done with this man, and the prompting he received from d'Albert, whom he afterwards raised to duke of Luynes, was all that was required to see the deed was carried out.[6]

NEWS FOR THE FOREIGN WOMAN, AND VERY BITTER

Noise from the shots that had ended Concini's life penetrated into the palace. The Queen-mother's dresser, Cathérine, *"leaned from the window, and, seeing, Vitry, called to him and asked what was the matter. 'The Maréchal d'Ancre is dead,' was the curt reply. Breathless, Cathérine repeated the news to Marie de' Médicis. 'God help me!' cried the queen-mother."*[7]

It was **NEWS** that proved **VERY BITTER FOR THE FOREIGN WOMAN** (Marie de' Medicis was the daughter of Grand Duke Francesco de' Medicis of Tuscany and Joanna of Austria.) It meant her power had ceased, and her exile was to follow. *"She was to leave behind her favourite son, Gaston Duc d'Anjou, and her young daughters, Christine and Henriette-Marie. Blois was to be her place of exile."*[8] At her departure, the Queen-mother's self-composure finally broke down: *"leaning against the wall between the windows, she wept most bitterly. The courtiers kissed her dress, their eyes streaming with compassion, but she could neither speak nor see them through her blinding tears."*[9]

MORE THAN FIVE HUNDRED OF HER OWN WILL BE KILLED

Marie de Medici's exile lasted until February 1619. With aid from the Duke of Epernon, she contrived an undignified escape by clambering though a window and lowering herself to the ground. Together with a guard of two hundred cavalry, she travelled to Angoulême in open rebellion against her son. It would be three years before Richelieu, having been recalled to government, was able to persuade the Council to sanction her return to Court. During those three years, backed by powerful magnates, she raised two revolts against the King: the first in 1619, and the second on 7 August 1620, in what became known as the '*Drôlerie des Ponts-de-Cé*' at Poitou.[10] This was where her fighting force was decisively beaten, with **MORE THAN FIVE HUNDRED OF HER SUPPORTING ARMY KILLED.**[11] It was left to the treaty of Angers (1620), to eventually restore a temporary peace between the King and his mother.

With his interest still centred upon events taking place in France from 1617 onwards, Nostradamus continues by revisiting Concini's murder, and Luynes *coup d'état*.

C.X: 45

L'ombre du regne de Nauarre non vray,
Fera la vie de fort illegitime:
La veu promis incertain de Cambray,
Roy Orleans donra mur legitime.

The pretence of Navarre's reign not legitimate,
He will make the life of destiny unlawful,
The intended accord of Cambrai uncertain,
The King will give Orleans a legitimate wall.

ombre, (O.Fr.) shadow, pretext, pretence; vray, (O.Fr.) true, just, legitimate; veu, (O.Fr.) accord.

THE PRETENCE OF NAVARRE'S REIGN NOT LEGITIMATE

Henri IV was King of France and *Navarre*. His assassination in 1610 left the kingdom in the hands of his widow and their underage son Louis XIII. *"During his minority, his mother, Marie de Medici dissipated practically all the authority and treasure that his father Henry IV, had built up after the French Wars of Religion."* [1] Plans for the smooth continuation of the reign had, in fact, been carefully put in place, should the King die, but attempts to follow what he had worked so hard to achieve were soon replaced by circumstances that Marie de' Medicis was unable to control.

> *Incapable of dominating the competing forces that divided France...*
> *[And] as only a Regent and a foreigner, she was unable to withstand the demands of Condé and his followers except by bribes and offices, which bankrupted the treasury and threatened to break up France into a confederation of provinces.* [2]

The **PRETENCE OF** continuing **NAVARRE'S REIGN** also proved to be **NOT LEGITIMATE** in other ways. Apart from the illegal practices that diminished the treasury, which included Concini's misadministration of funds to resource his personal wealth, the regency came to its own abrupt end by an equally unlawful *coup*. The murder of the Queen-regent's chief minister propelled Charles d'Albert, Louis' favourite, into the now vacant office with the title, duc de Luynes. [3] It was in this capacity that he became the virtual ruler of France, but in this role: *"He was to prove an increasingly pernicious influence on Louis."*

HE WILL MAKE THE LIFE OF DESTINY UNLAWFUL

Predestination is, in other words, *a life of destiny*, and this became the doctrine that Calvin advocated. It was his belief that there existed an *'Elect, ordained by God'*, who were predestined for heaven. In 1619, at the Synod of Dort in the Netherlands, this became a tenet, central to Calvinism, and one that was adopted by the Protestant Huguenots. Contrarily, Luynes, now with overall control of the government, set about removing every vestige of Huguenot influence from the land.

> *At home, he embarked on the policy of liquidating the independence of the . . . Huguenots. . . . Against the Huguenots, preliminary measures had already been taken in June 1617, when Luynes decreed that . . . Protestant Kingdoms of Navarre and Béarn in the Pyrenees were united with France. . . . this order entailed the restoration of Roman Catholic worship and the restoration of Church lands.*[4]

Inevitably, military action followed this decree; two-thirds of the Huguenot *'state-within-a-state'* were re-conquered and restored to Catholicism. A LIFE OF DESTINY, as set out by Calvin, became ILLEGAL in what had virtually become, once more, Catholic France.[5]

THE INTENDED ACCORD OF CAMBRAI UNCERTAIN

The peace settlement of 1559, signed by France, Spain, the Holy Roman Empire and England at Le Cateau-Cambrésis, took place fourteen miles from Cambrai.[6] It brought to an end the Habsburg-Valois War begun by Henri II in his attempt to subjugate Italy. Sixty years later, in the reign of Louis XIII, the planned promise of peace, held by the INTENDED ACCORD OF CAMBRAI, became UNCERTAIN: it having come under threat from the Thirty Years War, which broke out on 23 May 1618. *"Ferdinand II in alliance with Spain revived the apprehensions of France, and inaugurated another stage in the long Franco-Habsburg power-struggle."*[7]

In April 1624, Richelieu received his long-awaited recall to the King's Council. And by the following August, he had converted this appointment to one of supreme authority. Louis XIII's brother Gaston, over-ambitious for power, was moved to jealousy by the Cardinal's office, and the spark of rebellion began smouldering inside him. In 1626, this spark ignited into a blaze when Gaston openly refused to obey Louis' wish that he marry Marie de Bourbon-Montpensier. To make matters worse, Gaston then conspired with the Marquis de Chalais to assassinate Richelieu. The plot was uncovered before it could be implemented and Chalais was executed. Gaston, however, who was still heir to the throne, received only a reprimand. But to assuage his hurt, and to help motivate his sense of responsibility, he was made *duc d'Orléans*.

In a further bid to encourage his brother to adopt a more conciliatory attitude towards the realm, Gaston was also put in charge of redesigning the classical wing at the Château Blois, which was completed in 1635 by François Mansard.[8] This was in direct contrast to the irregular proceedings accompanying the task undertaken by Louis Le Barbier in Paris, which was to demolish the wall built by Charles V, and replace it with a protective wall.

> *Richelieu was in a hurry to build the new wall on the Right Bank, . . . because the old one obscured the view from his Palais Cardinal. A contract was signed in October 1631, but the contractors . . . were as unreliable as Le Barbier – whose front-men they turned out to be. Virtually nothing was ever completed. . . . Given the treatment meted out to the likes of Concini, he and his accomplices were lucky to escape with their lives.*[9]

Nostradamus's prediction that THE KING WILL GIVE ORLEANS A LEGITIMATE WALL stands out in direct contrast to certain illegalities involved in Le Barbier's sub-contractual operations involving the Paris wall. We therefore see that although the words used by Nostradamus are predominantly telegraphic, they are perfectly apposite at directing attention to the event predicted.

This oracle has been of special note because it identified Henri IV by his kingdom of NAVARRE, and Gaston, heir to the throne of Louis XIII, by his ducal title of ORLÉANS. Unless there was an heir to the throne, Gaston would be first in line of succession. But in 1638, the situation changed. Anne of Austria, wife to Louis XIII, gave birth to one of the nation's greatest monarchs, Louis XIV: aptly called the Sun King. Nostradamus correctly predicted the child's birth in one half of a split quatrain. For the other half of the verse, he referred to a dramatic incident at court, which involved the infant's mother some years before.

C.IV: 93

Vn ferpent veu proche du lict royal,
Sera par dame, nuict chiens n'abayeront:
Lors naiftre en France vn Prince tant royal,
Du ciel venu tous les Princes verront.

A serpent seen close to the royal bed,
It will be by reason of the woman, night time, the dogs will not bark;
In that time a Prince to be born in France, so regal,
All the Princes will observe he arrived from heaven.

abayeront, (O.Fr.) aboieront; Lors, (O.Fr.) in that time, season, age, etc.

The allusion to *a serpent* brings to mind the temptation of Eve in the Book of Genesis. Nostradamus's intention appears to have been exactly this, for a similar event occurred in France at the time of the marriage ceremony between Louis XIII's sister Henrietta Maria and Charles I of England.

Charles's representative at the proxy wedding was the dashing George Villiers, 1st Duke of Buckingham. When the Duke first saw Louis XIII's wife Anne of Austria an immediate attraction was kindled between them and for the first time in her life the Queen gave way to a flirtation. Thereafter, during Buckingham's short stay in France, he sought the company of Anne at every opportunity.

On the way back to England, the wedding party stopped at Amiens. It was there, while walking in the garden, that Buckingham made his first amorous approach. The Queen's attendants quickly intervened, and Anne retired to her bedroom leaving Buckingham to continue on his journey to Dover. However, contrary winds meant that sailing was deferred, this allowed Buckingham to give way to the temptation of seeing Anne for one more time, and he hurriedly returned to Amiens.

NIGHT TIME, IT WILL BE BY REASON OF THE WOMAN: THE DOGS WILL NOT BARK
Immediately upon arrival, although it was then NIGHT TIME, he sought audience with the Queen-mother, requesting permission to visit Anne in her bedroom.[1] After having obtained the royal consent; that is to say: THE DOGS WILL NOT BARK, the Duke of Buckingham entered the Queen's bedroom, and kneeling before Anne, he declared his love for her.

A SERPENT SEEN CLOSE TO THE ROYAL BED
The Queen's ladies-in-waiting, who had been informed of the Duke's movements, hurriedly appeared and being alarmed at the duke, SEEN CLOSE TO THE ROYAL BED, and being aware of the situation that was fast developing, they quietly persuaded the would-be lover to leave the room.[2]

SO REGAL

Nostradamus now takes this little episode in the life of the French Queen, and joins it to the birth of her son, the future Sun King, Louis XIV, whose reign would be **SO REGAL**. By using the word *lors* Nostradamus was also able to conceal the period of time involved, because the word originally meant anything from six months to twenty years.

IN THAT TIME, A PRINCE TO BE BORN IN FRANCE

It was in 1638 when the arrival of **A PRINCE, BORN IN FRANCE** caused joy to the population and great disappointment amongst the existing Princes. Before then, Gaston had been heir to the throne and had likely seen himself as the future King of France. Henri de Bourbon 3rd Prince of Condé, whose lust for power had so much troubled the regency of Marie de' Médicis, was also thwarted in furthering his political ambition.[3]

ALL THE PRINCES WILL OBSERVE HE ARRIVED FROM HEAVEN

Louis XIII was made aware of this possibility for future dissent amongst the Princes, and he wisely ordered that **ALL THE PRINCES** must **OBSERVE** true allegiance to the new Prince of France.[4]

Because the marriage between Louis XIII and Anne of Austria had long been barren, and the King preferred the company of men to that of women, their child was looked upon by many as having **ARRIVED FROM HEAVEN**. The baby's mother thought so too, and commanded that a chapel be built at Val-de-Grâce to *'immortalize the miracle'*. Thereafter, the infant was referred to as: *'Dieu-donné'* (the God-given).

Interestingly, there is a connection between Buckingham's amorous advances at the bedside of the French Queen, which occurred in 1625, and the birth of Louis XIV thirteen years later. This is because Buckingham's attempted seduction became so widely talked about that it was seriously suggested his features had become imprinted on the baby's face as a direct result of the mother's love for her English admirer.[5] *"Michelet says that Louis XIV resembled Buckingham, then dead ten years, as the consequence of a 'maternal impression'."* This may sound quite absurd to sophisticates in the present age, but it was widely rumoured in the many innuendos that circulated after the baby's birth.

Reference to Louis XIII's brother Gaston, and the envy he felt towards the King as well as his hatred for Cardinal Richelieu, has already featured in these oracles. The next prediction takes up the story of the quarrel that developed between the two royal brothers, and the open warfare that subsequently developed between them.

C.III: 98

Deuf royals freres fi fort guerroyeront
Qu'entre eux fera la guerre fi mortelle,
Qu'vn chacun places fortes occuperont:
De regne & vie fera leur grand querele.

*Two royal brothers will make such powerful war
That between them the conflict will be so deadly,
When each one will occupy powerful places:
Their great quarrel will be about the reign and life.*

TWO ROYAL BROTHERS WILL MAKE SUCH POWERFUL WAR

During the French Wars of Religion, Henri III and his brother Alençon had taken up arms on opposing sides, but without actually coming to blows. By contrast, the war that later took place between Louis XIII and his brother Gaston totally overshadowed the Valois brothers' earlier fratricidal impulse.[1]

THEIR GREAT QUARREL WILL BE ABOUT THE REIGN AND LIFE

The first WAR BETWEEN THE TWO ROYAL BROTHERS occurred as a result of Gaston's open defiance of the King; he had entered into a marriage that impaired his relationship with his brother Louis. The war was therefore initially ABOUT LIFE.

The trouble arose after Gaston's wife Marie de Montpensier died while giving birth to their daughter Anne-Marie-Louise (La Grande Mademoiselle). As a widower, he became morose, and this soon revealed a quarrelsome nature. Eventually, he incurred the King's wrath by remarrying without royal consent. In actual fact, his marriage was treasonable, because his new wife Marguérite de Lorraine was the sister of the Duc de Lorraine, a nobleman allied to Spain.[2]

The second WAR BETWEEN THE TWO ROYAL BROTHERS was fought when Gaston allied himself with the Spanish Infanta, Isabella Clara Eugenia. She provided troops for him to continue with his armed struggle against his brother, so that he might further his political ambition. This war was therefore ABOUT THE REIGN.[3]

This second reason for Gaston's anger sprang from his jealousy over the position held by Richelieu, and the power the Cardinal was able to wield over the King. Gaston believed this position was rightfully his, and he sought to obtain control of the reign by ridding France of its first minister.

WHEN EACH ONE WILL OCCUPY POWERFUL PLACES

Louis XIII had been quick to respond to Gaston's unauthorised marriage, and had marched his royal forces north to the town of Nancy, capital of Lorraine, and one of the POWERFUL PLACES referred to by Nostradamus; its powerful presence was due to its protective walls. *"In the 16thC the most modern defensive walls and bastions of the period were built to protect it."* Lorraine's troops poured over the French frontier to meet the King's army but were soon defeated, forcing Gaston to flee for his life. His destination was Brussels, another POWERFUL PLACE, and one that had renewed its status and importance in 1531, when it became capital of the Spanish Netherlands.

THAT BETWEEN THEM THE CONFLICT WILL BE SO DEADLY

Safe inside Brussels, the Infanta Clara of Spain not only offered him refuge and hospitality after his crushing defeat on the battlefield, but also supplied him with fresh troops, so that he might renew the *war against his royal brother*.[4] Reinforced by Spanish men at arms, Gaston led them into France, but was met by a royalist army, which inflicted a second defeat upon him.

The King, having earlier quelled Lorraine, was returning to Paris when he received news of his brother's alliance with the Spanish Infanta. He now sought an excuse to attack Brussels and dislodge his rebellious brother. The excuse he found is identified in the next quatrain.

Some of Nostradamus's prophecies attract more attention than others. This is likely to occur when names arise. One quatrain is seen to be of special interest because of the attention it has attracted in the past. Not only does it name the great Montmorenci, governor of Languedoc, but it also names Clerepeyne, the army officer appointed to be his executioner. Nostradamus has given names before, so this is not a unique example, but it has tended to act like a magnet for sceptics, anxious to find reasons to calm their unease that Nostradamus – despite their scorn – may have been speaking true all the time.

C.IX: 18

Le lys Dauffois portera dans Nanfy,
Iufques en Flandres Electeur de l'Empire,
Neufue obturee au grand Montmorency
Hors lieux prouez deliure à clere peyne.

The Man of Dauphiné will carry the lily into Nancy,
Even into Flanders: Elector of the Empire,
Unused, closed to the great Montmorency,
Outside the premises approved, delivered to Clerepeyne (assured punishment).

Dauffois, (syncope) Dauph[in]ois = person of Dauphiné; obturee, (Latinism) obtur/o, to close; clere, (O.Fr.) assuré; neufve, (O.Fr.) new, unused; peyne, (O.Fr.) punishment, penalty, forfeiture; clere peyne = Clerepeyne.

Dauphin was the title given to the eldest son of the French king. It was derived from the province of Dauphiné, which was ceded to Philip of Valois by Humbert III in 1349 on condition that it would always belong to the eldest Prince of the realm. After the death of Francis II in 1560, France had to wait until the birth of Louis XIII in 1601 before the title could be applied again.

THE MAN OF DAUPHINÉ

Although Louis XIII became king in his ninth year, and had abundant time to learn the profession of kingship, he never truly took the reins of power himself, preferring instead to allow others to act in his name. *"He was well aware that he lacked the ability and application to rule France, and he left the tedious detail to others."* [1] The first of the surrogate rulers was Louis' mother, Marie de' Medicis. She was followed by a favourite of the King, the duc de Luynes. Finally, Cardinal Richelieu took over as head of state. In this sense, Louis XIII remained a Prince throughout his life, never really making the transition from Dauphin to King. He was therefore, in a very real sense – the **MAN OF DAUPHINÉ**. [2]

WILL CARRY THE LILY INTO NANCY

It was in 1632 that Louis XIII **CARRIED** his royal standard, the Fleur–de–Lys – **THE LILY** – **INTO NANCY**. This was in response to his brother Gaston having married the Duke of Lorraine's sister, without first having obtained royal approval.[3] In the brief conflict that followed, Lorraine's troops were heavily defeated and the Duke was forced to concede terms to the King. Gaston sought refuge in Brussels.

The voluntary exile of the King's brother to the Spanish Netherlands, where his mother later joined him, posed a new threat to France. Louis therefore sought justification for invading Flanders, so that he could remove the danger posed by his brother. He found the excuse he was looking for when on *'May 19 1635'. – "France declares war on Spain on the pretext of Spaniards carrying off the Elector of Trèves."*

EVEN INTO FLANDERS

"The old international rule of declaring war by a herald was still in use. Louis XIII was the last to observe this custom, when in 1635 he sent a herald-at-arms to Brussels to declare war on Spain." **CARRYING THE LILY INTO FLANDERS** in order to declare war was the last opportunity for this oracle to be fulfilled.[4] Flanders was then part of the Spanish Netherlands and its capital was Brussels.

ELECTOR OF THE EMPIRE

Louis XIII's excuse for invading Flanders came when Philip Christoph von Sötern was forcibly removed to Tervuren in Flanders, and later imprisoned.[5] Sötern was *"elected elector-archbishop of Trier in 1623."* (*The Counter Reformation*, David M. Luebke, p.166). *"Initially, there were seven electors: the Count Palatine of the Rhine, the King of Bohemia, the Duke of Saxony, the Margrave of Brandenburg, and the Archbishops of Cologne, Mainz, and Trier."* (Wikipedia – Holy Roman Empire). Sötern was also a Francophile, and his support for Cardinal Richelieu in the Thirty-Years-War resulted in his abduction in 1635 by Spanish Hapsburg troops.

THE GREAT MONTMORENCY

Three years earlier in Languedoc, Henri, II duc de *Montmorenci*, its governor since 1614, who had been made Grand Admiral that year and appointed Marshal of France in 1630, was captured during the final stages of the Battle of Castelnaudary (1 October 1632). This immensely popular figure, known locally as **THE GREAT MONTMORENCY** – *"the greatest nobleman of France outside the royal family itself,"* [6] – had been inveigled by the King's brother, Gaston, to raise a rebellion in the south against the King. The uprising was intended to coincide with Gaston's own insurrection in Lorraine, but the Prince's part in the plan failed when he was defeated and forced to flee to Brussels. When news of the uprising in Languedoc reached Louis, a detachment of the King's army left Nancy and marched south to engage the rebels.

UNUSED, CLOSED

Once again, the King's army was victorious, and Montmorency was captured. However, because of his rank and title he was not thrown into a common gaol, but **ENCLOSED** under guard inside Toulouse's newly constructed, and as yet **UNUSED** Hôtel de Ville, where he awaited trial for treason.[7]

As an interesting aside, before his capture and when Montmorency saw the battle was lost, he continued to fight singlehanded, so that he might die with honour in full armour. His efforts failed; instead of death he received only dreadful wounds. Had he succeeded in his effort to die on the battlefield, this prophecy would have failed, or perhaps never have been made.

OUTSIDE THE PREMISES APPROVED

On 30 October, the Duke mounted the scaffold to meet his death. The execution was no longer a public affair. *'It was thought safer to carry out the sentence in private'*. Fearing the violence of the crowd and with deference to a request made by the condemned man's family, the venue was changed from the Place de Salin, and a scaffold erected **OUTSIDE THE PREMISES** newly **APPROVED**, which was *'in the quadrangle of the Parliament House, the Capitol of Toulouse'*.[8]

Armed troops lined the streets outside the building, and even ringed the raised platform on which the beheading was to take place. The verdict of guilty had not been well received, and the sentence of execution evoked such an outcry, even outside France, that had it not been for Richelieu's intractable opposition to a reprieve, the King would have spared Montmorency's life.

A little before the day of execution, the condemned man's family, one of the most noble in France, pleaded that the execution be not conducted by a local headsman, but by a serving officer from the King's regiment to reflect the status of the condemned nobleman. Louis consented. Moreover, because of the rebellious mood amongst large sections of the crowd, he also agreed to the family's further request that the sentence be carried out in private.

A contemporary print of Montmorency about to be beheaded confirms the status of his executioner. It shows the headsman dressed in the finery of a gentleman, quite possibly from the *gardes du corps*, and who is about to perform the act of decapitation with what appears to be a *'swept-hilt sword'*, as was used by cavalry officers at that time.[9] [*Author's Note:* The illustration at the front of this chapter recaptures the essential details of the original print.]

DELIVERED TO CLEREPEYNE, ASSURED PUNISHMENT

Seventeen years after the event, the Chevalier de Jant, an antiquarian attached to Louis XIV's Court and employed by the duc d'Orléans, became so interested in this prophecy that he travelled purposefully down to Toulouse in order to check the facts for himself. It was there that he discovered **CLEREPEYNE** to be not only the name of Montmorency's executioner, but also a soldier attached to the King's army sent to the district to restore order. (*Prédictions tirées des Centuries de Nostradamus:* 1673).

> It so happens that Clerepeyne's name is fully attested by Étienne Joubert and by the Chevalier de Jant, both contemporary with the event. Further than this, M. Motret has brought to light, after minute historic research, that the family, by solicitation of the King, could obtain only two concessions of mere formality – that the execution should be with closed doors, and by a soldier in lieu of the common headsman.[10]

It should also be noted that Nostradamus has deliberately avoided rhyming *peyne clere* with *empire*: choosing instead to write the words in the form of Clerepeyne's name; i.e., *clere peyne*, which translates as *assured punishment*. It is a tactic that has become typical of Nostradamus. Whenever he provides a name, he does so, only when a double meaning can be attached to it. However, the reader should by now be aware of the number of times that names have occurred in their correct historical context, despite alternative and appropriate meanings, and this far exceeds anything chance might throw up. Many more examples have still to be examined.

Before Louis XIII came to the throne, and for the greater part of his reign, The French monetary system was far from simple. It consisted of the écu, sometimes called the crown; this was divided into livres, which were divided into sous, which were divided into derniers. Before his reign ended, the King reformed the French currency by introducing the golden louis, which he divided into different denominations. For lesser values, the coins were made of brass.

Not long after the reorganization of the French currency, and with Louis' health failing, Spain seized this opportunity to break its peace treaty with France and march on Paris. It was left to the dashing duc d'Enghien to save the country. Both events are neatly combined in the following oracle.

C.V: 19

Le grand Royal d'or, d'ærain augmenté,
Rompu la pache, par ieune ouuerte guerre:
Peuple affligé par vn chef lamenté,
De fang barbare fera couuerte terre.

The great Royal (Louis) d'or augmented by brass,
The agreement broken, open warfare by a young man:
People afflicted through a lamented chief,
The ground will be covered by foreign blood.

Royal d'or, (synonym) Louis d'or = the gold louis; ærain, (O.Fr.) brass; pache, (O.Fr.) contract, agreement; barbare, (Greek), foreign tongue.

THE GREAT ROYAL, LOUIS D'OR

In 1640, Louis XIII – THE GREAT ROYAL of this prophecy – decided to overhaul France's monetary system. To do this, he introduced the golden louis, or LOUIS D'OR, designed and engraved by Jean Varin. Nostradamus has employed the name Louis for a double purpose. On the one hand it refers to Louis XIII, THE GREAT ROYAL; on the other hand, it concerns the name given to his new gold piece.

AUGMENTED BY BRASS

Amongst the other denominations established at the same time were those of two, four, eight, ten louis, and the demi-louis. These higher denominations were AUGMENTED BY BRASS coins of lesser value.[1]

THE AGREEMENT BROKEN

In 1643, Louis XIII became seriously ill and his demise seemed inevitable. Spain sought to take advantage of the King's failing health by sending an army into France from the Netherlands: the intention being to occupy Paris. This act **BROKE AN AGREEMENT** between the two countries (Peace of Vervins, 2 May 1598), signed by Henri IV and Philip II.[2]

At Rocroi in northern France, **A YOUNG MAN**, the twenty-three-year-old Duke of Enghien, at the head of the cavalry confronted the Spanish infantry with its dreaded *tercios*. In the **OPEN WARFARE** that ensued, this young hero's cavalrymen cut their way through the Spanish army, forcing those who escaped to flee into the marshes. France was saved from defeat. Only the resolute *tercios* stood their ground, but to no purpose for they were killed where they stood:[3] **THE GROUND COVERED BY FOREIGN BLOOD.**

Five days before the Battle of Rocroi (19 May 1643), the Court's worst fears were confirmed: Louis XIII breathed his last. Whilst reigning, the King had possessed that rare *'gift of appearing at ease with the common people'*:[4] for which he received the cognomen of *'Le Juste'*. It was this 'common touch' that was later reflected by the people's **AFFLICTION, THROUGH** the loss of **A LAMENTED CHIEF.**[5]

An event of some interest occurred several days before Louis expired, and which was recorded at the time. Apparently, the King suddenly awoke, and addressing the Prince of Condé, he said:

> *I was dreaming that your son, the Duc d'Enghien, had engaged the enemy, that the fighting was fierce and persistent, and that victory hung long in the balance, but that after a severe struggle it remained with our forces who achieved the mastery of the field of battle.*[6]

Louis did not live long enough to learn that his dream had been prophetic.

After invading France from the north, Spain's Commander-in-chief Francisco de Melo suffered appalling losses, totalling as many as eight thousand of his men killed and almost another seven thousand captured.[7] Added to this, France's victory filled the treasury with enough *louis d'or* to pay the army for a month.

Shortly before Louis XIII's final illness, the King's brother made a further attempt at realising his ambition of personally replacing Richelieu. And once again it involved a plot to kill the

Cardinal by bribing someone else to do the deed. On this occasion, Gaston also allied himself to Spain, so that in the event of his success, he would have backing from the Spanish militia. The story is told in the next oracle.

C.VIII: 68

Vieux Cardinal par le ieufne deceu,
Hors de fa charge fe verra defarmé,
Arles ne monftres double foit aperceu,
Liqueduct & le Prince embaufmé.

The aged Cardinal deceived by the young man,
Outside of his employment, he will see himself disarmed,
Arles, not denounced, duplicate well and truly understood,
The leader wasting away (led by water), also the Prince embalmed.

monftres, (Latinism) monstr/o; aperceu, (O.Fr.) connaître; Liqueduct, (portmanteau) Lique/sco + duct/or, also (Latinism and paragram) l'aquaduct/io.

THE AGED CARDINAL

When nearing the end of his life, Cardinal Richelieu – by then THE AGED CARDINAL – appointed *a young man*, Henri Coiffier de Ruzé Marquis de Cinq-Mars, as a personal attendant to Louis XIII. Cinq-Mars was only 17 years of age, but so successful did this arrangement become that by the age of 21 he had been appointed King's Grand Écuyer, (Master of the Horse). It was a position that entitled him to be addressed as Monsieur le Grand, and his appetite for further advancement was whetted. But Richelieu's response to any higher office was dismissive.

DECEIVED BY THE YOUNG MAN

Louis XIII's brother Gaston d'Orléans was always on the lookout for resentment against Richelieu, and he saw in this YOUNG MAN fertile ground for yet another plot aimed at deceiving the Cardinal. Together with the duc de Bouillon, Cinq-Mars was drawn into a devious plot, aimed at removing Richelieu from office and inviting military aid from Spain.[1]

OUTSIDE OF HIS EMPLOYMENT, HE WILL SEE HIMSELF DISARMED

At Narbonne, where Louis XIII was a guest of the Archbishop, a message was secretly conveyed to Cinq-Mars urging him to flee, as the plot he was involved in had been uncovered and his life was now in great danger. The young conspirator lost no time in leaving HIS EMPLOYMENT. In great haste, he hurried OUTSIDE, making for the city gates but found them barred. In desperation, he sought refuge in a farm worker's cottage where the occupant's two nieces were living, and with one of whom he had recently been intimately acquainted. But his effort to escape was short-lived. The owner returned unexpectedly, having heard the commotion of the search. Cinq-Mars was discovered, and he was quickly **DISARMED** by the guards who had been hastily summoned to arrest him.[2]

The disarming of Cinq-Mars is not without further interest, because the young captive made a big issue about giving up his sword. This weapon was part of a gentleman's attire: without it, those in the street would quickly recognize his disgrace. *"'Let me at least keep my sword as we pass through the streets,' begged the proud French-man."*[3] And the sword was returned to him.

The plot to assassinate Richelieu and ally Spain with France was apparently uncovered while examining Spain's diplomatic box. Inside was a secret document that revealed the conspirators intentions. This had been written in the form of a treaty between those named in the plot and the Spanish government.

ARLES, NOT DENOUNCED

After its discovery the document was replaced, but not before a duplicate had been made. The Secretary of State, Chavigny, then sent the copy to *Arles*.[4] But at **ARLES**, it was decided the conspiracy should **NOT** be **DENOUNCED** until the text had been thoroughly examined, and a proper case made against the conspirators.

DUPLICATE WELL AND TRULY UNDERSTOOD

Silence was therefore maintained as Richelieu began completing a court case against de Bouillon, Cinq-Mars and his friend de Thou. Once the **DUPLICATE** was **WELL AND TRULY UNDERSTOOD**, a charge of treason was brought against the three conspirators.[5]

LEADER WASTING AWAY, LED BY WATER

At the time of Cinq-Mars betrayal, Richelieu was fifty-seven, and the years had taken their toll. France's **LEADER** was **WASTING AWAY**. *"His body devoured by rodent ulcers, one of which paralysed his right arm; parchment faced, wasted to a skeleton, he seemed to be living by will-power alone."*[6]
It was because of his failing health that the Cardinal decided it would ease his discomfort if he travelled from Arles to Lyons for the forthcoming trial, using the French waterways.

In preparation for the trip:

His Eminence lay in a bed hung with purple taffeta. Before him went a little boat to mark the fairway, and immediately behind it a boatload of arquebusiers and their officers.[7]

Note especially, the oracle's ingenious use of the word *liqueduct*. This single hybrid word has allowed information to be conveyed that relates to both the Cardinal's means of travel; that is, LED BY WATER, and the poor state of his health; WASTING AWAY. In the twenty-first century, another hybrid word, *Raypoz* may produce a similar combination of factual evidence.

ALSO, THE PRINCE EMBALMED

Louis XIII died on 14 May 1643, eight months and two days after the execution of Cinq-Mars. Throughout his reign he had relied upon others to rule in his name. *"His reign can be studied under the names of those who ruled for him – Marie de Medici, Luynes, Richelieu."* In this sense he was more PRINCE than King. [8] Note also that in C.IX:18, Louis XIII was described as *the Man from Dauphiné*, rather than King. One other interesting fact about Louis XIII's death was that the body was so carefully EMBALMED that when his coffin was smashed open one hundred and fifty years later, during the French Revolution, his remains were discovered to be in a re-markably good state of preservation.

4

FROM SUPREMACY TO DECLINE

The birth of Louis XIV was referred to in the previous chapter as *a gift from heaven*. But a more earthly sign accompanied the arrival of the Sun King: he was born with two teeth in his mouth, and this attribute occurs within Nostradamus's *Centuries*. However, to include this fact in a prophecy would make it easily recognisable to members of his Court, thereby drawing attention to the rest of the prophecy before it was fulfilled. Nostradamus recognised the potential challenge to freewill this might pose, and to avert the threat, he has deliberately obscured the verse by extending its timescale over most of the King's long life. Even so, the prophecy still manages to retain a unified whole by linking the beginning and end of Louis XIV's reign to the many popes that occupied Rome during his lifetime.

C.III: 42

L'enfant naiſtra à deux dents en la gorge,
Pierres en Tuſcie par pluie tomberont:
Peu d'ans apres ne ſera bled, ne orge,
Pour ſaouler ceux qui de faim failliront.

The child will be born with two teeth in his mouth
'Peters' in Tuscany will fall down like rain:
Well fed for years, afterwards there shall be no corn, no barley,
For repleting those who will be failing from famine.

Pierre, (A rock; i.e., Peter, the first Pope); Tuſcie, (Latinism) Tuscus; i.e., Etruscan; par, (O.Fr.) in equal manner; peu, (O.Fr. past participle of 'paistre') repu, bien nourri.

THE CHILD WILL BE BORN WITH TWO TEETH IN HIS MOUTH

The birth [of Louis XIV] took place at twenty-two minutes past eleven on Sunday morning. The child was a big, well-formed boy, weighing forty-eight marks – nine pounds . . . Louis [XIII] . . . came up immediately to the bedroom . . . Then Dame Péronne, midwife in charge, handed him his son and proudly pointed out that the child had been born with two teeth.[1]

Reference to the state of *Tuscany*, whose boundary extended to the north of the Tiber, implies that *pierres* may be interpreted as 'popes', for Rome was the city formerly occupied by the Etruscan people, and it was they who laid the cultural foundations upon which the Eternal City grew.[2] *Pierre* (French for Peter, and Petros in Greek, meaning 'a rock') has biblical connotations: refer Matthew 16: *'You are Peter and on this rock I will build my Church'.* Popes in Rome are all descendents of Peter.

'PETERS' IN TUSCANY WILL FALL DOWN LIKE RAIN

Throughout the life of Louis XIV – he became king at the age of four – no less than nine popes occupied the seat of St. Peter; they were: Urban VIII, Innocent X, Alexander VII, Clement IX, Clement X, Innocent XI, Alexander VIII, Innocent XII and Clement XI.[3] Nostradamus's sense of dark humour can be discerned in the second line of the oracle: 'PETERS' FALLING DOWN LIKE RAIN. Although this is exaggerated beyond serious comment; nevertheless, as on other occasions, there exists an underlying reason behind this phrase. Firstly, by alluding to so many popes who died during Louis XIV's reign, it signals the span of years required for this oracle to be accomplished. Secondly, it indicates the longevity of Louis XIV's life, and thirdly, it introduces the final part of the prophecy, which directly concerns the rainfall in France.

WELL FED FOR YEARS

For most of the Sun King's time in power, perhaps with one exception, France enjoyed good harvests, and **FOR YEARS** his people were sufficiently **WELL FED** to occasion no complaint. But towards the end of Louis' reign the situation dramatically changed. France suffered the worst winter ever recorded. In Chapter Two, C.VI: 2, the correct year for this calamity is actually predicted, *viz.*

> *In the year '709, the skies shall be proof,*
> *When not without grief, he exchanges abroad its corn for gold.*

The frosts arrived early in October 1708, but it was during a brief respite in the first week of January **1709** that the countryside became saturated, with France undergoing a period of seemingly incessant rainfall. Then, immediately after the rain had stopped, the land was covered by a heavy frost, which instantly froze the rainwater into the ground, thereby vastly exacerbating the problems that were to come. For it heralded the beginning of what was to become the harshest winter on record, and it arrived with a severity that continued unabated until the middle of March. [4]

AFTERWARDS THERE SHALL BE NO CORN, NO BARLEY

Inevitably this caused the harvests to fail. Consequently, **WITH NO CORN** for bread, and **NO BARLEY** for brewing beer, a staple drink at that time, and the yield everywhere withering in the rock-hard ground, many thousands of people across France died: if not from hunger, then from hypothermia.

FOR REPLETING THOSE FAILING FROM FAMINE

In response to the famine, the French *Parlement* introduced emergency legislation, accompanied by levies to help cope with the crisis. Even the King was required to contribute – something previously unheard of. With the revenue collected, grain was purchased from *abroad*, and granaries were set up across the country, run by government officials **FOR REPLETING THOSE** who were **FAILING FROM FAMINE**. [5]

There is an interesting lesson to be learned from this quatrain involving translation and interpretation. Nostradamus employs the phrase: *Peu d'ans après*. This can mean 'a few years afterwards'. But context is all-important. In ancient French, 'peu' is the past participle of paistre (paître), and means 'well nourished' or 'satiated'. Hence, these words are capable of acquiring a different meaning: one that is more appropriate to the context of the prophecy.

Such ambiguities go ill with sceptics, for they fail to appreciate this type of word play, and may protest that words are being used to fit in with history. But such protests are simply an attempt to erect a smoke screen over Nostradamus's success. The point being that these words are definitely confirmed by history. Moreover, the translation is correct according to context. And, since Nostradamus's prognostications were published long before the event they describe, they are genuinely prophetic; in the present case, even the actual year has been predicted.

Louis XIV was born on 5 September 1638. On 16 May 1643 his father died, leaving the young boy at the age of 4 years and 8 months to become King of France. Ahead of the child lay a destiny that would mark him out as the Sun King and one of France's greatest and most illustrious monarchs. Nostradamus predicted his future greatness and his association with the Sun by giving him the appellation, 'Æmathien': a word that is capable of meaning either *'Amethea'*: one of the horses in Greek mythology that pulled the chariot of the sun across the heavens, or *'Amythaon'*: a Greek name from mythology that translates as, *'unspeakably great'*.

This has a bearing on the next oracle, which takes up the story of Louis XIV at the time of his father's death (see also Chapter 3, C.V: 19). It then proceeds to 7 November 1659, when at the age of twenty-one, he concluded the *Peace of the Pyrenees* with Philip IV. This span of sixteen years is not unusual when contemplating these oracles. Nostradamus habitually employs spans of time as a strategy for concealment, especially when there is a likelihood that attention will focus upon a particular oracle. During Louis XIV's reign, curiosity concerning the predictions made by Nostradamus would have been fashionable, as

Voltaire recognised: *"The court was still infatuated with the delusions of judicial astrology."*

C.X: 58

Au temps du dueil que le felin monarque,
Guerroyera le ieune Æmathien:
Gaule branfler, perecliter la barque,
Tenter Phoffens au Ponant entretien.

At the time of mourning when the cat-like monarch (Felip)
Shall wage war with the young Amethian / Amythaon:
France shaking, the barque in danger,
Endeavouring to attain boundaries at the Atlantic Ocean conference.

dueil, (deuil); felin, (Spanish paragram) Feli[p] = Philip; Æmathien, (Gk) Amythaon –
Unspeakably Great, also Amethea, (Gk) "One of the horses of the Sun"; Tenter, (O.Fr.)
chercher à atteindre, sonder; Phoffens, (Gk syncope) Phoss[at]ens (Φοσσατονς)
boundaries, also Greek anagram, - phossens - Φασ[ι]ανος (Pheasants).
Cross-references: Æmathien, C.IX: 38; C.IX: 64; C.IX: 93; C.X: 7.

AT THE TIME OF MOURNING

AT THE TIME when the Court in France was MOURNING the death of Louis XIII, Philip IV seized the moment for a surprise attack against its old enemy.[1] Victory seemed assured, because France had just come under the rule of a four-year-old boy, with his mother acting as regent.

THE CAT-LIKE MONARCH, PHILIP

Philip IV is referred to in the oracle as a MONARCH with feline tendencies: CAT-LIKE being a term of contempt for a human being [OED]. The Venetian ambassador reported that Philip had fathered 32 bastards by actresses procured for him through a network of agents. He was also prone to bouts of sexual debauchery, followed by religious remorse. On one occasion, he even appealed to the abbess at the convent of Àgreda to pray for him, that he be relieved of his lechery, but she was unsuccessful.[2]

Felin is also a well-chosen word for Philip IV because quite apart from describing this King's nature, it also forms an excellent paragram in the Spanish language; that is, Feli(p) is Spanish for PHILIP. This type of connection is typical of Nostradamus, as other examples will continue to show.

WAGING WAR AGAINST THE AMYTHAON

On 19 May 1643, Spain prepared for its assault on Paris, but was repelled by Enghien at the battle of Rocroi in the Ardennes. The conflict actually took place on the day of Louis XIII's funeral.

Consequently **AT THE TIME OF MOURNING, THE CAT-LIKE MONARCH,** whilst **WAGING WAR AGAINST THE YOUNG AMYTHAON,** lost up to 8,000 men dead, and almost another 7,000 captured. France suffered fewer casualties, having approximately 2,000 killed and as many again captured. The Battle of Rocroi is often referred to as one of France's greatest victories.[3]

Louis XIV began his reign with the triumph of Enghien's victory at Rocroi.[4] He had not long to wait for this piece of good fortune to suffer a reversal. In 1648 there began the first of the French civil wars known collectively as the *Fronde*.

It was the turmoil inside France, resulting from these civil wars that *'threatened to shake the fabric of the state to its foundations'.*[5] The First *Fronde* concerned the Revolt of the *Parlements* (1648-49), and was aimed against the extremism of Cardinal Mazarin as adviser to the Regent Anne of Austria. The Second *Fronde* known as The Fronde of the Princes (1651-52) was *"a series of riots, and skirmishes involving Paris, the provinces and the Spanish."*

At the time of this civil unrest, and for some years afterwards, the Catholic Church experienced a rise in Jansenism. The movement was a puritan division of orthodox Catholicism, mainly aimed at independent thinkers, and like Calvinism, it accepted the doctrine of predestination. It soon took a hold on French intellectual life during the early part of Louis' reign: even threatening the power of the Jesuits and their influential position close to the King. Moreover, it played a role amongst those who took part in the *Fronde*, thereby earning the detestation of Louis XIV. But in 1653 Pope Innocent X, perceiving the Church – **THE BARQUE** of Saint Peter – to be **IN DANGER,** publicly condemned Jansen's *Augustinus* by issuing his papal Bull, *Cum Occasione.*[6]

This oracle began with a war between France and Spain. It ends with the restoration of peace between both countries. In November 1659, Louis XIV was finally able to force Philip IV of Spain to the negotiating table. The *Peace of the Pyrenees*, as it became called, took place on the border between France and Spain, where the River Bidassoa divides the two countries. It was in the middle of this river, on the *Ile de Faisans* (Island of *Pheasants*), just a few miles upstream from the ATLANTIC OCEAN that the delegates held a CONFERENCE to ATTAIN the exact BOUNDARIES defining France's recent acquisitions. As a result of these negotiations, Louis obtained almost all of Artois; the Flemish towns, Gravelines and Landrecies; some places in Hainault and Luxembourg, notably Thionville by the Moselle, and Moyenvic and Stenay. Roussillon, in the south, was also acquired by France.[7]

One may also presume, in line with the occasional humour found in the final line of Nostradamus's oracles that the delegates TASTED PHEASANT during their time away from the negotiating table, since the island where they met was named after this culinary specialty.

The commencement of Louis XIV's reign was bedevilled by conflict. Apart from Spain's invasive force repelled by Enghien, there were the civil disorders known as the *Fronde*. Nostradamus alludes to these uprisings again in the next quatrain, and in doing so he implicitly dates his prediction by referring to the civil unrest occurring inside the British Isles; that is, the English Civil War. Moreover, by matching the phraseology found in C.IX: 49 (Chapter 5), to that found in this present quatrain, both of which refer to Britain's unrest during the middle of the seventeenth century, Nostradamus has been able to add to his strategies another, that of cross-referencing his prophecies. We shall discover more than a few instances where this has occurred.

C.X: 7

Le grand conflit qu'on apprefte à Nancy,
L'Æmathien dira tout ie foubmetz,
L'Ifle Britanne par vin, fel en folcy,
Hem. mi. deux Phi. long temps ne tiendra Metz.

The great conflict that one is preparing at Nancy,
The Amythaon will say, 'I subjugate everything,'
The British Isle by reason of wine, salt, in anxiety,
Express courier, war, between two Philips, long time he will not occupy Metz.

L'æmathien, (Gk) The Amythaon, also Amethea; folcy, (O.Fr.) souci; Hem. (Latin abbreviation) Hem[erodromus]; mi. (Latin abbreviation) mi[lites]; Hem + mi. (portmanteau paragram) [H]emmi, (O.Fr.) au milieu de; Phi. (abbreviation) Phi[lippe]; vin, fel, (biblical references). Cross-references: (i) Æmathien, C.IX: 38; C.IX: 64; C.IX: 93; C.X: 58. (ii) vin, fel, C.IX: 49.

The *Peace of the Pyrenees* in 1659 (see also C.X: 58) contained a number of clauses to ensure that France and Spain would continue to live peacefully together. As part of the insurance that these terms would be honoured, Louis XIV agreed to take the Infanta Marie-Thérèse for his wife. Another clause stipulated that swift action be taken jointly by the two nations against Charles IV Duke of Lorraine.

THE GREAT CONFLICT THAT ONE IS PREPARING AT NANCY

Despite both Spain and France having been at war with each other, Louis XIV and Philip IV had much to complain about regarding Lorraine's recent involvement in their affairs. Initially, the Duke had received money from Spain to take his troops into Paris, but he had then accepted a greater sum from France not to march them into Paris. As an act of reprisal against Charles, but moderated by a concession: *"France restored to him his estates, but razed Nancy to the ground."* [1]

THE AMYTHAON WILL SAY 'I SUBJUGATE EVERYTHING'

Louis XIV resolved from the very beginning of his rule to make the monarchy his profession. In the belief that Kingship was a divine office and its incumbent appointed by God, he positioned himself at the pinnacle of every state department. Ministers were appointed for their brains, and Louis used their talents and intellect for his own purpose, although always making the final decision his own. Consequently, when Nostradamus predicted that **THE AMYTHAON WILL SAY, 'I SUBJUGATE EVERYTHING,'** he presumably had in mind Louis XIV's famous dictum, *'L'État C'est Moi'*. (I am the State). [2]

The byname *Amythaon* given by Nostradamus to Louis, which translates as *unspeakably great*, forms an appropriate cognomen for a monarch whose subjects called him *'Louis le Grand'* (Louis the Great) and *'Le Roy Soleil'* (the Sun King). This second appellation, however, achieved significant meaning from the inscription engraved on coins minted in 1638 to celebrate Louis' birth. According to Greek Mythology, each day begins with *Amethea* making an appearance in the east as it pulls the Sun across the sky on its daily journey to the west.

In 1638 the Mint struck a coin with the zodiacal sign of September 5, 1638, and the inscription Orbus Solis Gallici (Thus Rises the Sun of France).[3]

THE BRITISH ISLE BY REASON OF WINE,

In the same year that the *Peace of the Pyrenees* was signed, 1649, the **BRITISH ISLE** committed regicide by beheading Charles I.[4] The monarchy was overthrown and a republic or commonwealth became the new political order under the leadership of Oliver Cromwell. At the same time, the nation was passing through a phase in which politics and religion had become more integrated than during any other period in its history. Nostradamus reflects this union between politics and religion by referring to **WINE**, a biblical metaphor (*Matthew* ix.17), which serves to denote the new style of government introduced into Britain by Oliver Cromwell.

SALT, IN ANXIETY

Nostradamus has very clearly recognized this union between religion and politics, because he uses another biblical metaphor, **SALT** (*Matthew* v.13), to symbolize the moral elite. These were members of the Church who were most troubled by Parliament's act of regicide. They believed it placed people like themselves, whom Jesus had referred to as the *salt* of the earth, in direct opposition to biblical teaching. Consequently, in their **ANXIETY**, they not only dreaded that divine retribution would follow, but that their own salvation was compromised.

EXPRESS COURIER, WAR

In France, in 1651, the same year that coincided with Cromwell's rule in Britain, an unfortunate incident took place that plunged the country into a renewal of its own civil war. The Prince of Condé was threatening to upset the fragile peace in France by raising insurrections in Guienne, Poitou, and Anjou. He was also begging help from Spain.[5] In an effort to placate the Prince, and avoid a fresh outbreak of civil war, the Queen-mother, while still regent for Louis XIV, dispatched an **EXPRESS COURIER** to Angerville with terms favourable to Condé.

But the courier blundered, and instead of going to Angerville, where the prince was, arrived at Augerville. The message came too late. Condé said that had he received it sooner, he would have accepted the peace proposals.

Thus through the error of a courier and the sheer caprice of the prince,
France was again plunged into civil war.[6]

At the commencement of Louis XIV's reign, Philip IV was King
of Spain, and he continued to rule the country until his death in
1665. There was then a lapse of 35 years before Philip V came to
power. It was in 1678-9, in the midst of this period BETWEEN the
TWO PHILIPS, that the *treaties of Nijmegan* were signed.

The treaties were important to Louis XIV because they enabled
France to finally complete its acquisition of METZ. This city had
originally been ceded to France in the reign of Henri II in 1552,
under terms agreed by the *Treaty of Chambord*. But it was not until the *Peace of Westphalia* in October 1648 that the transfer was
finally confirmed. This delay in agreement had occurred because
of disputes as to where the boundary lines lay. Attempts at re-
solving these difficulties were begun many times, but fresh outbreaks of war always intervened, and it was not until a further
thirty-one years, in 1679 – *between two Philips* – that questions
involving the precise location of these boundaries were finally
resolved.[7]

Nostradamus seemed well aware of the interest that the future would take in his oracles, and he took every possible pre-
caution to avoid a premature discovery of their meaning. One
method was to expand a prophecy over more than one decade.
Another was to employ parallel situations, using obscure references that would only later be recognized for their predictability.
In what follows, Nostradamus has combined both strategies
while adding a third: that of changing the order in which the
events predicted were to occur.

C.IX: 93

Les ennemis du fort bien efloignez,
Par chariots conduict le baftion,
Par fur les murs de Bourges efgrongnez,
Quand Hercules battra l'Hæmathion

The enemies of the fortress moved well back,
The fortification served with safe conduct by barrows,
For surety, the walls at Bourges reduced to pieces,
When Hercules will defeat the Amythaon.

eflongnez, (O.Fr.) reculer; conduict, (O.Fr.) servir de sauf-conduit; fur, (sûr); efgrongnez, (O.Fr. esgraigner) réduire en morceaux; chariot, (O.Fr. chariotte) a small type of Litter with an axle and two wheels; Haemathion, (Gk) Amythaon, also Amethea. Cross-reference: Hæmathion, C.IX: 38; C.IX: 64; C.X: 7; C.X: 58.

The interesting point about this particular prophecy is that it concerns some of the major building and structural operations undertaken during the reign of Louis XIV. Sebastien Le Prestre de Vauban was the engineering genius of his age, and a man who specialized in both making and breaking fortifications.

THE ENEMIES OF THE FORTRESS MOVED WELL BACK

In 1672, the fortress at Maastricht housed a garrison of six thousand troops fighting for the United Provinces. THE ENEMIES OF THE FORTRESS were the French who had taken Maastricht the year before, but had omitted to secure the fortress. Now, that obligation fell to Vauban.[1]

At the siege of Maastricht (1673) he used a complete system of 'parallels'—i.e., trenches dug parallel or concentric to the perimeter of the defenses and connected by radical zig-zag trenches that made the approach comparatively safe from the defenders' artillery fire.

On the night of 17 June, the sappers who were now MOVED WELL BACK and out of immediate danger, *'opened the attack trenches'*. On 30 June the fortress surrendered to Vauban who had been directing the siege.

In the spring of 1678, Vauban completed another great defence system. This was the fortification of Dunkirk, which Louis had acquired from Charles II in 1661.

In November 1670 Louvois allocated a task force of 22,000 men to accelerate the prodigious earthworks at Dunkirk, Tournai and Ath. The transport of earth from the excavations to the parapets was achieved by each soldier carrying a hod-load . . . Vauban applied for a large number of barrows . . . Louvois immediately rejected the idea . . . But Vauban's quiet persistence won the day, and 2,000 barrows were provided.

THE FORTIFICATION SERVED WITH SAFE CONDUCT BY BARROWS

On 10 May Colbert wrote to Vauban to congratulate him upon his achievement. Vauban had re-designed THE FORTIFICATION at Dunkirk, in order TO SERVE the vessels sailing in and out of this port WITH SAFE CONDUCT: the major part of the work having been achieved BY the use of BARROWS.

I have no doubt that you would consider this job as one of the finest things which you have ever done so far ... it seems that you have given to Dunkirk a port which will be capable of receiving vessels of up to 700 or 800 tons, so that the King could keep here a squadron as large as he pleases and, greatly increase his maritime strength.[2]

Nostradamus now goes back in time as part of his concealment strategy. On 8 October 1651, Louis XIV entered *Bourges*, receiving great acclaim from the people. The Governor of the city, the Prince of Condé, had recently begun negotiations with France's enemy, King Philip of Spain, and this had opened up the Second *Fronde*. At the same time, Condé's brother, the Prince of Conti, had been stirring up the people of *Bourges* against the King. But their attitude changed dramatically when Louis XIV entered the city; his arrival immediately won over the people.

THE WALLS AT BOURGES REDUCED TO PIECES, FOR SURETY

As reward for their loyalty, Louis ordered that THE WALLS of the *Grosse Tour*, a massive castle AT BOURGES, be razed to the ground. The castle had for long been a hated symbol of subjugation amongst the townsfolk, but after the Sun King's command, it was REDUCED TO PIECES.[3] The people of Bourges were therefore reassured, having now received FOR a SURETY, evidence that the King's actions had genuinely been for their benefit.

WHEN HERCULES WILL DEFEAT THE AMYTHAON

The final line of this prophecy involves a building project of another kind. '*The Strait of Gibraltar – Latin*, FRETUM HERCULEUM' is an existing channel '*connecting the Mediterranean Sea with the Atlantic Ocean*'.[4] This Strait, shortened to HERCULES, had DEFEATED THE AMYTHAON (Louis XIV) during France's war with the United Provinces. At the battle of Stromboli (8 January 1676) French losses mounted, reaching 400 killed, compared with an estimated eighty casualties suffered by the Dutch. Louis realised that to be a force in the Mediterranean, his ships on the west coast would have to avoid the 2,000-mile detour through the Strait of Gibraltar to reach the heart of the Mediterranean. The Sun King's solution was to plan the construction of a waterway that would eliminate the need to sail around the Spanish coastline. The engineer chosen for this enterprise was Pierre-Paul Riquet.

Riquet's solution was the construction of a channel running between the Atlantic Ocean and the Mediterranean Sea. This took the form of a canal between the River Garonne and the Golfe du Lion. The result of this massive exercise in engineering was the *Canal des Deux Mers* or *Canal de Languedoc*. It measures 279 kilometres in length, 20 metres in breadth and 2 metres in depth; it was finally completed in 1681, thus bringing it up to date with the previous predictions.

Nostradamus's next prophecy again concerns the Amythaon: this time involving his part in two events that were later included on the famous Gobelin tapestries. These huge works of art were intended to glorify the Sun King by showing incidents that were considered important during his reign.

The oracle also contains a brief reference to Louis XIV's chief minister, who for a short time was Nicolas Fouquet. Towards the end of his career, Fouquet built a magnificent dwelling place to add to those he already owned. But as the work neared completion, he began to realise the increasing likelihood that he would never enjoy the freedom to live there.

C.IX: 64

L'Æmathion paſſer monts Pyrenées,
En Mars Narbon ne fera reſiſtance:
Par mer et terre fera ſi grand menée.
Cap. n'ayant terre ſeure pour demeurance.

The Amythaon excelling [at the] Pyrenean Mountains,
In warfare, Narbonne will not make resistance:
By sea and land, he will make such a great prolonged outcry.
The chief not having property certain for dwelling.

Æmathion, (Gk) Amythaon – Unspeakably Great, also Amethea (Gk) No Loiterer [One of the horses of the Sun]; paſſer, (O.Fr.) excell; menée, (O.Fr.) cris prolongés; ſeure, (O.Fr.) certain, confiant, qui a de l'assurance, or sûreté; Cap. (Latin abbreviation) Cap/ut; Cross reference: Narbonne, C.IX: 38.

THE AMYTHAON EXCELLING AT THE PYRENEAN MOUNTAINS

In 1659 Louis XIV concluded the *Peace of the Pyrenees*: a treaty that took its name from the mountains that separate France from Spain. It was in their shadow that Louis XIV – THE AMYTHAON, [1] – secured a beneficial peace settlement with Spain: EXCELLING in the process by gaining Roussillon, Artois, parts of Luxembourg and Flanders; a new border with Spain was also fixed along the edge of THE PYRENEES. [2]

138

The treaty also led to Louis' marriage with Marie-Thérèse, the Spanish Infanta, and a binding agreement that he would renounce his right to claim, through marriage, the Spanish crown; for to have done otherwise would have made France too powerful.

IN WARFARE, NARBONNE WILL NOT MAKE RESISTANCE

In return for surrendering this right, the Sun King made valuable territorial gains (see C.X: 58). Included amongst these was the province of Roussillon. It was because of this acquisition that Carcassonne, the former capital of Languedoc, together with nearby Narbonne were no longer considered frontier towns. The fortifications at Carcassonne from then onwards were left to fall into decay. Consequently, **IN WARFARE, NARBONNE,** as the former capital of that region (*"The Romans made it the capital of their first colony in Gaul, Gallia Narbonensis, and it was a vital port both then and later in the Middle Ages,"*[3]) was **NOT ABLE TO MAKE RESISTANCE** against a future invasion.[4] This inability to defend the province was to become critical later in Louis XIV's reign, as we shall discover in a subsequent quatrain.

Two years after this conference, Nostradamus's prophetic eye was attracted by French interests across the Channel. In July 1661, the newly installed King Charles II sent a request to the French and Spanish ambassadors, asking that they not attend the arrival of the diplomatic party from Venice. The appeal was made because of what was known as 'the rights of passage' (*céder le pas*); Charles wanted to avoid a confrontation between Spain and France as to which of these two nations' ambassadors would take precedence in the parade.

OUTCRY BY SEA

When Louis XIV received news from England that France had agreed to this request and stood down, he was furious. And in August, his **OUTCRY** was sent **BY SEA** to Charles II in London. England was left in no doubt as to the pre-eminence of France when appearing on parade. Charles was even criticized for intervening in French affairs.

On 30 September, the French ambassador, d'Estrades, saw an opportunity to regain favour with his King. The Swedish ambassador was due to arrive in London, and the opportunity for

French carriages to take a leading position in the parade presented itself. Unfortunately, the Spanish ambassador had a similar idea. And to serve his purpose, he imported into England several thousand Spanish soldiers as 'servants'. The French had only five hundred. Therefore, when a fight broke out in this charged atmosphere, *"a number of French dead were left on the city streets."*

Louis raged when details reached him at Fontainebleau, and he vowed he would oblige all countries, *"to yield to my ambassadors the precedence in all the courts of Europe."* The French ambassador was recalled from Madrid, and Spain's ambassador in France was ordered to leave the country. Negotiations concerning the future of the Low Countries were also broken off, and a renewal of the war with Spain was threatened.

Louis XIV's displeasure lasted well into the next year, until on 24 March 1662 the Comte de Fuentes arrived in Paris on a special embassy. His mission was to offer Spain's apologies, and provide assurances that Spanish ambassadors would never again compete against the precedence of France.

Hardly had one diplomatic incident been resolved when another arose. On 2 June 1662, Louis' ambassador to Rome, the duc de Créqui, arrived at the French Embassy and found it situated close to the barracks housing Pope Alexander VII's Corsican guards. On 20 August, an argument developed between three Frenchmen and three of the Pope's men. Soon, swords were drawn and a fight began. In the excitement, others from the garrison, armed with harquebuses, joined the Corsicans and they began shooting at anyone suspected of being French. When de Créqui appeared on the balcony to see what the commotion was about, a volley of gunfire greeted him. He survived, but Louis' outrage, hardly quelled since the previous incident, now extended to the Pope, and an immediate apology was demanded for the behaviour of his guards.

The Pope vacillated for several days, during which time, thirty-two Corsicans were allowed to leave Rome and avoid punishment. Ten days after the fight, Louis wrote to Pope Alexander withdrawing his ambassador, declaring: *"that no one who concerns my dignity should remain any longer exposed to outrages such as have been unequalled even by the barbarians themselves."* He then ordered the papal nuncio to leave Paris and commanded French troops to seize the papal state of Avignon

Louis' **PROLONGED OUTCRY** (it began in 1661) was eventually pacified by the *Treaty of Pisa* (12 February 1664), in which Pope Alexander finally yielded to Louis XIV's demands.[5]

The final line of this oracle covers the same period of time, and includes a further example of Nostradamus's bitter humour. At the commencement of Louis XIV's reign Nicolas Fouquet continued to see himself as First Minister in charge of finances. But his time in office was about to end. Another minister, Jean-Baptiste Colbert dissembled Fouquet's accounts before the King, and demonstrated several inaccuracies. The disgraced minister was then arrested and charged with lèse-majesté.[6]

As finance minister during Cardinal Mazarin's period of government, Fouquet had acquired some expensive properties. Among these was his house at Saint Mandé adjoining the park at Vincennes; another was a château on Belle-Isle at the mouth of Quiberon Bay. But the most extravagant, and architecturally grand was his mansion known as Vaux-le-Vicomte.

> *On 2 August 1656, he signed an agreement with Louis Le Vau . . . Early in 1657 a task force of 18,000 was set to work. Levelling the ground for the immense gardens and laying the foundations for the château and its palatial outbuildings. Within a year the shell of masonry was completed.*[7]

CHIEF NOT HAVING PROPERTY CERTAIN FOR DWELLING

The entire construction, magnificently furnished, and with '*143 tapestries*' designed by Le Brun and manufactured in a special factory created for the occasion, was finally completed in 1661. But on 3 September, Fouquet was arrested. For the next three years, this former **CHIEF** finance minister of France – now **HAVING NOT THE CERTAINTY OF HIS PROPERTY** being available **FOR DWELLING** – was put on trial for embezzlement. In December 1664 he finally received his sentence. Initially his punishment was banishment, but Louis subsequently altered this to perpetual imprisonment. Fouquet was sent to the castle at Pignerolo on the borders of Piedmont, where he remained until his death twelve years later.[8]

The next quatrain concerning Louis XIV is accurately dated. But it was not included amongst Nostradamus's published prophecies. It first appeared in 1605 with a note attached – *'Added since the printing of 1568'*, and it made its first appearance in a copy made from Benoist Rigaud's first edition. Leffen's own reference to it (1650) stated – *'Adjousté depuis l'impression de 1568'*. The most likely explanation is that it was one of the missing quatrains from Century VII that emerged with its number missing.

Additional Quatrain

Quand le fourchu fera fouftenu de deux paux
Avec fix demy cors, & fix fizeaux ouvers:
Le trefpuiffant Seigneur, heritier des crepaux,
Alors fubiugera, fous foy tout l'univers.

When the fork shall be supported by two ends,
With six half horns, & six open scissors:
The exceedingly powerful Lord, inheritor of the toads:
Then he will subjugate, beneath him all the universe.

paux, (Latinism) paus/ae – ends, stops; fizeaux – ciseaux.

THE FORK SUPPORTED BY TWO ENDS WITH SIX HALF HORNS AND SIX OPEN SCISSORS

The first two lines commence with an instruction. By recording on paper what is written, the symbols: **IVI C C C C C C X X X X X** appear. After closing together **IVI**, to form M, a date can then be read in Roman Numerals; *viz.* M = 1000; C = 100; X = 10, which, combined, give the year 1660.[1]

According to the legalistic form of dating, widely used when these oracles were written, 24 March 1660 would have been followed by the first day of the New Year 1661. This was because the birth of Jesus had been fixed at 25 December, from which it was concluded that 25 March was the date on which the Virgin Mary conceived her God-child. Hence, 25 March became the first day of each New Year. Before then, the New Year had been celebrated on 1 January, and indeed, this convention still continued in many parts of the country for different reasons.

THE EXCEEDINGLY POWERFUL LORD

On 28 February 1660 (O.S.), the virtual ruler of France, Cardinal Mazarin, died: his death giving way to the reign of Louis XIV. *"Only then"*, the King wrote in his memoirs, *"did it seem to me that I was King: born to be King."* And, eventually, as history would show, he became ruler of *"the most absolute monarchy in Europe."*[2]

INHERITOR OF TOADS

Louis XIV's reign has since become inseparable from the palace he built at Versailles. He **INHERITED** the site from his father Louis XIII, who had used a small building there as a hunting lodge and retreat. On 25 October 1660, Louis XIV, accompanied by his wife, Maria Theresa, visited the Val de Galie next to the hamlet of Versailles in order to assess the potential of his inheritance. The King was clearly satisfied by what he saw, for upon returning to Paris he decided to construct a new palace on the site. However, the ground was low lying and consisted mostly of marshland: an ideal habitat for amphibians – hence, the **INHERITOR OF TOADS** (another piece of dark humour from Nostradamus). Consequently, before any building work could take place, the land had to be drained. By the time of its completion in 1687, the Palace of Versailles had become – *"one of the most massive architectural statements of political power in French history."*[3]

THEN HE WILL SUBJUGATE

Louis XIV desired above all other considerations to make his reign glorious. He therefore made it personally known that:

> *All power, all authority, resides in the hands of the king, and there can be no other in his kingdom than that which he establishes. The nation does not form a body in France. It resides entire in the person of the king.*[4]

BENEATH HIM ALL THE UNIVERSE

From this time onwards, France made important progress in every field of political, economic, scientific, philosophic, and artistic development, until eventually – *"Louis XIV appeared the most prosperous and powerful monarch in the world."*[5] By a series of wars, he had extended France's borders, acquired new territories, and spread his *'gloire'* across half the civilized world.

> *The king was at this time at the height of his greatness. Victorious since he had begun his reign, having besieged no place which he had not taken, superior in every way to his united enemies, for six years the terror of Europe … in 1680 the Council of Paris conferred the title of Great upon him.*[6]

There is no contradiction in using the word 'universe' as a synonym for 'world': because in the 17th century, the Copernican system was still in the throes of replacing the ancient belief that the earth was a fixed stationary body at the centre of the universe.

In this next quatrain, Louis XIV is again identified as *the child born with two teeth*. We therefore have, as before, another prophecy with an extended time lapse. In this case, the predictions have been separated by a seven-year interval, thus adding further to the difficulty of identifying events in advance of their fulfilment.

C.II: 7

Entre pluſieurs aux Iſles deportés,
L'vn eſtre nay à deux dents en la gorge:
Mourront de faim, les arbres eſbrotés,
Pour eux neuf roy nouel edict leur forge.

Amongst a great number exempted, to the Isles,
The one to be born with two teeth in his mouth:
They will die of hunger, the trees stripped bare,
For them a new king: a new edict their fabrication.

pluſieurs, (O.Fr.) a great number, many; deportés, (O.Fr.) priver, dispenser; eſbrotés, (O.Fr. broster) brouter, bourgeonner, prefixed with es, acts like es+fruitier = to make sterile; edict, (Latinism) edict/um; forge, (O.Fr.) fabrication en général.
Cross-reference: à deux dents en la gorge, C.III: 42.

AMONGST A GREAT NUMBER EXEMPTED

Louis XIV's revocation of the *Edict of Nantes* (Edict of Fontaine-bleau, 18 October 1685) caused A GREAT NUMBER of French citizens to be EXEMPTED from legal representation. These were Huguenots, and once deprived of the law, they were easy prey to the cruellest treatment, even possible execution.[1]

TO THE ISLES

AMONGST those leaving France to escape persecution were many skilled artisans who crossed the Channel TO THE British ISLES.[2]

A whole quarter of London was populated with French silk operatives; others brought to that city the perfected art of glass-cutting, an art that was henceforth lost to France.

THE ONE BORN WITH TWO TEETH IN HIS MOUTH

THE ONE TO BE BORN WITH TWO TEETH IN HIS MOUTH again identifies Louis XIV: foreseen by Nostradamus almost one and a half centuries earlier, as the King responsible for this huge migration. The scholarly Hugo Grotius also seems to have had a presentiment of Louis XIV's future intentions.

Neither the pope nor the lay princes appreciated the fears of the Swedish minister, the learned Hugo Grotius, who upon hearing that the child had been born with two fully developed teeth and that one wet nurse after another proved to be unable to sustain the punishment of feeding him, wrote to his master, "The Dauphin is not satisfied to dry up his nurses he tears them to pieces with his bites. It is for the neighbours of France to fear this precocious voracity." [3]

THEY WILL DIE OF HUNGER, THE TREES STRIPPED BARE

Seven years after Louis XIV's shattering persecution of the Huguenots, France was struck by *"a terrible winter [1693 – 94] followed by a poor harvest,"* which together, reduced the stock of available food, causing *'widespread famine'* across the land.[4] Nostradamus refers to **PEOPLE DYING FROM HUNGER** as the crops withered and the **TREES FAILED TO BUD** properly; this was brought about by a bitterly harsh spring that year, which devastated the food supply.

FOR THEM, A NEW KING

The Huguenot refugees who crossed over to England – **THE ISLES** – fared much better. **FOR THEM** there was **A NEW KING**. Instead of James II, who shared Louis XIV's Catholic faith and political ideals, William III was elected in 1689 to replace the unpopular James.[5] Like the refugees, this king was a Protestant who opposed *'French aggrandizement'*. Thereafter, *"France became and long remained Britain's enemy."*

A NEW EDICT THEIR FABRICATION

Nostradamus concludes by providing the reason for **THEIR** exemption from law: it was a **FABRICATION** invented by the King in the form of **A NEW EDICT**, which reversed Henri IV's earlier edict.

On Thursday 18 October 1685, the King signed the Edict of Fontaine-bleau, usually known as the Revocation of the Edict of Nantes. It forbade any exercise in public of la Religion Prétendue Réformée. To be a practising Huguenot was henceforth to be outside the law.[6]

With the fear of persecution, and lacking any legal redress – *"a prodigious number of people proscribed, naked, fugitive, wandered, innocent of any crime, seeking asylum far from their native land."*[7]

In the oracle that follows, Nostradamus provides another example of an extended view of the political situation in France at that time. On this occasion the quatrain covers twenty-one years, in order to include events that took place towards the end of Louis XIV's reign. In the previous quatrain the Sun King was identified as: *the one to be born with two teeth in his mouth*. This time, Nostradamus returns to the appellation of Amythaon. It is this consistency of historical facts, each time accurately correlated to the use of these identifiers, which must eventually wear away at even the most persistent doubt.

C.IX: 38

L'entrée de Blaye par Rochelle et l'Anglois,
Paffera outre le grand Æmathien:
Non loin d'Agen attendra le Gaulois,
Secours Narbonne deceu par entretien.

The entrance of Blaye, by reason of Rochelle and the English,
The great Amythaon will pass further:
Not far from Agen (Eugene), he will attend to the Frenchman,
Assistance, Narbonne deceived by the conference.

Æmathien, (Gk) Amythaon – Unspeakably Great, Amethea (one of the horses of the Sun); deceu, (O.Fr. decevoir) tromper, trahir; De Agen (paragram) [U]e [E]gen = Eugene; Cross-references: Aemathien, C.IX: 64; C.IX: 93; C.X: 7; C.X: 58; entretien, C.X: 58; Narbonne, C.IX: 64.

THE ENTRANCE OF BLAYE

Blaye is a town 45 kilometres north of Bordeaux, standing on the estuary of the rivers Garonne and Dordogne. Overlooking THE ENTRANCE to the estuary AT BLAYE is an imposing fortification built by Vauban for Louis XIV. Plans for the work outlining this construction were proposed to the King in a memoir dated 30 October 1685. The stronghold was finally completed in the autumn of 1689 at a cost of more than a million livres. Its purpose was to shield the approach to Bordeaux, which is situated further inland.[1]

BY REASON OF LA ROCHELLE AND THE ENGLISH

The reason for the King's sudden urge to construct a fortification at THE ENTRANCE OF BLAYE was because OF LA ROCHELLE AND THE ENGLISH. La Rochelle had been the centre and stronghold of the Huguenots ever since Calvin's protestant ideas were introduced into France. Louis' fear was that that *the English* might attack *La Rochelle* in an attempt to support, perhaps even repatriate, the Huguenot population that had fled France after having been denied legal representation under the newly decreed *Edict of Fontainebleau*. Consequently, in the same year that Louis revoked the *Edict of Nantes*, he began fortifying the *entrance at Blaye*.[2]

It was also *at Blaye,* on 30 December 1700 that Louis XIV's young grandson arrived on his journey to Bordeaux; later **PASSING** beyond the fortress town *en route* for the French frontier and the Spanish crown, which he was to accept under the guidance and rule of **THE GREAT AMYTHAON**. Spain's King Charles II had died without a natural successor, and Louis XIV's grandson had been nominated to succeed him as Philip V.

> *Europe seemed for a moment to stand paralysed, amazed and impotent, on seeing the Spanish monarchy come under the domination of France . . . one of his two grandsons was about to rule under his orders, Spain, America, half Italy and the Netherlands.*

Hence, through the rule of his sixteen-year-old grandson, Louis XIV – **THE GREAT AMYTHAON** – was able to extend his power and influence well beyond Iberia, into other parts of Europe, and across the Ocean to America.[3]

Since *Agen* is not the actual place where the event predicted in the third line occurred, but is said to be **NOT FAR FROM AGEN**, it leaves open the possibility that the town has been mentioned for another reason. This may have been the intention if we see *D'Agen* as a paranagram for Eugene (see above). Moreover, *Agen* is on the river Garonne, which flows down from *Blaye,* thus linking it to the previous part of the prediction. It also lies to the west of Provence in southern France, and it was there that this part of the oracle was fulfilled.

> *While his grandson was losing Naples, Louis himself was on the point of losing Provence and the Dauphiny. The Duke of Savoy and Prince Eugene had already crossed the Col of Tenda and entered Provence . . . the King of France perceived that the very Duke of Savoy who, the previous year had possessed little else than his capital and Prince Eugene who had been brought up in the French Court, were about to wrest Toulon and Marseilles from him.*

Since this oracle concerns France, there can be only one legitimate reason why emphasis has been given to **THE FRENCHMAN**, and that is because he would be recognized by that description; *viz.*

The first general to counterbalance the superiority of France was a 'Frenchman'; for so Prince Eugene may well be called, although he was the grandson of Charles Emmanuel, Duke of Savoy. His father, the Count of Soissons, had settled in France, was made Lieutenant-General of the armies and Governor of Champagne, and had married on 18 October 1663, Olympia Mancini, one of the nieces of Cardinal Mazarin. The fruit of this marriage . . . was the prince afterwards so dangerous to Louis XIV, who was born in Paris.[4]

On 22 August 1707, THE AMYTHAON did, indeed, ATTEND TO THE FRENCHMAN when Louis XIV broke the siege of Toulon. This provided the necessary means to secure Provence and liberate the Dauphiny.[5]

Prior to the Conference held on the Isle of Pheasants, which resulted in the signing of the *Peace of the Pyrenees* (1659), Narbonne, former capital of Gaul, had been under the protection of the fortress at Carcassonne. But when Roussillon became annexed to France, as part of this treaty, the frontier fortress was left to fall into disrepair. The consequences of allowing this to happen are expressed in the next part of the prophecy.

NARBONNE DECEIVED BY THE CONFERENCE

Roussillon originally formed part of the Roman province of Gallia Narbonensis, and NARBONNE is still known as *'the crossroads of southern Europe'*, having also been the capital of Languedoc. But it was DECEIVED BY THE Atlantic Ocean CONFERENCE, which gave Roussillon to France.[6] The acquisition of this region was considered a triumph. The downside was that the fortress at Carcassonne became neglected, since maintaining it no longer seemed necessary. This was to prove a mistake because the city was then unable to give the required ASSISTANCE to Louis XIV in his war against the *Frenchman*. For Toulon, where the siege took place, is a naval port inside the Golfe du Lion, and it shares the same stretch of coastline as its former medieval capital, *Narbonne*.

The next quatrain to be considered is very different from those previously met with, in that it is a continuation from the verse that precedes it. What has caused the seer to combine these two verses together is undoubtedly the connection provided by the failing moon: one symbolic, the other actual. If this interpretation is correct, then we see Nostradamus taking his final bow upon leaving the world stage. But, in doing so, he has left behind a civilization in the grip of terror: engulfed by a catastrophic, natural disaster, which leaves everyone fearful for their survival.

C.I: 48

Vingt ans du regne de la lune paſſés
Sept mil ans autre tiendra ſa monarchie:
Quand le ſoleil prendra ſes iours laſſés
Lors accomplir & mine ma prophetie.

Twenty years passed from the reign of the moon,
Seven thousand years another will hold his monarchy:
When the sun shall take up its days fatigued,
In that time, to accomplish and end my prophecy.

mine, (O.Fr. miner) finir.

In a letter addressed to his son (1 March 1555 O.S.), which formed the Preface to his first book of prophecies published some weeks later, Nostradamus stated that his predictions *'extend from now to the year 3797'*. However, for the moment, let us consider the verse below that leads from this. It makes a brief reference to the worldwide tumult that has been predicted for those alive in the fourth millennium, and then uses this to refer to the year 1700: a time when the War of the Spanish Succession was about to begin, and when Peter the Great was intent upon stamping his influence upon Russia, while at the same time conquering the northern corner of Europe. The verse is therefore notable for contrasting the lost power of the celestial moon (see above), with the lost power of the emblematic moon (see below), which symbolized the Ottoman Empire.

C.I: 49

Beaucoup beaucoup auant telles menées,
Ceux d'orient, par la vertu lunaire:
L'an mil ſept cent feront grands emmenées
Subiugant preſque le coing Aquilonaire.

Much, much before prolonged wails of this sort,
Those of the east, through the overthrown moon:
The year 1700, they will strike great blows,
Almost subduing the northerly corner.

telles, (O.Fr.) de cette nature, de ce genre; meneés, (O.Fr.) cris prolongés; vertu, (Latinism) verti (war) overthrown, destroyed; emmenées, (O.Fr. amenée) coup asséné, sommation; Aquilonaire, (Latinism) aquilonius.

149

The gospels refer to the end of the world as a time when the sun will be darkened and the stars will fall from the sky. There is reason to believe that Nostradamus was also talking of this period when he referred to the *'prolonged wails'* made by the people of that age.

> *There will be signs in the sun and moon and stars; on earth nations in agony, bewildered by the clamour of the ocean and its waves; men dying of fear as they await what menaces the world, for the powers of heaven will be shaken.* (Luke 21: 25-27).

At the time Nostradamus wrote the opening line of his oracle, the Ottoman Empire was at its peak. Its decline came later, towards the end of the seventeenth century when, between 1683 and 1699, Turkey fought the armies of the Holy League – Austria, Poland, Venice, and Russia. The war was finally brought to an end by the *Treaty of Karlowitz* (26 January 1699), which gave considerable concessions to the League, with Poland receiving a large part of what is now Ukraine. Russia's reward came in the following year, when Turkey signed the *Treaty of Constantinople* (1700). Under this agreement, Turkey was compelled to surrender the province of Azov in southwest Russia.

THOSE OF THE EAST, THROUGH THE OVERTHROWN MOON

Nostradamus has several times employed the phrase *those of,* and followed it by naming a particular region. Each time he has done this, it has directed attention towards the victors, or occupiers of that region, rather than to its native inhabitants. In 1699, Russia and Poland, as part of the Holy League, defeated the Ottoman Empire.[1] In this sense, Russia and Poland became **THOSE OF THE EAST, THROUGH THE OVERTHROWN MOON**; that is, the overthrow of the emblematic moon representing the Turkish Empire.

The analogy to events in 3797 AD, or thereabouts, is to the fatigued sun that rises in the east, and with its weakened gravitational field slowly releases the moon from its orbit. In fact the moon is even now, very slightly, moving away from the earth at the annual rate of 3.4 cm. A weakened sun would also affect the earth's orbit, causing the stars to appear to fall from their position in the sky (motion being relative). Moreover, the loss of the moon would have a devastating effect upon the tidal flow across the globe, giving new breath to Jesus' prophecy in the gospels, with its reference to the oceans in turmoil.

THE YEAR 1700

In **THE YEAR 1700**, the Great Northern War began. This involved Russia and Poland, assisted by Denmark, and was directed against Charles II of Sweden who had formed an alliance with Turkey.

THE GREAT ONES STRIKING BLOWS

In March that year, **THE GREAT ONES** of the northern region **BEGAN STRIKING BLOWS**. First was Christian V of Denmark who conquered the neighbouring region of Holstein-Gottorp: its ruling duke having allied himself to Sweden. Two months later, Poland struck at Livonia (now part of Estonia and Latvia); with the result that Riga became occupied. Another two months passed, and Charles XII sprang to the fore by invading Zealand, Denmark's largest island in the Baltic Sea. Charles then advanced on Copenhagen to force the Danes into handing back Holstein-Gottorp and compelling them to sue for peace (*Treaty of Traventhal*, August 1700). Victorious, he then turned his army towards occupied Riga, compelling Augustus II of Saxony-Poland to withdraw his forces. Buoyant with this further success, Charles turned his attention next to Peter I of Russia, and at Narva in Estonia, on 20 November 1700, with only 9,000 men he scattered a Russian army that was more than twice his strength.[2]

ALMOST SUBDUING THE NORTHERN CORNER

After suffering defeat at Narva, Czar Peter, another of the **GREAT ONES** in that part of the world, retaliated and retook the Baltic provinces from Charles XII. Later, in 1703, he founded the city of St. Petersburg, from where he was able to subdue the Cossacks in what became known as the Third Peasant War. Then, aided by Augustus, he went on to destroy the Swedish army sent to attack Moscow. Turning his attention to the northwest, he subjugated Finland before making several renewed and successful attacks by land and at sea against Sweden. Having **ALMOST SUBDUED THE NORTHERN CORNER**, Peter finally brought the War to an end. It was because of Czar Peter's efforts that Russia was able to take its first steps towards becoming one of the great political powers in the modern world.[3]

151

The reason for the seer's attention having been drawn to these countries outside of France is because it was his policy to predict for other nations that were destined to make a political impact on the world stage. He therefore focuses on Russia at the commencement of its emerging influence: at a time when the country was taking its first step towards becoming a world power. Later, we shall see how the seer has followed this up with further predictions for Russia, involving Catherine the Great, Czar Nicholas, the Russian Revolution, Lenin, the October Revolution, Gorbachev, Yeltsin, and the end of the communist system in Russia.

For the next oracle we return once more to France; to the court of Louis XIV, and to events that were taking place at the time Peter the Great was establishing himself *in the northern corner*. This time the oracle covers a time span of fourteen years. Nostradamus's preoccupation with twice seven seems invitingly close to the coincidental fact that Louis XIV died in his 77th year; in fact, just four days short of his 77th birthday. No claim is made that this is anything other than coincidence, even though what is contained in the quatrains and what is discovered to be historical fact often appear thought-based.

C.IV: 2

Par mort la France prendra voyage à faire,
Claſſe par mer, marcher monts Pyrenées,
Eſpaigne en trouble, marcher gent militaire:
De plus grand, dames en France emmenées,

Through death, France will make a journey to exploit,
Army by sea, marching [across] the Pyrenean Mountains,
Spain in trouble: the kindred soldier progressing:
For the greatest, the ladies of France conveyed away.

prendra, (O.Fr.) se passer; à faire, (O.Fr.) to exploit, to work, do, make &c. Claſſe, (Latinism) army, fleet; en (pronoun invariable) of it; gent (O.Fr.) kindred.

THROUGH DEATH

As the seventeenth century drew to its close, the approaching death of King Carlos II of Spain was occupying the thoughts of many European leaders. The reason was because the King had no heir, and a successor from outside Spain could possibly alter the balance of power in Europe. At the time, there were two principal claimants for the throne should it become vacant.

152

France and Austria were both anxious to add the Iberian Peninsula to their country's empire.

Carlos II eventually died in November 1700, and in his will he left the throne to Louis XIV's grandson, Philip d'Anjou. But the Holy Roman Emperor Leopold I disputed the bequest, proposing instead that his son Archduke Charles should succeed Carlos. It was THROUGH the DEATH of Spain's king, and the disagreement it bred between Louis XIV and Leopold I that the War of the Spanish Succession broke out: a conflict that was to bring in many other European countries.[1]

FRANCE WILL MAKE A JOURNEY TO EXPLOIT

When Louis' grandson left France to become Philip V of Spain, he took France with him. The fact that FRANCE was recognised at the time to have MADE THIS JOURNEY prompted the Spanish ambassador to remark – *"the Pyrenees had just melted away, and henceforth the two nations would no longer be separated."* Louis XIV clearly shared this sentiment, for he saw in his grandson's enthronement the opportunity TO EXPLOIT French interests in Spain.[2]

ARMY AT SEA

By 1704, the War of the Spanish Succession had not only begun, it had also spread to other countries, and Louis XIV's naval ARMY found itself confronted by the British and Dutch fleets AT SEA (Battle of Valez-Málaga).[3]

> *The 18th century (1704) saw one of the most important naval battles of the War of Succession. A Franco-Spanish fleet and the combined forces of the English and Dutch navies locked horns in a fierce battle involving 146 ships and almost 50,000 men. The confrontation failed to produce a clear victor and the Anglo-Dutch contingent withdrew to the port of Gibraltar, the French and Spanish heading for Malaga.*

MARCHING ACROSS THE PYRENEAN MOUNTAINS

Fighting on the Spanish mainland also began in 1704, when Archduke Charles arrived in Lisbon to gather support for his claim to the Spanish throne. Engaging him in battle were the forces of Louis XIV, whose army had recently MARCHED ACROSS THE PYRENEAN MOUNTAINS to back Philip V.[4]

SPAIN IN TROUBLE

SPAIN was soon IN TROUBLE. Barcelona was taken, and an Allied army advancing from Lisbon captured Madrid, forcing Louis' grandson Philip V to flee the capital.[5] As a consequence of this reversal, the Austrian Emperor upon seeing that he now held the upper hand, and backed by the United Provinces, insisted that Louis declare war on his grandson and provide help to drive him out of Spain. But, supported by the patriotism of the French people, Louis refused to comply with Leopold's demand, preferring instead to renew the war. The decision proved to be correct.

THE KINDRED SOLDIER PROGRESSING

"Regaining strength, the French made progress in Spain." That is, with **THE KINDRED SOLDIER PROGRESSING**, Philip V was able to recover most of his lost territory. Even so, the young King was unable to enter Madrid until 3 December 1710. While Barcelona had to wait until September 1714 before it was reclaimed.[6] The French also achieved military success outside of Spain, with Prince Eugene suffering defeat at Denain in the Netherlands (24 July 1712).

The War of the Spanish Succession finally came to an end in 1714, although it was June 1715 before a Franco-Spanish force was able to land on the island of Minorca and take possession. Two months later, France was mourning the death of its King.

THE GREATEST

Louis XIV was *'Le Grand Monarque'*: **THE GREATEST** monarch of that age, and it is with this title that the final line of Nostradamus's prophecy commences. In August 1715, the King lay dying from a leg infected with gangrene.[7]

THE LADIES OF FRANCE CONVEYED AWAY

On his death bed:

> *The King now turned to the princesses who were present. 'He summoned me next,' wrote Madame, 'as well as the duchesse de Berry and all his other daughters . . . He bade me adieu in words of such tenderness that I marvel that I did not fall over backwards unconscious.*

Also in attendance were Françoise Marquise de Maintenon, Louis' wife, and Mlle d'Aumale, both women had remained by the King's bedside for the greater part of his illness.[8]

Eventually, upon seeing that the King had passed into a state of unconsciousness, and perceiving the end was near and they could offer no further assistance, **THE LADIES OF FRANCE** were **CONVEYED AWAY** in tears, so that the King might be allowed to die in peace. Louis XIV passed from this life at 8:15 on the following morning (1 September).

Note the subtlety of Nostradamus when referring to the ladies of Louis XIV as *the ladies of France*. When Louis made his now famous announcement: *'L'État c'est moi'*. (I am the State), he identified himself with France. Hence the ladies of France were the ladies of Louis XIV.

Louis XIV was succeeded by his five-year-old great-grandson, the third son of the Duke of Burgundy. This enormous gap in the line of inheritance to the throne was caused by the sudden deaths of those in between. It seemed at one time as though the bloodline of the Bourbon kings would be completely extinguished in France. And this appeared even more likely when the little heir to the throne caught the same smallpox that had already killed his parents and his brother. But he survived to become Louis XV. Nostradamus evidently foresaw all this, because he predicted that the line will *not* fail. And, to confirm that he was talking about this particular time in France's future, he gave an astronomical date that would mark the year when this prophecy would begin its fulfilment.

C.IV: 97

L'an que Mercure, Mars, Venus, retrograde,
Du grand Monarque la ligne ne faillir:
Efleu du peuple l'vfitant pres de Gandole,
Qu'en paix & regne viendra fort enuieillir.

The year when Mercury, Mars, Venus are retrograde,
The line not failing for the great Monarch:
Raised in rank, inuring him for the people, near Gandia,
When in peace and reign he will come to wax painful old.

Efleu, (O.Fr. eslever) élever en rang; vfitant, (O.Fr. vsiter) to accustom, to inure; Gandole, (Gandia), also paranagram: Gand[n]le – England: Note that 'Gandole' fails to rhyme with 'retrograde'; fort, (O.Fr.) pénible; enuieillir, (O.Fr.) to wax old.

N.B. Gandole in the third line is taken from du Rosne's edition of 1557. Later editions such as that of Rigaud (1568), which was probably edited by Chavigny, give the word as Gagdole. Leffen's edition of 1650, copied from a 1558 edition printed at Lyon, but subsequently edited, cites the word as Graudale, and may, perhaps, be a printing error for Grandale (Grandul in Andalusia). In the edition containing the two forged anti-Mazarin quatrains, but also copied from an earlier edition, the word appears as Pactole, which is a river of Lydia.

155

As previously mentioned, when these verses were written, Europe was still calculating New Year's Day for legal purposes according to the Old Style of dating. It was also a practice favoured by the seer when assigning a date to his prophecies. Consequently, the year 1710 ran from New Year's Day on 25 March up until 24 March twelve months later.

THE YEAR WHEN MERCURY, MARS AND VENUS ARE RETROGRADE

On New Year's Day, 25 March 1710, the planet VENUS was in RETROGRADE motion. On 22 December 1710, MARS, too, went RETROGRADE. And on 2 February 1710 (O.S.), it was MERCURY'S turn to go RETROGRADE.[1] Thus; all three planets became retrograde in 1710 (O.S.). It is also interesting to observe how the oracle has correctly named the planets in the *reverse* order to that in which their *retrograde* motion occurred.

In April 1711, just two months after *Mercury* went *retrograde*, the Dauphin, aged fifty, contracted smallpox and died. This left Louis XIV's grandson, the Duke of Burgundy, as the new heir to the throne. Ten months later, the Duke's wife, Marie Adélaïde fell ill and was dead within five days. Her husband, who had been by her bedside for the short duration of her illness, caught the infection and he, too, quickly passed away. The inheritance of the crown therefore went to the eldest of his two surviving sons, the duc de Bretagne. But he, together with his brother the duc d'Anjou, both succumbed to the infection that had just killed their parents. Bretagne died on 7 March, leaving Anjou's death expected any day. But the little boy recovered to become King Louis XV.[2]

THE LINE NOT FAILING FOR THE GREAT MONARCH

In quick succession the next in line for the throne had passed through three generations, from Louis XIV's son to his grandson, to his eldest great-grandson, and then to his other great-grandson. But, as the oracle had correctly foretold for this time: THE LINE of succession NOT FAILING FOR THE GREAT MONARCH. As noted in the previous quatrain, Louis XIV was indeed called '*Le Grand Monarque*'.[3]

RAISED IN RANK

Louis XIV's other grandson, Philip, had earlier been RAISED IN RANK from Duke of Anjou to King Philip V of Spain. However, it was this acquisition of the Spanish title that debarred Philip from succeeding to the French throne. Consequently, it allowed the succession to pass down a generation to Louis' great-grandson.

INURING HIM FOR THE PEOPLE

Philip V was just sixteen years of age, and a Frenchman when he became King of Spain. It was therefore necessary for Louis XIV and his councillors to **INURE HIM** [4] **FOR** acceptance by **THE PEOPLE** over whom he would rule.[5] But there was a rival for the Spanish throne. This was the Archduke Charles, Emperor Leopold's son. It was because of this rivalry that the War of the Spanish Succession (1701–14) broke out. In the battle for preferment between these two men, France was able to take comfort from knowing that the greater part of Spain accepted Philip: only Catalonia, Aragon and Valencia preferred Charles.

NEAR GANDIA

The control of Valencia, a city **NEAR GANDIA**, was the aim of those fighting at the Battle of Almanza (25 April 1707). This conflict proved to be one of the most important in the War of the Spanish Succession, because it brought to an end Charles's hold on Valencia (8 May),[6] it also changed the direction of the war in France's favour. However, it is noteworthy that Gandia has been named instead of Valencia, and that by writing it as Gandole, Nostradamus has allowed the spelling to be seen as a paranagram, which when rearranged, spells England: one of the countries brought into the conflict.

In London, during March of that year, the Act of Union between Scotland and **ENGLAND** was passed. As one nation, Great Britain was now able to bring economic and cultural advantages to both countries. But, just as importantly, it also removed the threat that Scotland might one day choose a different king from England, and pursue policies contrary to those being followed in the War of the Spanish Succession.[7]

WHEN IN PEACE AND REIGN, HE WILL COME TO WAX PAINFUL OLD

In 1714, the War was finally brought to an end with a series of peace treaties. Philip V kept Spain, as well as Spanish America. The Emperor received Milan, Naples, Sardinia, and control over the Spanish Netherlands. Louis XIV's extensive **REIGN** continued just long enough for him to oversee the PEACE settlement reach its conclusion. But, as the oracle predicted: HE WILL COME TO WAX PAINFUL OLD. In an age when life expectancy was lower than fifty, the King had already reached the latter half of his seventies. He died a PAINFUL death on 1 September 1715, just four days short of his seventy-seventh birthday, with his leg black from gangrene.[8]

This oracle foreshadowed the unlikely event that Louis XIV's great-grandson would succeed him. The next prediction concerns the succession. It also introduces the first male to take on the role of regent since the publication of these prophecies in 1555.

C.III: 15

Cueur, vigueur, gloire, le regne changera,
De tous points, contre aiant fon aduerfaire.
Lors France enfance par mort fubiuguera.
Le grand regent fera lors plus contraire.

Heart, vigour, glory; the reign will change,
Having his adversary differing at all points,
In that time France, through death, will subdue a childhood.
The great regent will then be very contrary.

Cueur, (O.Fr.) heart, mind, courage.

HEART, VIGOUR, GLORY

In his Memoirs, Louis XIV wrote – *"In my heart I prefer fame above all else . . . Love of glory has the same subtleties as the most tender passions . . . "* In fact, Louis XIV – *"pursued his gloire, with such concentration that it became an even more fundamental theme of French policy."*[1] To this, one may add the report made by John de Witt, the Sun King's Dutch adversary – *"a twenty-six year-old king, vigorous of body and spirit, who knows his own mind and acts on his own authority."*[2] With just three words: HEART, VIGOUR, GLORY, Nostradamus has identified the character of Louis XIV, as seen by both himself and his contemporaries.

THE REIGN WILL CHANGE

In 1715, Louis XIV, the Great Monarch, died and the REIGN CHANGED. *"After the experience of his reign, there was a general determination never to be treated in the same manner again, and the Regency opened in a mood of full-scale reaction.* The Sun King's death had also come with France immersed in financial difficulty.

[An] intense social crisis caused by the burden of taxation ... almost twenty-five years of war was finally concluded by a state of mutual

158

exhaustion. ... [the] remainder of the eighteenth century ... was to be characterised by economic and demographic recovery, and long periods of internal peace and order.[3]

HIS ADVERSARY DIFFERING AT ALL POINTS

The King had left precise instructions in his will for a Council of Regency to rule France during his great-grandson's minority. But Philippe, duc d'Orléans, **HIS ADVERSARY** while he lived, continued to oppose him after his death, **DIFFERING AT ALL POINTS** of government. His first action was to remove the duc de Maine and the Comte de Toulouse from the Council, so that he alone could be Regent.[4]

Secondly, the groups representing Louis XIV had been: *"the Sword, the Parlements and the Jansenists."* D'Orléans opposed all three. *"In 1720 he was forced to exile the Paris Parlement to Pontoise ... He [also] insisted on enforcing the papal Bull Unigenitus (1713) against the Jansenists."* And thirdly, in 1718 he dissolved the *Polysynodie*, through which he had originally sought to give the nobility of the Sword a role in government.[5]

IN THAT TIME FRANCE, THROUGH DEATH, WILL SUBDUE A CHILDHOOD

It had been **THROUGH** the **DEATH** of his grandfather, his parents, and his only surviving brother that five-year-old Louis XV became King of France.[6] With so many recent deaths in the royal family, and he being the last in the bloodline, the country took the utmost care to ensure that the little boy reached manhood safely; because of this **HIS CHILDHOOD WAS SUBDUED.**

He had been brought up by obsequious courtiers, subject to tedious and rigid ceremonies. He ate in public, watched in worshipful silence by those who had the privilege of entering his presence. He rose and went to bed accompanied by elaborate ceremonies and disputes among nobles as to which duke had the right to hold his shirt, which the candlestick. . . . The boy became silent and withdrawn, increasingly moody and sullen.[7]

THE GREAT REGENT WILL THEN BE VERY CONTRARY

Philippe, duc d'Orléans, a nephew of Louis XIV, was **THE GREAT REGENT**. He was also the only male to have occupied the position of regent since these oracles were written. But Philippe was a flawed character. *"His irreverence, habitual drunkenness, and licentious behaviour had earned him an unsavoury reputation."* Nevertheless, he possessed ambition and political acumen. In the wake of Louis XIV's death, he made plans for the succession of his own dynasty, should his young charge die.

> On 2 September, the Duke of Orleans went to meet the parlementaires in the Grand-Chambre du Parlement in Paris in order to have Louis XIV's will annulled and his previous right to the regency restored. ... Philippe disapproved of the hypocrisy of Louis XIV's reign and opposed censorship, ordering the reprinting of books banned during the reign of his uncle. Reversing his uncle's policies again, Philippe formed an alliance with England, Austria, and the Netherlands, and fought a successful war against Spain that established the conditions of a European peace.[8]

This was VERY CONTRARY to the previous policies adopted by Louis XIV, who had engaged in many wars and maintained a tight control over the State, seeing himself as its embodiment.

In the oracle that follows, the regent to Louis XV is actually named, along with the length of time he was to serve in this capacity. As with previous prophecies, this too covers a fairly lengthy period, which tends to deflect attention away from its content. People by and large are inclined to lose interest in a prophecy if its fulfilment is too long delayed. The oracle also provides a second name, and one that was entirely relevant to the reign of Louis XV. This naming of names is a highly contentious part of Nostradamus's prophecies. Yet, in reality, the future is simply another man's history, and both political and social histories consist of the biographies of those who left their names imprinted on what happened in the world during their time. More will be said about this in the Afterword.

C.IX: 89

Sept ans fera PHILIP. fortune profpere,
Rabaiffera des BARBARES l'effort.
Puis fon midy perplex, rebours affaire,
Ieune ognion abyfmera fon fort.

Seven years will be PHILIPPE: a thriving success,
He will abate the effort of the foreign tongues,
Then his midi causes confusion, a wayward affair,
Young Gallic Hercules will abase his stronghold.

PHILIP. (abbrev.) Philip[pe]; fortune, (Latinism) success; profpere, (Latinism) thriving, prosperous; rebours, (O.Fr.) wayward; perplex (Latinism) perplex/or; BARBARES; (Greek: βαρβαρος) foreign tongues; ognion, Og[m]ios – the Gallic Hercules; abyfmera, (O.Fr.) to cast into a bottomless pit; fort, (O.Fr.) fort, stronghold, standing or settled camp.

N.B. This quatrain has been copied from the Vrayes Centuries published by Pierre Leffen in 1650, which was reproduced from the Lyon edition of 1558. It differs from that of Rigaud's 1568 edition at several points. Firstly, 'PHILIP.' has been written as Philip. Secondly, 'BARBARES l'effort', has been written as 'Arabes l'effaict', which then fails to rhyme with son fort, while also casting doubt on the meaning intended for l'effaict. Thirdly, midy perplex, is written as mydi perplex (without a comma). There is also a printing error in Rigaud; the number of the quatrain, 89 (LXXXIX) has been incorrectly shown as LXXXXI (91).

SEVEN YEARS WILL BE PHILIPPE

The period of SEVEN YEARS and five months that passed between September 1715 and February 1723 marked the time that PHILIPPE duc d' Orléans acted as Regent to Louis XV.

His rakish friends turned the seven years of his regency into a disorderly reaction against the sad, stiff austerity which characterised the last years of his uncle, Louis XIV's reign.[1]

A THRIVING SUCCESS

Upon becoming regent, Orléans' first act was to remove the little King from Versailles and house him at the *Palais de Tuileries*, in the heart of Paris. From this base, and with the circumstances favourable for reform, he set about transforming the capital into A THRIVING SUCCESS. *"His regency, unlike most preceding ones, passed off in relative tranquillity."* (Black and Porter, 2001, p.532)

An application of money and energy stimulated the development of an entire new district of the city, the faubourg Saint-Germain, where the nobility, freed from the constraints of life at Versailles, began to build elegant new town houses; Parisian society turned to the pursuit of pleasure, buying beautiful clothes and objets de luxe, discovering the delights of fine cuisine and lavish entertaining, and all the joys of la vie mondaine.[2]

HE WILL ABATE THE EFFORTS OF THE FOREIGN TONGUES

In 1715, Turkey was still anxious to engage Russia in war: the country's intention being to recover Azov from Peter the Great, but Turkey needed help from Charles XII of Sweden. In the midst of this intrigue there existed an anti-French alliance resulting from the War of the Spanish Succession. But, in the negotiations that took place, Philippe duc d'Orléans was able to secure: *"A subsidy treaty with France . . . [which] averted the danger to Sweden once Charles, in December 1715, had been forced to leave Stralsund and Wismar."* In the following year, he also ABATED THE EFFORTS OF Spain, THE FOREIGN TONGUES when: —

161

> ... the abbé (later Cardinal) Guillaume Dubois, concluded with Great
> Britain, France's traditional enemy, an alliance that secured British sup-
> port against Philip V's claim to the succession to the French throne.
> France and Great Britain went to war with Spain in 1719, and in the
> following year Philip V was forced to renounce his French claims and
> recognize Orléans as Louis XV's heir.[3]

HIS MIDI

France's Midi – *'Midi (de la France)'* – refers to the South of France
(Cassell's Dictionary). From this, it is but a single step to understand that *'his midi'* is Philippe's Midi, which was situated in
America. For it was in the state of Louisiana, in the Deep South,
that New Orleans [4] was named after Philippe d'Orléans. In this
sense, New Orleans became **HIS MIDI**.

CAUSES CONFUSION

It is this feature that takes us to 1720. Paris was in uproar. A
Scottish financier, John Law, with the Regent's approval, had
started a commercial bank, later the *Banque Royale*, using the
revolutionary idea of paper money. People were being encouraged to bring their gold and silver to the bank and exchange it
for banknotes. The precious metal received this way was then
invested to exploit America's resources.

Law's company had earlier obtained exclusive rights to develop
the vast French territories in the Mississippi river valley of North
America. As part of the enterprise the Mississippi Company was
established in 1717, primarily to deal with investments following
the founding of New Orleans. But the venture collapsed, **CAUSING**
widespread **CONFUSION**.[5] John Law fled to Brussels to escape the
wrath of those who had lost money. *"Those who had invested in the
'Mississippi' saw their savings gone, their security vanished, their hopes destroyed."*

A WAYWARD AFFAIR

At its high point, before the collapse, 500-livres shares were being exchanged for 18,000 livres, and an open-air stock market in
the centre of Paris was conducting business amidst frenzied
scenes of buying and selling. When the bank eventually collapsed, the Regent, who had made John Law the Controller-
General of Finance, took fright at this **WAYWARD AFFAIR**,[6] and removed Louis XV to the safety of Versailles.

Nostradamus now directs his attention to the King.

Shortly before his death in September 1715, Louis XIV appointed Fleury tutor to his five-year-old great-grandson and heir, who succeeded to the throne as Louis XV.

This appointment continued to be approved by d'Orléans after the King's death. Some years later, in June 1726, Louis decided to reward his old tutor, then aged 73, by firstly appointing him Minister of State, and then by arranging for his election to the College of Cardinals.

YOUNG GALLIC HERCULES

Now, there are occasions when it happens that a pupil receives the sobriquet of the master he learned from. For example, Louis XV might easily have been called 'young Fleury'. Because – *"Fleury [had been] the only father he had known"*,[7] and the child had grown-up totally under his influence. Nostradamus, with his preference for classical literature calls him instead: **YOUNG GALLIC HERCULES**. Why? Because Louis XV was **YOUNG**, he was **FRENCH**, and the full name of Louis XV's tutor, and surrogate father, was André-**HERCULE** de Fleury.

Interestingly, in Greek literature, Ogmios was portrayed as a balding, wrinkled old man gifted with eloquence. It was a therefore a perfectly apt description for the 73-year-old *Hercule* de Fleury, the King's minister, and former educator.

WILL ABASE HIS STRONGHOLD

The seer's deliberate use of *'abysmera'* (a verb derived from the abyss) provides an accurate, if religiously moralistic prophecy of Louis XV's reign. For this particular monarch was addicted to gambling, alcohol, and fornication, although with no preference as to order. *"Louis XV drank beyond measure so that his royal majesty was sometimes compromised upon leaving the table."* Madame de Pompadour, in later life: *"did everything she could to divert him from his passion for gambling but could not manage it."*

It was, however, his sexual appetite for teenage virgins, who he installed in his *'Birdcage'* until they became pregnant, as almost invariably they did, that affirmed his reputation for licentiousness. *"The Parc-aux-Cerfs at Versailles visited nightly by Louis for assignations arranged by Pompadour gained an infamous reputation."* [8] Versailles was the King's *stronghold* or settled camp, and, as the oracle predicted, Louis XV **ABASED HIS STRONGHOLD**.

163

There is an interesting aspect to this prophecy; it is the reference to Ogmios the French Hercules. The suggestion was made in Chapter One that Nostradamus did not always understand the prophecies he made, at least those far into the future. In this respect, he was in the same position as the Pythia at Delphi, who required a priest to interpret the prophetic utterances she gave to those consulting her. The reference made to Ogmios tends to confirm Nostradamus as a medium through which visions of the future passed, and which he recorded without necessarily understanding the story behind them.

For example, the scholarly Nostradamus would have recognized the name Ogmios as a synonym for the French Hercules. Upon seeing this written down in one of his prophetic verses, he may have imagined the appearance in France of a mighty warrior. The possibility that it referred to the name of a person in the circumstances described above is very far from being deducible before the event. Hence, the facility for error is evident, and this mistake appears to have been committed by Nostradamus in his letter to Henri II, where he confides:

> *The Gallic Ogmios will be accompanied by so great a number that the Empire of his great law will extend very far. For some time thereafter the blood of the Innocent will be shed profusely by the recently elevated guilty ones.*

If this was intended to refer to Louis XV, then serious objections can be raised. Firstly, Louis XV was not only debauched, he also avoided the daily grind of governing France at every opportunity: often allowing his mistress to attend to his duties. Moreover, there was no *Empire of his great law*. Yet, what follows in the letter is perfectly correct. Louis XVI succeeded to the reign, and with him came the French Revolution. *The blood of the Innocent* was *shed profusely* beneath the guillotine, and *the recently elevated*: those elected to govern France *were the guilty ones*.

It would appear that Nostradamus mistook Louis XIV for the French Hercules, for it was the Sun King: *"in a series of aggressive wars, [who] extended the realm and strengthened its frontiers, making France the leading power in Europe."* [9] Because some oracles overlap, as in the case where the reign of Louis XIV is succeeded by his great-grandson, the opportunity for mistaking one for the other is at risk. Consequently, someone without a full knowledge of the situation, yet attempting to make sense of what was written long before its fulfilment, could easily mistake the young French Hercules, so-called to identify Louis XV as a pupil of Hercule de Fleury, with Louis XIV who was in a very real sense the French Hercules.

This next quatrain provides a brief pen portrait of Louis XV's character. And, as with Oliver Cromwell whom we shall encounter in Chapter 5, the problems raised by describing the personality of someone many years before their birth, poses questions about the nature of time that neither science nor religion have been able to answer. It is therefore understandable that those who have devoted their lives and beliefs to these subjects will prefer to avoid the possibility of prophesy altogether, using their own particular premise to disavow whatever contradicts it.

C.V: 38

Ce grand monarque qu'au mort fuccedera,
Donnera vie illicite & lubrique:
Par nonchalence à tous concedera,
Qu'a la parfin fauldra la loy Salique.

That great monarch whom at the death, he will succeed,
He will give way to a life illicit and slimy:
Through nonchalance he will concede to everything,
So, at the end, the Salic law will be wanting.

lubrique, (Latinism) lubric/us; a la parfin, (O.Fr.) à la fin; fauldra = faudra, see falloir.

THAT GREAT MONARCH WHOM AT DEATH HE WILL SUCCEED

THAT GREAT MONARCH, *'Louis Le Grand'*, **WHOM** his great-grandson **WILL SUCCEED AT HIS DEATH,**[1] invites a comparison between the two monarchs. For example, Louis XV's *"personal rule (1743-74) made ministerial inability a permanent feature of the rest of the reign."* In this, he was the complete opposite of his great-grandfather, who made the rule of France his full-time profession.

HE WILL GIVE WAY TO AN ILLICIT LIFE

Part of the reason for Louis XV's ineptitude may have begun with the man who became regent during his minority. Philippe II duc d'Orléans proved to be no exemplar of morality. By the time he became regent he had already acquired the reputation for: *'irreverence, habitual drunkenness, and licentious behaviour'*. It is not surprising therefore that upon reaching adulthood, and with such a role model, the King followed Orléans' example. To his addiction for gambling and alcohol HE GAVE WAY TO A LIFE of ILLICIT sex with young girls, whom he maintained in his *'birdcage'* until pregnancy made it necessary for them to be replaced.[2]

SLIMY

The oracle also describes the King as *'slimy'*. This is understood to be a reference to his *'cabinet noir'*: a group of men who, among other practices, had devised a means for opening letters and re-sealing them without detection. Louis XV became totally addicted to reading the salacious gossip and intimate secrets of his courtiers, especially those of the clergy and the nobility, who were unwise enough to entrust secrets of a sexual nature to letters sent through the *Paris Poste*.[3]

The King also began a policy, which he set up in or about 1748, involving a complex system of underhand diplomacy known as *'le Secret du roi'*. French spies were stationed in major European capitals and ordered to secretly pursue political objectives that were frequently opposed to Louis' own publicly acclaimed policy.

NONCHALANT, CONCEDING EVERYTHING

Louis XV's ineptitude for government was another of his characteristics, for he had neither the interest nor the energy required for dealing with the day-to-day affairs of running the country. Instead, he preferred to fill his day with the delights of hunting, and the nights by attending to his mistresses. A power vacuum was therefore created, which allowed his ministers to form into factions, often with opposing viewpoints. It was this NONCHALANT attitude towards government, combined with the willingness to CONCEDE EVERYTHING involving state affairs to the competence of others,[4] that further contributes to the identity of Louis XV as the subject of this oracle.

AT THE END, THE SALIC LAW WILL BE WANTING

The final line refers to the *'Salic law'*. This operated in France, and was designed to prevent the succession of the monarchy passing into female hands.

Fleury died, aged eighty-eight, in 1742, the King allowed himself – and France – to be ruled by his mistresses, first Mme de Pompadour for two

166

decades, then after her demise, by the much hated vulgarian Mme du Barry.[5]

Madame de Pompadour (aka Mistress of France), *"exerted her influence over appointments, promotions, honours, and preferment's of all kinds."* She was therefore able to influence the course of France's affairs, both foreign and military. In addition, she gave regular audiences to visiting ambassadors. At the palace of Versailles, it was said she virtually achieved the position of Queen.[6]

The SALIC LAW was intended to prevent this from occurring. Nostradamus therefore resorts to the darker side of his humour by predicting that it would BE WANTING at the latter part of Louis XV's reign. This was because of the manner in which the King's mistresses had taken over the office of government.

Readers may have noted that no real attempt has been made to conceal the truth of this particular oracle. Even sceptics are reduced to dismissing it as a coincidental success. There is, of course, a reason for the oracle's lack of obscurity and this tends to throw extra light upon the construction of these predictions.

Louis XV lived during an age that had become gripped by the Enlightenment with its rationalism, and the writings of the *philosophes*. The rationalists regarded reason to be the only test of knowledge. They were also directly opposed to any system that claimed access to esoteric knowledge, whether from mystical experience, revelation, or intuition. In the reign of Louis XV, this climate of intellectual scepticism began with Voltaire and Montesquieu, but later fell under the wider influence of men like Diderot, Rousseau, Leclerc, de Buffon, Condillac, Turgot, and Condorcet. Since France was under the sway of these *philosophes*, with their denunciation of esoteric knowledge, the predictions made by Nostradamus were never going to be taken seriously. Hence, there was no need for obscurity. That was reserved for people of a different age: those who were prepared to give credence to prophecy. This explanation for the present oracle's openness does, however, imply prescient knowledge of the intellectual climate existing at that time, namely the Enlightenment.

Nostradamus leaves France for the next oracle, in order to focus upon events happening in Persia. Why Persia? The answer is disquieting. A study of these oracles reveals that the seer only predicted for countries outside of France if they were to make a major impact on the world at some later date. Therefore, by prophesying for Persia during its politically formative years in the early 18th century, Nostradamus is signalling that Persia will one day have a central role to play on the world stage. What that role will be is still awaited. Unfortunately, since the turn of the twentieth century, Persia – now renamed Iran – has been much in the news.

> *Iran is constructing a heavy water reactor that is designed to produce plutonium quite readily . . . Weapons experts say plutonium is often preferred to enriched uranium for compact warheads on missiles because it takes a smaller amount to produce a significant blast.*
> [Iranians Retain Plutonium Plan in Nuclear Deal – WILLIAM J. BROAD and ELAINE SCIOLINO 25 November 2004].

In the same report, it was said –

> *Non-proliferation experts see heavy water reactors as a danger because they are a relatively simple way to produce bomb fuel. These reactors use natural uranium, rather than the enriched form, which is difficult and costly to make.*

This reference to uranium, as we shall later see, is of potential concern, and could have future consequences for the world. Iran naturally denies any ulterior motive.

C.III: 77

> Le tiers climat foubz Aries comprins,
> L'an mil fept cens vingt & fept en Octobre,
> Le roy de Perfe par ceulx d'Egypte prins:
> Conflit, mort, perte: à la croix grand opprobre.

> *The third region between north and south, under Aries, comprehended,*
> *The year 1727 in October,*
> *The king of Persia bounded by those of Egypt:*
> *Conflict, death, loss: great opprobrium to the cross.*

climat, (O.Fr.) portion of the world between north and south; soubz, (O.Fr. sous) under; comprins, (O.Fr.) comprehended; prins, (O.Fr. prendre) se terminer.

THE THIRD REGION

David Ovason, an earlier commentator of this prophecy in 1997, discovered that *the third region* was a Babylonian reference to the seven bands of latitude devised by an Arabian astronomer named Alfraganus.[1] These bands stretched from the Equator to

168

the North Pole, and if taken to be approximately of equal width, (i.e., 0–13; 13-26; 26-39) **THE THIRD REGION** occurs between latitudes 26° and 39°. Both these lines encircle the globe, and between them they include many countries, but it is to Persia, modern-day Iran laying between these latitudes that attention is drawn.

UNDER ARIES

Continuing with astrology as the key to understanding this first line leads to the suggestion that Aries refers to the land of Syria and Palestine. Both countries, together with that part of the world, were deemed to be **UNDER** the influence of **ARIES**. Ovason has confirmed that Ptolemy's *Tetrabiblos* included a list of countries that were assigned to a sign of the Zodiac: among these was Aries, which included the region of Palestine and Syria.[2]

COMPREHENDED

Nostradamus has therefore identified a geographical region that extends from countries on the eastern shore of the Mediterranean to the land of Persia, lying in the third region between the Equator and the North Pole.

On 12 October 1722, Mir Mahmud, leading an army of Afghans, successfully conquered Persia from the east. The Ottoman Turks who already held Syria and Palestine seized this as an opportunity to add to their own empire. *"In 1723 ... the Ottomans invaded from the west [under Aries], ravaging western Persia."*[3] In Russia, Peter I responded to what was happening in Persia, and in return for lands on the southern and western shores of the Caspian Sea, he provided military aid to the beleaguered Persians.

Eventually, an agreement was reached that divided much of Persia between the Ottoman Turks and the Russians. And on 23 June 1724 the *Treaty of Constantinople* was formerly signed by Turkey and Russia against Persia. This extended their territorial gain to the west, where Persia was forced to cede the extensive borderlands captured by Turkey.

THE YEAR 1727 IN OCTOBER

In **1727**, Persia made an agreement with the Ottoman Empire: signing up to it **IN OCTOBER**.[4] Under this new alliance Persia now agreed to join forces with the Ottoman Turks against the Russian occupiers, in return for recognition by Turkey.[5]

KING OF PERSIA BOUNDED BY THOSE OF EGYPT

From as early as 1525, Egypt had been part of the Ottoman Empire, governed BY Turkish administrators. Hence, THOSE OF EGYPT were the country's Turkish occupiers.[6] This coincides with other verses where *those of* is intended for the occupying force, and not the indigenous people of the region or country named. From 1723, when the Ottomans invaded western Persia, up until 1730 when the *'Iranians drove the Turks out of Iran'*, THE KING OF PERSIA had been BOUNDED by the loss of his borderlands to the west.

CONFLICT, LOSS, DEATH

The entire period under review was one of CONFLICT between the Persians and the invading Afghans, Turks and Russians, resulting in the LOSS of large areas of territory and the DEATH of those who fell in the fighting.

The final phrase of this oracle is yet another of Nostradamus's enigmatic last lines, and refers to a satirical book portraying French life as seen through the eyes of two Persian travellers. The book was published in 1722, the same year that Mir Mahmud *overran Persia*. It was written by Montesquieu under the title: *'Lettres Persanes'* (Persian Letters).

GREAT OPPROBRIUM TO THE CROSS

In the years that followed its publication, the book's OPPROBRIUM TO THE CROSS did great harm to the Catholic Church. Derisory comparisons were drawn between Islam and Christianity, with the book satirizing Catholic doctrine as well as criticizing the papal bull, *Unigenitus*, which Pope Clement XI had directed against Catholic dissidents and the followers of Cornelius Jansen.[8]

Charles Louis Montesquieu, author of the *Persian Letters* and *De l'Esprit des Lois* (1748) was part of a new and growing intellectual movement called the Enlightenment (the Age of Reason). It was anti-religion, anti-revelation, and anti-inspiration; in fact, anti anything that failed a rational explanation. Its origins sprang from the growth of ideas that surrounded *'Newtonian materialism'*. In its time, it attracted many leading scientists, philosophers, politicians, and artists.

As part of the trend towards this new rationalism, a question central to the movement concerned the mechanics of perception.

Two British philosophers, John Locke and David Hume (*An Essay Concerning Human Understanding,* 1690: and *A Treatise of Human Nature* 1739 respectively) were to nurture the seeds of doubt sown by Isaac Newton and René Descartes: both having denied the ability of the senses to arrive at knowledge of the real world. Nostradamus, although ostracized by the Enlightenment, has nevertheless predicted what effect this would have upon religious observance.

C.IV: 25

Corps fublimes fans fin à l'œil vifibles
Obnubiler viendront par ces raifons:
Corps, front comprins, fens, chief & inuifibles,
Diminuant les facrées oraifons.

The bodies aloft, visible to the eye, without end,
They will come to obscure through these reasons:
Bodies, forehead included, senses, extremity also invisible,
Diminishing the sacred prayers.

fublimes, (Latinism) sublim/is, raised high; Obnubiler, (O.Fr. obnubler) obscurcir; front, (O.Fr.) front or forepart of a thing; chief, (O.Fr.) extrémité.

THE BODIES ALOFT, VISIBLE TO THE EYE

The opening line to this oracle refers to the stars in the night sky before the arrival of the telescope. There were, according to the Greek astronomer Ptolemy, in excess of a thousand **BODIES ALOFT, VISIBLE TO THE EYE** at any one time. [1]

WITHOUT END

The discovery of the telescope not only magnified these celestial bodies, it also brought into view even more that were invisible to the naked eye. The more powerful the telescope, the more stars there were to be seen. Soon, the celestial bodies began to appear **ENDLESS.** [2]

THEY WILL COME TO OBSCURE

The telescope did more than magnify the stars; it forced people to consider the implication of light travelling between these distant bodies and the eye of the observer. For the inescapable conclusion was, and is still, that the stars seen in the night sky cannot actually occupy the position where they appear. That is to say, since observers are dependent upon light reaching the eye, and because starlight often takes centuries, even millennia to arrive before affecting the retina of the eye with the image of its

171

celestial origin, then the images they produce may refer to stars that have since ceased to exist. It is like a traveller who sends a letter from the other side of the world. By the time the letter arrives, the sender will have moved to another location.

It is in this sense that when a scientific explanation is applied to vision, it will COME TO OBSCURE everything seen by the eye: replacing each object from which light has been reflected, by an image of its conjectured reality; conjectured, because what is actually seen is given shape and colour by the mind of the percipient, and this may be different to what exists.[3] Obvious examples of this are the magnification of an object compared with what is observed by unaided vision; reversal prisms that change the perceived polarity of the world from left to right to one of right to left; objects of vision that decrease in size with distance, when it is known that no such decrease has occurred. Nostradamus goes deeper into this subject with a single line of telegraphic words.

BODIES, SENSES, INVISIBLE

Natural philosophers living in the seventeenth-century, men like Galileo and Newton had recognised the problem posed by light, not just from the stars, but also from the world perceived through *the senses*. It was left to philosophers like René Descartes, John Locke, and David Hume to attempt to rationalize a person's perceptive faculty, while also attempting to preserve the essential features of what is understood to be the physical world. But, in doing so, their individual studies of *the senses* suggested, contrarily, that the world of corporeal substance; that is, the actual BODIES were directly unavailable to the SENSES.

Knowledge of the world, it was claimed, consisted entirely of mental imagery, which came to be called *ideas*, and as ideas, they existed only in the mind of the percipient. Locke was even forced to admit that - *"Matter is something we know not what."* By this, he meant that matter cannot be known by directly perceiving it. In short, what each person is presented with by the visual sense is a 3-dimensional video of mental pictures. Material objects are cognised by their colour and shape, which are always vulnerable to a perceived change, when no material change has actually taken place. This effect is therefore alleged to be a representation of the real thing; the real thing being INVISIBLE to direct vision.

Locke was therefore forced to make some attempt at restoring confidence in the scientists' quest for knowledge of matter, by defining substance in terms of its primary and secondary qualities. The former, he claimed, really did belong to substance; the latter was perceived to exist only in the mind of the beholder.[4]

FOREHEAD INCLUDED, FOR THESE REASONS

The scientific rationale for visual perception is based upon sound empirical research. Light waves reflected from objects existing in a three-dimensional world in which time passes in fleeting instants, enter the eye and affect the retina with inverted images of the surface from where these waves last rebounded. A formation of rods and cones behind the eye translates these impressed images into electro-chemical impulses, which are then sent to the cortex of the brain, **FOREHEAD INCLUDED**. The mind then actively, but subconsciously, decodes these cerebral signals to create a picture for the percipient, which is then seen by the 'mind's eye', so to speak; excessive alcohol, illness or drug abuse may, of course, affect the decoding of these signals, and therefore what ultimately appears in a person's field of vision. However, what is ordinarily seen in a person's illuminated field of vision is believed to replicate material objects existing in a black, invisible, world that regenerates itself at every instant. If it did not constantly regenerate itself at every instant, it would be a block universe existing eternally. The block universe is the subject of the Afterword, for which this prophecy of Nostradamus is an essential primer.

George Berkeley, Bishop of Cloyne, rejected the scientific explanation with a logical riposte that has never been successfully answered (*Principles of Human Knowledge*, and *Three Dialogues Between Hylas And Philonous*). Basically, if the mind did have the capacity to create mental images (ideas) of objects which it then projected onto the external bodies from which they originated, one would have to ask afresh for an explanation as to how these projections are seen and known, since the act of projection places them outside the mind. We have only to consider the possibility of images supposedly projected instantaneously onto bodies existing in outer space, distant galaxies for example, in order to acknowledge that however appealing this explanation may seem, it is logically indefensible. Indeed, the absurdity of even considering it leads one back to the field of vision created by the subconscious mind. Hence, given that knowledge of the world is obtained through a succession of mental images; from where did these images originate, if not from an invisible world of material bodies? Berkeley's answer was from the Mind of God. This possibility will be looked at again in the Afterword, when the prophecies of Nostradamus have been considered more fully, and an explanation for their accuracy is considered.

EXTREMITY ALSO INVISIBLE

Nostradamus now returns to the *bodies aloft without end*, and predicts that at the *extremity* of the universe, the celestial bodies there will *likewise* be *invisible*. By this he means that we will not even be able to see their images. This is now an acknowledged fact in astronomy. The reason for their invisibility is because the universe is expanding at such a fast rate that the light from stars at the EXTREMITY of the universe has not yet arrived on earth, and it is this that renders them, like the world of matter, ALSO INVISIBLE.

It was because of these scientific discoveries and the rationale attached to them that the final line of Nostradamus's prophecy became fulfilled. For as the Age of Reason increasingly gained authority, so the Church went into retreat.

The power of the Pope was reduced: taxes to Rome were cut; papal Bulls needed royal permission . . . agents from Rome lost their powers of visiting monasteries . . . the training and the work of the clergy were taken over by the State, which regarded priests more as agents of education, health and welfare than as a means of eternal salvation.[5]

Some monasteries were closed down, and censorship, which had formally been the prerogative of the Church, was taken over by the State.

DIMINISHING THE SACRED PRAYERS

The effect of this materialistic rationalism led to a DIMINISHING of THE SACRED PRAYERS, as congregations became less attended. Outside the Church, a growing divide between religion and science took hold of western thought, and its effect on the public has allowed an increase in hedonistic, secularism to occur in society.

Nostradamus next directs his prophetic gaze back to Russia: a country destined to achieve world prominence. It will be recalled that the seer's first introduction to the Russian people came at the commencement of the 18th century (C.I: 49), when Peter the Great subdued the northern corner of Europe, and laid the foundation for St. Petersburg to become his seat of government. The seer now predicts the emergence of another important figure in Russian history – Catherine the Great.

C.VIII: 15

Vers Aquilon grands efforts par hommaſſe,
Preſque l'Europe & l'vniuers vexer,
Les deux eclypſes mettra en telle chaſſe,
Et aux Pannons vie & mort renforcer.

Towards the North, great exertions by a manly woman,
Vexing nearly all Europe and the universe,
She will ascribe the two eclipses as like banishment,
And for Pannonians, life and death increasing.

Hommaſſe, (O.Fr. - hommesse) virago, manly woman; mettra, (O.Fr.) imputer; chaſſe, (O.Fr.) bannissement; Pannons, (Latinism) Pannoni/a;
Cross-reference: vie & mort, C.II: 90.

TOWARDS THE NORTH

Nostradamus describes the scene of this oracle as: **TOWARDS THE NORTH** and this takes us to Russia, the adopted country of German-born Catherine the Great, Empress, and the *'All-wise Mother of the Fatherland'*.[1]

GREAT EXERTIONS

As the unopposed ruler of Russia, Catherine was free to begin her reign with **GREAT EXERTIONS** in the management of the country's state affairs; it was these that were to bring her fame. Her first accomplishment was to turn Russia into a prosperous and powerful state. She achieved this by establishing order and justice across the land. In short: *"she reformed the administrative system, plundered the Church, liberalized the economy, emancipated the nobility, and helped it absorb Western culture."* She also made plans for improving the spread of education, and then set about creating a court that would rival Versailles.[2]

BY A MANLY WOMAN

As for her appearance, described by Nostradamus as being that of **A MANLY WOMAN:** *"Even Catherine's admirers sometimes noticed . . . that she looked her best in masculine attire."*[3]

It was, however, her foreign policies that caused concern to Europe, and to many other parts of the world. This began with an extension of Russia's boundary to the west, taking in Poland, Lithuania, Byelorussia and Western Ukraine; to the south, she wrested the Crimea from Turkey's grasp, and to the east, brought Alaska into the Russian fold, thereby involving America. Few countries in Europe failed to feel the effects of Catherine's rule.

VEXING NEARLY ALL EUROPE AND THE UNIVERSE

With the acquisition of the Crimea, Russia was able to exert its influence in the Mediterranean and reach Central and Western Europe. An alliance with Austria, coupled with the renouncing of treaties made with Prussia and England; the division of Poland, between Russia, Austria and Prussia; an excursion into Persia to lay the foundations of her Empire in Central Asia; and an alliance with Denmark in the war against Sweden: [4] these were enough to fulfil the seer's prediction that she would VEX NEARLY ALL EUROPE AND THE UNIVERSE. In Nostradamus's time the world was the centre of the universe.

ASCRIBING THE TWO ECLIPSES AS LIKE A BANISHMENT

Catherine initially came to Russia as the wife of Czar Peter III. But when her husband showed signs of feebleness, which he coupled with an open admiration for the Prussian army, thereby losing the respect of his people, she saw in this a means by which she could replace him. Her opportunity came when he further antagonised his subjects by attempting to cajole the Russian Orthodox Church into adopting Lutheran ideas.

In a *coup d'état* assisted by Grigory Orlov, and joined by other members of the guard, Peter III was seized and forced to abdicate (10 July 1762). He was then *banished* and sent to the village of Ropsha, where he was strangled a week later by Grigory's brother, Aleksey Orlov. This was the first ECLIPSE that began AS A BANISHMENT.

A similar plight had befallen Ivan, Peter III's predecessor. In November 1741, the child-Emperor Ivan VI had been seized by the Grand Duchess Elizabeth in a palace *coup*, and banished to Schlüsselburg. He remained there until July 1764, when a young officer, Vasily Mirovich, launched a rescue attempt designed to

176

restore him to his rightful position as Emperor of Russia. But Catherine had already given orders that if anyone tried to liberate the former Emperor, he was to be killed. Her orders were meticulously carried out, for when Mirovich found Ivan, he was already dying from multiple stab wounds.[5] This was the SECOND ECLIPSE that had begun AS A BANISHMENT.

Within the span of Catherine's rule, from 1762 to 1796, TWO Czars, Ivan VI and Peter III had been ECLIPSED: both men having undergone SIMILAR BANISHMENTS, and afterwards been murdered by order of the Empress.

FOR THE HUNGARIANS DEATH INCREASING

The final line of this oracle focuses upon Hungary. During the eighteenth century, the country formed part of the Habsburg Empire. Its territory had once been part of the Roman province known as Pannonia: hence Nostradamus's classical reference to this part of the world. But in the early part of the 18th century THE HUNGARIANS' DEATH toll steadily INCREASED as the country became rocked by 'Fierce fighting that raged for decades'; this was caused by patriots, striving to free their land from Turkish control. In the event, their attempt at liberation brought in Austria, which then became locked in conflict with Hungary's freedom fighters. Peace was finally achieved through a compromise agreement at Szatmár in 1711.

LIFE INCREASING

Exhausted by years of fighting the country welcomed the intervention of the Habsburgs and recovery was swift.

> *Hungary made an impressive recovery, both material and cultural, from the sorry state to which it had earlier been reduced. The population more than doubled, to reach 8 or 9 million by 1800.*[6]

Most aptly, Nostradamus has concluded this oracle with a prediction of LIFE INCREASING. It is a theme with which he also commences C.II: 90: a quatrain that continues foretelling the future of Hungary during the century that followed. The reader should note that Nostradamus quite often connects one oracle to another by using a phrase or word that is common to both.

From Russia's development in the north, Nostradamus now turns to the west, and America's beginning as a nation state.

VII: 80

L'Occident libres les Ifles Britanniques,
Le recogneu paſſer le bas, puis haut:
Ne content trifte Rebel. corſſ. Eſcotiques,
Puis rebeller par plus & par nuict chaut.

The British Isles free [of] the West,
The acknowledged suffering the low point, then eminent:
Not pleased, standing in wait, Revolution, Scottish privateers,
Furthermore, rebelling for more, and by reason of a fierce onset at night time.

recogneu, (O.Fr.) recognisance, acknowledged; passer, (O.Fr.) to suffer; haut, (O.Fr.) eminent; triste, (O.Fr. homonym) sadness, stand in wait; Rebel. (abbreviation) Rébellion; corss. (abbreviation) corsairs; chaut, (O.Fr. homonym, chaude) warm, fierce onset.

THE WEST

The context of this prophecy requires that **THE WEST** be taken literally, so as to include America.

THE BRITISH ISLES FREE

The **BRITISH ISLES** became free of its colony in North America as a result of the American War of Independence, fought between 1775 and 1783: although it was a freedom sought only by America.

THE ACKNOWLEDGED

After war broke out in April 1775 at Lexington, George Washington presented himself in uniform to Congress, indicating that he was ready to do battle.

> *Washington had the prestige, the military experience, the charisma and*
> *military bearing, the reputation of being a strong patriot, and he was*
> *supported by the South, especially Virginia. Although he did not explic-*
> *itly seek the office of commander and even claimed that he was not equal*
> *to it, there was no serious competition. Congress created the Continental*
> *Army on June 14, 1775; the next day ... Washington was appointed Ma-*
> *jor General and elected by Congress to be Commander-in-Chief.[1]*

SUFFERING THE LOW POINT

By the end of the following year, the Commander-in-Chief found himself **SUFFERING A LOW POINT** in his fight for American independence: being at the time –

> *... desperately short of men and supplies Washington almost despaired.*
> *He had lost New York City to the British; enlistment was almost up for a*
> *number of the troops, and others were deserting in droves; civilian morale*
> *was falling rapidly; and Congress, faced with the possibility of a British*
> *attack on Philadelphia, had withdrawn from the city.[2]*

Nevertheless, for the remainder of the war against the British, his force of character and strength of personality compensated for any lack of greatness as a general that may have contributed to these earlier setbacks in battle. Instead, it was his charisma that proved instrumental in keeping the Revolution active up until victory was finally achieved, although not without some assistance from the French.

THEN EMINENT

Following independence from Britain, Washington resigned from the army on 23 December 1783 and went into retirement. But four years later he was persuaded to attend the Constitutional Convention, whereupon he was elected to the office of President of the Convention. Thereafter, *"Such was his prestige that agreement over a chief executive was reached only because he agreed to fill the position."* [3] On 30 April 1789 he became the first President of the United States, and the only president to receive 100% of the electoral votes. In fact, *"The delegates designed the presidency with Washington in mind, and allowed him to define the office once elected."* He was returned to office in the elections of 1792, but declined a third period in office.

NOT PLEASED, STANDING IN WAIT

From 1759 to the outbreak of the American Revolution, Washington managed his lands around Mount Vernon and served in the Virginia House of Burgesses. Married to a widow, Martha Dandridge Custis, he devoted himself to a busy and happy life. But like his fellow planters, Washington felt himself exploited by British merchants and hampered by British regulations. As the quarrel with the mother country grew acute, he moderately but firmly voiced his resistance to the restrictions. [4]

Although NOT PLEASED with an oppressive British rule, which included the 1765 Stamp Act: effectively the first tax on the colonies, he bided his time, preferring to STAND IN WAIT until the opportunity for direct action presented itself.

REBELLION

That time arrived with the *American War of Independence*, which was also known as the *American Revolutionary War*. It began as a REBELLION directed against British policies, and involved the thirteen states that border America's east coast. The powder keg was ignited at Lexington in Massachusetts during April 1775, and the fighting would continue for almost nine years.

John Paul Jones was born 6 July 1747 at Kirkcudbright on the southern coast of Scotland. He learned his seamanship as a boy: later emigrating to America, which became his adopted home. At the time of the Revolutionary War, America had no navy, and needed to acquire one quickly. In December 1775 Jones became America's Continental Navy's very 1st Lieutenant aboard the frigate USS Alfred, with orders to attack British merchant ships. *"During this six week voyage, Jones captured sixteen prizes and created signifi- cant damage along the coast of Nova Scotia."* Despite this success, his disagreement with higher authority led to him being assigned a smaller command:

> *the newly constructed USS Ranger ... After making the necessary prepa- rations, Jones sailed for France on November 1, 1777 with orders to as- sist the American cause however possible ... Throughout the mission, the crew, led by Jones's second-in-command Lieutenant Thomas Simpson, acted as if they were aboard a privateer, not a warship.[5]*

Indeed, *"in Britain at this time, he was usually referred to as a pirate."* [6] But, to avoid the charge of *piracy* after having captured a ship, the *Serapis,* while sailing under an unknown flag: the Dutch, being friendly to America, entered the *'John Paul Jones flag'* in their records.

FURTHERMORE, REBELLING FOR MORE AND BY REASON OF THE FIERCE ONSET AT NIGHT TIME
Nostradamus now switches attention to the cause of the Revolu- tionary War. *'No taxation without representation'* captures the mood at the time. The colonies were being taxed by a government in a distant land, in which politicians in America had no representa- tives. **THEY WANTED MORE** control over their affairs, particularly in the manner which their country was ruled. **REBELLION** was in the air, and weapons were already being imported from France and stock piled. The British learned of this and sent a detachment of troops to seize the illegal arms.

> *On the night of April 18, 1775, General Gage sent 700 men to seize muni- tions stored by the colonial militia at Concord, Massachusetts. Riders in- cluding Paul Revere alerted the countryside, and when British troops en- tered Lexington [at 6 a.m.] on the morning of April 19, [having marched through the night] they found 77 minutemen formed up on the village green. Shots were exchanged, killing several minutemen. The British moved on to Concord, where a detachment of three companies was en- gaged and routed at the North Bridge by a force of 500 minutemen. As*

the British retreated back to Boston, thousands of militiamen attacked them along the roads, inflicting great damage before timely British reinforcements prevented a total disaster. With the Battles of Lexington and Concord, the war had begun.[7]

The *night time* ride of Paul Revere from Boston to Lexington in order to warn the citizens that the British were on the march to seize weapons is now part of America's history. The onset of the Revolutionary War for American independence, freeing the country from the British Isles, therefore began AT NIGHT TIME, as Nostradamus predicted.

On 10 May 1774, Louis XV lay dying of smallpox: the disease he had survived as a boy and which had destroyed his parents and his elder brother. A single candle burned at the window of his bedroom. The moment it became extinguished, his third grandson, together with his wife, would become the new King and Queen of France. The two who stood in wait were the ill-fated Louis XVI and his wife Marie Antoinette.

Although their reign was to end in tragedy, with the royal couple executed beneath the blade of the guillotine, and their little son wasting away as a prisoner of the Revolution, the beginning was very different. Even so, opponents of the monarchy were always on the lookout for scandal, and the Queen proved a ready target with her frivolity and lavish lifestyle. The 'Affair of the Diamond Necklace' has since entered the history books as a piece of calumny directed against the Queen. Nostradamus alludes to this before predicting Louis XVI's sad end.

C.X: 43

Le trop bon temps, trop de bonté royale,
Faicts & deffaicts prompt, fubit, negligence:
Leger croira faux d'efpoufe loyale.
Lui mis à mort par fa benevolence.

The very many good times, excess of royal kindness,
Hasty actions and mishaps, unexpected, negligence:
Lessening the charges, he will believe [it] false concerning [his] loyal wife.
He, put to death on account of his goodwill.

trop, (O.Fr.) beaucoup, excès; deffaict, (O.Fr.) mal, malheure; negligence, (O.Fr.) injustice, outrage; Leger, (O.Fr. as Legier) diminuer les charges; benevolence, (O.Fr.) bienveillance.

THE VERY MANY GOOD TIMES

Marie Antoinette's entry into the social whirl of French court life soon drew notice, and was to set the standard by which THE VERY MANY GOOD TIMES were judged. Elaborate hairstyles, the latest fashion, parties, dancing, masked balls, visits to the theatre and the opera, were often preceded by attendance at race meetings run at the Bois de Boulogne. She also became addicted to gambling, and her participation in card games would go on through the night, with her losses paid out of the King's purse, while her winnings were collected for herself from distraught courtiers. At Versailles, a little village was constructed set amidst meandering streams and rustic bridges, where she was able to dwell in a sylvan paradise of her own fantasizing.[1]

EXCESS OF ROYAL KINDNESS

By 1776, the Queen's dress allowance had grown from 150,000 livres to half a million. *"The King paid up 'at her very first word' according to Mercy. Again when she bought a pair of diamond bracelets for 400,000 livres, she had to borrow from the King, who* [with EXCESS OF ROYAL KINDNESS] *did not complain."* Added to these extravagances were those of the Queen's household: it was a privilege of the maids at that time to acquire her *'garments once discarded but hardly worn'*.[2]

Charles Auguste Böhmer and his partner Paul Bassenge were the official Court Jewellers. Some time prior to 1785, they had produced *"an elaborate, many-looped diamond necklace . . . It consisted of 647 diamonds, gemstones of the highest quality; its weight was 2800 carats."* The necklace, worth between one-and-a-half and two million francs, was offered for sale to Marie Antoinette, but she declined to buy it. Thereafter, a maze of confused assumptions followed.

HASTY ACTIONS

Cardinal Rohan, who was descended from one of the more illustrious families of France, received a letter, allegedly from the Queen, requesting that he purchase the necklace for her. In fact, a woman, Nicole d'Oliva – *aka* le Guay – had impersonated the Queen. And in doing so, had successfully duped the Cardinal into believing he was to act secretly as Marie Antoinette's agent. The Cardinal HASTILY obliged, thinking to enjoy royal favour as a reward.

UNEXPECTED, AND MISHAPS

Unaware of what was happening behind her back, Marie Antoinette was surprised to receive a letter from Böhmer, who had lately become worried that the Queen had not yet worn the necklace: for which he had still not been paid (12 July 1785). Unable to comprehend the content of this letter, the Queen unwisely used it as a lighter to melt the wax on her correspondence.

When Böhmer received no reply to his letter, and then learned that it had been burnt, he complained to Madame Campan (First Lady of the Bedchamber) that Her Majesty owed him the balance for the necklace, mentioning that he had so far been paid only 30,000 francs through the hands of Cardinal Rohan. At this point, it is fair to say that no one involved in this affair actually knew the truth of what had happened. Everyone had been given to **HASTY ACTIONS**, based upon false assumptions, and with no awareness of the *trouble* these were soon to cause. [3]

When the Queen was informed of Cardinal Rohan's involvement in the matter and the trouble this had caused by implicating her, she said she was unable to *"conceive of the Cardinal being involved in such a business."* Declaring that the *"whole affair was 'a labyrinth' to her."* The King, too, was amazed that a member of the House of Rohan could have allowed himself to become deceived so readily. [4]

NEGLIGENCE

Marie Antoinette had obviously been made the innocent victim of a conspiracy to defraud Böhmer. Behind it was the Comtesse, Jeanne de Lamotte Valois (impoverished, but claiming to be descended from Henri II). She had forged the signature of Marie Antoinette on the letter she sent to Cardinal Rohan, requesting that he purchase the necklace on the Queen's behalf. Regrettably,

> . . . *although the total innocence of Marie Antoinette was obvious, standard accounts of the affair viewed her as guilty 'because large numbers of people wanted to believe in her guilt.'*

Marie Antoinette's supposed guilt in the affair now gripped the public imagination, and this was contrasted with the plight of the *'famished peasants'*. As the full story finally unfolded, the facts became twisted, and the Queen's **NEGLIGENCE** in the affair took a turn for the worse. She became transformed from *"innocent victim to vindictive harpy . . . damag[ing] the monarchy to an incalculable degree."* [5]

At noon on 15 August, Louis XVI took action. He summoned the Queen and Cardinal Rohan to his inner cabinet. There, the full truth was disclosed. The Cardinal had been duped into believing the signature of the Queen was genuine, and from thereon, he, had acted improperly, hoping to ingratiate himself in the eyes of the Queen. Marie Antoinette was exonerated from total blame, thus **LESSENING THE CHARGES** directed against her.

Louis was now content to **BELIEVE FALSE** the damaging and defamatory stories that were being repeated **CONCERNING HIS LOYAL WIFE**. Cardinal Rohan was less fortunate. He was imprisoned in the Bastille, and upon release, banished. Jeanne de Lamotte Valois was dealt with more harshly. She was stripped naked and whipped by the public executioner before being branded with hot iron as a thief, and given a life sentence.[6]

The affair of the diamond necklace had undoubtedly damaged the reputation of the Queen, and by extension, the monarchy. Coming, as it did in 1786, just three years before the first outbreak of trouble that was to herald the beginning of the French Revolution, the affair added fuel towards the hatred and antagonism building up towards Marie Antoinette and her frivolous lifestyle. Even so, no one could then have believed possible that this was to lead to the abolition of the monarchy and the public execution of both the King and Queen.

The oracle concludes with the fate of Louis XVI. It does so by linking the kindness he showed towards his wife, with the same goodwill that so much contributed towards his eventual death at the hands of the revolutionaries seven years later.

Louis XVI (23 Aug 1754–21 Jan 1793) King of France (1774), whose kind heart and good intentions proved inadequate to deal with the mounting crisis of the Ancien Regime . . . He was guillotined in Paris.[7]

HE, PUT TO DEATH ON ACCOUNT OF HIS GOODWILL: – but note how close the French word 'Lui' resembles **L**(o)**ui**(s), or even **Lui**(s) in Spanish. Also, the two words 'Lui' and 'Louis' are virtually indistinguishable when vocalised.

5

ENGLAND'S CENTURY OF TURMOIL

The seventeenth-century was particularly noticeable in England for the fluctuation it brought to the monarchy. At the
beginning of the century, James VI of Scotland was invited to
leave his homeland and settle in London as King James I of England. After his death, the throne passed to his son Charles I, who
by the middle of the century had lost first the crown, and then
his head.

We therefore begin this chapter with Nostradamus tracing
the fate of England at the stage where Oliver Cromwell emerges
to change the direction of both politics and the English monarchy. The seer does this with a prophecy that is entirely disposed
to the Englishman who attempted to mould the government of
Britain into an image of his own liking. Politicians of every hue
have the same objective, but not all have been as successful as

Oliver Cromwell. The following verse contrives to produce a verbal outline of this man, for he is recognizable in every phrase.

C.VIII: 76

Plus Macelin que roy en Angleterre,
Lieu obſcur nay par force aura l'empire:
Laſche ſans foy, ſans loy ſaignera terre,
Son temps approche ſi pres que ie ſouſpire.

More Macellinus than king in England,
Born in an obscure place, by force he will have the empire:
Shameful (Charles) without faith, without law, the land will bleed,
His time approaches so near that I sigh.

Macelin, (Latinism) Macellin/us; Laſche, (O.Fr.) Lâche, also paranagram (Lasche[r]) for Charles.

Macellinus was the epithet for Marcus Opilius Macrinus. He had formerly been an army officer, but became Rome's Emperor after initiating the death of the reigning Emperor, Caracalla.[1]

MORE LIKE MACELLINUS THAN A KING IN ENGLAND

IN ENGLAND, Oliver Cromwell became LIKE MACELLINUS, for both men had begun their careers as army officers. Then, in 1649, as Macrinus had done in 217 AD, Cromwell initiated the death of his king. For eleven years after the execution of Charles I, there would be no more kings *in England*. Cromwell had become the nation's chief: preferring to adopt the title of Lord Protector rather THAN that of KING.[2]

BORN IN AN OBSCURE PLACE

On 25 April 1599, Elizabeth Steward, wife of Robert Cromwell, GAVE BIRTH to her second son Oliver. His arrival in the world took place inside a very ordinary house, IN AN OBSCURE PLACE that lay on the main High Street of a small town called Huntingdon.[3]

BY FORCE, HE WILL HAVE THE EMPIRE

Between 1640 and 1646, Cromwell made his mark as a member of parliament, and from then onwards became the most successful commanding officer in the Parliamentary army. It was from this power base, achieved BY FORCE in the English Civil War, that HE WAS ABLE to influence the House of Commons, which eventually led the governing body to put the King on trial for treason. Charles I was executed in January 1649, leaving the way open for Cromwell to replace him, and TO HAVE THE EMPIRE (i.e., the country, and the nation's possessions abroad) at his command.[4]

The oracle then inserts a few brief, well-chosen words that are meant to describe the character of Cromwell, but their negative connotations will not please his admirers. For example, was Cromwell's treatment of **CHARLES SHAMEFUL**?

> *As one of the generals on the parliamentary side in the English Civil War against King Charles I, Cromwell helped to bring about the overthrow of the Stuart monarchy.*

To complete the overthrow, Charles I was made to stand trial, and charged with *"high treason . . . [and] other high crimes against the realm of England."* On January 27, the court trying the King declared him to be *'a tyrant, traitor, murderer, and public enemy'*. He was executed two days later.[5]

WITHOUT FAITH

Upon matters of religion, Cromwell remained independent, and **LACKED** the **FAITH** of either Anglicans or Roman Catholics. When questioned upon matters of religion, he replied that it was easier to say what he was against than what he was for. And, although he declared his belief in God, this did not prevent him killing Catholic priests, ejecting Anglican clergy from their parishes, proscribing the Prayer book, and forbidding the December celebration of Christ's birth.[6]

WITHOUT LAW

The oracle is also correct in predicting the **ABSENCE OF LAW** during Cromwell's reign. By announcing the abolition of the monarchy, and by declaring that England would become a Free State, or Commonwealth, he distanced the nation from its *'last tenuous link with legality'*. The Rump Parliament that took over Britain represented no more than a few eccentrics, and it operated entirely without constitutional respectability. Furthermore, upon dissolving the Barebones Parliament of picked supporters, because even they were unable to agree with Cromwell, he duly informed them of his reason for disbandment – *"Necessity hath no law."*[7]

THE LAND WILL BLEED

The English Civil War is referred to allegorically as a time when **THE LAND WILL BLEED**. In the conflict between King and Parliament, Cavalier and Roundhead, Cromwell quickly rose to prominence. Victorious in more than thirty battles fought during the nine years between 1642 and 1651, he delivered a convincing and decisive blow against the royalist armies opposing him, thus preparing the way for the overthrow of the English monarchy.[8]

HIS TIME APPROACHES SO NEAR THAT I SIGH

Cromwell's life span extended from 25 April 1599 to 3 September 1658. Nostradamus's own life ended thirty-three years before Cromwell's birth, therefore justifying HIS SIGH, and the reference he made to the TIME APPROACHING when Cromwell would fulfil his prophecy.

The next oracle offers four lines of apparently unconnected events concerning Great Britain. However, with a little guile concerning numbers and sequences, Nostradamus has contrived to unify them. This is achieved by allowing the dates on which each event became fulfilled to contribute to the year in which the last of the four predictions took place.

C.II: 68

De l'Aquilon les efforts feront grands:
Sus l'Ocean fera la porte ouuerte,
Le regne en l'Ifle fera reintegrand:
Tremblera Londres par voile defcouuerte.

From the North the efforts will be great:
At the side of the Ocean the port will be opened,
The reign in the Isle will be reinstated:
London will tremble through discovered sail.

Aquilon, (Latinism) Aquil/onis – north; Sus, (O.Fr.) du côté de; porte, (epenthesis) port[e].

The key to interpreting this oracle is indicated by *London* in line four. This suggests the preceding lines are likely to relate to the British Isles, and, indeed, the word *Isle* appears in the third line.

FROM THE NORTH THE EFFORTS WILL BE GREAT

In 1648, the Scottish parliament voted for a force of 30,000 men to be enlisted: *'to rescue the king's person'*. Cromwell's Roundheads had taken King Charles I prisoner during the English Civil War, and Scotland was intent upon rescuing him. Once across the border, 5000 Englishmen joined them with the same aim in mind. But Cromwell's Ironsides countered this threat by hurrying *north* to Preston. In August 1648 the two sides met head on, and in the battle that followed, the Scots and their English allies were heavily defeated. FROM THE NORTH THE EFFORTS HAD BEEN GREAT, but were not great enough to overcome Cromwell.[1]

AT THE SIDE OF THE OCEAN THE PORT WILL BE OPENED

Fast forward now by six years, and we find: *"The Anglo-Portuguese alliance, offering the English fleet the splendid harbour of Lisbon."* This occurred in July 1654. *'Lisbon is the key to the Mediterranean'.* It is also situated AT THE SIDE OF THE ATLANTIC OCEAN, and with its PORT OPENED to British ships, it enabled them to repair and restock, instead of making an extra day's journey to either Plymouth or Portsmouth.[2] This was important to the navy's ships for it helped them maintain a commanding presence in the Mediterranean.

THE REIGN IN THE ISLE WILL BE REINSTATED

Fast forward another six years: THE REINSTATEMENT OF THE REIGN IN THE British ISLE has occurred only once since Nostradamus penned these oracles. Cromwell abolished the monarchy in 1649 at the time of Charles I's execution. But after his death in 1658, Richard Cromwell's attempt to follow in his father's footsteps was neither popular nor successful. Consequently, in May 1660, Charles II, son of the executed King, was invited to return to England from his exile in the Netherlands and resume the British monarchy.[3]

LONDON WILL TREMBLE THROUGH DISCOVERED SAIL

Finally, we go forward seven years to 8 June 1667, this time to find LONDON TREMBLING with fear. News had been brought to the capital that SAILS had been DISCOVERED belonging to the Dutch fleet, and its ships were already entering the mouth of the Thames. This was a time when England was at war with the Dutch, and it was feared that an invasion of the capital was about to begin. Widespread panic quickly followed, and the roads leading out of the city were soon clogged with barrows and carts laden with the belongings of those seeking refuge in the country. But, in the event, the Dutch fleet left the Thames, preferring instead to sail up the River Medway, where several ships at anchor were then destroyed close to the port of Chatham.[4]

The events predicted in this oracle are spread over nineteen years. Yet, there is a unity of purpose in both content and dating. Firstly, lines one and three refer to the British monarchy: its overthrow followed by its restoration; while lines two and four refer to the British navy: its success followed by its failure. Secondly, by taking each of the four years in which these predictions were fulfilled; that is, 1648, 1654, 1660 1667, and differencing them – a mathematical term for finding sequences of a certain type – the numbers 6 6 7 are obtained. And '667 is the year in which the final line of this oracle was fulfilled. Coincidence...?

The English Civil War, the execution of the King, and the dissolution of the British monarchy occurred during a momentous period in the nation's history. Any seer wishing to demonstrate a precognitive ability would naturally be drawn to this period of time. Nostradamus's next oracle does precisely that by focusing upon the capture and subsequent death of Charles I.

C.VIII: 37

La forterefle aupres de la Tamife
Cherra par lors le Roy dedans ferré,
Aupres du pont fera veu en chemife,
Un deuant mort, puis dans le fort barré.

*The fortress close by the Thames
Will fall, in that time [when] the King is locked inside,
Close to the ferryboat, he will be seen in a shirt,
One before death, then confined inside the fort.*

serré, (O.Fr.) enfermer; pont, (Latinism) pont/o = ferryboat; barré, (O.Fr.) clouer.

THE FORTRESS CLOSE BY THE THAMES

Discounting palaces, there are two fortresses on the banks of the river Thames; they are the Tower of London and Windsor Castle. **THE FORTRESS CLOSE BY THE THAMES** at Windsor has been the home of the royal families of England ever since Edward III converted part of the building into royal apartments in 1348, and it is to this castle that Nostradamus has directed his prophecy.[1]

WILL FALL

If Windsor Castle were to be captured by an opposing army, it would signal the end of the reigning monarch. This, in fact, is what happened during the English Civil War when the fortress **FELL** to Cromwell's model army.[2]

IN THAT TIME WHEN THE KING IS LOCKED INSIDE

In December 1648, **THE KING**, then a captive of Cromwell, was taken under guard from Hurst Castle on the Isle of Wight to Windsor Castle, whereupon he was **LOCKED INSIDE**. He remained a prisoner there until 19 January, when he was transferred to St. James Palace at Westminster to stand trial for High Treason.[3]

The complex of government buildings that run adjacent to the Houses of Parliament along Whitehall, and which occupy the site where Charles I was executed, can today be reached from the southern shore of the Thames by crossing Westminster Bridge. But in 1649, Westminster Bridge did not exist. In its place was the Stangate ferryboat, which crossed the Thames from Lower Marsh to Westminster.

London's busiest crossing point other than at London Bridge was from Stangate, the ferry of Lambeth Marsh, to Westminster and near the point that the Romans crossed with a ford to link with Watling Street.[4]

Its main competitor was the Horse Ferry that crossed at a point farther upstream, outside Lambeth Palace. Today, Horseferry Road, running from Lambeth Bridge to Victoria, still bears the name of that particular crossing point.

CLOSE TO THE FERRYBOAT

It was a grey, icy-cold January day in London when the King prepared to leave St. James Palace for his execution. What follows is a story told many times by historians. The King requested permission to wear an extra shirt, lest the chill in the air should make him shiver, and this should be misinterpreted as a tremble of fear.[5] His plea was granted, and the King was then escorted to the scaffold, which had been set up outside the Banqueting Hall in Whitehall, **CLOSE TO THE FERRYBOAT**.

ONE SEEN BEFORE DEATH IN A SHIRT

Charles I was executed on 30 January 1649, appearing in public as **ONE** who was **SEEN BEFORE** his **DEATH IN** the extra **SHIRT** he had requested to wear.

THEN CONFINED INSIDE THE FORT

After this act of legalized regicide, Charles's body was carried to Windsor Castle where it was **THEN CONFINED INSIDE THE FORT** ready for burial.[6] Nostradamus's bitter humour is once again evident in this final phrase, for it was the King's eternal confinement within the fort that he has referred to.

On 17 March, only forty-six days after the government had sentenced the King to death, the British Parliament abolished the monarchy.

The next quatrain is another of the seer's split prophecies. On this occasion, Nostradamus has devoted only one line to the first part of his prediction. Yet, the date on which this became fulfilled was to act as a signal for what occurred exactly one year later to the very day. The second part of the oracle refers to the tragedy that followed, while also providing reasons for its occurrence.

C.IX: 49

Gand & Bruceles marcheront contre Enuers,
Senat de Londres mettront à mort leur roy,
Le fel & vin luy feront à l'enuers,
Pour eux auoir le regne en defarroy.

Ghent & Brussels will trade contrary to Antwerp;
The government in London will put their king to death,
The salt and wine will be on the wrong side to him.
On account of them, getting the kingdom into disarray.

Enuers, (Anvers); marcheront, (O.Fr. syncope – marcheeront) négocier, trade.
Cross-references: fel & vin, C.X: 7; à l'enuers, C.I: 3. (This expression is consistent with its use in describing the political opposition to both Charles I and Louis XVI at the time of their show trials and beheading.)

N.B. The verb marcher is used by Nostradamus to mean 'making progress; i.e., to move forward' in C. IV: 2 and C.VIII: 19

Although the event described in the opening line appears to have no connection with what follows, a subtle link exists. It is the date on which the legislation governing the *treaty of Münster* was signed.

TREATY OF PEACE concluded on January 30th of this present year 1648 in the city of Münster in Westphalia, between his Most Serene and Mighty Prince PHILIP, fourth of the name, King of Spain, etc., on the one side and the High, Mighty Lords States General of the United Netherlands, on the other.

GHENT AND BRUSSELS WILL TRADE CONTRARY TO ANTWERP

The date, 30 January 1648 proved to be auspicious. It was one year to the very day before *the government in London put their king to death*. And that is precisely the prediction that follows on from this. But what of the French word *marcheront*? In old French, as in the modern language, it has the same meaning: to march, tread, step, make progress, etc. It can also mean to ply (to make one's way). But *marcheront* may also be said to have been syncopated from *marcheeront*, which means to trade or negotiate, and GHENT AND BRUSSELS WERE NEGOTIATING a peace treaty, which included a TRADE agreement that was CONTRARY TO the commercial interests of ANTWERP. But, if preferred, one can still read this as: GHENT & BRUSSELS WILL MAKE PROGRESS CONTRARY TO ANTWERP.

On 30 January 1648, one year to the day before Charles I was executed outside Westminster Hall, Philip IV signed *'the Treaty of Münster'*. Under the terms of this treaty, the waterways connecting *Antwerp* to its commercial interests in the cities of Bruges, *Ghent, Brussels* &c were closed. The boats that formerly transported goods to and from the seaport of *Antwerp* were no longer able to serve the cities mentioned in the prophecy, and had to *ply* for *trade* using a different port.[1]

The persistently devious, but never illogical efforts made by the oracle to obscure the meaning of a prediction until after the event, explains the use of this syncope. The line taken at face value appears to predict that Ghent and Brussels will march against Antwerp: which never happened, and in any case, would have no bearing upon the next three lines which concern England. However, add one letter to *marcheront*, and the prediction is at once electrified, as we shall now see.

THE GOVERNMENT IN LONDON WILL PUT THEIR KING TO DEATH

In the aftermath of the English Civil War, and with Charles I held in captivity, *Parliament* decided the King should stand trial for his life. In the days following this decision, Charles was charged with treason, tried before a tribunal, found guilty, and on 30 January 1649, THE GOVERNING BODY IN LONDON PUT THEIR KING TO DEATH.[2]

Confronted by this direct evidence of Nostradamus's precognitive powers, cynics have resorted to dismissing this prophecy as pure guesswork: ignoring, of course, the *Treaty of Münster* and its date. There are, however, other major obstacles to a sceptic's denial. In the first place, Nostradamus lived at a time when monarchs ruled under the authority of God, and by what was also believed at that time, to be their 'divine right'; they were therefore answerable only to Him. In France, during the middle of the sixteenth century, there was no known precedent to suggest this situation would ever change. Secondly, from all the capital cities in Europe, Nostradamus actually picks *London* as the place where this act of political regicide will occur. Added to this, the rest of the oracle has still to be considered as further evidence of prevision.

THE SALT AND WINE WILL BE ON THE WRONG SIDE TO HIM

Salt and *wine* are the same two biblical metaphors that occurred in C.X: 7, where they also provide a neat cross-reference to what was occurring in France during the middle of the 17th century. The *salt* of the earth refers to the moral elite: people by whose standards of behaviour the world is kept in check. The *wine* represents new principles of government. These biblical metaphors are entirely apt for this period of English history, in which politics and religion had become intensely interwoven.

> *For twenty years, from 1640 to 1660, religious enthusiasm and political idealism so swept English thought that by comparison for the following twenty years they seemed almost to disappear.*

In the middle of the 17th century, the nation's moral elite – THE SALT (see, Matthew v: 13) – turned against its divinely ordained king. In taking this stand, *the salt* agreed to a set of new political ideas – the WINE (see, Matthew ix.17) – which a caucus of politicians deemed to be justification for their anti-royalist strategy.[3] Or, as Nostradamus put it: THE SALT AND WINE WILL BE ON THE WRONG SIDE TO HIM.

ON ACCOUNT OF THEM, GETTING THE KINGDOM INTO DISARRAY

And it was ON ACCOUNT OF THEM, (the *salt and wine*) that THE KINGDOM was brought INTO a state of DISARRAY.

> *The nation [became] divided along a series of irregular jagged lines which defy simple interpretation in clear-cut social, religious, geographical, or economic terms.*[4]

The English gentry were just as equally split, some expressing allegiance to the King, and others to Parliament; even members of the same family might be found in disagreement. *"In general, in most areas there were two parties – one supporting the King and the other Parliament."*

194

The execution of King Charles I was a truly historic occasion. In the religious climate of Nostradamus's time, regicide was a crime against God's chosen instrument, and liable to divine punishment. Consequently, when London was struck by the most virulent outbreak of Plague in its entire history, and this was followed one year later by a fire of such intensity that the heart of the city was incinerated, many people believed it to be divine judgement, akin to that visited on the cities of Sodom and Gomorrah.

Nostradamus deals with both the *Plague* and the *Fire* in a split quatrain. This manages to include all three tragedies to hit London during the middle of the seventeenth century. For amongst the faithful of that period, there was a deep-rooted belief that they were connected. Nostradamus also deals a little more fully with Charles's trial.

C.IX: 11

Le iufte à tort à mort l'on viendra metre
Publiquement & du millieu eftaint:
Si grande pefte en ce lieu viendra naiftre,
Que les iugeans fouyr feront conftraint.

*The 'Just One' to injustice; one will come to put him to death
Publicly, and in the centre, extinguished:
Such great pestilence will arrive to appear in this place,
That the judgements [and] hearth will be compacted in the commotion*

Eftaint, (O.Fr. estainct) extinguished, spent; naiftre, (O.Fr.) poindre, apparaître; iugean, (O.Fr. – jugier) judgments; fouyr, (O.Fr. syncope – fouyer) hearth; cook-room; conftraint, (O.Fr.) serré par l'émotion.
Cross-references: jufte, C.II: 53; C.II: 51; mettra à mort, C.IX: 49

THE JUST ONE

Charles I was the legitimate King of England, therefore THE JUST ONE ('just' is referred to several times in connection with Charles I: see cross-references above).

TO INJUSTICE

As the English Civil War drew to a close, and with Charles now captive (30 November 1648), it was decided he should stand trial for treason and other high crimes. Without support from the House of Lords, the House of Commons was forced to appoint a High Court to try the King. But TO this INJUSTICE Charles responded by refusing to acknowledge either the legitimacy of the tribunal, or the lawfulness of the charges brought against him.

The government being made aware of its own dubious legality, and with the Lords mounting a protest at being excluded from all further proceedings relating to the trial, the Commons prorogued further consultations, and summarily declared the monarchy abolished.[1]

ONE COMING TO PUT HIM TO DEATH

At his trial, Charles was charged with high treason and *"other high crimes against the realm of England."* But when he refused to plead, Cromwell decided to accept the trial as an act of justice, and signed the death warrant.[2] Predictably, **ONE HAD COME TO PUT HIM TO DEATH.**

PUBLICLY, AND IN THE CENTRE, EXTINGUISHED

The execution was scheduled to take place **PUBLICLY**, outside the Banqueting Hall of Whitehall Palace at Westminster: the spectacle having been arranged **IN THE CENTRE**. This consisted of an unrestricted gathering of onlookers who had arrived to witness the beheading of a king. Inside the actual Banqueting Hall were crowds of soldiers, privileged visitors, and foreign ambassadors – *"[an] abundance of men and women . . . to behold the saddest sight England ever saw."* Outside the Hall, on the roofs of adjacent buildings, other onlookers had scrambled to find a position. And on the ground, massed around the scaffold, were several ranks of foot soldiers. To the rear of them were more troops on horseback, and then a mass of spectators behind barricades, all drawn to the scene. At 2 pm on 30 January 1649, the axe fell and Charles I was immediately **EXTINGUISHED.**[3]

SUCH GREAT PESTILENCE WILL ARRIVE, TO APPEAR IN THIS PLACE

Sixteen years passed by, during which time there had been a resumption of the monarchy in England. The Plague, however, was never far away, and **SUCH GREAT PESTILENCE ARRIVED, TO APPEAR** in London during 1665 – **THIS PLACE** of injustice and regicide – that for the space of eleven months, close to 100,000 people perished.[4]

AND HEARTH

In the following year London suffered another blow, when a fire broke out in the **HEARTH** of Thomas Farrynor's **COOK-ROOM** in Pudding Lane. The flames quickly spread, covering an area ranging from the Tower to Temple Church. For three days, London was affected as the fire spread, threatening to engulf the entire capital. During that time:

> . . . *eighty churches, several of the city gates, and thirteen thousand two hundred dwelling houses [were destroyed]. The ruins covered a space of four hundred and twenty six acres.* [5]

THE JUDGEMENTS WILL BE COMPACTED IN THE COMMOTION

For some Londoners who were regular church-goers, the *Great Fire*, following within a year of the *Great Plague*, caused many of the faithful to COMPACT these two disasters. And IN THE COMMOTION that followed this loss of life and property, the JUDGEMENTS they made were that London was suffering punishment by God for allowing the execution of their lawful king.[6] Their worries also included the City's relaxed attitude to the liberal pleasures that had been ushered in after the re-instatement of the monarchy.[7]
Nostradamus's reference to *judges* may also have connotations with the *book of Judges* in the Bible. This refers to Israel abandoning God and being punished for its sin. The similarity to England having also abandoned God by executing its King, and then suffering two disasters shortly afterwards, may have invited this comparison.

The execution of Charles I occupied Nostradamus's thoughts over several quatrains, and in another verse he again refers to this, while more openly predicting the Great Plague of London. However, as already mentioned above, some members of the Christian community saw the Plague as divine retribution for the capital city's crime of regicide. Nostradamus acknowledges this piece of factual history by using the word *avenge*. He also predicts the reintroduction of a strategy used by the ancients: that of symbolizing a particular country by identifying it with a female figure which personifies the traits and characteristics it is intended to represent. In the course of these oracles we shall encounter two famous examples of this occurring: the first being Britannia. This ancient lady of Roman antiquity was revived during the time of Charles II as a fitting symbol for the people of Britain. The second example occurs much later, when we shall discover the Statue of Liberty being used to represent the U.S.A.

C.II: 53

La grande peſte de cite maritime
Ne ceſſera que mort ne ſoit vengée
Du iuſte ſang, par pris damne ſans crime
De la grand dame par feincte n'outraigée.

The great plague of the maritime city
Will not cease from death, nor be it so avenged,
For the Just Blood, through [being] seized, convicted without crime
By the great dame, by pretence, not having offended.

damne, (O.Fr.) convicted.

THE GREAT PLAGUE OF LONDON

London has long been known as a *maritime city* as the Port of London bears witness. In the past this was the cause of many outbreaks of Plague, which spread the infection across London and beyond. Rats infested with fleas carrying the disease were apt to scurry aboard ships in Eastern ports, eventually disembarking at London's docks. In May 1665, England's great capital city began to experience the first signs of what would become one of the most devastating outbreaks of the disease in the city's history: **THE GREAT PLAGUE OF LONDON** had arrived.[1] Identifying the *maritime city* as London is also justified by the third line of the oracle, which refers to the *Just Blood*: a cognomen used by Nostradamus for Charles I who was unjustly executed.

WILL NOT CEASE FROM DEATH

For eleven months, *'The Great Plague of London'* took its toll on the population; and it **WOULD NOT CEASE FROM DEATH** until it had carried off an estimated: *'one hundred thousand souls'.*[2]

NOR WILL IT BE AVENGED FOR THE JUST BLOOD

It is not unusual in some societies, even in these modern times, for terrible calamities to be seen as 'Acts of God'. Indeed, the Bible records God's anger at the disobedience of His people, and the punishments they were made to suffer. In London, at the height of the Great Plague, it was likewise suggested that the city was undergoing a similar sentence for having executed Charles I: a monarch descended from the lawful Stuart bloodline, hence *the Just Blood*. (Charles I had actually been given the cognomen *'the man of blood'* although for a different reason). Many therefore believed that the mounting death toll **WOULD NOT BE AVENGED FOR** the crime against their lawful King – **THE JUST BLOOD** –

until the city had been severely punished for its disobedience.[3]

BEING SEIZED AND CONVICTED WITHOUT CRIME

The King, **HAVING BEEN SEIZED** on 30 November 1648,[4] and then two months later executed, had at first been an embarrassment to his opponents. Had they released him, there was a danger he would later punish them. On the other hand, unending imprisonment would invite attempts to release him, as had already happened with the army sent from Scotland. The alternative was execution, but only after a legal trial had justified the death sentence.

> *On 6 January, the Rump of the commons set up a 'High Court of Justice' to try the King; the hitherto obscure John Bradshaw was to preside . . . Bradshaw's tribunal, its legality highly questionable, duly found Charles guilty of 'High Treason and other High crimes', and ordered that he be put to death by the severing of his head from his body.*

In fact, the verdict was a contradiction in terms. High treason is an offence committed against the King, and since Charles was the King, he was effectively **CONVICTED WITHOUT CRIME.**[5]

BY THE GREAT DAME

Nostradamus then blames this act of regicide upon the British people by equating them with Britannia, claiming that the crime against the King was **BY THE GREAT DAME**. Nostradamus actually enlarges upon this definition of Britannia in the next quatrain, by calling her the *Dame of Antiquity*. Importantly, this reference to Britannia is itself prophetic, because it was during the reign of Charles II that plans to symbolise the British people by this Roman figure were finally completed.

> *She has never been absent from the coinage since the reign of Charles II and now, she is universally recognised as the personification of Britain.* [6]

THROUGH PRETENCE

It was, of course, the British people represented by their elected government that sentenced the King to death. Because there was no constitutional means for ridding the kingdom of its legitimate monarch, it had to be accomplished **THROUGH PRETENCE**. The *pretence* being that the King had engaged in a cruel and costly war against Parliament and in doing so had actively committed treason.[7] In fact, Charles had been forced to take this action in order to defend what he believed to be his divine right to rule; that is, being answerable only to God. This was also the teaching of

Nostradamus, and we can see how his beliefs, as well as his occasional humour, have become integrated into his prophecies.

NOT HAVING OFFENDED

Although Charles I had indeed been engaged in a civil war, the majority of people in Britain confessed to a liking for the King, and he was **NOT** seen as **HAVING OFFENDED** them.[8] His fate was to come up against the wishes of Parliament's forceful and ambitious leader, Oliver Cromwell. As can often happen at such times, the population found itself swept along by the sheer force of one man's personality.

The Plague was not the only tragedy to strike London in the 1660s. Scarcely had the pestilence subsided when the capital was struck by another calamity. A fire left to smoulder in the hearth of Thomas Farrynor's bake house in Pudding Lane at the weekend, re-ignited during the early hours of Sunday morning. Very soon the flames had spread. By Monday morning, fanned by the wind, there was no stopping it. Nostradamus actually gives the exact date for the Great Fire of London, albeit in subtle terminology, concealing it in a reference to Charles II's Dutch Wars, which were being fought at the same time.

C.II: 51

Le fang du iufte à Londres fera faute,
Bruflés par fouldres de vint trois les fix.
La dame antique cherra de place haute:
De mefme fecte plufieurs feront occis.

The blood of the 'Just One' will make a mistake in London,
Burnt by sudden calamities of twenty-three the sixes.
The antique dame will fall from her high place:
Of the same sect many will be killed.

Bruflés, (O.Fr.) brûler; vint, (O.Fr.) vingt; antique, (Latin) in the old style; cherra, (future tense of choir); occis, (Latinism) occi/do = kill; plusieurs, (O.Fr.) many, a great number. Cross-references: fang du iufte and La dame, C.II: 53; du iufte, C.IX: 11.

THE BLOOD OF THE JUST ONE

The blood of the Just One literally means the natural child of the Just One. In previous quatrains, the *Just One* has been identified as Charles I, who succeeded to the throne as the lawful King of England: he being the son of James I. But he was executed in 1649, and replaced by Cromwell. As a usurper, Cromwell's rule was unlawful in the seer's eyes. Nostradamus is therefore able to refer to Charles I as *the Just One*, and to his son Charles II as: **THE BLOOD OF THE JUST ONE.**

It was in March 1665 that Charles II **MADE A** costly **MISTAKE**. He embarked upon a needless and fruitless war with Holland. It not only cost the treasury many millions of pounds to pursue, thereby draining the country's finances, but it also united France, Spain and Denmark in their hostility towards England. Worse still, Charles was eventually defeated. This cost Britain the only colony held by England on the mainland of South America. The King was also forced to relinquish Nova Scotia, as well as several strategic forts in Africa. He did, however, manage to retain New Amsterdam, which he renamed New York. At home, he was required to meet the compensation claims of English merchants and to agree concessions for Dutch carriers arriving at English ports.[1] Taken as a whole the war had proved to be a disastrous mistake.

Charles II had declared this war on the Netherlands in March 1665, while still resident **IN LONDON**. Prophetically, this is important, because two months later, the capital was hit by the worst outbreak of Plague in its history: whereupon: *The king, on its first appearance, withdrew to Hampton-court; but that being thought too near the capital, he afterwards removed to Salisbury.*[2]

One can see how parsimonious, yet pregnant with meaning each phrase is within these oracles. In this instance, the emphasis is on the *mistake made* by the *blood of the just one* occurring *in London*. Two months later, the King left London for the safety of the country. Thereafter, *London* is made to serve the next part of the prophecy, which was fulfilled a year later.

In 1666, Charles II suffered a further blow. **LONDON** ignited into a furnace that burned out of control for four days. Few people died, but many premises were **BURNT** to the ground **BY THE SUDDEN CALAMITIES** that followed. Amongst these *calamites* were 89 parish churches, 13,200 dwellings, shops and warehouses, the great Livery Halls; even St. Paul's Cathedral did not escape the inferno.[3]

The Fire began in the bakery of Thomas Farrynor of Pudding Lane. The oven fire had not been properly damped down on the night before, and the next day, it being Sunday, the flames were able to spread to other parts of the bakery unnoticed. Soon there was no stopping it. A wind had also blown up overnight and was fanning the fire, causing it to spread quickly and in several directions at once. Sparks then swept through the air in great profusion, and these fell onto the timbered houses and thatched roofs of premises nearby, spreading flames at an alarming rate.

As previously mentioned, according to the legalistic style of dating, which operated when this prophecy was made, New Year's Day began on 25 March, and this did not change in Britain until 1752.

The British decreed that the day following Sept. 2, 1752 should be called Sept. 14, a loss of 11 days. All dates preceding were marked O.S. for Old Style. In addition New Year's Day was moved to Jan. 1 from Mar. 25 (e.g. under the old reckoning, Mar. 24. 1700 had been followed by Mar. 25. 1701). [The World Almanac and Book of Facts: 1977, p.784].

TWENTY-THREE THE SIXES

Consequently, Week One ended on 1 April; Week Two ended on 8 April, and by continuing this count, we eventually arrive at Week **TWENTY-THREE**, which ended on 2 September. Add to this **THE SIXES**; i.e., **1666**, and Nostradamus has foreseen the exact date of the Great Fire of London, **2 SEPTEMBER 1666**.[4]

	1666	Weeks
March	25 (New Years' Day)	-
April	1, 8, 15, 22, 29,	5
May	6, 13, 20, 27,	9
June	3, 10, 17, 24,	13
July	1, 8, 15, 22, 29,	18
August	5, 12, 19, 26,	22
September	2,	**23**

THE ANTIQUE DAME

The Dame of Antiquity was discussed earlier, and identified as Britannia: *"it was the Romans who first named the island of England and Scotland Britannia . . . It was the Romans too who . . . first portrayed Britannia on coinage."* Hence, we have the reason for Nostradamus referring to her as **THE ANTIQUE DAME**.[5] During Charles II's reign, the idea of

202

representing the British people by Britannia was revived, and the King's great love Frances Steward was asked to pose for Britannia in what was to become: *"a fitting symbol used on the reverse of copper coins of Charles II."*

WILL FALL FROM HER HIGH PLACE

The oracle's reference to *falling from a high place* is biblical. It occurs several times in the Bible and refers to idols being toppled. Once again, this is apt. Britannia was an idol, and one that was intended to be a symbol for Britain's growing power at sea. For this reason the spear, originally held by Britannia, was replaced by Neptune's trident.

It was during Charles II's Dutch Wars that **BRITANNIA FELL FROM HER HIGH PLACE**; that is, the high regard in which she was held. *"Whoever deserved to rule the waves in Charles II's first Dutch wars, it was not Britannia."* In June 1667, Dutch ships entered the Thames unchallenged, and then sailed up the River Medway, even as far as Upnor Castle to inflict terrible damage on the King's ships anchored at Chatham.[6]

OF THE SAME SECT, MANY WILL BE KILLED

This naval setback came only one year after Admiral De Ruyter had achieved a glorious victory over an English fleet commanded by Sir William Berkley. In a four-day battle that took place in the English Channel, the Dutch inflicted over 8,000 casualties on the English. Tragically, a great number of the victims were family men who had been pressed into service as they left church. After the battle, their bodies *"were found floating in the water dressed in their Sunday black just as they had been caught after church by the press gang."*[7]

Nostradamus, being himself Catholic, has specifically identified the **MANY** who **WILL BE KILLED FROM THE SAME SECT** as those from the Anglican Church, which he saw as a breakaway sect from the true Catholic faith. Historical records have since confirmed the truth of his choice of words.

England's identity as a Protestant country was established in the reign of Henry VIII: it having been achieved through the King's desire to marry Anne Boleyn at the expense of divorcing his wife, Catherine of Aragon. But after his death, the nation's religious persuasion wavered. And for many years afterwards, questions surrounding the legitimacy of *the divorce,* which had been so much central to England's change of religion, were never far from men's thoughts. In the reign of James II, England's religious affinity once again became the focus of attention.

C.X: 22

Par ne vouloir confentir au diuorce,
Qui puis apres fera cogneu indigner,
Le roy des Ifles fera chaffé par force
Mis à fon lieu que de roy n'aura figne.

Through not being willing to consent to the divorce,
Who, then, afterwards will be recognized as unworthy,
The King of the Isles will be expelled by force,
Put in his place, when as King, he will not have [the] seal.

cogneu, (Latinism) cogn/osco = recognized; indigner, (Latinism) indign/us; figne, (Latinism) sign/um = seal.

In 1685 Charles II died without leaving a legitimate heir, although the duke of Monmouth (whom we shall meet later) did declare that Charles had secretly married his mother Lucy Walters, thereby legitimising his claim to the throne. This was ignored, and the crown passed to Charles's brother, who became James II.

UNWILLING TO CONSENT TO THE DIVORCE

Unhappily for English Protestants, before taking over the reign, James had converted to Catholicism, and was therefore one of a number who remained UNWILLING TO CONSENT TO THE legitimacy of Henry VIII's DIVORCE. As with all practising Catholics, James continued to believe that Henry's *divorce* had been illegal, and that England had become a Protestant nation under false pretences. He therefore began his reign with the fullest intention of returning the nation to the Catholic country it had once been before the contentious issue of *the divorce.*[1]

This ambitious project soon encountered opposition from both Whigs and Tories, especially when the King systematically began dismissing Protestants from positions of authority, only to replace them with Catholic sympathisers. Further antagonism arose when, across the Channel, Louis XIV repealed the legislation that had given Huguenots freedom to practise their religion. Thousands of refugees flocked to England. And this encouraged fear that James would follow Louis' example. Protestant anxiety finally reached crisis point when, on 10 June 1688, the Queen gave birth to a male heir, James Edward, thus signalling a Catholic succession to the throne.

WHO THEN AFTERWARDS WILL BE RECOGNIZED AS UNWORTHY

Historical appraisals of James II have tended to agree with the oracle; that is, after his succession, **HE WILL BE RECOGNIZED AS BEING UNWORTHY**. What really antagonised the people was James' persistence in believing the biblical tenet, which asserts the absolute power of the monarch; moreover, he set about implementing this in a way that was considered to be obstinate, short-sighted, and mulish; even the Pope counselled greater caution. Innocent XI advised him to beware of alienating the very people he wished to win over. But the papal advice was ignored. And, quite apart from his preference to place Catholic favourites in positions of power, he also dissolved Parliament (July 1687): his intention being to reopen it with men who were sympathetic to his aims.[2]

Powerful forces at once united to oppose the King. Emerging from these was a decision made by Prince William of Orange to invade England: a resolution that had the backing of members of parliament. James II panicked and tried to reverse the unpopular measures that had brought this about. But it was too late. Realizing this, he fled for the safety of France and the protection of Louis XIV. But at Faversham in Kent, he was apprehended and brought back to Whitehall.

THE KING OF THE ISLES EXPELLED BY FORCE

The prophecy now focuses upon Prince William, to whom the throne of England was offered, so that it might be shared jointly with his wife Mary. Before this could be legitimised, James II, despite everything, was still legally the King of England and Scotland – that is, **KING OF THE ISLES** – and it was imperative that he be removed. He was therefore ordered to leave the country. On 23 December 1688, under guard, James was **EXPELLED BY FORCE**. At Rochester in Kent, he was placed on board a ship heading for the French coast and sanctuary in Picardy, where upon arrival he received the protection of Louis XIV.[3]

Interestingly, in Nostradamus's time, there was no 'King of the Isles', since England and Scotland each had its own monarch. This did not change until Queen Elizabeth's death in 1603, when

James VI of Scotland was invited to take the English crown as James I. Nevertheless, Britain is clearly intended as the subject of this oracle through its reference to *the Isles*. (The use of 'Isles' when referring to Britain has been employed on a number of other occasions; e.g., C.II: 68, C.VIII: 64, C.X: 39, and this has set a precedent.) Of equal interest is the fact that James II was the first, and so far only King of England and its associated territories, to be *expelled* from the country *by force*. His expulsion left the way clear for his replacement to be elected into office.

> *Seven eminent Englishmen, among them the Tory Earl of Danby and Henry Compton, bishop of London, [had written] inviting William of Orange to come over with an army to redress the nation's grievances.*

PUT IN HIS PLACE AS KING

When news of this invitation reached the Prince in Friesland, he accepted the offer subject to certain conditions being met. Thereafter, in a successful, and unopposed invasion that took place in November 1688 (the Glorious, or Bloodless Revolution), William arrived in England to TAKE HIS PLACE AS KING, alongside his sovereign wife Mary.[4]

HE WILL NOT HAVE THE SEAL

Nostradamus ends the oracle with an interesting piece of prophecy. During King James' moment of panic; that is, before taking flight from the capital, he first burnt all the writs he had made out for electing his new Catholic parliament. Then, taking the great *seal of England* with him, he threw it into the River Thames. Consequently, when William III replaced James II AS KING, he discovered that HE DID NOT HAVE THE SEAL. This lay somewhere in the mud, at the bottom of the river Thames near Vauxhall.[5]

William's arrival in England as the future King Consort did not meet with universal agreement. Although England offered little resistance to the idea, the stubborn Scots continued to raise objections, siding with the deposed James II who was still James VII of Scotland. In an effort to overcome these protests, William called a meeting in London, inviting the Scottish noblemen present at the time to discuss how progress could be made to win their country's acceptance. This meeting is indicated in the following quatrain, and is accompanied by a brief description of the King, and what took place to bring him to England. The verse also contains a reference to the death of the Duke of Monmouth, the son of Charles II, who was also William's chief opponent for the Crown. Nostradamus has, however, reversed the order in which the history occurred, leaving the final line for his description of William III.

C.IV: 89

Trente de Londres fecret coniureront,
Contre leur Roy fur le pont l'entreprife:
Luy, fatelites la mort degoufteront,
Vn Roy efleu blonde, natif de Frize.

Thirty in London will adjure in private,
The enterprise on the sea against their King:
Regarding him, attendants will sicken [at] the death,
A King elected, susceptible, native of Friesland.

fecret, (Latinism) secreto; coniureront, (O.Fr.) adjurer; pont, (Latinism) pont/us; fatelites, (Latinism) satell/itis; blonde, (O.Fr.) susceptible; degousteront , (O.Fr.) desgouster, to loath, disgust or abhor; Frize, (Latinism) Frisii.

At the beginning of 1689, Prince William of Orange was King in all but name. He still needed to persuade Scotland to accept him as the country's monarch. In the previous December, William's father-in-law, James II, had abandoned the thrones of England and Scotland by seeking asylum in France. But, until Parliament decreed otherwise, he was still legitimately the King of both countries, and Scotland remained reluctant to accede to English demands.

IN LONDON, THIRTY WILL ADJURE IN PRIVATE

To resolve this problem, William called a meeting IN LONDON, consisting of THIRTY Scottish sympathizers, with the aim of ADJURING IN PRIVATE, so that a consensus might be obtained concerning how best the present difficulties might be resolved.

There being at that time many Scotsmen of rank in London, he summoned
them together, and asked their advice in the present state of affairs. This
assembly, consisting of thirty noblemen . . . chose duke Hamilton for their
president.[1]

Whereupon, after much discussion, an agreement was reached that William should arrange a convention north of the border in order to settle the matter. This was convened in Edinburgh on 22 March 1689.

THE ENTERPRISE AGAINST THEIR KING ON THE SEA

Before William of Orange arrived in England to become King, it had been necessary for Parliament to take action against James II. This involved several members of the British government sending an invitation to Prince William, requesting that he invade England and take the Crown.[2]

To ensure success of **THE ENTERPRISE AGAINST THEIR KING**, the British government even provided the Prince with a fleet of ships to facilitate his journey **ON THE SEA**. Up to fifty men-of-war were eventually assembled along the coast of Holland, together with a large number of transports, so that when the Prince left Helvoet Sluice bound for England, he had under his command almost five hundred vessels. On 5 November 1688, William landed safely and unopposed at Torbay in Devon.[3] A picture of the fleet's arrival and the disembarkation of Prince William and his armed forces can be seen in a contemporary print owned by the Ann Ronan Picture Library.

REGARDING HIM,

Attention now turns to the Duke of Monmouth, King Charles II's illegitimate son. **REGARDING HIM** – Monmouth had previously made an attempt at seizing the Crown for himself, and to help accomplish this, he raised a small army against James II, but was heavily defeated (Battle of Sedgemoor, 6 July 1685). While trying to escape, he was captured and sent to the Tower of London. At his trial, he was found guilty of treason and on 15 July 1685, he was beheaded.

THE ATTENDANTS WILL SICKEN AT THE DEATH

Monmouth's execution was a particularly gruesome affair. The headsman suffered an attack of nerves at the critical moment, and his first blow was so weak that Monmouth was able to look up at his executioner with a reproaching stare. Twice more the axe fell, but without achieving any real progress. At this point, the headsman threw down his axe and said he could do no more, leaving Monmouth semi-conscious, kneeling in a swamp of his own gore awaiting the next move. The sheriff, who was there to see the sentence was properly carried out, remonstrated with the headsman, demanding that he return to the task before him. Reinforced by the sheriff's words the executioner picked up the axe and struck once more, but again without effect. At last, overcoming his nerves, the headsman managed to deliver the fatal blow, but it was only after the sixth strike that the head at last fell away from the body, with THE ATTENDANTS at the execution SICKENED AT THE DEATH.[4]

ELECTED KING

As for the Prince of Orange, his accession to the throne came on 13 February 1689, after having been ELECTED by Parliament as the nation's new KING.

> ... the so-called Convention Parliament, summoned in January 1689, declared that James had abdicated and offered the vacant throne, with an accompanying Declaration of Right, to William and Mary. They were proclaimed in February and crowned on April 21.[5]

SUSCEPTIBLE

Once on the throne, William III quickly proved himself SUSCEPTIBLE to the task ahead by defeating James II in the battle of the Boyne (1690). He then devoted considerable energy to fighting "a gruelling war against France at sea and in the Netherlands, eventually forcing France to sign the Treaty of Rijswijk (1697) in which she abandoned all her war aims."[6] He was also successful in defeating several counter-revolutionary attempts made by James II, which gained their support from both Ireland and Scotland.

A NATIVE OF FRIESLAND

Nostradamus also predicted that England's ELECTED KING would be A NATIVE OF FRIESLAND. William Prince of Orange was indeed a native of Friesland. Friesland or Frisia was the ancient name given to the Netherlands where William was 'Stadholder'. And it was the place where he had lived for the first thirty-eight years of his life.[7]

The need for maintaining secrecy often involves ingenious methods of concealment in order to stay one step ahead of the interpreter. This is evident in the first line of the next quatrain, in which Nostradamus employs a homonym in 'The land of the great celestial temple'. Britain is the land implied by the reference to London in the next line; hence the temple could refer to Stonehenge, described in William Stukeley's book as: A Temple Restored to the British Druids (1740). But Stukeley was a friend of Isaac Newton, and he wrote a memoir of the scientist's life in 1752. And therein lays the connection to the homonym.

C.VI: 22

Dedans la terre du grand temple celique,
Nepueu à Londres par paix faincte meurtry:
La barque alors deuiendra fcismatique,
Liberté faincte fera au corn & cry.

Within the land of the great celestial temple,
Nephew in London, through feigned peace, killed:
The barque then will become divided,
Feigned liberty will be in the proclamation / hue & cry.

temple, (O.Fr. anatomical) tempe; celique, (O.Fr.) celeste; faincte, (O.Fr.) feinte; meurtry, (O.Fr.) tuer; corn & cry, (O.Fr.) hue and cry, proclamation.

The word 'temple' is a homonym. One definition points to a place of worship; another definition indicates the flat portion of the head above the cheekbone. Nostradamus's use of *celestial* as a defining adjective would normally place the question of its intended meaning beyond doubt, but the intelligence behind these prophecies is subtle, cryptic and of a different order. Just once in the history of England – and London is referred to in the second line – *celestial temple* was capable of taking its alternative meaning.

WITHIN THE LAND OF THE GREAT CELESTIAL TEMPLE

This occurred in 1687, when England's great scientific genius, Isaac Newton, published his famous *Principia*. It was a book that expounded the *celestial* laws of the universe. And it was the mathematical description of these laws that first took shape inside the author's *temple*. In other words: WITHIN THE LAND OF THE GREAT CELESTIAL TEMPLE refers to England: *the land of the great Isaac Newton*, the genius, whose brain was responsible for formulating the laws that govern the motion of the *celestial* bodies.[1]

THE NEPHEW

James Scott Duke of Monmouth, the illegitimate son of Charles II, was by birth a NEPHEW of King James II. But he also believed himself to be legitimate, and the rightful heir to the English throne. In June 1685, in pursuit of this goal, he landed at Lyme Regis in Dorset at the head of a rabble army. Several days later, at Taunton in Somerset, he proclaimed himself King of England. But on 6 July, John Churchill, future Duke of Marlborough, intercepted him on his way to London. Monmouth's army was defeated, and after a brief flight he was taken captive and imprisoned in the Tower of London.[2]

IN LONDON, THROUGH FEIGNED PEACE, KILLED

From his prison cell **IN LONDON**, Monmouth wrote a contrite letter to his uncle. It was full of remorse, begging the King to be lenient and to overlook his past disloyalty; promising, instead, to repay him with his total allegiance.[3] (The Victorian artist John Pettie has painted a dramatic canvas of Monmouth's penitent appeal). The King responded to his nephew by giving the impression of being won over, and Monmouth was re-admitted to court. However, this move towards peace proved to be no more than a ruse by which the King hoped to discover information concerning Monmouth's accomplices. But when Monmouth refused to divulge names, he was returned to his cell in the Tower.[4] It was **THROUGH** the failure of this **FEIGNED PEACE** that Monmouth was **BEHEADED** a few days later; his death is referred to in the previous oracle (C.IV: 89).

The barque of Saint Peter – as previously explained in C.X: 58 – is intended to represent the Church, and this brings us to the next part of the oracle. Before succeeding to the throne, James II had converted to the Catholic faith. Consequently, as soon as he became King (6 February 1685), he set about returning England to the Catholic fold. Unfortunately for his aspiration, the attempts he made achieved only division: England having become a predominantly Protestant country.

THE BARQUE WILL BECOME DIVIDED

Prominent amongst James' more divisive schemes was the appointment of Catholics to military commands. Parliament objected to this policy, but the courts upheld the King's right to make the appointments. James also tried to gain admission for pro-Catholic administrators to the universities. This, too, was met with strenuous opposition. Another of his objectives was the *Declaration of Indulgence*, which suspended the penal code against Catholics. This incited bishops across the country even more, and many refused to announce it to their congregations. For this act of defiance they were arrested and imprisoned.

The conflict between a Catholic king and a Protestant country resulted in THE CHURCH BECOMING even more, DIVIDED, [5] and in 1688; James II was forced to leave the country because of his policies.

FEIGNED LIBERTY IN THE PROCLAMATION

The Glorious Revolution that followed James II's deposition promised to herald a new era of liberty. But in the event, it proved to be only a FEIGNED LIBERTY, for very little changed. William III simply reversed the policy of James II. Whereas, the former King had packed Catholics into positions of authority, William filled these positions with Protestants. In May 1689, the *Toleration Act* was passed; despite its name, the PROCLAMATION was a false friend: one that *failed to provide true* religious *liberty* for Catholics, for it *denied them the right of full citizenship.* [6]

HUE AND CRY

The oracle has ended with an alternative: one that undoubtedly points to the HUE AND CRY which greeted the Protestant King, and made by people believing they had been freed from the tyranny of papal supremacy.[7] Nostradamus has used this expression before in C.I: 38, where he writes: *'Par cor ne cri harnois n'arreteront'* (By horn nor voice the harness (or equipment) will not be restrained). However, coincidentally, a literal translation of *horn and voice* can also be construed as a prophetic spin-off for 1685. This was the year that Handel was born – he of HORN AND VOICE. Handel, though born in Saxony, became a naturalized Englishman in 1726, and later took up residence in London, thus connecting him to the quatrain's location. 1685 also relates to this oracle because it was the year when Isaac Newton presented Edmund Halley with his *"nine page treatise entitled De Motu Corporum in Gyrum – On the Motion of Revolving Bodies . . . It was this paper which led, in little more than two years, to the appearance of the completed manuscript of the Principia."* But what also connects Newton's *celestial temple* with the *horn and voice* of Handel is that both men were united by a single phrase – **'The heavens are telling'**. For Newton this was the Principia, telling how the heavens moved; for Handel it was *The Messiah* in which the choir sing the same words: *'the heavens are telling'*. *"This, the most famous of all Handel's oratorios (1742), must be regarded as one of the greatest and most consistently inspired works written in*

English words." It is a commendation that may also be applied to Newton.

Returning to the fate of the Kings and Queens of England, one must ask: Did Nostradamus foresee the end of the British monarchy? For traditionalists and republicans alike, the following oracle may give pause for thought. The seer does not say the monarchy will end, but he does limit the number of changes that will take place over a stated period of time to just seven: all of which have since come to pass. Moreover, as confirmation of the timescale involved, the oracle concludes with a separate prediction of the unrest encountered in Romania following the seventh change.

C.III: 57

> Sept fois changer verrés gent Britannique,
> Taintz en fang en deux cens nonante an:
> Franche non point par apui Germanique.
> Aries doute fon pole Baftarnan.
>
> *You will see the British people changing seven times,*
> *Stained in blood within two hundred and ninety years:*
> *Not at all exempt from German support.*
> *Aries fears his Bastarnae people.*

verrés (vous verrez); Taintz, (O.Fr.) teint; Franche, (O.Fr.) libre; non point, (adverb used with negative) not at all; apui, (appui); pole, (O.Fr.) peuple, foule.

Nostradamus begins this quatrain with an unambiguous assertion. He tells his own people, the French, and others who read his words that THEY WILL SEE SEVEN CHANGES taking place, all of which involve THE BRITISH PEOPLE. He also provides the precise number of years over which these seven changes will occur. He then concludes the prophecy with a prediction involving the people of central-eastern Europe, which on the face of it, appears to be disconnected from what has gone before.

YOU WILL SEE THE BRITISH PEOPLE CHANGING SEVEN TIMES

The probability of fulfilling this prophecy by chance is too remote for consideration. Only a true prophet could have looked into the forthcoming three centuries, and given the exact number of years when the final change would take place. Since Nostradamus published this oracle in 1555, at a time when the Tudors ruled England, the seven changes referred to must necessarily begin from the time of their reign.[1]

213

House of Tudor (1485 – 1603); changes from this period forward:

1 Stuarts: James I; Charles I.
2 Cromwell: Oliver; Richard.
3 Stuarts: Charles II; James II; Mary II.
4 Orange: William III.
5 Stuarts: Anne.
6 Hanover: George I; George II; George III; George IV; William IV.
7 Windsor: Victoria; Edward VII; George V; Edward VIII; George VI; Elizabeth II.

In 1917, during the seventh change, the monarchy altered its dynastic name but there was no change to the bloodline which began with Victoria and Albert.

> In 1837 the Crown descended to Queen Victoria, six generations removed from George I, while Hanover, where female succession was forbidden, passed to a male descendant of George III. In 1849, Victoria married Prince Albert of Saxe-Coburg-Gotha, whose family name was Wettin. In 1917, when Britain was at war with Germany, George V adopted the name Windsor for his dynasty.

STAINED IN BLOOD

The oracle next predicts that during these *seven changes*, *the British people* will be **STAINED IN BLOOD**. Ever since the reign of Edward VI (1547 – 1553), when this oracle appears to have been written, blood has been spilt in great profusion by the British. It began with the slaughtering of religious martyrs in the 16th century, and then proceeded to the war with Spain. This was followed by the Civil War of 1642, and those fighting for their independence in Ireland. Across the Channel there was even more carnage when England fought against Spain, Holland, France, Germany, Italy, Portugal, and further afield, Canada, North America, India Egypt, China, etc.

Nostradamus wraps these bloody conflicts up into a passage of *290 years*: this being the time he predicted would elapse to bring about the *seven changes* referred to. Hence, based upon the list given above, the precise number of years can be calculated.

WITHIN TWO HUNDRED AND NINETY YEARS

On 28 January 1547, Edward VI became King of England following the death of his father Henry VIII. Since the preface in the first book of Nostradamus's prophecies is dated 1 March 1555, just nineteen months after the death of Edward (6 July 1553), there is every reason to believe that the majority of these oracles were written at the time of Edward VI's reign. Consequently, the count will commence from 1547.

On 20 June 1837, Victoria ascended the throne. This brought about the seventh and final change, because it allowed her to marry into the House of Wettin: the House of Hanover having split from the succession in 1837. If we subtract 1547 from 1837, the result is **290 YEARS**: the precise number foretold by the seer.[2]

NOT AT ALL EXEMPT FROM GERMAN SUPPORT

Nostradamus then delves further into the future of the English monarchy by predicting that the succession will **NOT BE EXEMPT FROM GERMAN SUPPORT**. The marriage of Queen Victoria in 1840 to Albert, son of Duke Saxe-Coburg-Gotha, retained the German connection that began with the House of Hanover. This line of German succession, having endured since 1714, eventually terminated when the next in line for the throne, William IV's brother Ernest, chose the Hanover crown. His choice was made necessary because succession in Germany was forbidden to a woman (Salic law). Thereafter, the Hanoverian connection with England's monarchy ceased with the Queen's marriage.[3]

After the coronation of Queen Victoria (28 June 1838), parts of Europe became caught up in the turmoil of political change. Nostradamus concludes his prophecy by referring to one outbreak in particular.

In 1848, the Transylvanian part of Eastern Europe, including Hungary rose up in revolt against the landowners. There existed amongst these revolutionaries a group of young intellectuals led by the poet Sandor Petofi. Together, the rebels were successful in abolishing censorship and formulating a set of laws that became known as the *'April Laws'*.[4] This piece of legislation, with its intention of removing serfdom and unifying Hungary, adds to the reason for Nostradamus referring to **ARIES**, since the sun traditionally appears in this constellation between March 21 and April 20.

Many conservatives resented what the *April Laws* stood for, and the objectors found willing allies among Romanians; that is, *the Bastarnae* who refused to accept the new administration. *The Bastarnae* were a German tribal people known to the Romans,

215

and who had formerly *"settled in Europe east of the Carpathian Mountains from the upper valley of the Dniester River to the Danube River delta."* This area is presently occupied by Romania, and includes the *Aries* River and *Aries* Valley.

ARIES FEARS HIS BASTARNAE PEOPLE

On 2 December 1848, Emperor Ferdinand I of Austria, King of Hungary and Grand Prince of Transylvania, **FEARING HIS BASTARNAE PEOPLE**, which was in a state of revolt over the *April Laws,*[5] was persuaded to abdicate in favour of his nephew Franz Josef. Under this new regime, the recent *April Laws* were abolished.[6] Nostradamus calls Ferdinand **ARIES**, because this was his birth sign. He was born on 19 April 1793. *Aries* also complements the *April Laws,* so named because they were signed on 11 April 1848: under the sun sign *Aries.*

This brief mention of Emperor Francis Joseph of Austria acts as a prelude to the creation of the Austro-Hungary alliance, predicted by Nostradamus in C.II: 90. But more importantly, the oracle weaves together a connection between England, Germany and Franz Josef, for the Austrian Emperor was destined to play an important role in the outbreak of the First World War, in which Great Britain and Germany became enemies.

> *In the period 1908-14 Francis Joseph held fast to his peace policy in the face of warnings by the chief of the general staff, Franz, Count Conrad von Hötzendorf, who repeatedly advocated a preventive war against Serbia or Italy. Yet, without having fully thought out the consequences, he let himself in July 1914 be persuaded by Count Leopold Berchtold, the foreign minister, to issue the intransigent ultimatum to Serbia that led to World War I.*[7]

It can therefore be seen how two, apparently unconnected parts of this prophecy have ultimately become united. For as Nostradamus steadfastly maintained, his prophecies were 'continuous'. This theme of continuation is the subject of the next chapter, which recounts the major events that occurred, during the French Revolution.

6

THE FRENCH REVOLUTION

One of the most momentous and historically important events of the eighteenth century took place appropriately enough in France. The French Revolution broke out in 1789, and was not officially declared over until a decade later. During those ten hectic years many dramatic incidents occurred, the most important of which were chronicled by Nostradamus almost two and a half centuries before they happened. The story begins where most histories commence, with the Storming of the Bastille. Like the prediction for the Great Fire of London, the seer confines this event to a single line, accompanying it with other historically recorded happenings of that time. Also, like the oracle predicting the Fire of London, Nostradamus has provided a concealed date for the fall of the Bastille: one that is just as accurate, and subtle, as those he has previously given.

C.IX: 23

Puiſnay iouant au freſch deſſouz la tonne,
Le hault du toict du milieu ſur la teſte,
Le pere roy au temple ſainct Solonne,
Sacrifiant ſacrera fum de feſte.

The next born under the barrel, passing time in the chill,
The top of the fortress, in the midst, over the bricks,
The Father King at the temple, Saint Solano,
Sacrificing, he will sanctify the smoke of the festival.

iouant, (O.Fr.) passing time, dallying; tonne, (apocope) tonne[rre]; toict, (O.Fr.) forter-esse; teſte, (Latinism) test/ae – bricks; Solonne, (Spanish, Solanne) Solano.
Cross-reference: milieu, C.I: 65.

THE NEXT BORN

In 1789 Louis XVI was King of France. He was also the eldest surviving member of three brothers. The second eldest, **THE NEXT BORN**, was *Provence*.[1] As we shall now see; Nostradamus uses the title of the King's brother to direct attention, not to the man but to the region in southern France that has the same name.

PASSING TIME IN THE CHILL

It was in 1789 that Provence suffered its worst winter for eighty years. This led to a shortage of bread, since the mills had frozen in the icy conditions and they were no longer able to grind flour for bread.[2] The people in the mills and the bakers were among those unable to work: **PASSING** their **TIME IN THE CHILL** instead.

UNDER THE BARREL

It was in January, during these wintry conditions that the Comte de Mirabeau was elected as the representative of Aix-en-Provence. Nostradamus has punned on the Count's nickname, *Tonnerre:* this being the name he had actually given to himself, *'Mirabeau–Tonnerre'.*[3] For by his own recognition, he had the physique of a **BARREL**. Hence, the first line, once the veil has been lifted to uncover its cryptic construction, reads: *'Provence* i.e., *the next born, passing time in the cool, under* its newly elected representative, *the barrel* (Mirabeau-Tonnerre).

It is noteworthy that one of Mirabeau's first tasks, as representative of *Provence,* was to issue a report to the Assembly in Paris concerning the dreadful weather conditions in the south, and the effect this was having upon his constituents. This parliamentary report therefore connects Provence, Mirabeau and the cold weather to the prediction appearing in line one.

On 14 July 1789, the great Parisian *fortress* known as the Bastille, and which formed part of the old city walls, was invaded by an angry mob. IN THE MIDST of the affray the governor was killed and the building torn down, brick by brick. Nostradamus has described the scene that was later painted by Pierre Antoine Demachy: '*The Demolition of the Bastille*'. It shows the invading mob clambering OVER THE BRICKWORK (*sur la teste*) AT THE TOP (*le hault*) OF THE FORTRESS (*du toict*), in the process of demolishing it.[4]

The mob who raided the Bastille acted on the assumption that the King was bringing armed troops into Paris to disband the newly constituted National Assembly. Seizing the Bastille was meant to diminish the fortress's importance, and send a warning to the King. It achieved its purpose. Louis ordered his troops to withdraw, while also agreeing to accept the '*new constitutional development*'.

THE FATHER KING

Three days later, on 17 July, Louis XVI was asked to attend the *Hôtel de Ville* in Paris and accept the Assembly's formal approval of his willingness to comply with the new political order. The King left Versailles under heavy escort and arrived in Paris amidst cheers from the people and cries of: *"Our King, our father!"* When Louis reached his destination at the centre of Paris, he saw that these chants were confirmed in writing. For in large letters above the archway ran the slogan: 'LOUIS XVI; FATHER OF THE FRENCH; THE KING OF A FREE PEOPLE'.[5]

One year later, in 1790, festivals celebrating the new political order were taking place in many towns and regions across France. Paris decided to hold a celebration of its own, choosing July 14th to commemorate the fall of the Bastille.

AT THE TEMPLE

In less than a month the *Champ de Mars* to the west of the city had been transformed into what was called a *Temple* to the Federation. At the centre was a large raised dais. This was to be the Altar of the Fatherland, where political oaths would be sworn before a bishop of the Revolution. Encircling this were the enclosures to seat the congregation. At the far end of the field, a tall triple arch eighty feet high had been erected with a platform for spectators. Below, *the Father King* had been allocated his own seat **AT THE TEMPLE**, but it was one that had been deliberately placed amongst other invited guests.[6]

Saint Solano has no obvious connection with the French Revolution, for he had acquired his reputation as a miracle worker in Peru during the sixteenth century, His inclusion in this oracle, especially *at the temple* is because his feast day coincides with *'Bastille Day'* on *'July 14ᵗʰ'*.[7] Quite remarkably, we therefore have a prophecy within a prophecy, for *Solano* was not beatified until long after Nostradamus was dead. The seer therefore had no way of knowing by ordinary means that *Solano* would be beatified, nor had he any normal means of knowing the date that would be selected for his feast day.

SACRIFICING, HE WILL SANCTIFY THE SMOKE OF THE FESTIVAL
At the temple, the father king was required to approve the vows given at the ceremony with a personal declaration to the new constitution. He did this by raising his hand and swearing that as – *"King of the French . . . [he would] use the power entrusted to him by the constitutional law of the State, to maintain and see the decrees of the National Assembly were upheld."* [8] Essentially, what Louis XVI had done was to **SACRIFICE** his royal power by **SANCTIFYING THE SMOKE**; that is, the *fumum vendere* (empty promises) **OF THE FESTIVAL**.

The old English adage: to give someone an inch and they will take a yard (sometimes referred to as a mile) was no less true in France. Louis XVI had complied with the initial wishes of the Third Estate (a group in society made up of *'lawyers, functionaries and professional men'*,) and in return they demanded still more from him. The next oracle deals with the worsening situation for the monarchy, as a sequence of dramatic events followed one after the other in quick succession.

C.VI: 23

D'efprit de regne munifmes defcriées,
Et feront peuples efmeuz contre leur Roy:
Paix, faict nouueau, fainctes loix empirées,
Rapis onc fut en fi tres dur arroy.

Concerning the spirit of the reign, munificence decried,
Also, people will be stirred up against their King,
Peace, a new act, sacred laws made worse;
Paris (kidnap) at one time was in such very harsh array.

Muniſmes, (Latinism) munis; Rapis, (anagram) Paris: also, (O.Fr. syncope – Rapi[neu]s) Ravisseur; empirier, (O.Fr.) gâter; onc, (O.Fr.) une fois, en certaine circonstance; dur, (Latinism) dur/us; arroy, (O.Fr.) ranger.

After the fall of the Bastille, the King's position had become increasingly precarious. He no longer commanded enough power to defend his friends and family. But, on the other hand, the move towards a republic had been too fast. Its supporters had yet to come to terms with the role of the monarch in this new power shift. Their solution was a new constitution. In this, Louis would be known as the King of the French, instead of by his hereditary title King of France and Navarre. He would also be given a veto to be used at the Assembly, but this would only be valid for four years.

CONCERNING THE SPIRIT OF THE REIGN, MUNIFICENCE DECRIED

It was the King's reply CONCERNING these new arrangements to his REIGN that fulfilled the opening line of this oracle. For, although Louis declared himself to be in full agreement with *'the spirit'* [1] of the document's intentions, he qualified his obliging MUNIFICENCE with a small number of reservations, and it was these personal preferences that caused his response to be DECRIED.[2]

PEOPLE WILL BE STIRRED UP AGAINST THEIR KING

The Press responded by mounting a continuous attack against Louis. By 2 October 1789, these outbursts had descended to the level of a character assassination. With its power to circulate political bias *via* the printed word, THE PEOPLE WERE BEING STIRRED UP AGAINST THEIR KING.[3] Louis' situation began to look increasingly perilous.

PEACE

Concerned at the international attention France was now receiving, the Assembly moved to calm international fears by announcing to the world (22 May 1790), its resolve for PEACE. France, it was declared, would never wage war or seek conquest or use its military might against the freedom of any people.[4]

A NEW ACT

A month later, on 19 June, the Assembly passed **A NEW ACT**, which ended the nobility's right to pass on their titles and coats of arms to their children.[5] This was a direct blow against the privileges enjoyed by the Ancient Regime, and as the Abbé Maury cleverly pointed out: *"If there is no nobility, there is no monarchy."* Time was beginning to run out for the royal family. But first the power of the Church had to be weakened.

SACRED LAWS MADE WORSE

On 12 July 1790, it was announced that priests and bishops were to be elected, and all men of the cloth were to become civil servants. To pay for the clergy's upkeep, the Church's assets, including its lands, would be placed under state control. Moreover, there would also be a reduction in the number of dioceses, so as to bring them into line with the number of departments.[6] As predicted: **THE SACRED LAWS** will be **MADE WORSE**.

KIDNAPPED

In June 1791 a new drama unfolded. The government announced to the people that the King had been **KIDNAPPED**, but he had been rescued before he could be taken out of the country.[7] In fact Louis XVI and Marie Antoinette had attempted to leave Paris secretly, and escape across the Belgian frontier. But at Varennes, just forty kilometres from safety, they were recognized and detained. Under guard, the royal couple were brought back to the capital. The report of their kidnap was in fact a cover story to avoid the embarrassment of admitting publicly, that the King had tried to escape the clutches of his government.

PARIS AT ONE TIME WAS IN SUCH VERY HARSH ARRAY

As a result of the King and Queen's attempt to secretly leave for Belgium, and with the cover story of their kidnap still only partly believed, it was just this **ONE OCCASION**, when **PARIS WAS IN SUCH A VERY HARSH ARRAY**. *"The streets were lined with National Guards, their arms reversed as though for a funeral procession."* The crowd was huge, but in obedience to a government decree it remained utterly silent as the King and Queen were driven through the streets to their palace. Notices were everywhere on display – *"Whoever applauds the King shall be flogged. Whoever insults him shall be hanged."*[8]

As early as November 1789, the government had made its first move towards sequestering Church lands. This sudden acquisition of property gave the Assembly a new idea for raising funds. The land could be turned into money by valuing it and then issuing interest bearing bonds with each certificate guaranteed by the value of the land upon which it was drawn. However, after the issue of these bonds, the holders realised that they could be used as currency, changing hands in the same way that money is exchanged. Nostradamus neatly ties these events together in the following quatrain.

C.I: 53

Las qu'on verra grand peuple tourmenté,
Et la Loy faincte en totale ruine:
Par aultres loyx toute Chreftienté,
Quand d'or, d'argent trouue nouuelle mine.

Alas that one shall see a great people tormented,
And the sacred law in total ruin:
By other laws all Christendom,
When for gold, money discovers a new source.

ONE SHALL SEE A GREAT PEOPLE TORMENTED

Legislation attacking the Church was passed in two stages, in 1789 and then with greater severity in 1790. The second piece of legislation introduced the Civil Constitution of the Clergy,[1] and its announcement split the country in two: at which point, **ONE WAS ABLE TO SEE A GREAT PEOPLE TORMENTED** at having to behold France's religious heritage being torn apart. (Nostradamus always refers to his nation as *a great people*).

THE SACRED LAWS IN TOTAL RUIN

Under this new legislation, the clergy were required to swear, on oath, their allegiance to the new Constitution. Many refused, taking courage from those in their congregation who supported them. On 10 March 1791, Pope Pius VI condemned the Civil Constitution of the Clergy. But this only brought fresh outbreaks of violence against the papacy, and those supporting it. Louis XVI added to the ferment by declaring that his conscience forbade him receiving Holy Communion from a constitutional priest. For this, he was declared a traitor, but he stuck to his decision. Amongst the population, controversy continued, often accompanied by violent demonstrations. Effigies of the Pope were made and then set alight, convents were attacked and the nuns assaulted, churches were daubed with revolutionary graffiti, and the King was repeatedly importuned to sanction the constitutional priests.[2] Everywhere it seemed, THE SACRED LAWS WERE IN TOTAL RUIN.

BY OTHER LAWS

Behind this change in attitude to the Church was the legislation passed by the National Assembly in 1790; that is to say, OTHER LAWS were now governing the Church. These included the requirement that priests and bishops had to be elected, and thereafter to swear their allegiance to the new Constitution. Those who preached outside the law were to be arrested for civil disturbance. At the same time, the privileges of the monarchy were also being diffused. The King no longer had the power to make decrees. In place of this was France's first written constitution based upon the Rights of Man.[3]

ALL CHRISTENDOM

On 13 April, Pius VI again denounced the Civil Constitution, urging ALL CHRISTENDOM not to collaborate with anyone obedient to these *other laws*. The Constitution, he declared, was *'schismatical'*, and he condemned those priests and prelates who had taken the oath of allegiance in defiance of his order.[4] Interestingly this was the same pope that in 1781 had also condemned Nostradamus.

The lands belonging to the Church in France were nationalised on 2 November 1789. It was intended that money raised from this acquisition of land would pay the wages of the constitutional clergy; that is, those who had sworn to abide by the government's ruling.

WHEN FOR GOLD, MONEY DISCOVERS A NEW SOURCE.

The land acquired in this way therefore led to A NEW SOURCE of MONEY. Initially, Church property to the value of 400 million *livres* was offered for sale. Unlike money whose value was based on gold, these bonds (*assignats*; i.e., 'assigned') were guaranteed by land, and bore interest. *Assignats* then began changing hands, as money changes hands in the present day. In 1790, the government bowed to pressure and *assignats* were declared legal currency.[5]

In this next oracle we come to one of the most dramatic and far-reaching events in the history of France: the arrest of the King and Queen at Varennes. It has been said by historians that by attempting to flee France and the Revolution, Louis XVI finally lost the support of those who had once been prepared to defend him. Nostradamus seemed fully aware of the many ramifications arising from the King's attempted escape, because he was at his most adept in packing the four lines of this verse with as much detail as he could muster, including several names. The interest in this oracle has acquired for it a long history of commentaries relating to its fulfilment, for the name Varennes, which Nostradamus actually gives, has acted like a magnet to those interested in the history of what took place on that June day in 1791. But it is only now that the full story of what has been predicted can be fully appreciated.

C.IX: 20

De nuit viendra par la foreſt de Reines,
Deux pars vaultorte Herne la pierre blanche,
Le moine noir en gris dedans Varennes.
Eſleu cap. Cauſe tempeſte feu, sang tranche

At night it will come through the forest of Queens (Ardennes),
Two roles, indirect flight (escaping adversaries), Woodland Hunter, the white stone,
Lemoine, the monk (king) black, in grey inside Varennes.
Elected chief (Capet), causes storm, passion, blood slice.

de Reines, (paranagram) d[a] Ren[n]es = Ardennes; pars, (Latinism) par/s – stage part, role; vaultorte, (portmanteau) vaul + torte, [vaul, alternative spelling of vol; torte, (O.Fr.) détourné], also vaultont, (O.Fr. infinitive form of vaulter, volter) 'changer de place pour éviter les coups de son adversaire', see Dictionnaire de L'Academie français; Herne, (folklore) The Woodland Hunter; noir, (paranagram) [n]roi; cap. (abbreviation) Cap[et]. Cross-references: pars, C.IX: 34; cap, C.IV: 11; C.VIII: 19; C.IX: 26.

The royal family's bid to flee Paris was planned for the night of 20 June 1791. Shortly after midnight, the little group clinging to the shadows made their way out of the palace to an awaiting coach. This took them to the luxurious *berline de voyage* that was to take them to the border. All through the night of the 20th and the next day, the royal party made its way unrecognised and unimpeded through the French countryside, where wayside inns in little towns and villages provided them with fresh horses. All seemed to be going according to plan.

AT NIGHT IT WILL COME THROUGH THE FOREST OF QUEENS: ARDENNES

On the *night* of June 21, the *berline* reached the vast area of wood-land that was once part of the ancient *forest of Ardennes*. **THE FOREST** had been the choice **OF** the **QUEEN** when determining the route they were to take: *the Queen* having planned every part of the direction that would take the family to freedom. Ambassador Mercy had already written to Vienna explaining: *"Marie Antoinette was arranging the whole thing."* Important, too, is the fact that it was **AT NIGHT IT CAME THROUGH THE FOREST OF ARDENNES**, because nightfall set the scene for one of the most dramatic events in the history of France.[1] Unbeknown to the occupants inside the *berline,* a chase through the surrounding woodland had just begun. The success or failure of that pursuit would result in either their capture or their freedom. Either way, the future of France was at issue.

TWO ROLES ESCAPING ADVERSARIES

Inside the coach were the King and Queen, accompanied by the Dauphin, his sister, the children's aunt (Madame Elisabeth) and their governess, the Marquise de Tourzel. To help prevent rec-ognition, Louis had decided he would dress-up and act the part of a valet to the Baroness von Korff (the Marquise de Tourzel). The Queen was to play the role of a governess: her charges being her two children. It was dressed in these **TWO ROLES**, valet and governess that the King and Queen of France set off on that fate-ful night: **ESCAPING** their **ADVERSARIES** by moving to another place.[2]

INDIRECT FLIGHT

"The route they had chosen . . . [was an **INDIRECT FLIGHT***] less frequented than the main way through Chateau Thierry and Epernay."* It also avoided Rheims where the King was known by sight.[3] But at Sainte-Ménéhould, the first mishap in a developing tragedy occurred: the King care-lessly allowed himself to be seen at the carriage window. The postmaster standing close by, an ex-dragoon named Jean-Baptiste Drouet, who had been eying the coach with suspicion, thought he recognized the face, and reported what he had seen to the local mayor. Plans were hastily made. Drouet was to ride ahead and raise the alarm in the next town so that the identities of those inside the *berline* could be verified. The postmaster took with him the local innkeeper, another ex-dragoon named Gil-laume, and together they set off towards Verdun in pursuit of

the coach. But, after some miles, without gaining sight of their quarry, it occurred to Drouet that they were on the wrong road. He now suspected that the coach must have turned off at the crossroads some way back, and was heading for *Varennes*.

WOODLAND HUNTER

It was at this point in the pursuit that Drouet became the Oracle's *woodland hunter*.[4] He left the road, with or without Guillaume (one account says that Guillaume rode on to Verdun, in case the coach was still on the road ahead), and headed for a shortcut through the forest that led to *Varennes*. It was a moonless night, but not yet completely dark. The chase had begun. Drouet must reach *Varennes* before the coach ahead left town.

THE WHITE STONE

As Drouet galloped through the forest, the next part of the prophecy became fulfilled. Ahead of him, the **WOODLAND HUNTER** saw *"the glimmer of a known white stone, a landmark."* Drouet *"sheered down a ride to the right: the wood ended abruptly, and [he] saw below . . . the lights of Varennes."* [5] Had **THE WHITE STONE** been missed, Drouet would have become lost in the forest, and the royal coach would have continued on its uninterrupted journey to the frontier. But, there, still in town was his prey – the *berline*, with its occupants quite unaware of the great drama that was beginning to unfold.

LEMOINE

Meanwhile, in Paris, Louis XVI's senior *valet:* a man named **LEMOINE** was the first person to discover that the King had left. *"It was 7 a.m. precisely at the Tuileries when the royal manservant, Lemoine, drew the curtains of the bed to wake the King up. The bed was empty!"* [6] Louis had, of course, escaped in the night *disguised as his valet.*

> *Since the Revolution was in the process of reducing them to common citizens, how fitting it would be to depart reversing roles with their servants . . . the King, in round hat, wig and plain coat, was to play the valet.* [7]

THE MONK KING BLACK

'Black' was formerly used in art to signify *'evil, falsehood, error'.* [8] Nostradamus has used *noir* to mean **KING BLACK** before, when describing Charles IX's part in the St. Bartholomew's Eve Massacre (C.IV: 47). Louis XVI's flight to Varennes was arguably the gravest error he ever made. It lost him valuable support, and was to

cost him, the Queen and the Dauphin their lives. Louis' devotion to his religious faith – hence THE MONK KING – is indicated by his biographer: *"he never ceased praying to God ... for Louis XVI Christ was an immediate reality ... he was at one with ... the thousands of loyal priests."* [9]

IN GREY, INSIDE VARENNES

Having caught up with the *berline* INSIDE VARENNES, Drouet quickly raised the alarm. The bridge leading out of town was blocked by a cart, and the procurator was summoned to the scene. A crowd, growing all the time, quickly gathered around the royal party whose travel papers were being examined in the light of glowing lanterns. The King, still incognito as the baroness' valet, stood in the lantern light dressed IN GREY – *"a grey coat, satin waistcoat, grey breeches and stockings, shoes with buckles and a three-cornered hat."* [10]

> *At that period, when it took six or seven days by diligence to go from Varennes to Paris, it was a remarkable thing to see the King . . . And thus there was great stupefaction when Louis XVI showed himself . . . pale, fat and silent, with a dull eye, a hanging lip, a shabby wig and a grey coat.* [11]

ELECTED CHIEF, CAPET

Within the hour, Louis XVI was identified by a former courtier, and his bid to escape came to an abrupt end. Next day the coach was turned round, and under guard, Louis XVI and Marie Antoinette were returned to Paris. The King was then suspended while both the Assembly and the nation argued amongst themselves concerning the monarchy's future. Finally, on 3 September 1791, Louis XVI was given another chance to take an active role in government, this time as the nation's constitutional head, when the Assembly ELECTED him as France's CHIEF Executive.[12] But this did not stop criticism. In the Press, as elsewhere, Louis XVI began to be called by the derogatory title, *'Louis Capet',* [13] sometimes even *'Citizen Capet'*. (The name, CAPET, was obtained from his ancestors, but he personally deplored its use).

CAUSES STORM, PASSION

For the three months following his return to Paris, the King had remained suspended from office while the Assembly debated in private what the country continued to discuss publicly – Was the King a traitor to his people? As a result, France *'seethed like a sea in a storm',* [14] while the monarchy, now virtually powerless, tottered towards its inevitable destruction. Inside parliament, *"Passionate debates tore the Assembly asunder."*[15] While outside the political arena, these protests were repeatedly voiced aloud, condemning the King as a traitor to his country. Eventually, on 10 August 1792, the intensity of emotion boiled over, and a band of revolutionaries, inspired by the oratory of Danton, marched towards the royal palace intent upon murder.

BLOOD SLICE

Outside the Tuileries, a company of Swiss bodyguards were on duty. News was brought to the King of the threatened strike against the royal palace. Safe inside the Assembly Hall with his family, Louis sent a written message to the Swiss guards not to fire on the people. The order proved to be another *error* by the **BLACK KING.** *"The Swiss were massacred and then cut to slices. Their heads and arms were severed from their bodies . . . Eight hundred Swiss and gentlemen lost their lives because Louis XVI could not bear the thought of violence."*[16] In the evening, the remains of the Swiss, and many of the palace servants caught up in the frenzy of killing, were burnt; the bonfires casting a macabre glow across the scene of carnage that lay all around.

This oracle has covered a lot of ground, but leaves the attack on the royal palace to be dealt with in greater detail in a subsequent oracle. The next verse, with the King still in Varennes, predicts the royal family's ignominious return to Paris. Nostradamus also foresees the consequences that were to follow.

C.I: 5

Chaffés feront fans faire long combat,
Par le pays feront plus fort greués:
Bourg & cité auront plus grand debat,
Carcas. Narbonne auront cœurs efprouués.

They will be pursued without making a long struggle,
In the country they will be tormented more shockingly:
Borough and city will have the greatest debate,
Because of the disaster (Carcassonne), Narbonne, will have hearts tested.

greués, (O.Fr.) tourmenter, blâmer sévèrement; Carcas. (portmanteau and abbreviation) car + cas; [cas, (O.Fr.) chute], also Carcas[sonne].

THEY WILL BE PURSUED

When Paris awoke on the morning of June 21st to find that the King and Queen had left during the night, panic broke out. Riders were dispatched in every direction with orders to PURSUE and detain the fugitives until an escort party could be arranged to bring them back. In the early hours of the morning of June 22nd, two envoys, Romeuf and Bayon, arrived in Varennes having successfully followed the trail of the *berline* through the towns it had passed through.[1]

WITHOUT MAKING A LONG STRUGGLE

The appearance in Varennes of the two dusty riders from Paris coincided with the arrival of a detachment of troops loyal to the King. The army officers at once offered to escort the royal family to the Belgian border. A heated discussion followed between the National Guard who had also been summoned and the troops, during which a shot was fired, swords were brandished, and a man was wounded in the mêlée. But the King, WITHOUT wishing to cause further bloodshed by MAKING A LONG STRUGGLE, relented and agreed with Romeuf and Bayon that he and his family would return to Paris. It was to prove a fatal decision.[2]

IN THE COUNTRY THEY WILL BE VERY MUCH TORMENTED

On their return journey through the countryside, angry demonstrations and a barrage of insults met the royal party at every stop. Acts of atrocious disrespect were aimed at the King and Queen each time the coach stopped over for the night. And this continued throughout the four-day journey back to Paris. At Sainte-Ménéhould, the mayor, who had sent Drouet to detain the travellers, publicly BLAMED the King for leaving Paris. At Dormans, THEY WERE TORMENTED by a hostile crowd that kept them awake all night with their anti-royalist chanting. At Épernay there was a threat to assassinate Marie Antoinette, and during a struggle that developed inside the hotel her dress was ripped. At Châlons, the dregs of Rheims arrived to intercept the coach, and then confront the royal party with their obscenities: most of which were directed at the Queen. At Chouilly, a hostile crowd surrounded the Berline, shaking their fists at the occupants; one man even leaned into the coach and spat at the King's face.[3]

BOROUGH AND CITY WILL HAVE A GREAT DEBATE

Once Louis XVI reached the comparative safety of the Tuileries, every BOROUGH AND CITY across France became embroiled in A GREAT DEBATE. Could the King be considered a traitor for having tried to leave the country? And, had it been his intention to prepare the way for an invasion of France in order to restore him to power? Different answers were suggested, including his deposition in favour of the Dauphin and a Regent. But this was countered by another argument that the suspension of the King had already made the monarchy redundant.[4]

BECAUSE OF THE DISASTER

Louis' flight to Varennes had been a tragic failure, and **BECAUSE OF THIS DISASTER** the monarchy now seemed doomed to fall.[5] However, for a short period of time the King was given a reprieve in the form of an experimental role as the country's Chief Executive.

CARCASSONNE AND NARBONNE WILL HAVE HEARTS TESTED

In concluding this oracle, Nostradamus has named two towns situated close together in the south of France, *Carcassonne and Narbonne,* and he uses them as examples of places where the general clamour that gripped the country was occurring at the time. But both have double meanings. Carcassonne, in its abbreviated form, produces the reason for *hearts* being *tested.* The city is also symbolic: it being renowned as having once been the strongest fortification in France prior to it being abandoned in the seventeenth century. The monarchy too had once been the strongest establishment in France, but was now being systematically demolished, causing those involved in defence of the King to **HAVE THEIR HEARTS TESTED.**

Narbonne, which had once been the Roman capital of Gaul and the crossroad of France, is also associated by name with the Comte de **NARBONNE** who, on two notable occasions, **HAD HIS HEART TESTED.** Twice he gave way to his conscience and made a move towards defending the King, but on each occasion he was dissuaded from doing so.[6] *Narbonne* will reappear in these prophecies later.

At the time that Louis XVI was returning from Varennes in disgrace, the remains of Voltaire were being brought back to Paris in triumph. Nostradamus comments upon the incidence of the two events by actually naming both the King and Voltaire. One is therefore excused wondering at this great writer's reaction, had he realised that both his name and a recognizable description of the procession taking his remains to the Pantheon

existed in print two centuries before he was even born. His vigorous denial for such beliefs was given expression in his *Age of
Louis XIV* (pp. 271, 272). *"The court was still infatuated with the delusions
of judicial astrology; more than one prince imagined with arrogant superstition
that nature honoured him to the point of inscribing his destiny in the stars."*

C.IX: 26

> Nice fortie fur nom des lettres afpres,
> La grande cappe fera prefent non fien:
> Proche de Vultry aux murs de vertes capres,
> Apres plombin le vent à bon effien.

> *Foolish exit by the name from the bitter letters,*
> *The great Capet will make manifest not his own:*
> *For appearance / Voltaire close to the walls by the green shrubs,*
> *Afterwards lead: the opinion with plausible certainty.*

Nice, (O.Fr.) niais: originally from the Latin word *nescius*; afpres, (O.Fr.) aigre; fur, (O.Fr.)
at, by, hard by, toward, about; à effien, (O.Fr. escient) avec certitude; cappe, (paranagram), Cap[t]e CAPET, also capper, (O.Fr.) prendre; present, (O.Fr.) qui est là manifeste;
de Vultry, (paranagram) [a]e V[o]ltry – VOLTAYRE, also Vultry, (Latinism) vult/us; plombin,
(Latinism) plumb/um – lead, bullet; bon, (O.Fr.) plausible; Cross-reference: La grande
cappe, C.IV: 11; C.VIII: 19; C.IX: 20.

> N.B. 'Vultry' is spelt with a small 'v' in the Rigaud edition of 1568, but
> with a capital 'V' in the 1558 Lyon edition, which was reproduced at
> Leyden in 1650. Note, too, that Nostradamus spells the town of Nice, as
> Nisse in C.X: 87 (Chapter 7).

FOOLISH EXIT

The oracle opens with an apt description of Louis XVI's FOOLISH
attempt to EXIT Paris. The flight ended with his arrest at Varennes, and marked the real beginning of the monarchy's downfall.[1]

BY THE NAME FROM THE BITTER LETTERS

THE BITTER LETTERS were those Louis XVI signed BY NAME, and left
behind, reproaching those who had taken away his powers. The
King anticipated his escape to the border would be successful.
He was therefore quite candid when explaining the reasons for
his unannounced departure. But the escape failed, and the letters
were quickly discovered. In writing, Louis had accused the political clubs of promoting anarchy; he also admitted that his devotion to the revolution was made only under extreme duress.
And that his stipend was totally insufficient to maintain the
honour and dignity of his position. The recriminations resulting
from these missives were never forgotten, and added greatly to
his disgrace.[2]

THE GREAT CAPET

CAPET was the derogatory name given to Louis XVI after his arrest at Varennes, where he became THE TAKEN ONE. This name soon caught on amongst the revolutionaries, and thereafter he became referred to as *'Citizen Capet'*, or plain *'Louis Capet'*.[3] Nostradamus acknowledges this, but distinguishes its derogatory nature by calling him THE GREAT CAPET, using a word that can also refer to THE TAKEN ONE.

WILL MAKE MANIFEST, NOT HIS OWN

Louis XVI remained suspended from office until the Constitution had been completed. By 14 September 1791, the document was ready, and the King was called upon by the Constituent Assembly to swear to uphold and defend it; that is, MAKE MANIFEST to the nation his support. But, as Nostradamus predicted, the instrument of government to which Louis was required to swear was NOT HIS OWN, for although he was King, he had been denied any part in its preparation.[4]

FOR APPEARANCE, VOLTAIRE CLOSE TO THE WALLS BY THE GREEN SHRUBS

Louis XVI's *foolish exit* from Paris is now contrasted with the triumphant entrance of *Voltaire*. Although long dead, *Voltaire's* body was to be interred in the Pantheon, alongside that of Descartes. The coffin with its remains began the journey to Paris from Romilly-sur-Seine during the second week of July 1791. FOR APPEARANCE, it was attended by a huge procession, which included the National Guardsmen. The cortège reached the outskirts of the city on the 11th July.

From there VOLTAIRE was taken CLOSE TO THE WALLS of the Bastille.[5] Although a major part of these fortifications had been reduced to rubble in the 1789 uprising, the Bastille was still considered to be an important stopping point, because during his lifetime *Voltaire* had twice been imprisoned there. Upon reaching the site of this former fortress: *'The coffin was then placed behind a barrier of poplars and cypresses;* or, as Nostradamus said: BY THE GREEN SHRUBS.[6] An address was then read to declare that *Voltaire* had endured, whereas the walls that once enclosed him had not. Finally, at 10 o'clock that evening, his body arrived at the Pantheon where it was laid to rest.

Five days **AFTERWARDS**, on 16 July, the people of Paris were invited to put their names to a petition on the *'altar of the patrie'* at the Champ de Mars. The next day, a confrontation occurred between a crowd of demonstrators, numbering about 50,000, and the National Guardsmen sent to restore order. Stones were thrown at the guards who responded with **LEAD** (*bullets*).[7] As many as fifty people died in the resulting gunfire.

The petition, to which the people had been invited to put their name, expressed **THE OPINION WITH PLAUSIBLE CERTAINTY** that Louis XVI *'had deserted his post'* and through his *'perjury'*, had effectively abdicated. Unless the nation indicated otherwise, Louis should no longer be recognized as King. The petition was effectively calling for Louis XVI to be deposed.[8]

As may be expected in verses that are logogriphs, Nostradamus has devised several strategies for concealing the names of those whose fate it was to participate in the great events of history. One such strategy consisted of providing the byname given to an individual. This was then used to predict a major event associated with that person. An example of this method in action occurs in the next quatrain, which is wholly concerned with the dissolution of the *Ancien Regime*.

C.VII: 14

Faux expoſer viendra topographie,
Seront les cruches des monumens ouuertes:
Pulluler ſecte, ſaincte philoſophie,
Pour blanches, noires, & pour antiques vertes.

Faux will come to make known topography,
The outer casings of tombs will be opened:
A sect sprouting, philosophy consecrated,
On account of whites, blacks, and for ancient greens.

Faux, (Byname) 'Louis le Faux'; cruches, (O.Fr.) coquilles; monument, (O.Fr.) tombeau.

FAUX was the derisory nickname given to Louis XVI by a Paris newspaper after his mistaken attempt to flee Paris (20 June 1791). The name quickly caught the public imagination, and the King became identified as: *"the man whom Père Duchesne now habitually called 'Louis le Faux'-or sometimes just 'le Faux-Pas',"*[1]

During the French Revolution, the names of the old provinces: Aquitaine, Burgundy, Lorraine &c were consigned to history. In their place, the country became divided into departments (*départements*): the names of which were incorporated into the Constitution of 1791. On 14 September, *"Louis [came] to the Constituent . . . to swear 'to maintain it at home and defend it against attacks from abroad and to use all the means which it places in my power to execute it faithfully.'"* [2]

Included in this new Constitution was the division of France into departments. By swearing to uphold the Constitution, the King agreed **TO MAKE KNOWN THIS NEW TOPOGRAPHY** to the nation.

Before the revolution the royal families of France had been interred inside the mausoleum at Saint-Denis. On 1 August 1793, a decree, passed by the Convention, authorised the **OPENING** of **THE OUTER CASINGS OF** the royal **TOMBS** in order to transfer the remains of the bodies to a communal grave. For several days afterwards, tombs were opened *'in churches, temples and other parts of the Republic'*, but particularly at Saint-Denis, where the desecration of the mausoleum took place in what can only be described as a macabre pantomime. The skeletal remains of the nation's former kings, queens and princes were gruesomely displayed, even toyed with, before being thrown unceremoniously into a common pit close by. [3]

It is of some interest to note that in the midst of this grisly scene, the embalmed body of Louis XIII was extricated from his tomb and observed to be almost unaffected by the century and a half that had elapsed since his embalmment. (C.VIII: 68, chapter 3, specifically refers to his embalmment).

After religion had effectively been abolished (this movement began to gather force during the early days of revolutionary fervour), and the de-Christianising of the country was almost complete, it became apparent that a new philosophy was needed to replace what was lost. The **SECT** that **SPROUTED** to fill this void was the cult of the Federation with its oaths to liberty, its temples of concord, and its festivals of celebration. [4]

At an intellectual level, the mainspring of this revolutionary creed was Rousseau's treatise of 1762: *'Du Contrat Social'*. Festivals were held across the country to celebrate France's new Constitution, in which the high priests of the Federation swore to uphold it; effectively mimicking the priesthood, they CONSECRATED Rousseau's PHILOSOPHY,[5] and it became the country's new gospel.

Another feature of the Ancient Regime that became subject to replacement was the importance formerly given to coloured cockades. WHITE (blanche)[6] was the traditional colour of the Bourbon dynasty to which Louis XVI belonged. BLACK was the colour adopted by the Queen.[7] This led to her followers becoming dubbed *'les noires'*. AND GREEN was the colour adopted by the dukes of Artois for their cockade.[8] The duc d'Artois was Louis XVI's brother who became King Charles X in 1824. Once the revolution was underway, a new cockade was designed to announce the coming change; displaying the cockade became virtually obligatory. GREEN had been the revolutionaries' first choice; until it was pointed out that this was the colour of d'Artois' cockade. Hence, *'the tricoleur'* replaced ANCIENT GREEN.

Part of Nostradamus's strategy to convince posterity of his prophetic ability was that of providing cross-references between oracles. He achieved this many times by the use of a word, a name or a phrase: one that was capable of being applied to the same subject or idea in different quatrains. This practice is apparent in the next verse. He begins with *'la part'*; a word in singular form, but which calls to mind the plural, *'deux pars'* that began the quatrain describing the King and Queen's attempt to escape from Paris (see C.IX: 20).

Also in this next verse, the seer employs the phrase *over the tiles*. This again is very similar to another phrase he used in C.IX: 23, *over the bricks*. In that oracle, the seer was referring to the storming of the Bastille; but in the oracle below, he is referring to the storming of the Tuileries. The *Palais de Tuileries* was built in the sixteenth century on the site of a tile works. *"Tuileries was actually a literal reference to . . . an enormous, polluted excavation pit from which Parisian contractors mined clay to manufacture the city's famous red roofing tiles*

– or tuiles." The oracle we are to consider is also famous for including the names of two men: both of whom lived lives that were worlds apart. They were, however, united by a single act: one that they each carried out separately; to wit, in their own special way they each stood accused of handing over the monarchy to its enemy.

C.IX: 34

La part foluz, mary fera mittré,
Retour conflict paffera fur le thuille:
Par cinq cens vn trahyr fera tiltré,
Narbon & Saulce par coutaux auons d'huille.

The female party alone, the husband will be mitred,
Return conflict will pass over the Tuileries:
Through five-hundred, a betrayer will be titled,
Narbonne and Sauce, by knives: [we] have oil.

mittré, (O.Fr.) to hood, to crown, to mitre; thuille, (O.Fr. tuile & apocope, see note) thuille[ries]; Narbon, (apocope) Narbon[ne]; Saulce, (epenthesis) Sauce. Cross-reference: part, C.IX: 20.

The first two lines of this oracle foretell with signal words three separate occasions when the royal palace was invaded by a mob of angry revolutionaries. That is to say, Nostradamus has identified each one of these occasions by using distinctive keywords that point directly to what happened when each incident took place. The two lines, however, read as though they are referring to a single occurrence, and this has misguided past attempts at understanding what happened.

THE FEMALE PARTY ALONE

From the expression *deux pars*, by which the King and Queen were identified in quatrain C.IX: 20, it may be concluded that *la part*, the female party or role, refers to Marie Antoinette. On 5 October 1789, a mass of people, numbering about 5,000, mostly comprised of market women (*poissardes*), arrived at Versailles on foot having walked from Paris. Outside the palace walls they began shouting: *"Bread or to the gallows!"* La Fayette who was in charge of the National Guard arrived on the scene, and in an attempt to calm the women, he promised that the King and Queen would appear before them. It was evening when Louis XVI and Marie Antoinette eventually emerged onto the balcony overlooking the Marble Court. The crowd stared up at them, and began shouting: *"The Queen alone!"* The King was persuaded to go indoors, and Marie Antoinette – **THE FEMALE PARTY** – stood on the balcony **ALONE**, facing the mob below.[1]

The husband of the *female party* is therefore Louis XVI, which introduces the second assault on the royal palace. This took place inside Paris on 20 June 1792, at the *Palais de Tuileries*, where Louis XVI and his family had been forced to remove after the incident at Versailles. A crowd that had earlier gathered to celebrate the Oath of the Tennis Court suddenly turned violent and directed their mounting ire at the royal palace. Brandishing an assortment of pikes, hatchets, knives and clubs they broke into the building, hacking down doors in their effort to locate the King. He was eventually found alone in the Oeil de Boeuf, a room overlooking the courtyard and garden.

THE HUSBAND WILL BE MITRED

The King was not wanting in courage, and remained impassive as the mob approached him. Having cornered their prey, the leaders were slightly at a loss as to what they should do next. First came the abuse, then the demands: prominent amongst which, was: *"Drive out your priests!"* This referred to the King's stubborn insistence to attend Mass said only by priests who had refused to take the oath of allegiance to France. Then, taking a red revolutionary cap (*le Bonnet Rouge*) one of the men placed it on the King's head. Nostradamus's bitter humour comes into play at this point. Since the demands being made concerned the priesthood, he referred to the revolutionary cap of liberty on Louis' head as a mitre: **THE HUSBAND WILL BE MITRED**.[2] Critics among the nobility later described it as his *'Crown of Thorns'*. When the National Guardsmen eventually arrived to rescue the King, he was found safe, but perspiring, and with the red cap still askew on his powdered hair.

RETURN CONFLICT WILL PASS OVER THE TUILERIES

For the whole of July the *Palais de Tuileries* was left alone, and for those few weeks some semblance of normality was established. But on the 10 August 1792, in blistering heat, the violence **RETURNED** as a fresh wave of **CONFLICT** surged **OVER THE TUILERIES**:[3] eventually drowning the monarchy in its swell. It was during this orgy of violence and murder that the gallant Swiss guardsmen, together with many of the palace servants were cut to pieces (see C.IX: 20). A monumental plaque to the gallant Swiss who died that day was erected in Geneva, where it can still be seen.

Fortunately for the royal family, the King and Queen had been forewarned, and they were given shelter inside the Assembly Hall. Nostradamus now identifies the culprits.

Upon the evening of Sunday, the 29th of July the dusty 500 of Marseilles with their guns, crossing the bridge at Charenton, saw the distant towers of Notre Dame above the roofs of Paris. [4]

These were the **FIVE HUNDRED** from Marseilles, eager to take part in the overthrow of the monarchy. Inspired by the recent speeches of Danton, they joined in the invasion of the Tuileries, murdering everyone unfortunate enough to cross their path.

With no safe residence remaining, the royal family was taken under guard to the Temple Tower. There they were confined for a short while until the Republic of France could decide their fate (the Republic had declared itself on September 21st). After some consideration, and to legitimise their actions, the government came to the conclusion that the King should be tried for treason, and executed. By December of that year, the court proceedings were under way, and this brings us to the next part of the prophecy.

A BETRAYER WILL BE TITLED
Louis XVI's cousin, the Duke of Orleans, had seen the Revolution as an opportunity for obtaining power. Using the sobriquet Philip Égalité he had been elected to the Assembly. Now, at the trial of the King, he was to become his **BETRAYER**.

The Duc d'Orléans was greeted with cries of a very different type. On the preceding evening he had voted for the King's death: when he advanced, the sweat standing on his brow, and mumbled his 'No' to the question of the reprieve, the Right yelled mercilessly at him: 'We cannot hear you!' and Égalité had to repeat his 'No'. [5]

NARBONNE, BY KNIVES
Louis, Comte de *Narbonne*, whom Louis XVI made Minister of War (7 December 1791), sought to raise the King's esteem in the public eye. *"Instead of holding the line at peace, he began to prepare actively*

for war." [6] 'Par coutaux', **BY KNIVES**, indicates Narbonne's role in government; the phrase: *'aiguiser ses couteaux'*, means 'sharpening knives', and is used in French to mean: *'preparing for war'*. But when **NARBONNE** was sacked from the Ministry as a result of his intrigues, the Catholics accused him of: *'handing over the monarchy to the demagogues'.* [7]

SAUCE, WE HAVE OIL

Sauce, on the other hand, was to earn his place in history as the man who did, quite literally, hand over the King to his enemies. Jean-Baptiste Sauce was the Procurator of Varennes, and the official to whom Drouet made his approach after galloping through the forest to overtake the royal coach. **SAUCE** was also the town's chandler and the owner of a small oil shop that sold candles and similar merchandise; hence, **'WE HAVE OIL'**. It was in an upper bedroom of this building that the King and Queen were persuaded by Sauce to spend the night of June 21st. On the following day, envoys arrived from Paris to detain the King, and *Sauce* handed over the royal family to the National Guard. [8]

> N.B. Historian Carlyle spelt Sauce's name as Sausse. But Dumas was able to verify the correct spelling as 'Sauce', by examining the man's own signature. [9]

With the authority of the King reduced to almost nothing, the opportunity presented itself for others to fill the power vacuum. Amongst the first to emerge was Georges Danton. It was his rousing speech to the *Five Hundred* from Marseilles that led to the slaughter inside the palace grounds (see C.IX: 34). In the next quatrain, Nostradamus foresees Danton's election as the new Minister of Justice. And it was while holding this appointment that he allowed the September Massacres to occur.

C.IV: 11

Celuy qu'aura gouuert de la grand cappe,
Sera induict à quelque cas patrer:
Les douze rouges viendront fouiller la nappe.
Soubz meurtre, meurtre fe viendra perpetrer.

The one that will obtain government from the great Capet
Will be induced by some to achieve ruin:
The twelve reds will proceed to soil the cloth,
Under murder, murder will come to perpetrate itself.

gouvert, (syncope) gouver[nemen]t; cappe, (paranagram) Cap[t]e – Capet, also capper,

(O.Fr.) prendre; cas, (O.F.) chute; patrer, (Latinism) patr/o; venir, (O.Fr.) proceed;
Cross-reference: la grand cappe, C.VIII: 19; C.IX: 20; C.IX: 26.

THE ONE THAT WILL OBTAIN GOVERNMENT FROM THE GREAT CAPET

Georges Jacques Danton began his career as a lawyer but soon acquired popularity for his political ideas, which he debated as a member of the radical Cordeliers Club. It was in this capacity that he was able to draw support from the Paris Commune. His rousing speech to the Five-Hundred from Marseilles, prior to their attack on the Tuileries, led to him being offered a government post, and he was: *"Appointed justice minister in the provisional executive council set up on the overthrow of Louis XVI in August 1792."*
The King by this time had been placed under guard inside the Temple. Outside, on the streets of Paris, activists were busily distributing pamphlets with the heading: *'The Great Treason of Louis Capet'.*[1] It was because of this incitement against the King and the recent murders inside the Tuileries that: − *"The Assembly, terrified by the slaughter, took the king into protective custody, [and] turned executive power over to a committee of six ministers led by Danton."* Hence, of the six ministers appointed, **THE ONE THAT WILL OBTAIN GOVERNMENT FROM THE GREAT CAPET** *'was more powerful than any of them, Georges Jacques Danton'.*[2]

WILL BE INDUCED BY SOME TO ACHIEVE RUIN

It was while in this position of power that Danton was **INDUCED BY SOME** of the more bloodthirsty revolutionaries to legitimise the notorious September Massacres.[3] In effect all that he **ACHIEVED** by this act of mass murder was yet more **RUIN** to the clergy. This further act of bloodletting also attracted international condemnation for the Revolution. Nevertheless, to justify the murders committed during the September massacres Danton deemed them to be the dispensation of *'people's justice'*, and they were given a flimsy veil of legality by allowing the hasty formation of citizens' tribunals. These were composed of groups of revolutionaries, sitting in judgement so as to give each prisoner the formality of a hearing before their sentence of execution was passed; death often being administered by a sword thrust.[4]

THE TWELVE REDS

Earlier that year, on 23 April, Antoine Merlin de Thionville had suggested to the Legislative Assemble that all non-juring priests should be deported. In response to his suggestion, it was decided that a committee of **TWELVE** revolutionaries (**REDS**) should be

241

formed in order to investigate the degree of unrest caused by non-juring priests.[5] (This committee is not to be confused with another committee of twelve, convened on 17 June 1792, with the directive to oversee the activities of new ministers.)

WILL PROCEED TO SOIL THE CLOTH

One month after studying their remit, *the twelve reds* reported back, having AGREED that non-juring priests were enemies of the Revolution. A motion was then passed that any priest failing to swear the required oath could be deported if twenty active citizens requested it. This ruling was to be enforced by the department in which the plea was made. Thereafter, the prisons slowly filled up with non-juring priests.[6] These were men of THE CLOTH who would soon find their CLOTH SOILED, quite literally, by their own blood as the September Massacres began to swiftly decrease their number.

It is interesting to observe how the word *soil* has been incorporated into Nostradamus's prediction. After the massacre of the priests had been completed, the Minister of the Interior, Jean-Marie Roland de la Platière, who shared in the guilt of what had happened, expressed his concern by announcing: *"the children of liberty"* (those who had murdered the men of *the cloth*) *"must not soil themselves."* Coincidence? There is more. Roland had earlier written a book on the mechanical production of cotton, and he *"knew the cloth industry to perfection."* Is this another coincidence? Or is it an example of the Oracle using Nostradamus's vocabulary for the purpose of using words associated with what happened?

The massacres began on 2 September 1792, and in the course of five days, approximately 1,400 prisoners were murdered: the majority being men of *the cloth*. Often they were no more than simple clerics who had been forcibly removed from their seminaries, their churches or their colleges.

UNDER MURDER, MURDER WILL PERPETRATE ITSELF

Inside the Temple Tower, Marie Antoinette was allowed the companionship of the Princesse de Lamballe, who acted as her lady-in-waiting. The revolutionaries very quickly decided that this loyalty to the Queen was suspicious, and in less than a week after arriving at the Temple, the Princess was arrested and taken to the prison of La Petite Force for questioning. From there, on 3

THE FRENCH REVOLUTION

September, at the height of the massacres, the Princesse de Lamballe was transferred to the murder centre at L'Abbaye.

Inside a room strewn with the corpses of murdered priests, she was asked to swear an oath of her hatred for the King and Queen. She declined. A door opened and the Princess was pushed through. It closed behind her.[7] In the street outside were a group of men in wait. They stripped her, raped her, cut off her breasts, impaled her genitals on the end of a pike, charged a cannon with one of her legs and paraded her severed head on the end of a pole past the windows of the Temple cell where the Queen was imprisoned, so that she could gaze on her former companion's face for one last time.[8]

The Princesse de Lamballe was born Marie Thérèse de Savoie–Carignan. *"Her rank at court [was] derived from her marriage into a legitimated princely house, not her birth."* It was because of her royal connections, and her reputation for purity that the revolutionaries decided to use the September Massacres as a convenient means for disposing of her; that is, without the bother of a court trial,[9] which, legally she was perfectly entitled to. It was therefore UNDER cover of the widespread MURDER of France's clergy, that, another MURDER CAME TO PERPETRATE ITSELF.

The victims of the September Massacres were mainly priests, monks, nuns and novices drawn from monasteries, seminaries, churches, etc. The intention of the revolutionaries was to complete the de-Christianising of France that had begun a few years earlier. Nostradamus devotes the next quatrain to the effect that this persecution of the Church had on France.

C.I: 44

En brief feront de retour facrifices,
Contreuenants feront mis à martyre:
Plus ne feront moines abbés ne nouices:
Le miel fera beaucoup plus cher que cire.

In short, there will be a recurrence of renunciations,
Contraveners will be put to martyrdom:
There will be no more monks, priests, nor novices,
Honey will be plentiful, more liked than beeswax.

cher, (O.Fr.) aimé.

A RECURRENCE OF RENUNCIATIONS

The Enlightenment, which had begun to gather force during the early part of the eighteenth century, was the initial reason for some members of the clergy to abandon their vows. As a result, both the training and the work of priests gradually became the responsibility of the State. *"Monasteries – particularly purely contemplative houses – were dissolved, and their wealth confiscated. . . . In many states, the Jesuits were expelled."* The opening line of Nostradamus's prediction above refers to A RECURRENCE of priests and other religious abandoning their vows.

The move towards completely de-Christianising France began on 2 November 1789 when the National Assembly voted by 568 to 346 that Church property be transferred to the nation. This led the Constituent Assembly to abolish all monastic vows and to place a banning order on congregations. Priests and other religious were strongly urged to RENOUNCE THEIR VOWS and become productive citizens. An oath of allegiance to nation, law, king and constitution was subsequently required from any French priest wishing to remain active in the Church.[1]

CONTRAVENERS PUT TO MARTYRDOM

On 26 August 1792, a law was drafted requiring all dissident priests; that is, CONTRAVENERS, to leave the country or be deported to Guyana.[2] One week later, priests still in Paris were rounded up and imprisoned. Their fate was to be victims of the September Massacres described in C.IV:11 above. But this still did not eliminate all priests. Therefore, on 23 April 1793, a new decree was passed, condemning to death within 24 hours all non-juring priests remaining in France. This was followed in the autumn of that year by a new wave of atrocities, with religious PUT TO MARTYRDOM wherever they were found. In Nantes, on the River Loire, Jean-Baptiste Carrier drowned eighty-four non-juring priests by confining them below decks in a river transporter, and then scuttling the boat. At Lyons, Marseilles, Bordeaux, and other towns and cities across the country, murder, the guillotine and the Great Terror added to the Paris death toll.[3]

THERE WILL BE NO MORE MONKS, PRIESTS NOR NOVICES

A significant number of clergy refused to swear the oath, preferring instead to obey the Pope who had condemned the Civil Constitution. These recalcitrant priests left France to take refuge in Spain, England and Ireland. In Spain alone, an estimated 6,000 priests sought asylum in that country. In France, monasteries and convents lay silent, with church services conducted only by state registered clerics. NO LONGER WERE THERE ANY MONKS, PRIESTS OR NOVICES in France.[4]

HONEY WILL BE PLENTIFUL, MORE LIKED THAN BEESWAX.

Nostradamus, with his bitter humour, ends this prophecy by comparing the country's religiosity prior to the Revolution, with its subsequent decline. Church candles, for example, were made from expensive *beeswax*. But with demand for this type of candle rapidly diminished, the resources of the hive switched to *honey*.[5] The product of the hive is therefore used as a moral indicator, signalling the social change taking place within French society. HONEY, representing self-indulgence and the abandonment of religious morality, became MORE LIKED THAN BEESWAX, which represented the Church. In this respect, HONEY was MORE PLENTIFUL THAN BEESWAX because demand for the latter had been reduced.

With the Revolution now in full swing, Nostradamus continues with his detailed predictions of its progress. In the next quatrain the seer once again refers to *the great Capet,* thus allowing it to continue to cross-reference with Louis XVI, whose fate was now very much a part of revolutionary France. Also, as with the previous 'great Capet' quatrain, Danton makes another appearance, if only to exit. In this respect, we shall later see Nostradamus alluding to the deaths of other prominent revolutionaries; e.g., Marat, Robespierre, Couthon and Saint-Just.

C.VIII: 19

A foubftenir la grande cappe troublee,
Pour l'efclaircir les rouges marcheront,
De mort famille fera prefque accablee.
Les rouges rouges le rouge affomeront:

For upholding, the great Capet troubled,
As for explaining it, the reds will make progress,
Concerning the fatal family, it will be all but crushed,
The red reds will kill the red one.

foubftenir, (O.Fr. soustenir) to uphold, tolerate; cappe, (paranagram.) cap[t]e – Capet, also, capper, (O.Fr.) prendre; mort, (O.Fr.) funeste; affomer/ont, (O.Fr.) charger, tuer. Cross-reference: la grande cappe, C.IV: 11; C.IX: 20; C.IX: 26.

THE GREAT CAPET TROUBLED FOR UPHOLDING

Louis XVI, now addressed by the revolutionaries as Louis CAPET, became greatly **TROUBLED** after his arrest at Varennes.[1] Unwisely, before leaving the Tuileries, he had written a letter (see C.IX: 26) **UPHOLDING** his reasons for leaving France.[2] This letter was quickly delivered into the hands of his enemies, and its content made uncomfortable reading, even for the King's most loyal supporters.

AS FOR EXPLAINING IT

AS FOR EXPLAINING IT, there was little his followers could say, since Louis continued to *uphold* the old traditions of monarchical rule. To make matters worse, he admitted that the support he had given for the new order had been made under duress. And he questioned the truth of the claim that Frenchmen really did want to replace fourteen hundred years of monarchical government with the *'anarchy and despotism'* arising from the present political situation.[3]

THE REDS

The reds were the revolutionaries. The red flag adopted by the revolutionaries came about *"in 1791, when the crowd attacking the Tuileries picked up a blood-soaked royal standard. Henceforth, 'red' and 'white' were the accepted color codes for revolution and counter-revolution."*[4]

WILL MAKE PROGRESS

After the ignominy of his arrest in Varennes, and the embarrassment of having his grievances made known to his enemies, support for Louis XVI dwindled, even amongst moderate politicians. In July, a petition was circulated, which declared that Louis XVI had *'deserted his post'* and, in effect, abdicated. Tom Paine, author of *Rights of Man,* claimed that the King's attempt to leave France had already *'instituted a Republic'.* In this atmosphere of unrest, the political club known as the Cordeliers demanded that their members take a solemn vow of *'tyrannicide'* to protect the liberty of France. To make matters worse, the failure to explain the contents of the King's letter as anything other than pique, further allowed **THE REDS TO MAKE PROGRESS** towards their aim of abolishing the monarchy.[5]

THE FATAL FAMILY ALL BUT CRUSHED

It was now becoming increasingly clear that the King and Queen were doomed: **ALL BUT CRUSHED** beneath the gathering weight of opposition to their existence. On 20 June 1792, a mob of armed rioters had broken into the palace and threatened Louis with violence if he did not obey their demands. On 3 August the Paris sections voted for Louis' deposition. Two weeks later, a mob of rioters more violent than before invaded the Tuileries for a second time, slaughtering the Swiss Guard and every palace worker they came across. With no place safe to go, Louis XVI, Marie Antoinette and their two children, now described by Nostradamus as **THE FATAL FAMILY**, since three fatalities were soon to befall them, were taken under guard to the Temple Tower.[6]

In 1793 Georges Danton, Minister of Justice during the September Massacres, received a new appointment to sit on the Committee of Public Safety. But ill health caused him to leave Paris, and spend time recuperating in the country. Nursed by his sixteen-year-old wife Louise, his political views became more restrained. And it was with this turn of mind that he returned to political life in Paris, appealing to his fellow revolutionaries for greater moderation. However, in his absence, the reds had become much redder in their desire to shed blood: seeing this as the only means of furthering their objectives; which is to say, they were now *the red reds*.[7] They therefore rejected Danton's appeal for restraint, perceiving it to be a weakness.

THE RED REDS WILL KILL THE RED ONE

History has had little trouble affirming that *'the memory of Danton is red with violence'*. But though still, politically, *a red*, he viewed the carnage taking place as excessive, and sought further to persuade his former colleagues to reduce this bloodletting. The *red reds* were unmoved and now saw Danton's plea as an act of betrayal against the Republic. Reaction was swift. On the night of 30 March 1793, Danton was arrested and charged on very weak evidence compiled by Robespierre and Saint-Just. Three days later, the former Minister of Justice experienced the same fate he had meted out to so many unfortunates in the past. He was made to stand trial for his life. Revolutionary justice was swift, and he was executed on 5 April.[8] **THE RED REDS HAD KILLED THE RED ONE.**

The second invasion of the Tuileries in August 1792 had made it wholly impossible for the royal family to return to the palace. For their own safety, they were taken to the Temple. This was an old, dark, austere complex of buildings in Paris that had formally been the residence of the Knights of Malta. Louis XVI's brother Artois had subsequently acquired it, and turned part of the building into his palace. But he was later forced to abandon it after the Revolution took hold. The oracle below tells of the time spent inside the Temple by the King, and the charge of incest that was brought against the Queen.

C.IX: 22

Roy & ſa court au lieu de langue halbe,
Dedans le temple vis à vis du palais
Dans le iardin Duc de Mantor & d'Albe,
Albe & Mantor poignard langue & palais.

King and his court at the place of lodgement language,
Inside the temple, opposite to the palace,
In the garden, Duke Normandy, and Blanch,
Blanch and Normandy, dagger language and in public.

halbe, (O.Fr. apocope) halbe[rc] – hotel, lodging house; Mantor, (Latin portmanteau) Mant/o + or/a; also de Mantor (anagram and paragram) d[y]) Man[n]or – NORMANDY; Albe, (Latinism) Alb/eo – to become white; palais, (O.Fr. homonym) – palace, also, open, in public.

KING AND HIS COURT AT THE PLACE OF LODGEMENT LANGUAGE

After the *Palais de Tuileries* had been ransacked, and the Swiss guardsmen murdered in a frenzy of killing that also included many of the palace staff, the King and Queen together with their children were *lodged* inside the *Temple tower*. It was a dark, sombre building in which two floors had been assigned to the royal party. Attending them was a catering staff of thirteen and a valet. In effect, this was now **THE PLACE OF THE KING AND HIS COURT**. No longer was there any privacy. Armed guards occupied the **LODGEMENT** at all times, and the crudity of their **LANGUAGE** became the means of frequent insults aimed at the King and Queen.[1]

INSIDE THE TEMPLE, OPPOSITE TO THE PALACE

The Temple, which was now the royal family's prison, had once been a medieval keep. When Louis arrived there several days after the sacking of the Tuileries, he naturally expected to be lodged in the palace that had formerly housed his brother the duc d'Artois.[2] Instead, he and his family were given rooms **INSIDE THE TEMPLE** Tower. This was a building sited directly **OPPOSITE TO THE PALACE**.[3]

DUKE OF NORMANDY IN THE GARDEN

On 27 March 1785, at the time of his baptism, the Dauphin, Louis

Charles had been proclaimed DUKE OF NORMANDY. He was there-
fore *"the first son of France to bear that title in three hundred years."* [4] But
now, though still aged only eight, he was confined behind the
Temple walls, a child prisoner of the State. For some time he was
not seen by those visiting the Temple, causing the Committee to
become aware of rumours that he was no longer inside the keep.
After that, his guardian, Antoine Simon, took him for regular
walks IN THE GARDEN.[5]

AND BLANCH

The *Duke of Normandy's* mother, Marie Antoinette, is appropriately referred to in this oracle as BLANCH: this was because her
hair had turned white as a result of her ordeal – *'blanchis par la
douleur'*.[6] Although separated from her son, and confined to her
room, the Queen managed to find a crack in the woodwork of
the turret, and there she would stand for hours every day, peep-
ing through in the hope of catching just a single glimpse of her
little son *in the garden* below.

On 3 August 1793, Marie Antoinette was removed from the
Temple and taken to the Conciergerie. Her husband Louis XVI
had been guillotined earlier that year (we shall read more of this
in another oracle). The time had now arrived for the Queen to be
dealt with in a similar manner. But for such an important event:
one with international consequences, a legal case had first to be
made against her for the court hearing.

BLANCH AND NORMANDY, DAGGER LANGUAGE AND IN PUBLIC

In an attempt to defame Marie Antoinette to the fullest possible
extent, her chief prosecutor devised a story in which the Queen
stood accused of an incestuous relationship with her eight-year-
old son. The oracle's phrase: *dagger language* is sexual innuendo
for this piece of calumny.[7] Robespierre rejected the story completely, and the Committee of Public Safety ordered it to be
suppressed. But a juror demanded that it be made known, and
so the accusation of incest (DAGGER LANGUAGE) between BLANCH AND
NORMANDY, was read out IN PUBLIC.[8]

Because the next quatrain did not appear in any of the surviving publications prior to 1643, doubt has been cast upon its au-
thenticity. However, upon examination, it is in Nostradamus's

style; it also correlates perfectly with the history it predicts. The quatrain concerns Louis XVI at the time of his trial and execution, and concludes by referring back to the major cause of his downfall: his flight from Paris. The oracle calls it *wrong*. Interestingly, this is also the judgment made by modern historians. Many take the opinion that had Louis remained in the capital, both he and the Queen would have survived the Revolution.

C.VII: 44

Alors qu'un bour fera fort bon,
Portant en foy les marques de justice,
De fon fang lors portant fon nom,
Par fuite injufte receura fon fupplice.

That time when a Bourbon (younger brother) will show good strength,
Bearing in himself the signs of justice,
Carrying the name of his kindred at the time,
Through wrong flight, he will receive his ordeal.

bour (O.Fr. syncope) bour[sal] – a younger brother; also: bour . . . bon – Bourbon.

THAT TIME WHEN A YOUNGER BOURBON BROTHER

Prior to becoming Louis XVI, this ill-fated monarch was the Duke of Berry, a grandson of Louis XV and the third son of the Dauphin. He was therefore **A YOUNGER BROTHER**. Louis XVI was also a member of the **BOURBON** dynasty: a family that succeeded to the throne more than thirty years after Nostradamus's death.[1]

After his flight from Paris in June 1791, and the failure to reach the Belgian frontier before being arrested in Varennes, Louis' role as King gradually deteriorated. After being brought back to the capital in ignominy, he was compelled to relinquish much of his inherited power and settle for an executive role: one in which he was allowed the limited use of a veto in return for swearing to uphold the new Constitution. It was a stopgap measure that soon turned to violence against the crown. This, in turn, quickly led to his incarceration inside the Temple, and from there to his trial for treason.

WILL SHOW GOOD STRENGTH

It was during his trial while in the face of adversity that Louis, having previously appeared as a rather inadequate monarch, began to distinguish himself by his dignity, resourcefulness and a **SHOW** of **GOOD** inner **STRENGTH**.[2]

250

The trial took place between December 1792 and January 1793. During the whole of that time, the King stood before the court appearing quite unruffled: *'showing the calmness of a man who actually believes he is irreproachably in the right'*. Each time an accusation was made against him, he responded by: *"flatly denying that he had done anything illegal either before or after 1791."* [3] Essentially, at all times, **BEARING IN HIMSELF THE SIGNS OF JUSTICE.**

Before being taken from the Temple to face trial, the Mayor of Paris, Aubin-Bigore Chambon, had arrived with a summons for the man named Louis Capet. *"I am not Louis Capet,"* retorted the King indignantly; *"My ancestors had that name but I have never been called that."* [4] It was, nevertheless, a fulfilment of Nostradamus's prediction, for he had foretold that **AT THAT TIME** he would be **CARRYING THE NAME OF HIS KINDRED.**

It was **THROUGH** Louis XVI's failed attempt to escape from France in June 1791, which the oracle, in complete agreement with historians, condemns as a **WRONG FLIGHT** that a legal case for treason was made possible. The charge was that he had secretly left France to raise troops abroad.[5] Once the guilty verdict had been obtained, there was no further place in government for a convicted king, and Louis was forced to **RECEIVE HIS ORDEAL** beneath the blade of the guillotine.[6]

The first surviving reference to this quatrain appeared in a publication by Claude Garcin of Marseilles in 1643, which he claimed was copied from a printed impression made some time after Rigaud's edition of 1568. This same quatrain also appeared in Leffen's edition of the prophecies in 1650, although Leffen stated that it had been copied from the Lyons edition of 1558. There is, however, one significant difference between the two printings; Leffen writes 'son nom', in the third line, whereas in Garcin's edition it appears as 'long nom'. Garcin does not name his source.

Before attending his trial, Louis XVI had remained confined inside the Temple Tower alongside his wife, his sister and his two children. Nostradamus continues with the theme of the royal family's incarceration, but expands upon it by referring to an event at the beginning of the revolution, and which was to eventually lead to the Dauphin being denied succession to the Crown.

C.I: 65

Enfant fans mains iamais veu fi grand foudre:
L'enfant royal au ieu d'œfteuf bleffé.
Au puy brifes: fulgures alant mouldre:
Trois fous les chaines par le milieu trouffés.

Child without safeguards, never seen so great a calamity:
The royal child injured at the game of tennis.
Broken by the mountain; thunderbolts proceeding to grind down,
Three in bonds (with the white hairs) trussed-up in the midst.

mains, (O.Fr., judicial meaning) sauvegarde; œfteuf, (O.Fr.) balle à jouer; puy, (O.Fr.) mountain; fulgures, (Latinism) fulgur/is – thunderbolts; chaines, (O.Fr. homonym) cheveux blancs = white hairs, also bonds.

CHILD WITHOUT SAFEGUARDS, NEVER SEEN SO GREAT A CALAMITY

The CHILD WITHOUT SAFEGUARDS, as we shall now determine, was the Dauphin, Louis Charles. He was confined to the Temple Tower in the summer of 1792, aged seven. After being separated from his mother (3 July 1793) it was decided to re-educate him as a 'citizen' of the Revolution, and he was placed in the care of Antoine Simon and his wife. Although only a child, he was encouraged to drink wine, given brandy to stop him crying, and for his amusement, he was provided with pornographic picture books. At other times, he was taught how to blaspheme and curse at his own family: *"Haven't those confounded bitches* [his mother, sister and aunt] *up there been guillotined yet?"* The prostitutes that entertained the palace guards were also brought to him. This caused a doctor to examine the child for signs of any sexually transmitted diseases, but nothing was found. After the guillotining of his parents in 1793, Louis Charles's welfare became ignored, and he was left to waste away in a dirty, lice-infested little room inside the Tower block. He died there from tuberculosis and neglect on 8 June 1795, aged ten and a quarter.[1] NEVER SEEN SO GREAT A CALAMITY, wrote Nostradamus.

THE ROYAL CHILD INJURED AT THE GAME OF TENNIS

The oracle now looks back to where this abuse against THE ROYAL CHILD began, and lights upon the Oath of the Tennis Court as the

252

original instrument that INJURED the boy. The Oath was sworn by deputies of the Third Estate at a meeting held in Versailles in 1789. The deputies had originally intended to meet inside the Assembly Hall but upon arriving, they found it locked. Fortunately, someone remembered an indoor tennis court nearby, and it was inside the 'Jeu de Pomme'; i.e., AT THE GAME OF TENNIS that members of the Third Estate swore never to separate until a 'constitution of the kingdom' had been established.[2] Historians have long pointed out that this was the definitive beginning of the revolution that followed. For, in effect, they were declaring war against the old regime and the absolute power of the monarch, which in turn was to affect the *royal child* as heir to the throne.

BROKEN BY THE MOUNTAIN

THE MOUNTAIN was the name given to the political party peopled by revolutionaries voicing extremist views, and whose members were seated at the highest point in the Assembly Hall. It was through legislation, inspired by their inflammatory oratory that won for them the approval of the people, and which afterwards translated into the violent acts that BROKE the monarchy.[3]

THUNDERBOLTS PROCEEDING TO GRIND DOWN

What was left of the old order was blown away in the tourbillion that followed. From having once occupied the ultimate seat of French power, Louis XVI's position was systematically reduced by a series of sudden, devastating blows. These began with the Oath of the Tennis Court; then the Storming of the Bastille; next the women's march to Versailles; the King's arrest at Varennes; the assault on the Palais de Tuileries; the slaughter of the Swiss guards and palace staff; the September Massacres; then finally, the royal family's incarceration in the Temple Tower. Combined, they were THUNDERBOLTS, with each fresh blow PROCEEDING TO GRIND DOWN the King's power base until nothing further remained.[4]

THREE IN BONDS, WITH THE WHITE HAIRS, TRUSSED UP IN THE MIDST

In the final phrase to this oracle, a somewhat bitter reference is made to THREE prisoners IN BONDS, including one WITH THE WHITE HAIR. These are identified as Louis XVI, Madame Elisabeth the King's sister, and Marie Antoinette, ungraciously identified by her *white hair*. All three were imprisoned inside the Temple. It was after returning to the palace following her capture at

Varennes that the Queen removed her cap, *"to reveal hair that had gone quite white through her sufferings."* (Fraser). All *three* were imprisoned together in the Temple, and all *three* were guillotined at the *Place de la Révolution*, IN THE MIDST of a crowd gathered to watch.

This method of execution involved the condemned person being strapped to a plank held vertically. This was then swung down to a horizontal position, with the victim's neck clamped between two halves of wood, so that the head protruded. Suspended high above was the blade of the guillotine. Prior to this, the victims were first TRUSSED-UP, with their hands tied tightly behind their back. When the King's turn came, he vehemently protested at this indignity, but there was no exception.[5]

For Nostradamus, the execution of a king at the hands of his own subjects was an event totally alien to the society in which he was raised. We therefore find him returning to the subject on several occasions, each time referring to the event within a different prophecy. This strategy also acts as a timing device, for by referring to what happened at Varennes, the remaining part of the prophecy can be dated close to that incident. In the next oracle, it is the colour of the King's clothes worn during his flight from Paris that enables the remaining lines of the quatrain to be understood. This includes count Narbonne-Lara, Louis' one-time Minister for War, together with Gorsas, the first deputy to be guillotined. Both men had one thing in common, they were at one time sympathetic to Louis XVI's predicament, but were later swayed by the arguments of others.

C.VIII: 22

> Gorſan, Narbonne, par le ſel aduertir,
> Tucham, la grace Parpignam trahye,
> La ville rouge n'y vouldra conſentir.
> Par haulte vol drap gris vie faillie.

> *Gorsas, Narbonne, through the salt (Staël), turning,*
> *You! Bourbon: forgiveness, Perpignan betrays,*
> *The red city will not be willing to consent to it.*
> *Through haughty flight, grey cloth, life finished.*

Gorſan, (paragram) Gorsa[s] (also anagram) gosar[a]n (O.Fr.) necklace; le ſel, (paranagram) [t]e s[a]l – Stael; aduertir, (Latinism) adver/to; Tucham, (apocope, Tu Cham[pi]; i.e., O.Fr. Champi = Bourbon): also (Greek) Τυχα[μ]; Parpignam, (Latin portmanteau) – Par/o + pign/us, also Perpignan; hault, (O.Fr.) haughty, arrogant; faillie, (O.Fr.) finir.

At the time of the Revolution, Antoine-Joseph *Gorsas* was a journalist for the *Courrier de Paris à Versailles,* and one of the few men who were willing to write articles in support of the monarchy. He was subsequently elected as a deputy to the Assembly, and at the King's trial voted for detention as a preference to execution. But on 7 October 1793 he was arrested, tried, and executed, all in a single day.[1] **GORSAS** was the first deputy to die beneath the Paris blade, therefore the first deputy to wear the guillotine's wooden *necklace.* This was the framework clamped around the condemned person's neck in order to hold the head firmly in place prior to decapitation.

NARBONNE, TURNING THROUGH THE SALT (STAËL)

The Comte de **NARBONNE** has received mention before. He was appointed by Louis XVI as Minister for War. He also believed the King might be restored to favour by going to war against the émigré army that had gathered at Coblenz, believing this would induce an atmosphere of patriotism across the country.[2] But as the revolution progressed, he came increasingly under the influence of others; referred to by the seer as *the salt.* This usually refers to the moral elite (see see C.IX: 49 and C.X: 7), but in this particular case it also provides a paranagram for *Staël.* Narbonne was planning to speak at the King's trial, but **THROUGH** the persuasive arguments of his mistress and mother of his child, Madame de **STAËL**,[3] **TURNING** him from his resolve, he remained silent.[4]

YOU! BOURBON

The subtle interplay between '*tucham*' and '*tu champi*' is particularly noteworthy, for it employs both the paragram and an apocope. This word play therefore enables Louis XVI to be identified by both his **BOURBON** name and **TU**; this singular form of address had been adopted by citizens of the Revolution; *viz. – "[As a mark of] greater social equality . . . tu replaced vous."* (Littlewood).

CHANCE

CHANCE had an important role to play in the failure of Louis XVI to escape Paris.[5] His bad luck began with the **CHANCE** observation made by Drouet, the postmaster in Sainte-Ménéhould, who caught sight of the King inside his stationary coach, causing the alarm to be raised. It was also good fortune that accompanied

Drouet on his night time pursuit through the forest, made without mishap, and without losing his way. It was again by **CHANCE** that the dragoons, sent to escort the King's carriage to the safety of the Belgian border, lost their way in the forest. They had ridden there to seek cover from prying eyes while they waited for the royal runaways to arrive, but in the forest gloom they became lost, and did not reach Varennes until the next morning: too late to save the King and Queen in their bid to reach the border.

FORGIVENESS

After the King's enforced return to Paris, and in the wake of much debate, Louis was **FORGIVEN** his attempt to escape the Revolution. And in September 1791, he was restored to office with assurance for his safety.[6]

PERPIGNAN BETRAYS

Three months later in December, the pro-Royalist officers at the garrison in *Perpignan* mutinied, and an attempt was made to raise a force strong enough to support the monarchy. But most of the soldiers billeted there refused to take part in the uprising. It was because of **PERPIGNAN'S BETRAYAL** to the King that the revolt failed.[7]

THE RED CITY

Following the elections of September 1791, Paris became **THE RED CITY**. It is not difficult to see why. *"It was among the hundreds of 'new men' . . . that some of the most extreme revolutionaries were to be found."* These 'new men' were far more revolutionary than their predecessors, and they favoured turning France into a republic as soon as possible.[8]

WILL NOT BE WILLING TO CONSENT TO IT

For the beleaguered monarchy, the situation was now grim. The majority of politicians who had previously given the King assurances for his safety had been replaced during these elections, and the new deputies were of a different mould. They were eager to build a new order upon the policies of the previous administration, and were **NOT WILLING TO CONSENT TO** the **FORGIVENESS** given to the King by their predecessors.[9] Within very little time, this impatience to rid France of its monarchy found expression in mob violence, when gangs of revolutionaries twice overran the royal residence. On the second of these occasions, all pretension of a monarchy in France ceased, and the King and Queen were taken away to the Temple to await their fate.

THROUGH HAUGHTY FLIGHT, GREY CLOTH, LIFE FINISHED

Nostradamus completes this oracle by looking back at what brought the monarchy to its terrible end, and in telegraphic language he picks out the words that most aptly refer to it. THROUGH HAUGHTY FLIGHT can be seen as an obvious reference to the King's *flight* from Paris, after having left behind that *haughty* letter complaining of the way he had been treated.[10] The GREY CLOTH worn by Louis XVI during his arrest at Varennes confirms the King's identity, for it will be recalled that *grey* was the colour of the cloak, breeches and stockings he wore while dressed as a valet (C.IX: 20).[11] LIFE FINISHED is where it ended, a little over eighteen months later, beneath the guillotine.[12]

The September elections ushered in a new breed of men. They arrived in Paris to take their seats with the zeal and purpose of determined reformers. It was their intention to abolish the monarchy and make France a republic. The following oracle reflects the importance of this endeavour, for it is given first place in Century One.

C.I: 3

Quand la lictiere du tourbillon verfée
Et feront faces de leurs manteaux couvers:
La republique par gens nouveaux vexée,
Lors blancs & rouges iugeront à l'envers.

When the litter is overturned by the whirlwind,
And faces will be covered by their cloaks:
The republic is vexed by new people,
Then whites and reds will judge on the wrong side.

Cross-reference: à l'envers, C.IX: 49.

WHEN THE LITTER IS OVERTURNED BY THE WHIRLWIND

This aptly constructed allegory foretells the coming of the French Revolution: a time when political turmoil is so sudden and so ferocious, that it can only be compared to a *whirlwind*. The nobility in France are identified by the *litters* used for conveying them on short journeys. Nostradamus then foretells that an approaching WHIRLWIND WILL OVERTURN these LITTERS, sweeping the occupants away.[1]

THEN FACES WILL BE COVERED BY THEIR CLOAKS

Continuing with the same allegory, Nostradamus next identifies the nobility *by their cloaks*. At the time of the Revolution, it was only the upper classes that were rich enough to afford these. But after laws proscribing the nobility were passed, those affected by the legislation were compelled to COVER THEIR FACES WITH THEIR CLOAKS, metaphorically speaking, in order to conceal their identities.[2] All this was far removed from life in Nostradamus's time, and it would be two hundred years before the social changes in France occurred to make this reality.

THE REPUBLIC IS VEXED BY NEW PEOPLE

The monarchy in France was formerly replaced by a REPUBLIC on 21 September 1792. After the elections of September 1791, in which members of the previous Assembly had legislated against their own re-appointment, the NEW PEOPLE elected to office were the revolutionary figures that would later form the first *Republic*. *"Inside the Convention, the struggle for power developed between the Girondins and the more active and extreme Mountain, so called because its members took their seats on the highest tiers of benches."* It was therefore: *'The Conflict of Girondins and Jacobins'* that VEXED THE REPUBLIC.[3] Between November 1793 and July 1794: *"the Jacobins tried to set up a system of government based on the absolutist aspects of Rousseau's Contrat Social."* But the growing instability this created was to ultimately lead to the Great Terror.

THEN WHITES AND REDS WILL JUDGE ON THE WRONG SIDE

It will be recalled from C.VIII: 19 that *"'red' and 'white' were the accepted color codes for revolution and counter-revolution:"* white being the King's colour.[4] Nostradamus uses these colours for the trial of the King.

Louis XVI was put on trial for his life following the abolition of the monarchy. After the hearing, three votes were taken to determine his guilt and punishment. At the first vote, a verdict of guilty was read out. A second ballot was then called for in order to decide if his sentence should be death or exile. The result was death. There was then a third vote to settle the question of a reprieve. Nostradamus makes a political judgement, based upon his prediction, by asserting that the voters on both sides – the REDS AND the WHITES – WILL JUDGE the King guilty; that is, be ON THE WRONG SIDE to him.[5] As a piece of cross-referencing, Nostradamus uses these same words when predicting the outcome of Charles

I's trial in 1649; although instead of *reds and whites*, he employs *salt and wine* (see C.IX: 49).

The King received his death sentence with a placid show of inner courage. He did however harbour the regret that his own relative, the newly named Philip Égalité, had voted for his death. He felt this had been a great betrayal.

The next oracle is split between father and son. It begins with the Dauphin Louis Charles, whom the revolutionaries renamed, Prince Royal: having dispensed with the title of Dauphin along with everything else that was associated with the Ancient Regime. The oracle then abruptly deviates to focus upon the King. The unity between these two lines, apart from the relationship of father and son, is centred upon their faces.

C.VI: 92

Prince de beauté tant venuſte,
Au chef menee, le ſecond faict trahy:
La cité au glaiue de poudre, face aduſte,
Par trop grand meurtre le chef du roy hay.

A Prince of beauty, so greatly attractive.
Conducted to the principal, the second act has betrayed:
The city to the blade: the face burnt with powder,
Through excessively great murder, the head of the King despised.

tant, (Latinism) tant/us; venuſte, (Latinism) venust/us; aduſte, (Latinism) adust/us (from adur/o).

A PRINCE OF BEAUTY, SO GREATLY ATTRACTIVE

By the time Louis Charles's features had developed, it was obvious that he had inherited the attractive looks of his mother. The oracle's words: **SO GREATLY ATTRACTIVE** are therefore especially appropriate. Moreover, the oracle specifically refers to him as **A PRINCE**. This is also apt, because once the young child had been placed inside the Temple prison, an order was passed decreeing that in future he be referred to as the *'Prince Royal'*.[1]

The structure of this oracle is similar to that of C.VII: 11, which concerned another royal child, Louis XIII. This oracle began by describing the royal child's bad relationship with his mother. It then proceeded to the second line by describing the characteristics of the Queen-regent's chief minister. Nostradamus has adopted a similar strategy for this oracle. He commences by describing the well-attested *beauty* of Marie Antoinette's son, the future Louis XVII. The seer then subtly changes the subject to events leading towards the execution of the boy's father, Louis XVI. However, the underlying theme that unifies these two opening lines is the comparison between the facial beauty of the Prince and the facial disfigurement of the King following his execution.

CONDUCTED TO THE PRINCIPAL

On the morning of 11 December 1792, Louis XVI was CONDUCTED from his prison quarters inside the Temple TO THE PRINCIPAL – Citizen Aubin-Begorre Chambon, Mayor of Paris.[2] The purpose of this enforced visit was to submit the King to a lengthy period of questioning before an assembled tribunal, so that a way might be found to bring a prosecution against him. As a direct result of this meeting, Louis XVI was brought to trial later that month. As part of the outward show, the King was granted permission for legal representation, this of course proved ineffective, and by a unanimous vote he was found guilty of treason.

THE SECOND ACT HAS BETRAYED

Trying the King and finding him guilty as charged was only the first of *three acts* in this courtroom drama. *The second act* required a vote to be taken in order to determine the nature of his sentence; the options were: death, detention or exile. It was during THE SECOND ACT that the King was BETRAYED. The duc d'Orléans, a cousin of Louis XVI, but now calling himself Philippe Égalité was amongst those who voted for death.[3] Louis later confessed to his manservant how much Orléans *betrayal* had grieved him.

THE CITY TO THE BLADE: THE FACE BURNT WITH POWDER

On 21 January 1793, it seemed the whole of THE CITY of Paris had been drawn TO the *Place de la Révolution*, where THE BLADE of the guillotine hung menacingly in the air, awaiting its royal victim.[4] Immediately after the execution, the King's head, together with his decapitated body were conveyed to the cemetery of the Madeleine. A deep pit had been dug to receive the remains. The head and torso were then *"laid in a coffin, which was put in the grave, and immediately covered with quicklime."* [5] That is to say, THE FACE was BURNT WITH POWDER. This can now be contrasted with the *beauty* of his son, with which the prophecy began.

The world stood amazed: aghast at the beheading of Louis XVI. London referred to it as: *"the foulest and most atrocious act the world has ever seen."* Nostradamus called it simply: **AN EXCESSIVELY GREAT MURDER.** The courts of Europe, no less outraged, were vociferous in condemning those responsible, whom they labelled the *'assassins of Paris'.* [6]

Nostradamus has added a conclusion to this prophecy. After the execution, Louis' head was held aloft for the watching crowd to bear witness. They greeted the spectacle with an enormous, *derisory* cheer. Soon afterwards, pictures of **THE** King's severed **HEAD** appeared on prints and on crockery as a crude reminder **OF THE KING** they had so much **DESPISED.** [7]

For Nostradamus, the beheading of France's King was too great a subject to be left to a single prophecy. It had to be approached from several different directions: as, indeed, had been the case with the execution of Charles I. And with each new approach, fresh prophecies appear. One of the architects behind Louis XVI's overthrow was Jean Paul Marat. In the next oracle there is a passing reference to his murder as the seer views the King's execution from a different viewpoint.

C.I: 57

Par grand difcord la trombe tremblera.
Accord rompu dreffant la tefte au ciel:
Bouche fanglante dans le fang nagera:
Au fol fa face ointe de laict & miel.

Through great discord the waterspout will shake,
Accord broken, raising the head to the sky:
Bloody mouth will swim in his blood,
To the soil, his face anointed with milk and honey.

fol, (Latinism) sol/um – soil.

Eventually, the French Revolution reached the stage when the destructive forces within it began spiralling out of control; **THROUGH GREAT DISCORD THE WATERSPOUT** – equivalent to *the whirlwind* in C.I: 3 and a metaphor for the Revolution – began to **SHAKE.** The fateful year was 1792: a time when the elections of the previous September had given voice to men like, *Robespierre, Marat, Robert,*

261

Santerre, Danton, Fabre, Desmoulins and the actor Collot d'Herbois'. Before their election, the previous administration had been in accord with the monarchy, and had even given assurances that if Louis XVI swore to uphold the Constitution it would remove any cause for further injury. But it was not to be. In the summer months of 1792, the royal palace in the centre of Paris was twice overrun; the second time with such carnage and ferocity that the royal family were only saved by their timely removal to the Assembly Hall. In the following month, the September Massacres opened the prison doors to the slaughter of the clergy and other inmates.[1] The Revolution was shaking and about to spiral out of control.

THE ACCORD BROKEN

THE ACCORD, so carefully planned, and which was intended to avoid any further interruption in the French capital, was **BROKEN** by the physical attacks made against the King, and there would be no turning back. The monarchy was officially abolished on 21 September 1792, and three months later, the King was put on trial for his life.[2]

RAISING THE HEAD TO THE SKY

The verdict was completely predictable; the assembled deputies voted for the King's execution. The beheading of Louis XVI took place on 21 January 1793 at the *Place de la Révolution*. As a final gesture to this act of regicide, and in keeping with the practice of the time: *"The executioner leaned over the basket and firmly picked up the severed head. He raised it on high and walked along the four sides of the platform showing it to the sovereign people."*[3]

BLOODY MOUTH

One of the principal fomenters of unrest at that that time was Jean Paul Marat. His popular paper, *L'Ami du Peuple*, the forerunner of modern tabloid journalism, acted as a disseminator for his sanguinary views. A favourite saying of his had been: *"We must cement liberty in the blood of the despot."* Previously, in the summer of 1790, he had declared to his readers that five or six hundred heads cut off would be a price worth paying if it bought them freedom and happiness. During the September Massacres, it was Marat who urged the good citizens of Paris to go the prison where the priests were being held, and a run a sword through them. But Marat's bloodthirsty speeches had also attracted enemies; some were already calling for Marat's own blood to be spilt. *"In Caen, Pézenas wrote 'Purge France of this man of blood [who] sees the Public Safety only in a river of blood.'"* [4]

On 13 July 1793, Marat's opponents had their wish granted when a well-educated and attractive young woman of 24, Marie-Anne-Charlotte Corday d'Armont, arrived in Paris from Caen. Her objective was to seek an interview with Marat under the pretence of informing him of some plots that were being planned by the Girondins in her hometown.

WILL SWIM IN HIS BLOOD

Marat suffered from prurigo, a skin complaint he had contracted in the past while hiding in the Paris sewers. To alleviate his discomfort, he took to having frequent baths. It was while bathing, and still immersed in a tub of water, that he agreed to see Charlotte Corday. The decision was to prove fatal. After entering the room and engaging Marat in conversation, Charlotte Corday drew a knife from the fold of her dress and stabbed him below the neck, severing an artery. **BLOODY MOUTH**, as the seer has named Marat, was now **SWIMMING IN HIS BLOOD**. His cries for help, as he threshed about in the water, were to no avail. Nothing could be done for him, and he died from loss of blood. [5]

HIS FACE, ANOINTED WITH MILK AND HONEY TO THE SOIL

Six months previously, Louis XVI's body and severed head had been interred in a deep grave dug for him at the Madeleine, and the remains covered with quicklime. In later years, an attempt was made to recover his body, but **THE SOIL** around the grave, to which the head and trunk had been committed, revealed only a grey chalky compound. [6] In this respect, it was suggested by James Laver (*Nostradamus: The Future Foretold*, p.155) that a clue exists in Nostradamus's phraseology for dating the King's execution. Louis XVI was beheaded on 21st January, the Feast Day of St Agnes; she, like Louis XVI, was also executed. But the connection appears to go deeper, for the words taken from the Church's celebratory 'Office of St Agnes' read: *"Mel et lac ex ore ejus suscepi, et sanguis ejus ornavit genas meas . . ."* [7] That is to say, they contain the same words as those appearing in this oracle; that is, 'mel et lac' – **MILK AND HONEY**; 'ore' – **FACE** or **MOUTH**; sanguis –

BLOOD.[8] Clues as subtle as this are not unusual in these prophecies, and tend to raise the level of scholarship well above that of any previous commentary, whether by advocate or sceptic. There is also the distinction between Marat and Louis XVI: the former Nostradamus calls *bloody mouth*, signifying bloodthirsty oratory; the latter he refers to as having been *anointed by milk and honey*, which suggests a person born within the privileged surroundings of the nobility. In short, they are not the same person, although a superficial reading might allow this error to be made.

1793 was a particularly gruesome year for those caught up in the French Revolution. The King was executed in January, and Marie Antoinette followed her husband to the guillotine nine months later. Outside Paris, the impact of changing from monarchy to a republic began to be felt across the country, and nowhere more than in Lyons and the Vendée. In the next quatrain Nostradamus foretells events for that year in both localities, at the same time providing further names, and the particular day of the year that was to prove particularly gruesome.

C.IX: 68

Du mont Aymar ſera noble obſcurcie,
Le mal viendra au ioinct de Saone & Roſne:
Dans bois cachez ſoldatz iour de Lucie,
Qui ne fut onc un ſi horrible throſne.

Of the Mountain, Amar, Marat: the high born will be obscured,
The evil will come at the junction of the Saône and Rhône,
Soldiers hidden in woodland: day of Lucy,
Which, never was there ever one such horrible throne.

Aymar, (paranagram) A[t]mar = Marat, also, A[ ]mar.

OF THE MOUNTAIN, AMAR

The Mountain, as we have seen, was the name given to the political body that occupied seats high above the floor of the Assembly Hall.[1] Seated amongst these new arrivals to the newly constituted Convention was André *Amar*, the representative for Isère, who took his seat beside those OF THE MOUNTAIN. AMAR had famously called the guillotine: *'the holy altar'*, and its operation: *'a celebration of the red Mass'*. In this sense, his sanguinary vocabulary had much in common with that of *Marat*, with whom he has become linked.[2]

264

Marat, as revealed above, also practised a bloodthirsty rhetoric. But there was another link that brought these two men together. After the murder of **MARAT, AMAR** was chosen by the Convention to investigate and prepare an official report on his murder.[3]

On 19 March 1793, just six months after *Marat,* and *Amar,* had taken their seats in the newly constituted Convention, *the Mountain* demanded the proscription of all noblemen. On 28 March and again on 5 April, all émigrés were sentenced to perpetual banishment. That is to say: **THE HIGHBORN WERE OBSCURED** (put out of sight).[4]

Lyons lies *at the junction of the Saône and Rhône.* The city is not actually named in the oracle, but its location is unmistakeable. Quite possibly, this omission was deliberate, and was intended to signal the city's forthcoming loss of name. Lyons had earlier rebelled against the new constitution. An irate Convention in Paris responded by dispatching troops to restore order. When this had been accomplished, Couthon declared that the name Lyons should be wiped off the map, and a column erected to declare: LYON N'EST PLUS (Lyons is no more). The city was then renamed: Ville-affranchie (Freed City).

As a still more exacting mark of the Convention's anger, Lyons was forced to endure a Terror that is regarded, still, to have been even worse than that suffered in Paris. In other words: **THE EVIL WILL COME AT THE JUNCTION OF THE SAÔNE AND RHÔNE.** Joseph Fouché was put in charge of executing the city's rebels, and he remained in Lyons until 2,000 of its citizens had been executed: some of these were young men that he bound together and used as targets for cannon fire.[5] More will be said about this in a subsequent oracle.

In that same year, 1793, another rebellion broke out, this time in the Vendée, part of western France. The bocages or *woodland,* mostly comprising of copses and groves, proved to be an excellent battleground for the armed guerrillas who were fighting for the royalist cause. These militant Vendéans and Bretons, known as Chouans, would conceal themselves amongst the trees; that is,

SOLDIERS HIDDEN IN WOODLAND: and from there, they were able to ambush the republican forces sent to confront them.[6]

DAY OF LUCY

At first these tactics were enormously successful. But in October, the Vendéan rebels were falsely led to believe that a ship was arriving at Granville with an army of émigré volunteers. 30,000 armed men, followed by more than a 100,000 citizens of all ages, made their way to the Normandy port to greet the arrivals. It was a trap. There was no ship. Realizing they had been the victims of a cruel deception, this huge flock of people began to straggle back the way they had come. Alas, there was an army in wait for them. During their 120-mile trek, the Vendéan rebels, including women and children, were raped, robbed and killed without mercy.

> *The last confused horde of La Vendée had been driven from the walls of Granville in Normandy, to which it had erred and drifted rather than retreated. At Mans on 13th December it was cut to pieces.* (Belloc)

In the Roman Catholic Calendar of Saints, 13th December is Saint Lucy's Day – **DAY OF LUCY.**[7] Nostradamus has now dated three prophecies by stating the name of a saint whose feast day falls on the same day as the fulfilment of a particular prophecy; they are Saint Solano (14 July), Saint Agnes (21 January) and Saint Lucy (13 December). Some coincidence for sceptics to swallow!

THERE WAS NEVER ONE SUCH HORRIBLE THRONE

1793 began in January with the guillotining of Louis XVI. Before the end of the year, the Queen, too, would go to the guillotine. Both their children, the heir to the throne, ten-year-old Louis-Charles, and his sister Marie-Thérèse were kept separate from each other, orphaned, locked away and alone inside the Temple prison. The little Prince would soon die from tuberculosis and neglect. Nostradamus's description of this period in French history is surely incontestable: **THERE NEVER WAS EVER ONE SUCH HORRIBLE THRONE.**[8]

The tragic events surrounding the French throne in 1793 are further retold in the next oracle, but from a different perspective. In this, we shall see key words signalling the sequence of events that began with the execution of the King, and ended with the beheading of his grandfather's paramour, Madame du Barry. Her death beneath the guillotine followed very soon after that of Marie Antoinette; the coincidence relating to their times of death plays upon the fact that the two women were archenemies. By predicting their executions in sequence, Nostradamus has indicated an awareness of this connection.

C.IX: 77

Le regne prins le Roy conviera,
La dame prinſe à mort iurez à ſort,
La vie à Royne fils on deſniera,
Et la pellix au fort de la conſort.

The captured reign will convey the King,
The captured wife to a death sworn by lot,
One will deny the son life, with the Queen,
And the kept mistress to the stronghold of the consort.

conviera, (O.Fr. epenthesis – conv[e]iera) convey; pellix, (Latinism) pellex = kept mistress.

THE CAPTURED REIGN

In the summer of 1792, the monarchy's long REIGN in France was finally brought to an end, having been replaced – CAPTURED – by a republican government.[1]

CONVEYING THE KING

On 21 January 1793, members of the Convention were finally ready to remove the last vestige of France's old monarchical system from the political scene. On a grey winter's morning a coach arrived outside the Temple to CONVEY THE KING to the *place de la Révolution* where he was to be guillotined.[2] The conveyance in which Louis XVI made his final journey is not without significance. Of the many thousand men, women and children that were guillotined in Paris during the French Revolution, all except the King were *conveyed* to their deaths in a tumbrel (a dung cart). Louis XVI was the only person to be afforded the special privilege of being *conveyed* to his execution by coach.

THE CAPTURED WIFE TO A DEATH SWORN BY LOT

Marie Antoinette was THE CAPTURED WIFE of the King. From her place of captivity inside the Temple Tower, she was transferred to a cell inside the Conciergerie, situated on the Île Saint Louis. There, she was to remain for the duration of her trial, having been charged with treasonable activities against the state.[3] At her trial, the evidence was heard by fifteen jurors who retired to cast their votes – THEIR LOTS. A verdict of guilty was SWORN in, and the former Queen was sentenced TO DEATH. She was executed on the following morning (16 October 1793).[4]

ONE WILL DENY THE SON LIFE, WITH THE QUEEN

Three months earlier on the evening of 3 July, six Municipals arrived at the Temple to address the Queen. Their mission was to remove her son and place him in the care of Antoine Simon. Marie Antoinette became defiant. *"She stood in front of his bed, and she said 'never' . . . they could kill her but she would never consent."* But the child was removed, *"and all night long and for two whole days he cried for his mother."* But he never saw her again.[5] Two years later, alone and ill inside his prison cell, he was allowed to die from neglect; ONE HAD DENIED THE SON LIFE; it being thought convenient to permit this.

THE MISTRESS TO THE STRONGHOLD OF THE CONSORT

The final line of the quatrain concerns another death: one that occurred just seven weeks after the execution of Marie Antoinette. The victim was Madame du Barry, a former prostitute who later became the concubine; that is, KEPT MISTRESS of the King's grandfather, Louis XV.[6] The important part about this prophecy is that her death was not entirely unconnected with that of Marie Antoinette – THE King's CONSORT. This relationship between the two women is best explained by du Barry's biographer, Stanley Loomis.

> *The curve of destiny had brought the one time enemies together again at the end of their lives. They had entered history within a year of one another; they were to die upon the same scaffold within a few months. The two women had been enemies at Court.*

"On December 4th, Madame Du Barry was transferred . . . to the grim prison of the Conciergerie:" THE STRONGHOLD, which only recently had been occupied by the King's CONSORT.[7] She was guillotined on 8 December 1793 amidst appalling scenes of hysteria.

Attention is now directed to Lyons, the city that revolted and became renamed Ville-affranchie (Freed City). Reference has previously been made to the atrocities carried out there by Fouché, and the 2,000 deaths inflicted upon its citizens (see C.IX: 68).

Nostradamus now adds to this by predicting the mass drowning that took place at Nantes.

C.V: 33

Des principaux de cité rebellee,
Qui tiendont fort pours liberté rauoir:
Detrencher maſles, infelice meſlee,
Crys hurlemens à Nantes piteux voir.

Concerning the principals of the city [that] rebelled,
Who will strongly hold out for recovering liberty:
Males cut to pieces, an unhappy affray,
Shrieks, howling at Nantes, piteous to see.

tiendont, – tiendront; infelice, (Latinism) infelic/o.

CONCERNING THE PRINCIPALS OF THE CITY THAT REBELLED

In contrast to the sans-culottes, whose name has since become synonymous with the revolution, it was not they who rebelled inside Lyons in May 1793, but the professional elite – *"men who considered themselves the natural political and cultural leaders of the city."* [1]

WHO WILL STRONGLY HOLD OUT FOR RECOVERING LIBERTY

For five months the people of Lyons held out under siege conditions against troops sent by the Paris based Convention to restore order. The principal citizens of the city were protesting against a diminution of their former liberty, which had resulted from the recent revisions made to the Constitution. [2]

MALES CUT TO PIECES

In retribution for what the Paris government saw as a counter-revolution, the Convention exacted its revenge on some of the greatest people of the city. These included many of the Lyonnais notables. All were executed. But the severest measure taken against the citizens of Lyons was the act of savagery inflicted upon their young **MEN** who were **CUT TO PIECES**. [3]

What happened [in Lyon] was far worse than the Paris terror... the volleys on the plain of Brotteaux, where on the 14th Frimaire, [4th December] sixty-four young men, all firmly bound, were mown down by grape shot and then dispatched with sword thrusts. (Madelin)

UNHAPPY AFFRAY

"Fouché remained in Lyons till he had murdered 2000 persons 'whose blood-stained corpses,' he writes 'cast into the Rhône... inspire a feeling of terror and a picture of omnipotence of the people on either bank.'" [4] – **AN UNHAPPY AFFRAY** had been Nostradamus's description.

The final line of the oracle continues the theme of counter-revolution, but switches attention to *Nantes*. Like Lyons, *Nantes* was also the scene of a revolt against the Paris government, but with motives more aligned with those who were fighting for the royalist cause in the Vendée.

SHRIEKS, HOWLING AT NANTES, PITEOUS TO SEE

In October 1793, the siege at *Nantes* was broken, but only after the Republican Army surrounding the city had been heavily reinforced by regiments taken from the Grand Army at Mainz. Retribution swiftly followed: *"The most notorious massacres were at Nantes, where . . . Jean-Baptiste Carrier, supplemented the guillotine with what he called 'vertical deportations' in the river Loire."* In short, guillotining was *'supplemented'* by mass drowning. *Nantes* was a slave port, and there was an abundance of shallow boats on the Loire, which had been used to convey their human cargo down river. These boats gave Carrier the idea for his 'noyades'. Men and women that had been sentenced for execution were first stripped naked (victims' clothes were considered a perquisite), then bound together *vis-à-vis* in what were termed *'Republican Marriages'*. In this state they were put on board the boats. Once the vessels were far enough from the shore, they were scuttled, and the condemned pairs sank beneath the waves: the river finally silencing the terrified **SHRIEKS** and **HOWLING**, which Nostradamus found so **PITEOUS TO SEE**.[5]

Instrumental in bringing Marie Antoinette to the guillotine was Maximilien de Robespierre. His rise to power began with his election to the Third Estate in 1789 as the representative for Artois. During the next five years he achieved total power in France. Nostradamus provides a brief pen portrait of this man.

C.VIII: 41

Esleu fera Renard ne fonnant mot,
Faifant le faint public vivant pain d'orge,
Tyranizer après tant a un coup,
Mettant a pied des plus grands fur la gorge.

The sly man of malice will be elected, not a word ringing out,
Playing the public saint, living on barley bread,
Afterwards, tyrannizing so many by a blow,
Putting with foot on the neck of the greatest ones.

Renard = sly, also paragram – Renar[t] (O.Fr.) malice.

Before Robespierre came to power, *"No one who knew him then pictured him as a revolutionary. He professed – and for several years continued to profess – his belief in the King as a 'young and wise monarch', part of whose 'august character' was a 'sacred passion for the happiness of the people'."* Once in public office, his attitude and opinions dramatically changed, betraying the **SLYNESS** of his former attitude. As one of his political opponents commented: *"He possessed a truly Machiavellian skill . . . in dividing men and sowing differences between them, of enticing others to test the ground for him and then either abandoning them or supporting them as prudence or ambition dictated."* The **MALICIOUS** side to his nature soon after became apparent: – *"he had for every dissenter from his narrow creed the one and simple remedy of the guillotine . . . which in Paris alone cost two thousand six hundred victims."* [1]

Although Robespierre took no part in the attack on the Tuileries (10 August 1792), *"that same afternoon his section (an administrative subdivision of Paris), Les Piques, nominated him to the insurrectional Commune."* Three weeks later, the terrible September Massacres took place. And on 5 September, without having done more than excuse these crimes: *"the people of Paris elected him to head the delegation to the national Convention."* It was as their representative that: *"The National Convention elected him president, on June 4, by a vote of 216 out of 220."*

It is an interesting fact that although Robespierre was the *elected* President of the National Convention, *'His voice was weak,'* and he often struggled to make himself heard: **NOT A WORD RINGING OUT.** [2]

Despite the revolutionaries' anti-Christian fervour, Robespierre publicly acknowledged the existence of a Supreme Being, and for his own part received the sobriquet of *'the incorruptible'.* Later, in a display of sanctimonious passion, he organized the *'Festival of the Supreme Being'* (8 June 1794), during which, in the role of: *'true priest of the Supreme Being';* that is, **PLAYING THE PUBIC SAINT**, he delivered a sermon to the people, explaining to them: *"the relations between moral and religious ideas with republican principles."* [3]

Robespierre's sister Charlotte confirmed that her brother ate only *"a meagre breakfast of bread and milk . . . He seems to have been almost completely uninterested in food, living mainly on bread, fruit and coffee."* We see from this, that for solid food, apart from fruit, he was LIVING almost solely ON BREAD.[4]

TYRANNIZING SO MANY BY A BLOW

Once installed as the virtual dictator of the nation, Robespierre set about eliminating those whose republican ideas failed to match his own. In the space of six months, three opposition groups were sent to their deaths. First to go were the twenty-two leading members of the Girondin party; they were executed on 31 October 1793. On 24 March 1794 it was the turn of the Hébertists, with Jacques Hébert, and nineteen of his supporters guillotined. Less than a fortnight later (5 April) Robespierre turned his malice in the direction of the Dantonists, and another nineteen political opponents were sent to the guillotine. AFTER WHICH, his *Law of Suspects* (17 September) introduced a period that became known as the *Great Terror*. During this phase, the guillotine worked relentlessly, TYRANNIZING SO MANY BY A BLOW. Presumably, *by a blow* is meant to suggest a *blow* to the back of the neck by the falling blade of the guillotine. Certainly, the execution machine worked unceasingly during that time, until the gutters in the surrounding streets ran red with the lifeblood of those it had beheaded.[5]

PUTTING WITH FOOT ON THE NECKS OF THE GREATEST ONES

Robespierre *"entered the Committee of Public safety on July 28, 1793 . . . and for one amazing year . . . was the real ruler of France."* It was while in this position of power that he was able to PUT his FOOT ON THE NECKS OF THE GREAT ONES; e.g., Marie Antoinette (16 October); the Girondin leaders (31 October); the duc d'Orléans, (6 November); Madame Roland (8 November); Jean-Sylvain Bailly (11 November), Antoine Barnave (29 November); Jacques Hébert (24 March); Georges Danton, Camille Desmoulins, Charles Delacroix, Fabre d'Églantine, Hérault de Séchelles (5 April).[6] Moreover, the seer's reference to *the neck* tends to draw particular attention to the guillotine. For, it was *the neck* that lay directly beneath the blade.

The year 1793 saw the number of executions in France steadily increase. Amongst those who went to the guillotine was the Queen; her death was referred to earlier. But, as with other great events in history, Nostradamus finds reason to return to this subject again and again: each time presenting the facts from a different angle. In the next quatrain, the seer describes not only the Queen's emotional state as she approached the guillotine, but also the instrument of her death itself, which did not come into use until 1792.

C.I: 82

Quand les columnes de bois grande tremblée,
D'Aufter conduicte couuerte de rubriche:
Tant vuidera dehors grand affemblée,
Trembler Vienne & le pais d'Auftriche.

*When the columns of wood have trembled [the] great lady,
Conducted by the merciless one, clothed with rubric,
He will purge so many out from the great Assembly,
Vienna trembling and the land of Austria.*

Columnes, (Latinism) column/a; grande, (great one, feminine); aufter, (O.Fr.) âpre – cruel, austere; Tant, (Latinism) tantum; vuidera, (O.Fr.) vuidier – purger de.

WHEN THE COLUMNS OF WOOD

The guillotine became the official method of execution in France after the penal code became law in October 1791. It consisted of two upright **COLUMNS OF WOOD** with a trapezium shaped blade suspended beneath a crossbar at the top. At the base were two slats of wood, with semicircles cut from each edge: when closed, they formed a circle – Sanson's little window as it became called. A plank of wood was laid lengthwise before the slats, upon which the victim's body lay flat, so that when the slats were clamped together, the victim's neck lay directly beneath the blade. The entire machine was placed on an elevated platform to provide a better view for those watching.

HAVE TREMBLED THE GREAT LADY

On the morning of 16 October 1793, Marie Antoinette, the former **GREAT LADY** of France, left the Conciergerie to be taken to the guillotine. The artist, Jacques-Louis David sketched her as she travelled in a tumbrel to the *Place de la Révolution*. Upon arrival, she bravely mounted the platform, but upon seeing the great blade suspended between **THE COLUMNS OF WOOD** her nerve failed, and it was *"only at the last minute on the scaffold itself did she begin to tremble."* [1]

CONDUCTED BY THE MERCILESS ONE

Between October 1793 and April 1794, Maximilien de Robespierre, aided by Georges Couthon and Louis Antoine de Saint-Just,

273

rose to become the virtual dictator of France. Known as *'the Incorruptible'*, he was austere, MERCILESS and quite ruthless in pursuing his single-minded ambition, which was to mould the country according to his wishes. For dissenters, he had a simple solution – the guillotine.

At the trial of Louis XVI, Robespierre had urged the court not to give special consideration to the Queen: *"send her before the courts, like all other persons charged with similar crimes,"* he insisted. On 27 March 1793, having accused Marie Antoinette of being: *'no less guilty'* than the late King, Robespierre *"suggested to the Convention that the former Queen should be brought before the new Revolutionary Tribunal, which had been set up on 10 March, for her crimes against the State."* This proposal BY THE MERCILESS ONE was acted upon, and on 3 August the Queen was CONDUCTED to the Conciergerie to await her trial.[2]

CLOTHED WITH RUBRIC

As further confirmation that Robespierre was, indeed, *the merciless one*, Nostradamus has provided a little more detail. For example, when making his speeches, Robespierre gained the reputation of being *'a fanatical believer in the inspired text'* and the public adored his oratory. It is also interesting to note that the word *clothed* has been chosen to describe his *rubric*. Robespierre was known to be a fastidious dresser. *"Green was the shade he most often favoured in the choice of the clothes he wore, with such attention to their immaculate neatness and precision of cut."*[3] Together, CLOTHED WITH RUBRIC is a phrase wherein both words apply specifically to Robespierre.

HE WILL PURGE SO MANY OUT FROM THE GREAT ASSEMBLY

Among the political factions at the time were a group known as the Girondins. They were a loosely formed party of moderates from the Gironde department who made up part of the Legislative *Assembly*, and who had joined together in 1791. In 1793 the Girondins began mounting attacks against the Mountain, whose chief spokesman was Robespierre. But these attacks led to their unpopularity, and *twenty-two* of their number were PURGED FROM THE ASSEMBLY and prosecuted.

In March 1794, Hébert invited the enmity of Robespierre. Hébert had been the vigorous instrument in bringing to trial both Marie Antoinette and the Girondin leaders. But his anti-Christian campaign angered Robespierre, who accused the Hébertists of a counter-revolutionary conspiracy. Hébert, together with *nineteen* of his friends, were thereafter PURGED FROM THE ASSEMBLY. On 24 March, they were guillotined.

In the following month, it was the Dantonists who fell under Robespierre's vengeful eye. Convinced by his belief that liberty could only be obtained if criminals lost their heads, the *austere one* saw Danton's indulgent attitude as a dangerous opportunity for counter-revolution. On the 30 March, the Committee of Public Safety ordered Danton's arrest, and on 5 April, after a trial cut short to ensure a conviction, Danton, and *seventeen* of his followers were taken in three red tumbrels to the place de la Révolution, and guillotined.

In the space of just six months, following the execution of Marie Antoinette, Robespierre, *the austere orator* of the revolution had PURGED SO MANY FROM THE Legislative ASSEMBLY, the Girondins, the Hébertists, and the Dantonists; a total of sixty in all.[4]

VIENNA TREMBLING AND THE LAND OF AUSTRIA

On 16 October 1793 VIENNA was TREMBLING as the inhabitants of the city allowed their thoughts to dwell upon what was taking place in Paris that day. Marie Antoinette, the daughter of Maria Theresa and Francis I, also the sister of Emperors Joseph II and Leopold II, having been transferred to the Conciergerie to stand trial for treason, had been found guilty and was to be beheaded at midday.

That same day, 16 October, outside of Vienna, THE LAND OF AUSTRIA was likewise TREMBLING. Josias of Coburg commanding the Habsburg Austrian army was suffering defeat at the hands of Jean-Baptiste Jourdan and Lazare Carnot in the battle of Wattignies, near Maubeuge in France. As a result, Austria was forced to lift the siege of Mauberge for the loss of 2,500 men.

The Great Terror was one of the bloodiest periods in French history. It brought the whole revolution to one fearsome climax. Nostradamus foretells how it ended.

C.II: 98

Celuy du fang refperfe le vifaige,
De la victime proche facrifiée:
Tonant en Leo augure par prefaige:
Mis eftre à mort lors pour la fiancée.

275

Behold, he of blood, the face splattered,
Of the victim, soon sacrificed:
Thunderer in Leo, a sign for a presage:
To be put to death at that time outside of assurance.

Celuy, (O.Fr. from the Latin – ecce ille); reſperſe, (Latinism) respers/us; proche, (O.Fr.) prochaine; Tonant, (Latinism) epithet of Jupiter; pour, (O.Fr.) dehors, en avant; fiancée, (O.Fr. epenthesis on the word fiance) assurance.

BEHOLD! HE OF BLOOD

Nostradamus introduces this prophecy by boldly announcing his subject: **BEHOLD! HE OF BLOOD**. It was Robespierre who ascended the political ladder to become virtual dictator of France, and who frequently spoke of that *'cleansing bath of blood'* as a means for achieving his goal. In his time as dictator of France, it was estimated he was responsible for guillotining 17,000 persons: many of whom were innocent victims that had been wrongfully accused.[1]

HIS FACE SPLATTERED

His own life came to its timely close with **HIS FACE SPLATTERED** in blood. A gendarme named Charles-André Méda, who had been sent to arrest him, shot at him, hitting him in the face: *"the bullet struck Robespierre, passed through his cheek, and shattered his jaw."* (Madelin). The next morning *'the incorruptible'* was hauled before the court with a blood soaked bandage holding his shattered jaw in place.[2]

THE VICTIM SOON SACRIFICED

How perfectly ironic it was that Robespierre should have concluded his major speeches with the words: *"I offer my personal sacrifice for the good of the patrie."* Because, on 28 July 1794, he was allowed to do just that: upon being found guilty, he was sentenced to immediate execution.[3] The sentence was carried out that same evening, with **THE VICTIM SOON SACRIFICED**. Nostradamus's bitter humour can be seen at play again.

THUNDERER IN LEO, A SIGN FOR A PRESAGE

Nostradamus next provides the period of the year when Maximilien Robespierre met his end. 28 July occurs at the time when the sun is **IN LEO**, and for good measure he names the dictator, **THUNDERER**. The Latin word 'Tonant' means *'Thunderer (epithet for Jupiter)'*. Jupiter was the Roman god for whom *"the cult of Jupiter Optimus Maximus ('the best and greatest') began under the Etruscan kings."*[4]

Note Jupiter's cognomen: – Maximus. By using this, **THUNDERER IN LEO** becomes equivalent to *Maximus in Leo*. But *"Maximilian . . . is derived from the Latin word maximus."*[5] And so, by translation, we obtain *Maximilien in Leo*, which, as Nostradamus predicted would be **A SIGN FOR A PRESAGE**. For Maximilien Robespierre, **THUNDERER IN LEO** was indeed a *sign*, since it *presaged* his death.

TO BE PUT TO DEATH AT THAT TIME, OUTSIDE OF ASSURANCE

One month earlier in June 1794, the Committee of Public Safety had passed Robespierre's *'law of 22 Prairial'*. This was the law that finally brought down the legislator – 'hoist by his own petard'. What it did was to hasten the process of execution, but it also threatened the safety of almost everyone.

> *Defence lawyers were dispensed with; so were witnesses unless the 'formality' of calling them was considered 'necessary to discover accomplices' . . . The Tribunal was no longer required to interrogate the accused before their public trial, since this merely 'confused the conscience of the judges'; now, in the absence of positive proof, juries must be satisfied with 'moral proof'.*

As Couthon remarked, *"For a citizen to become a suspect, it is sufficient that rumour accuses him."* Or, as Nostradamus rephrased it: **TO BE PUT TO DEATH AT THAT TIME, OUTSIDE OF ASSURANCE.**[6]

With the guillotine working full time, and the Revolution already consuming its underlings in what became known as the *'Grande Terreur'*, it would not be long before those at the very top became victims too. By 1794, Robespierre had cleared the way for what was increasingly seen as his tyrannical dictatorship. Lesser members of the government began to grow frightened, and in a dramatic *coup*, Robespierre and his two satellites, Couthon and Saint-Just, were arrested, summarily tried, and sent to the guillotine, all within the space of twenty-four hours. The next quatrain sets the scene of the Great Terror, and ends with some well-chosen descriptive phrases that were totally apt at the time this oracle became fulfilled.

C.II: 42

Coq, chiens, & chats, de sang seront repeus,
Et de la plaie du tyrant trouué mort.
Au lict d'vn autre iambes & bras rompus,
Qui n' auoit peur mourir de cruelle mort.

Cock, dogs and cats will be fed with blood,
And with the wound of the tyrant, death is judged:
On the bed of one other, legs & arms broken,
Somebody not having fear, dying by a cruel death.

repeus, (past historic) repaitre; lict, (O.Fr.) bed, couch, pallet; Qui, (O.Fr.) somebody

The opening line presents a perfectly recognizable picture of France during the Terror. This was a time when the revolution finally peaked with an orgy of decapitations resulting from Robespierre's *'Law of Suspects'*. This piece of legislation authorized the arrest of anyone suspected of counter-revolutionary involvement. The death sentence was usually applied as a matter of course.

COCK, DOGS AND CATS FED WITH BLOOD

The Latin word 'gallus' is a homonym, and means both 'Gaul' and COCK. Hence: *"the 'Red Cock' – that symbol of pillage and arson of the French Revolution."* [1] For this is a prediction of the time when THE COCK was FED by a BLOODLUST. So many heads were being daily sliced from their bodies during the Great Terror that DOGS AND CATS in the neighbouring surround WERE FED WITH BLOOD,[2] as they eagerly lapped up the human life force, spilt in such profusion from the systematic falling of the Paris blade.

THE WOUND OF THE TYRANT

But in July 1794 Robespierre, himself, was taken into custody by deputies who feared they might be next in line for the guillotine. The circumstances of his arrest are given in the previous oracle, including a reference to THE WOUND OF THE TYRANT. Robespierre received a bullet through the cheek, claimed to have been fired by Constable Méda who was first on the scene.[3] However, an alternative version suggests that the *wound* was actually caused by Robespierre, himself, in a bungled suicide attempt.

DEATH IS JUDGED

After a painful night spent suffering his injury, during which several teeth were removed, Robespierre was brought before the court next morning. Although unable to speak, he was tried upon recognition, and in accordance with the *Law of Suspects*, DEATH WAS JUDGED to be the appropriate sentence. It was carried out that evening, but only after the guillotine was hastily re-erected at the *Place de la Révolution*, especially for his execution.[4]

Robespierre was not alone. His two closest companions, Couthon and Saint-Just: men who shared his views and his power joined him on the scaffold. Both appear in this oracle.

ON THE BED OF ONE OTHER, LEGS AND ARMS BROKEN

Georges Couthon, although politically active, was a paraplegic. At some stage in his life he had suffered paralysis in both legs – probably as a result of meningitis – and could only move around **ON A** mobile **BED**; possibly a horizontal tricycle type of wheelchair that supported his legs but with a raised back. At the time of Robespierre's arrest, Couthon was with the dictator inside the Hôtel de Ville. But, alarmed at seeing his own arrest was imminent, he attempted to escape by manoeuvring his *bed* down a flight of stairs. He failed, with terrible consequences. His wheelchair hurtled out of control, and he ended up helplessly at the foot of the stairs: *"in appalling pain, his bent limbs smashed from the fall."* [5]

SOMEBODY NOT HAVING FEAR, DYING BY A CRUEL DEATH

The third member of this trio was Louis Antoine Léon de Saint-Just, young, handsome, and with a reputation for icy coolness in any situation. He was arrested, along with Robespierre and Couthon, and next day was executed **NOT HAVING** shown the least **FEAR,** even though **DYING BY A CRUEL DEATH.** *"Saint-Just went to his death every bit the Roman stoic, in which role he had evidently cast himself."* [6] (Schama).

This next oracle moves the clock forward to the lone survivor of the royal family, locked away inside the Temple tower. Marie Thérèse, daughter of Marie Antoinette and Louis XVI. She is identified by reference to her mother, and to her cousin, whom she eventually married after her release from prison. Once again, Nostradamus slips in a name that is exactly right for the time of the oracle's fulfilment.

C.X: 17

La royne Ergaſte voiant ſa fille bleſme,
Par vn regret dans l'eſtomach enclos,
Crys lamentables ſeront lors d'Angoleſme,
Et aux germains mariage forclos.

The Foreign Queen (a prisoner, devastated) seeing her daughter pale,
Through a lament during the stomach enclosure,
They will make distressing wails in the time of Angoulême,
And marriage for the cousins, finally.

Ergaſte, (Latinism) Ergastul/um, also (2 anagrams: gaster[e], (O.Fr.) dévaster, & es-tra[n]ge, (O.Fr.) foreign); regret, (O.Fr.) plainte; enclos, (O.Fr.) enceinte; forclos, (O.Fr.) finalement.

THE FOREIGN QUEEN DEVASTATED, A PRISONER

The capitalization of 'Ergaste' emphasizes its importance. From it, we obtain three key words that describe the situation of Marie Antoinette during the months before her execution. The French QUEEN was Austrian, and therefore FOREIGN. She was being held under house arrest inside the Temple Tower, and therefore a PRISONER. And on 16 January 1793 she had every reason to be DEV-ASTATED, for on that day her husband Louis XVI had been sentenced to die beneath the blade of the guillotine.[1]

SEEING HER DAUGHTER PALE

On the evening of 20 January, the night before the execution, the King was allowed to visit his family for one last time. It was during this final farewell, with the emotional stress of parting proving too stressful for the QUEEN'S DAUGHTER, that the little girl GREW PALE. The King was about to leave the room, *"when the Princesse Royale, the King's daughter, suddenly threw herself at her father and collapsed in a dead faint. Bringing her round was the family's last embrace."*[2]

A LAMENT DURING THE STOMACH ENCLOSURE

From the moment of the King's death onwards, Marie Antoinette remained bowed down with a grief that went too deep for words. . . . She wanted suitable mourning clothes . . . [and] asked for [and received] a black taffeta cloak, fichu, skirt and gloves.

She also asked for black curtains and a black coverlet but these were refused. Nostradamus's phrase does, however, conceal a remarkably clever piece of timing, because the words: *a lament during the stomach enclosure* provides the exact date of Marie Antoinette's own execution. The period of her *lament* began with news of her husband's death sentence on 16 January and it continued for exactly nine months, until her own death on 16 October, which is the nine-month period of THE STOMACH ENCLOSURE during pregnancy.[3] But instead of enclosing a child, she was nursing a LAMENT. At the end of this period, precisely to the day, the Queen was guillotined.

THEY WILL MAKE DISTRESSING WAILS IN THE TIME OF ANGOULÊME

The French Revolution began in 1789 and ended in 1799; hence the DISTRESSING WAILS of its victims throughout this decade. But, this same period marks THE TIME OF ANGOULÊME. In 1789 at Versailles, Louis XVI's enforced removal to Paris signalled to his brother, the duc d'Artois, that it was time to leave the country. He did so with immediate effect, taking with him his wife and two sons, the dukes of *Angoulême* and Berri.

Marie Thérèse, having remained with her parents, was later held inside the Temple until 26 December 1795. Four years after her release, she married Artois' son, and became the duchesse d'ANGOULÊME. Hence, *Angoulême's* departure from France coincided with the start of the Revolution; his marriage reunited him with France and coincided with the end of the Revolution.[4]

MARRIAGE FOR THE COUSINS, FINALLY
Angoulême might well marry his first cousin, the daughter of Louis XVI who left the prison of the Temple for Vienna in December 1795 . . . Finally, on 10 June 1799 she was married to the Duc de Angoulême at Mittau.[5]

The marriage between THE COUSINS had been arranged before the *Princesse Royale* was taken to the Tower, but their MARRIAGE only FINALLY became possible after her release.

This next oracle is one of special interest because of its cryptic, yet unique way of naming the little boy who should have become Louis XVII. The quatrain also dates this period of time according to the Revolutionary Calendar. The Republic had designed this new dating system to replace the Gregorian calendar, because under that system, the number of years dated back to the birth of Christ: something a de-Christianised country did not want to be reminded of.

C.IX: 17

Le tiers premier pis que ne fit Neron,
Vuidez vaillant que fang humain refprandre:
R'edifier fera le forneron,
Siecle d'or, mort, nouueau Roy grand efclandre.

The third foremost worst, which Nero never did,
Exempted from great qualities, as human blood pours out:
It will make to re-educate the baker's boy,
Period of [d]or, death, new king, great scandal.

Vuidez, (O.Fr.) exempted from; vaillant, (O.Fr.) doué de grandes qualités; r'edifier, (O.Fr.) instruire, enseigner; forneron, (O.Fr. fournier[e]) a baker, a woman baker, hence, fourneron: baker's boy; efclandre, (O.Fr.) scandale.

In France during the *Ancien Regime*, the reigning monarch had ruled by divine right. It was therefore his prerogative to summon together the Estates General to discuss any pressing problems, but only if it was considered necessary. There were three estates: the first was the clergy, the second the nobility and *the third* included professional men. In 1788, a fiscal crisis occurred in France, and it was decided, for the first time since 1614, to convene the Estates General. They met at Versailles in June 1789, and it was from the disruption occurring during this convention that the seeds of the French Revolution were sewn.

THE THIRD FOREMOST WORST

Once the overthrow of the monarchy had been achieved, the nobility was dispersed and the Second Estate disappeared. At the same time a programme of de-Christianising France swept through the land, and this brought to an end the power of the First Estate. With the first and second estates removed from power, THE THIRD Estate became FOREMOST.[1] It also became the WORST. The catalogue of crimes against both clergy and ordinary citizens, committed by the Third Estate, is far too long to be contained in a single paragraph. For brevity, one may simply call to mind the September Massacres of 1792, in which many hundreds of priests, nuns and novices were put to the sword, or the mass drowning carried out at Nantes, where *'Republican Baptisms'* involved locking priests into the belly of a boat before sinking it in the river Loire. At Gonnord, thirty children were deliberately buried alive. Sentences of death were passed for the most trivial of reasons; and trials, if they can be called that, made Justice hide her head in shame.

> *Hundreds of innocent people suffered . . . some of them through clerical and administrative errors, or even because their accusers chose not to spare them. Others were sentenced on the strength of denunciations by jealous or vindictive neighbours.[3]*

WHICH NERO NEVER DID

Nero has acquired a much deserved reputation for brutality against Christians.

> *Nero had begun the persecution of Christians (daubing them with pitch and burning them alive as torches for his nightly garden parties or sewing*

them in the skins of wild animals to be hunted by dogs) [although] this was limited in duration and location.[2]

EXEMPT FROM GREAT QUALITIES AS HUMAN BLOOD POURS OUT

In the midst of this heinous carnival of judicial carnage were the politicians who, being **EXEMPT FROM GREAT QUALITIES** finally yielded to poetic justice and handed out death sentences to each other: **AS HUMAN BLOOD POURED OUT** from those caught up in this frenzy of political madness.

> *... day after day, the guillotining continued. Unsuccessful generals suffered with fallen politicians, men convicted of publishing counter-revolutionary writings or of airing royalist opinions with deserters and traitors. . . . Throughout the autumn and winter of 1793 the Terror was maintained unabated. . . . Nearly 3,000 executions took place in Paris; about 14,000 in the provinces.*[4]

Inside the Temple tower at that time was the heir to the French throne, eight-year-old Louis Charles. He had begun life as the younger brother of the next in line for the throne, but his brother Louis Joseph died 4 June 1789, and so Louis Charles became the new Dauphin. By then he had already received a preliminary education in writing, drawing and natural history from his tutor, the Abbé d'Avaux who: *"filled him full of moral maxims and classical anecdotes."*

IT WILL RE-EDUCATE

But during his incarceration inside the Temple, it was decided *"to retrain – or brainwash – the former Dauphin . . . The Commune's prosecutor, Chaumette, had declared the previous year: 'I wish to give him [Louis Charles] some education. I will take him from his family to make him lose the idea of rank.'"* The tutor appointed to **RE-EDUCATE** the little boy was Antoine Simon, a cobbler. *"Dirty books, rowdy songs, blasphemy and brandy—that was the regime which Simon found perfectly natural for his pupil, since it was his own."*[5]

THE BAKER'S BOY

Nostradamus has identified Louis-Charles as **THE BAKER'S BOY**. The Dauphin obtained this nickname from the *'poissardes'*. These were the market women and fishwives who demanded that the royal family remove to Paris and take up residence in the *Palais de Tuileries* (5 October 1789). During the royal family's enforced journey to the capital, the cheering women, who were celebrating their triumph at removing Louis XVI, Marie Antoinette and Louis Charles from Versailles, sang that they were bringing: *"the* *baker, the baker's wife and 'the baker's boy' to Paris."*[6] The women's emphasis on baking was because of the shortage of bread at that time caused by a poor harvest.

The final line of this quatrain – if Nostradamus's cryptic tendencies are ignored – appears to speak of a 'golden age' (*Siecle d'or*). The time of the French Revolution was anything but that. Instead, what the oracle is really referring to is the Republican Calendar, in which each month was renamed so that it would correctly reflect the nature of the season in which it occurred.

PERIOD OF 'DOR'

THE PERIOD OF 'DOR' therefore occurred in the summer months of MESSIDOR, THERMIDOR and FRUCTIDOR.[7] And indeed, it was the summer of 1795 that coincided with the fulfilment of the last part of this oracle.

DEATH

In the summer of 1795, ten-year-old Louis-Charles, *the baker's boy,* died from tuberculosis; his DEATH was *"exacerbated by conditions that were at best neglectful, at worst brutal."*[8]

NEW KING

After the death of Louis Charles, nominally Louis XVII, the Comte de Provence, who at that time was in exile in Verona, at once declared himself to be the NEW KING, taking the title, Louis XVIII. *"He [also] announced that on his return to the throne he would restore the traditional three orders in France."*[9]

GREAT SCANDAL

Plans were soon underway for the restoration of the monarchy. On 27 June 1795 (9 Messidor III) an émigré army financed by English money, and aided by Chouan forces from the Vendée, landed on the southern coast of Brittany. But General Lazare Hoche and his Republican Army were there to meet the insurgent army. In the fierce battle between the two sides, seven hundred combatants, including ennobled members of the Ancient Regime, were taken prisoner. It was then that the GREAT SCANDAL took place. The captives, together with many titled members of the nobility, were executed by firing squad for high treason. The repercussions this caused in Europe was to continue for many years, further blackening the revolutionary movement.[10]

By 1795 the severity of the Revolution had almost run its course. Robespierre was dead, and deprived of their leader, the Jacobins faltered. It was during this political loss of direction that plans were made for returning France to its monarchical roots. This inevitably involved conflict, and it was while engaged in a street battle to replace the Republican parliament that a new player appeared on the world stage — Napoleon Bonaparte.

C.IX: 51

Contre les rouges fectes fe banderont,
Feu, eau, fer, corde par paix fe minera,
Au point mourir ceux qui machineront,
Fors vn que monde fur tout ruynera.

Sects will bind themselves together against the reds,
Fire, water, iron, rope: will diminish themselves through peace.
Those who will organize a conspiracy, dying at the occasion,
Except one who will lay ruin on the whole of the world.

banderont, (O.Fr.) lier; fe minera, (O.Fr.) décrôitre; point, (O.Fr.) occasion; Fors, (O.Fr.) hors; machineront, (O.Fr.) organiser un complot.

SECTS WILL BIND THEMSELVES TOGETHER AGAINST THE REDS

The fall of Robespierre brought to an end the reign of terror. All across France bands of people began to rise up against the excess of brutality that had been making victims of so many innocent people. In Paris, deprived of their leaders, the Jacobins became disorganized, and DIFFERENT SECTS; e.g., the Monarchists, Federalists, Girondists were among those who BOUND THEMSELVES TOGETHER in loose coalitions [1] AGAINST THE REDS. [2]

FIRE, IRON ROPE, DIMINISHING THROUGH PEACE

The end of the Terror, which had gripped France for more than half a decade, affected the number of EXECUTIONS, causing them to DIMINISH THROUGH the spread of PEACE. The materials used for meting out death sentences are mentioned in the oracle. FIRE refers to gunfire and the houses of the aristocracy that were torched, often while the occupants lay sleeping inside; WATER calls to mind the mass drowning – the *noyades* – that occurred, particularly at Nantes. ROPE needs little explanation; even less to those unfortunate enough to hear the blood-curdling yells directed at them: '*à la lanterne*' (a lamp-post that served as a gibbet in the early part of the Revolution). IRON refers to the guillotine, the cannon and the sword.

285

An opportunist attempt at **ORGANISING A CONSPIRACY** was made soon after the death of Robespierre. Royalists tried to seize power by taking advantage of a distracted administration. But their attempt was countered by stiff opposition from troops still loyal to the revolution. In a bloody battle that took place outside the *Palais de Tuileries* on 5 October 1795 – *'journées de Vendémiaire'* – the royalists came under massive firepower, many **DYING AT THE OCCASION.** By evening: *"when two or three hundred men had been killed or wounded on both sides, the fighting was over."* Napoleon Bonaparte, who had been appointed second in command under General Barras, later wrote: *"We killed a large number of them. They killed thirty of our men, and wounded sixty."*[3]

Here, for the first time, we encounter Napoleon Bonaparte. His famed *'whiff of grapeshot'*, which he afterwards claimed had scattered the insurrectionists and restored order, quickly brought him to the notice of the Directory. Three weeks later he had been put in charge of France's internal affairs.

There is an implied suggestion in the oracle's final phrase; it is that the **EXCEPTED ONE** not *dying at that occasion* will, himself, be a conspirator. Although Bonaparte was instrumental in putting down the October insurrection, his own conspiracy, the *coup d'état* of Brumaire (9 November 1799) had still to wait another four years before it was implemented. But when it did arrive, it brought with it a new era, involving **ONE WHO WILL LAY RUIN ON THE WHOLE WORLD.**[4]

As a closing note to this chapter, statisticians amongst the readership may be interested to note that of the 28 quatrains concerning events that occurred during the French Revolution, 9 are from Century IX and 7 from Century I. That is more than one half ($^4/_7$) from just these two sources.

7

THE NAPOLEONIC ERA

The present chapter begins with an oracle foretelling the emergence of Napoleon Bonaparte at the time of Louis XVI's declaration of war against Austria. This makes for a fitting start, because it was at Toulon in southern France where the artillery expertise of Bonaparte first came to prominence. This, in turn, led to the young artillery officer being given a role in defeating the Royalists during their attempt to seize control at the time of the Paris uprising in 1796. It was from this further success that Napoleon was promoted to command the Army of Italy. The conquests he made in northern Italy swiftly followed, but with it, came his invasion of Rome, and the ruin of the papacy. The oracle ends with Napoleon's coup d'état of 1799, which gave him control of France. Thus, in four lines, Nostradamus has provided an outline of Napoleon's rise from Republican soldier to First Consul.

C.VI: 25

Par Mars contraire fera la monarchie.
Du grand pefcheur en trouble ruyneux:
leune noir rouge prendra la hierarchie,
Les proditeurs iront iour bruyneux.

Through war, the monarchy will be contrary.
Concerning the great fisherman in ruinous trouble:
The young man, black, red, will take the priestly government,
The traitors will eject fiercely: day of mists.

prodicteurs, (Latinism) prodit/ors; iront, (O.Fr.) rendre furieux; bruyneux, (O.Fr.) mists.

THROUGH WAR, THE MONARCHY WILL BE CONTRARY.

In 1792, Louis XVI and Marie Antoinette were still nominally King and Queen of the French, but were also under mounting pressure from those who wanted to see France become a republic. The royal couple's plight was recognized abroad. Both the King's brothers, Provence and Artois, together with their sister, urged Austria to invade France. But despite agitating for this action, it was actually France that declared war on Austria (April 1792). Three months later, this declaration was followed by another, when France declared itself against Prussia.

Although opposed to war with the country of his wife's birth, even though it was aiming to restore him to his former power, Louis XVI *"felt compelled to give way to the demands for war which were now almost universal."* His brother had said if you make this declaration we will know that you have been forced to do so. In other words, **THROUGH WAR, THE MONARCHY WILL BE** holding a **CONTRARY** position to its declaration.

The disastrous beginning of the war led to the most violent demonstrations in the capital: rumours of counter-revolution were rife, the King and Queen were accused of conspiring with the enemy and an 'Austrian Committee' at the Tuileries was supposed to be betraying military intelligence to Vienna. [1]

CONCERNING THE GREAT FISHERMAN

The great fisherman is an aptronym for the pope, and dates back to St. Peter, the fisherman who followed Christ as his apostle and became a fisher of men's souls. The Roman Church therefore adopted Peter as its first pope.

IN RUINOUS TROUBLE

Pope Pius VI soon found himself in most **RUINOUS TROUBLE** at the hands of Napoleon. After the young conqueror had invaded the

Papal States and routed the papal army at Ancona, *"[Pius VI] was forced to surrender Ferrara and Bologna together with valuable manuscripts, at the Treaty of Tolentino."* To add to his *trouble*, Pius was ordered to pay France a huge indemnity, and then made to vacate Rome. He never returned, and died at Valence on 29 August 1799.[2]

THE YOUNG MAN

THE YOUNG MAN is Napoleon Bonaparte, the instrument of Pius VI's *ruinous trouble*. In 1795, at the age of 26, he had been given command of the artillery at Toulon. His success there, in forcing the English to retreat, led Barras to appoint him brigadier-general and to employ him in defence of the Tuileries against the Royalists (13 Vendémiaire). This was the occasion of his celebrated *'whiff of grapeshot'*, which scattered the insurgents; it also rewarded him with command of the Army of Italy, and ultimately — *"a series of stunning victories over the Austro-Russian armies."*[3]

BLACK, RED, HE WILL TAKE THE PRIESTLY GOVERNMENT

Nostradamus has used the word *noir* in this oracle: a word he uses to signify: *'evil, falsehood, error'*, especially when applied to kings or leaders of men who cause the deaths of innocent people. It was in Italy that Bonaparte first exposed the more ruthless side of his nature: *"he bled them white by his taxation and military requisitions; he repressed with merciless severity the slightest resistance to his authority; he murdered the ancient and historic freedom of Venice."*[4] It is likely, however, that Nostradamus would have seen Bonaparte **BLACKENED** by his treatment of the Pope. After his military success in northern Italy, the Directory ordered their commander-in-chief to occupy Rome and disarm the papal army. In the course of this operation, the eighty-year-old pope, Pius VI, was arrested, and then ordered to leave the Vatican under escort. He never returned. His dismissal from Rome therefore allowed the Directory to **TAKE OVER THE PRIESTLY GOVERNMENT**.[5]

'Bonaparte was [also] a child of the revolution' and a former acquaintance of the Robespierre family. He was therefore — *"Regarded by the Montagnards, as politically reliable,"*[6] and every bit as **RED** as those who had brought down the monarchy.

THE TRAITORS WILL EJECT FIERCELY

In 1799, a group of politicians discontented with the nation's affairs suggested to Napoleon that he might *'purge'* the Assembly.

He agreed, and a plot was put together. It began with *'the false pretext of a Jacobin conspiracy'*. In response to this, and as a safety measure, the various Councils were transferred to the Orangery at St. Cloud. Lucien Bonaparte, President of the Council of Five Hundred, then put in place the next part of the plan. This required him to summon troops to CLEAR THE HALL AT BAYONET POINT by falsely declaring that daggers had been drawn against his brother. The plot worked. *"All through France the coup d'état of Brumaire (November 9) was acclaimed as the dawn of a new era."* [7]

DAY OF MISTS

Nostradamus had already foreseen the new revolutionary calendar introduced in 1792, which he referred to in his letter to Henri II (27 June 1558), and which he used in C.IX: 17. It will be recalled that during the de-Christianising of France, it was decided to rename the months in line with the seasons. Consequently, THE DAY OF MISTS according to the new calendar occurred in *"Brumaire (Month of Mist")*: [8] the date of Napoleon's *coup*.

Bonaparte was the first ruler of France since the publication of these prophecies to bear a name that had not previously been used by any earlier king. An intelligent guess could have come up with the same prediction that this would one day happen. But what places this prediction apart from inspired guesswork is the accurate detail that accompanies it, and for which history has since provided adequate confirmation.

The French Revolutionary Wars were an important part of the history of this period. Some mention has already been made of these, and it is to the *Battle of Fleurus* (1794), in which France defeated the Austrians, thereby providing the victors with an easy entrance to the Southern Netherlands that we now turn.

Fleurus is of special interest because it was one of the first battles to use a hot air balloon as an observation device. This next oracle refers to the balloon's inventor by name, barely disguising it in a split quatrain that introduces two subjects in the very first line.

C.V: 57

Iftra du mont Gaulfier & Auentin,
Qui par le trou aduertira l'armee:
Entre deux rocz fera prins le butin,
De Sext. manfol faillir la renommee.

Make way for Montgolfier and Aventine,
Which by reason of the orifice, one will direct the army:
Between two popes the booty will be taken,
Of the Sixth, lonely absentee, (seeming disabled) failing his renown.

Iſtra, (O.Fr.) s'écarter; mont Gaulfier, (mont G[o]lfier) = MONTGOLFIER; advertira, (Latinism) adver/to; roc, (synonym) pierre; i.e., Peter; Sext. (Latin abbreviation) Sext[us]; mansol, (Latin and O.Fr. portmanteau) L. man/sio + sol/us; O.Fr. mans + ole.

MAKE WAY FOR MONTGOLFIER

The opening words of this oracle indicate travel. The name **MONTGOLFIER** should therefore be instantly recognizable as the surname of two brothers: Joseph Michel and Jacques Etienne. Both men were co-inventors of the hot air balloon, for which the first publicly demonstrated flight took place as early as 1783.[1] It was, however, in 1793 and again in1794 that its military use became recognized.

AND AVENTINE

AVENTINE is one of the Seven Hills of Rome, and in this instance a metonymy for the papacy. The Pope's connection with travel began in 1798. This was the year that Napoleon's army invaded Rome and captured Pius VI. Being uncertain what to do next, other than separate the Pope from his influence inside the Vatican, the Directory sent the Holy Father through Italy and into France, on an extended journey lasting eighteen months. The Pope's travels took him through Siena, Florence, Parma, Piacenza, Turin, Briancon, Grenoble, and finally to Valence, where he died.[2]

WHICH BY REASON OF THE ORIFICE, ONE WILL DIRECT THE ARMY

Ten years after the discovery of the hot air balloon, its military capabilities were being explored for observation purposes. It was first tried at the Battle of Maubeuge (1793). And at the Battle of Fleurus (1794) – *"A French reconnaissance balloon, l'Entreprenant, continuously informed General of Division Jean-Baptiste Jourdan about Austrian movements."*[3] **THE ORIFICE** is the inlet for the hot air required to raise the balloon off the ground.

BETWEEN TWO POPES

The two popes referred to are Pius VI and Pius VII. Pius VI died in August 1799, but it was not until March 1800 that his successor, Pius VII was elected.

THE BOOTY WILL BE TAKEN

During the six month interval BETWEEN these TWO POPES Rome was sacked of its treasures; that is, THE BOOTY TAKEN.

Palaces, galleries and churches were stripped; antique sculptures, Renaissance paintings, tapestries, and precious stones and metals were packed up and loaded on to wagons . . . On one day gold and silver bars worth 15 000 000 scudi were carried off; on another 386 diamonds, 333 emeralds, 692 rubies, 208 sapphires and numerous other precious stones and pearls, many of them prized off papal tiaras, were sent to Paris. [4]

OF THE SIXTH, LONELY ABSENTEE, SEEMING DISABLED

Pius THE SIXTH became the LONELY ABSENTEE, forced to suffer eighteen months *alone* while separated from his seat in Rome. He was also very ill at this time, and died shortly after arriving in Valence.

FAILING HIS RENOWN

Pius VI was elected to the throne of St. Peter on 15 February 1775. Towards the end of his reign, he had become *renowned* in the Christian world as the longest serving pope since the commencement of the papacy. But, on 29 August 1799 he died, aged 82, thereby FAILING HIS RENOWN.[5]

C.IV: 54

Du nom qui onques ne fut au Roy gaulois,
Iamais ne fut vn fouldre ſi craintif,
Tremblant l'Italie, l'Eſpagne, & les Anglois,
De femme eſtrangiers grandement attentif.

By a name which at any time was not for a French King,
No never was a thunderbolt so fearful,
Italy, Spain and the English trembling,
Concerning female foreigners, handsomely attentive.

Iamais ne, – not ever = never; femme, (O.Fr.) femelle.

BY A NAME WHICH AT ANY TIME WAS NOT FOR A FRENCH KING

Napoleon was the first ruler of France, since Francis I came to power in 1515, to bear a name that was different from those who had reigned before him. After France became a republic, it was first the Convention, and then the Directory that governed the country. But in 1799, Napoleon's *coup d'état* changed the power structure, and within the space of a few years he had become Emperor of the French.[1]

NO, NEVER WAS A THUNDERBOLT SO FEARFUL

The era termed Napoleonic defines a succession of wars from

1798 to 1815 in which, proportionately, more people were killed than during the First World War, with its estimated military deaths of 8·5 million. Many of the battles fought by France during this era of almost continuous warfare have since given their names to history; e.g. Nile, Marengo, Trafalgar, Austerlitz, Jena, Borodino, Wagram, Waterloo; etc.[2] NEVER before in the history of France HAD THERE BEEN SUCH A THUNDERBOLT as Napoleon; and with A NAME THAT WAS NEVER BEFORE GIVEN TO A FRENCH KING.

ITALY, SPAIN, AND THE ENGLISH TREMBLING

Nostradamus next singles out the three countries that were to be especially affected by Bonaparte's rule. ITALY was invaded and conquered by Napoleon on two occasions. The first campaign was undertaken in 1796 and the second in 1800.[3] SPAIN was forced to endure the Peninsula War from 1808 until 1815.[4] And between 1799 and 1815, THE ENGLISH were engaged is a series of five separate coalitions against France: during which, two outstanding victories were achieved: one at sea (Trafalgar), the other on land (Waterloo).[5] All three countries, *Spain, Italy and England* subsequently lent their names to Napoleonic armies; they were: *L'Armée D'Italie* (April 1796), *L'Armée de l'Angleterre* (1803), *L'Armée D'Espagne* (November 1808). Once again, as in C.I: 82, Nostradamus uses the word 'TREMBLING' to mean an awareness of approaching danger.

CONCERNING FEMALE FOREIGNERS, HANDSOMELY ATTENTIVE

The Oracle now shifts attention to Bonaparte's sexual interests. Napoleon married twice. His first wife Joséphine was born into an aristocratic Creole family on the island of Martinique. His second wife, Marie-Louise was an Austrian princess: daughter of the Emperor Francis II. The mistress, by whom he had a son, was the Polish countess Maria Walewska. His other mistress, Giuseppina Grassini, was an Italian opera singer, whose career he continued to sponsor, even long after their affair had ended. He also fostered a close friendship with the Swiss intellectual, Germaine de Staël.[6]

Nostradamus next takes a prophetic look at Napoleon as Emperor. In doing so, he remarks upon the ruler's practice of raising those humbly born to princely titles. At the same time, he foresees Napoleon's ruthless streak. It is by no means a flattering description that is painted in this verse, but it is Bonaparte that fits the quatrain to a T.

C.I: 60

Vn Empereur naiftra pres d'Italie,
Qui à l'Empire fera vendu bien cher:
Diront auec quelz gens il fe ralie,
Qu'on trouuera moins prince que boucher.

An Emperor will be born close to Italy,
Who, to the Empire, will be sold very expensively:
They will remark with what people he rallies with,
When one will discover, less a prince than a butcher.

AN EMPEROR WILL BE BORN CLOSE TO ITALY

THE EMPEROR Napoleon Bonaparte was BORN on 15 August 1769 at Ajaccio in Corsica.[1] The Island lies in the Mediterranean, directly to the west of Rome and south of Genoa. It is therefore sufficiently CLOSE TO ITALY to be a fulfilment of this prophecy. In fact, it is closer to the Italian coastline than it is to mainland France.

WHO WILL BE SOLD VERY EXPENSIVELY TO THE EMPIRE

It was by a series of spectacular battles in which he repeatedly emerged victorious that Napoleon was able TO establish AN EMPIRE. It eventually stretched from Spain to the Baltic, and included Italy and the Illyrian provinces as well as much of what is now Poland.

In 1804, Bonaparte accepted the title of Emperor.[2] But the people of France paid a heavy price for their Empire. *"Estimates of casualties over the eleven years fluctuate enormously; some authorities place them as high as 1,750,000."* (Chandler). As well as lives lost, the cost in money was equally massive. On one occasion: *"At least [three-hundred-million francs] for the army alone,"* was requested from the Treasury. Even this amount was considered *"paltry compared with the vast revenues Napoleon had been used to."* (Coote). In 1812, it was reported that he spent nearly three times that sum.[3]

THEY WILL REMARK WITH WHAT PEOPLE HE RALLIES WITH

Unlike rulers in the past, Napoleon did not fraternize with members of the existing nobility. Instead, he chose talented individuals from working-class backgrounds as his close companions: individuals who shared his ideals. He recognized their value, and the contribution they were capable of making to the French Empire, and so he rewarded them with positions of power. Pierre Augereau rose from being the son of a stonemason to become Duke of Castiglione; André Masséna was a cabin boy whom Napoleon made Prince of Rivoli; Joachim Murat started life in an inn, but subsequently rose to become King of Naples, and Michael Ney, the son of a blacksmith, received the title, Prince of Moscowa.[4]

This oracle has so far presented Bonaparte in fairly uncritical terms. The final line veers away from this appreciative approach, and points accusingly at the man's taste for human butchery. Before 1804 Bonaparte was still a king in waiting, consequently, reference to him as a PRINCE must therefore predate his coronation.

WHEN ONE WILL DISCOVER HIM LESS A PRINCE THAN A BUTCHER

It was while conducting his military expedition in Egypt, from May 1798 to October 1799, that evidence of his *butchery* began to emerge. In October 1798, he ordered his chief of staff to cut the throats of all the prisoners, and dispose of their bodies in the Nile. While in Cairo, his Correspondence recorded that he was cutting off heads at the rate of five or six a day. But it was in March of the following year that the worst excess of butchery occurred. Three thousand men, holding out against Bonaparte, agreed to surrender on condition their lives would be spared. The French officer in charge of these negotiations agreed terms, but Napoleon countermanded these, and ordered that the rebels be executed. For good measure, he added another 1400 prisoners to this list of condemned men. *"He later attempted to explain this foul butchery in terms of military necessity."*[5]

Napoleon was a fatalist who saw himself as a man of destiny. This may be of help to someone attempting to understand his character. Quite whether the Emperor believed Laplace – the French mathematician who removed God from Newton's scheme of the universe, and who thought that: were the location and velocity of every particle in the universe known, natural laws could then be used to calculate future events – is not known. Napoleon did question Laplace about God's role in the universe, but the mathematician replied that he had no need for that hypothesis. Nostradamus was aware of Napoleon's fatalistic trait, and this is referred to it in the next oracle.

C.I: 76

D'vn nom farouche tel proferé fera,
Que les troys feurs auront fato le nom:
Puis grand peuple par langue & faict duira,
Plus que nul autre aura bruit & renom.

By a wild name, such a one will be pronounced,
Which the three sisters will obtain [as] the name for destiny:
Then a great nation will govern by tongue and deed,
More than no other, he will have fame and renown.

farouche, (O.Fr.) sauvage; fato, (Latin, ablative case from fat/um) destiny; duira, (O.Fr.) gouverner.

BY A WILD NAME, SUCH A ONE WILL BE PRONOUNCED

Stewart Robb, a former commentator of this oracle made the following observation: the emperors Napoleon (pronounced in French as Na-poll-y-on) and A-poll-y-on (a Greek name that interprets as 'Destroyer': see *Book of Revelation*: ix, 11) sound sufficiently close when **PRONOUNCED** in the French tongue for a comparison to be drawn. The poet Lord Byron was also aware of this similarity, and referred to Napoleon in *'Childe Harold's Pilgrimage'* – *"Conqueror and captive of the earth art thou! / She trembles at thee still, and thy wild name."* [1]

WHICH THE THREE SISTERS WILL OBTAIN THE NAME FOR DESTINY

In Greek Mythology it was believed that the Fates, who took human form as **THREE SISTERS**, were responsible for deciding each person's destiny. Napoleon accepted this fatalistic viewpoint. For, as he once admitted: *"All that is to happen is written down. Our hour is marked and we cannot prolong it a minute longer than fate has predestined."* [2] It is in the light of this admission that his biographers often like to portray him as a **MAN OF DESTINY**.

THEN A GREAT NATION WILL GOVERN BY TONGUE AND DEED

As one would expect from a Frenchman, France is referred to as **A GREAT NATION**. In the age of Napoleon, France certainly did **GOVERN** its growing Empire **BY TONGUE**; that is, by its administration, **AND** enforced its proclamations by **DEED** of force, if necessary.

Certain areas . . . were simply incorporated into the Grande Nation: Avignon (1791), Belgium (1795), Nice and Savoy (1796), Geneva and Mulhouse in Alsace (1798). The left-bank Rhineland, annexed . . . Other areas, Dutch, Swiss and Italian, submitted to the organization of satellite republics under constitutions worked out by local admirers of the Revolution . . . Practically everywhere they went, from Amsterdam to Mainz

*and from Basel to Naples, the armies of France could count on a welcome
from critics of the Old Régime in each locality.* ³

MORE THAN NO OTHER, HE WILL HAVE FAME AND RENOWN

Nostradamus concludes this oracle by foreseeing the greatness
of Napoleon as expressed by the majority of his biographers.

*The greatest personality of all time, superior to all other men of action by
virtue of the range and clarity of his intelligence, his speed of decision, his
unswerving determination, and his acute sense of reality, allied to the
imagination on which great minds thrive.* ⁴ (Aubry).

Perhaps great leaders cannot be divorced from great evil. In
Napoleon's case this often appears to have been true, and Nostradamus does not let us forget it. In this next oracle, the seer
paints a much darker side to Bonaparte's character, at the same
time identifying the Emperor by his preferred hairstyle.

C.V: 60

Par tefte rafe viendra bien mal eflire,
Plus que fa charge ne porter paffera:
Si grand fureur & raige fera dire,
Qu'à feu & fang tout fexe trenchera.

*By reason of the crop head, he will arrive choosing great evil,
Not bearing more than his charge, he will acquit himself:
He will express such great fury and rage,
That in fire and blood he will wear out an entire sex.*

Bien, (O.Fr.) vraiment; eflire, (O.Fr.) choose, elect; paffera, (O.Fr.) s'acquitter – to pay off
one's debts; trenchera, (O.Fr. trenchiera) decider, miner; i.e., to wear away.
Cross-reference: teste rase, C.I: 88; C.VII: 13

BY REASON OF THE CROP HEAD

Identifying Napoleon Bonaparte as **THE CROP HEAD**, or *'Le Tondu'* ¹ as
he was called by his men, is entirely consistent with Nostradamus's choice of words. In an age that flaunted elaborate hairstyles, the Emperor of the French chose instead to wear his hair
close cut. To great acclaim, he was **ELECTED** First Consul and *de
facto* ruler of France in 1799, and in 1804 he was made Emperor.

HE WILL ARRIVE CHOOSING GREAT EVIL

Thereafter, the Napoleonic wars continued almost without let
for the duration of Bonaparte's reign. But always with war there
ARRIVES GREAT EVIL. Quite apart from the pillaging, the rapes and the
murders of women and children, which inevitably accompanied
his territorial conquests, there were the judicial killings that he

authorized, most amounting to no more than butchery. More-over, as earlier remarked, the succession of battles that were fought in his name cost more lives (estimated at 1·75 million), proportionally, than were lost during the First World War.[2]

NOT BEARING MORE THAN HIS CHARGE, HE WILL ACQUIT HIMSELF

Napoleon was also a liar. Sometimes his falsehoods were delib-erate misrepresentations, and sometimes they were acts of self-deception, but they were always designed **TO LESSEN THE CHARGE** against him. Even when he had given written instructions for an action to take place, he was quite capable of **ACQUITTING HIMSELF** from any suggestion of involvement, particularly if the conse-quences turned out to be unpopular. Any blame for failure would be explained away as the fault of his underlings.[3]

HE WILL EXPRESS SUCH GREAT FURY AND RAGE

Bonaparte's fits of *rage* also need to be considered when assess-ing his character. These were moments when the Emperor lost his composure and gave way to *'hystero-epileptic attacks'*. These epi-sodes have been well documented. At times he would use his riding whip to thrash unfortunate servants, and even officers if they angered him. On one occasion, while in a fit of rage, he hammered Marshal Berthier's head against a stone wall. On an-other occasion he kicked a minister of State in the stomach.[4] But this impassioned part to his nature also had its positive side, and this was apparent in the speeches he gave to his fighting men. His inspirational address to the ragged army that he led into It-aly is referred to in C.III: 37. But he could be quite devastating in his condemnation of a poor performance.

> *Soldiers, I am not satisfied with you. You have shown neither bravery, discipline nor perseverance . . . You have allowed yourself to be driven from positions where a handful of men could have stopped an army . . . you are not French soldiers. General, Chief-of-Staff! Let it be inscribed on their colours: 'They no longer form part of the army of Italy!'*[5]

THAT IN FIRE AND BLOOD HE WILL WEAR OUT AN ENTIRE SEX

The final line of this oracle contains an implicit reference to **THE FIRE AND BLOOD** which was part of the numerous battles and con-flicts he fought. War requires an enormous number of men serv-ing in the field. It has been estimated that between March 1804 and April 1815, that is, after his *election*, which is referred to in the first line, and the *real evil* that followed, as many as *'two million native-born Frenchmen saw active service in his successive armies'*. There were also: *'no less than thirty-two levies on the various classes over the same period'*.[6] Yet still these numbers fail to take account of the millions more pressed into service from other countries. Without the least shadow of doubt, the Napoleonic wars gave rise to the largest armies the world had ever seen. And to accomplish it, in Nostradamus's words: HE WORE OUT AN ENTIRE SEX.

In the next quatrain the seer predicts yet another side to Napoleon's character, that of his role as a legislator. The quatrain also contains a further reference to his having promoted to the nobility many of the lowborn men who fought alongside him. The prophecy also foresees the Emperor's inability to make successful agreements with Church leaders.

C.V: 79

La facree pompe viendra baiſſer les aiſles,
Par la venue du grand legiſlateur:
Humble haulſera vexera les rebelles,
Naiſtra ſur terre aucun æmulateur.

The sacred pomp will come to lower its wings,
Through the arrival of the great legislator.
He will raise the humble; he will anger the rebellious,
Not one emulator will be born on earth.

Aisles, (O.Fr.) compare: rongner les aisles à = to bring down, to weaken; æmulateur, (Latinism) aemulatio – emulation.

THE SACRED POMP and high-flown splendour that had for so long been part of the Roman Catholic Church in Rome was eventually brought down to earth during the Napoleonic Era, when it was FORCED TO LOWER ITS WINGS. This was achieved THROUGH THE ARRIVAL OF THE GREAT LEGISLATOR.

THE SACRED POMP WILL COME TO LOWER ITS WINGS

Pius VII entered Rome as the newly elected Pope on 3 July 1800, and was immediately confronted by a draft of the Concordat containing Napoleon's preferred ideas concerning the relationship that should exist between State and Church. The document demanded from the Pope that all French bishops be directed to give up their sees; the number of dioceses be reduced; the Papacy must cease to claim back the booty taken from the Vatican following Pius VI's arrest (C.V: 57 refers); the State would then accept responsibility for paying the clergy their wages. Negotiations took a year, during which, *'ten successive drafts'* were argued over before the Pope eventually signed the agreement (15 July 1801). But in April of the following year, Napoleon withdrew the concessions used as an inducement to persuade Pius to sign up to his proposals. In their place, he issued a set of Organic Articles; these tightened the State's control over the Church, and restricted papal intervention in France.[1]

THROUGH THE ARRIVAL OF THE GREAT LEGISLATOR

It was at this time, when Bonaparte was drafting the Concordat that he turned his attention to framing the Code Civil: often presiding over the council as it debated the future course of French law. These efforts led to the Civil Code being produced in 1804, and, two years later, to the Code of Civil Procedure. From 1807 onwards, these Codes became known as: *'Code Napoléon'* and they still form the basis of much that comprises French law.[2]

HE WILL RAISE THE HUMBLE

This part of the prophecy was fulfilled when Napoleon RAISED to THE peerage men born in HUMBLE circumstances. Pierre Augereau, the son of a stonemason became duke of Castiglione; André Masséna, an orphan and former cabin boy became prince of Rivoli; Joachim Murat, the son of an innkeeper became king of Naples; Michael Ney, the son of a blacksmith became prince of Moscowa; Jean de Bernadotte, a private soldier became king of Sweden; Louis-Alexandre Berthier, an engineer became prince of Wagram; Jean-Baptiste Bessières, a cavalry trooper became duke of Istria; Armand-Augustin-Louis Caulaincourt, another cavalry trooper became duke of Vicenza . . . etc.[3]

HE WILL ANGER THE REBELLIOUS

Rebel forces had been operating inside France, particularly in the west and in the south, since the Revolution. These were populated by monarchist sympathizers and backed by recalcitrant priests. On 28 December 1800, Napoleon issued a proclamation that was intended to bring an end all rebellious dissent. In the document, he drew attention to original grievances that had since been redressed, and offered a pardon to those who agreed to end their struggle. In the same breath, he threatened punishment for all those who continued to rebel. Within weeks, a full scale clearing-up operation had begun, which included *his threat to execute* any *"villagers carrying arms or preaching rebellion."* In the south, the rebels were dealt with by reorganizing the gendarmerie into brigades a hundred strong. They were then ordered to clear the countryside of its rebels and brigands. [4]

NOT ONE EMULATOR WILL BE BORN ON EARTH

The final line repeats a similar prediction given above, that never again will there be one born on earth to emulate the deeds of this man. [5] – *"No other career seems to embody quite so strikingly the dynamism of what Oswald Spengler was later to call 'Faustian man' – tireless in his activity, at once intelligent and unscrupulous in his choice of means, ruthless in his egoistic will to power."* (Ford). *"He forgot that a man cannot be God; . . . "* (Marshal Foch).

Napoleon's successful military career has already been compared to his lack of real achievement in dealing with Church matters. This next oracle sees Nostradamus once again correctly anticipating this failing, while also predicting Bonaparte's rise from soldier to emperor.

C.VIII: 57

De fouldat fimple paruiendra en empire.
De robe courte paruiendra à la longue,
Vaillant aux armes en eglife ou plus pyre,
Vexer les preftres comme l'eau fait l'efponge.

From a simple soldier he will attain his end in empire,
From a short robe, he will attain to the long one,
Valiant at arms: in church, where, much worse,
Vexing the priests, as water does the sponge (vexes free will).

parvenir, (O.Fr.) atteindre le but; vaillant, (O.Fr.) de grande valeur; fait (from faire also O.Fr.) exploit: this verb, when followed by a noun, can take the place of almost any verb, hence, vex; efponge, (O.Fr. homonym) sponge, libre arbiter = free will

FROM A SIMPLE SOLDIER

Napoleon began his military career as a second lieutenant stationed at Valence in the Régiment de la Fère du corps royal d'artillerie. [1]

HE WILL ATTAIN HIS END IN EMPIRE

Later, through military action at Toulon and again in Paris, he came to the notice of the Directory; this led to him being appointed commander-in-chief of the Army of Italy. A succession of victories followed, both in Italy and later in Egypt. Having secured the adoration of the French people, he sprang a *coup* to remove the corrupt Directory and take control of the government (1799). Five years later, he was able to proclaim himself **EMPEROR OF THE FRENCH**.[2]

FROM A SHORT ROBE, HE WILL ATTAIN TO THE LONG ONE

Before the Revolution, *'Noblesse de Robe'* referred to magistrates who had attained their title of nobility through having bought or inherited it. By contrast, **THE SHORT ROBE** indicated a person who was not of that order. For good measure, the artist, Jacques-Louis David, when painting those present at Napoleon's coronation, showed *the Emperor in a* **LONG ROBE**. François Gérard also painted a portrait of Napoleon in his *long* coronation gown.[3]

VALIANT AT ARMS

Nostradamus correctly predicts Bonaparte's **VALOUR ON THE BATTLE-FIELD**. Legends surrounded his victories, *"and he encouraged it. The legend of Lodi, the legend of the Pyramids, the legend of St. Bernard, the legend of Marengo."*[4] (Thompson).

IN CHURCH, WHERE, MUCH WORSE

Despite Napoleon's achievements in government and on the battlefield, he was never able to repeat this success when dealing with the Church, except by force. In 1796 Pope Pius VI was compelled to bow to Napoleon's military supremacy and agree the terms set out in the Treaty of Tolentino. This cost the papacy Ferrara, and Bologna as well as a collection of valuable manuscripts. Five years later, Pius VII, too, was forced into submission when he agreed under pressure to the Concordat of 1801. This required the papacy: *"to accept the revolutionary reforms in clerical matters, including the abolition of tithes, the sale of church property and the suppression of many dioceses."* (Sutherland). Eight years later, Bonaparte confiscated the papal territories completely, and exiled Pius VII because he would not agree to their annexation.[5]

VEXING THE PRIESTS

After languishing for three years in exile at Savona, Bonaparte ordered the Pope to be brought to Fontainebleau. The Emperor had recently become irritated at his failure to obtain Pius' signature to an agreement he was preparing (the *Concordat of Fontainebleau*). The Pope's arrival failed to ease the situation. Instead, it began many long, drawn out periods of argument, in which Napoleon **VEXED THE PRIESTS** with proposals that Pius refused to consider. *"Day after day cardinals, bishops, and state officials repeated in his ears arguments he had grown tired of refuting."*[6]

AS WATER VEXES FREE WILL

Nostradamus's allusion to *water* refers to the palace of Fontaine-bleau, originally called *Fontaine Belle Eau*. Views of the palace reveal a wide expanse of *water* running almost the length of the building, and this commences the one kilometre canal built by Henri IV. It was at this WATER *palace* that Napoleon attempted to bend the Pope's *will* to his own. But Pius remained resolutely opposed to the Emperor's demands, and it was not until January 1813 that he finally faltered. Bonaparte was quick to realise the vulnerable state of the Pope's resolve, for it was only after *"three years' of attacks that it was ready for the final assault."* Drained of his usual energy and VEXED by the same arguments continually being put forward, Pius finally capitulated, and allowed his FREE WILL to be exploited by Napoleon's wishes. However, a few days later, having recovered his composure, Pius withdrew his consent, but Napoleon declined to accept any retraction, and the Concordat was published.[7]

In the next oracle, Nostradamus repeats his earlier warning to the Papacy, but adds to it by predicting the exact number of battles that would be fought during this period.

C.I: 15

Mars nous menaſſe par ſa force bellique,
Septante foys fera le ſang eſpandre:
Auge & ruyne de l'Eccleſiaſtique,
Et plus ceux qui d'eux rien voudront entendre.

Mars menaces us by reason of his martial strength,
Seventy times he will cause blood to spill:
Increase and ruin for the Ecclesiastic,
And those moreso who will want to hear nothing from them.

Mars, (Greek Myth.) god of war; eſpandre, (O.Fr.) répandre. Ecclesiastique, (O.Fr.) Latin – ecclesia = church, but note the capital E.

MARS MENACES US BY REASON OF HIS MARTIAL STRENGTH

Napoleon's military conquests began in the spring of 1796 with his appointment as Commander of the Army of Italy. By the following year he had established himself as one of the foremost military and political figures in Europe. Thereafter, until 1815, he repeatedly led France into a series of wars.

... between March 1804 and April 1815 practically two million native-born Frenchmen saw active service in his successive armies; there were no less than thirty two levies on the various annual classes over the same period, and probably a further million men were procured from allied or satellite states. [1]

SEVENTY TIMES HE WILL CAUSE BLOOD TO SPILL

At the time Napoleon left the field at Waterloo he had, during his career, **CAUSED THE BLOOD TO SPILL** in battle no less than **SEVENTY TIMES**. Alan Palmer records the names of all *seventy battles* in *An Encyclopaedia of Napoleon's Europe*: viz.

Aboukir Bay; Acre; Albuera; Alexandria; Almeida; Arcis-sur-Aube; Arcole; Aspern; Auerstädt; Austerlitz; Badajoz; Bassano; Bautzen; Baylen; Bayonne; Berezina; Bidassoa; Borghetto; Borisov; Borodino; Burgos; Caldiero [2]; Castiglione; Champeaubert; Ciudad Rodrigo; Corunna; Dego; Dresden; Eckmühl; Eylau; Friedland; Fuentes de Oñoro; Hohenlinden; Jena; Katzbach; Krasnoe; Kulm; Laon; La Rothière; Leipzig; Ligny; Lodi; Lützen; Maloyaroslavets; Mantua; Marengo; Montmirail; Oporto; Orthèz; Polotsk; Pultusk; Pyramids; Quatre Bras; Salamanca; San Sebastian; Saragossa; Smolensk; Talavera; Toulouse; Ulm; Vauchamps; Vilna; Vimiero; Vitebsk; Vitoria; Wagram; Waterloo; Wavre; Zurich. (p.xxiii). [2]

N.B. Two battles occurred at Caldiero. The first of these was fought on 12 November 1796 in a failed attempt at preventing the Austrian General, Joseph Alvintzi, reaching Verona. The second battle took place on 30 October 1805, and was fought between Archduke Charles of Austria and Bonaparte's Marshal, André Masséna.

INCREASE AND RUIN FOR THE CHURCH

Pius VII began his ministry six months after the unhappy demise of Pius VI, and with an **INCREASE** in fortune **FOR THE CHURCH**. The Concordat of 1801, agreed between Bonaparte and the Pope, acknowledged Catholicism to be the preferred religion of France. It also guaranteed every citizen the freedom of worship. The French government also arranged to pay the clergy from state funds, and it redrew the boundaries of many dioceses to help implement this arrangement. But in 1808, the predicted **RUIN FOR THE CHURCH** was fulfilled, when Rome became incorporated into the French Empire. Pius VII objected by excommunicating those responsible. Napoleon retaliated by ordering the Pope's arrest. Pius VII was subsequently deported and taken to Grenoble; from there he was transferred to Savona. He did not see Rome again until 24 May 1814. [3]

AND THOSE MORESO WHO WILL WANT TO HEAR NOTHING FROM THEM

During the final decade of the 18th century France had attempted to de-Christianise the nation using legislation based
upon rationalist viewpoints; in this respect, the Napoleonic Age
was heir to the Enlightenment. Supernatural revelation continued to be decried, while historical comment and literary criticism were increasingly disposed towards secularist views. This
had the effect of diminishing attendances at church services. This
trend away from organised religion, and to take up arms, was to
result in **MORE** ruin **FOR THOSE WHO WILL WANT TO HEAR NOTHING FROM
THEM**; that is, *for those who will not want to hear from the Church*.[4]
And so it proved to be, with casualties that numbered hundreds
of thousands in land battles fought at Austerlitz, Jena-Auerstadt,
Eylau, Friedland, Wagram, Berezina, Borodino, etc.

The foregoing oracles have provided a general overview of
Napoleon Bonaparte's character during his term as Emperor of
the French. It was, however, as a warrior chief that Napoleon
first achieved international acclaim. In 1796, the Directory gave
him a bedraggled army with which to invade Italy. By his inspired leadership, he led his soldiers from one victory to another, until finally the north of Italy was in French hands. The
oracle that follows gives an account of Bonaparte's First Italian
Campaign, and in doing so, the Commander-in-Chief is given a
byname that will be used by the seer to identify him in five further verses.

C.VI: 79

Pres du Tefin les habitans de Loyre,
Garonne, & Saonne, Seine, Tain, & Gironde:
Outre les monts drefferont promontoire,
Conflict donné, Pau, granci, submergé onde.

Near the Ticino, the inhabitants of Loire,
Garonne, and Saône, Seine, Tarn, and Gironde:
Over the mountains they will lay out a promontory,
Conflict given, Pau (the short one) grabbed, submerged [in] water.

Pau, (O.Fr.) petit = short, also diminutive of Na[pau]leon (note capital P): granci, (Italian)
granc/ire, also, granc/io. Cross-references: Pau, C.II: 33; C.II: 94; C.III: 75; C.IV: 70; C.VIII: 1;
dresseront promontoire, C.I: 77

N.B. Napoleon Bonaparte was popularly known as 'LE PETIT CAPORAL'
(THE LITTLE CORPORAL) see Note 5.

NEAR THE TICINO

Milan was Bonaparte's first objective. *"But to reach Milan he would have to cross the most formidable river of Italy, the Po: and also its left hand tributary, the Ticino, and each crossing would be disputed by Beaulieu's army."* [1]

THE INHABITANTS OF LOIRE, GARONNE, AND SAÔNE, SEINE, TARN AND GIRONDE

Napoleon Bonaparte's first invasion of Italy was notable for its *'many river crossings'*. The oracle reflects this by referring TO THE IN-HABITANTS OF THE DIFFERENT RIVER REGIONS ACROSS FRANCE, and from which soldiers of the Army of Italy had been drawn.

> *The dominating natural feature [of the First Italian Campaign] was the great River Po with its series of Alpine tributaries – the Sestia, Ticino, Adda, Oglio and Mincio watercourses, and beyond them the rivers Adige and Brenta, flowing independently into the Adriatic. . . . A series of smaller streams similarly linked the Apennines with the Po.* [2]

OVER THE MOUNTAINS THEY WILL LAY OUT A PROMONTORY

Having taken his liberating army ACROSS THE MOUNTAINS that divide France from Italy,[3] Bonaparte literally drove a wedge – that is to say, he LAID OUT A PROMONTORY between the combined forces of the opposition, the Piedmontese and the Austrians.[4] This strategy proved extremely successful, and resulted in King Victor Amadeus III of Sardinia-Piedmont being forced to cede the transalpine provinces to France. It also required him to grant safe passage to the French armies at the *Peace of Paris* (May 15, 1796). Napoleon's divisive strategy in achieving this victory is still considered a textbook classic in military warfare. It is noteworthy that a similar strategy of dividing the opposition by *'laying out a promontory'* was also employed by the English navy at the Battle of Trafalgar, where Nostradamus uses the same phrase (C.I: 77), when predicting Admiral Nelson's death.

CONFLICT GIVEN

It was during Napoleon's first Italian campaign that a dramatic incident occurred: one, which had the outcome been different, would have changed the face of European history. In November 1796, while still in the process of subduing Northern Italy, Napoleon reached the town of Arcola on the River Alpone. It was there that a fierce CONFLICT BROKE OUT between the French and an Austrian detachment that had positioned itself to defend the bridge. Further advance was immediately brought to a standstill.

Impatient at the delay, and believing that a joint charge across the bridge would solve the problem, Napoleon seized a flag and began to lead a party of men across the canal. A volley of gunfire met his appearance.[5]

SERIOUS BLUNDER, GRABBED

The charge had proved to be A SERIOUS BLUNDER. One of Bonaparte's men quickly saw the peril in which the Commander had placed himself, and GRABBED hold of him, urging that he take cover. But Napoleon resisted.

SUBMERGED IN WATER

In the ensuing *"confusion the commander fell into the deep dyke at the side."* and being SUBMERGED IN WATER was in real danger of drowning. Two aides-de-camp, Louis Bonaparte and Antoine Marmont, dived into the water to rescue their Commander, and Napoleon was brought safely to shore.[6] Had it not been for their quick intervention, as well as the reaction of the officer on the bridge, who was shot dead a moment later, the Napoleonic era might never have begun.

The next oracle continues with its prediction of Napoleon's First Italian Campaign, focusing upon the army's entry into Milan. This prophecy also provides the first instance of Nostradamus referring to Napoleon as *'the Eagle'*.

C.III: 37

Auant l'aſſaut oraiſon prononcée:
Milan prins d'Aigle par embuſches deceuz:
Muraille antique par canons enfoncée,
Par feu & ſang à mercy peu receuz.

Before the assault, a speech pronounced:
Milan taken by the eagle, deceived through ambushes:
The old high wall forced open by cannons,
By fire and blood, with little mercy received.

deceuz, (O.Fr. decevoir) deceived;   Cross-reference: Aigle: C.I: 23; C.IV: 70; C.VIII: 4; C.VIII: 46

BEFORE THE ASSAULT, A SPEECH PRONOUNCED

Napoleon's first appointment of command began with an inspirational SPEECH to his ragged and dispirited army in Nice. It was PRONOUNCED BEFORE embarking upon THE ASSAULT against Milan.

Soldiers! You are hungry and naked; the government owes you much but can give you nothing. The patience and courage, which you have displayed among these rocks, are admirable; but they bring you no glory - not a glimmer falls upon you. I will lead you into the most fertile plains on earth. Rich provinces and opulent towns will be in your power, and in them you will find honour, glory and wealth. Soldiers of Italy, will you be lacking in courage or steadfastness? [1]

MILAN TAKEN BY THE EAGLE

Within a matter of weeks this same army had become the new conquerors of Italy, ENTERING MILAN on 15 May 1796. THE EAGLE was to become a symbol of Napoleon's power. *Eagles* were subsequently given to the commanders of his Imperial Army. An *eagle* with outstretched talons was also placed on the wall above the emperor's desk at Fontainebleau, and a cast of the bird was made for his sceptre. It was while directing his campaign in Italy that: *"The young eagle had found his wings; the future lay with Destiny."* [2]

DECEIVED THROUGH AMBUSHES

Napoleon's entry into Italy was later explained to have been successful THROUGH the early use of AMBUSHES. Colonel Thomas Graham, a British officer attached to the 90th Foot, and an observer at the time, wrote an account of its successful practice, which he included in his biography. *"Some French sharpshooters, concealed by the bushes at the edge of the river . . . kept up a very constant and annoying fire on the fine regiment of Kehl (three battalions) . . . 150 men killed and wounded was the consequence."* [3]

THE OLD HIGH WALL

The success of Napoleon's entry into *Milan* was nevertheless incomplete. This was because the retreating Austrian army had left behind a detachment of troops. They had firmly established themselves behind the OLD HIGH WALL of the city's ancient citadel, the *Castello Sforzesco*: built in the fifteenth century by Francesco Sforza. Unable to dislodge the besieged Austrians, the main body of Napoleon's army left *Milan* in pursuit of General Beaulieu, who had retreated to Mantua. It was while in Tuscany that the French army were able to capture some *cannons* from Fort Urban.

FORCED OPEN BY CANNONS

Napoleon realised these *cannons* would aid Marshal Sérurier's assault on Mantua, *"but first the guns were sent to Milan to enforce the capitulation of the castello."* (Chandler). On 29 June 1796, the strategy succeeded. The castle was finally **FORCED OPEN BY** the newly arrived **CANNONS**, and the Austrian garrison, besieged since Beaulieu's departure, surrendered their position.[4]

It had been after the main bulk of the French army left Milan that opposition to the city's occupation gathered force and the unrest this caused spread to towns and villages surrounding the city. Within a very short time, the authority established by Bonaparte had almost disappeared.

BY FIRE AND BLOOD WITH LITTLE MERCY RECEIVED

Upon discovering this lapse in command, Bonaparte lost no time in re-establishing his authority. He also decided to teach the people a lesson in brutality. The village of Binasco was punished **BY** setting it on **FIRE** and its men folk shot.[5] In Pavia, the French army was given free rein to loot, rape and destroy at leisure; *"many innocent townsfolk died in the process,"* **WITH LITTLE MERCY RECEIVED.**[6]

After the success of his Italian campaign, and while holding court in the palace of Mombello near Milan during the summer of 1797, Napoleon received orders from the Directory to enter Rome. This was intended to be a prelude to wider ambitions, which included the planned invasion of England and the spread of the French empire across the sea to the eastern shores of the Mediterranean. The next quatrain, covering the space of two years, has predicted what happened.

C.II: 94

GRAND. Pau, grand mal pour Gaulois recevra,
Vaine terreur au maritin Lyon:
Peuple infiny par la mer paffera.
Sans efchapper vn quart d'vn milion.

GREAT MAN, Pau: for the French, he will receive a great evil,
Vain terror for the maritime Lion
Innumerable people will cross by sea,
Without escaping, a quarter of a million.

Pau, (O.Fr.) petit, also diminutive of Na[pau]leon; recevra, (O.Fr.) accepter. Cross-references: Pau, C.II: 33; C.III: 75; C.IV: 70; C.VI: 79; C.VIII:1

GREAT MAN, PAU

NAPOLEON'S reputation as a **GREAT MAN** was obtained after returning from his successful conquest of Italy. *"In March 1796 Napoleone Buonaparte was known only to comparatively restricted circles within France,* *but a year later his name had become a household word throughout Europe."* [1]

In Paris, the Directory issued fresh orders to their triumphant Commander-in-Chief, telling him to destroy the papal government in Rome. This conflicted with Bonaparte's preferred option, which was to invade Austria. But, obedient to his masters in Paris, he ACCEPTED his orders. The French army then marched on Rome, and entered the city on 11 February 1798, forcing Pope Pius VI to sign the *Treaty of Tolentino*. This ceded to France the major papal territories of Bologna and Ferrara. His next GREAT EVIL was to force the Pope to make a cruel journey across Italy and France. *"He [Pius VI] was then eighty years old, very frail and mortally ill."* He died after reaching the citadel in Valence.[2]

In October of the following year, the Directory gave Bonaparte a new command: he was to head the *'Armée d'Angelterre'* and make plans for the invasion of England. The oracle refers to Britain as THE MARITIME LION, thus joining the nation's symbolic *lion* with its growing mastery at sea: something that was far from obvious when this prediction was written.

Convinced that an invasion was soon to take place, Martello towers were constructed along the southeast coast of England, and the military were given preparatory training for the expected attack. Bonfires were also prepared on a chain of hilltops to signal the invasion when it came. But these precautions turned out to be in VAIN, the TERROR threatened by the French never materialized. Napoleon, having visited the Channel ports on a tour of inspection, discovered that the French navy would be no match FOR THE MARITIME LION. He therefore abandoned his intended invasion of England, and instead, turned his attention towards Egypt and the Holy Land.[3]

On 19 May 1798, at the head of a great fleet, Napoleon left Toulon bound for the eastern end of the Mediterranean. After setting sail, he was joined by even more ships from Corsica, Genoa and Civita Vecchia. His armada eventually numbered approximately 300 ships, with an estimated 55,000 men on board. Eight months later, he wrote to Tipu Sultan at Seringapatam, informing him:

'an innumerable and invincible army' had left France **BY SEA** to liberate him from: *'the iron yoke of England'.*[4]

A little more than a month after the French arrived in the East, there occurred one of the greatest disasters in that country's naval history. On 1 August 1798, Horatio Nelson's squadron discovered the French ships anchored in Aboukir Bay. What followed was the annihilation of Napoleon's armada.

A QUARTER OF A MILLION WITHOUT ESCAPING

"This terrible disaster . . . imprisoned Bonaparte in his conquest, without hope of escape." (Lefebvre). It would be two years before the estimated 30,000 men who survived Bonaparte's eastern venture were able to return.

Meanwhile in France, the absence of French soldiers at home caused General Jourdan to propose to the Directory that a new *levée en masse* be introduced to replenish the country's armed forces. *"The mass conscription . . . was expected to lead to the enlistment of 223,000 men."* (Sydenham). In the summer of 1799, legislation was passed requiring all young men to register for military service. Under a previous law it had been possible for conscripts to *escape* military service by paying someone else to take their place. This practice was now forbidden and there would be **NO ESCAPE** for the expected 223,000 men who were to be called-up for service.[5] 220,000 conscripts, plus 30,000 men left stranded in Egypt (calculated to the nearest 10,000), meant that a **QUARTER OF A MILLION** men were **WITHOUT ESCAPE** at that time, for one reason or another.[6]

Quite apart from predicting Bonaparte's military expeditions, Nostradamus was also fascinated by the character of the man. Several quatrains have already dealt with this subject, and in doing so, they have collectively given an accurate pen portrait of the person he was.

In the next oracle, which is a split quatrain, Nostradamus attaches a previously used aptronym to his subject, thus allowing continuity *via* the use of cross-references.

C.I: 88

Le diuin mal furprendra le grand prince,
Vn peu deuant aura femme efpoufée,
Son puy & credit à vn coup viendra mince,
Confeil mourra pour la tefte rafée.

The divine sickness will surprise the great prince,
A little before, he will have wed a married woman:
His support & esteem, by a coup, will become small,
Prudence will fail regarding the crop head.

puy, (O.Fr.) appui; conſeil, (O.Fr.) sagesse; mourra, (O.Fr.) faire mourir; raſer, (O.Fr.) tondre de près; teſte, (O.Fr.) tête.   Cross-reference: teste rasée, C.VII: 13; C.V: 60

THE DIVINE SICKNESS WILL SURPRISE THE GREAT PRINCE

Most biographies of Bonaparte confirm that he suffered from 'petit-mal'—the divine sickness. *"At worst the turns could only have been of the lesser, petit mal, type."* On one notable occasion, prior to his becoming Emperor of the French – hence, GREAT PRINCE – THE DIVINE SICKNESS SURPRISED him. It occurred in 1802, while enjoying an intimate moment with Mlle George (Josephine Weimer aged fifteen), an actress from the Comédie Française, he *"passed into a dead faint in bed."* His conquest screamed in horror, pulled the bell-chord, and ran naked from the bedroom, passing Joséphine and other concerned members of the household who were hurrying to investigate the cause of the commotion.[1]

A LITTLE BEFORE, HE WILL HAVE WED A MARRIED WOMAN

Bonaparte's sexual interests are continued in this prophecy by referring to his marriage with Joséphine de Beauharnais, whom HE WED on 9 March 1796. Joséphine was A previously MARRIED WOMAN. Her first husband was guillotined during the Revolution and his estate forfeited. She therefore found herself alone and destitute in Paris with two children to support. It was while in this state that she first met Napoleon in October of 1795.[2]

This oracle is one of a small number of split-time prophecies. These have been constructed with intervals of more than a decade between two related subjects. Their purpose is to dispel interest in understanding the remaining part of a prophecy after the first part has been recognized. In the present instance, a gap of fourteen years passes by before Nostradamus rejoins Napoleon's life story as it began to enter its final stage.

HIS SUPPORT AND ESTEEM

Napoleon became First Consul as the result of a *coup* in 1799. In 1802 he accepted the title Consul for life, and in 1804 he was raised to Emperor. *"From 1799 to 1814 he was the autocrat of France and the dependent territories his conquests secured for her."* And he achieved this with full support from the people of France.

BY A COUP

A *coup* had brought him to power, and it was a *coup* that removed him from power. Following a succession of reversals in Russia, Spain and Leipzig, he was confronted by his chief minister Charles Talleyrand, who had the backing of the Senate and the military. Bonaparte was then told that a Provisional Government had been formed to replace him, and he no longer had support from the military. *"This Provisional Government issued [an] Address to the army absolving it from allegiance to Napoleon."* [3]

WILL BECOME SMALL

As consolation to his former status, Napoleon was allowed to retain the title of Emperor, although with a dominion and authority that was confined solely to the SMALL island of Elba in the Mediterranean. [4]

PRUDENCE WILL FAIL

Bonaparte's lack of PRUDENCE was confirmed by his FAILING powers at the close of his reign. His failure in Russia, followed soon after by his decision to escape from Elba in the hope of regaining his position as Emperor of the French were *imprudent,* and showed his *failure* to come to terms with the changing reality of Europe's united stand against despots. [5]

REGARDING THE CROP HEAD

As previously stated: Napoleon's men frequently referred to their Commander-in-Chief by his familiar nickname: *'Le Tondu'.* Keeping his HAIR CLOSE-CROPPED had become the Emperor's preferred hairstyle at a time when others chose a more fashionable appearance. [6]

Nostradamus next turns his attention to the fortunes of Napoleon's defeated enemy, the Piedmontese. To guard against invasion, Piedmont had allied itself to the Austrians. But in 1796, Bonaparte invaded Italy, and drove a wedge between the two armies (see C.VI: 79). The following verse is another split prophecy concerning the fate that befell Piedmont's defeated King.

C.VIII: 88

Dans la Sardeigne vn noble Roy viendra,
Qui ne tiendra que trois ans le royaume,
Plufieurs coulleurs auec foy conioindra,
Luy mefmes apres foin fomeil marrit fcome.

313

A noble King will arrive in Sardinia,
That but [for] three years, he will not hold the kingdom,
He will unite several colours with himself,
The same He, afterwards, heed, drowsiness, lamented end.

ſoy, (3rd person reflexive); conioindra, (O.Fr.) unir; marrit, (O.Fr.) chagriner; ſcome, (O.Fr.) extremité; soin (O.Fr.) heed, circumspection

Sardinia became a kingdom of the House of Savoy only in 1720. Before then it had been a Spanish possession. The change in ownership came about through the *Treaty of London* (1718), which compelled Victor Amadeus II to surrender Sicily to Austria. In exchange, he received *Sardinia*. Importantly, therefore, it was only after 24 August 1720 that *"he and his successors were known as kings of Sardinia."*

A NOBLE KING WILL ARRIVE IN SARDINIA

Charles Emmanuel IV, whose biographical details fit this oracle, became **KING OF SARDINIA** and Piedmont on 14 October 1796, following the death of Victor Amadeus III. His accession coincided with the French Revolution, to which he was bitterly opposed. In the following year, the uprising in France intruded into his kingdom, and he responded by executing the insurgents, including many Jacobins who were intending to introduce their revolutionary ideas to his people.

At the time of Charles Emmanuel's succession, Piedmont was allied with Austria. But his kingdom became diminished when, during a strategically brilliant ten-day campaign, Napoleon divided the two armies, taking Piedmont, and scuttling the Austrians. Further losses occurred on 9 December 1798, when the French general, Barthélemy-Catherine Joubert, forced the King to surrender all his mainland possessions to France. In the following year Naples, too, was overrun and Charles was forced to concede that there was now no foreseeable hope of recovering his possessions. Bowed down by these losses, Charles Emmanuel **RETIRED TO THE ISLAND OF SARDINIA**, the only part of his kingdom that remained free from Napoleon's grasp.[1]

THAT BUT FOR THREE YEARS, HE WILL NOT HOLD THE KINGDOM

For the next **THREE AND A HALF YEARS**, he remained *King of Sardinia*. But the death of his wife Marie Clotilde, daughter of the French dauphin, on 2 March 1802 so grieved him that three months later he abdicated in favour of his brother Victor Emmanuel.[2] There is

314

an interesting postscript to this part of the prophecy: for although Charles Emmanuel held the Kingdom for just over three years, he retained the title of King until the end of his life.

HE WILL UNITE SEVERAL COLOURS WITH HIMSELF

The loss of Piedmont occurred in April 1796, six months before the death of Victor Amadeus III. He and his forty-year-old son had allowed the Piedmontese to *unite* with the Austrians under General Colli. And it was during their combined battle with the French that Napoleon achieved his great victory: driving a wedge between their two armies (refer C.VI: 79). By 25 April 1796, Cherasco, too, had been captured, and the King of Sardinia-Piedmont was forced to admit the total defeat of his armies in the field. Paris was quickly notified of these successes, and its streets were thronged with cheering onlookers when General Andoche Junot entered the city: *"carrying a trophy of twenty-one captured flags."* These were the SEVERAL COLOURS which THE KING of Piedmont-Sardinia had UNITED WITH.[3]

THE SAME HE, AFTERWARDS

By emphasizing THE SAME HE, Nostradamus has acknowledged his previous deviations from one subject to another, made without warning. But now he confirms this strategy does not apply in the present case. It was AFTER abdicating in 1802 that Charles Emmanuel became a novitiate of the Jesuits in Rome. He remained there until his death on 6 October 1819, aged sixty-eight.[4]

HEED, DROWSINESS, LAMENTED END

The stress of past defeats, the death of his beloved wife, and the loss of his kingdoms appear to have played upon his mind. In his new life with the Jesuits, he would sometimes be overcome by an excess of piety. In this state, he would HEED others' needs, and leave his cell in a state of DROWSINESS and wander into the streets begging for alms.[5] It was a sad, and much LAMENTED END for a king descended from the noble House of Savoy.[6]

Nostradamus now returns to the subject of Napoleon Bonaparte and his campaigns. In this next oracle the seer introduces one of the commander's chief lieutenants: a man he identifies by predicting his outstanding facial feature. One is therefore driven to accept that genetic endowments are every bit as predictable as are the positions of the stars that correlate to events on Earth.

C.II: 67

Le blonde au nez forche viendra commettre,
Par le duelle & chaſſera dehors:
Les exiles dedans fera remettre,
Aux lieux marins commetrant les plus forts.

The susceptible one with the pitchfork nose will arrive to carry out,
In the struggle, he will expel abroad:
The exiles within he will push back,
Committing the strongest to maritime places.

blonde, (O.Fr. homonym) fair, susceptible; forche, (O.Fr.fourche) pitchfork; commettre, (O.Fr.) exécuter; duelle, (Latinism – duellum) battle, warfare; remettre, (O.Fr.) re-pousser.

THE SUSCEPTIBLE ONE WITH THE PITCHFORK NOSE

General Augereau first made his reputation as a soldier in the conquest of Northern Italy. *"Contemporaries described him as . . . an able tactician and thorough soldier . . . his towering height and huge hooked nose made him an imposing figure."* (Chandler).[1] It was because of his proven capability in the field that Napoleon saw him as being SUSCEPTIBLE to *carrying out* a *coup d'état* against the moderates in Paris.

WILL ARRIVE TO CARRY OUT

Augereau ARRIVED in the capital at the head of his troops, prepared TO CARRY OUT the *coup.* With customary candour he declared that he had arrived *'to kill the royalists':* men that his Commander-in-Chief had said were too dangerous to be allowed to live.[2]

IN THE STRUGGLE, HE WILL EXPEL ABROAD

After Augereau's *coup d'état,* known by its Revolutionary Calendar date as Fructidor (4 September 1797), more than 130 royalists and counterrevolutionaries from the *Corps Législatif,* together with many non-juring priests were rounded up in THE STRUGGLE and forcibly EXPELLED ABROAD.[3] Interestingly, the oracle uses the word *'duelle',* which, as *'duel'* in modern French, has the same meaning as in English. Before embarking upon his military career, Augereau had been a *'duellist':* earning his living as a fencing master in Dresden.

THE EXILES WITHIN, HE WILL PUSH BACK

Before Augereau's *coup,* the government had tolerated the gradual return of THOSE EXILED under the harsher regime of France's former revolutionary government. Augereau sought to reverse

316

this by re-enforcing the hard-won gains of the Revolution: to do this, **HE DROVE BACK INTO EXILE** those with pro-Royalist sympathies.[4]

COMMITTING THE STRONGEST TO MARITIME PLACES
"Among the victims of this September violence were some of the noblest names in France." **THE STRONGEST** amongst their number, who were identified as those agitating for a return of the monarchy, were banished to Guiana and the coastal town of Cayenne; that is to say, they were **COMMITTED TO MARITIME PLACES.**[5]

It will have been noticed that Nostradamus has several times used the name, 'Pau', by which he means Napoleon. 'Pau', describes Napoleon Bonaparte because of his short stature. His height of 5 feet 2½ inches (1·587 metres), measured by his valet, Gourgaud, soon earned him the byname of: *The Little Corporal*.

This same cognomen is repeated in the next quatrain, which covers five events extended over a period of five years. This length of time presents an obvious difficulty for those attempting to understand these prophecies before their time of fulfilment. Consequently, as with other oracles, this is best appreciated retrospectively.

C.II: 33

Par le torrent qui defcend de Verone,
Par lors qu'au Pau guidera fon entrée:
Vn grand naufrage, & non moins en Garonne,
Quant ceux de Gennes marcheront leur contrée.

By reason of the rapid stream that descends from Verona,
In that time when Pau will direct his entrance:
A great shipwreck, and not less in Garonne,
When those of Genoa will pace their region.

defcend, (Latinism) descendo; Pau, (O.Fr.) petit, peu; Quant, (O.Fr.) dans le temps où. Cross-references: Pau, (Na *pau* leon, the short one) C.II: 94; C.III: 75; C.IV: 70; C.VI: 79; C.VIII: 1.

BY REASON OF THE RAPID STREAM THAT DESCENDS FROM VERONA
During Napoleon's First Italian Campaign, the city of *Verona* (situated in a loop of the *river Adige*), became Bonaparte's headquarters. From there he planned *'to rush all available troops from Verona to seize Villa Nova'*. On 14 November 1796, leading 18,000 men, he **DESCENDED FROM VERONA.** His destination was Ronco, 18 miles **ALONG THE ADIGE,** where a pontoon bridge had been built to take his army across the river on its way to relieving Mantua.[1]

With detachments led by Augereau and Masséna pouring across the river to secure the marshlands on the north bank, Napoleon was able to mount an assault against Joseph d'Alvintzi at Arcola. The Austrian General had earlier arrived in the town, intent upon retaking *Verona* as a means of relieving Mantua, which had been besieged since July. But d'Alvintzi's subsequent defeat at Arcola put an end to this plan, and ultimately led to Austria's General Würmser surrendering Mantua to Bonaparte.

IN THAT TIME WHEN NAPOLEON WILL DIRECT HIS ENTRANCE

It was therefore **IN THAT TIME WHEN** the army *descended from Verona*, to follow the course of the Adige to Ronco, that **NAPOLEON** first defeated the Austrians at Arcola. From there he **WAS ABLE TO DIRECT HIS ENTRANCE** into the besieged city of Mantua, which had been holding out against the French army for eight months.[2]

A GREAT SHIPWRECK

The prophecy now moves forward to the evening of August 1st 1798, when Horatio Nelson led his British squadron into the bay at Aboukir, where Napoleon's fleet lay at anchor. In what became known as the *Battle of the Nile*, Nelson totally destroyed the French fleet in what can only be described as **A GREAT SHIPWRECK**.[3]

NOT LESS IN GARONNE

The River *Garonne* is not navigable. The oracle is therefore referring to the region of *Garonne* where, in the summer of 1799, a royalist uprising occurred. From June through to August, the rebels achieved some notable successes. But from the 5th to the 20th of August, a counter-revolutionary force led by General Aubugeois and aided by General Commes, successfully crushed the uprising with a series of ruthless operations directed against the royalist forces. The rebellion finally came to an end at Montréjeau in Haute-**GARONNE**.[4]

The prophecy next moves forward to April 1800. The French had captured the city of *Genoa* in 1796, the same year that *Verona* was taken. But the Austrians were determined to retake the city as a preliminary to invading France. In the spring of 1800, General Ott launched a surprise attack against Masséna, the victor of Arcola, and the French were forced to take cover inside *Genoa*. Ott then threw a cordon of 24,000 men around the city to begin a siege, not unlike that which had occurred at Mantua.

WHEN THOSE OF GENOA WILL PACE THEIR REGION

The expression *those of*, is a reference yet again to the occupiers, rather than to the Genoese. In which case, **THOSE OF GENOA** refers to the 24,000 Austrian troops besieging the city, and the French soldiers inside the city who were holding out: both armies were therefore forced **TO PACE THEIR REGION** for the duration of the siege. The French managed to hold the city for three months before starvation forced Masséna to surrender.[5]

The foregoing oracle has covered five major events, partitioning them on a year by year basis. In November 1796, Napoleon led his army out of Verona to win the Battle of Arcola. In February 1797 he broke the siege of Mantua, and entered the city. In August 1798 his fleet was destroyed in the Battle of the Nile. In August 1799, the royalist rebellion that broke out in Haute-Garonne was ruthlessly put down. And in May 1800, the French army was besieged by Austrian troops inside Genoa.

In our next oracle, Nostradamus once again returns to his aptronym for Napoleon, calling him the *'crop head'*. In doing so, he takes up the story of Napoleon's voyage to the eastern shores of the Mediterranean (see C.II: 94), and the French conquest of Egypt. It begins with the Commander-in-Chief's arrival at Alexandria in 1798.

C.VII: 13

De la cité marine & tributaire,
La tefte raze prendre la fatrapie:
Chaffer fordide qui puis fera contraire,
Par quatorze ans tiendra la tyrannie.

From the maritime city and tributary,
The crop head will capture the satrapy:
Pursuing the sordid one who then will be contrary,
For fourteen years he will hold the tyranny.

tefte, (O.Fr.) tête; raze, (O.Fr.) tondre de près; fatrapie, (Latinism) satrap/es.
Cross-reference: tefte raze, C.I: 88; C.V: 60

FROM THE MARITIME CITY AND TRIBUTARY

The *maritime city* is Alexandria, described today as *'an oriental Marseilles'*. When Bonaparte arrived in the summer of 1798, little of the old city remained.[1] It was after successfully launching an attack on Alexandria, and securing it for occupation that Napoleon took a detachment of 25,000 men on a march to Cairo.

"From Alexandria . . . an old canal led past Damanhour into the western branch of the Nile at El-Ramanieh. The natural line of march was along this canal." [2]

The oracle identifies this canal as A TRIBUTARY FROM THE MARINE CITY; which, indeed, was the case. And it was by following this waterway that Napoleon's army was led directly into Egypt's capital city.

THE CROP HEAD

"Bonaparte, now 30 years old, [i.e. in 1799] was thin and short and wore his hair cut close - le petit tondu, the 'little crop-head,' as he was called." [3]

WILL CAPTURE THE SATRAPY

In ancient times, Egypt had been a SATRAPY of Persia: *"after Alexander's death in 323 . . . [Ptolemy] became satrap of Egypt."* Nostradamus uses this same word, *Satrapy* to emphasize what now follows.

From Alexandria, Cairo was promptly reached, and the city CAPTURED, but only after a particularly bloody encounter had cost 6,000 Mamelukes their lives for the loss of only 10 French. As victor, THE CROP HEAD lost no time in proclaiming himself to be the new governor OF THE SATRAPY. [4]

PURSUING THE SORDID ONE

The French army's next goal took them eastwards towards Syria, occupying the towns of El-Arish, Gaza and Jaffa, as they made their way eastwards. The governor of Syria was Djezzah Pasha, also known by his nickname, *'The Butcher'*: a name derived from his sadistic and SORDID practices. Relentlessly, Napoleon PURSUED him from one town to the next, until eventually he was driven back to the fortress at Acre: the last secure foothold in his dominion. [5]

WHO THEN WILL BE CONTRARY

It was at Acre that Djezzah Pasha became the contrary force that would ultimately resist the French onslaught, and force them to retreat. In the course of this opposition to dislodge him, he resisted eight direct assaults. But it was also at Acre that evidence of his SORDID nature became apparent. In order to motivate his troops to their greatest effort, Djezzah Pasha promised a reward for every French head brought to him. This gruesome operation then had the effect of both delaying and disrupting the fighting, because each time a French soldier was killed, his assailant would stop to cut through the man's neck, and take the severed head to Pasha for payment. By next morning the scene in the gardens outside the Syrian governor's seraglio was littered with the corpses of headless French soldiers.[6]

FOR FOURTEEN YEARS HE WILL HOLD THE TYRANNY

Nostradamus now states precisely the number of years that Napoleon was destined to remain at the head of government, and by positioning it at the end of this oracle it is perfectly placed. After retreating from Acre, Napoleon returned to Cairo, and from there, left Egypt for the shores of France. He arrived home in October 1799. One month later, he organized the *coup d'état* that made him First Consul and virtual ruler of France: after which, he became Consul for Life and finally, Emperor of the French. He abdicated on 6 April 1814. **HIS** period of **TYRANNY WAS** therefore **HELD FOR FOURTEEN YEARS**, four months and 28 days.[7]

Before leaving Egypt, Napoleon's Army of the Orient fought several important battles, as well as being involved in numerous skirmishes. The next quatrain finds Nostradamus again calling the French Commander by the now familiar Pau. The Oracle also predicts an incident, which at the time, as it does now, caused much controversy—mercy killing.

C.III: 75

PAV. Veronne, Vicence, Sarragouſſe,
De glaives loings, terroirs de ſang humides:
Peſte ſi grande viendra à la grand gouſſe,
Proches ſecours, & bien loing les remedes.

*PAU (the short one). Verona, Vicenza, Saragossa,
Of far distant blades, humid lands of blood:
Plague so great will arrive with the large pod,
Help nearby, and the medicines very far away.*

PAV. (O.Fr.) petit, also diminutive of Na[pau]leon; loing, (O.Fr.) A une grande distance; terroirs, (O.Fr.) territoires. Cross-references: PAV: C.II: 33; C.II: 94; C.IV: 70; C.VI: 79; C.VIII: 1

NAPOLEON (THE SHORT ONE)

The prophecy begins by capitalizing '**PAV**', thus emphasising **NAPOLEON** as the intended subject ('v' and 'u' being equivalent in the classical Latin alphabet). *Pau*, meaning the 'short one' refers to Bonaparte's height of 5 feet 2½ inches (1·587 metres).

VERONA, VICENZA, SARAGOSSA

All three cities listed in the opening line of this oracle figured in campaigns directed by Napoleon. But since the predictions in this quatrain concern lands at the eastern end of the Mediterranean, rather than continental Europe, the intention must be to draw parallels between the two. For example, during Bonaparte's First Italian Campaign, VERONA was captured, subsequently lost, and later recaptured. Similarly, in Egypt, ALEXANDRIA was captured, subsequently lost, and later recaptured.[1]

In the same Italian campaign, the occupation of VICENZA allowed the French to go on and make further conquests. Likewise, when CAIRO was occupied, it allowed the French to go on and make further conquests.[2]

In Spain, at the Siege of SARAGOSSA, the French were eventually forced to withdraw. Likewise, in Syria, at the Siege of ACRE, the French were eventually forced to withdraw.[3] In short, VERONA and *Alexandria*; VICENZA and *Cairo*; SARAGOSSA and *Acre*, pairwise, share the same characteristics.

By comparing them, Nostradamus has doubled the prophetic content of the oracle.

OF FAR DISTANT BLADES, HUMID LANDS OF BLOOD

The words that comprise the second line of this quatrain call to mind Napoleon's invasion of the orient. The battles fought in Egypt, Palestine and Syria to extend France's empire eastwards were, indeed, fought upon FAR DISTANT HUMID LANDS where, *"the sabre, with the addition of a dagger in the other hand, proving more than a match for the bayonet."* (Thompson).[4] As for the BLOOD spilt there, this was the result of battles fought by Napoleon's army at Alexandria, Cairo, El-Arish, Gaza, and Jaffa.[5]

PLAGUE SO GREAT WILL ARRIVE

It was during the French occupation of Jaffa that the PLAGUE struck with frightening rapidity. In a matter of days the death toll had mounted to nearly 300 dead or dying. And even after the soldiers left Jaffa, the death toll continued to diminish their number.[6]

WITH THE LARGE POD

Upon reaching Acre, but failing after several vain attempts to take its heavily defended fortress, Bonaparte realised that his ambition to emulate Alexander the Great and continue on to India was now impossible. He therefore resolved to return to Cairo. But with many of his men victims of the plague, and unable to make the journey back across the desert sands, Bonaparte *"gave orders that they should be given a fatal dose of opium."* (Thompson). A broth laced with the *"narcotic drug that is obtained from the [large] unripe seedpods of the opium poppy"* was administered to the *plague* victims, and their deaths followed quickly.[7]

HELP NEARBY AND THE MEDICINES VERY FAR AWAY

At the time this was taking place, HELP was CLOSE AT HAND. Admiral Perrée had recently arrived at Acre with a small flotilla, and his ships were in a position to transport many of the sick and wounded men back to Alexandria. But he declined to do so: presumably for fear that he and his crew might become infected by plague.[8] The main body of French troops were therefore left to carry their sick and injured comrades on the long trek back across the desert to Egypt, knowing that THE MEDICINES were VERY FAR AWAY.[9]

The next oracle reminds one of Napoleon's arrival in Egypt; it ends with his departure. In between, Nostradamus predicts Turkey's reaction to Bonaparte's invasion of Egypt, and the equally direct response the country made to combat plans for an armed insurrection. Had the rebels been successful, they would have replaced the old monarchical system of the Sultan, with the politics of French Republicanism.

C.I: 98

Le chef qu'aura conduit peuple infiny
Loing de son ciel, de meurs & langue estrange:
Cinq mil en Crete, & Thessale finy,
Le chef fuiant sauué en marine grange.

The chief that will have conducted innumerable people
Far from his sky, for foreign customs and language:
Five thousand by Crete, and Thessaly finished,
The chief fleeing, concealed in a nautical barn.

Cross-reference: peuple infiny, C.II: 94

THE CHIEF THAT WILL HAVE CONDUCTED INNUMERABLE PEOPLE

THE Commander-in-CHIEF [1] WHO CONDUCTED INNUMERABLE PEOPLE across the sea has previously been identified as Napoleon, for that was how he described his Army of the Orient in a letter sent to the

Sultan Tipu in January 1799 (see C.II: 94).

FAR FROM HIS SKY

The phrase: **FAR FROM HIS SKY** is similar to that used in C.III: 75 (*'far distant blades, humid lands of blood'*), which predicted events from Napoleon's odyssey to Egypt and Syria. It therefore tends to affirm the location inferred when reading the first line.[2]

FOR FOREIGN CUSTOMS AND LANGUAGE

Napoleon encountered many **FOREIGN CUSTOMS** upon arriving in the Moslem world. After capturing Alexandria and then Cairo, he made his famous Arabic Declaration – his **FOREIGN SPEECH**. In this, he addressed the people of Egypt, assuring them that he was, and would continue to be, a friend to the Islamic religion. He then set up a council of Moslem leaders to ensure that full cooperation was maintained with his administration, and to reassure them that the existing *customs* of their people would be preserved.[3]

The oracle, while still concerning *foreign customs and speech*, next turns its attention to Crete and Thessaly: both of which belonged to the Ottoman Empire. In 1798 Turkey had declared war on France because of the concern it felt at Napoleon's invasion of Egypt. At the same time, Turkey was coming under increasing pressure from a different direction. Rigas Velestinlis, a Thessalonian, had been enthralled by the success of the French Revolution, and he wanted Turkey to adopt *The Rights of Man*.

FIVE THOUSAND BY CRETE

With Turkey officially at war with France, the Sultan dispatched:
– *"Turkish Reinforcements from Rhodes [numbering] 5,000."* The fleet passed **BY** Ottoman-held **CRETE** heading for Napoleon's army at Haifa.[4]

THESSALY FINISHED

Turkey also struck against: –

> *Rigas Velestinlis . . . [and his] plan for an armed revolt against the Turks. Rigas . . . had come under the influence of the French Revolution, as is manifest in a number of revolutionary tracts he had printed, intending to distribute them in an effort to stimulate a Pan-Balkan uprising against the Ottomans.*

Among his targets for political reform were *"the principalities of Moldavia and Wallachia.' The latter proposed the establishment of what, in essence,*

would have been a revived Byzantine Empire, . . . in which monarchical institutions would have been replaced by republican institutions on the French model."[5]
The Emperor, Diocletian, had made *Thessaly* part of this *Byzantine Empire*, hence the connection made by Nostradamus. Much later, after the arrival of the Walachians: *"Thessaly came to be called Great Walachia. (Megale Vlachia)."* But in the summer of 1798 Rigas was strangled by Ottoman assassins in Belgrade, and his political ambition for **THESSALY** was **FINISHED**.

THE CHIEF FLEEING

Having begun with Napoleon's arrival in Egypt, the Oracle concludes with his retreat from Acre. It was there that news reached **THE CHIEF** that his conquests in Italy were being reversed. Eager to immerse himself once more in the political life of Paris, he collected together a few chosen officers, and left Egypt in secret, **FLEEING** by ship to France: leaving behind: *"the splendid soldiers who for his sake, under strange and tropical skies, had faced hunger and thirst, wounds and death [but now] found themselves deserted by their chief."*

CONCEALED IN A NAUTICAL BARN

While at sea, Bonaparte remained ever wary of the British navy patrolling the Mediterranean, as well as the ships passing by; he therefore **CONCEALED** his presence below deck. The vessel he used for the voyage is described as **A NAUTICAL BARN**. Bonaparte had in fact acquired two ships; of these, *the commander* chose the frigate *Muiron*: *"But both frigates were Venetian-built and very bad sailors."* (Oman). Nostradamus's description of the ship is noticeably contemptuous.[6]

Napoleon left Egypt in August, but it was not until October that he arrived back in France. His arrival was not anticipated, and when his ship the *Muiron* appeared in full view of those on the French shore, it was greeted with suspicion. Fortunately, news of the army's recent victory at Aboukir had already arrived, and a hero's welcome was quickly organized to celebrate the Commander-in-Chief's safe return.

C.I: 30

La nef eftrange par le tourment marin
Abourdera pres de port incongneu,
Nonobftant fignes de rameau palmerin,
Apres mort, pille: bon auis tard venu.

The foreign ship, by reason of the marine torment
Will arrive close to port unrecognised,
Not obstructing the signs of the palm bough,
Afterwards a death, bereft of all: good intelligence arrived late.

Abourdera, (epenthesis) Abo[u]rdera, also Arabic phonetic – Abourdera for Abour[k]era (Aboukir); incongneu, (Latinism) incognitus; Nonobſtant – Non + obstant, (Latinism) obst/o; signes, (O.Fr.) enseigne for pilgrimage, or war; pille, (O.Fr. pillé) bereaved of all.

THE FOREIGN SHIP, BY REASON OF THE MARINE TORMENT

THE FOREIGN SHIP refers to the Venetian-built galley that brought Napoleon back to France from his eastern campaign in October of 1799.[1] It was THROUGH the loss of his fleet (Battle of the Nile, August 1798), referred to by Nostradamus as THE MARINE TORMENT that Napoleon found himself stranded in Egypt. By the time he was ready to leave, he had acquired two vessels, the *Muiron* and *Carrère*, and these carried him and his officers back to France.[2]

WILL ARRIVE CLOSE TO PORT UNRECOGNISED

On Wednesday 9 October, Napoleon's ship ARRIVED at the French coastal town of Frejus. The *Muiron* had been UNRECOGNISED when it first appeared CLOSE TO PORT. But upon learning that Bonaparte was on board, news of his return quickly spread across the country.[3]

NOT OBSTRUCTING SIGNS OF THE PALM BOUGH

In medieval Europe, the *palm bough* was traditionally carried by a *'palmer'*: a pilgrim returning from the Holy Land. Napoleon and the members of his party were also returning from the Holy Land. But the palm also has another meaning: *'To bear the palm'* is to be the best. *"The allusion is to the Roman custom of giving the victorious gladiator a branch of the palm tree."* (Brewer). Both descriptions serve to describe Napoleon's return from the east. He had returned from the Holy Land, where on one occasion he *"had set up his quarters in the Monastery of Nazareth, and had read the Bible to his officers under a Syrian sky in places sanctified by Christ and His apostles."* Secondly, he had returned as a recent victor from his triumph *'against the Turks at Aboukir'*. In each of these respects, he bore the SIGNS OF THE PALM BOUGH, and for which, there would be NO OBSTRUCTING his disembarkation, despite having arrived on board a foreign ship without papers.[4]

AFTERWARDS A DEATH, BEREFT OF ALL

Bonaparte's departure from Egypt on 22 August left General Jean-Baptiste Kléber in overall control of France's conquests in the east. But, soon **AFTERWARDS** (14 June 1800), he was assassinated by *"a Syrian Muslim, Sulayman al-Halabi."* [5] After Kléber's **DEATH**, Cairo was overrun by a British-led invasion force, and the city retaken. Three months later Alexandria too was recaptured, causing the French army to finally lay down its arms. Kléber's death had left France **BEREFT OF ALL** its conquests in the east. [6]

GOOD INTELLIGENCE ARRIVED LATE

Following the capitulation of Cairo, peace negotiations were begun between France and England. However, because of the extra distance required for information to travel from Paris to London, news of the fall of Alexandria was able to be delayed by several days. France realised its negotiating power would be severely compromised once the loss of Alexandria was discovered. Hence, by skilful political manoeuvring, the French managed to get the preliminaries to the peace treaty signed, before Whitehall received news of the British victory at Alexandria. In short: **GOOD INTELLIGENCE ARRIVED LATE**. [7]

The next quatrain is split between events in Egypt and the changes to the political situation in France, which occurred at the beginning of the Revolution, and lasted up until the time of Napoleon.

C.I: 16

> Faulx à l'eftang ioinct vers le Sagitaire,
> En fon hault AVGE de l'exaltation:
> Pefte, famine, mort de main militaire,
> Le fiecle approche de renouation.

> *Saturn in Aquarius joined towards Sagittarius,*
> *AUGEREAU at his height, from the raising up:*
> *Plague, hunger, death by the military hand,*
> *The century approaches renewal.*

Faulx, (O.Fr.) a scythe: the astrological symbol for Saturn; eftang, (O.Fr.) a pool, pond, standing water: the astrological sign for Aquarius; ioinct, (O.Fr.) joined, coupled, put; vers, (O.F.) dans la direction de; AVGE, (abbreviation) – AUGE[REAU] also, AUGE[AN] – 'To clear away an accumulated mass of corruption.' (Brewer).

SATURN IN AQUARIUS JOINED TOWARDS SAGITTARIUS

The orbit of Saturn around the Sun measures 29·458 years, and when it appears in Aquarius, it may remain there on average for 2·45 years: there being twelve signs of the Zodiac. Nothing therefore can be determined from the first line of this oracle. It is only when the remaining three lines are examined, and it is recognised that the events predicted refer to the end of the 18th century that the first line reveals its secret. Saturn was in Aquarius for the whole of 1789: [1] the year when the French Revolution began. The phrase that follows this: *'towards Sagittarius'*, simply means towards the period of Sagittarius; this occurs between 23 November and 21 December. The oracle is apparently directing attention to the month or months leading up to and including that period.

It is therefore TOWARDS SAGITTARIUS that one must seek for what happened. The Oath of the Tennis Court was sworn in June 1789, paving the way for the Third Estate to dispel from government the First and Second Estates. To rid France of the First Estate, a process of de-Christianising the nation began. This was greatly helped by the perilous state of the country's finances. On 2 November the vast property held by the Church was nationalised to fund the State's treasury. Five days later it was decreed that deputies were to be excluded from the Ministry; effectively, the First Estate had been removed from its former position in government and dispossessed of its wealth. *"On December 19 it was decided to auction off up to four hundred million livres' worth of ecclesiastical property through the agency of the municipality of Paris,"* [2] in exchange for assignats, *"which were to become the currency of the Revolution."* [3]

The assault on the nobility and its role in government also emerged TOWARDS SAGITTARIUS. On 6 October, the royal family was forced by the market women and fish wives to leave the palace of Versailles and take up residence in Paris. Four days later, Louis XVI was demoted from King of France and Navarre to just King of the French; [4] *"the parlements were declared to be henceforth in abeyance. In sweeping reforms of the judicial system, judges were to be selected by the people and paid by the state; local government was transformed following upon the creation of new provisional assemblies and the abolition of intendants."*

AUGEREAU AT HIS HEIGHT, FROM THE RAISING UP

Nostradamus now moves across these ten years of revolutionary government that ruled France, to arrive at the *coup* that ended it. *"On September 4th the Jacobin Directors helped by Bonaparte's nominee, General Augereau, who was put in command of the troops in Paris carried through the coup d'état of 15th Fructidor* (4 September 1797, see also C.II: 67)." By 1799, AUGEREAU, was AT HIS HEIGHT of achievement (he had begun life as a street urchin), having been made a deputy and secretary of the Directory.[5] But shortly before the turn of the century, Napoleon sprang his own *coup*, which replaced Barras' corrupt government. This was essentially an *Augean* act. With Paul de Barras in power, *"and with him a Jacobin government so bad and purposeless that only fatigue and indifference could have preserved it,"* (Fisher), there was a real need for the Herculean act of sweeping clean the '*Augean* Stables' (a metaphor for sweeping away corruption). Thereafter, Bonaparte became the military dictator of France, putting behind him the revolutionary governments that had earlier replaced the Estates-general of the *Ancient Regime* a decade earlier.

PLAGUE, HUNGER

Before returning to France in the autumn of 1799, and prior to conducting his *coup d'état*, Napoleon had been forced to retreat from Acre, having failed to take the Syrian fortress. It was during this retreat from Acre that the French army: *"Plague ridden, burdened by wounded, starved,"*[6] at last reached Katia, where they *"fell like starved vultures on the drink and supplies stored there."*[7]

DEATH BY THE MILITARY HAND

Shortly before the close of Bonaparte's campaign in Egypt (July 1799), his *Armée d'Orient* was forced to repel a Turkish expeditionary force that had landed at Aboukir Bay.

> *It was not a bloodless victory: . . . the French lost 150 killed and 750 wounded . . . of the Turkish force 2000 were killed on the field . . . and no less than 10,000 shot or drowned as they vainly attempted to swim to their ships. Another 1800 were found killed and 300 wounded in the fort.*[8]

THE CENTURY APPROACHES RENEWAL

This final line requires little explanation. The political events described above occurred in 1789, and again in 1799, the year that THE CENTURY APPROACHED RENEWAL. It was also the year Pope Pius VI died in exile.

C.VIII: 46

Pol menfolee mourra trois lieuës du rofne,
Fuis les deux prochains tarafc deftrois:
Car Mars fera le plus horrible trofne,
De coq & d'aigle de France freres trois.

Citizen, Southerner of France will decay three leagues from the Rhône,
The two neighbours Pius – flee! A fabulous monster destroyed,
Because Mars will make the most horrible throne,
For the cock and for the eagle; three brothers for France.

Pol menſolee, (Medieval Latin) Pol/ita mensol/is; mourra, (O.Fr. future tense of mourir) die, decease, decay; Fuis, (O.Fr. paranagram & imperative) [P]ius, also fuis = flee, escape; tarasc, (Medieval Latin) tarasc/us. Cross-references: aigle, C.I: 23; C.III: 37; C.IV: 70; C.VIII: 4; cock, C.II: 42

CITIZEN, SOUTHERNER OF FRANCE

After Napoleon's Army of Italy had invaded Rome and carried away Pius VI, the ageing, invalided pope was given the new and revolutionary title of *'Citizen Pope'*. He was then taken on an extended journey that ended with his death in Valence in *southern France*. Nostradamus acknowledges both these facts by calling him **CITIZEN, SOUTHERNER OF FRANCE**.[1]

WILL DECAY THREE LEAGUES FROM THE RHÔNE

It was while stopping over for the night at a town called Romans, which is located exactly **THREE LEAGUES FROM THE RIVER RHÔNE** that Pius VI's fragile health deteriorated even further.

The Pope produced a lot of blood without in the least acknowledging any further discomfort: the medicine prescribed for his paralysis having prevailed upon his interior. To conclude the course of this last illness, the pulse not conspicuous at all from fever but beating naturally with extreme faintness . . . The steward charged with his conveyance, without heeding to the requests of the inhabitants of Romans, who were hoping very much that the Pope would pass the following day in the midst of them, had decided that the departure would take place the next day at the most convenient hour so as to avoid the tumultuous mob. The Holy Father was thus transported on the 14 July from Romans to Valence. (L'Abbé Baldassari).[2]

THE TWO NEIGHBOURS PIUS – FLEE!

By coincidence, both Pius VI and his successor Pius VII were born in the same town of Cesana in the Romagna: moreover, the Braschi and the Chiarmonti were *'family friends'*. Hence, they are referred to as **THE TWO NEIGHBOURS**,[3] **PIUS**.[4] Both Popes were also the victims of Napoleon's occupation of Rome during their term in office, having on different occasions objected to France's quest for expansion. Both were made to pay the price, which was exile. Pius VI was sent to Valence, where he died; Pius VII was sent to Savona. Nostradamus therefore advises both popes to escape, or **FLEE** the city before they are captured.

A FABULOUS MONSTER DESTROYED

The French flag ship, the *Bucentaure*, (βουξ + κενταυροξ) – half ox and half man – is the **FABULOUS MONSTER** referred to by Nostradamus. The ship was commanded by Admiral Ville-neuve, who led the French and Spanish fleets against Nelson's British squadron off Cape Trafalgar in October 1805. But during the battle, the *Bucentaure* was raked by cannon shot from Nelson's ship Victory, and it took no further part in the action. An attempt to salvage the wrecked vessel was made after the fighting ceased, but this failed, and the ship was **DESTROYED** when it sank on its way to Cadiz.[5]

BECAUSE MARS WILL MAKE THE MOST HORRIBLE THRONE

MARS, god of war and strife, mythologically speaking, **MADE THE SEAT OF GOVERNMENT** in France **MOST HORRIBLE** during the time of the French Revolution and Napoleonic Era. A decade of revolution and war, followed by a further decade and a half of battles fought across Europe, even into Asia, ensured the fulfilment of this prophecy.[6] Nostradamus now predicts those who will occupy the seat of government at this time, naming first the Cock.

FOR THE COCK

The **COCK** became a symbol of France during the revolution. The Latin word '*Gallus*', translates as either Gaul or a cock. It can therefore be understood to represent the French Republic after the fall of the monarchy (see also C.II: 42).[7]

AND FOR THE EAGLE

The **EAGLE** was adopted by Napoleon as a symbol of his power, and is used by Nostradamus as a byname for the Emperor in other quatrains (see C.I: 23; C.III: 37; C.IV: 70; C.VIII: 46).[8]

FOR FRANCE, THREE BROTHERS

FRANCE'S THREE BROTHERS during this troubled time were Louis XVI, who was guillotined during the French Revolution, his brother, Stanislas Xavier, the duc de Provence, who became Louis XVIII, (following the abdication of Napoleon in 1814 and again in 1815) and their younger brother, the Comte d'Artois, who succeeded to the throne in 1824 as Charles X. All three were grandsons of Louis XV, whose own son, the Dauphin died before he could inherit the Crown.[9]

After returning from Egypt, and learning of the reversals made by Austria to his earlier conquests in Italy, Napoleon decided to embark upon a second invasion of that country. This bred thoughts of Hannibal and his surprise attack on Rome. The French Commander therefore decided to follow the Carthaginian Commander's example by taking his own army over the Alps. The prophecy below describes the progress made by the French, as they marched over the mountains towards the besieged city of Genoa where André Masséna, under siege, was slowly being starved into submission.

C.IV: 37

Gaulois par faults, monts viendra penetrer:
Occupera le grand lieu de l'Infubre:
Au plus profond fon oft fera entrer:
Gennes, Monech poufferont claffe rubre.

The Frenchman, by bounds, will arrive to penetrate the mountains:
He will occupy the celebrated place of the Insubres:
To the greatest depth his army will succeed in entering,
Genoa! Monaco will repulse the red fleet.

Gaulois, (O.Fr.) Of France, French, a Frenchman; penetrer, (Latinism) penetr/o; oft, (O.Fr.) armée; Monech, (Latinism) Monœcis; rubre, (Latinism) rub/ri. Cross-reference: Gaulois, C.X: 34

THE FRENCHMAN

"Napoleone di Buonaparte (he habitually signed his name after the Italian fashion until 1796)" was entitled to French nationality because Corsica had been annexed by France shortly before his birth.[1]

BY BOUNDS, WILL ARRIVE TO PENETRATE THE MOUNTAINS

In May 1800, accompanied by an army of 50,000 soldiers, the First Consul began the long climb over the Alps: PENETRATING THE MOUNTAINS that separate France from Italy. But the snow was still deep in the higher regions, and his personal decent from the Great St. Bernard Pass was unconventional, which is to say: he descended BY BOUNDS. According to the official bulletin, *"The First Consul came down from the top of the St. Bernard Pass, sliding and rolling in the snow."* (Chandler).[2]

HE WILL OCCUPY THE CELEBRATED PLACE OF THE INSUBRES

After successfully crossing *the mountains*, Bonaparte was able to OCCUPY the Po Valley, which was once THE CELEBRATED PLACE OF THE INSUBRES. *The Insubres* were an ancient people who had inhabited the region close to the River Po. They were also a race that had previous links with Hannibal; he, having urged them to free themselves from Rome's domination.[3] Presumably, it was this parallel that had caused Nostradamus to name these people. From there, the French army moved on to Milan, arriving in the city on 2 June.

On 14 June, approximately 25 miles north of *Genoa*, the French army of the Reserve met and fought the Austrians at Marengo. The battle was fiercely contested, and might have been lost by the French, but for Bonaparte's reserve force. Nonetheless, by the end of the day the First Consul was able to emerge victorious.

TO THE GREATEST DEPTH, HIS ARMY WILL MAKE ENTRY

In the wake of this success, and with the recapture of *Genoa*, Napoleon was able to drive the Austrians out of Italy. By December, Joachim Murat, leading the FRENCH ARMY down the leg of Italy, had recovered the Papal States, and occupied Tuscany: having ENTERED the Carolingian kingdom of Italy – which occupied the northern and central peninsula down to Rome – TO THE GREATEST DEPTH.[4] Further south was the Kingdom of Naples, and beyond that, the Kingdom of Sicily.

GENOA

On the day of Napoleon's arrival in Italy, *Genoa*, which had been besieged since the middle of April, was forced to admit defeat. The Commander-in-Chief, André Masséna, had held out as long as possible, but a shortage of food eventually compelled his surrender, and he was allowed by General Ott to withdraw to Nice.[5]

MONACO WILL REPULSE THE RED FLEET

One month earlier, on 23 May, the British fleet under Lord Keith's command; that is, *"Keith-Elphinstone, George, (viscount Keith, K. B. – Admiral of the Red, &c.),"* which until then had been occupying the Ligurian Sea in order to blockade *Genoa,* and prevent supplies reaching the besieged city, turned to attack MONACO.[6] But Lord Admiral Keith's RED FLEET WAS REPULSED.[7] As a result of Monaco's staunch naval defence; Nostradamus was able to point out to *Genoa*, which had succumbed to attack, that *Monaco* had been more successful in withstanding assault.

The next quatrain moves forward to the time when Napoleon

333

had reached the pinnacle of his power. Once again, the enormity of this man's deeds, in having taken prisoner first Pius VI and then Pius VII, has occupied Nostradamus's prescient powers: and in doing so, the region where the pontiffs were once held is named. This prophecy is also remarkable for containing a cryptic reference to Napoleon by both name and title.

C.VIII: 1

PAV, NAY, LORON plus feu qu'à fang fera,
Laude nager, fuir grand aux furrez.
Les agaſſas entree refuſera.
Pampon, Durance les tiendra enſerrez.

NAPOLEON ROI (Pau, Ney, Erlon), will be more fire than blood,
Swimming in praise, shunning a great man at the raisings-up:
He will refuse the Piuses entry,
Possessing all: Durance will hold them enclosed.

Pau, (O.Fr.) petit, also diminutive of Na[pau]leon; Nay, (O.Fr.) rough, also paragram – Ney; Loron, (O.Fr. syncope) lorion, also Loron (paranagram) Erlon; feu, (O.Fr. homonym) one who accepts his destiny, also fire; furrez, (Latinism) surre/xi; agaſſa, (synonym) pie (synonym) Pius; Pampon, (Greek syncope) παμπ[αν]ον, i.e., Pamp[an]on, possessing all; enferrez, (O.Fr.) enfermer. Cross-references: Pau, C.II: 33; C.II: 94; C.III: 75; C.IV: 70; C.VI: 79

N.B. The letters of Pav, Nay, Lor[i]on, together form the anagram — **Na Pav Lyon Roi**: phonetically, this creates the sound – NAPOLEON ROI. There is no distinction between 'u' and 'v' in imperial Latin. It is also to be noted that Napoleon was King of Italy as well as Emperor of the French.

NAPOLEON, KING: HE WILL BE MORE FIRE, THAN BLOOD

The first line predicts that NAPOLEON WILL BE KING, although NOT BY BLOODLINE. His rise to power was accomplished THROUGH THE FIERY nature of his character. *"Miot de Melito, who met him at Brescia on June 5th [1796] described in his Mémoirs . . . his strong features, keen questioning look, and quick decisive gestures revealed a flame-like spirit (âme ardente)."*[1]

(NEY, ERLON)

Michael NEY and Jean Baptiste, Comte d'ERLON were both members of Napoleon's team of commanding officers who fought with him at Waterloo. These names, combined with 'PAU', provide the basic letters for the Emperor's full name and title. It is also to be observed that the verb 'sera' is in the third person singular, and therefore serves a single subject; not three, as implied by the opening triple.

Three times, in 1800, in 1802, and in 1804, he sought and obtained authority from the people. In quick succession the popular voice made him First Consul for ten years, Consul for life, and finally Emperor. No European monarch could claim so good a title.[2]

SHUNNING A GREAT MAN AT THE RAISINGS-UP

Pope Pius VII had been persuaded, although not without difficulty, to officiate at Napoleon's coronation. Eventually, he agreed to attend, but with the full expectation that it would be he, alone, who placed the crown upon the Emperor's head. It was not to be. As the critical point in the coronation ceremony approached, when the crown was to be placed upon the emperor's bead, Bonaparte realised this was an act of submission to higher authority. His vanity would not allow it. Seizing hold of the crown himself, he placed it upon his own head; crowning his wife Joséphine Empress of France immediately afterwards. Pius VII – THE GREAT MAN of this oracle – fuming with inner anger at having been brought to Paris to officiate, and then SHUNNED at the crowning moment, or as Nostradamus foresaw: AT THE RAISING-UP (plural from *aux*), was forced to step back and take his seat amongst the onlookers.[3]

HE WILL REFUSE THE PIUSES ENTRY

The predicted exile of the two *Piuses* by Napoleon is again mentioned. In February 1798, Pius VI was taken into custody and removed from Rome. Thereafter, he spent the remainder of his life being moved from town to town until he finally died inside the citadel at Valence. Ten years later, (July 1809), Pius VII was also removed from Rome. He spent the next five years in exile at Savona on the Italian coast. BOTH PIUSES [4] WERE therefore REFUSED ENTRY to Rome by order of Bonaparte.[5]

POSSESSING ALL

By the terms laid out in the *Treaty of Tilsit* (July1807), Napoleon was able to establish control of the western and central mainland of Europe. In July of the following year he again entered Rome; this time, with the intention of adding the papal territories to his list of occupied territories so that he might then POSSESS ALL.[6]

DURANCE WILL HOLD THEM ENCLOSED

Pius VII objected strongly to Napoleon's proposed acquisition, and responded by ex-communicating the French soldiers who were carrying out the annexation order. Napoleon retaliated by seizing the Pope and transporting him to Avignon, a city that lies INSIDE the fluvial curve of the River DURANCE. It was from there that he was subsequently sent to Savona. Ten years earlier, Valence, which also lies INSIDE the fluvial curve of the DURANCE, had been the city to which Pope Pius VI was taken shortly before his death.[7]

Although Napoleon was undisputed Emperor of the French, and saw himself superior to any man on earth, he also retained the fear of losing that power. This may have motivated him to commit one of the greatest crimes of the nineteenth-century: that of having the duke of Enghien executed. Enghien was the –*"Last member of the distinguished French family of Condé and . . . first cousin of the later King Louis Philippe."* By authorising his kidnapping and execution: *'Napoleon had made himself a regicide'*. The quatrain in which this is foretold contains another split prophecy.

C.II: 76

Foudre en Bourgoigne fera cas portenteux,
Que par engin ne pourroit faire:
De leur ſenat ſacriſte fait boiteux,
Fera ſauoir aux ennemis l'affaire.

A calamity within Bourgogne will make a portentous event,
Without by a stratagem, (Enghien), he would not be able to do:
Of their governing body, a sacristan made lame,
He will explain the affair to the adversaries

Bourgoigne, (epenthesis) Bourgo[i]gne; engin, (O.Fr. engien) artifice, also (syncope) for Enghien; pourroit, (conditional form of pouvoir); fera savoir = to explain.

Apart from indicating a region of France, *Bourgogne* was also the name of a quite remarkable sergeant in Napoleon's army (A. J. B. F. Bourgogne). What made him significant was the vivid, first-hand, personal history of his experiences, which he recorded while serving under the Emperor Napoleon. Louis Philippe, King of the French from 1830 to 1848, later honoured the old soldier with the commission of *Major de Place* in his hometown of Valenciennes, and it was there that he wrote his memoirs, which include the following event.

WITHIN BOURGOGNE

In his book, literally WITHIN BOURGOGNE, the ex-sergeant recounted a sudden, dramatic incident that he had personally witnessed during Napoleon's Russian campaign of 1812. It is his description of this event, which appears very similar in detail to the incident predicted in the second half of this oracle that makes it *a portentous event;* for it can be said, it was an incident portended by this earlier happening.[1]

A CALAMITY WILL MAKE A PORTENTOUS EVENT

What *Bourgogne* described, was the emergence of A sudden CA-LAMITY – *a bolt from the blue.* A troop of Cossack riders suddenly appeared without warning, and made directly for a small group of French militia surrounding Bonaparte. It was a planned attack by the Russian cavalry to take the French by surprise, kidnap the Emperor, and take him into captivity. The attempt only just failed. Nevertheless, Napoleon was haunted by the possibility that another attempt might be more successful, and from then onwards he kept a phial of poison hung round his neck, believing that suicide was preferable to capture.

Nostradamus foresaw this attempted kidnapping as 'MAKING A PORTENTOUS EVENT'. This can imply a previous incident had existed, to which the attempted kidnapping of Bonaparte is compared.

WITHOUT BY A STRATAGEM (ENGHIEN), HE WOULD NOT BE ABLE TO DO

Eight years earlier, in March 1804, a party of French cavalry officers suddenly and unexpectedly appeared at Ettenheim, where the Duke of *Enghien,* prospective heir to the French throne, was in exile. The plan was for the cavalry to kidnap the Duke and bring him back to France. The *stratagem* worked. *Enghien* was captured, and taken to the Chateau of Vincennes, where he was summarily tried for conspiracy, and executed by firing squad.[2]

EXCEPT BY this STRATAGEM against ENGHIEN, Napoleon WOULD NOT HAVE BEEN ABLE TO remove the heir to the French throne, whom he saw as a potential rival to his power.[3] The repercussions of this murder not only shook France, but also horrified all Europe.

OF THEIR GOVERNING BODY, A SACRISTAN MADE LAME

Behind the *stratagem* to kidnap *Enghien* was a leading member OF THE GOVERNING BODY: someone who was also both A SACRISTAN AND LAME (sacristan: a person in charge of Church property). Charles Maurice de Talleyrand, Napoleon's Foreign Minister, had become crippled after a childhood accident, and this may have steered him towards his early career in the Church. During the French Revolution, he changed sides and became involved in politics. His abilities, and past career in the Church were soon recognized, and he was put *in charge of Church property*; that is, he became *a sacristan*. And, importantly, it was Talleyrand in 1804 that calmed Napoleon's concerns regarding a possible Royalist threat by kidnapping the Duke of *Enghien* and having him executed.[4]

HE WILL EXPLAIN THE AFFAIR TO THE ADVERSARIES

Eventually, Talleyrand betrayed Napoleon to the Czar of all the Russias. He did so **BY EXPLAINING** to Czar Alexander **THE** details of a secret **AFFAIR** that he had been advising Bonaparte upon. Czar Alexander was therefore being fed with advance knowledge of what was intended for his forthcoming talks with the French. *Affair* is also the word that Napoleon used to describe the secret treaty he wished to negotiate with Czar Alexander. *"It was an affair, he added, which must be treated between themselves."* But, unbeknown to Bonaparte, after each session with Alexander, the Czar would arrange to meet with Talleyrand in order to discuss the proposals that had taken place earlier that day. *"There can be no doubt that by any usual standard, Talleyrand's behaviour at Erfut constituted treason to France and treachery to Napoleon."*[5]

With his foresight still focused upon the Napoleonic Era, Nostradamus turns his attention next to the *Battle of Trafalgar* and the death of Admiral Nelson.

C.I: 77

Entre deux mers dreſſera promontoire
Que puis mourra par le mords du cheual:
Le ſien Neptune pliera voyle noire,
Par Calpre & claſſe aupres de Rocheual.

Between two seas he will lay out a promontory
Who then will die by the sting of the jailbird / man at arms:
His own Neptune will fold the black sail
Into Gibraltar, and the fleet close to Rochefort.

Que, (O.Fr.) who; mords, (O.Fr.) bite, nibble, sting; cheual = lout, jailbird, (Harraps Dictionary & Harraps Dictionary of Slang and Colloquialisms) but cheval can also be a syncope for cheval[ier], which has the meaning of 'man ar arms'; Calpre, (Latin epenthesis) Calpe; val/eo is Latin for 'fort' in French, hence: Roche + val = Roche + fort = Rochefort. Cross reference: dreſſera promontoire, C.VI: 79.

BETWEEN TWO SEAS

The Strait of Gibraltar flows **BETWEEN TWO SEAS**, the Mediterranean and the Atlantic Ocean.[1] In October 1805 this area became the scene of the *Battle of Trafalgar*, an affray that took its name from Cape Trafalgar on the Spanish mainland nearby. At the head of the British fleet was Horatio Nelson in the *Victory*. His adversary was Admiral Villeneuve in the *Bucentaure*.

HE WILL LAY OUT A PROMONTORY

Nelson's battle formation was unusual in that he lined up his ships in the form of a spear: the oracle refers to this formation as *a promontory*. At its head, he placed his own ship *Victory*, and with the *Temeraire* on one side and *Neptune* on the other, he led his fleet into battle. It will be recalled that Nostradamus predicted Napoleon would also *'lay out a promontory'*. This was fulfilled when Bonaparte drove a wedge between the Austrian army and the Piedmontese during his first Italian campaign. Nelson's plan was also designed to **LAY OUT A PROMONTORY** and to drive a wedge between the enemy's ships.[2]

WHO WILL THEN DIE

The French flagship *Bucentaure* was amongst the first to be put out of action by cannon fire, but this early success was quickly followed by tragedy. Nelson had been seen on deck by one of the sharpshooters high up on the mast of the *Redoubtable*. The marksman fired, and Nelson fell to the deck fatally wounded. **HE DIED A LITTLE WHILE AFTERWARDS**, holding on to life just long enough to be told that the battle had been won.[3]

BY THE STING OF THE JAILBIRD [OR MAN AT ARMS]

During the Napoleonic Wars, men were still being pressed into naval service on both sides of the Channel. The oracle refers to the *man at arms* who killed Nelson as *a ruffian* or *jailbird*. In fact, the men used by the French, if not swept up from the gutters, were often released from jail on condition that they would fight in the navy. *"The work of the press gangs went on continuously, in France . . . for many of these men-unskilled, vagrants, jailbirds – life on land had been even harder than life at sea."* (Ford). The snipers perched precariously on the mast tops fell into this category: having been placed there because this was one of the most dangerous, accident-prone places to be, whilst on board a fighting ship.[4]

HIS OWN NEPTUNE WILL FOLD THE BLACK SAIL INTO GIBRALTAR

Nelson's body was taken on board HIS ship, H.M.S. NEPTUNE, and carried in solemn state TO GIBRALTAR.

Reference to *the black sail* has been included in the prophecy because of the similarity it has to a familiar tale from Greek Mythology. Theseus, the son of Aegeus, king of Athens, hoisted *a black sail* before setting off to destroy the Minotaur, a fabulous beast; half bull, half man. Now compare this to the French ship, *Bucentaure*: a name meaning half bull half man, which was destroyed by Nelson. Theseus said: if he returned alive, only then would he change *the black sail* for a white one. Nelson, of course, did not return alive, hence the reference to *the black sail*. Theseus, however, did return: *"on the eighth day of Pyanepsion – (a period in October)."* Again, compare this with the date of Nelson's victory at Trafalgar – *'21 October'*. Unfortunately, upon his return voyage, Theseus forgot to hoist a white sail. When those on land saw his ship approaching with a black sail, they fell into mourning for the death of their hero. Once again, compare this to the reception which greeted the body of Nelson, when *his Neptune* brought their hero's body INTO GIBRALTAR.[5]

A painting of this scene by William Clarkson Stansfield R.A. (1793–1867) hangs at the National Maritime Museum in Greenwich. It shows *"Lord Nelson's flagship, with much of her masts and rigging shot away, being towed by H.M.S. Neptune into Gibraltar Bay on 28 October 1805."*

THE FLEET CLOSE TO ROCHEFORT

After the Battle of Trafalgar, Rear-Admiral Dumanoir le Pelley, with a small FLEET of four French ships under his command, took evasive action to avoid being detected by the British Navy. As he crossed the Bay of Biscay, he encountered a lone British frigate. This was the *Phoenix*, searching the Bay for a squadron of ships that was known to have left ROCHEFORT under the command of Rear-Admiral Allemand. With odds of four to one, le Pelley gave chase, but as his ships headed south in pursuit, they encountered five British ships commanded by Captain Sir Richard Strachan in the 80-gun *Caesar*. In the sea battle that followed all four of the French ships were captured and badly damaged. They were later taken back to Plymouth and refitted for further use by the British Navy.[6]

The next oracle introduces Napoleon as Emperor of France, and King of Rome and all things Roman. But this is merely a preamble to a prediction of the reasons that led to Napoleon's abdication.

C.VIII: 60

Premier en Gaule, premier en Romanie,
Par mer & terre aux Anglois & Paris,
Merueilleux faits par celle grand mefnie
Violant, Terax perdra de norlaris.

Foremost in France, foremost in Roman territory,
By reason of sea and land, by the English, and Paris,
Marvellous deeds by that Grande Armée.
Violating agreement: the Monster will lose in the north land.

Romanie, (Latinism, adjective) Roman/us; mefnie; (O.Fr.) armée; Terax, (Greek) Τερας and Teras, (Medieval English); Violant, (Latinism) viol/o – to violate an agreement; norlaris, (portmanteau and anagram) nor' + laris (O.Fr.) north land, also Lorrain[e]. Cross reference; norlaris, C.IX: 50

FOREMOST IN FRANCE, FOREMOST IN ROMAN TERRITORY

The oracle commences by introducing Napoleon as the man who, in 1804, became FOREMOST IN FRANCE.[1] He had rejected the title of King because of its revolutionary connotations. Instead, he chose the title Emperor, following the tradition of the Romans. After subjugating Rome, then declaring himself King, he demanded from Pius VII that he hand over the Papal States. By then, Bonaparte had obtained such *"a concentration of power comparable only to that of the Roman Caesars, of Charlemagne and of the Holy Roman Emperors."*[2]

BY REASON OF SEA AND LAND, BY THE ENGLISH

Napoleon's reign beginning as First Consul and then as Emperor was dominated by war at SEA AND on LAND: with *the English* as his main adversary. The War of the Second Coalition was led BY THE ENGLISH and involved the battle of the Pyramids (21 July 1798); the Nile (1 August 1798); Marengo (14 June 1800), and Hohenlinden (3 December 1800). The War of the Third Coalition was again led BY THE ENGLISH and involved battles at Ulm (20 October 1805); Trafalgar (21 October 1805), and Austerlitz (2 December 1805). The War of the Fourth Coalition was again led BY THE ENGLISH. This time it involved the battles of Jena and Auerstedt (14 October 1806); Eylau (8 February 1807), and Friedland (14 June 1807). Then, between 1808 and 1815 Napoleon's army was involved in the Peninsula War, in which Wellington led a coalition of *English*, Spanish and Portuguese that slowly drove the French back over the Pyrenees.[3]

The overthrow of Napoleon came at the end of sixteen years of endeavour **BY THE ENGLISH**, with battles fought *on land and sea*; **AND** it came with the fall of **PARIS**. In the third week of March 1814, Russian troops entered the suburbs of the capital from the east. Napoleon had made a brave and strategic defence of the city. *"But no amount of skill could do more than postpone defeat."* By the last day of the month, Paris was forced to capitulate. Inside the city Talleyrand's, *"opportunity had come to free France from the tyranny of Napoleon. . . . . On the morning of the 31st . . . he drafted a Declaration, which was approved by Alexander and published the same night."* This effectively confirmed the occupation of Paris by allied forces, and that no negotiations with Napoleon would be undertaken. On 6 April, Napoleon, while still resident at Fontainebleau found himself without support, and *"signed an unconditional abdication."*[4]

"La Grande Armée – Officially came into existence in September 1805." The **MARVELLOUS DEEDS** accomplished by it, particularly in the campaigns of 1805-7 are very well known: –

> . . . *after marching through Germany at a prodigious speed, Napoleon at the head of the Grande Armée had trapped a whole Austrian army at Ulm and received its surrender. By 14 November he was entering Vienna in triumph. Two weeks later . . . he then turned and defeated the vastly superior combined forces of Austria and Russia. The Battle of Austerlitz, one of the most perfectly conceived and executed in the history of warfare . . . would always remain the jewel of all military jewels in Napoleon's crown.*[5]

Its end came *"After Napoleon had sacrificed the whole of the Grande Armée in Russia in 1812, abandoning its shattered remnants as he scurried home to a disbelieving and restive Paris."* And with its end came another defeat in October 1813, in the Battle of Nations at Leipzig, *"in the bloodiest encounter Europe would know until 1914."*[6] Bonaparte's abdication and his exile to Elba came less than six months later with the fall of Paris.

"The Treaty of Fontainebleau, signed on April 12th by the representatives of

Russia, Austria Prussia, and France (but not England), provided for the future of the deposed Bonapartes." A clause in this *agreement* stipulated: – *"For Napoleon the island of Elba was to 'form during his lifetime a separate principality which he shall possess in full sovereignty and property'"* [7] But Bonaparte **VIOLATED THE AGREEMENT** by escaping from his exile on Elba as soon as the opportunity arose. [8]

THE MONSTER

Napoleon's covetousness for empire, and his reputation as a conqueror had by this time earned him the widely known sobriquet of *'Ogre'*, or *'the Corsican Ogre'.* This *"image lingered well into the Victorian period. English mothers, for instance, reputedly chastened their recalcitrant offspring with the dire threat that 'Boney will come and get you'."* [Confirmed by the author]. [9]

Nostradamus translates *Ogre* as **THE MONSTER.**

WILL LOSE IN THE NORTH LAND (LORRAINE)
"For several centuries Lorraine was part of the Belgian province of the Roman Empire." Waterloo is in Belgium, and it was at Waterloo in **THE NORTH LAND**, on 18 June 1815, that Napoleon was to **LOSE** his final battle: [10] bringing to an end his astonishing career.

Still intent upon predicting events for Napoleon, Nostradamus next looks at the Emperor's policy of expanding French influence in adjacent countries. This quatrain is also noticeable for its employment of a similar strategy to that found in C.IV: 37, where it will be recalled how the seer admonished Genoa's failing by praising Monaco's success.

C.VI: 12

Dreſſer copies pour monter à l'Empire,
Du Vatican le ſang Royal tiendra:
Flamans, Anglois, Eſpaigne auec Aſpire,
Contre l'Italie & France contendra.

Raising armies in order to serve the Empire,
Concerning the Vatican, the Kingly blood will possess:
Flemish! The English aspire with the Spanish (Persia),
And France will contend against Italy.

monter, (O.Fr.) servir; tenir, (O.Fr.) posséder; Aſpire, (3rd person singular) aspire, and Aspire (anagram) Persia.

RAISING ARMIES IN ORDER TO SERVE THE EMPIRE
Under Napoleon, the French Empire expanded its boundaries from the Baltic to the Mediterranean and from the Atlantic to the western borders of Austria and Prussia. A constant input of men

was therefore required to maintain this dominant position. In 1808, Bonaparte, *"disposed of some 300,000 troops in Spain, 100,000 in France, 200,000 in the Rhineland, and 60,000 in Italy."* It has been calculated that during the whole time in which Bonaparte remained Emperor of the French, the number of men called to serve in his armies reached two million.[1]

By using the word EMPIRE, Nostradamus has predicted the decree made on 18 May 1804 by the *Sénatus-Consulte*. This placed the Republic in the hands of an Emperor. The decision had been made, not simply to follow a precedent set by the Roman Empire, but as a practical means of keeping the French Emperor apart from Royalist plots intent upon returning France to a monarchist state.

CONCERNING THE VATICAN, THE KINGLY BLOOD WILL POSSESS

In 1808, French troops entered Rome. Napoleon, now King of Italy,[2] ordered General Miollis TO POSSESS THE VATICAN, seize control of the government, and mount guard over the entrances to the papal palace. Napoleon's plan was to annex the Papal States, and incorporate them into France's expanding political system, thereby adding to *"his passionate aim to be Rex Totius Italiae [King of all Italy]."*[3] In the early hours of the morning of 6 July, *"detachments of troops with scaling-ladders forced their way into the Quirinal, broke down door after door in the dark, echoing palace."* The Pope was at last found seated at a table attended by five cardinals. *"I am sent by His Majesty the Emperor Napoleon to ask whether your Holiness is disposed to agree to the treaty whose terms have been presented to him."* The Pope replied that he was unable to comply. *"'Then', said the General, 'I must put you under arrest.'"*[4]

The year, 1808 also saw the commencement of the Peninsula War. In April, that year, the *Spanish* royal family was summoned to Bayonne, and forced to abdicate in favour of Napoleon's brother Joseph. But, by the time summer arrived, Spain was in revolt against their new King, and Joseph was forced to leave Madrid. England saw Spain's uprising as their opportunity to establish a bridgehead in Portugal. Towards the end of the year an army was dispatched under the command of Sir Arthur Wellesley, (subsequently Duke of Wellington) to achieve this objective.

The **Flemish** people were not nearly so concerned. Since 5 June 1806, Napoleon's third brother Louis had become King Lodewijk I, and both Belgium and Holland had settled comfortably down under his rule.[5] Whereas the **Spanish** had rebelled against the imposition of a Corsican king, and the **English** had joined them in their opposition to the Bonapartes:[6] with both countries **aspiring** to rid their countries of Napoleon's influence,[7] the **Flemish**, in complete contrast, remained noticeably apathetic.

In the third line of the quatrain, *Aspire* has been given a capital letter. This usually implies that a second meaning may be involved: quite possibly concealing a name.

In 1808, Napoleon was still engaged in an attempt to persuade the Shah of **Persia** to join him in an offensive against Georgia. The Emperor had sent General Gardanne to see the Shah, carrying with him a promise of material aid if the plan he had in mind was undertaken. Accompanying the promise was Bonaparte's agreement to equip the Shah with: *"4,000 infantry, commanded by chosen and experienced officers, 10,000 muskets and 50 pieces of cannon."* But in the event, very little aid materialized.[8]

Prior to 1808, the kingdom of Italy comprised only the northern and eastern plains of the peninsula from Lombardy to the Adriatic. But in 1808 this was extended, when France added the March of Ancona down to the border of Naples. Pius VII had naturally remained hostile to the occupation of Rome, and the loss of the Papal States. He also disapproved of *"Napoleon's attempts to remodel North Italy's legal and administrative systems on those of France."* [9] And it was in the strongest possible terms that he *"denounced French demands for the immediate closure of Italy's ports to British trade."* [10]

Napoleon's poor relationship with the Catholic Church has been the topic of several previous quatrains. In the next oracle, Nostradamus returns to this subject but from the Cardinal of France's point of view. This verse is of special interest because the Cardinal in question was also Napoleon's uncle, and was therefore expected to be compliant to his nephew's wishes.

C.VIII: 4

Dedans Monech le Coq fera receu,
Le Cardinal de France apparoiftra
Par Legation Romain fera deceu,
Foibleffe à l'Aigle, & force au Coq naiftra.

Inside Monaco the Cock will be received,
The Cardinal of France will prove himself,
The Roman will be deceived by the Legation,
Weakness by the Eagle, & authority will be issued to the Cock.

Monech, (Latinism) Monœcis; apparoiftra, (O.Fr.) se montre; Legation, (Latinism) legati/o; Foibleffe, (O.Fr.) Faiblesse; force, (O.Fr.) autorité; Cross-references: Aigle: C.I: 23; C.III: 37; C.IV: 70; C.VIII: 46; Cock & Aigle: C.VIII: 46

N.B. 'Legation' appears in the 1650 edition of the Centuries published by Pierre Leffen of Leyden, which was reproduced from the Lyons edition of 1558. Unfortunately, Rigaud's edition of 1568 prints this word as 'Logarion'. This would seem to be a typesetting error, with 't' misread as 'r', and 'e' misread as 'o'. Rigaud also prints 'Aigle' and 'Coq' without capital letters.

INSIDE MONACO THE COCK WILL BE RECEIVED

Prior to 1861, *Monaco* occupied more than twice the land it now covers. The reduction in size occurred under Prince Charles III, who sold off half the Principality to France in exchange for independence. This oracle concerns *Monaco* before the sell-off. *"On 15th February, 1793, the Convention decided upon the incorporation of the Principality into France."* **THE COCK** was therefore **RECEIVED INTO MONACO** for a period that extended from the French Revolution up until the close of the Napoleonic Era, when territorial acquisitions were restored to their former boundaries.[1]

At this point, Nostradamus focuses his predictive power onto the problem that Napoleon was having with Pope Pius VII. In pursuit of his aim, which was to cower the Pope into submission and thereby compel him to sign an agreement limiting his power, Bonaparte believed he had found a way to achieve this. He therefore *"summoned a comité ecclésiastique . . . to advise him about the Pope's bull of excommunication, and other matters."*

Napoleon's aim was to force Pius VII to agree a new Concordat: one that invested only bishops with whom he approved. The Pope refused, holding out until June 1811, when, due to his silence upon a particular clause intended for the Concordat, he allowed this to be construed as consent. Twenty-four hours later Pius made it known that he withdrew any support that may have implied consent to this decree.

THE CARDINAL OF FRANCE WILL PROVE HIMSELF

Napoleon promptly countered by ordering Pius' denial to be suppressed. He then summoned the National Council and directed them to *"endorse the decree embodying the Pope's concession."* It was then that THE CARDINAL OF FRANCE PROVED HIMSELF by rallying members of the Council into supporting the Pope, in defiance of the Emperor. (The Archbishop of Lyon, Cardinal Joseph Fesch, was France's representative at the Vatican: he was also Napoleon's uncle.[2]) Each member of the papal LEGATION swore on oath their allegiance and true obedience to the *Roman* Pontiff, and to the Roman Catholic Church.[3]

THE ROMAN WILL BE DECEIVED BY THE LEGATION

Bonaparte responded to this mark of dissent by immediately dissolving the Council, preferring instead to intimidate each member personally until they had individually given him their signature of acceptance. As a result of Bonaparte's underhand strategy, Pius VII – THE ROMAN – was DECEIVED BY THE LEGATION. For the Council members' signatures now appeared on the document confirming concessions that the Pontiff had been assured they would resist.[4]

WEAKNESS BY THE EAGLE

In the year following the Pope's unintentional submission to a new Concordat, Bonaparte – THE EAGLE (this being his adopted emblem) – began to show signs of WEAKNESS. This became apparent when he embarked upon a gravely misguided invasion of Russia. It ended in failure, and a decisive retreat from Moscow. One year later Bonaparte suffered his second reversal at Leipzig: a battle that freed Germany from French domination. And in 1814, Wellington pushed the French army back over the Pyrenees to free Spain and Portugal from *the Eagle's* grasp.[5]

AND AUTHORITY WILL BE ISSUED TO THE COCK

In Bonaparte's weakened state, those poised against him were able to force him to abdicate, and to accept exile on the island of Elba. Louis XVIII was therefore able to return to France as King, in the knowledge that the coalition had given him full AUTHORITY TO rule France – THE COCK. The country once more came under monarchist rule.[6] The Congress of Vienna, which was convened by the victorious nations that had opposed revolutionary France and the Napoleonic Empire, met in September 1814, and *"approved the final peace treaty with France limiting it to its 1792 borders."* It was the legal rebirth of the Gallic Cock.

As Napoleon's military insight grew steadily weaker, so Nostradamus's prophetic eye was drawn to gaze ever more intently upon the dramatic events that were to end his authority as Emperor. Chief amongst these was his war against Russia. It began with an error of judgment for which, as described in the next verse, the consequences became daily more apparent, until eventually, the entire campaign ended in retreat.

C.IV: 75

Preſt à combatre fera defection,
Chef aduerſaire obtiendra la victoire:
L'arrieregarde fera defenſion,
Les defaillans mort au blanc territoire.

Prepared to do combat, he will make a defection,
Chief adversary will obtain the victory:
The rear guard will make a defence,
The faltering ones dead in the white territory.

Preſt, (O.Fr.) Prêt; defenſion, (Latinism) defensi/o.

PREPARED TO DO COMBAT

In his preparation for war with Russia, Napoleon began the massive task of planning what would be needed for the battles ahead: *"The aim of all my moves will be to concentrate 400,000 men at a single point. We can hope for nothing from the countryside and accordingly must take everything with us."*

> *Twenty-six transport battalions were formed accordingly, four consisting of 600 light carts (each with a capacity of 600 kilos), another four of 600 heavy wagons (1,000 kilos apiece), the rest being equipped with 252 four-animal wagons (loading 1,500 kilos apiece) . . . For meat rations, vast herds of cattle and oxen were collected ready to accompany the army eastwards . . . In round numbers, the Grande Armée was accompanied by no less than 200,000 animals . . . besides a total of some 25,000 vehicles . . . He also placed great reliance on restocking his convoys and forward magazines by means of the great rivers of western Russia, and accordingly two naval squadrons, each of 100 river boats, were held in readiness to convey stores from Tilsit to Kovno, by way of the River Niemen.[1]*

HE WILL MAKE A DEFECTION

The treaty of Tilsit (7–9 July 1807) was signed after Napoleons' victories at Jena, Auerstadt, Eylau and Friedland. In the treaty there was a secret article made between Napoleon and Tsar Alexander I of Russia, which agreed to their alliance against Great Britain, should it be called upon. In the event, Napoleon soon became disappointed. It appeared that Alexander was not complying with this agreement, and when several terse diplomatic exchanges between the two brought no improvement, his patience ended. On 22 June 1812, Napoleon made the following address. *"Soldats! . . . At Tilsit, Russia swore eternal friendship with France and also war against England. Today she has broken her undertakings!"* Czar Alexander's *laissez-faire* attitude towards confronting the British caused Napoleon to MAKE A DEFECTION from the treaty, and to prepare for war.[2]

CHIEF ADVERSARY WILL OBTAIN THE VICTORY

Bonaparte's *chief adversary* was Czar Alexander I the *'little father'* of the Russias.[3] His ambassador in London, Vorontzov, wrote a letter on 5 June 1812, which provided in remarkable detail the eventual course that the war would take.

> *Even if, at first, military operations go against us, we can win, by persistent defence and retreat. If the enemy pursues us, it is all up with him: for, the further he advances from his bases of supply and munitions into a trackless and foodless country, starved and encircled by an army of Cossacks, his position will become more and more dangerous; and he will end by being decimated by the winter, which has always been our most faithful ally.*

During the next six months Vorontzov's prediction was accurately fulfilled. On 5 December 1812, at Smorgoni near Vilnius, Bonaparte *"dictated the 29th Bulletin announcing the defeat and dissolution of the Grand Army."* He had finally been compelled to formally concede VICTORY TO Czar Alexander, HIS CHIEF ADVERSARY.[4]

THE REAR GUARD WILL MAKE A DEFENCE

A prominent feature of Napoleon's retreat from Moscow was Marshal Ney's REAR GUARD DEFENCE against the Cossack forces who repeatedly attacked the tail of the French army. *"Ney, who had fought a series of stubborn rear-guard actions since Krasnoi on November 7th, was the last Frenchman to leave Russian soil."* It was Ney's gallantry in providing a defence for the retreating French army that subsequently earned him the title: *'bravest of the brave'.*[5]

349

In temperatures as low as minus 30 degrees *the* STRAGGLERS, numbering as many as 30,000, were at their weakest and most vulnerable. The first snow fell on 3 November and this was followed by severe frosts. In the midst of this WHITE TERRITORY, vast numbers, literally thousands of men, FROZE TO DEATH.[6]

> *The sufferings of the retreat were now as horrible as anything imagined in Dante's Circle of Ice . . . men dropped and froze by the roadside, or lay down and froze around the camp-fires at night. . . . The 350 tattered and exhausted men who returned with him over the ice were all the effectives left of the 250,000 who had led the invasion across the river six months before.*[7]

In the next oracle, Nostradamus continues with Napoleon's calamitous war against Russia, and in doing so, the seer provides the precise date on which the invasion took place.

C.VI: 24

> Mars & le ſceptre ſe trouuera conioinct,
> Deſſoubz Cancer, calamiteuſe guerre.
> Vn peu apres ſera nouueau Roy oingt,
> Qui par long temps pacifiera la terre.

> *Mars and Jupiter will find themselves united,*
> *Under Cancer, calamitous war.*
> *A little afterwards, a new King will be anointed,*
> *Who will pacify the land for a long time.*

le ſceptre, (synonym) Jupiter.

At the end of June 1812, A CONJUNCTION BETWEEN MARS AND JUPITER occurred. Those familiar with horoscopes will know that the period UNDER CANCER, extends from 22 June to 22/23 July. Consequently, the information provided by this oracle can be dated to the last week of June 1812. On 22 June Napoleon was on the banks of the River Niemen in what is now Lithuania, surveying the prospect of crossing the river and taking his *Grande Armée* into Russia. On the evening of the 23rd, the crossing began; it continued all through the 24th of the month and into the 25th. The position of *Mars and Jupiter* on 24 June 1812 was within 7½ minutes of arc to each other; that is, they were separated by just one eighth of a degree.[1]

In the event, the Emperor's WAR against Russia proved to be CA-LAMITOUS. The Battle of Borodino, fought on 7 September 1812, proved to be the most costly of all France's victories. At its close 30,000 Frenchmen perished, although the loss to the Russian Army was greater, totalling approximately 58,000 dead. And when Bonaparte did reach Moscow, he met only disappoint-ment. The city was set on fire to deny his troops both provisions and shelter, and any hope he had of establishing a treaty with Czar Alexander came to nothing. Gloomily, Napoleon was forced to retrace his steps back to Poland, having accomplished nothing, except the deaths of nearly a 100,000 men. Even the re-treat was disastrous, for it coincided with the fierce onset of a Russian winter, and many thousands among Napoleon's starv-ing men fell dead from malnutrition and hypothermia, or as vic-tims of the Cossack skirmishes against the straggling party at the tail end of the French army.[2]

SIXTEEN MONTHS AFTER re-crossing the river Niemen, with what was left of his *Grande Armée*, Napoleon's reign was over.[3] France ac-cepted Louis XVIII as its NEW KING, and this signalled the coun-try's return to a monarchical system of government.[4]

From 1792 up until 1815, France had been almost continuously at war. But in 1815, the King was able to agree peace terms with the country's former enemies. Based upon treaties signed in Vienna (9 June 1815) and in Paris (20 November 1815), France was able to enjoy A LONG PERIOD OF PEACE. *"Under Louis, French industry prospered, the Army was reformed, and France recovered international confidence after sup-pressing a revolt in Spain (1823)."* Louis XVIII died in 1824, leaving France to remain largely at PEACE until 1854, when the country joined with England against Russia in the Crimean War.[5]

The failure of Napoleon's Russian campaign was only a prel-ude to further setbacks. In Spain, the French army was gradually being forced back to the mountain frontier that divided the two countries. English and Spanish armies had united under Wel-lington, and in a prolonged war, Spanish territory was gradually being reclaimed. Nostradamus's next oracle directs attention towards the closing stages of the Peninsula War.

C.IV: 70

Bien contigue des grans monts Pyrenees,
Vn contre l'aigle grand copie addreſſer:
Ouuertes veines, forces exterminees,
Que iusque à Pau, le chef viendra chaſſer.

Entirely contiguous with the great Pyrenean Mountains,
One against the eagle directing a great army:
Veins open (water courses), troops exterminated,
When the Chief will come pursuing, only as far as to Pau.

Cross-references: Pau, C.II: 33; C.II: 94; C.III: 75; C.VI: 79; C.VIII: 1; aigle, C.I: 23; C.III: 37; C.VIII: 4; C.VIII: 46

This combination of cross-references can only point to the Emperor Napoleon Bonaparte, referred to in this prophecy as *the eagle*. In 1808, the British Government sent Sir Arthur Wellesley (later made Duke of Wellington) to the Iberian Peninsula to lead an Anglo-Spanish assault against the French War Lord, Bonaparte. The Peninsula War, as it became labelled, lasted five years. In the end, France was defeated, and its army driven back across the Pyrenees.

ENTIRELY CONTIGUOUS WITH THE GREAT PYRENEAN MOUNTAINS

As the year 1813 drew to a close, the Emperor was to find his occupation of Spain under threat: *"Amid the Pyrenees, the armies of Marshal Soult and Suchet (sharing 100,000 men between them) were steadily giving ground before the advance of Lord Wellington's Anglo-Spanish forces (125,000 strong)."* [1]

ONE AGAINST THE EAGLE

The ONE referred to in this prophecy is undoubtedly the future Duke of Wellington. *"When in 1808 the Portuguese rose against Napoleon, Wellesley was ordered to support them."* In the event: *"[The Iron Duke] won nineteen pitched battles and innumerable combats . . . sustained ten sieges and [took] four great fortresses . . . twice expelled the French from Portugal, once from Spain."*

THE EAGLE, as with Caesar before him and Hitler afterwards, became Napoleon's adopted symbol. The tapestry that once decorated Bonaparte's study at the Tuileries, and which is now at Malmaison, is decorated by an eagle clutching thunderbolts in its talons, and the symbolic letter 'N' around it. [2]

DIRECTING A GREAT ARMY

In the final stages of the Peninsula War: —

[Wellington] rode over to San Sebastian to discuss with Graham how

352

best to renew the siege . . . A little later he instructed a troop of Horse Artillery from Santa Barbara to move to Sumbilla . . . Wellington was back at Lesaca in time for dinner at eight and approved the precautions that Murray had taken . . . Wellington wrote to Graham before going to bed instructing him to re-embark the bulk of the siege material which would be an encumbrance . . . He also sent orders for one of the two Spanish divisions blockading Pamplona to move north to support Picton and Cole and for the cavalry to move to Pamplona . . . The Sixth division was to send two of its brigades to touch in on Hill's new position. The third division was to remain in Santesteban to secure the town . . . the Seventh division was to march to Sumbilla where it would be closely in touch with the Sixth. The Light division will place itself on the left bank of the Bidassoa . . . Having made these dispositions, Wellington at four in the morning, rode over to the valley of Baztan where he found Hill strongly posted with 9000 men in hand and no contact with the French. [3]

VEINS OPEN

In the 19th century, British armed forces were known by their numbers, and not by the county names they later acquired. It was also common for some brigades to be given nicknames: *"Regiments also acquired nicknames, some of which have stuck and some have not . . . the 29th Foot . . . were known as 'The Vein Openers."* [4]

TROOPS EXTERMINATED

Actually, the *Vein Openers* suffered particularly badly during Wellesley's efforts to remove the French from Spanish soil. In one memorable battle, the 29th Foot lost four-fifths of their number – **TROOPS EXTERMINATED**. Quite apart from this one regiment, were those *"killed, wounded or captured [numbering] two hundred thousand enemies – leaving of their own number forty thousand dead, whose bones whiten the plains and mountains of the Peninsula."* (Napier).[5]

By employing the words *'ouvertes veines'* (veins open), the oracle has allowed two different interpretations to be made, both of which were highly significant to events occurring during the Peninsula War. The second interpretation allows this same phrase to be understood as *water courses open*. These were to feature in Wellesley's final efforts to push the French back over the mountains.

WATER COURSES OPEN

A description of the final Anglo-Spanish assault against Marshal Soult contains several reports of the **MANY RIVERS** Wellesley crossed, as he made his way towards the city of Toulouse for the final battle of the Peninsula War.[6]

Rivers and waterways are the natural feature of any terrain at the foot of a huge mountain range. And the largest of those footing the Pyrenees is the *Gave de* **PAU**. This was reached by Wellesley at the same time the coalition forces were converging upon Paris (March 1814).[7] In this sense *Pau* allows a double meaning, for it represents both Napoleon *in absentia*, whom Wellesley – **THE CHIEF** – **HAD COME PURSUING**, [8] and it also describes the *Pau* region in southern France, reached by Wellesley's army at the time Bonaparte was abdicating.

An event that occurred towards the end of Napoleon's reign received attention in the New York Times on 4 January 1942. Author Stewart Robb wrote that Professor Jacques Barzun – later to become dean and provost of Columbia University – had been persuaded to view Nostradamus's prophecies seriously on the strength of the oracle below. Professor Siceloff, an associate mathematician, also confided that the probability of these particular predictions combining in the manner which they had, solely by chance alone, was so close to zero as to be considered impossible. But then the same could be said for the other oracles.

C.X: 34

Gauloys qu'empire par guerre occupera
Par fon beau frere mineur fera trahy,
Par cheual rude voltigeant traynera,
Du fait le frere long temps fera hay.

The Frenchman that will occupy the empire by war,
By his lesser brother-in-law, he will be betrayed,
He will languish for a rough prancing horse,
For the deed, the brother will be hated a long time.

Gaulois, (O.Fr.) Of France, French, a Frenchman. Cross-reference: Gaulois, C.IV: 37.

THE FRENCHMAN

Napoleon was born **A FRENCHMAN** through the good fortune of Corsica having been acquired from the Genoese two weeks before his birth. It was this legal nicety that bestowed French citizenship upon him, and therefore qualified him for a military education on the mainland.

THAT WILL OCCUPY THE EMPIRE BY WAR

Napoleon's reign as Emperor of France lasted from 1804 until 1814. During that period, and a little before, when he was First

Consul, five separate and opposing coalitions OCCUPIED THE EMPIRE BY WAR. The nations that took part in these were drawn from Britain, Austria, Russia, Turkey, Naples, Portugal, Prussia, Sweden, Saxony and Spain. As a result of these coalitions, France fought a great number of battles, which at the time became household names; e.g., Pyramids, Nile, Marengo, Hohenlinden, Ulm, Trafalgar, Austerlitz, Jena, Eylau, Friedland, Aspern, Wagram, Smolensk, Borodino, and these are given without mention of those fought in the Peninsula War. In fact, the expression *'Napoleonic Wars'* soon became a recognized generalization for this period in history, for the conflicts were – *"massive in their geographic scope, ranging . . . over all of the five continents."*[1]

BY HIS LESSER BROTHER-IN-LAW

In 1800 Napoleon's youngest sister, eighteen-year-old Caroline, married the dashing cavalry leader Joachim Murat. Seven years later, the Emperor rewarded HIS sister and *brother-in-law* with the throne of Naples. In this sense, Murat was Napoleon's LESSER BROTHER-IN-LAW.[2]

WILL BE BETRAYED

The betrayal referred to by Nostradamus occurred in 1814. It also became the motivation for a book *The Betrayers: Joachim and Caroline Murat,* by Hubert Cole. *"Sire, I have just concluded a treaty with Austria,"* Joachim wrote to Napoleon on January 15, 1814. *"He who for so long fought at your side, your brother-in-law, your friend, has signed an act which appears to give him a hostile attitude towards you."* Murat was referring to a treaty he had entered into with Austria at the time he and his wife were King and Queen of Naples. The treaty was intended to unify central and southern Italy by bringing the Neapolitans into Rome at the expense of evacuating Napoleon's occupying forces inside the eternal city. Murat realised too late that he had been outmanoeuvred.[3]

HE WILL LANGUISH FOR A ROUGH PRANCING HORSE

Murat had become despondent through this change of occupation, and LANGUISHED FOR his former life as a cavalry leader, and victor of many memorable battles. Instead, he was now a politician and administrator in the Court of Naples. *"'The King appears to be extremely bored and seeks every opportunity to escape from the inactivity which wearies him to death,' reported Aubusson."*

It may be noted, in passing, that the Louvre in Paris owns a huge portrait of Joachim Murat astride **A PRANCING CAVALRY HORSE.**[4]

FOR THE DEED, THE BROTHER WILL BE HATED A LONG TIME

When Napoleon heard what had happened, he raged against *his brother-in-law's betrayal,* and never forgave him for his treachery, refusing even to call upon him for aid when the Emperor's need was at its greatest. Even, *"the allies showed little consideration for Murat, who in their eyes was still only the defaulting henchman of Bonaparte."*[5]

By 1814, the tide had turned against Napoleon, and he found himself attacked on all sides: retreat from Russia, retreat from Spain, retreat from Germany. Even his own minister, Talleyrand, was conspiring with the allies to effect his abdication. There was no recourse but to comply; he abdicated on 6 April. Napoleon was then exiled to the island of Elba in the Mediterranean. As a concession, he was allowed to retain the title Emperor of Elba and granted a pension with which to administer his rule. The oracle below foresees this happening.

C.I: 32

Le grand empire fera toſt tranſlaté
En lieu petit, qui bien toſt viendra croiſtre:
Lieu bien infime d'exigue comté,
Ou au milieu viendra poſer ſon ſceptre.

*The great empire will soon be transferred
Into a little place, which very soon will come to increase:
The place very tiny, of scanty reckoning,
Where in the midst he will come to lay down his sceptre.*

THE GREAT EMPIRE WILL SOON BE TRANSFERRED

In 1804, Napoleon Bonaparte was made Emperor of the French. At its height, his empire stretched from the Mediterranean to the Baltic, and eastwards to encompass parts of Poland. But in 1814 Napoleon was forced to abdicate.

By the Treaty of Fontainebleau, the allies granted him the island of Elba as a sovereign principality with an annual income of 2,000,000 francs to be provided by France and a guard of 400 volunteers; also, he retained the title of emperor.[1]

INTO A LITTLE PLACE WHICH, VERY SOON WILL COME TO INCREASE

Elba has an area of 86 square miles.[2] Although the land, itself, might not be able to *increase,* Napoleon's personal magnetism made sure that his following did. General Cambronne joined him in exile and brought with him seven hundred men to add to the four hundred that had earlier arrived; ostensibly they were there to act only as his personal guard.[3]

THE PLACE VERY TINY, OF SCANTY RECKONING

SCANTY RECKONING provides a fitting description for Elba,[4] judging by the number of times it changed hands. During the Middle Ages, Elba was ruled by Pisa, who then passed it on to Genoa. Afterwards, it became the property of the dukes of Piombino, but they had no use for it and transferred ownership to Cosimo I. Then Spain acquired partial ownership. After which, Naples became its new ruler. Finally, in 1802, France took possession.[5]

WHERE, IN THE MIDST, HE WILL ARRIVE TO LAY DOWN HIS SCEPTRE

The *sceptre* refers to the staff of imperial authority. It therefore confirms the possessor to be an emperor. After having had his title of Emperor of the French *transferred* to that of Emperor of Elba, Napoleon took control of the island's affairs. For the few months he remained in exile, he devoted considerable energy towards expanding the island's economy. This was achieved by reviving the iron-ore industry, and by encouraging the islanders to increase their agricultural output. New roads were planned and constructed, and sanitation was introduced.[6]

Bonaparte's exile soon became a cause for unrest amongst many citizens. A genuine desire for the old days of empire began to emerge. On Elba, Napoleon was informed of this unease, and he discerned from this an opportunity to regain his lost power. The next quatrain deals with this subject, but the time sequence of his leaving for exile and then returning to France has been reversed to obfuscate prior interpretation.

C.X: 23

Au peuple ingrat faictes les remonftrances,
Par lors l'armee fe faifira d'Antibe,
Dans l'arc Monech feront les doleances,
Et à Freius l'vn l'autre prendra ribe.

The remonstrances made by the ungrateful people,
From that time, Antibes will arrest the army:
Within the curve (Cannes), Monaco, they will make lamentations:
And at Fréjus, the one will take the other shoreline.

fe faifir, – arrest; L arc, (possible anagram) [n]e a[n]c – Canne; Monech, (Latinism) Monoecis; ribe, (O.Fr. rive) coast, shoreline.

On 3 May 1814 Louis XVIII entered Paris. The monarchy had been restored in France and Napoleon Bonaparte was an exile on the island of Elba. The end of the Napoleonic period was expected to herald a period of relief after almost continuous warfare during the past two decades.

Instead, there were protests. These came predominantly from the country folk. The French Revolution had driven out the nobles, and divided up the land amongst the people. But with the return of the monarchy came talk of land reform, and this was accompanied by fear that the government might reverse the gains made by the people. Some became resentful, harking back to an earlier time of French greatness, and the man who had ruled them. To add to this, the huge armies employed by Napoleon had since been reduced for economic reasons, and many soldiers, with years of service, suddenly found themselves unemployed, unwanted, and very hungry. Paris soon became a hotbed of dissent, especially amongst disaffected officers on half-pay, who were airing their grievances to each other.

THE REMONSTRANCES MADE BY THE UNGRATEFUL PEOPLE

On 27 February 1815, Napoleon, having been informed of the rising level of dissent, left Elba secretly, heading for the French coast and one last gamble at regaining his lost empire. When news of his escape reached Paris it was met with a barrage of painted slogans. *"Down with the Priests!" "Down with the nobles!" "Death to the Royalists!" "Bourbons to the Scaffold!"* THESE REMONSTRANCES BY AN UNGRATEFUL PEOPLE became so threatening that Louis XVIII was forced into a hurried withdrawal from the capital city, and he sought refuge in Ghent.[1]

FROM THAT TIME, ANTIBES WILL ARREST THE ARMY

On the first day of March, Napoleon's flotilla dropped anchor in the *Golfe Jouan*, which lies between *Antibes* and *Cannes*. Captain Lamouret, accompanied by a party of twenty soldiers, set off to capture an observation post outside *Antibes*. Captain Henri Bertrand followed this up by entering the town to deliver Bonaparte's proclamation and collect passports. It was a misjudgement. Inside *Antibes*, the military commander lost little time in *arresting* Bertrand and taking him away for interrogation. This led to Lamouret taking his troops into ANTIBES and seizing the garrison. But the local commander quickly surrounded the fortress, leaving the French **ARMY** penned up inside **UNDER ARREST**. It was a poor start to Napoleon's ambitions, especially since *"efforts to free the soldiers under arrest in Antibes . . . proved nugatory."*[2]

After setting foot on land, and being advised of the advance party's arrest, Bonaparte headed away from *Antibes*, along the shoreline to Cannes, where he set up camp among the dunes. Cannes lies on the crescent coastline of the Gulf of Napoule, and the **CURVE** of its sandy beach has given distinction to an excellent promenade (*Promenade de la Croisette*) lined with palm trees.[3]

It was while encamped outside Cannes that a local butcher devised a plot to murder Bonaparte. Armed with a musket, he declared that he would assassinate the former Emperor. But the **CITIZENS OF CANNES** became fearful that the attempt might result in terrible repercussions, even their murder, or their houses burnt down. After hearing their wails and protests – **LAMENTATIONS** – the would-be assassin relented, and gave up the idea.[4]

A further incident, also of note, occurred while Napoleon was encamped outside Cannes. The Prince of **MONACO** happened to pass by in his carriage. Napoleon at once summoned him to his tent and invited the Prince to join his expedition. But the Prince warily replied that he was going home. To which Napoleon responded: – *"So am I."*[5]

The final line to the oracle names *Frejus*: a town adjacent to Cannes. This might seem to predict what happened next, but Nostradamus has once more laid a false trail to throw commentators off the scent. The timescale has been reversed. The event in the fourth line was fulfilled less than a year before the predictions in lines one to three came to pass.

For example, the second and third lines predict Bonaparte's arrival in France after his escape from Elba. But, to complicate an interpretation in advance of the predicted event, the fourth line has foreseen what was to happen when Bonaparte was about to depart for Elba in the previous year. This has guaranteed that understanding will not occur until after it has taken place.

Nine months earlier, Napoleon had been on his way to Elba. A British ship, the *Undaunted*, lay at anchor in wait for his arrival. But as the exile's carriage approached port:

> *Napoleon begged to be allowed to make a small change of route and make for Frejus . . . This was allowed, and Campbell ordered Captain Ussher to sail the frigate Undaunted across to nearby Saint Raphael from where they would depart the following morning.*[6]

In this way, the prophecy that: AT FRÉJUS THE ONE (Napoleon) WILL TAKE THE OTHER SHORELINE became fulfilled.

Napoleon spent nine months on the island of Elba before escaping to France: *'to make one more bid for Empire'*. Nostradamus foresaw this happening, and predicted the incident from more than one viewpoint. In the next oracle, the seer indulges in his bitter humour by writing the prophecy in his native Provençal.

The reason for this can be attributed to the following sequence of events. When Napoleon came ashore near Antibes, a long march to Paris lay before him. To ensure the success of his mission, he deliberately chose: *"the difficult mountain route to Grenoble – purposely avoiding Marseilles and the department of Provence with its traditional Royalist sympathies."* (Chandler). Foreseeing Napoleon would take steps to avoid Provence, the seer predicted the Emperor's intention by writing the prophecy in Provençal: the language of the people Napoleon most wished to avoid. That said, the quatrain encompasses a split prophecy, with each half dealing with a different Bonapartist *coup*.

C.IV: 26

> Lo grand eyſſame ſe leuera d'abelhos,
> Que non faran don le ſiegen venguddos:
> De nuech l'emboſque, lou gach deſſoubz las treilhos,
> Ciutad trahide per cinq lengos non nudos.

> *The great swarm of bees will arise,*
> *When none know the place they came from:*
> *At night the ambuscade, the muddle under the trellis,*
> *City betrayed by five tongues, not naked.*

THE GREAT SWARM OF BEES WILL ARISE

As ruler of Elba, one of Napoleon's first tasks was to design a flag for his little empire: *'Napoleon's Elban flag with its red stripe on a white background and three golden bees'* was his choice. Thereafter,

"Bonaparte's personal standard, ornamented with bees [became the] imperial symbol."[1]

WHEN NONE WILL KNOW THE PLACE THEY CAME FROM

Nostradamus has connected the Emperor's Elban *bees* with his escape from exile, and the *swarm* of men along the way who left their homes and villages to join him on his long march to the capital, so that in the end **NONE KNEW WHERE SO MANY HAD COME FROM.** *"At every stop Napoleon harangued assemblies of local people, adapting the tone of his addresses to suit the tastes of his varied audiences."* And when Marshal Ney was sent by Louis XVIII to bring Napoleon to Paris in an iron cage: *"the old attraction again proved too strong and the men once more deserted en masse, followed by their commander."*[2]

On 19 March 1815, the King and his court hurriedly left Paris for the Belgian border, and a return to life in exile. The next day Napoleon entered the *Tuileries* to resume his role of governing France. Nostradamus uses this *coup d'état* to switch the time frame back to November 1799, when Napoleon engineered a similar *coup* as a step towards becoming emperor. Nostradamus foresaw history repeating itself, and he has acknowledged this with his split quatrain. This change of timeframe is far from unique in these prophecies, for the same tactic of using history to predict the future will be encountered again in C.X: 64, when the German army entered Rome during World War II.

AT NIGHT THE AMBUSCADE

Bonaparte's first *coup d'état* on 19th Brumaire was concluded **AT MIDNIGHT.** It began with a plot to move the councils (the Ancients and the Five Hundred) from Paris to Saint-Cloud. This succeeded. Then, on the following afternoon, (10 November) Bonaparte was forced out of the hall with daggers drawn. His brother, Lucien, reacted to this by summoning the guards, and they cleared the hall at bayonet point. This purging of deputies brought the Ancients to the conference, and they *"voted the suppression of the Directory, [and] the creation of an executive commission of three."* By nine p.m. that evening: *"a 'rump' of the Five Hundred, Lucien presiding . . . named Sieyès, Ducos and Bonaparte as provisional Consuls of the French Republic. Before midnight the three took an oath of loyalty to the Republic."* **THE AMBUSH** had achieved the desired result. By *midnight,* Napoleon had become one of the Consuls; it was a position from which he would thereafter rule France.[3]

"The events of [that] following day, November 10, were almost catastrophic, and responsibility for the near-débâcle lies heavily at Bonaparte's door." His speech to the Ancients in the *Galérie de Mars* was ill-received, some reports even called it 'incoherent'. Bonaparte then left the hall to attend a meeting of the Five Hundred in the Orangery, where he was received with shouts of: *'outlaw him'*, and *'down with the military dictator'*. At this point, with the situation now in a total MUDDLE, Bonaparte was forced to withdraw into the courtyard below, dishevelled and perspiring, protesting that stilettos had been pointed at him. It was this complaint that brought Joachim Murat and his Guards into the assembly hall, with drums beating and bayonets fixed. The Deputies fled through the open windows, allowing Bonaparte to return and complete his *coup*.[4]

And so – *"On a dull November evening the last scene of the French revolution was enacted in the orangery and park of St. Cloud."* The Orangery had been originally designed to grow fruit in a cool climate. Grape vines, together with their supporting *trellis* work are indicated to identify the function of the building in which the coup took place.[5]

From August 1795 up until Napoleon's *coup d'état de Brumaire*, France was governed by the Directory. This consisted of *"five 'Directors', jointly responsible for the conduct of affairs."* However, *"Many of the Directors were personally corrupt."*

The City, by convention, is Paris unless Nostradamus has provided evidence to the contrary. On 9 November 1799, THE CITY WAS BETRAYED BY its FIVE Directors: four of whom (Gohier, Moulin, Sieyès and Ducos) gave both their TONGUES and signatures to a conspiratorial decree. This was their agreement to move proceedings from Paris to Saint-Cloud. The fifth Director, Paul Barras, resigned office leaving the way clear for what was to happen. For it was only by moving the government to Saint-Cloud that Bonaparte was able to proceed with his *coup*, which he had planned would take place there.[6]

The final phrase to this quatrain represents another subtle

piece of perfect black humour, so typical of Nostradamus.

When preparing his *coup d'état* of November 9th –

> *Bonaparte found himself almost necessarily drawn into consultation with*
> *three men who, like himself . . . were now convinced of the need for a new*
> *constitution. . . . . By a curious chance the three men upon whom Bona-*
> *parte relied to make him master of the state were all ex-ecclesiastics.*

These three ex-ecclesiastics had been *unfrocked* during the Revolution, they were: *"Fouché, Talleyrand, and Sieyès."* Though *unfrocked*
by the Church, they found new attire in service to France. Sieyès
joined the Consulate as one of its three members; Fouché was
made Minister of Police and Minister of Interior; Talleyrand accepted the post of Minister for Foreign Affairs; *unfrocked* they
may have been, but Napoleon ensured they were **NOT NAKED**.[7]

The next oracle continues the story of Napoleon's escape
from Elba, and follows with the consequences this brought to the
people of France. It concludes with Bonaparte's life as an exile in
the Antipodes, and a warning that everything achieved during
the previous quarter of a century were soon to fade into obscurity.

C.X: 87

Grand Roy viendra prendre port pres de Niſſe,
Le grand empire de la mort ſi enfera,
Aux Antipolles poſera ſon geniſſe,
Par mer la Pille tout eſuanouira.

A great King will arrive, taking a port close to Nice,
The great empire, from its death, he will so much furnish with iron,
At the Antipole, his heifer will lay down,
By reason of the sea, the pillage / the felt cap: all will vanish.

prendre, (O.Fr.) se passer; enfera, (O.Fr.) garnir de fer; ſi, (O.Fr.) autant; Pille (Latinism)
Pille/us – felt cap also (syncope) Pill(ag)e eſuanouira, (O.Fr.) disparaître.

A GREAT KING WILL ARRIVE, TAKING A PORT CLOSE TO NICE

On 1 March 1815 Napoleon, **THE GREAT KING, ARRIVED** back in France,
having left Elba accompanied by a small army of men who had
been with him during his exile. The party of men landed at Juan
Bay, **A PORT CLOSE TO NICE**. *"The imperial invasion of France was about to be-*
gin."[1] From there the former Emperor began his long march towards Paris. By the time he arrived, the numbers supporting
him had swelled to a multitude. King Louis XVIII wisely left the

capital to seek sanctuary in Ghent.

From the moment of his arrival on French soil, Napoleon revived the title: *'Empereur des Français'*. He then issued a manifesto declaring: *"his abdication had been a voluntary retirement, and that he returned by invitation . . . In future, the aim of all my thoughts will be the happiness and the consolidation of the French Empire."* After Bonaparte's exile to Elba, a medal had been struck by the Allied powers with the motto, *'Gallia reddita Europae'* (France restored to Europe). The medal was intended to mark the death of THE GREAT EMPIRE, but that was soon to change with Bonaparte intending to bring it back FROM ITS DEATH.[2]

Realising that Europe would oppose his voluntary release from exile Napoleon began preparing his newly assembled *Armée du Nord* for war, which involved SO MUCH FURNISHING WITH IRON.

> *Every week a million and a half cartridges were manufactured; every day the Paris workshops produced 1,250 uniforms. Arsenals and depots were ransacked for firearms, however ancient, and teams of ordnance experts worked night and day to adapt the old weapons and refurnish them.*

Manpower had also been a problem. But, within two months of arriving in France: *"a force of 280,000 soldiers was produced . . . [with] a prospect of a further 150,000 once the Class of 1815 had been re-conscripted and put back in uniform."*[3]

It was to prove but a brief moment of glory. England, Austria, Prussia and Russia quickly formed a new alliance, determined to rid Europe of the 'Corsican Ogre'. A collision course between the two was inevitable, and the clash of wills came about on a field to the south of Brussels where the battle of Waterloo took place, and which is the subject of a separate oracle.

After losing at Waterloo, Napoleon was again forced to accept exile; this time it was to be the remote rocky island of St Helena in the South Atlantic Ocean. Upon arriving in the southern hemisphere (AT THE ANTIPOLE), an old farmhouse was set aside for his living quarters: *"Longwood House, the damp, unhealthy, rat-infested wooden farmhouse that became Napoleon's home."*[4] It had once been joined to a cattle stall, hence the verbal connection to *heifer*.

Heifer refers to *'a young cow that has not had calf'*. It also provides an unflattering but rather deserved description of Bonaparte's young wife. At the time they were married (11 March 1810), Marie-Louise had only just celebrated her eighteenth birthday, and with her upbringing as a princess of the royal Austrian household, she was therefore untouched:[5] unlike Napoleon's first wife, who had already given birth to two children when they married. But after Napoleon's removal from power, Marie-Louise abandoned her husband to live with Count Neipperg. Nostradamus's acidic reference to the empress as HIS HEIFER is a further example of the seer's bitter humour. Especially, since after Bonaparte's first exile to Elba, Prince Metternich sent Count Neipperg to escort Marie-Louise back to Vienna. This led to an amorous relationship forming between Neipperg and the Austrian princess, subsequent to which, she allowed herself to LAY DOWN with the Count. He subsequently fathered four children by her: two at least, and possibly three, being sired while her husband was on St Helena.[6]

BY REASON OF THE SEA, THE PILLAGE, THE FELT CAP: ALL WILL VANISH

BY REASON OF THE SOUTH ATLANTIC OCEAN, Napoleon Bonaparte was separated from all further involvement in the affairs of France. Moreover, the word, PILLAGE,[7] with its association to material and territorial gain from war, provides an unflattering association with Napoleon and the seventy battles he fought to build his empire. There is also, THE FELT CAP – *le bonnet rouge* – worn throughout the French Revolution, to symbolise the period in this country's history that preceded the Napoleonic age. But, with the reinstatement of the monarchy in France, the Republic ended, and the territorial gains made under Napoleon were returned to their former boundaries; that is to say: of THE PILLAGE AND THE FELT CAP, ALL WILL VANISH.[8]

The Battle of Waterloo has become synonymous with the end of Napoleon's reign as Emperor. In the next and final quatrain of this chapter, Nostradamus provides sufficient detail, albeit couched in his usual cryptic manner, to indicate that he had prescient knowledge of the time and the place where this conflict would occur.

C.I: 23

Au mois troifiefme fe leuant le foleil,
Sanglier, liepard au champ mars pour combatre:
Liepard laiffe au ciel extend fon œil,
Vn aigle autour du foleil voyt f'efbatre.

In the third month, the sun rising,
Boar, leopard, in the martial field in order to do combat:
Leopard quits; extends his vision to the sky,
An eagle is seen to caper around in the sunshine.

Liepard, (O.Fr. liepart) leopard; combatre, (O.Fr.) lutter; laiffe, (O.Fr. laisser) to put off; extend, (Latinism) exten/do. Cross-reference: Aigle, C.III: 37; C.IV: 70; C.VIII: 4; C.VIII: 46

IN THE THIRD MONTH

The third month usually indicates March, but Nostradamus re-peatedly uses the earlier, legalistic form of dating in which 25th March began the New Year. Consequently, THE THIRD MONTH is un-derstood to mean June.[1]

THE SUN RISING

On the morning of 18 June, the SUN ROSE above the countryside at Waterloo. Torrential rain over the past eighteen hours had wa-terlogged the ground, but by next morning the clouds were gone and the sky was clear.[2]

BOAR

Apart from the *boar* being a legendary beast, it is also associated with northern Europe, in particular Prussia.[3] Interestingly, the *boar* also signifies one of the twelve years in the Chinese horo-scope; the case at hand being of special notice because 1815 was the year of the *boar*.

LEOPARD

The *leopard*, like the *boar*, is another heraldic beast. It was identi-fied by the French as a creature related to England, because Eng-lish heralds had described their device as a: *'fion feopardé'*.[4]

IN THE MARTIAL FIELD

The battlefield of Waterloo is extremely small in area. The opposing ar-mies occupied two low ridges, separated by a gentle valley extending over a distance of some 1,500 yards. In width, the battle zone barely extended over 5,000 yards.

IN ORDER TO WAGE WAR

On the day of the battle, the whole area was filled by *"almost 140,000 troops and more than 400 guns."* Fighting began at midday on the 18th, with Wellington – **THE LEOPARD** – pitting his troops against Napoleon – **THE EAGLE**. It was not until Blücher – **THE BOAR** – arrived that evening, with his Prussian troops still fresh, that the exhausted French realised the battle was lost.[5]

Napoleon lost the Battle of Waterloo because he delayed the start. The hold-up gave Blücher and his troops enough time to reach the battlefield, and this changed the course of events. But although the reason for delay was the weather, it was not only the weather on the day of the battle; it was also the weather on the eve of battle. Had Napoleon not been hindered by rain on the 17th, the Battle of Waterloo would have been replaced by a victorious Bonaparte defeating the Iron Duke, as the British army retreated from Quatre Bras to take up their position on the field at Waterloo.

LEOPARD QUITS; EXTENDS HIS VISION TO THE SKY

On the eve of Waterloo, with Wellington – the **LEOPARD** – having **QUIT** Quatre Bras with the French in pursuit, *"a colossal thunderstorm burst overhead, and within minutes the ground was turned into a quagmire. This ruled out any moves across country, and the French pursuit was consequently confined to the roads."*

Depite the adverse conditions, the French attempted to make up the ground that lay between the two armies, and almost caught up with Lord Uxbridge's rear guard. But *"'The tracks were so deep in mud after the rain that we found it impossible to maintain any sort of order in our columns,' noted Sergeant Mauduit of the Imperial Guard."* By 6.30 in the evening it had become clear that Wellington, having **EXTENDED HIS VISION TO THE SKY**, and taken advantage of the elements, had escaped to the safety of a ridge at Mont-St.-Jean. It was from there that he made plans to engage the French in battle next day.[6] *"What would I not have given to have had Joshua's power to slow down the sun's movement by two hours,"* said Napoleon afterwards. Little did he realise the effect the sun would have upon his own strategy, come the next day.

AN EAGLE IS SEEN CAPERING AROUND IN THE SUNSHINE

On the morning of the 18th, Bonaparte – **THE EAGLE** – was informed of intelligence just received, revealing that Wellington and Blücher intended to join forces. But the Emperor dismissed the account as nonsense. In a similar mood, he declined to recall

Grouchy. It was only when General Drouot suggested delaying the battle to let the sun dry out the sodden ground, that he took note.

> *Napoleon immediately agreed, and ordained that the main action should commence only at 1:00 p.m. This decision proved the most fatal one of the day for the French. For had even an adequately supported infantry attack been launched against Wellington during the morning, the French must surely have won; for Blücher would have been too late arriving on the field to affect the issue.* [7]

Nostradamus's bitter humour, which he usually reserves for the final line, again comes to the fore. By delaying the planned attack until midday, Bonaparte left the morning free for other activities: – **CAPERING AROUND IN THE SUNSHINE**, as Nostradamus derisorily put it.

The previous chapter closed with a note regarding the distribution of the quatrains that were used. It will be recalled that of the 28 oracular verses, 9 were from Century IX; that is almost one third. In the present chapter 38 quatrains have been identified as belonging to the Napoleonic era. Of these, the number of prescient verses taken from Century IX is exactly zero. While it is generally held that Nostradamus shuffled his verses like a deck of cards before allocating the result to individual sets of one hundred: the so-called Centuries, it is difficult to accept this explanation. To have placed most quatrains pertaining to the French Revolution in Century IX, and then to have followed this with prophecies for the Napoleonic era, and avoided Century IX completely, appears deliberate. In which case, Nostradamus would have been aware of the dating applied to his prophecies, which of course, he did claim was the case.

8

FROM RESTORATION TO REPUBLIC

Napoleon's 'One Hundred Days' has become familiar to everyone with a claim to be well-read. This refers to a time beginning 20 March 1815 when the Emperor, having escaped from exile on Elba, returned to Paris and his former seat of power at the *Palais de Tuileries*. The first major task he set himself was to secure France's border with Belgium. On 12 June he left the capital to join his newly assembled *Armée du Nord* mustered near the northern frontier. Six days later, on the fields outside the village of Waterloo, ten miles south of Brussels, he was defeated by the joint efforts of Wellington and Blücher. On 22 June, he formally signed his second abdication, and in the following month left France to live out the remainder of his years in exile on the rocky outpost of St. Helena. It is with Napoleon's exit that a new chapter in the life of France began, and the first quatrain in this chapter predicts its beginning.

C.X: 90

Cent fois mourra le tyran inhumain.
Mis à fon lieu fcauant & debonnaire,
Tout le fenat fera deffoubs fa main,
Fafché fera par malin temeraire.

One hundred courses: the inhuman tyrant will expire.
Put in his place one shrewd and of good ancestry,
All the senate will be under his authority,
He will be angered by an evil reckless person.

fois, (O.Fr.) a time, turn, course or bout; debonnaire, (O.Fr.) de bonne race; main, (O.Fr.) autorité.

ONE HUNDRED COURSES

At first sight, the word 'fois' suggests 'times'. But 'fois' has a wider meaning and can also refer to a 'course', such as that taken by the sun as it makes its daily transit across the sky. **ONE HUNDRED COURSES** can therefore be read as *'One Hundred Days'*.[1] That is: one hundred times for the sun to take its daily course across the sky.

THE INHUMAN TYRANT WILL DECEASE

The inhuman tyrant is a description that found fulfilment in the public outcry: *'the Devil is unchained'*. This chorus of disapproval spread right across Europe when it was learned that Bonaparte had escaped from Elba. Protests were quickly converted into action, and his second term of office ended with Blücher completing at Waterloo what Wellington began.[2] After the **ONE HUNDRED DAYS** had run their course, and **THE INHUMAN TYRANT** had lost his final battle, and safe conduct to America had been denied, a British ship took him to St Helena, where he **DIED** on 5 May 1821.

PUT IN HIS PLACE ONE SHREWD

On 8 July 1815, Louis XVIII returned to Paris as King: having been **PUT IN PLACE** of the deposed Bonaparte by a people at last willing to return to a monarchical government. Louis XVIII proved to be a **SHREWD** monarch, being very careful to moderate the ambitions of the ultra-royalists: a party of extremists who were intent upon removing everything the Revolution had achieved. Had they not been kept in check by the King, they would have divided the country. But he was able to subdue their excesses by choosing only moderate royalists as his ministers: men who would not attempt to return the country to its pre-revolutionary state.[3]

OF GOOD ANCESTRY

Among Louis XVIII's forefathers were two of France's greatest kings, Henri IV and Louis XIV: he was therefore a Bourbon by birth and **OF GOOD ANCESTRY**.[4]

ALL THE SENATE WILL BE UNDER HIS AUTHORITY

During the reign of Louis XVIII, France began to experiment with a new parliamentary system of government. The King was given full executive powers, and this placed **ALL THE SENATE UNDER HIS AUTHORITY**. *Sénatus-Consulte* was the actual name given to this governing body. It consisted of 141 members: these being men who had opposed Napoleon in April 1814. Under this revised system of government, laws continued to be passed by parliament, and budgets were still subject to its approval; but, with such a strong monarchist support, the King was able to exercise full control of the country's affairs.[5]

HE WILL BE ANGERED

The anger felt by Louis XVIII began with the murder of his nephew, the duc de Berry. His irate feelings were then further exacerbated by the resignation of his favourite, Élie Decazes, whom the King had only just appointed as France's Premier. Decazes was forced to submit his resignation five days after the duc de Berry's murder, in response to repeated censures by the ultra-royalists. They had placed the blame for the assassination on his *'too liberal attitude'*.[6]

BY AN EVIL RECKLESS PERSON

De Berry's murderer was *"a little weasel-faced mongrel,"* named Louis-Pierre Louvel: a saddler by trade and a Bonapartist by persuasion. On 13 February 1820 he mortally wounded the Duke as he was leaving the *Paris Opéra*, and his death followed next day.[7]

Ten years earlier, in Vienna on 11 March 1810, Napoleon Bonaparte had married by proxy the Archduchess Marie-Louise, daughter of the Austrian Emperor. One year later, in March 1811, she gave birth to a son to whom Bonaparte gave the title,

King of Rome. But after Bonaparte's abdication, it was left for Marie-Louise to argue her son's case for his continued recognition as the rightful heir to her titles. It is her plea, together with a complex range of other matters that are now predicted.

C.V: 39

Du vray rameau de fleur de lys iſſu,
Mis & logé heritier d'Hetrurie:
Son ſang antique de longue main iſſu,
Fera Florence florir en l'armoirie.

Descended from the true branch of the fleur-de-lis,
The heir of Etruria, taken and lodged:
His ancient blood issued from a long-time power,
Will cause Florence to blossom on the coat of arms.

heritier, (O.Fr.) heir, inheritor; longue, (O.Fr.) longtemps; main, (O.Fr.) puissance; armoirie, (O.Fr.) coat of arms.

N.B. The Rigaud edition of 1568 has the final word in the third line as 'tissu' (woven). However, the extant du Rosne edition (1557) gives the word as 'issu'.

The *fleur-de-lys* has a long association with the rulers of France. As far back as the twelfth century, either King Louis VI or King Louis VII (sources disagree) became the first French monarch to use the *fleur-de-lys* on his shield. After the French Revolution and the Napoleonic Era, *"The fleur-de-lys was restored to the French flag in 1814."* (Wikipedia).

In 1731, Louis XIV's great-grandson; that is, Philip V's eldest son by his second marriage, became the Duke of Parma, thereby creating the House of Bourbon-Parma – a *true branch of the fleur-de-lis.* The *"House of Bourbon - Spanish BORBÓN . . . provided . . . kings or queens of Spain from 1700 to 1808, kings of Etruria from 1801 to 1807."*

Parma became annexed to France through the *Treaty of Aranjuez* (21 Mar 1801). After which, as compensation for having taken Parma, the Grand Duke Ferdinand's son and successor, Charles Lodovic, was given Tuscany, which became known as the *Kingdom of Etruria.* It was therefore Napoleon who first created this *'new Kingdom of Etruria out of Tuscany and Parma'.*

DESCENDED FROM THE TRUE BRANCH OF THE FLEUR-DE-LIS

On 10 Dec 1807, Charles Lodovic (22 Dec 1799 – 16 Apr 1884), son of Grand Duke Ferdinand of Parma, and of Bourbon descent – that is, DESCENDED FROM THE TRUE BRANCH OF THE FLEUR-DE-LYS – was forced to abdicate. Eight years later, by article 101 of the *Treaty of Vienna* (9 Jun 1815), the Duke was given the Duchy of Lucca, as compensation for the loss of Parma.[1]

THE HEIR OF ETRURIA

By the same treaty, Napoleon's former Empress, Marie-Louise, was granted the Duchies of Parma, Piacenza, and Guastella; in other words, this included *Etruria*. But the grant was for the duration of her lifetime only; after her death, the lands were to be returned to the House of Bourbon-Parma; that is, returned to *the true branch of the fleur de lys*. Marie-Louise appealed against this decision, and requested that her son by Napoleon I: *'principe of Parma, Piacenza e Guastella'*, be recognized as the HEIR OF ETRURIA, and that he should inherit the duchies granted her. But the appeal was unsuccessful, and *"her son's right of succession was overruled (1817), the duchies being secured to her for her lifetime only."*[2]

TAKEN AND LODGED

By the time this ruling was reached, Marie-Louise had already TAKEN her son, still prospective *heir of Etruria*, to Vienna. There, he was received into the court of her father, the Emperor Francis I, and given the title Duke of Reichstadt. He remained LODGED in the Schönbrunn Palace until his death from tuberculosis in 1832.[3]

This connection with the Habsburg dynasty of Austria introduces the third line of the oracle. In Italy, the break-up of Etruria by the Congress of Vienna gave Parma to Marie-Louise, and returned Tuscany to Ferdinand III. As a consequence of this: *"Members of the house of Habsburg ruled over Parma, Modena, and Florence."* It is with this in mind that Nostradamus proceeds to his next subject.

HIS ANCIENT BLOOD ISSUED FROM A LONG-TIME POWER

Ferdinand III was the grandson of Maria Theresa, and Emperor Francis I of Lorraine, from whom their descendants created the House of Habsburg-Lorraine. Ferdinand III was therefore ISSUED FROM AN ANCIENT BLOODLINE OF A LONG-TIME POWER. This was because, historically, the reign of the Habsburgs in Germany dated back to the thirteenth century.[4]

WILL CAUSE FLORENCE TO BLOSSOM

Florence was the capital and most important city in Tuscany; it was also the residential home of its dukes. Despite the political and revolutionary unrest in Italy at this time: *"Tuscany under Ferdinand III of Habsburg-Lorraine,"* became a centre for the arts. Intellectual life BLOSSOMED IN THE CITY OF FLORENCE, particularly with the establishment of the *Gabinetto di Lettura ('Literary Club')*, which boasted several famous writers, amongst its members.[5]

There is, however, a further and significant addition to this prophecy. *"[Pope] Leo XI, Alessandro de' Medici was, before his election, Archbishop of Florence and he rebuilt the Bishop's Palace in Piazza del Duomo. A gigantic coat of arms celebrates this fact."* What is important about this *coat of arms* are the three gold *fleur-de-lis* on a blue background – *'symbols of Florence,'*– for together with *"three roses and the motto: 'Sic Floruit' (he blossomed in this way), these are a reference to the fact that Leo XI was pope for only a few days. Elected on April 1, 1605, he died on April 27."* From this information, the remaining part of the prophecy follows quite smoothly.

IN THE COAT OF ARMS

In 1823, following the death of Pius VII, the new pope took the title Leo XII. This title was specifically chosen to honour the memory of Pope Leo XI, who had ennobled his family. *"Leo XII – Born at the Castello della Genga in the territory of Spoleto, 22 August, 1760; died in Rome, 10 February, 1829. His father's family had been ennobled by Leo XI in 1605."* It was therefore not only *Florence* that *blossomed* under Ferdinand III, but also the floral COAT OF ARMS in *Florence*, with its inscription that mentions BLOSSOMED. It had been put there in 1605 to celebrate Pope Leo XI, and centuries later, in 1823 the memory of this particular pope *blossomed* again with the election of Leo XII.[6]

With his prophetic eye still focused upon Italy, Nostradamus devotes a whole quatrain to the disturbances that broke out across the country during the early part of the nineteenth century. These occurred within the same timeframe as the events in the previous oracle.

C.III: 74

Naples, Florence, Fauence, & Imole,
Seront en termes de telle fafcherie,
Que pour complaire aux malheureux de Nolle,
Plainct d'auoir faict à fon chef moquerie.

Naples, Florence, Faenza & Imola,
Will be in states of so much angry feeling,
When, on account of being pleasing to the unfortunate ones of Nola,
Given to regret, for having made mockery to his chief.

Fauence, (Latin) Faventia; complaire, (O.Fr.) to please, like, serve, be obedient to, Plainct, (O.Fr.) donné à regret.

NAPLES, FLORENCE, FAENZA & IMOLA

FLORENCE, FAENZA AND IMOLA are three major cities located in what was formerly known as the Papal States. Together with **NAPLES** in the south they were centres for lodges of the Carbonari: a political movement that came into being during the early part of the nineteenth century.[1]

WILL BE IN STATES OF SO MUCH ANGRY FEELING

In 1820, members of the Carbonari, especially within the locations mentioned by Nostradamus, found themselves **IN STATES OF SO MUCH ANGRY FEELING**. Their members had only recently emerged from secret meeting places to campaign for greater political freedom, with open demonstrations being held against Austrian influence. Included amongst their several grievances were appeals for political reform: at the heart of which, was a call for a representative government: one that was free from foreign influence and interference.[2]

WHEN, IN ORDER TO BE PLEASING TO THE UNFORTUNATE ONES OF NOLA

To add to their anger, the Carbonari had been **SUPPORTING** General Guglielmo Pepe, a disaffected officer garrisoned at *Nola:* only to discover that King Ferdinand had deceived Pepe by reneging on an agreement made between the two for a new constitution.[3] Pepe had initiated an armed uprising at *Nola* in pursuit of political reform. The revolt had been successful, and King Ferdinand was forced to accede to the rebels' demands. But under the pretext of obtaining international approval for the new constitution, Ferdinand visited Prince von Metternich in Laibach, and appealed to him for military aid. The Austrian statesman responded by sending troops into Italy to confront General Pepe and his army of rebels. On 7 March 1821, at Rieti, the two sides met, and in the ensuing conflict, **THE UNFORTUNATE ONES OF NOLA** were defeated.[4]

GIVEN TO REGRET FOR HAVING MADE A MOCKERY TO HIS CHIEF

The final line of the oracle looks further into the reasons for what happened at Rieti. Ferdinand I believed Pepe HAD MADE A MOCKERY OF his position as King, by forcing him to accept the rebel army's demands. *"[He] saw Pepe as the criminal leader of a criminal movement, and it was with the strongest mental reservation, and under what he considered duress, that he consented to swear to a Constitution he abhorred."* [5] For this reason, he sought revenge against the general, and found in Metternich a willing ally. In the end, Pepe was GIVEN TO REGRET the confrontation he made TO HIS CHIEF, and for his own safety he fled to Spain; later he sought asylum in England.[6]

The prophecies of Nostradamus now return to France, and the last of the country's kings to rule the French; that is, unless there is a revival of monarchist rule at some time in the future. Louis Philippe was the son of the duke of Orleans, the royal cousin of Louis XVI, who betrayed the King at his trial by voting for his death. Citizen Égalité, as the duke chose to be called in his desire to identify with the revolutionaries, lost his head some months later. His son did not, and survived to take the crown as Louis-Philippe.

His predecessor, Charles X proved to be the last of the Bourbon rulers, and when given a choice between fighting for the throne with a prospect of losing his head, or a carriage to England, he chose the latter. Unfortunately, he is the one king in the line of monarchs from Nostradamus's time that appears to be absent from the Centuries. Quatrains have been suggested to fill this gap, but they have so far failed to match the rigorous standards required for inclusion. Since I cannot believe that Nostradamus would have omitted this king from his prophecies, then either the exclusion is due to my own inability at failing to recognize the quatrain, or else the absent verse is in the missing part of Century VII.

C.X: 16

Heureux au regne de France, heureux de vie,
Ignorant fang mort fureur & rapine,
Par mon flateurs feras mys en enuie,
Roy defrobé trop de foy en cuifine.

Happy in the reign of France, happy with life,
Ignorant of blood, death, fury and plundering:
By my flatteries you will be placed in envy,
King disrobed too much faith in cuisine.

HAPPY IN THE REIGN OF FRANCE, HAPPY WITH LIFE

Louis Philippe was proclaimed King on 9 August 1830, following the abdication of Charles X. He immediately set about popularising himself.[1] In this endeavour, he became the Citizen-King; always ready with a cheery word to rich and poor alike, and regularly to be seen strolling along the Paris boulevards with an umbrella on his arm. People would sometimes gather beneath his window and call for him to appear. The King would then emerge with his family, wave a tricolour and sing the Marseillaise. Everyone loved him for his charm and splendid good humour.[2]

IGNORANT OF BLOOD, DEATH, FURY AND PLUNDERING

Louis Philippe was born in Paris in 1773, but avoided; that is, was IGNORANT OF the BLOOD, DEATH, FURY AND PLUNDERING, which marked the French Revolution and Napoleonic Era. He was spared these atrocities by choosing exile and service in the Austrian army. He later moved to Switzerland, where he became a tutor. Restless, he travelled to the United States of America, where he spent two years before returning to Europe in 1800. For a short while he stayed in England: later joining the Neapolitan royal family in Sicily. It was there that he met and married Marie-Amélie, the daughter of King Ferdinand IV. It was not until the abdication of Napoleon, and the restoration of the monarchy in 1815 that he returned to France.[3]

BY MY FLATTERIES YOU WILL BE PLACED IN ENVY

Nostradamus predicts for this king: *By my flatteries you will be placed in envy*. But, note how the seer also addresses his subject in the 2nd person singular, '*seras*'. This familiarity of address is customarily restricted to family, close friends and small children. Yet, Nostradamus employs it to speak to the King of France, albeit down the centuries. Of all French monarchs, only the last, Louis Philippe, would have been content to be addressed with such familiarity, for he openly and actively encouraged this type of geniallity. *"He called workmen 'my friends', and the National Guardsmen 'my comrades'."*[4]

But, despite THESE FLATTERIES, and the subject BEING PLACED IN ENVY of others less fortunate, the verse concludes by predicting the abdication of the monarch. It also gives the cause; and, once again, the last line is not without a hint of that dark humour for which Nostradamus was well known in his day.

KING DISROBED

In 1848, Louis Philippe was forced to abdicate. The reason was entirely political. The first sign of trouble began in 1846, with poor harvests, industrial unrest and peasant protests. The mood of the country was also made worse by a large number of bankruptcies. And on 23 February, under pressure from his sons, the KING ABDICATED.[5]

The King's dethroning became necessary because of the growing unrest in the country. In his attempt to counter this, Louis-Philippe placed a banning order on public meetings. But this led to the political opposition retaliating by arranging *'banquets'*, for these were seen as a legitimate means of getting-together. And at these functions, diners could then freely meet to express their discontent.

TOO MUCH FAITH IN CUISINE

"It is I," said the King, *"I personally whom the banquets are aimed against. We shall see who is the strongest."* The King's trust in his ability to withstand the stratagems of his opponents was soon put to the test. A banquet had been arranged for 22 February 1848, but at the last minute it was cancelled. Louis Philippe received the news with raised spirits. *"Didn't I tell you it would all end in smoke? It is a regular April Fool's Day."* He was mistaken; the King had placed TOO MUCH FAITH IN CUISINE as the only means open to the protesters. On the day of the banquet, crowds of people paraded through the streets, waving banners and shouting their protests. Next day, the barricades went up, and when soldiers fired into protesters, killing some twenty men and women, the mob howled for vengeance. Louis Philippe attempted to make his way to the safety of Saint-Cloud, but the National Guardsmen barred his way. Under pressure, he was forced to abdicate.[6]

In the next oracle, Nostradamus returns to an earlier interest: the future of Great Britain, and predicts its growing empire, and the Queen and Empress who ruled over it.

C.VIII: 97

Aux fins du VAR changer le Pompotans,
Pres du riuage les trois beaux enfans naiſtre.
Ruyne au peuple par aage competans,
Regne au pays charger & plus voir croiſtre.

Within the limits of VAR, the ostentatious masters changing,
Close to the river, three fine children born.
Ruin to the people by a competent age,
Burdening the realm in the country, and more to see increasing.

VAR, (abbreviation); Victoria Alexandrina Regina; Pompotans, (Latin portmanteau)
pomp + potens, i.e., ostentatious masters.   Cross-reference: Pompotans, C.X: 100.

WITHIN THE LIMITS OF VAR

The reign of **Victoria Alexandrina Regina**, Queen of England, ruler
of the British Empire and Empress of India, lasted from 1837 to
1901; these are therefore **THE LIMITS OF VAR**. Victoria dropped the
name Alexandrina after becoming queen.[1]

THE OSTENTATIOUS MASTERS

The oracle has used the hybrid word '*Pompotans'*, to describe the
British people. At the time of the British Empire, its people were,
indeed, **MASTERS** of the world. Even today, the *pomp* and ceremony that once attended both royal and formal occasions can
still be discerned in the **OSTENTATIOUS** display of historical costume
and pageantry.[2]

CHANGING

Under Queen Victoria's rule, the country saw more **CHANGES** than
at any other time in its history. The monarchy was transformed:
brought about by the delegation of power to Parliament; this has
since become a standard model for the system presently in place
within the U.K. Victoria's reign also saw an advance in new
technologies. Steam trains appeared, and the internal combus-
tion engine was introduced, both of which were to revolutionize
the then existing means of transport.[3]

CLOSE TO THE RIVER

Windsor Castle, standing **CLOSE TO THE RIVER** *Thames*, has been the
home of the royal families of England ever since Edward III converted part of the fortress into royal apartments in 1348. Queen
Victoria lived there at the beginning of her reign, but later removed her court to Buckingham Palace. Despite this change of
abode, she retained Windsor as an occasional residence.[4]

379

Queen Victoria's first child was a daughter who took her mother's name, Victoria, and became known as 'Vicky': — *"Windsor, 21 November 1840. The queen gave birth to a princess here today, three weeks prematurely."* Four years later, Alfred arrived: – *"Windsor, 6 August 1844. Queen Victoria's expanding brood gained a new member today with the birth, at Windsor Castle, of a new prince. He will be christened Alfred Ernest Albert."* Last of the three to be born at Windsor was Leopold, born in 1853. This birth was remarkable because Victoria opted to be given chloroform during delivery. This was administered by Dr John Snow.

> *The decision of the queen to use chloroform during the birth of Prince Leopold, on 7 April has done a great deal to popularise what has hitherto been a controversial form of medication . . . knowing full well the suffering of giving birth, she welcomed the arrival at Windsor of the famous Dr. John Snow.* [5]

Of Victoria's other children, all six were born at Buckingham Palace.

The wealth of the British Empire during Victoria's reign has been contrasted by Nostradamus with the plight of the working class. Those familiar with the novels of Charles Dickens will have read his pen pictures of the destitution to be found amongst the poor of the land. In fact, the term 'working class' was invented to describe the wage earners of that time. Rates of pay were poor, and to supplement a living wage, families were forced to send their children to work. Child labour was rife, with infants employed to climb chimneys as sweeps, or else sent into the mines where the stronger ones hauled trucks and the weaker ones stood for hours, ankle deep in water, while they operated the pumps.

> *Many of the Victorian poor were people who had no hope of ever doing more than picking up a few days' or a few weeks' money here and there, existing in the intervals as best they could . . . And so they jolted down an uneven road of poverty to old age in the workhouse, if they lived so long.* [6]

As the oracle correctly states, this was **A COMPETENT AGE**. The British Empire was at its pinnacle, bringing in wealth from the lands it occupied. Industry expanded beyond all expectation, and literature, science and the arts flourished as never before.[7]

380

"One of the most glaring abuses of the labour of English women and children was the agricultural 'gang labour' system prevalent in East Anglia and the Midlands." Agricultural workers were often employed on a subcontractual basis. This meant that the money paid by the landowner was given to a gang leader, who took his commission and then passed over the little that remained to those who had actually worked the fields. Once again, children became part of the labour force in order to add to the meagre wages that a hard day's work brought home. In 1867, the government's conscience was partially touched by the necessity of child labour, which was **BURDENING** people **IN THE COUNTRY**, and a law – *The Gangs Act* – was passed, forbidding the employment of any child below the age of eight.[8]

Finally, the Oracle predicts the extraordinary advancement that was made in transport and optics. *"Queen Victoria . . . ruled over an era of tremendous change . . . Photography, moving pictures, electric light, the motorcar and the telephone have transformed people's view of the world."* In short, there was **MORE TO SEE**, and this was **INCREASING** all the time, whether by the speed of travel or through the invention of new optical instruments.[9]

With his eye still on what was happening outside France, Nostradamus returns to another of his favourite subjects, the papacy. In the middle of the nineteenth century, the Roman Church was under attack. Once again, as in 1798 and 1809, the Vatican was vacated, although not through the arrest of the pontiff, as had happened twice under Napoleon, but from the Pope's need for self-preservation.

C.V: 56

Par le trefpas du tres viellart pontife,
Sera efleu Romain de bon aage:
Qu'il fera dict que le fiege debiffe,
Et long tiendra & de picquant ouuraige.

Through the decease of a very aged pontiff,
A Roman will be elected of fine age:
When it will be said that the seat is spent,
And long will he hold, and with biting performance.

viellart, (O.Fr.) vieux; debiffe, (O.Fr. debiffé) razed, scraped out, far spent

381

THROUGH THE DECEASE OF THE VERY AGED PONTIFF

The first line of this verse is so general it could apply to many Roman pontiffs. But as the clues unfold, one is left in no doubt that the Oracle was directing its opening words at THE VERY AGED PONTIFF, Gregory XVI. He was born in September 1765 and DIED 1 June 1846, AGED EIGHTY.[1]

A ROMAN WILL BE ELECTED OF FINE AGE

THE POPE ELECTED to succeed him was Giovanni Maria Mastai-Ferretti who, at fifty-four, WAS OF FINE AGE. In 1814, he had been admitted to Pope Pius VII's court, where he studied theology in a Roman seminary. Between 1825 and 1827 he received his first major appointment, taking charge of the city's Hospice of Saint Michel; afterwards, he was appointed Archbishop of Spoleto. In 1840, he was elevated to the rank of cardinal. Finally, upon being elected to the papacy on 16 June 1846, he chose the title, Pius IX.[2]

WHEN IT WILL BE SAID THAT THE SEAT IS SPENT

In 1848, Pius IX became caught up in the revolutions sweeping across much of Europe. The outcry was for liberal reform, especially in the Papal States, where repression was at its severest.

> *Riot followed riot, the pope was denounced as a traitor to his country, his prime minister Rossi was stabbed to death while ascending the steps of the Cancelleria, whither he had gone to open the parliament, and on the following day the pope himself was besieged in the Quirinal. Palma, a papal prelate, who was standing at a window, was shot, and the pope was forced to promise a democratic ministry. With the assistance of the Bavarian ambassador, Count Spaur, and the French ambassador, Duc d'Harcourt, Pius IX escaped from the Quirinal in disguise, 24 November, and fled to Gaëta where he was joined by many of the cardinals. Meanwhile Rome was ruled by traitors and adventurers who abolished the temporal power of the pope, 9 February, 1849, and under the name of a democratic republic terrorized the people and committed untold outrages. [3]*

AND LONG WILL HE HOLD

The Pope appealed to France, Austria, Spain and Naples. On 29 June French troops under General Oudinot restored order in his territory. On 12 April, 1850, Pius IX returned to Rome, no longer a political liberalist. Pius IX's reign ended in 1878. After thirty-two years in office, he had become the longest serving pope in the history of the papacy.[4]

On 20 September 1870, Rome was once again occupied, this time by Italian troops intent upon making the capital city part of their kingdom. As a result of this insurgence, the Pope and his successors were allocated exclusive authority over Vatican City (a small separate area inside Rome). In return, the papacy was required to relinquish its control over the Papal States: a vast region that it had held since 756. Pius remained obdurate, refusing to recognize this loss of territory. As a further act of defiance, he prohibited Church members from voting in the state elections, aiming to reduce the authority of the government.

Pius had begun his term of office with liberal views. Bitter experience, however, subsequently forced upon him a different realism, to wit, that giving way to liberal thought only serves to lower standards of public behaviour and morality, and will ultimately undermine the foundations of the very system that allowed it. In response to this realization, Pius became the implacable enemy of political reform, hence, his **BITING PERFORMANCE**. His *"liberal stance was now discarded, and . . . he set up a paternalistic regime in the Papal States which alienated the educated and frowned on national aspirations."* As a consequence, the Church and the State became divided. In a desperate attempt to consolidate Catholic thought:

> *he published (8 Dec. 1864) the encyclical Quanta cura, with the 'Syllabus of Errors' attached, which denounced 'the principal errors of our times.'*

He also introduced the dogma of Papal Infallibility, and made known the Church's teaching regarding Mary's Immaculate Conception.[5]

Nostradamus's attention now returns to France with a chain of related prophecies concerning Napoleon III. The first prophecy provides a brief overview of this Emperor's reign.

C.VI: 74

La defchafee au regne tournera,
Ses ennemis trouués des coniurés:
Plus que iamais fon temps triomphera,
Trois & feptante à mort trop affeurés.

The exiled one will turn round for the reign,
His enemies discovered, composed of plotters :
More than ever his time will triumph,
Seventy-three: to a death being most certain.

trop, (O.Fr.) much, greatly; affeurés, (O,Fr.) etre certain.

THE EXILED ONE

After Napoleon's defeat at the battle of Waterloo, and the restoration of the monarchy in 1815, the former Emperor's closest relatives were forced into EXILE. Charles Louis-Napoleon, though only a child, was taken by his mother to Switzerland and lodged in their new castle home at Arenberg. By 1836, and now a young man, he become fired with political ambition. He saw himself as the natural heir to the French throne. In pursuit of this goal, Louis-Napoleon sought to win over the Strasbourg garrison as a first step towards displacing the reigning King. But the attempt failed and he found himself again an EXILE, this time at the mercy of Louis Philippe, who sent him to the United States. A year later, his mother suffered a serious illness, and he returned to Switzerland to be with her. From there, in 1838, he was taken into custody, and again sentenced to EXILE. This time he went to England. But, two years later, overcome by restlessness, he returned to France for another attempt at dislodging Louis Philippe. And, yet again, he was arrested: this time his sentence was life imprisonment inside the fortress at Ham in northern France. However, in May 1846, he managed to escape from the castle disguised as a mason. From France, he fled to England, where he remained in EXILE, awaiting some new opportunity to seize power.[1]

WILL TURN ROUND FOR THE REIGN

In 1848, news of an uprising against Louis Philippe was brought to Louis Napoleon from across the Channel. Seeing this as another prospect for achieving power, he quickly travelled to Paris, only to discover that a provisional government had taken control. The opportunity seemed lost, especially when he received orders to return to his *exile* in England. But help was at hand, a group of supporters nominated him for a place in the Constituent Assembly. During the September elections that followed, five *départements* voted for him, and this allowed Louis-Napoleon – *the exiled one* – TO TURN ROUND, and travel back to Paris. As an elected member of the Assembly, he was now eligible to run for the presidency. His name and popularity with the people, combined with the fact there was little opposition, won him the vote. From President, he became Prince-President, and in 1852 he took over THE REIGN of France as Emperor Napoleon III.[2]

HIS ENEMIES DISCOVERED, COMPOSED OF PLOTTERS:

Louis-Napoleon's reign also attracted ENEMIES. These were principally members of the Legitimist Party of royalists. They were divided into two groups, one supporting a Bourbon succession, the other preferring Orleans. The Republican Party, too, opposed Louis-Napoleon, and during the first four years of his presidency they met privately in groups across France: sometimes even using voluntary organizations to mask their political activities. In the crackdown that followed, thousands of these political PLOTTERS were DISCOVERED, and either jailed or sent to Algeria. In 1852, Prince-President Napoleon was even forced to take action against members of the Orleans family as a safeguard against their secretive *plotting*. A decree was issued, and they were banished from France.[3]

MORE THAN EVER HIS TIME WILL TRIUMPH

Napoleon III's Second Empire enjoyed unprecedented prosperity. Gold flooded into the country from French owned mines in California and South Africa. Railways were built, bringing the Riviera within reach of Parisians. Industrial production doubled; foreign trade did the same. Paris was reborn as a new city. The decaying remnants of former times were replaced with the great boulevards, mansions, stores and public buildings that brought the city into line with modern thinking. Under direction from the Emperor, Baron Haussmann created much that was to make Paris one of the most beautiful cities in the world. The humanities also flowered with a great blossoming of talent, in music, in literature and in the visual arts. To the world at large, it must have seemed that Napoleon III's Second Empire represented the summit of prosperity, gaiety and culture: MORE THAN EVER HIS TIME TRIUMPHED.[4]

SEVENTY-THREE: TO A DEATH BEING MOST CERTAIN

Louis Napoleon, otherwise Napoleon III, died 9 January 1873. For many years he had been suffering excruciating pain from bladder stones. With the weight of power removed from his shoulders, following his defeat and captivity in the Franco-Prussian War, he agreed to have the gallstones removed. But having survived two operations, he died while being prepared for further surgery.[5] It is noteworthy that this prophecy succeeds by nine days, for had he died during an earlier operation, the prediction of *seventy-three* would have failed.

Napoleon III's reign was most noticeable for the rebuilding of Paris. The old section, dating back centuries, was torn down; constructed in its place were the modern boulevards that still remain an attractive feature of the capital. This massive renovation was only made possible because it occurred within the fifty-seven peaceful years predicted for Paris by Nostradamus.

C.X: 89

De brique en marbre feront les murs reduicts
Sept & cinqaunte annees pacifiques,
Ioie aux humains, renoué l'aquedict,
Santé, grandz fruicts, ioye & temps melifique.

From brick into marble (rubble), the walls will be reduced,
Fifty-seven pacific years,
Joy to mankind, the aqueduct resumed,
Health, abundant results, happiness and a mellifluous time.

marbre, (O.Fr. homonym) caillou, marbre; melifique, (Latinism) mellifer – honey-making.

FROM BRICK INTO MARBLE (RUBBLE), THE WALLS WILL BE REDUCED

After winning the presidential election of 10 December 1848, Louis-Napoleon Bonaparte took the first step to realizing his dream. *"I want to be a second Augustus,"* he had earlier declared: *"because Augustus made Rome a city of marble."*[1] With the aid of Georges-Eugène Haussmann: *"Paris became one immense building site of mud, dust and rubble."*[2] In the centre of the city 20,000 houses were pulled-down and twice that number rebuilt. The old alleys and side streets gave way to great boulevards: which, with their wrought iron balcony fronted mansions soon became the homes of the Paris bourgeoisie. The *marble* halls of the Louvre were finally completed; a new *Palais d'Industie* was built, and massive renovations were made to the Hôtel de Ville.[3] Before the arrival of Haussmann, Paris had been a semi-medieval city; after his period of renewal the capital that emerged from the brick dust reflected both the commercial needs and social requirements of a modern society, much of which remains in evidence today.

FIFTY-SEVEN PACIFIC YEARS

In March 1814, during the reign of Napoleon I, 170,000 allied troops, drawn from Prussia, Austria and Russia entered the out-skirts of Paris, with the intention of unseating the Emperor. On the 30th, the capital came under cannon fire, and the city capitu-lated. The conquering armies that marched into Paris were headed by Czar Alexander of Russia, King Frederick-William of Prussia, and Prince Schwartzenberg of Austria. Napoleon I abdi-cated on 6 April; one month later the monarchy was restored with Louis XVIII taking on the role of the nation's King. Thereaf-ter, 1814 marked the commencement of FIFTY-SEVEN PEACEFUL YEARS for the capital city of France. But in March 1871, the *fifty-seven peaceful years* – almost to the exact day – came to an end. 30,000 Prussian troops once again entered Paris, as they had done in 1814, but this time to celebrate victory over France in the Franco-Prussian War. Nostradamus's *pacific years* refer to the absence of an invading army inside the capital, and not to an occasional outbreak of unrest, as occurred in Paris in 1830, with the three-day revolution that ended the reign of the Bourbon kings.[4]

JOY TO MANKIND

Parisian society during the reign of Napoleon III was a veritable JOY TO MANKIND. It was a period particularly noted for the introduc-tion of nineteenth-century gaiety to the capital. Masked balls, opera and the theatre became frequent leisure activities for those caught up in the social whirl. Art prospered with works from Monet, Delacroix, Berlioz, Chopin, Offenbach, Gounod, Balzac, Stendhal, Dumas, Flaubert, and many others.[5]

THE AQUEDUCT RESUMED

Napoleon III also revived the idea of uniting the Mediterranean with the Red Sea. His uncle Napoleon I had discovered earlier excavation attempts to achieve this during his Egyptian Cam-paign in 1798-9. Plans for redeveloping THE AQUEDUCT were RE-SUMED. After ten years of construction work under the direction of Ferdinand de Lesseps, the Empress Eugénie was able to open the Suez Canal on 16 November 1859.[6]

HEALTH

Health was another issue that came under the Emperor's gaze, so that: *"By the end of the reign the number of free hospitals in France had grown from 9,332 in 1852 to 13,278, of laying-in hospitals from 44 to 1,860."* In addition to this, the streets, the Gothic alleyways of old medieval

Paris were "*horribly unhealthy . . . filthy open drains ran down the middle of each thoroughfare. There was no proper water supply, everyone drinking from dubious wells: thousands died in the cholera epidemics of the 1830s.*" Napoleon III's response was to have Haussmann '*install modern drainage*'. This considerably reduced the incidence of disease in the city.[7]

ABUNDANT RESULTS

By the time the Emperor's plans were near completion, the **RE-SULTS** of his industry were **ABUNDANT**. Chief amongst many were:

> *. . . the rue de Rivoli, then . . . the avenue Napoleon III (now avenue de l'Opéra) . . . then came the 'grands boulevards', radiating out from the great squares. . . . Among the tall, white buildings that went up were the huge markets of Les Halles, the Polytechnique, the Ecole des Beaux Arts and such government offices as the Ministry of Foreign Affairs . . . The Louvre was completed, the Bibliothèque Nationale rebuilt and a new op-era house begun. Two vast parks were laid out at each end of the city . . . Paris also acquired its first department store, the Bon Marché, which opened in 1853.* [8]

HAPPINESS AND A MELLIFLUOUS TIME

"*In Paris nothing characterized the mood of the epoch more than those masked balls so cherished by Louis Napoleon. . . . Each ball was more sumptuous than the last and throughout the reign . . . took place with such regularity that they almost resembled a never-ending carnival.*" Elsewhere in the Second Empire, society became as keen as ever to follow the ways of their '*pleasure-loving Emperor*'.

For the working man, Louis Napoleon introduced beneficial social reforms. These included – "*institutions of maternal welfare, societies of mutual assistance, workers' cities and homes for injured workers; he proposed shorter working hours and health legislation; and he got rid of the degrading prison hulks.*" The Great Exposition of 1867 completed the picture. It attracted crowds from around the world, and contributed towards the Emperor's so-called, '*bread and circuses*' regime.[9]

The next quatrain contains a split prophecy covering two episodes in the reign of Napoleon III. It was first interpreted with some success by a former commentator, Anatole Le Pelletier, who succeeded three years before its fulfilment. This gives the lie to those who claim there are no examples of a prediction being understood before it takes place. His English acolyte Charles Ward, writing two decades after the event, was able to improve upon Le Pelletier's version by explaining the hybrid word '*lec-toyre*' as an anagram for 'Le Torcey', a suburb of Sedan.

C.VIII: 43

Par le decide de deux chofes baftars,
Nepueu du fang occupera le regne:
Dedans lectoyre feront les coups de dars,
Nepueu par peur pleira l'enfeigne.

Through the ending of two illegitimate matters,
A nephew of the blood will occupy the realm:
Inside (Sedan), (deprived of) Le Torcey, there will be blows from bolts,
The nephew through apprehension will fold his ensign.

decide, (Latinism) decid/o – cut off, put an end to; chofes, (O.Fr.) affaires; dars, (O.Fr.)
arme de trait; Dedans, (anagram & paragram) De[d]ans – Sedan; lectoyre, (anagram) Le
Torcey, also le[c] toyre, = toire,(O.Fr.) ôter; pleira, (from plier).

THROUGH THE ENDING OF TWO ILLEGITIMATE MATTERS

THE FIRST ILLEGITIMATE MATTER occurred in February 1848 with the uprising in Paris, which **ENDED** Louis Philippe's reign. As a result of the King's abdication, a new republic was declared in which Louis Napoleon took over the presidency. Three years later in 1851, **THE SECOND ILLEGITIMATE MATTER** occurred when Louis Napoleon overthrew this newly created republic and declared himself to be: *'Prince-President'*.[1]

A NEPHEW OF THE BLOOD

The *'Prince-President'* was indeed **A NEPHEW OF THE BLOOD**. Louis Napoleon was the third son of Napoleon I's brother, Louis Bonaparte (King of Holland from 1806 to 1810), and his wife Hortense de Beauharnais Bonaparte (daughter of Napoleon's first wife, the Empress Joséphine).[2]

WILL OCCUPY THE REALM

On 2 December, one year after having made himself Prince-President, Louis Napoleon proclaimed France to be the Second Empire: taking for himself, as its ruler, the title: Emperor Napoleon III.[3]

Nostradamus has this far been very open with his prediction that France's future ruler would be the *nephew* of a famous uncle, and that he would *occupy the kingdom* after two *illegitimate matters*. To offset this, he confounds further expectation by creating a gap of eighteen years: enough time for critics of Nostradamus to decry the oracle's initial fulfilment as a chance occurrence. But when the seer resumes, he does so with panache.

INSIDE SEDAN, DEPRIVED OF LE TORCEY

The Franco-Prussian War began in July 1870, and continued into August with four major battles being fought. On 1 September the battle of *Sedan* commenced, with Napoleon III having joined his men in the engagement. Three relatively small clashes had taken place by the side of the River Meuse on 29 and 30 August. These forced the French marshal Patrice Mac-Mahon to order his troops into the town of *Sedan*, where refuge was offered by the town's 15th century fortress.

> *The only part which its defences played, or might have played, in the ensuing battle lay in the strategic possibilities of the fine and roomy bridgehead of Torcy, covering the elbow bend of the Meuse whence the whole French army might have been hurled between the German III.* [4]

But the French, having DEPRIVED themselves OF LE TORCEY, were forced to seek cover INSIDE SEDAN.

THERE WILL BE BLOWS FROM BOLTS

Inside the fortress Mac-Mahon became injured. The Emperor was also suffering excruciating pain from gallstones. Without efficient command and with the continuous bombardment of shells exploding around them from the Prussian artillery – THERE WILL BE BLOWS FROM BOLTS – the French army fell into disarray. The only course of action was for soldiers to seek shelter from the barrage of exploding shells wherever cover could be found. [5]

THE NEPHEW THROUGH APPREHENSION WILL FOLD HIS ENSIGN

At about 5 o'clock in the evening, Napoleon III – THE NEPHEW of Napoleon Bonaparte I – realizing that the battle was lost, and THROUGH APPREHENSION for his men's safety, for they were being slaughtered at an alarming rate, FOLDED HIS ENSIGN, and replaced it with a white flag, which he hoisted above the citadel. He then informed King Wilhelm I – *"Having been unable to die in the midst of my troops, there remains nothing for me but to deliver my sword into your Majesty's hands. I am Your Majesty's true brother, Napoleon."* On 2 September 1870, at about 11 o'clock, Napoleon III signed the document prepared by Bismarck acknowledging his personal surrender. [6]

The Second Empire, although associated principally with Napoleon III, was greatly influenced by the Emperor's Spanish wife Maria Eugenia Ignacia Augusta. She was known at first as: '*La Reine Crinoline*', but later, as the Empress Eugénie she *"grew more concerned with influencing her husband's policies, than with making them. No woman had wielded such power in France since the sixteenth century."* The intellectual foresight behind Nostradamus seldom misses a major player in the politics of France, as we shall discover from the following prediction, which foresees Eugénie's rise to prominence.

C.III: 28

De terre foible & pauure parentele,
Par bout & paix paruiendra dans l'empire.
Long temps regner vne ieune femele,
Qu'oncq en regne n'en furuint vn fi pire.

From feeble estate and poor kindred,
By pushing forward, and accord, she will attain her aim in the empire.
Long time reigning, a young female,
That one time in the reign, one so bad not surviving from thence.

Parentele, (O.Fr.) kindred; bout, (O.Fr.) bouté, also boutant, pushed or pushing forward, paix, (O.Fr.) peace, quiet, accord, parviendra, (O.Fr.) atteindre le but; furvint, (O.Fr. syncope - survi[va]nt) surviving, outliving.

FROM FEEBLE ESTATE AND POOR KINDRED

Eugénie's father was Don Cipriano de Guzmán y Palafax y Portocarrero, Count of Teba. Despite the impressive title, and an ancestry that went back to the Visigoth kings, *"he inherited very little."* Soon after Eugénie's birth, he came close to ruin. This was because of his earlier support for a Liberal revolt, for which he was placed under house arrest at his *'little estate'* at 12 Calle de Garcia in Granada. His wife, Doña Maria Manuela Kirkpatrick de Closeburn was the daughter of a Scottish fruit merchant who had taken up residence in Spain, but who subsequently went bankrupt. Eugénie's biographer explains how: *"Cipriano made his children wear the same linen dresses winter and summer and would not buy them silk stockings for parties. Nor would he keep a carriage."* [1]

BY PUSHING FORWARD

After several years of searching for a suitable husband for Eugénie, her mother realised that Louis Napoleon, France's new ruler, and Europe's most eligible bachelor might yet be won. With her title derived from her husband's position in the Spanish nobility – *"Doña Maria Manuela immediately set about obtaining invitations to the Prince President's official receptions at the Elysée and Saint-Cloud, and found no difficulty in doing so."*

AND ACCORD

Napoleon had met Eugénie before. In the summer of 1849, he

had attempted to seduce her following a private dinner party arranged for that purpose. Mother and daughter were offended, and left France soon afterwards. Reconciliation with Napoleon after an absence of three years was quickly accomplished, and it allowed Eugénie to play her role to perfection, AND an ACCORD began to grow between the two. For Napoleon had discovered that his new friend was intelligent in conversation, politically astute, and attentive to his wishes in all except that of compromising her position by agreeing to become his mistress. The Prince President soon found his thoughts contemplating marriage.[2]

SHE WILL ATTAIN HER AIM IN THE EMPIRE

News of Napoleon's intentions soon became widely known. The British Ambassador, Lord Cowley, reported to London: *"[Eugenie] has played her game with him so well, that he can get her in no other way but marriage, and it is to gratify his passions that he marries her."* On the day before the civil wedding, Cowley *"informed London that the emperor 'has been captured by an adventuress'."* The civil marriage took place in the royal palace of the Tuileries on 29 January 1853. Next day it was solemnized in the Cathedral of Notre Dame. Eugénie had finally ATTAINED HER AIM IN THE EMPIRE by becoming Empress of the French.[3]

LONG TIME REIGNING

"From 1853 to 1870 Eugénie de Montijo was Empress of the French, sharing the Second Empire with her husband Napoleon III." She therefore REIGNED as Empress for seventeen years. Three times during the Emperor's absence she was appointed Regent (1859, 1865, and 1870), possessing absolute power and *"chairing the Council of Ministers once a week . . . besides receiving copies of reports on internal and external affairs."* Her control of the government at the time France was facing defeat in the war against Prussia was acclaimed by all, and: *"The Second Empire belonged as much to her as it did to him (Napoleon III)."*[4]

A YOUNG FEMALE

Eugénie was born on 28 May 1826. She was therefore 26 years-of-age when she became Empress.[5]

THAT ONE TIME IN THE REIGN

14 January 1858 was THE ONE TIME IN THE REIGN that proved most life-threatening for the Empress. Upon arriving at the *Paris Opéra* that evening with her husband, for a performance of Auber's

Gustave III "three grenades packed with bullets were thrown at their carriage, exploding in succession under the wheels." Seventeen lancers accompanying the royal carriage were wounded, as were another one hundred and forty in the crowd lining the street. Of these, ten died, including one of the lancers. From amidst the debris of the broken carriage, Eugénie and Napoleon emerged almost unscathed, although a glass splinter had grazed her eyelid and the Emperor sustained a cut lip.[6]

ONE SO BAD

The criminal mind behind the assassination attempt was an Italian patriot named Felice Orsini. The plot in which he was involved was intended to trigger a revolution in France that would transform it into a republic, capable of uniting Italy under a similar system of government.[7]

NOT SURVIVING FROM THENCE

Orsini **DID NOT SURVIVE** the effect of his criminal action. He was arrested, sentenced to death, and *"guillotined on 13 March."*[8]

Nostradamus continues to pursue his interest in the Empress Eugénie with a further quatrain. Those acquainted with her double wedding to Napoleon III may possibly recognise the opening lines of the following verse as a description of that event. Interestingly, it has only been recently that historians have given renewed prominence to Eugénie's role in French political affairs. By allotting the Empress a second prophecy, Nostradamus has anticipated her importance.

C.X: 19

Iour que fera par Royne faluée,
Le jour apres le falut, la priere:
Le compte fait raifon & valuée,
Par avant humble oncques ne fut fi fiere.

The day that she will be bowed to [as] for a Queen,
The day after the salutation, the prayer:
The unlikely tale made the subject of conversation, and evaluated,
Through previous humbleness, at one time was never so proud.

valuée, (syncope) evaluée; compte, (O.Fr.) an unlikely tale; raifon, (O.Fr.) sujet d'une conversation; oncques, (O.Fr.) une fois, en certains circonstances.

N.B. The text is from Leffen's copy of the 1558 edition published at Lyons. Rigaud's edition of 1568 differs with royne for Royne; iour for jour; valbuee for valuée, and feut for fut: accents are also omitted.

THE DAY THAT SHE WILL BE BOWED TO AS FOR A QUEEN

The civil wedding ceremony between Eugenia and Napoleon III was conducted in Paris on the evening of 29 January 1853, and took place inside the Tuileries Palace. She later wrote to her sister describing how *"[she] felt she was acting in a play when people addressed her as 'Your Majesty'."* For almost an hour after the marriage ceremony, **HAVING BEEN PROCLAIMED EMPRESS**, Eugénie received a **SALUTATION** from each leading member of the French government and from the elite of society.[1]

THE DAY AFTER THE SALUTATION, THE PRAYER

THE DAY AFTER THE SALUTATION, *'Eugénie (no longer Eugenia)'* and Napoleon attended the Cathedral of Notre Dame for the religious ceremony to bless their marriage.

> *The service is taken by the archbishop of Paris Monseigneur Sibour . . . During the wedding Lady Cowley has sketched the new empress inside her prayer book. Kneeling at a prie-dieu [praying stool], Eugénie's chin rests pensively on her hand."* [2]

THE UNLIKELY TALE MADE THE SUBJECT OF CONVERSATION

The marriage between Napoleon III and Eugénie had been such **AN UNLIKELY TALE,** that it became **THE SUBJECT OF** frequent **CONVERSATION.** In fact: *"the emperor had changed the date from 10 February on account of so much opposition to the marriage."* As late as early January: *"Many people at the highest level were still convinced that the marriage would never happen."* The London ambassador to Paris, Lord Cowley reported: *"It was, of course, ill received in Paris even by the emperor's friends, and it has set all the women against him. Clergy and army disapprove."* Gossip about the marriage had also caused news of it to travel across the Channel, where it was reported in the *Illustrated London News: "alas for the gallantry of Frenchmen . . . they find nothing better to do than repeat the scandals originating in the boudoirs of the fairer part of creation."* [3]

AND EVALUATED

In London, the foreign secretary's response to Lord Cowley's opinion of Eugénie as *'an adventuress'* was made with similar aloofness: *"to put this 'intrigante' on the throne is a lowering of the imperial dignity with a vengeance."* Napoleon, realising how his wife was being **EVALUATED,** was forced to counter the growing apprehension with a positive attitude. At the Tuileries on the eve of his wedding, he called together the Council of State and Assembly to hear a speech he had prepared concerning his marriage, *"copies of* *which were distributed throughout France. . . . His future wife, he told them was of high birth, French by education and a devout Catholic. He promised she would bring back 'the virtues' of his grandmother, Empress Joséphine."* Not everyone was convinced, as one learns from Baron Hübner's report, sent to his masters in Vienna. *"However democratic people may be, they would have preferred a princess."* [4]

THROUGH PREVIOUS HUMBLENESS

In complete contrast to becoming Empress of the French, Eugénie's **EARLY CHILDHOOD** had been considerably **HUMBLE**. Although descended from a noble Spanish family, the financial circumstances of her father had initially been poor: at one time, while under house arrest, he had even faced bankruptcy. Eugenie's mother was of lesser stock. She was the daughter of a Scottish fruit and wine merchant who had settled in Malaga, and then lost his money in a failed business venture. The contrast between the expectations of France for its charismatic Emperor, and the woman he had chosen to be his wife is therefore most evident.[5]

AT ONE TIME WAS NEVER SO PROUD

After the wedding ceremony at the Tuileries, Eugénie wrote to her sister, describing how: *"For three-quarter of an hour they filed past her, cardinals, generals and ministers bowing, ladies curtseying."* Next day at the Cathedral she appeared at Notre Dame, dressed:–

> *in white velvet sewn with diamonds; her full three-layered skirt is trimmed with priceless old English lace, her tight bodice is sewn with sapphires and orange blossom, and around her waist is Empress Marie-Louise's sapphire girdle—her three-quarter length sleeves reveal long, jewel-studded gloves. Her red hair has been arranged by the famous coiffeur Félix, curls flowing down the neck from the chignon to which her veil is fastened, and she wears the diamond and sapphire tiara that Empress Joséphine had worn at her coronation in 1804.* [6]

In retrospect, after long periods in exile, Napoleon III had at last been able to take the path towards becoming Emperor of France by walking out of the great fortress at Ham disguised as a workman. Coincidentally, he ended his term as Emperor by walking out of another great fortress, this time at Sedan, where he had been forced to capitulate to his German adversary, William I. Nostradamus was seemingly aware of this coincidence, for he makes it the opening comment in this next oracle.

C.IV: 65

Au deferteur de la grand forterefſe,
Apres qu'aura ſon lieu abandonné:
Son aduerſaire fera ſi grand prouefſe,
L'Empereur toſt mort fera condemné.

To the deserter of the great fortress,
That afterwards will have abandoned his position:
His adversary will acheieve such great prowess,
The Emperor soon dead will be condemned.

TO THE DESERTER OF THE GREAT FORTRESS

This surely relates to events involving two great fortresses in the life of Napoleon III. The first of these was the **GREAT FORTRESS** of Ham in northern France. In August 1840, Charles Louis Napoleon was arrested for a failed *coup,* and sentenced to life imprisonment. For six years he remained confined behind the walls of Ham fortress. Then, on 25 May 1846, **HE DESERTED THE FORTRESS.** *"He successfully accomplished his design by the simple expedient of walking out of the gaol disguised as a workman."* [1]

THAT AFTERWARDS WILL HAVE ABANDONED HIS POSITION

The other great fortress involving Louis-Napoleon stood in the French town of Sedan, and was reputed to be the largest in Europe. In September 1870, during the Franco-Prussian War, it became the scene of one of France's most ignominious defeats. Louis-Napoleon, **AFTERWARDS** Emperor Napoleon III, having suffered terrible casualties amidst a hail of continuous shelling, and finding his army cornered inside a fortress that was visibly shaking under this continuous bombardment, **ABANDONED HIS POSITION** and surrendered himself to the Prussian army. [2]

HIS ADVERSARY WILL ACHIEVE SUCH GREAT PROWESS

Napoleon III's **ADVERSARY WAS:** *'Wilhelm I of Germany',* the victor of Sedan. Outside Paris, he not only set up his Royal Headquarters inside the Palace of Versailles, but on 18th January, inside the Hall of Mirrors, he had himself proclaimed *'Kaiser'* of the German Empire. [3] By the end of September, the French governing body was compelled to concede to terms for peace laid down by Germany's new Emperor. These involved the loss to France of Alsace and most of Lorraine; a payment of five billion francs, and the cost of maintaining a German presence in the east until the indemnity had been paid in full. Finally, before pulling out of Paris, Kaiser Wilhelm insisted upon a victory parade. On the morning of March 1st, 30,000 triumphant German soldiers either marched or rode on horseback down the Champs-Elysées to the steady beat of their drums. In the afternoon, to the accompaniment of more military music, a second victory parade took place, this time with the massed troops striding onto the *Place de la Concorde*.[4]

THE EMPEROR SOON DEAD

Soon after his captivity by the Prussian Army, following the surrender at Sedan, THE EMPEROR Napoleon III was released. He sailed to England on 20 March 1871, once more an exile, and took up residence with his wife and son at Camden Place, in Chislehurst, Kent: occupying himself with plans for a fresh *coup d'état*. But LESS THAN TWO YEARS LATER, on 9 January 1873, while preparing to undergo a third operation to remove bladder stones, his condition suddenly deteriorated, and he DIED.[5]

WILL BE CONDEMNED

"Sedan was a defeat even more bitter than Waterloo . . . it delivered France into the hands of Prussia, and generations of Frenchmen have never forgiven Napoleon III for their country's humiliation." [6]

After Emperor Napoleon's surrender at Sedan, the Third Empire was declared, and a provisional government formed. Elections followed on 26 March 1871, but these failed to calm a situation that had ignited eight days earlier, when the government attempted to disarm the Paris National Guard. By attempting this, bloodshed and rebellion ensued. It was from this turmoil that the Commune was born. It came together as a political alternative to the conservative administration led by Adolphe Thiers. In the violence that followed, Thiers was forced out of Paris. But Bismarck stepped in with an offer to help him by releasing French soldiers captured in the Franco-Prussian War. Thiers responded by setting up his headquarters at Versailles, from where he was able to muster an army – the *Versaillais* – whose mission it was to recapture Paris.

C.V: 30

Tout à l'entour de la grande cité,
Seront foldartz loges par champs & ville:
Donner l'affault Paris, Rome incité,
Sur le pont lors fera faicte grand pille.

397

All around the great city,
Soldiers will be quartered in fields and town:
Paris giving the assault, Rome incited,
Over the bridge at that time an action will make great ruin.

Par (O.Fr.) as Latin per; pille, (O.Fr.) despoil, ransack, ruin; faicte, (O.Fr.) deed, action.

This prophecy concerns the second siege of Paris. The Prussian Army had conducted the first siege as a strategic follow-up to their victory at Sedan in September 1870. But after the armistice signed in January, and the removal of Napoleon III, an attempt was made to fill the political void by the Commune of Paris. This was a party of anti-religious left-wing socialists who seized power in March 1871.

ALL AROUND THE GREAT CITY SOLDIERS WILL BE QUARTERED IN FIELDS AND TOWN

From his base at Versailles, Adolphe Thiers, former head of the French government, deployed the prisoners-of-war released by Bismarck to lay siege to Paris, so that ALL AROUND THE GREAT CITY WILL BE SOLDIERS. The plan necessitated billeting the men close to the capital. Consequently, some were QUARTERED IN THE TOWN of Versailles, and others in camp sites erected IN THE FIELDS outside Paris.[1]

PARIS GIVING THE ASSAULT

On 22 May, 70,000 French troops poured through a breach in the city wall to the southwest of Paris, and street-by-street the insurgent *'Versaillais'* began retaking their capital.[2]

ROME INCITED

It was while Paris lay surrounded by troops loyal to Thiers that the Commune leader, *"Raoul Rigault ordered the taking of hostages. These were headed by no less a person than the Archbishop of Paris, Monseigneur Darboy."* But as *Paris gave way to assault,* Rigault realised the ineffectiveness of holding hostages. Nevertheless, he refused to release them. Instead, he had Archbishop Darboy brutally murdered. A further seventy hostages shared the same fate, among whom were *'dozens of monks and priests'.* This unnecessary slaying of Catholic clergy INCITED ROME to remonstrate at the time, and the murders have continued into the present day to be considered one of the Commune's most infamous crimes.[3]

OVER THE BRIDGE AT THAT TIME AN ACTION WILL MAKE GREAT RUIN

Meanwhile, as the battle for Paris continued, the fiercest fighting was occurring on the other side of the river Seine; that is, OVER

398

'the new Pont Royal, linking the Tuileries to the Left Bank'. There, the Communards were fighting **AN ACTION** with government troops. *"On the Left Bank, Communards fought at Montparnasse Station until their ammunition ran out . . . At the other end of the front, the Versailles troops were advancing rapidly towards Montmartre."* Estimates of those killed vary, from 6,500 to 40,000. After Thiers had put down the revolt, Paris descended into a strange quietness. *"Théophile Gautier noted the city's oppressive silence, and was particularly struck by the Rue de Lille, on the Left Bank . . . 'it seemed to be deserted throughout its length, like a street of Pompeii'."* [4]

Amongst the more prominent buildings that suffered destruction from the fighting were: *"the Tuileries, a large part of the Palais Royal, the Palais de Justice, the Prefecture of Police and the Conseil d'Etat. Whole sections of streets were ablaze; so was the Ministry of Finance."* Even the great column in the *Place Vendôme*, erected to celebrate Napoleon's victories of 1805, was knocked down.[5]

Of all the buildings destroyed during Thiers retaking of Paris from the Commune, perhaps the one having greatest historical significance was the *Palais de Tuileries*. Nostradamus appears to have recognized its special importance, for he makes its destruction the opening line of the following oracle.

C.IV: 100

De feu celefte au royal edifice.
Quant la lumiere de Mars deffaillira:
Sept mois grand guerre, mort gent de malefice,
Rouan, Eureux au Roy ne faillira.

Concerning the celestial fire at the royal building,
When the light of Mars will be wanting:
Seven months a great war, people dead by misdeed,
Rouen! Evreux will not fail the King.

deffaillira, (O.Fr.) manquer – to be wanting; malefice, (O.Fr.) méfait, délit.

CONCERNING THE CELESTIAL FIRE AT THE ROYAL BUILDING

On the night of 23 May 1871, **THE SKY** above Paris **LIT UP** with such a brilliant light that it dwarfed all the firework displays seen recently in the capital. **THE ROYAL BUILDING** in the centre of Paris, the *Palais de Tuileries,* was **ON FIRE**, and its glow could be seen for miles around. A Communard leader, Jules Bergeret, only recently released from prison, had decided upon the vengeful act of blowing up the royal palace. Barrel upon barrel of gunpowder was stacked inside the palace, and then ignited to send a huge fireball into the night sky. The central dome of the royal palace vanished in an instant, and another prediction by Nostradamus was about to become history.[1]

WHEN THE LIGHT OF MARS WILL BE WANTING

At the time of the palace's destruction, Mars was invisible to the naked eye; that is to say, THE LIGHT OF MARS WILL BE WANTING. The explanation for this was quite natural: the planet was appearing overhead only during the hours of daylight. Its light was therefore invisible to the naked eye.[2]

SEVEN MONTHS A GREAT WAR

The GREAT WAR mentioned by Nostradamus is therefore the Franco-Prussian War that preceded the destruction of the Tuileries. On 19 July 1870, Napoleon III had declared war on Prussia. The decision proved to be a disaster for France. During the conflict, French soldiers were so decisively defeated that the nation was compelled to accept the demanding terms set out in Bismarck's armistice agreement. This was signed on 27 January 1871.[3] The time period referred to in the prophecy is therefore the SEVEN named MONTHS from July to January, during which the conflict occurred.

After the armistice had been signed, French anger and suspicion at the humiliation dealt out by Bismarck's success turned inwards, and Paris underwent an intense period of civil strife. The capital was taken over by the Paris Commune, and the legitimate government retreated to Versailles. During the infamous 'semaine sanglante' (bloody week), which put an end to the Commune during the last week of May, between 20,000 and 25,000 people were killed inside the capital.

PEOPLE DEAD BY MISDEED

Added to this atrocity was the fate of those Communards who were taken prisoner; they had been so savagely treated that many failed to survive long enough to be shot by the firing squad.

> That Whitsun morning, in revenge, the Versailles troops marched 147 of the captured Communards out to Père Lachaise and summarily shot them against a wall of the cemetery. Inside La Roquette . . . some 1,900 prisoners are said to have been shot in two days, and at the Mazas prison another 400.

The London Times (1 June 1871) described the fate of these PEOPLE: DEAD BY the MISDEED of their captors as *"wholesale executions inflicted by the Versailles soldiery, the triumph, the glee, the ribaldry . . . sicken the soul."*[4]

ROUEN!

ROUEN is a port city and capital of Seine-Maritime in northwestern France; it lies to the northwest of Paris on the River Seine. During the Franco-Prussian War, *"[General] Manteuffel's forces continued to advance westward, capturing Rouen on 5 December."*[5] This acts as an introduction to one of Nostradamus's last lines, in which he concludes with a prediction that is meant to tease. In this case, he is rebuking Rouen for having been captured; comparing the city with its neighbour, Evreux, which assisted the besieged city of Paris.

EVREUX WILL NOT FAIL THE KING

During Bismarck's *Siege of Paris*, the citizens inside the capital adopted the idea of using balloons to communicate with the rest of the country. On 23 September, the Prussian army was astonished to see a balloon passing overhead – *"Its pilot Durouf landed safely at Evreux beyond the enemy's reach with 125 kilograms of despatches, after a three-hour flight."* *Evreux* is an old medieval town situated 25 miles to the south of *Rouen*. EVREUX HAD therefore NOT FAILED THE KING, for it was able to deal with the dispatches from Paris, whereas neighbouring *Rouen* had been forced to succumb to the invading army.[6]

This ploy has been used twice before. In C.IV: 37, Nostradamus rebuked Genoa for failing to match Monaco's efforts. And in C.VI: 12, it was the turn of the Flemish to be reprimanded for not resisting Napoleon as the Spanish and English had done.

In the next oracle Nostradamus returns his attention to the emerging development of the United States of America. The prediction includes implied references to the victory of the North over the South in the *American Civil War*, Thanksgiving Day, and the nation's growth towards becoming a superpower.

C.I: 50

De l'aquatique triplicité naiftra
D'vn qui fera le ieudy pour fa fefte:
Son bruit, loz, regne, fa puiffance croiftra,
Par terre & mer, aux orients tempefte.

It will be born composed of the aquatic triplicity,
For one that will take Thursday for its festival:
Its renown, reputation, rule, and its power will grow,
By land and sea, violent combat to the easterners.

triplicité, (Late Latin: triplicitatem) – tripllicity; los, (O.Fr.) honneur, reputation; bruit, (O.Fr.) renomée, gloir; tempelte, (O.Fr.) combat violent.

IT WILL BE BORN COMPOSED OF THE AQUATIC TRIPLICITY

The United States of America, Hawaii excepted, are bounded by **THE AQUATIC TRIPLICITY**. This comprises the Pacific Ocean on the west coast, the Atlantic Ocean on the east coast, and the Gulf of Mexico fed by the Caribbean Sea to the south.[1] Along America's northern border lies Canada. The term: 'United States' was **BORN** from a phrase used in the Declaration of Independence (1776), and later repeated in the preamble to the Federal Constitution of 1787.[2]

FOR ONE THAT WILL TAKE THURSDAY FOR ITS FESTIVAL

In 1863, President Abraham Lincoln, while still engaged in the American Civil War, decreed that the last **THURSDAY** in November should be celebrated as the nation's *'Thanksgiving Day'*. It was not until 1941 that this was amended, so that the **FESTIVAL** of Thanksgiving would always fall on the fourth *Thursday* of November.[3]

ITS RENOWN, REPUTATION, RULE AND POWER, WILL GROW

In recent times, America's **RENOWN, RULE AND POWER HAVE GROWN** enormously, and the country presently enjoys the **REPUTATION** of a super-power. The nation's political rule and military might are therefore impressive, and its influence has spread around the globe affecting many people's lives, in lands ranging from the smallest to the largest.[4] But this has not always been welcome.

VIOLENT COMBAT TO THE EASTERNERS BY LAND AND SEA

Currently, America's *reputation* for military fire-power **BY LAND AND SEA** is sufficient to secure its supremacy – *its renown* – in any part of the world where it has established its influence or *rule*.[5]
In December 1941, the Japanese air force made a surprise attack on the American fleet anchored at Pearl Harbour, thereby impelling the nation to declare war against Japan: *the easterners*. In June 1950, war broke out between North and South Korea, with the US becoming engaged in the conflict. Once again, the nation found itself pitted against *the easterners*, by taking up arms against North Korea: a country heavily supported by Chinese

soldiers and weaponry. In 1955, another war broke out, this time between North and South Vietnam. Again, America became involved in fighting against *the easterners*; this time it was the communist guerrillas of North Vietnam. Then, in January and February of 1991, the United States led a coalition force against Iraq – more *easterners* – in an effort to curtail the territorial ambitions of Saddam Hussein. In 2001, it became the turn of *the easterners* inside Afghanistan to bear the weight of American force, as aerial onslaughts were undertaken to root out and destroy the terrorist organization thought to be responsible for attacking the World Trade Center in New York. And, in March 2003, America once again declared war against *the easterners:* when they targeted Iraq for a second time. Nostradamus's prediction of VIOLENT COMBAT FOR THE EASTERNERS, is, if anything, a trifle understated.[6]

If wars, bloodshed, revolution, starvation, plunder, oppression and murder proliferate within these oracles then it can be seen as an indictment against mankind's failure to learn from history. The oracles of Nostradamus simply predict what will later come to pass. Fortunately, his interests do occasionally light upon more peaceful themes. In particular, the next oracle would likely have been of special interest to the seer. It concerns Louis Pasteur: a man who features among the world's greatest medical practitioners, and who was, at the same time, a Frenchman.

C.I: 25

Perdu, trouué, cache de ſi long ſiecle,
Sera paſteur demi Dieu honoré,
Ains que la lune acheue ſon grand cycle
Par autres veux ſera deſhonoré.

Lost, found, hidden for such a long period of time.
Pasteur (a pastor) will be honoured a demy-god,
Whilst the moon completes its great cycle;
By other luminaries he will be dishonoured.

ſiecle, (O.Fr.) une longue période de temps; Paſteur, (surname of the famous chemist, also 'pastor') Ains que, (O.Fr.) whilst; veux, (O.Fr.) lumières.

N.B. The third word of the fourth line, 'veux' is reproduced here according to Macé Bonhomme's spelling. However, Antoine du Rosne, has spelt it 'veutz,' and Benoist Rigaud gave it as 'ventz' (breaths).

To those familiar with the life of Louis Pasteur, the second and fourth lines will immediately suggest comparison. The third line is clearly an astronomical reference, and may be expected to relate to Pasteur's life in some way. This leaves only the opening line, which appears to point towards an archaeological discovery of some considerable importance. If this conjecture is valid, then that too will have some connection with *Pasteur*.

LOST, FOUND, HIDDEN FOR SUCH A LONG PERIOD OF TIME

One of the greatest archaeological finds of all time was undoubtedly the discovery of the LOST Rosetta stone in August 1799. It was FOUND during Napoleon Bonaparte's conquest of Egypt. Ancient hands using three writing systems – hieroglyphics, demotic script and Greek – had inscribed the stone with a decree made by Ptolemy V (Epiphanes) at some time during the second century BC. Thereafter, the stone had remained HIDDEN FOR 2,000 years; that is, SUCH A LONG PERIOD OF TIME. But, after it was discovered at Rosetta, a location some 35 miles from Alexandria, the inscription was able to provide scholars with a key to understanding many ancient and hitherto indecipherable hieroglyphs.[1]

Decipherment of the stone was far from simple, despite one third of it being in Greek. In fact, several decades elapsed before a Frenchman, Jean-François Champollion, discovered the key. It was entirely due to the breakthrough he made in 1822 that led to the new science of Egyptology.

PASTEUR

Nostradamus's next sentence introduces Louis PASTEUR. This world famous chemist was born in 1822: the same year that Champollion *found* the key to deciphering the Rosetta Stone. It may therefore be said that the oracle has cleverly combined one of the greatest archaeological discoveries of the age with the birth year of one of France's greatest scientists.[2]

(A PASTOR)

Pasteur proved to be an excellent scholar, and it was not long before he was appointed Dean at Lille University, and later Director of Scientific Studies at the *École Normale Supérieure*. This was also the time when he took on a *pastoral* role – *"by instituting evening classes for the many young workmen of the industrial city, conducting his regular students around large factories in the area, and organizing supervised practical courses."* [3]

404

In 1892: *"the whole of France assisted by representatives of many nations united to honour her greatest scientist."* The festival of appreciation took place at the Sorbonne in Paris, and was attended by delegates *"from London, Ireland, Brussels, Liege, Ghent, Leyden, Stockholm, Copenhagen, Genoa, Berlin, Cologne, Posen, Warsaw, Geneva, Berne, Lausanne, Athens and Bucharest."* By then, he had been given a seat *"among the 'Immortals': the forty Frenchmen most distinguished in letters and in science."* And when a popular vote was taken amongst the people of France, Louis *Pasteur* was voted *'the greatest Frenchman of all time'*. [4]

Between the commencement of Pasteur's international recognition in 1876, when he disposed of the myth of Spontaneous Generation, and his death in 1895, aged 73, nineteen years elapsed. This explains the astronomical reference in the third line. Nineteen years marks a *'Metonic Cycle'*; that is, the time taken WHILST THE MOON COMPLETES ITS GREAT CYCLE. The Greek astronomer Meton made this astronomical discovery in the 4th century BC, when he observed that the various phases of the moon continuously repeat themselves every 19 years. The oracle has therefore used this timing device to mark the passage of years during *Pasteur's* lifetime: a period when he enjoyed international recognition. [5]

In January 1887, almost midway through the Metonic Cycle that marked Pasteur's years of fame. A spate of criticisms broke out aimed at the chemist. These concerned the serum he used to cure Rabies: *'many were sceptical and a few were positively hostile'*. Monsieur Peter, prominent amongst the medical LUMINARIES who took part in DISHONOURING Pasteur, led the main attack. He publicly declared: *"that the anti-rabic cure was useless [even] dangerous when applied in intensive form."* The Press took up the attack, and very soon Pasteur found himself at the focal point of *'all that envy and hatred could invent'*, as wave after wave of protests poured in from across the country.

It was while at Bordighera, during a period of convalescence, that the Academy of Sciences retaliated on Pasteur's behalf. They did so by issuing a pamphlet exonerating him from any blame. These leaflets were delivered to every village across France, and proved very successful. By the time the chemist returned to Paris in March that year, the controversy had faded away.[6]

During the past two centuries France has experienced several changes in the way its empire is run. The next quatrain refers to one of these changes, and by doing so, makes it a precursor to what follows; to wit, the erection of Paris' great landmark, the Eiffel Tower. Nostradamus likens the Tower to Porphyrion. In classical literature, Porphyrion was a Giant that rebelled against Zeus, and was struck by lightning as punishment. To confirm the identification, Nostradamus refers to its place of location, the *Champ de Mars*. Interestingly, at the time it was erected, plans were being made for the construction of the Paris Metro, and this fact, too, seems not to have eluded the foresight of our seer.

C.I: 43

Avant qu'aduienne le changement d'empire,
Il aduiendra vn cas bien merueilleux:
Le champ mué, le pillier de porphire,
Mis, tranſlaté fus le rocher noilleux.

The change of empire that happens previously,,
A most marvellous event will occur:
The Champ modified, the pillar of Porphyrion;
Placed, transported on high: the underground caves, joints / spaghetti.

Avant (O.Fr. adverb) before, or ere, and forward; aduiendra, (O.Fr. advenir) happen, befall, chance, come to pass; cas, (O.Fr.) événément; mué, (O.Fr. verb, muer) modifier; porphire, (Latinism, Porphyrion) one of the giants; tranſlaté, (O.Fr.) transporter; sus, (O.Fr.) en haut; rocher, (O.Fr.) cave, maison, souterrain; noilleux, (O.Fr. noüailleux = noüageux) bunches, joints, *c.f.* nouilleux (nouilles) = spaghetti, noodles.

THE CHANGE OF EMPIRE THAT HAPPENS PREVIOUSLY

The end of the Second Empire was precipitated by the capture of Napoleon III at the battle of Sedan in September 1870. *"The news of Sedan precipitated the fall of the Second Empire and the proclamation of the Third Republic in Paris."* But the actual date of the Third Empire is subject to doubt, and is given by Claude Lebédel in his *Chronologie de l'Histoire de France* as, *'La IIIᵉ République: 1875–1940'*. He states that it is difficult to date the début of the Third Republic, since three dates have been suggested. The first is 4 September 1870, because of the military defeat and invasion of France. The second is February 1871, through the reunion at Bordeaux of the new National Assembly under the presidency of Adolphe Thiers. The third is January 1875, when the Assembly voted the

Wallon amendment with a scanty majority. This limited the mandate of the President of the Republic to a period of seven years. Before then there had been a compromise of between five and ten years.[1]

Nostradamus next reveals what will happen *before long*, following this prolonged *change of empire*. To commemorate the centenary of the French Revolution, and to create a signpost for the Great Exposition planned for 1889, an idea was proposed that was intended: *"To distract minds and hearts from France's territorial loss, the central theme was the colonial empire."* (The theme of *empire* links the opening two lines of this oracle). It was decided to hold a competition for the display of a landmark monument to mark the exhibition. The winning entry – clearly foreseen by Nostradamus more than three centuries earlier – was the Eiffel Tower.

A MOST MARVELLOUS EVENT WILL HAPPEN

At the time of its completion, the Eiffel Tower was the tallest manmade construction in the world: *'twice as high as the dome of St. Peter's in Rome or the Great Pyramid of Giza'*. It weighed 7,000 tonnes and was held together by half a million rivets, and altogether represented: *"[a] technological masterpiece in building-construction history."*[2]

THE 'CHAMP' MODIFIED

The location chosen for the monument was *the Champ de Mars*. The Field still occupies a huge area of open ground on the left bank of Paris, stretching back to the *École Militaire*. In the past, the field had been the scene of several rallies during the French Revolution; the first of which was the Festival of the Federation (1790); another was the Festival of the Supreme Being (1794). But before the Tower could be constructed, THE *CHAMP* had to be MODIFIED. Two acres of ground were therefore levelled for the site, in order to allow the foundations to be put in place.[3]

THE PILLAR OF PORPHYRION

PORPHYRION appears in Greek Mythology as the giant offspring of Uranus and Gaia. Nostradamus likens the giant's stature to a PILLAR, equating it with the Eiffel Tower, which reaches more than 300 meters up to the sky.[4]

PLACED

The Tower was PLACED at the far end of the field: the giant arches at the base were to act as entranceways to the exhibition.[5]

TRANSPORTED ON HIGH

Another feature of the Eiffel Tower's construction was *"the glass-cage machines designed by the Otis Elevator Company of the United States,"* and which became *"one of the principal features of the building."* The oracle predicts the importance of these lifts, for they proved to be a great attraction for the thirty million visitors who arrived at the Exposition, and who were then TRANSPORTED ON HIGH to experience a bird's eye view of Paris from the top of the Tower.[6]

UNDERGROUND CAVES, JOINTS, SPAGHETTI

Although the Exposition and the Tower were hugely successful, the attraction was also a continual cause of traffic congestion close to the site. A solution was therefore proposed. *"1889 . . . The traffic problems created by some thirty million visitors to the exhibition give rise to the project for building an underground rail network, the Paris métro."* The first line was opened in 1900. Further UNDERGROUND stations – CAVES – followed, JOINED to a network of interconnecting lines, *spaghetti-like*, crisscrossing the city.[7]

For those who accept Nostradamus's precognitive ability, there is an interesting aspect to his prophecies. He only predicts for countries outside of France if they have some important and lasting contribution to make to world history. And when this is foreseen, he traces that country's political history from its point of change. The next oracle represents an instance of this occurring. It concerns the rise of the Austro-Hungarian Empire during the years immediately prior to its involvement in the First World War.

C.II: 90

Par vie & mort changé regne d'Ongrie:
La loy fera plus afpre que feruice,
Leur grand cité d'vrlemens plaincts & crie:
Caftor & Pollux ennemis dans la lyce.

Through life and death, the reign of Hungary is changed:
The law will be harsher than a state of servitude,
Their great city with howls, complaints and outcry:
Castor & Pollex adversaries in the tiltyard.

afpre, (O.Fr.) cruel, harsh; fervice, (O.Fr.) état de servage. Cross-reference: life and death, C.VIII: 15.

It is a significant fact, and one relevant to these oracles, that Hungary played a major role in the events leading to World War

One. To acknowledge this, Nostradamus moves away from his customary involvement with France, in order to acquaint his readership with a second prophecy concerning the political beginnings of Hungary. He referred to this country earlier in Chapter 4 (see C.VIII: 15), which has a final line that cross-references to the one above by using three identical words: – *'for Pannonians,* LIFE AND DEATH *increasing'.*

The verse therefore begins where the previous one left off as it continues to plot Hungary's rise from a state of relative obscurity, to one in which it became part of the vast Austro-Hungarian Empire. It was while in this elevated position that Hungary played a crucial part in the events leading to the outbreak of the First World War.

THROUGH LIFE AND DEATH, THE REIGN OF HUNGARY IS CHANGED

On 8 June 1867, Emperor Francis Joseph of Austria was crowned king of Hungary. One year later, the Nationalities Law decreed that all citizens of Hungary, whatever their nationality, were to become a political part of *"a single nation, the indivisible, unitary Hungarian nation."* For the previous twenty years Hungary had been in a state of political unrest, having rebelled against its Habsburg rulers, and for a short time having gained independence. But Vienna had retaliated, and with the aid of its ally Russia, Hungary was restored to Austria. Weeks of bitter, bloody fighting followed, with savage reprisals against the rebel leaders.[1] The final outcome was the *'Ausgleich'*, which, THROUGH the rebels resolve to fight for a better LIFE, AND the DEATHS of those who fell trying to achieve it, CHANGED THE REIGN IN HUNGARY to that of the Dual Monarchy – Austria-Hungary.[2]

THE LAW WILL BE HARSHER THAN A STATE OF SERVITUDE

One feature of the new regime was the infamous Agricultural Law of 1876, which covered farm workers of both sexes. This legislation, *"not only curtailed their legal equality and personal freedom, but placed the often inadequately accommodated, low-paid labourer . . . under the 'authority of his master."* Not surprisingly, THE LAW was seen to be HARSHER THAN A STATE OF SERVITUDE, especially when it was succeeded by the notorious *'Slave Law'* (Law II of 1898).[3]

During this period of time, problems in the labour market began to cause growing anger, and this became directly related to the *harsh* treatment dealt out to the country's workforce. The legal rights of manual workers had been deliberately restricted, and personal freedom curtailed. Employers were even allowed to administer corporal punishment to a worker if the circumstances warranted it; and a troubled employer could always call upon the police to maintain order if workers protested, or if they wished to change their place of employment.

THEIR GREAT CITY WITH HOWLS COMPLAINTS AND, OUTCRY

In May 1905, the first signs of mass defiance against the hardships experienced under these *slave laws* appeared. Manual workers poured onto the streets of Budapest. 30,000 Metal workers joined forces with 25,000 agricultural labourers demanding higher wages and more civil rights. The military and the gendarmerie responded with multiple arrests and enforced conscription. For a little while the trouble was suppressed. But, in May 1912, a new wave of street battles broke out in Budapest. Once again, **THEIR GREAT CITY** descended into a scene of **HOWLS, COMPLAINTS AND OUTCRY**, as disgruntled workers clashed with the police force. This time the workers' protest was in response to the country's electoral reform programme and its defence bill.[4]

CASTOR AND POLLUX

Castor and Pollux mark the astrological sign of Gemini, which, as a sun sign, commences on 22 May. It is therefore noteworthy that the uprising in Budapest began on 23 May. However, the twinning of **CASTOR AND POLLUX** has another significance, for it also alludes to the twinning of Austria and Hungary; i.e., the *'Dual Monarchy'*, otherwise referred to as: *'König und Kaiser'* (King and Emperor).[5]

ADVERSARIES IN THE TILTYARD

The Oracle predicts a dispute will occur behind closed doors concerning military matters; that is to say, the two will be **ADVERSARIES IN THE TILTYARD**. A confrontation between the two halves of the Austro-Hungarian Empire did eventually take place, and it occurred behind the closed doors of their military establishment.

(Law XII of 1867, para. 11) not only caused friction between Vienna and Budapest, but also occasioned increasingly acrimonious internal quarrels within Hungary about the nature and role of the army. The mutual antipathy, which existed between the Hungarians and the army . . . was the

cause of continual conflicts which weakened the cohesion of the Dual Monarchy.[6]

The dispute was finally resolved with the dissolution of the twin monarchy in 1918, following the disastrous loss of life in the First World War.

In England the age of Queen Victoria epitomises the time of the British Empire. At its peak, it encircled the globe. To maintain this position of supremacy, huge armies were sent abroad to keep the peace and maintain order. The chapter now concludes with a quatrain predicting the length of time the British Empire would endure. In doing so, Nostradamus foresees an event that occurred during World War One, and which, itself, augured the British Empire's subsequent decline.

C.X: 100

Le grand empire fera par Angleterre,
Le Pempotan des ans plus de trois cens:
Grandes copies paſſer par mer & terre,
Les Luſitains n'en feront pas contens.

The great empire will be from England.
Mark you, the convoying, for three hundred years plus:
Great armies crossing by sea and land,
Those of Lusitania will not be pleased by it.

Pempotan, (Greek portmanteau) Πεμπω + ταν (Pempo – sending forth, convoying, as applied to troops + tan – a form of address to several persons, e.g. 'Mark you! Or, Look! Refer: *Liddell & Scott*); copies, (Latinism) copi/a; Luſitains, (Latinism) Lusitan/ia. Cross-reference: Pempotan, C.VIII: 97.

THE GREAT EMPIRE WILL BE FROM ENGLAND
"Queen Victoria reigned over a worldwide empire, which at its peak in 1914 included about one-fifth of the world's land surface and one-quarter of its population." Yet, when this prophecy was written, which was more than thirty years before England withstood Spain's great armada of 1588, there was no reason whatever to suspect that at some future date, one quarter of the world's population would be under the rule of ENGLAND'S GREAT EMPIRE.[1]

MARK YOU, THE CONVOYING, GREAT ARMIES CROSSING BY SEA AND LAND
The maintenance of a *great empire* can only be sustained by the occupation of GREAT ARMIES within the countries it governs. The enormous number of troops CROSSING BY SEA AND LAND – THE CONVOYING – that was required to accomplish this end, may easily be imagined.[2]

411

The story of the British Army in the 19th Century is the story of the Empire's wars. The army fought Chinese, Afghans Abyssinians, Maoris, Zulus and Sudanese, Boers and Canadians. Its battle-honours are nothing less than a roll-call of Empire; or more prosaically a gazetteer of Africa, the Near East and Asia. Indeed the British professional army owes its very existence to the growth of the British Empire. [3]

FOR 300 YEARS PLUS

The British Empire consisted of various territories all over the world conquered or colonized by Britain from about 1600. . . . The Empire faded gradually into the Commonwealth from the 1930s onward. [4]

THOSE OF LUSITANIA WILL NOT BE PLEASED BY IT

In the fifteenth century, Pope Alexander VI issued a Bull, *Inter Caetera* (May 1493), which divided the New World between Spain and Portugal: *Lusitania* was the name given to a major part of these two countries. *"By the time the British began colonizing overseas, the Portuguese and Spaniards had already divided a considerable part of the earth's land surface between them."* But the subsequent emergence of England as a naval power greatly threatened these country's territorial ambitions, especially after Sir Francis Drake's buccaneering exploits, and the English navy's resounding victory over Spain's armada. **THOSE OF LUSITANIA** therefore had good reason to be **NOT PLEASED BY IT**, as England's formidable sea power began to lay the foundations for its empire.[5]

Let it not be forgotten, however, that Nostradamus has a proven record of applying the phrase, *those of* to people who are temporary occupiers, rather than to those who are permanent dwellers. Reference to *Lusitania* is therefore equally likely to apply to those on board the liner *RMS Lusitania* at the time it was torpedoed by the German Navy on 7 May 1915. In which case, **'THOSE OF LUSITANIA WILL NOT BE PLEASED BY IT'** has a double meaning. Some may feel this is far-fetched. But, why else should Nostradamus emphasise *those of Lusitania*? There were many others *not pleased* at England's vast empire.

The tragic sinking of *the Lusitania* happened soon after the start of the First World War, and it cost the lives of 1,200 passengers and crew. Moreover, its relevance to this oracle is bound up with the approaching decline of the British Empire. This was recognised by the German government, who commemorated the sinking of the Lusitania by striking a medal depicting their naval success. To the German people, and to observers elsewhere around the world, this single event foreshadowed the approaching end of England's domination of the seas, and the first step in the gradual decline of its once *great Empire*.[6]

9

THE WORLD AT WAR

In common with C.II: 90, which refers to the emergence of Hungary as an important European power, and covers that country's history, from 1867 up until the First World War, the opening quatrain to this chapter also covers an extensive period of time, and, it too leads to the outbreak of the same war.

Bulgaria's loss of territorial rights in Macedonia in 1912, served to heighten tension throughout the Balkan States; it also increased King Ferdinand's desire to recover Macedonia at the first opportunity. In 1913, he launched an attack against Greek and Serbian forces in Salonika as a means of accomplishing his ambition, but was unsuccessful. The failure, however, continued to be such a contentious issue that one year later, it led Bulgaria into the First World War.

C.IX: 35

Et Ferdinand blonde fera defcorte,
Quitter le fleur fuyure le Macedon.
Au grand befoing defaillira fa routte,
Et marchera contre le Myrmidon.

Likewise, susceptible, Ferdinand will be in discord,
Leaving the fleur-de-lys to pursue Macedonia.
At the great battle, his route will fail;
Also, he will proceed against the holder of Thessaly.

Et, (O.Fr.) and, likewise, also, as well, both; blonde, (O.Fr.) susceptible; defcorte, (O.Fr.) contester, désaccorde, discorde; Macedon, (Latinism) Maced/onia; befoing, (O.Fr.) lutte, combat; defaillira, (O.Fr.) manquer, faire défaut; Myrmidon, (Latin) followers of Achilles [Achilles was the son of the mortal Peleus, king of the Myrmidons, a people occupying Thessaly].

LIKEWISE, SUSCEPTIBLE

This quatrain runs on from the preceding oracle, which terminates with the Comte de Narbonne and Jean-Baptiste Sauce, each in their own way and amidst bitter *discord*, having proved themselves *susceptible* to handing over Louis XVI to his enemies. Thus, despite scrambling his oracles into a non-sequential order, Nostradamus appears to have understood the connection between theses two verses by linking them with the old French, *Et*.

When Russia engineered the removal of Prince Alexander of Battenberg from his seat of power in Bulgaria, the regency, which had been set up to rule in place of the Prince, found great difficulty in obtaining a suitable candidate to replace him. This was primarily because of fears concerning Russian hostility. Eventually, *Ferdinand* of Saxe-Coburg-Gotha became **SUSCEPTIBLE** to the advantages of the appointment, and the Grand National Assembly elected him Prince of Bulgaria in July 1887.

FERDINAND

FERDINAND quickly proved himself capable of dealing with those opposed to his appointment; resentment coming not only from the Russians, but also from within Bulgaria, itself. Eventually, *"in March 1896 Ferdinand finally received international confirmation of his rule."* [1]

WILL BE IN DISCORD

Initially, *Ferdinand's* appointment as Bulgaria's Prince led to considerable **DISCORD** and a barrage of opposition.

Russia accused Ferdinand of being a usurper, while Europe simply refused to recognize his appointment, even the bishops of the Holy Synod declined to pay him homage; everywhere, it seemed, conspiracies were flourishing. [2]

Ferdinand was the son of Princess Clementine of Orleans and Prince Auguste; he was therefore the maternal grandson of the French King, Louis Philippe. Although **FERDINAND** left France; that is to say, he **LEFT THE FLEUR-DE-LYS** to become Prince of Bulgaria, his attachment to the French royal family, and his own ancestry were very evident, even from his table setting.

> *On every fork and spoon, on every piece of the massive silver plate was engraved the French fleur-de-lys. They marked the descent of the royal couple; the prince as grandson of Louis Philippe, [his wife] the Princess Marie Louise as granddaughter of Charles X.* [3]

In 1903, the Macedonian people rose up in protest against their Ottoman rulers in what became known as the St. Elijah's Day Uprising, but the revolt was brutally suppressed. *Ferdinand,* who had seen the recovery of this country, his **PURSUIT OF MACEDONIA**, as a priority, was compelled to bide his time and wait for another opportunity. It came five years later, with the activities of the 'Young Turks' (ideologists and discontented members of the 3rd Army Corps in Macedonia). Their discontent gave *Ferdinand* the chance he wanted, and together with other Balkan states, he decided the time was ripe to free *Macedonia* from Turkish rule. On 8 October 1912, together with Serbia, Greece and Montenegro, *Ferdinand* declared war against the Ottoman Empire.[4]

AT THE GREAT BATTLE fought between the Balkan States and the Ottoman Empire, the Alliance won a resounding victory, leaving Turkey to sue for peace (3 December 1912). But the victors were not satisfied. *Ferdinand,* in particular, urged the Bulgarian army to continue its assault on the defeated empire and capture Constantinople.[5] But *Ferdinand* was stopped short in his tracks: *"the assault on the Çatalca line failed, leaving the Bulgarian army in a weakened state."* The Prince's **ROUTE** to Constantinople **HAVING FAILED**, he was impelled to retreat. This led to his enforced acceptance of a much weaker armistice deal.[6]

At the negotiating table Turkey conceded nearly all of its European territory. However, because of Ferdinand's weakened position, the way was left open for Serbia and Greece to claim

416

the greater part of *Macedonia*. Ferdinand's annoyance at the terms of the settlement caused a political quarrel with his former allies. And it was Bulgaria's inability to resolve these differences that eventually led their King to embark upon his next venture.

ALSO HE WILL PROCEED AGAINST THE HOLDER OF THESSALY

On the night of 29 June 1913, King *Ferdinand* ordered his troops to **PROCEED AGAINST** Greece and Serbia (Second Balkan War). His plan was to attack the Greek and Serbian armies who were occupying territory they had recently captured. Three days earlier, Greece had captured the Macedonian capital Salonika; that is, Thessaloníki (named after Thessalonike, a half-sister of Alexander the Great) *Thessalo-nikē* means *'victory over the Thessalians'*. Hence, by capturing Salonika, Greece became **THE HOLDER OF THESSALY**. In the ensuing battle, both the Greek and Serbian armies fiercely resisted the Bulgarians' attempt to displace them. At the same time, neighbouring Romania, together with Turkey joined the quarrel by marching on Sofia. Amidst all this political and military upheaval, Bulgaria was defeated. In the new peace settlement, which was devised to resolve past grievances, the top half of *Macedonia* was given to Serbia, and the southern half to Greece, leaving *Ferdinand* with just a fraction of his former gains.[7]

Nostradamus now shifts attention to the First World War, and he does so by moving his prescient gaze first to England, which again he refers to as the Isles. He then broadens his outlook to encompass what was happening across Europe, and where it would ultimately end.

C.II: 100

Dedans les ifles fi horrible tumulte,
Rien on n'orra qu'vne bellique brigue,
Tant grand fera des predateurs l'infulte,
Qu'on fe viendra ranger à la grand ligue.

Within the Isles such a terrible stir,
Nothing one will hear without a warlike canvass,
So very great will be the insult of the predators,
That men will agree to have recourse to the great league.

tumulte, (O.Fr.) stir, commotion; brigue, (O.Fr.) canvass; predateurs, (Latinism) praedator; se venir (O.Fr.) convenir – to agree, to admit; ranger, (O.Fr. syncope: ran[i]ger), se refugier: to take refuge, to have recourse to.

WITHIN THE ISLES, SUCH A TERRIBLE STIR

It was 28 June 1914, when Archduke Franz Ferdinand and his wife, Countess Sophie Chotek were assassinated. One month later, the major countries of Western Europe were at war. *"Austria-Hungary declared war on Serbia on 28 July 1914 . . . Germany declared war on Russia on 1 August and on Russia's ally, France, on 3 August, invading Belgium on the same day as part of the Schlieffen Plan; Britain declared war on Germany on 4 August."*

Within the British Isles, the announcement of war caused SUCH A TERRIBLE STIR that it seemed to act as a magnet; its ghastly fascination drawing to it the cream of youthful Britain.

> *Five hundred thousand volunteered in the first month; and the recruitment rate ran at over one hundred thousand a month for eighteen months thereafter. Altogether, Great Britain raised more than three million volunteers. . . . Leading politicians stumped the country, winning popularity for themselves and implanting the passion of war in their audiences. . . . By such means, public feeling in England was brought to white heat.* [1]

NOTHING ONE WILL HEAR WITHOUT A WARLIKE CANVASS

"All over Europe conscripts were joining their units. Troop trains were rolling to their allotted destinations. Crowds demonstrated enthusiastically in every capital, crying 'To Paris' or 'To Berlin'" But it was in Britain that the WARLIKE CANVASS was most extreme. *"Therefore the British talked, from the beginning, in idealistic terms. This was 'a war to end all wars'; 'to make the world safe for democracy'."* Posters decorated the walls in every town and city with Lord Kitchener's forefinger pointing at each onlooker. His imperious declaration 'Your country needs YOU' was answered by the ever-growing numbers of young men it drew to the recruiting office. It is fair to say that most of those responding to this call to arms, believed the war would be over by Christmas, and very soon they would all be back at work having given the Hun a bloody nose. [2]

SO VERY GREAT WILL BE THE INSULT

Having begun with a prediction of the preparations being made for war, Nostradamus now moves to its cause, which was THE VERY GREAT INSULT suffered by Austria-Hungary; to wit, the assassination in Sarajevo on 28 June 1914 of the future King of Hungary and Emperor of Austria, Archduke Franz Ferdinand. *"It was more than a crime. It was a challenge to the position of Austria-Hungary as ruler of Bosnia; a challenge also to her prestige as a Great Power, which had been declining in recent years."* [3]

OF THE PREDATORS

The assassin was Gavrilo Princip, one of a group of seventeen young men calling themselves 'Young Bosnia' and with connections to a secret organization called the *Black Hand*. They had gone onto the streets of Sarajevo as **PREDATORS**, fully armed with the intention of seeking out and killing their prey, Archduke Franz Ferdinand and his wife who were visiting the city that day. One member of the gang, upon encountering the Archduke as he rode by, attempted to shoot, but his pistol jammed. Another took aim, but was overcome with pity for the Countess Sophie Chotek, sitting beside her husband, and he went home instead. Another tossed a grenade, aimed to fall inside the Archduke's car: instead, it hit the side, bounced off and exploded, injuring many bystanders. Princip was dealt the fateful hand. The Archduke's car took a wrong turning. While reversing, the car stalled close to where Princip had just emerged from a café. The assassin mounted the side of the car and shot dead both the Archduke and the Countess.[4] Austria immediately insisted that the Serbian government was behind the assassination, and on 23 July delivered an ultimatum to the country. Serbia refused to meet its demands. Five days later Austria declared war on Serbia, thus precipitating the First World War.

N.B. Wikipedia names Princip's companions as: *"Nedjelko Čabrinović, Trifun Grabež, Muhamed Mehmedbašić, Vaso Čubrilović, Cvjetko Popović, Lazar Djukić, Danilo Ilić, Veljko Čubrilović, Nedo Kerović, Mihaijlo Jovanović, Jakov Milović, Mitar Kerović, Ivo Kranjcević, Branko Zagorac, Marko Perin, and Cvijan Stjepanović."*

THAT MEN WILL AGREE TO HAVE RECOURSE TO THE GREAT LEAGUE

After predicting the build-up to hostilities, followed by the cause of the war, Nostradamus leaves the actual fighting to other quatrains. Instead, the final line is devoted to the formation of the League of Nations, which he calls **THE GREAT LEAGUE**. This was set up at 1919 at Geneva, following the end of hostilities. After the carnage of the First World War, **MEN** finally **AGREED TO HAVE RECOURSE TO** an international body to guard against national grievances and disputes ever again breaking out into deadly conflicts. *"The constitution of the League ('Covenant') was adopted by the Paris Peace Conference in April 1919 and written into each of the peace treaties."*[5] Nostradamus deals with the League of Nations and its ultimate failure in a separate quatrain (see C.I: 47).

The First World War is chiefly remembered in the west for having been fought in northern France and on the fields of Flanders. It was the first warfare to be fought from positions below ground. By using a system of trenches, soldiers remained hidden from the enemy until ordered to 'go over the top'. Artillery was also concealed below ground. From this subterranean position, and with monotonous regularity, a battery of shells aimed at enemy lines were fired across the 'no man's land' that divided the two armies. Disastrously, this new type of warfare was so efficient that it mostly resulted in situations of stalemate. Fighting became prolonged over lengthy periods of time and the resulting casualty figures soon reached astronomical numbers.

C.X: 13

Soulz la pasture d'animaux ruminants,
Par eux conduicts au ventre herbipolique,
Soldatz caichez, les armes bruit menants,
Non loing temptez de cité Antipolique.

Beneath the pasture for ruminant animals,
For the sake of them brought to the grassy administrative belly
Soldiers hidden, the weapons noisy, menacing,
Not far, having sought to reach the ancient administrative city.

herbipolique, (Latin portmanteau & syncope), i.e., herbi[dus] + pol[it]ique; menants, (syncope) men[aç]ants; temptez, (O.Fr.) chercher à atteindre; Antipolique, (O.Fr. portmanteau & syncope) Anti + pol[it]ique: anti, = antique, ancient, aged;. Cross-reference: par eux, C.II: 1

BENEATH THE PASTURE FOR RUMINANT ANIMALS

The French farming country that runs from Armentières to Lens, with its meadows and *pasture* land FOR cattle — RUMINANT ANIMALS — is indicated in the opening line of this oracle. During the First World War, this tract of land became part of the Western Front. Both the Germans and the British dug massive systems of interconnecting trenches BENEATH THE PASTURE.[1]

FOR THE SAKE OF THEM BROUGHT TO THE GRASSY ADMINISTRATIVE BELLY

Troops were regularly shipped over from England then transported by train to within marching distance of the battlefield. Upon arrival, the soldiers took up positions in the trenches that had previously been dug FOR THE SAKE OF THEM BROUGHT TO THE GRASSY battlefield. The trenches on both sides soon developed into a

420

labyrinth of intercommunicating passageways. First, there were the main fire trenches, with perhaps a shorter advance line to the forward position. Several alleys then led back to another trench running parallel with the first one. This was used for command, communications and support. Behind these were further trenches for supplies and a reserve force. At the centre of each complex was an **ADMINISTRATIVE BELLY**. It was there that orders were received from 'high command': generals who were running the war at a safe distance, using 'cigar butt ideas', intelligence reports and 'trial and error' judgments.[2]

SOLDIERS HIDDEN

Both the Germans and the Allied forces were engaged in a conflict that placed **SOLDIERS** out of sight, below ground level where they were **HIDDEN** from the enemy's sight and from the sniper's bullet. Trench warfare was quite unlike any other major battle that had been fought in the past.[3]

THE WEAPONS NOISY, MENACING

Noise, terrible at times, was a fairly unremitting feature of the Great War, and often resulted in soldiers returning to their homeland *'shell-shocked'*. In the end: *"Artillery did not win the war, but the noise and surreal landscape it produced defined war on the Western Front. Nothing like it had ever occurred before."* The *weapons* employed were those developed in line with the approach of the technological age. Rifles could be loaded and fired in seconds. Machine guns, with their loud, seemingly incessant nattering, could fire seven or eight rounds every second. Howitzers were also firing shrapnel shells, timed to explode in mid-air so as to scatter hundreds of lead balls in every direction. **THE WEAPONS** were, as predicted, **NOISY** and very **MENACING**.[4]

NOT FAR, HAVING SOUGHT TO REACH THE ANCIENT ADMINISTRATIVE CITY

Paris was the goal of the enemy's *'Schlieffen Plan'*: it being Germany's intention to secure the French capital as part of its invasion strategy. Led by General Moltke at command headquarters, Alexander von Kluck's forces arced their way across northern France towards the capital. On 5 September 1914, they crossed the River Marne and reached Meaux, about 20 miles from Paris; that is, **NOT FAR** from the outskirts of the capital, **HAVING SOUGHT TO REACH THE ANCIENT ADMINISTRATIVE CITY**.[5]

During the First World War, Paris, apart from being *ancient,* was also an *administrative city.* Developments in radio and telephone communications had, by 1914-15, reached a stage when plans and strategies for battles could be sent from one administration centre to another, as implied by this oracle. Fortunately for Paris, the rear of Kluck's assault party was left unguarded, and after a successful counterattack, his men were forced to retreat.[6]

Among the many great tragedies of the First World War were the huge numbers of deaths resulting from the impasse caused by trench warfare. Armies were bogged down (literally during the rainy season) unable to advance because of the effectiveness of the trench defensive system. Unremarkably, therefore, the war dragged on for four years, with the fields of Flanders seeing little change in the forlorn, desolate landscape. Nostradamus, usually so active at times of great political drama can therefore only give an overall picture of that largely, unchanging scene. In the next oracle, perhaps because of their many similarities, he groups together the more memorable battles fought in the Great War, linking them with the plight of the soldiers in the trenches.

C.II: 1

Vers Aquitaine par infults Britanniques,
De par eux mefmes grandes incurfions.
Pluies, gelées feront terroirs iniques,
Port Selyn fortes fera inuafions.

Towards Aquitaine, by reason of British assaults,
With great forays by the same them.
Rains, frosts will make the territories iniquitous;
The entrance to Turkey will bring about robust invasions.

infults, (O.Fr.) assaults; incurfions, (O.Fr.) forays, invasions, incursions; terroirs, (O.Fr. terreoir) territoire; Port, (Latinism) port/a; Selyn, (paragram & synecdoche), Sely[m] – Turkey. Cross-reference: par eux, C.X: 13.

TOWARDS AQUITAINE, BY REASON OF BRITISH ASSAULTS

Aquitaine was the Roman name for Gaul. Originally, it was identified by the land from the Pyrenees to the River Garonne. The relevance of *Aquitaine* to this oracle is its association with the British Expeditionary Force that had joined up with the French army in 1914, as it retreated before the onslaught of the German advance. The enemy had swept through Belgium and into France with the intention of capturing Paris. It was BY REASON OF

THE BRITISH ASSAULTS that failed to prevent this advance that *"the French government left the capital for the safety of Bordeaux."* Bordeaux is situated on the river Garonne, **TOWARDS** the northern border of **AQUITAINE.** Meanwhile, the German First Army had advanced to within thirty miles of Paris, before being halted at the battle of Marne. A gap dividing the German forces was exploited, and with the arrival of 6,000 reservists from Paris, the German army was forced to retreat and take up trench positions in the north.[1]

During the First World War a large expanse of northern France became the scene of unbelievable carnage as the German army sought to extend its hold on France from a position across its northern frontier. For four years, war on the *'Western Front'* – a battle line stretching from Switzerland to the sea – was fought with such ferocity that deaths and mutilations were sometimes counted in thousands per second.

WITH GREAT FORAYS BY THE SAME THEM.

At Mons, where the two opposing armies met in August 1914, the fighting ended with the British being forced to retreat. At Ypres, the first battle took place during the months of October and November when the two armies arrived outside the town at the same time. The second battle of Ypres took place in April of the following year, with poison gas making its opening début in what became euphemistically called the 'theatre of war'. The battle of the Somme began in July 1916, and lasted for two and a half months. After pounding the German line with mortar shells for a week, supposedly to diminish the opposition, the *British* – **THE SELF SAME THEM** – launched a major **ATTACK** from the trenches, and very quickly lost 20,000 men on the first day. By the end of the battle the number of British casualties had risen to more than 420,000, whereas the German casualty figure was put at 190,000. Passchendaele, also known as the third battle of Ypres, was fought during the late summer of 1917. After weeks of fighting, and repeated **ATTACKS**, the *British* forces managed to advance five miles for the loss of 325,000 men – equivalent to 37 men dead for every yard (0·9144 of a metre) forward.[2]

RAINS, FROSTS, WILL MAKE THE TERRITORIES INIQUITOUS

To make matters still worse, there was the **RAIN**. In October, during the battle of the Somme, torrential rain turned the battlefield into a quagmire. At Passchendaele the RAINS were even worse. Men floundered up to their waists in mud; heavy artillery sank beneath the surface of the ground, and tanks were submerged in the mire. The effect upon the human body from continuously standing in mud and water was *'trench foot'*, with the possibility of the toes, or even the foot, being amputated.

FROSTS, too, proved hazardous to trench life. Apart from many incidences of frostbite, a sudden thaw could melt the frost, causing the parapet of the trench to collapse, with potentially dangerous consequences for those attending to its repair. It was also difficult to dig trenches in ground that had frozen solid. During the course of the Great War, the number of British soldiers admitted to hospital suffering from either trench foot or frostbite totalled 75,000.[3]

The final line of the prophecy continues with events of the First World War, but shifts the scene to Turkey. Both Selim I and Selim II were rulers over the Ottoman Empire at the time of Nostradamus: the second of that name ruling during the Empire's greatest achievements.

THE ENTRANCE TO TURKEY

The ENTRANCE TO THE TURKISH CAPITAL is through the Dardanelles, a narrow strait in the northwest of the country that leads to the Sea of Marmara. In fact, the Strait and the Sea combined give it the appearance of a *port*, although many times enlarged.[4]

WILL BRING ABOUT ROBUST INVASIONS

In February and March 1915, an Anglo-British fleet launched a preliminary attack upon the fortifications lying on both sides of the Strait. The plan was to reach Constantinople and make contact with Russia. The first landings occurred on 25 April at Cape Helles on the tip of the Gallipoli peninsula. Another landing was made about 15 miles to the north, at Ari Burnu, by the Australian and New Zealand Army Corps (ANZAC). The French, on the other side of the Strait, made a further landing; all told, THE ENTRANCE TO TURKEY was intended to BRING ABOUT ROBUST INVASIONS.[5]

After three months of bitter fighting, three more British divisions landed with the intention of making a coordinated assault against the defending Turks. But the campaign was not successful, and casualties totalled 252,000 amongst the Allies, and as many again for the Turks.

The Great War in northern France is again the subject of this next oracle. As the conflict drew to its close, the German army made a significant breakthrough in the town of Saint-Quentin. In what became known as the Second Battle of the Somme, German forces managed to capture the town, thus allowing troops to penetrate further into France. An important feature of this victory, and one predicted by Nostradamus, was that it coincided with a sudden long-range artillery assault directed against Paris. Huge guns emplaced behind German lines, and situated nearly 100 km from the city, pounded the Paris rooftops with shells: greatly alarming the citizens, and filling them with dismay and consternation. The following prophecy is therefore split between Paris and St Quentin, but united by the single fact that both events occurred at the same time.

C.IV: 8

La grand cité d'affaut promt repentin,
Surprins de nuict, gardes interrompus,
Les excubies & veilles faint Quintin
Trucidés, gardes & les pourtails rompus.

The great city from assault, disclosed, regretting,
Surprised at night, the guards interrupted,
The sentries and night vigil [at] Saint-Quentin
Slaughtered, defences, and the entrances, broken.

promt, (Latinism) prom/o; excubies, (Latinism) excubi/ae; Trucidés, (O.Fr.) massacrer.

By convention, *the great city* is always Paris. However, the town of *Saint-Quentin* in northern France is also mentioned. And it is the connection between the two that precisely times the fulfilment of this prophecy. For both venues became directly linked by the events that took place in March 1918, during the closing stages of the First World War.

THE GREAT CITY FROM ASSAULT, DISCLOSED

On the 23rd of the month, **PARIS CAME UNDER ASSAULT**; that is to say it was laid open – **DISCLOSED** – to a barrage of artillery shells, which were fired from the forest of Coucy, behind German lines. The distance covered was almost one hundred kilometres (65 miles). In fact, seven *'Paris Guns'* were employed. The bombardment was specifically timed to commence immediately after the fall of

Saint-Quentin; hence the connection between these two cities.[1]

REGRETTING

Accuracy was, of course, impossible at such a range, and the indiscriminate fall of exploding shells: *"seriously hurt the morale of the Parisians."* [2] The bombardment continued until August and killed 250 people, wounding a further 620. The idea behind the shelling was to weaken the morale of the capital city.

SURPRISED AT NIGHT, THE GUARDS INTERRUPTED

The Battle of *Saint-Quentin,* also known as the Second Battle of the Somme, began **AT NIGHT** on 20 March 1918. Four and a half hours after midnight. **THE GUARDS** on night watch were suddenly **INTERRUPTED** by the instantaneous firing of six-thousand German guns.[3]

THE SENTRIES AND NIGHT VIGIL AT SAINT-QUENTIN SLAUGHTERED

Within moments, the **SENTRIES AND NIGHT VIGIL** patrolling the city's outposts were in a desperate situation. Apart from a steady hail of machinegun fire, there was also poison gas to contend with.

> *The back areas especially being drenched with gas which hung like a pall in the moist and heavy air . . . The men on the outpost line, beaten to the ground by the bombardment, and struggling amid clouds of gas were in desperate case . . . Presently the outposts were gone.* [4]

DEFENCES AND THE ENTRANCES BROKEN

"On the 22nd [March] the enemy broke right through into open country north-west of St. Quentin;" that is, **THE DEFENCES AND ENTRANCES BROKEN.** The German army having taken and secured the city was then able to move deeper into northern France. *"[Next] morning (23 March 1918) as if to signalise their triumph, they had begun the shelling of Paris with long range guns."* [5]

A country that came to prominence during the twentieth-century was undoubtedly Russia. Nostradamus had already begun charting this nation's rise to power with prophecies for Peter the Great and Catherine the Great. Now he returns to Russia to focus on the people's revolution.

C.I: 14

De gent efclaue chanfons, chantz & requeftes,
Captifs par princes & feigneur aux prifons:
A l'auenir par idiots fans teftes
Seront receus par diuins oraifons.

Concerning the slavish people, songs, chants and demands,
Captives by reason of princes and the Seignior to prisons:
In the future, through idiots without heads,
They will be greeted by divine speeches.

eſclaue, (O.Fr.) slavish; teſtes, (O.Fr.) têtes.   Cross-reference: gent eſclaue, C.V: 26.

CONCERNING THE SLAVISH PEOPLE

The word slavish – *'servilery following or conforming'* – is derived from the Old French word *'esclave'*, originally a Slav. (Chambers English Dictionary). In Medieval Latin it is: *'Sclavus'* from which we get the word Slav – people of Russia; OED. Hence: *'The Russian people have long been inured to tyranny'.* [1]

SONGS, CHANTS AND DEMANDS

In just three words, Nostradamus correctly describes the three events that signalled the outbreak of the Russian Revolution. In Petrograd, *"discontented workers began a demonstration carrying banners that said 'We want bread.'"* This was accompanied by shouts of: *"Down with the war . . . soon there were speeches on street corners, choruses of the French revolutionary song and national anthem, the Marseillaise - sung in Russian* [2] *. . . By Monday March 12 the tide of revolution was at its full, and there would be no stopping it."* [3]

CAPTIVES BY REASON OF PRINCES

Up until this time, Nicholas II had been Czar of Russia. But, within the space of seven violent days he was forced to abdicate as the upsurge in public protest became a full-scale revolt. In his place, he named *Prince Mikhail* as his successor; [4] he also appointed *Prince Georgy Lvov* to preside over the Council of Ministers. Both appointments were intended to save him from captivity, but this did not happen. PRINCE MIKHAIL refused the succession, and PRINCE LVOV'S provisional government resolved to place the deposed CZAR, together WITH HIS FAMILY, UNDER house ARREST. [5]

THE SEIGNIOR TO PRISONS

Czar Nicholas, referred to here as THE SEIGNIOR, was a feudal lord, [6] therefore an apt portrayal for the ruler of Russia at that time. He was taken, with his wife and children, to Czarskoe Selo: the FIRST OF THREE PRISONS in which he was held under guard. From there, he was transferred to a mansion house in Tobalsk, where he remained under arrest for eight months. At the end of April 1918, he and his family were again transferred, this time to a merchant's house in Ekaterinburg. A high wooden fence had been hurriedly placed around the property, including the garden. The windows were also painted over to shield the occupants from public view. The Romanov family arrived there on May 3rd to begin their final days as *captives* of the Revolution.[7]

IN THE FUTURE, THROUGH IDIOTS WITHOUT HEADS

Soon after the brutal murder of the Romanov family, a long period of Communist rule replaced Czarist Russia, and with it came the proposal that all men were equal. Committees began to appear: each with the intention of administering local rule.

> *Russia was seized with a passion for talk; army committees at every level were no exception and spent endless hours in desultory and often purposeless debate . . . and no motion was too preposterous or foolish not to be carried by unanimous vote.*

These committees were mainly attended by an uneducated proletariat. That is to say, since no one person was allowed to act, or be seen as superior to their comrades, debates were frequently conducted by ignorant, uneducated people; IDIOTS, as Nostradamus described them: acting WITHOUT HEADS; that is, without a chairman to officiate at the meetings. Nevertheless, this idea quickly took hold, and was soon apparent among the workforce, where, unlike western capitalist countries, there were *no heads* or supervisors.[8]

THEY WILL BE GREETED BY DIVINE SPEECHES

The final part of this prophecy predicts the coming of Lenin, although not without a tinge of Nostradamus's characteristic wit. For as one former Soviet citizen remarked: *"We were taught at school that we had no need of God because Lenin provided us with everything."* Historians were not slow to agree: *'semi-divine honours were readily paid'* to his every speech. Or, as Nostradamus said: THE PEOPLE WILL BE GREETED BY DIVINE SPEECHES. And for the entire generation that followed – *"The works of Karl Marx and Friedrich Engels were like prophetic works in the Bible for most [Bolsheviks]; and Lenin as well as Marx and Engels were beatified."* [9]

Using the same two words, *gent esclaue*, Nostradamus predicts the political changes that were to take place in Russia after the overthrow of the Czar. The February revolution of 1917, referred to above, was followed by the October Revolution eight months later, which gave Lenin his power base.

C.V: 26

La gent efclaue par vn heur martial,
Viendra en hault degré tant efleuee:
Changeront prince, naiftre vn prouincial,
Paffer la mer copie aux montz leuee.

The slavish people through a martial hour,
He will come raised in such high degree:
Born a provincial, they will change the prince,
Crossing the sea; an army raised at the heights.

copie, (Latinism.) copia; esleuee, (O.Fr.) promoted. Cross-reference: gent efclaue, C.I: 14.

THE SLAVISH PEOPLE

THE SLAVISH PEOPLE again refers to the Russian people, for the reasons given above in C.1: 14.[1]

THROUGH A MARTIAL HOUR

The *'October Revolution'* – it was called the October Revolution because, according to the Julian calendar then in use inside Russia, it occurred on 25/26 October 1917 – took place in Petrograd. It began on the 6th November (N.S.) and on the next day, **THROUGH A MARTIAL HOUR**, it was all over.

The uprising was directed by the Bolshevik Military-Revolutionary Committee headed by Lenin. The Committee had actually planned its moves several weeks earlier. The first act was to order Trotski's Red Guards to secure control of the post and telegraph offices; this was followed by securing the railway stations, and finally the military garrisons. Only then was the Winter Palace – *'the home of the Provisional Government'* – placed under siege.[2]

HE WILL COME RAISED IN SUCH HIGH DEGREE
"Lenin was a fanatical visionary whose effective power was multiplied threefold by an inner conviction that he was designed by fate to be the commander of a victorious Russian Revolution." [3] After the overthrow of the government inside the Winter Palace, the delegates voted overwhelmingly to accept full power and *"elected Lenin as chairman of the Council of People's Commissars, the new Soviet Government ... Overnight, Lenin had vaulted from his hideout as a fugitive to head the Revolutionary government of the largest country in the world."* [4]

THEY WILL CHANGE THE PRINCE

Since July, Alexander Kerenski had been allowed control over *Prince* Lvov's Provisional Government; this arrangement provided the *Prince* with time to give more attention to the Soviets;

429

that is, the elected bodies that stood for workers' rights. But, on November 7th, Lenin seized power for himself, effectively taking control of *Prince* Lvov's government. Realizing that he had not the manpower to withstand the Bolsheviks, Prime Minister Kerenski secretly vacated the Winter Palace in disguise. Hours later, in a united assault, Lenin's forces were able to break through the Palace defences and arrest the remaining government officers. This final act completed their *coup d'état*, and they were able to **CHANGE THE PRINCE** for a government headed by Lenin that would thereafter be based upon the political philosophy of Karl Marx.[5]

BORN A PROVINCIAL

Lenin was **BORN A PROVINCIAL**. His family name was Vladimir Ilyich Ulyanov, and he was raised in the *provincial* town of Simbirsk. The town was founded in 1648, and lies along the Volga River amidst agricultural surroundings. It has since been renamed Ulyanovsk in honour of its famous son.[6]

CROSSING THE SEA

During the months preceding the uprising that brought him to power, Lenin sought refuge in Helsinki. But, with the prospect of overthrowing the Provisional Government appearing increasingly probable, due mainly to Kerenski's mounting problems with the First World War, he secretly returned to Russia, **CROSSING THE SEA** from Finland. Once on Russian soil, sympathisers in Petrograd concealed his presence until it was time to strike.[7]

AN ARMY RAISED AT THE HEIGHTS

But there was opposition to Lenin. A small **ARMY** of Cossacks in favour of returning Kerenski to power was **RAISED**, and once armed, the men marched on Petrograd under the command of General Pyotr Krasnov, an anti-Bolshevik army officer who had previously served in the Imperial Guard. Soldiers belonging to Lenin's newly formed Sovnarkom (a Russian acronym for the Council of People's Commissars) rallied to defend their leader, and the two opposing armies met at **THE** *'Pulkovo Heights'*, which overlook the capital. The subsequent defeat of the Cossacks, and the capture of Krasnov, finally left the way clear for Lenin to continue as Premier until his death in 1924.[8]

A world war; a revolution, and finally a pestilence combined to complete the second decade of the twentieth century. 'Spanish Flu,' the last mentioned of the three, reached pandemic proportions in the year after the First World War ended. Together with the civilian and military deaths on both sides, (approximately 13,000,000), Spanish Flu took a further 50,000,000 people to their graves. If people were intent upon slaughtering each other, *Nature* (or God's punishment – depending upon which age makes the judgement) demonstrated far greater ability to do the same.

C.IX: 55

L'horrible guerre qu'en occident f'apprefte,
L'an enfuiuant viendra la peftilence,
Si fort terrible que ieune, vieil, ne befte.
Sang, feu, Mercur. Mars, Iupiter en France.

The horrible war that in the west advances,
The consecutive year, the pestilence will arrive,
So powerful [and] terrible, whether young, aged, [but] not beasts:
Blood, fire, Mercury, Mars, Jupiter in France.

f'apprefte, (O.Fr.) s'approcher; enfuivant, (O.Fr.) consecutive; vieil, (O.Fr.) vieux.

THE HORRIBLE WAR THAT IN THE WEST ADVANCES

On 3 August 1914, Germany declared war on France, while at the same time invading Belgium. Great Britain, under obligation to beleaguered Belgium, declared war on Germany. The next day, Austria-Hungary declared war on Russia and, the day after, Serbia declared war on Germany. Montenegro then declared war on Austria-Hungary, and five days later extended this declaration to include Germany. France and Great Britain responded by declaring war on Austria-Hungary. On the 23rd of the month, Japan joined in the fray by declaring war against Germany. Austria-Hungary responded by declaring war on Japan, and two days later, on the 25th, it declared war against Belgium.[1] Thereafter, the war was at its bloodiest and most deadly. *"Everyone expected the decisive campaign to be in the west; and they were right,"* the killing was to continue for four long years, and *"was virtually unprecedented in the slaughter, carnage, and destruction it caused."*[2]

THE CONSECUTIVE YEAR, THE PESTILENCE WILL ARRIVE

Hostilities finally came to an end on 11 November 1918. **IN THE YEAR** [i.e., twelve months] **FOLLOWING** – *"came the biggest pandemic visited on Europe since the Black Death. The 'Spanish Flu' killed more Europeans than the War did."* The first spate of this new strain of influenza virus

431

was comparatively mild when it appeared in July 1918, and exacted only a minor death toll. In October, it reappeared, but with greater severity. Finally, in February 1919, the virus mutated with deadly consequences.[3]

SO POWERFUL AND TERRIBLE, WHETHER YOUNG, AGED BUT NOT BEASTS

The infectious disease proved **SO POWERFUL AND TERRIBLE**, that: *"Altogether an estimated 30 million persons throughout the world perished."* No one was immune from the contagion, **WHETHER YOUNG** or **OLD**; although cattle were not affected by the disease. The elderly with their weakened immunity were always vulnerable, but the epidemic also *"specialized in prime young adults, particularly women . . . about half the deaths were among 20-to-40-year-olds, an unusual age pattern for influenza."* [4]

BLOOD, FIRE

As Nostradamus is occasionally prone to do when he wishes to divert attention away from those who try to anticipate his meaning in advance, he reverts back to his first subject. In this oracle, it is the war in France, with its **BLOODLETTING**. Years of trench warfare, futile bayonet charges, the constant **FIREPOWER** across 'no-man's-land' have fulfilled this prediction many times over.[5]

MERCURY, MARS, JUPITER, IN FRANCE

By referring to these three planets together, quite a rare occurrence, Nostradamus has provided a form of astronomical dating for the timing of the oracle's fulfilment. The conjunction between **MERCURY, MARS AND JUPITER**, with only minutes of arc separating them, occurred in January 1913: the year before the *horrible war will arrive in the west.* [6] But, as usual with the seer's prophecies, there is also a political interpretation to be understood from this triple union. **IN FRANCE**, on 17 January 1913, Raymond Poincaré was elected President of the Republic: whereupon, in August, he ordered that military service be extended to three years. One year later, 1 August 1914, he decreed that a general mobilization must begin in preparation for war, following the assassination of Archduke Franz-Ferdinand of Austria on 28 June.

Decades of international tension had divided the major European powers into two rival camps: on the one side, the Triple Alliance of Germany, Austria-Hungary and Italy; on the other the Triple Entente of France, Russia and Great Britain. No more than a spark – Franz Ferdinand's assassination – was needed to set the continent alight.

Nostradamus has used this triple conjunction of **Mercury, Mars and Jupiter,** in order to unite it with the **Triple** Alliance and the **Triple** Entente: for **in France,** it was these that were to lead the country into World War I.[7]

The 1914–18 War was to be: *'The War to end all wars'*, so terrible had been the carnage. But no sooner had it ended than a new breed of dictators emerged: men who would soon give the lie to the politician's dream. Nostradamus begins his countdown to the Second World War by introducing Benito Mussolini – Il Duce. The close resemblance between the Italian 'Duce' and the French 'Duc' allows the prophet to employ a paragram to disguise the one by the other. And since Nostradamus consistently uses this strategy in no less than four quatrains, each one undeviating in its description of the major events in Mussolini's life, there can be no reasonable doubt that this was the seer's intention.

C.IX: 80

Le Duc voudra les fiens exterminer,
Enuoyera les plus forts lieux eftranges,
Par tyrannie Pize & Luc ruiner,
Puis les Barbares fans vin feront vendanges.

The Duce (head of war) will want to exterminate his own kind,
He will send the strongest ones to inhospitable places,
Ruining Piacenza and Lucca through tyranny,
Then, the foreign speakers, without wine, will go grape picking.

Duc, (O.Fr. and apocope; note particularly, the capital 'D' indicating a name or title) chef de guerre, also (Italian) Duc[e]; Pize; (syncope) – Pi[acen]ze; Luc, (apocope) Luc[ca]; Barbares, (Greek) βαρβαρος - foreign speaking. Cross-references: Duc, C.VI: 31; C.IX: 95; C.X: 64.

> N.B. *"Barbarians is certainly not derived from the Latin barba (a beard), as many suppose. It is, instead a Greek word, and has many analogous meanings. The Greeks and Romans called all foreigners barbarians; meaning they were babblers:"* men who spoke a language not understood by them.

THE DUCE, HEAD OF WAR

The Duce (Benito Mussolini) was brought up as the member of a staunchly socialist family. In his youth he was a ready convert to his father's socialism, and while still young, became actively involved in arguing for socialist policies. Only later did political ambition overcome his working-class background, and he began to reject the socialist philosophy of his upbringing. In its place,

433

he turned his attention to fascism. It was this policy that eventually led to him becoming the fascist dictator of Italy, and which placed him in the position of **HEAD OF WAR**. Appropriately, his invasion of Abyssinia provided historical verification for this title.[1]

WILL WANT TO EXTERMINATE HIS OWN KIND

Mussolini's rise to leadership brought with it a heavy price. To secure his position from attacks by the opposition, he became responsible for the gangs of black-shirted *'Squadristi'* who carried out the murders of his former socialist colleagues; that is to say: **THE DUCE WILL WANT TO EXTERMINATE HIS OWN KIND.**

> *They made fifty-seven raids between January and March 1921 and burned down twenty-five buildings. They killed twelve Socialists . . . and as Mussolini relied on the Fascists, and had no alternative but to rely upon them, he implicitly at least, allowed them to murder.[2]*

HE WILL SEND THE STRONGEST ONES TO INHOSPITABLE PLACES

The Duce's response to attempts that were made against his life was to place the blame on the socialists. After gaining power in 1922, he lost little time in sending the leading members of their party into exile: transporting them to some of the remotest parts of the country. The victims of his purge, the *'confine'* –

> *. . . were originally interned in the Isle of Lipari off the north coast of Sicily. In later years, places of internment were opened on the Isles of Tremiti off the Adriatic coast and of Ponza and Ventotene in the Gulf of Gaeta, and on the mainland at Amalfi, Cava dei Tirreni and elsewhere.[3]*

RUINING PIACENZA AND LUCCA THROUGH TYRANNY

PIACENZA, on the banks of the River Po, subsequently became the scene of repeated, murderous attacks at night, perpetrated against members of the socialist farm-workers' union.[4] While in **LUCCA**, the citizens were also to experience the **TYRANNY** that essentially identified Mussolini's brand of Fascism. This was exemplified by the Fascist Party activists who targeted the Catholic People's Party.[5] The CPP had, up until then, enjoyed full support from the majority of residents in *Lucca*. But this sharply declined as a result of the repeated attacks made upon its supporters.[6]

THEN THE FOREIGN SPEAKERS, WITHOUT WINE, WILL GO GRAPE PICKING

In the final line to his oracle, Nostradamus provides a further example of his cryptic humour. *The foreign speakers* are the Germans who, as part of the peace negotiations following the First

World War, were forced to relinquish the 30-mile wide zone known as the Rhineland: a region that, in part, is famous for its grapevines. Hence, the Germans, or **THE FOREIGN SPEAKERS**, were, apropos Nostradamus's humour, **WITHOUT WINE**. But in 1936, Adolf Hitler saw an opportunity to recover the Rhineland. World attention was at the time still focused upon *the Duce* and his invasion of Abyssinia. Seizing this opportunity, and in defiance of both the *'Versailles'* and the *'Locarno'* treaties, Hitler ordered his troops to occupy the Rhineland; or, as Nostradamus predicted, with tongue in cheek: **THE FOREIGN SPEAKERS WILL GO GRAPE PICKING.**[7]

The two decades of peace between the end of the First World War and the commencement of the Second World War was a period of intended unity among nations, with a desire to avoid conflict by discussing contentious issues before they erupted into conflict. Policing this unity, although only at a political level, was the League of Nations. It has been well said that 'the road to hell is paved with good intentions', and so it proved. Bickering, defiance, unilateralist policies and political vanity eventually blighted many of the important issues that the League was designed to resolve. In the end, the entire fabric of this international organization collapsed, allowing the Second World War to redress the League's failure. By doing so, the deaths of a further forty-seven million of the world's population were added to those killed in the First World War.

C.I: 47

Du lac Leman les fermons facheront:
Des iours feront reduicts par les fepmaines,
Puis mois, puis an, puis tous defailliront,
Les magiftrats damneront leurs loys vaines.

Concerning Geneva, the speeches will anger:
Of the days, they will be dimmed by the weeks,
Then months, then a year, then all will fail,
The officials will condemn their ineffectual laws.

lac Leman, (Latin) Leman[nus] lac[us] – Geneva; fermons, (O.Fr.) discours; magiftrats, (Latinism) magistrat/us; fepmaines, (O.Fr.) semaines.

CONCERNING GENEVA

The four lines of the oracle predict the decline of the League of Nations: an international peacekeeping body whose headquarters were situated at **GENEVA**. The League was important because

435

it was formed after the First World War: its intention being that member states would air their grievances inside an international forum, and seek solutions that secured a peaceful settlement.[1] But, as the oracle foretold, this noble idea was doomed to failure.

THE SPEECHES WILL ANGER

The first Assembly met on 15 November 1920, with forty-one nations represented. More than twenty nations later joined, but there were also numerous resignations: notably, those resulting from **ANGRY DISAGREEMENTS** voiced by countries wanting to act independently; e.g., Brazil, Spain, Japan, Paraguay, Germany, Italy and USSR.[2]

OF THE DAYS, THEY WILL BE DIMMED BY THE WEEKS, THEN MONTHS, THEN A YEAR

Prolonged attempts at settling disputes bedevilled the League. Meetings frequently made little progress, and matters of immediate concern in international politics were deliberated upon endlessly without resolution. The political questions and issues occurring after 1931 readily fall into this category, and were to become the subject of many endless disputes: an example was the Japanese occupation of Manchuria in 1931. This preceded a decade of political turmoil among the nations affected, and the disputes challenged the League's principles down to its very roots. Added to which, the League was also ineffective at coping with the rising power of Germany; or with Italy's invasion of Ethiopia, and Albania; or with the economic distress caused by the Great Depression.[3]

THEN ALL WILL FAIL, THE OFFICIALS WILL CONDEMN THEIR INEFFECTUAL LAWS

By the late 1930s, the principles of the League's covenant had been abandoned. The League of Nations finally folded in 1939 with the outbreak of World War II. Further meetings of the member states ceased, and the League was officially disbanded in April 1946. **ALL WILL FAIL.**[4] **THE OFFICIALS** responsible for the statutes governing the League's operation had effectively conceded that **THEIR LAWS** were **INEFFECTUAL.**[5]

Three years before the League of Nations came to the end of its effective existence, the British Isles found itself engaged in a constitutional crisis. The nation's monarch, Edward VIII was about to abdicate in order to pursue marriage with an American divorcee. Nostradamus has correctly predicted what happened during this crisis. But, one wonders if there is an underlying reason for devoting an entire quatrain to this subject. For one cannot help but call to mind the predicted 'seven changes' that were to occur within the British monarchy, spread over a period of '290 years' (see C.III: 57). The seventh change came about with the accession and marriage of Queen Victoria. Since then, there have been no further changes in the descent of the royal family in Britain. But, there was also no prophecy for an eighth change.

C.VIII: 58

Regne en querelle aux freres diuifé,
Prendre les armes & le nom Britannique,
Tiltre Anglican fera tard aduifé,
Surprins de nuict mener à l'air Gallique.

The kingdom in dispute with the brothers disunited,
Doing without the armorial bearings and the British title,
The English title will be endorsed later,
Unexpectedly at night, going to the French air.

Prendre, (O.Fr.) se passer; aduifé, (O.Fr. aviser) viser; nom, (O.Fr.) titre.

On 20 January 1936, King George V died, and a crisis hit the British monarchy. The King's eldest son, the Prince of Wales, known familiarly as David in royal circles, was the natural heir. Unfortunately, at least from his family's point of view, and the government's, he had met and fallen passionately in love with a twice-married American woman, Mrs. Wallace Simpson. To further complicate matters, England's newly appointed King intended to marry as soon as the lady's second divorce had been legalized. A constitutional crisis followed, and one that placed THE KINGDOM IN DISPUTE.

THE KINGDOM IN DISPUTE

As King of England and its remaining Empire, Edward VIII would also be the Church of England's Defender of the Faith. It was this that made his intended marriage to a divorcee unacceptable, for the Church's ruling forbade remarriage. Moreover, according to tradition, Wallace Simpson, although having no aristocratic pedigree would still become Queen of England if the marriage took place. Not all British people were persuaded to accept this state of affairs, and the country; that is, the *kingdom*, became *divided* over the issue. *"Small crowds gathered outside No. 10 waving placards inscribed 'Hands Off Our King' and 'Abdication Means Revolution.'* But, the British Parliament and the Royal family remained obdurate: The King must renounce his intention to marry Wallace Simpson, or he must abdicate.[1]

THE BROTHERS DISUNITED

It was the fallout from this *dispute* that led to disunity between the two brothers. David's younger sibling, Albert, was the natural successor should the throne become vacant, but it was not a position that he relished occupying, or felt comfortable with. And when Edward VIII resolved to abdicate rather than separate from the woman he loved, the ramifications led to a split between the brothers. Their quarrel began the same week in which the abdication took place, and concerned *disputes* involving the precise amount of the proposed financial settlement. *"By the end of 1937, they were no longer on speaking terms."* [2]

DOING WITHOUT THE ARMORIAL BEARINGS AND THE BRITISH TITLE

On 11 December 1936, Edward VIII publicly announced over the radio that he was *abdicating, and passing* THE BRITISH TITLE to his brother. The oracle refers to the British crown in terms of ARMORIAL BEARINGS, that is, the *Royal Coat of Arms*; this is in agreement with what had become the custom in England since the reign of Queen Victoria. During her period of rule, the monarchy had increasingly become a figurehead of the State, rather than a decision-making office. The Royal Coat of Arms therefore came to represent the public face of the British monarchy. It is of some interest to note that by abdicating, which he did on the day prior to his public announcement; Edward VIII became the only monarch ever to have voluntarily given up the crown of England.[3]

Some years previously, in July 1911, as the eldest son of George V, David had been invested with the title, *'Prince of Wales'*. He retained this distinction until the death of his father, whereupon he became: *"King of Great Britain and Ireland and British Dominions Overseas, Emperor of India."* This was the official title by which he was known for the entire eleven months of his reign.

THE ENGLISH TITLE WILL BE ENDORSED LATER

After relinquishing the crown and the titles that went with it, he was given THE ENGLISH TITLE: *'Duke of Windsor'*, which was ENDORSED by his brother on 12 December 1936. In other words, it was only

438

LATER, after all his non-English titles had expired or been removed that he was invested with a wholly *English title.*[4]

The final line of the oracle concerns Edward's *surprise* at the rapid development of events following his abdication. He had expected to remain in England, together with his new wife at Fort Belvedere, near Sunningdale in Berkshire. The 18th century manor house had been a gift from his father George V, and he had since renovated it and made it a home. But his popularity in the country contrasted too well against the nervous, ineffectiveness of his younger brother, now King George VI; therefore, to avoid competition, England and Fort Belvedere were denied him.

UNEXPECTEDLY AT NIGHT, GOING TO THE FRENCH AIR

Instead of enjoying married life in Berkshire, the duke of Windsor found himself **UNEXPECTEDLY** ushered out of the country. He was escorted from his home **AT NIGHT**, and put on board HMS Fury. The ship left Portsmouth harbour during the early hours of Saturday 12 December, bound for the French coast, or **THE FRENCH AIR**, with the former king about to begin the life of an exile. *"For the next two years the duke and duchess lived mainly in France."* [5]

Another major event occurring at this same time was the Spanish Civil War. Nostradamus predicted the beginning of this conflict, and even managed to identify three of the participating parties. As a result, this quatrain has received much attention from past commentators, although not everything has been gleaned from the seer's precognitive references. The following narrative will attempt to redress these previous omissions.

C.IX: 16

De caftel Franco fortira l'affemblee,
L'ambaffadeur non plaifant fera fcisme:
Ceux de Ribiere feront en la meflee,
Et au grand goulphre defnier ont l'entree.

Concerning Castile, Franco will depart from the ruling body,
The ambassador, not pleased, will make a schism:
Those of Rivera (the River) will be in the conflict,
And at the great gulf, denying entrance there.

caftel, (Spanish syncope) castel[lano] – Castilian, hence Castile; ont, (O.Fr.) adverb of place, Où; Ribiere, (Spanish paragram) Ri[v]ière = Ribera, (paragram) = Ri[v]era.

Nostradamus begins his prediction by describing events that took place shortly before the Spanish Civil War began. For although the revolt started in Morocco, before spreading to garrisons on the mainland: *"The Civil War took place because the rising was successful only in Old Castile."*[1]

Nostradamus next pinpoints the precise event that was to bring about the Spanish Civil War: **FRANCO'S DEPARTURE FROM** mainland Spain to take up the post of Military Commander and Governor of the Canary Islands. The move was intended to remove him from political influence amongst members of **THE RULING BODY**, but it was to have the opposite effect. On 18 July 1936: *"while serving as Governor of the Canary Islands he led the anti-Socialist revolt which began the Spanish Civil War."*[2]

THE AMBASSADOR referred to in this oracle was a Russian diplomat, Marcel Rosenberg. One month after civil war broke out, Spain agreed to resume diplomatic relations with Russia, and an *ambassador* was sent to Madrid from Moscow. Rosenberg's arrival in Spain coincided with Franco's rise to prominence.[3]

Franco soon became deeply suspicious of the Russian ambassador's growing influence amongst Spain's socialists. He therefore ordered Moscow to recall Rosenberg. **THE AMBASSADOR** was clearly **NOT PLEASED** at receiving this sudden recall. Consequently, before leaving Spain, he devised a plot involving key members of the opposition parties.[4]

"Skilfully, Rosenberg, while he was still in Valencia . . . cultivated good relations with Largo Caballero's great socialist rival, Indalecio Preto." This relationship eventually **CAUSED** the predicted **SCHISM**, with its mass resignations which followed. *"On 13th May [1937] the Spanish Communist Party brought matters to a crisis."* Two of the party members who held government office demanded that Cabellero dissolve the PUOM. The demand was refused and the two ministers walked out of the cabinet meeting. This appears to have been a prearranged signal because: *"Simultaneously, the Russians let it be known that that they would not provide aircraft for an offensive in Extremadura, which Largo Caballero had long been planning."* A ministerial crisis immediately followed

in which moderate socialists, who had been backing Caballero, went over to the Communists. With his party *divided,* that is, the predicted SCHISM having been brought about, *"Largo Caballero was forced out of office."* [5]

The oracle then continues by predicting an actual scene from the conflict that took place during the Spanish Civil War: it does so by cleverly constructing a double meaning to produce the name of another Spanish combatant, José Antonio *Rivera*.

THOSE OF RIVERA WILL BE IN THE CONFLICT

José Antonio RIVERA was the founding-leader of a political party called the *'Falange Española'*. The party's intentions were initially peaceful, but this failed to prevent its members becoming involved in the fighting. *"José Antonio had lost all ability to steer his followers away from the path of violence . . .Though it was not the Falangists who had started the firing, they continued it with a vengeance."* [6]

THOSE OF THE RIVER WILL BE IN THE CONFLICT

Rivera, however, can also be interpreted as *river,* and during the civil war, the *River* Manzanares, which flows through Madrid, became the scene of a desperate, bloody and heroic stand by the citizens of the capital. On 8 November: *"the Army of Africa suffered casualties on a scale hitherto unknown as it battled to cross the Manzanares."* The opposition – THOSE OF THE RIVER – were the ordinary citizens of Madrid, who, being armed only with old rifles and little ammunition, yet managed IN THE ensuing CONFLICT to halt the Nationalist forces in their bid to cross the *river*.[7]

AND AT THE GREAT GULF, DENYING ENTRANCE THERE

THE GREAT GULF describes a bird's-eye view of the Mediterranean Sea. This had to be crossed by Franco from Morocco to mainland Spain, in order to supply his forces with the large shipments of armaments needed for the war. However, all attempts to carry these arms into Spain by ship were resisted. The Republican Navy had set up a blockade, DENYING him ENTRANCE to the mainland. *"One by one, the ships of the Republican Navy, led by the battleship Jaime I, were steaming towards Tangier. Once anchored there, they might make it impossible for the Army of Africa to cross the Strait."* [8] The blockade proved so efficient that Franco was forced to convey his armaments by air.

It was seen earlier how Nostradamus provided details of

Mussolini's rise to political prominence. In the next oracle, Nostradamus does the same for Adolf Hitler. The second line begins with his election to the leadership of the Nazi (Nationalist) party. By a series of changing circumstances, this led to his election as Chancellor of Germany. During his period of office, three separate incursions into other countries are predicted: each successive one being more extensive than the last. The first was a relatively small scale raid across the border into Switzerland; the second was a much larger armed incursion into the Rhineland, and the third, the greatest of all, was his invasion of the Lowlands in order to occupy Paris.

C.III: 53

Quand le plus grand emportera le pris,
De Nuremberg, d'Aufpurg, & ceux de Bafle,
Par Agripine chef Frankfort repris,
Tranfuerferont par Flamans iufques en Gale.

When the greatest shall carry off the prize,
Concerning, Augsburg, Nuremberg, and those of Basel.
The chief, by reason of Cologne, Frankfurt recovered;
They will go through Flanders, even into France.

emportera, (O.Fr.) carry off, get; le pris, (O.Fr.) recompense; Agripine, (Latin) Cologne; tranfverferont, (O.Fr. - future tense of traverser); Gale, (Latinism) Gall/us – Gaul, i.e., France.

WHEN THE GREATEST SHALL CARRY OFF THE PRIZE

On 30 January 1933, Adolf Hitler was made Reich Chancellor of Germany following the resignation of the Schleicher cabinet two days earlier. In the turmoil caused by the cabinet's resignation, leading politicians were counselled for their preferences; it was from these soundings that an agreement was reached among them, naming Hitler as the one politician most members would be willing to serve under. Up until then, only Nazi fanatics had believed this could happen. Nevertheless, against the odds, Hitler emerged to be seen as **THE GREATEST** to **CARRY OFF THE PRIZE**.[1]

Hitler's rise to power began with his dictatorial control of the NSDAP (abbreviated to Nazi Party). His appointment occurred on 26 July 1921, but only after he had first resigned from the party, and then allowed its administrators to persuade him to reconsider his decision. It was the promise of leadership with *'dictatorial powers'* that induced him to return: as we shall now see.

Representatives of: *'the Augsburg and Nuremberg branches of the Deutsche Werkgemeinschaft'* had earlier caused Hitler irritation when he learned they were engaged in talks with Dr Otto Dickel, author of *The Resurrection of the Western World*, and a potential party leader. Hitler was invited to attend the NSDAP to consider the merger proposal favoured by Dickel. Unwilling to consent to this proposal, Hitler flew into one of his rages, and threatened: *"the Augsburg and Nuremberg representatives that he would see a merger was stopped."* Dickel, however, persisted in having his way, causing Hitler to storm out of the meeting in disgust, having first tendered his resignation. The NSDAP, soon realised that Hitler, with his personal magnetism and considerable rhetorical power, was too valuable a member to lose, and so a way was paved for his return as the Nazi Party's Führer.[2]

It has several times been pointed out that when Nostradamus uses the words *those of*, he very seldom refers to the actual inhabitants of the place mentioned. Instead, the words are intended as a reference to its occupiers or invaders. *Nuremberg* and *Augsburg* have already figured in Hitler's rise to power; it is the city of *Basel* that we turn to now.

Six months after becoming Chancellor (9 August 1933), Hitler ordered his *'Nazi police'* to cross the Swiss border into **BASEL** and search for Communist propaganda. Demonstrations by Nazi supporters on both sides of the frontier followed. This was the first international incident involving Hitler's *'Nazi Polizei'*, and it sent a clear signal to other countries of what was to follow.[3]

The city of Colonia Claudia Ara Agrippinensium, shortened to *Cologne*, was named after the birthplace of *Agrippina* the younger. She married the Emperor Claudius, and became mother to Nero, who repaid her in adult life by having her murdered. Nostradamus has concealed Cologne's name behind that of Agrippina.

In March 1936, *Cologne* made international news. Hitler had torn up two treaties, those of *Versailles* (1919) and *Locarno* (1925), and was preparing to march his army into the demilitarised zone of the Rhineland. His point of entry was the *'Hohenzollern Bridge in Cologne'*. Thirty thousand regular troops were amassed there, waiting to be sent by Hitler into the forbidden zone with orders to take up positions along the banks of the Rhine. Some 3,000 of their number were then ordered to venture further into the region and secure it.[4]

THE CHIEF

Eighteen months earlier, Hitler had been appointed CHIEF; that is, *'Führer of the German Reich'*, following Hindenburg's death on 2 August 1934. His move toward reclaiming the Rhineland was hailed by the German people as a triumph, particularly following the country's humiliation after the First World War.

FRANKFURT RECOVERED

Frankfurt has been used by the seer as a synecdoche for the recovery of the Rhineland. As long ago as 843 AD the Rhineland had become the western border region of the East Frankish, or German kingdom: hence, the name *Frankfort*, which originally meant *'Ford (crossing place) of the Franks)'*. Consequently, Nostradamus's reference to FRANKFURT has allowed the Rhineland's Frankish origins to be substituted for the territory RECOVERED in 1936 by the Germany Chancellor.[5]

THEY WILL GO THROUGH FLANDERS, EVEN INTO FRANCE

Hitler's invasion of the Lowland will be familiar to anyone acquainted with the history of the Second World War. *"From 14 May 1940, the German Panzer forces bridged the River Meuse and poured into Belgium"* on their way to *France*. Hence, THEY WILL GO THROUGH FLANDERS, EVEN INTO FRANCE. Hitler's territorial ambitions for a *'Greater Germany'* had begun,[6] and the Second World War was about to make history.

With the coming of Hitler, Nostradamus now turns his attention to the Second World War, and the events that took place during the first months of its declaration. What is described as taking place in the quatrain below must have baffled earlier commentators. For the seer has predicted the transportation of children. Prior to the Second World War, transportation had connotations only with the criminal class and political exiles: to have imagined that one day children would be transported would have defied belief. Nor would such incredulity have been tempered by the further prediction that this would occur inside the British Isles. But it did happen, although 'transportation' took on the much politer word of 'evacuation'.

C.VIII: 64

Dedans les Ifles les enfans tranfportez,
Les deux de fept feront en defefpoir,
Ceux du terroüer en feront fupportez,
Nom pelle prins des ligues fuy l'efpoir.

Within the Isles, the children transported,
The second of September, they will be in despair,
Those of the burrowing for shelter will be supported within,
Title, spear, terminated; the hope of the confederacies gone.

deux, (Cassells French Dictionary) second (of the month); fept, (Latinism) septem, from which we get Septem[ber]; terroüer, (O.Fr. terrier) to burrow for shelter; pelle, (O.Fr. pel) spear; prins, (O.Fr. prendre) se terminer.

WITHIN THE ISLES, THE CHILDREN TRANSPORTED

The Isles is a term Nostradamus has frequently applied to THE British ISLES and the present case is no exception. At the outbreak of the Second World War, CHILDREN in England living in the major towns and cities within range of German bombers were, quite literally, TRANSPORTED: either across the sea to America, to Canada, to South Africa, or else by train to remote rural locations in Great Britain. *"1939: London, 3 September. The mass evacuation of children from cities to the reception areas considered safe from air attacks has been proceeding for three days. By tonight nearly 1,500,000 will have been moved."* [1]

THE SECOND OF SEPTEMBER, THEY WILL BE IN DESPAIR

War between England and Germany was declared on 3 September 1939. The oracle, however, refers to the day before; that is, THE SECOND OF SEPTEMBER. It was on this day that the British Parliament waited IN DESPAIR for a reply to their ultimatum to Hitler. If the German Chancellor failed to concede to the proposals contained in the government's compromise formula, war would be inevitable. *"September 2 ... The Cabinet met that afternoon without Churchill. Its members were unanimous that an ultimatum should be sent to Germany, to expire at midnight."* But, Hitler ignored Neville Chamberlain's offer of peace, and a state of war was declared between the two countries next morning.[2]

With many vulnerable children evacuated, their parents and the people who remained behind were now the likely targets of aerial bombing. Government *support* was therefore offered to every household in the form of an *underground shelter:* nicknamed, collectively, as dugouts. For those living in high rise flats, a communal shelter was built underground, but with brick sides above ground, and a thick concrete slab on top for cover; fatal to all inside if the shelter suffered a direct hit. The need for these shelters had been anticipated some months earlier. On 5 April 1939, the British House of Commons was told by the minister in charge that 279,435 *shelters for use underground* had already been delivered to houses in the city, giving cover for one and a half million people, and another 80,000 were being made weekly. Since February 1939, these Anderson shelters (named after the Home Secretary) had been delivered to homes in the metropolitan boroughs of London and other provincial towns and cities thought to be at risk.

THOSE OF THE BURROWING FOR SHELTER WILL BE SUPPORTED WITHIN

In order to erect an underground shelter – *"one began by digging a hole 7ft. 6in. long by 6ft. wide . . . to a depth of 4ft. into which were inserted six curved steel sheets, bolted together at the top to form an arch. At either end were flat steel plates . . . Outside, an Anderson had to be covered with at least fifteen inches of earth."* The oracle refers to the people using these, and to their purpose as: THOSE OF THE BURROWING FOR SHELTER [i.e., those excavating the ground] WILL BE SUPPORTED WITHIN. In other words, safely ensconced below ground, the shelters offered some measure of support if a bomb should fall nearby.[3]

In the same year, on 13 December 1939, whilst on patrol in the South Atlantic, three British cruisers encountered the German battleship *Admiral Graf Spee*, and gave chase. What followed became known as the Battle of the River Plate, and it resulted in the German ship becoming seriously damaged. After seeking temporary refuge in Montevideo, it was expelled by the Uruguayan government, and the German warship was forced to return to sea. In wait was a British cruiser squadron under Commodore Harwood. On 17 December, under orders from Hitler, the German commander, Admiral Langsdorff scuttled the Graf Spee rather than face defeat.

TITLE, SPEAR, TERMINATED

Graf is a *title* of nobility in Germany, comparable to *Comte* in French, or *Earl* in English. *Admiral Graf* is therefore equivalent to

'Earl Admiral' and clearly a *Title*. 'Spee', from the German stem 'Spee(r)', means a spear; 'Pel' in Old French also meant 'spear'. Hence, *Nom pel prins* in German, becomes 'Graf Spee(r) endte' or, **Graf Spee terminated.**[4]

THE HOPE OF THE CONFEDERACIES GONE

The oracle concludes by predicting that the treaties and alliances formed after the First World War, and which were designed to prevent further wars breaking out, would prove ineffective; that is, **THE HOPE OF THE CONFEDERACIES GONE**. Between 1925 and 1939 there were at least ten pacts or peace treaties made between the major countries of Europe.[5] Yet, despite the *hope* these had initially held for peace, none were sufficient to avert the world war that broke out in 1939.

Not content with having provided the date of the eve on which the Second World War was declared, Nostradamus now gives an astronomical point in time, which marks the precise day, month, and year on which France and England would declare war against Germany. The seer also provides a paragram for Hitler's name, and it is one that he repeats with equal consistency in two further quatrains. This has proved a contentious issue with commentators and sceptics alike. Yet, it is a necessary fact that if prophecy is true, then it is no different in principle to history. For every prophecy becomes history eventually. Therefore names in history can be no different from those in prophecy. Although to share this view, one must see past, present and future as being coexistent (the Afterword explores this in greater detail).

C.IV: 68

En l'an bien proche efloigné de Venus,
Les deux plus grans de l'Afie & d'Affrique:
Du Ryn & Hifter, qu'on dira font venus,
Crys, pleurs à Malte & cofté Lyguftique.

In the year truly approaching, elongation of Venus,
The two greatest of Asia and of Africa:
Concerning the Rhine and Danube (Hitler), which one will say are accesses,
Screams, tears at Malte, and the Ligurian Coast.

efloigné, (O.Fr.) allonger; grans, (Italian) grand; Hifter, (paragram + transposition) Hit[l]er; venus, (O.Fr. syncope) venuës; cofté, (O.Fr.) côte. Cross-references: Hifter, C.II: 24; C.V: 29.

IN THE YEAR TRULY APPROACHING, ELONGATION OF VENUS

On 3 September 1939, *Venus* and Earth were in superior conjunction; that is to say, Earth, Sun and *Venus* were in a straight line, with *Venus* behind the Sun. *Venus* was therefore at full length, which is to say: an ELONGATION OF VENUS had occurred. It was also on 3 September 1939 that England and France separately declared war on Germany.[1]

The oracle may have intentionally provided a clue to one identity in the next line by using the Italian word *'grans'*. In the timeframe of World War II, this points to Mussolini, not just because he was Italian, but more importantly because since May 1936, his conquest of Eritrea, Ethiopia and Somalia had given Italy an East African empire. Hence, Mussolini had become *the great man of Africa*.

At the same time as the Italian army was fighting to gain control in *Africa*, Japanese troops were marching into Peking to support a *coup* organized by Tokyo (26 November 1935). The successful outcome of this incursion allowed Japan to begin a full-scale invasion of northern China, and by October 1938, the entire eastern seaboard was in Japanese hands. Coincidental with the outbreak of war in Western Europe, General Tojo Hideki, the former Chief of Staff of the Kwantung Army, became Japan's War Minister, and *the great man of Asia*.

THE TWO GREATEST, OF ASIA AND OF AFRICA

On 27 September 1940, the two war ministers Mussolini and Hideki; that is, THE TWO GREATEST, OF AFRICA AND ASIA, joined Hitler in Berlin to sign up to the Tripartite Act. This made the three participating countries of Italy, Japan and Germany, comprising more than 250 million people, the mightiest alliance in the world.[2]

CONCERNING THE RHINE AND DANUBE, WHICH ONE WILL SAY ARE ACCESSES

Having introduced both *Africa* and *Asia*, which were to become major battlegrounds in the Second World War, Nostradamus next brings in two of Europe's mightiest rivers, the *Rhine* and the *Danube*. Both of these waterways flow through the countries of mainland Europe that were caught up in World War II; e.g. Austria, (Danube and Rhine); Czechoslovakia, (Danube); The Netherlands, (Rhine); France, (Rhine), Romania, (Danube); Bulgaria,

(Danube); Hungary, (Danube); Yugoslavia, (Danube); Germany (Danube and Rhine); Ukraine, (Danube); the USSR. (Danube).[3] The two rivers RHINE AND DANUBE WERE therefore ACCESSES to the countries that became participants in World War II.

HITLER

In addition to this, by using the River Danube's ancient name of *Hister*, it allows the name Hitler to emerge as a paragram: formed by transposing 't' and 's', with 'l' substituted for 's'. Equally noteworthy is the fact that Hitler's name became so closely identified with Nazi Germany during the war that it was used in England as a synonym for that country. One would speak of fighting *Hitler*, or of bombing *Hitler*, etc., when, in fact, Germany was the intended target. In this sense, Hitler, too, was a *venue*.

There is also a further connection between Hitler and the Danube. In 1894, Hitler's father moved the family to a little farmhouse in Leonding on the outskirts of Linz, and it was in Linz that Hitler received his education. The river Danube, or *Hister*, flows through the centre of Linz.

The Mediterranean was another major venue in the Second World War, with *Malta* situated halfway between two Allied land bases: one at Alexandria, the other at Gibraltar. Because of its strategic position, the island was recognised to be of immense importance to both sides.

SCREAMS, TEARS AT MALTA

The first bombing raid targeting the Maltese occurred in June 1940. *"Malta was first attacked by Italian aircraft on 11 June 1940."* After the Luftwaffe arrived on the island of Sicily, raids against *Malta*, especially between January and April 1941 intensified. Attacks by the Italian Navy were also made against Valetta harbour, but these failed to achieve a breakthrough. *"[Air] raids were renewed in December with even greater intensity. During January 1942 there were 262, during February 236, and in March and April twice the tonnage of bombs that London had suffered during the Blitz was dropped on Malta."* [4]

AND THE LIGURIAN COAST

It was not long after the bombing of *Malta* that the LIGURIAN COAST suffered a similar pounding. In February 1941, the British Navy joined with the Royal Air Force in carrying out a massive assault upon Genoa. On 24 October 1942, this attack was repeated, when it was reported that – *"Last night 100 Lancasters attacked Genoa."* Further attacks followed: *"For many months the Allies had been bombing Genoa, Turin, Milan and other Italian ports and cities."*[5]

The Second World War was quite unlike any that had been previously fought. In World War I, the opposing sides were soon entrenched in a stalemate position across northern France and Belgium. And this continued for almost the entire duration of the conflict, costing millions of lives. But in the 1939-45 warfare, hostilities spread across the occupied countries, and this allowed Nostradamus to cover events with a larger number of predictions. In the next oracle, he foresees some important incidents that occurred during the onset of hostilities.

C.V: 85

Par les Sueues & lieux circonuoifins,
Seront en guerre pour caufe des nuees:
Camp marins locuftes & confins,
Du Leman faultes feront bien defnuees.

Through the Sueves and circumjacent places,
They will be at war on account of the cause from the clouds,
Flat land, marine locations, and borders,
Concerning Geneva, the faults will be very apparent.

Sueues, (Latin) Suev/i – People of N. E. Germany; Camp, (O.Fr.) bataille, pays plat; nuees, (O.Fr.) nuages; locustes, (Latinism & epenthesis) locus(t)es; confin, (O.Fr.) position, limitrophe, voisinage; Leman, (Latin) Leman/nus lac/us – Geneva. Cross-references: camp, C.II: 24; Leman, C.I: 47.

N.B. Du Rosne published the original of this particular version in 1557. It differs from a later edition published by Rigaud in 1568, which gave the first and final words of line three as 'Gamp' and 'cousins'. Leffen's copy taken from a different source gives these words as 'Camp' and 'cousins'. The confusion seems to stem from a typesetting error; i.e., the inversion of 'n' to give 'u' which naturally leads to seeing 'f' as 's'. The 'G' for 'C' can be attributed to the typesetter's carelessness.

THROUGH THE SUEVES AND CIRCUMJACENT PLACES,

THE SUEVES were a *Germanic people* who occupied the land to the east of Hamburg, and whose central tribe was situated in what is now Brandenburg: a region lying to the west of Berlin.[1]

THE CIRCUMJACENT PLACES can therefore be identified as those that surround the heartland of Germany, namely: Austria, Poland, Czechoslovakia, France, England, Belgium, Netherlands, Denmark and Norway.

It was, indeed, countries CLOSEST TO GERMANY that were AT WAR. And it was ON ACCOUNT OF THE CAUSE, which came FROM THE CLOUDS.

> *There were, of course numerous hazards inherent in airborne operations, but until now the Germans had known only successes. Their use of paratroopers in Norway, Belgium and Holland during 1940 had brought striking results. . . . The Luftwaffe's airborne supremo was Kurt Student, a World War I fighter pilot and squadron leader. He had keenly studied the potential of airborne techniques in Russia. . . . Not only did he have troops leaping from flying aircraft but also equipment-bearing soldiers carried in gliders, and 'air mobile' forces, men trained in the art of going into action straight from the door of a landed plane.[2]*

On 10 May 1940, the German air force bombed *"Dutch and Belgian airfields while airborne troops landed ahead of ground forces."* During the next four days *"Airborne troops attacked The Hague and secured bridges near Rotterdam."* At the same time, *"glider-borne troops captured the Fort of Eban Emael and bridges over the Albert Canal."* But most importantly, it was FROM THE CLOUDS that the first ever parachute battalion invaded another country. On 9 April 1940, German parachutists captured the airfields at Oslo and Stavangar during Hitler's invasion of Norway.[3]

The FLAT LAND, also known as the lowlands of Belgium and Holland, were at the centre of Germany's invasion plans during the Second World War. At the beginning of May 1940, Hitler's armed forces crossed into the Low Countries, thus avoiding France's Maginot Line, which did not stretch into Belgium.

> *The invasion of Belgium and Holland on 10 May 1940 opened seven weeks of 'lightning war' (Blitzkrieg) in which penetration by German tank columns ('panzers') and use of air power encompassed the fall of the Netherlands and Belgium by the end of May and of France by 22 June.[4]*

On 13 October 1939 a German submarine penetrated the defences at Scapa Flow in the Orkneys and sank HMS Royal Oak with the loss of 833 lives. On 13 December the battle of the River Plate took place at Uruguay. On 16 March 1940 it was the Luftwaffe's turn to bomb the naval base at Scapa Flow. On 5 April, the RAF retaliated with a strike at German shipping in the Kiel Canal. On the 10th and 13th of April, two naval battles were fought at Narvik in Norway between the Royal Navy and the Kriegsmarine. By 24th May, German victory on the continent seemed assured. The soldiers of the British Expeditionary Force sent to assist France had been beaten back to the French coastline, leaving France unsupported. It was at Dunkirk – ANOTHER MARINE LOCATION – that war was at its fiercest during that month. The shoreline became a battle zone as retreating British troops attempted to board the flotilla of small boats sent over from Dover to rescue them. On 4 June Dunkirk fell to the Germans. Ten days later Le Havre also fell. In August 1942 a commando raid was made on the port of Dieppe, involving more than 6,000 men, but of those who crossed the Channel only half returned.

During the same period of time, the invading German army crossed the BORDERS at Czechoslovakia, Poland, Denmark, Norway, Holland, Belgium, Luxembourg, France, Romania, Yugoslavia and Greece.[5]

CONCERNING GENEVA, THE FAULTS WILL BE VERY APPARENT

The prophecy ends with a condemnation of the League of Nations, with its headquarters IN GENEVA.[6] The League had been formed after the First World War as a means of preventing disagreements between countries escalating out of control. But the United States Congress refused to ratify the Treaty of Versailles and disassociated itself from the League. Then, in the 1930's, the fragile agreement between member nations began breaking down. Japan invaded China; Italy invaded Ethiopia; Germany invaded the Rhineland; in each case the League was at a loss to make more than a token response of disapproval. In the midst of all this political upheaval a disarmament conference was convened, in which Germany failed to achieve the parity it was seeking. Attempts made to remedy the situation were ineffective. And by the time they eventually reached the table, Hitler was already Chancellor of the German Reich. On 14 October 1933, he formally withdrew Germany's support for the League. In the same year Japan also withdrew. The remaining member of the Axis, Italy, pulled out in 1937. The League eventually disbanded — THE FAULTS BEING VERY APPARENT.[7]

The German invasion of France was successful because Hitler wisely avoided crossing the Maginot Line. This was a series of fortresses constructed along the French frontier separating the two countries. It had been built as a protective measure against sudden invasion. But in the event, it proved ineffective. When the time came, Hitler simply took his troops around the end of the line, and into the lowlands. From there, he was able to make his way towards France using blitzkrieg warfare. Nostradamus predicts the construction of the Line, and the fall of Paris, which resulted from its failure.

C.IV: 80

Pres du grand fleuue, grand foſſe, terre egeſte,
En quinze pars fera l'eaue diuiſee:
La cité prinſe, feu, fang, crys, conflit meſte
Et la plus part concerne au colliſee.

Close by the great river, a huge trench, earth carried away,
In fifteen parts, the water will be divided:
The city taken, fire, blood, shouts, [a] sad conflict,
And the greatest part relates to the coming into conflict.

egeſte, (Latinism) ege/ro – from egestus; conflit, (Latinism) conflict/us; meſte, (O.Fr.) triste; colliſee, (Latinism) collis/us from collido.

CLOSE BY THE GREAT RIVER, A HUGE TRENCH, EARTH CARRIED AWAY

The great river refers to *"the Rhine, the second most important river in Europe . . . [It] touches French territory along the Alsace-Baden frontier for about 125 miles (200 kilometres)."* In 1927, André Maginot, the French Minister for War, sought approval to begin excavating for the construction of an underground line of fortifications, CLOSE TO THE GREAT RIVER alongside its left bank. The proposed undertaking was enormous, consisting of a massive trench approximately fourteen miles long. The excavation and construction of these fortifications were to continue until 1936, with every type of facility catered for to ensure the comfort of those occupying the Line. These included: *"air conditioning, clean messes, shower baths, reading rooms and cinemas."* [1]

IN FIFTEEN PARTS

The completed construction consisted of a line of *"fortified regions for about twenty kilometres of front, on 15 depths."* [2]

THE WATER WILL BE DIVIDED

Alongside THE WATER, the Line was DIVIDED into sections, with each subdivision overlooked by separate observation casements and machinegun nests.[3] Despite these massive preparations, when hostilities did break out between the two nations, as they did in 1940, Germany simply sidestepped this line of fortresses, and attacked France through the Low Countries.

THE CITY TAKEN

The German army advanced through Belgium, Holland and then into France. The goal was Paris, and **THE CITY** was **TAKEN** on 14 June 1940.[4]

FIRE, BLOOD, SHOUTS

In an effort to frustrate the German advance towards Paris as much as possible, the oil refinery situated on the outskirts of Paris was deliberately set on **FIRE** to deny the German army access to fuel.[5] And, of course, the taking of Paris inevitably involved **BLOODSHED**. Victims who fell were either shot as the German army advanced into Paris, or bombed, as happened on 3 June with the cost of 250 lives. There was also some sniper fire.[6] Then, as the triumphant German army marched into Paris, and along the Champs Elysées beneath the emblem of the swastika, they were met by **SHOUTS** of derision and abuse from the angry crowd that gathered to watch the fall of their city.[7]

A SAD CONFLICT

"For the third time in seventy years, Paris was under siege." Inside the capital everywhere closed down as people sought to leave the city – *"an endless stream of refugees poured out along the Boulevard Raspail."* Along the Champs Elysées, a similar bleak appearance could be observed, as buses were positioned along the normally bustling thoroughfare, as obstacles to deter airborne troops invading the city from the clouds. Finally, on the night of 11 June: *"General Maxime Weygand declared Paris an 'open city'."* The great capital had given up with little struggle.[8]

AND THE GREATEST PART RELATES TO THE COMING INTO CONFLICT

Up until the time Paris fell, the French people had felt perfectly safe behind the Maginot Line. *"They developed a 'Maginot line complex'."* It was born from a *"confidence that these fortifications would stop the Germans the next time with little loss of life to the defenders."* As historian, William Shirer said: *"The complex took hold of almost everyone."* It therefore came as a total shock to the French people when the Line failed to prevent the German invasion. Hence, **THE GREATEST PART** of the offensive being discussed was not the occupation of Paris, but it RELATED instead TO THE WAY in which THE CONFLICT BEGAN.[9]

The fall of France and the capture of Paris clearly captivated Nostradamus's attention, for he has now referred to it several times. In the next oracle he provides further information: this time naming the tanks used by the German Panzer Divisions for their blitzkrieg operations. In addition, Hitler's name reappears under the now familiar guise of *Hister*.

C.II: 24

Beſtes farouches de faim fleuues tranner:
Plus part du camp encontre Hiſter ſera,
En caige de fer le grand fera treiſner,
Quand Rin enfant Germain obſeruera.

Ferocious beasts with a hunger to cross rivers,
Greater part of the flat land will be against Hitler,
In an iron carriage, the great man will want to delay,
When the Rhine infantryman shall observe the German.

faim, (O.Fr.) désir, a great longing; camp, (O.Fr.) pays plat; Hiſter, (paragram + transposition) Hit[l]er; caige, (epenthesis - cage & syncope for O.Fr.) c[ari]age; treiſner, (O.Fr. – trainer) retarder; enfant, (O.Fr.) enfant de pié, fantassin; Germain, (Latinism) German/i. Cross-references: Hiſter, C.IV: 68; C.V: 29; also, camp, C.V: 85.

FEROCIOUS BEASTS WITH A HUNGER TO CROSS RIVERS

Hitler's use of Blitzkrieg tactics during the Second World War involved a ground assault force headed by armoured tanks. These came to be aptly named: *Tigers* and *Panthers*. The development of the TIGERS proved to be particularly useful when crossing a large expanse of land. This was because they were capable of CROSSING RIVERS, even to the extent of remaining submerged for up to two and a half hours. The PANTHERS, however, were considered to be Germany's best tanks in terms of their speed, weight and firepower.[1] *Crossing rivers* was an essential feature of blitzkrieg warfare, because large regions of territory were often crisscrossed by rivers, and the whole terrain had to be covered in one continuous sweep. The ability for tanks to remain operational while submerged in water was therefore vital for success.

THE GREATER PART OF THE FLAT LAND WILL BE AGAINST HITLER

The *flat land* (see C.V: 85) refers to the lowlands of Belgium and Holland, and was conquered, with little opposition, in May 1940. But, as the oracle correctly predicted: THE GREATER PART of the Dutch and Belgian people WILL BE AGAINST HITLER. *"When the Germans*

455

invaded the Low Countries in 1940, they did not find large groups of people who supported their aims . . . the vast majority . . . were utterly hostile to Germany's plan to absorb them into the Pan-German Reich." [2]

The linking of Hitler to *Hister*, the ancient name for the Danube, associates the Führer's education and formative years in Linz (the Austrian town through which the Danube flows), with the spelling of his surname. It achieves this, because Hister conveniently forms a paranagram with the name Hitler. In a similar manner, Napoleon's epithet of *Pau* (the short one) was linked to his association with Italy's mighty river, the Po, as well as *Po* being derived, phonetically, from the middle part of Bonaparte's name. The Oracle therefore shows a measure of consistency when identifying Europe's two most recent warlords by associating them with two rivers that had a direct bearing upon their personal history, as well as their names.

IN AN IRON CARRIAGE

In June 1940, France fell to the German invaders, and Hitler was able to travel to Rethondes in the forest of Compiegne, and seat himself inside *"the railroad car in which Marshal Foch had forced the Germans to surrender"* in 1918, after the First World War.
INSIDE the same **IRON CARRIAGE** the roles were now reversed, and it was *Hitler* who dictated the terms of surrender to the French.[3]

THE GREAT MAN WILL WANT TO DELAY

At the head of the French delegation was General Charles Huntziger, acting on behalf of France's new Prime Minister, Philippe Pétain: the former hero of Verdun: an appointment that propelled him into becoming **THE GREAT MAN** of France. In obedience with orders, Huntziger **WANTED TO DELAY** proceedings by negotiating a more favourable settlement. The whole day, and well into the next were spent protesting that the German terms were too *'merciless'*, and far harsher than those imposed by France in 1918. But the German deputation rapidly grew tired of these delaying tactics and threatened to resume hostilities unless a settlement was reached. At this, France capitulated, and the terms of surrender were quickly agreed.[4]

WHEN THE RHINE INFANTRYMAN SHALL OBSERVE THE GERMAN

The Old French language has subtly concealed the predicted failure of the Maginot Line. For the **INFANTRYMEN** stationed inside

456

the fortresses along the banks of THE RHINE could do no more than OBSERVE GERMANY in case a secondary attack was launched from across the river: the main thrust of the invasion force having circumvented the Line to pour men and armaments into the lowlands.[5]

The commencement of the Second World War brought with it a fresh initiative against the British Isles. Hitler resolved upon a naval policy of preventing ships reaching UK ports, thus depriving the people of food and the essential raw materials needed for fighting a war. Since Great Britain was approachable by foreign shipping from the Atlantic Ocean, the German Navy set up a system of submarine patrols, euphemistically called 'Wolf Packs'. These did enormous damage during the first years of the war. The next quatrain refers exclusively to what was happening on the Ocean.

C.IV: 15

D'ou penfera faire venir famine,
De la viendra le raffafiement:
L'œil de la mer par auare canine,
Pour de l'vn l'autre donra huile froment.

From where one will think to make famine appear,
From there will arrive the satiety:
The eye of the sea, by reason of the wolfish canine,
For the one, the other will give oil [and] wheat.

auare, (Latinism) avar/us = avaricious, rapacious, wolfish.

FROM WHERE ONE WILL THINK TO MAKE FAMINE APPEAR

During the Second World War, Germany attempted to starve England into submission. The oracle points to the great expanse of ocean as the place FROM WHERE ONE WILL THINK TO MAKE FAMINE APPEAR, as indeed Hitler also thought, when he proposed to destroy all shipping headed for the British Isles: effectively besieging the nation. In February 1940, German submarine commanders were ordered to sink without warning all ships bringing food and supplies into Britain. This strategy began the Battle of the Atlantic; and it commenced with German U-boats destroying almost one hundred vessels every month.[1]

FROM THERE WILL ARRIVE THE SATIETY

The United States responded to Britain's need for food and fuel during this crucial time by passing the *'Lend-Lease Act'* (March

1941). Although America was officially a neutral country, the Act allowed food and arms to be sent to any nation whose protection was deemed to be vital to the defence of the US. The problem therefore became not one of supply, but of transportation. To reach Britain, ships had to cross the Atlantic Ocean, since FROM THERE WILL ARRIVE THE SATIETY.[2] It is this that introduces the next part of the prediction.

THE EYE OF THE SEA, BY REASON OF THE WOLFISH CANINE

German submarines were lying in wait for all merchant ships heading for Britain. Under the command of Admiral Dönitz, fleets of U-boats, called 'wolf packs'; hence, THE WOLFISH CANINE, would situate themselves out at sea, but within radio contact of their headquarters at Kerneval in northwest France. Once a convoy had been sighted, information was then relayed to Admiral Dönitz and his staff. This enabled the German Admiral to notify commanders in that area, giving them the convoy's position and their orders to intercept. *"This was the process known as 'the forming of the wolf pack', the gathering together of as many U-boats as possible."*[3] Remarkably, too, the oracle has also referred to the periscope: the *lens above the waves*, used for observing ships while staying submerged, Nostradamus calls it: THE EYE OF THE SEA.[4]

FOR THE ONE, THE OTHER WILL GIVE OIL AND WHEAT

At the time of the Second World War, Great Britain was not an oil-producing nation. Its need for this commodity had therefore to be met from imports. The United States, with its Lend-Lease Agreement was therefore THE ONE ABLE TO GIVE THE OTHER OIL AND WHEAT.

The most serious danger was the loss of the UK's oil supply, which by 1942 came almost entirely from the USA and the Caribbean, 65% of it shipped from the eastern seaboard of the USA where it was, at that time, particularly vulnerable to interception by submarines.

In September 1940, German submarines intercepted convoy SC7, and subsequently sank 27 ships with the loss of *"10,000 tonnes of food [and] 5,000 tanks of petrol."* In October, a further 32 ships were torpedoed, and soon the allies were losing, on average, 96 ships every month.[5] It was not until the spring of 1943 that successful counter measures became effective.

In Nostradamus's time, oil was not the essential commodity that it later became. The essential need for oil only arose with the mechanization of society. Therefore, in terms of pure guesswork, the necessity of oil to a besieged people would not have been viewed as a priority in sixteenth century France. Those reading this quatrain at the time of its publication would have made nothing of what was predicted.

Amongst the foulest atrocities of the twentieth century were Germany's 'death camps'. The names of Dachau, Treblinka, Buchenwald, and Belsen still retain a chilling ring to them. But most notorious of all was Auschwitz, which alone was responsible for the murders of between 1,500,000 and 2,250,000 victims: the vast majority of whom were Jewish. Nostradamus was himself descended from that race of people, and his description of what took place there is telling, for he wrote: **'nothing like it was ever seen before'**. His clairvoyant vision of this place is the subject of the next oracle.

C.II: 6

Aupres des portes & dedans deux cites,
Seront deux fleaux oncques n'aperceu vn tel,
Faim dedans pefte, de fer hors gens boutés,
Crier fecours au grand Dieu immortel.

Close to the gates, and within two towns,
Will be two scourges, a likeness never once perceived,
Hunger, disease inside; outside, the people forwarded by iron,
Crying help to the great immortal God.

fleaux, (O.Fr. flael (singular) scourges, also châtiment envoyé par Dieu); oncques; (O.Fr.) une fois – once; boutés, (O.Fr. – bouter) force, thrust, forward, push. Cross-reference: fleaux, C.I: 63.

CLOSE TO THE GATES

"The entrance gate that prisoners called the 'Gate of Death' was located in the main SS guardhouse building. Trains carrying deportees entered here after May 1944 on the railroad spur that extended into the camp."

Before then, the trains had stopped outside the entrance *gate*. Inside the compound were two further *gates*, over which was cast the most infamous message in history:

ARBEIT MACHT FREI – *(Work Brings Freedom) was the sign above the iron gates of Auschwitz. It was placed there by [SS-Hauptsturmführer] Rudolf Höss, commandant of the camp. He seems not to have intended it as a mockery, nor even to have intended it literally, as*

a false promise that those who worked to exhaustion would eventually be released, but rather as a kind of mystical declaration that self-sacrifice in the form of endless labour does in itself bring a kind of spiritual freedom.[1]
(Friedrich, pp.2-3).

AND WITHIN TWO TOWNS

CLOSE TO THE GATES; that is to say, leading from them, was the German prison compound of Auschwitz: Hitler's largest extermination camp. The hyphenated name, *'Auschwitz-Birkenau'* was obtained from TWO Polish TOWNSHIPS: Auschwitz from, Oswiecim; Birkenau from neighbouring Brzezinka. It was inside this hugely extensive prison compound, with its electrified fences, that row upon row of prison huts had been erected to house the masses, as they spilled each day from the cattle trucks arriving from across occupied Europe; men, women and children: families torn from their homes to end their lives degraded, numbered and despised.

WILL BE TWO SCOURGES

KL Auschwitz I – Gas Chamber I. Beginning in 1942, Auschwitz began to function in another way. It became the center of the mass destruction of the European Jews. The Nazis marked all the Jews living in Europe for total extermination, regardless of their age, sex, occupation, citizenship, or political views. They died only because they were Jews. After the selections conducted on the railroad platform, or ramp, newly arrived persons classified by the SS physicians as unfit for labor were sent to the gas chambers: the ill, the elderly, pregnant women, children. In most cases, 70-75% of each transport was sent to immediate death.

KL Auschwitz II – Birkenau. The Crematorium II building, which contained a gas chamber and furnaces for burning corpses. Several hundred thousand Jewish men, women and children were murdered here with poison gas, and their bodies burned. The bodies of Jewish and non-Jewish prisoners who died in the concentration camp were also burned here. According to calculations by the German authorities, 1,440 corpses could be burned in this crematorium every 24 hours. According to the testimony of former prisoners, the figure was higher.[2]

As to whether Nostradamus intended the full meaning of *fleaux* to be read as 'chastisements of God' or simply 'scourges' which can also mean instruments of divine punishment, is unknown. One must bear in mind that alluding to God as the cause of travail has a strong biblical foundation. In the seventeenth-century, Londoners were still inclined to believe the Great Plague and the

Great Fire the year after, were punishments from God for their government's act of regicide. Even in the early 1970s, the irreligious uttering from the Archbishop of York, followed very soon after by York Minster being set alight from a bolt of lightning was thought by some to be rather strangely coincidental.

A LIKENESS NEVER ONCE PERCEIVED

As for the hell on earth that was Auschwitz, this defied even Dante's imagination – *"There has never been a more horrific place than Auschwitz, the Nazi concentration camp in Poland where the biggest mass murder ever took place. More than a million men, women and children died there."* These words seem to be rather eerily like those uttered by Nostradamus four centuries earlier. The camp was a death factory, with purpose-built gas chambers for exterminating as many men, women and children as could be accommodated inside. Immediately upon arrival, inevitably by cattle wagons, the passengers would be divided between those who were to be killed, and those who were to be used for enforced labour. Some were chosen for experimentation in the medical laboratories of Josef Mengele and his prison doctors. Most of those in the condemned group were unaware of what lay ahead as they filed past a small ensemble of musicians playing classical music on a grassy lawn. Their destination was a building containing showers for delousing – or so they were told. Once they had been stripped naked and forced inside the building, the doors were barred, and Zyklon B tablets were then inserted into a chamber in the roof that led down to the people pressed together below. When mixed with air, the tablets converted into a lethal gas, which proved fatal when inhaled. The bodies of the dead were then removed for cremation in one of a number of ovens nearby, specifically designed to accommodate as many corpses as possible.[3]

HUNGER

Feeding those who were allowed to live and work was not considered a priority at Auschwitz, and what passed for food was scarce. When, finally, Russian soldiers stumbled across the site in January 1945, *"they saw living skeletons moving slowly in a landscape of corpses sprawled in the snow."* [4]

Disease, too was rife among those detained, with scabies most prevalent. When the Germans finally abandoned the camp, they *"left only a few hundred inmates behind in the camp's hospital block, most of them sick with diphtheria, scarlet fever or typhus."* [5]

OUTSIDE the extermination camp, in the occupied countries of Europe, **THE PEOPLE** with immediate Jewish ancestry were being systematically and forcibly rounded-up under gunpoint – *forced by iron.* Those arrested were then collected together in groups, and housed in ghettoes to await transportation, either to Auschwitz, or one of the other death camps. *"Trains brought Jews to Auschwitz-Birkenau from as far north as Norway, as far west as the Atlantic coast of France, as far south as Rome, Corfu and Athens, as far east as Transylvania and Ruthenia."* It is estimated that, *"More than two and a half million Jews were deported to Birkenau, and at least two and a quarter million murdered there."* In addition, it may be noted that the French word for railway is *Chemin de Fer* (**PATH OF IRON**): a clear allusion to the fate of those **FORWARDED BY IRON** to the death camps. [6]

The Bible is a rich source of many stories from ancient times that tell of God's help, and His intervention in the history of the Jewish people. E.g. *"And Judah gathered themselves together, to ask the Lord* (Chronicles 20:4) . . . *If when evil cometh upon us, as the sword, judgement or pestilence, or famine, we stand before this house, and in thy presence, (for thy name is in this house,) and cry unto thee in our affliction, then thou wilt hear and help* (20:9) . . . *for God hath power to help and to cast down."* (25:8).

The final line to Nostradamus's prediction refers to these appeals. But the Jewish people at Auschwitz, who prayed and cried to God for help, called out in vain. Help lay still in the future.

Inside the compound at Auschwitz, Jewish religious ceremonies continued to be observed by the work force, although an increasing number were to find their faith insufficient to support former beliefs. Inside the locked death chamber, the pleas, prayers and **CRIES FOR HELP TO THE GREAT IMMORTAL GOD** from those condemned to slowly suffocate in the poisonous blue haze they were forced to inhale, became a haunting memory in the minds of the *Sonnerkommandos.* These were compatriots of the condemned, but who had been assigned to remove and dispose of the corpses after the gas had cleared. The anguished screams of those dying, and their fading cries for help were a chilling part of the horrors taking place inside.[7] Today, *"[many] Jews can no longer subscribe to the biblical idea of God who manifests himself in history, who, they say with Weisel, died in Auschwitz."* (Armstrong). Curiously, as if to anticipate this falling away from belief, Nostradamus, or his angelic mentor, has used an old French word to indicate that the torment of Auschwitz was capable of being defined as an instrument sent by God as a judgement, or chastisement, every bit as severe as other punishments recorded in the Bible.

From the horrors of Auschwitz, Nostradamus returns his attention to Italy's role in the Second World War. Under Mussolini's rule, the country had supported Germany, but by 1943, the climate of opinion changed, and Mussolini found himself outnumbered at government level. King Victor Emmanuel III had initially been forced by public opinion to concede to Mussolini's popularity when confirming his appointment as Prime Minister. But political recognition can be fickle, and upon realizing that the public mood had turned against the Duce, Italy's King quickly stepped in to recover control. The next oracle tracks Mussolini's downfall during the final two years of the war.

C.VI: 31

Roy trouuera ce qu'il defiroit tant,
Quant le Prelat fera reprins à tort:
Refponce au duc le rendra mal content,
Qui dans Milan mettra plufieurs à mort.

The King will detect that which he would so much have desired,
When the Chief in General shall be returned to change direction:
A reply to the Duce will show him badly pleased,
Who, inside Milan, will put a number to death.

Prelat, (O.Fr.) chef in general; defiroit, (conditional tense); tort, (O.Fr.) détour; trouuera, (O.Fr.) découvrir; rendra, (O.Fr.) exposer; duc, (O.Fr.) chef de guerre, also, Italian and paragram – Duc[e]. Cross-references: duc, C.IX: 80, C.IX: 95; C.X: 64.

THE KING WILL DETECT THAT WHICH HE WOULD SO MUCH HAVE DESIRED

Victor Emmanuel III of Italy had bowed to public pressure when appointing Benito Mussolini as Italy's Prime Minister. It was an action **THE KING** had not wished to take, but the Duce had been too powerful at the time to ignore. However, after the outbreak of the Second World War, a number of political and military failures had diminished Mussolini's support amongst the people, and the opportunity was at last DETECTED for the King to dismiss Mussolini from office. Victor Emmanuel therefore disclosed to his Prime Minister THAT WHICH HE SO MUCH WOULD HAVE DESIRED, had the circumstances been different.[1]

WHEN THE CHIEF IN GENERAL SHALL BE RETURNED, TO CHANGE DIRECTION

In place of Mussolini, King Victor Emmanuel reappointed Pietro Badoglio, his former CHIEF OF THE GENERAL Staff,[2] and a man who had originally opposed Italy's entry into the Second World War.[3] Two months after Badoglio WAS RETURNED to office, Italy's new leader took action TO CHANGE the DIRECTION in which the country was headed. On 13 October 1943, Italy declared war against its former ally, Germany.[4]

Nostradamus now turns his precognitive powers to predict events that took place later *inside Milan,* as Mussolini's life drew towards its end.

A REPLY TO THE DUCE WILL SHOW HIM BADLY PLEASED

Eighteen months after his dismissal by King Victor Emmanuel, *the Duce* attended a meeting with Italy's Resistance leaders inside Cardinal Schuster's palace *in Milan.* The purpose was to discuss the possibility of his surrender in exchange for his life being spared. *"Mussolini asked if the Resistance and the Allied commanders would guarantee his life and the lives of his ministers and their families if they surrendered."*

The Duce was replied to in no uncertain terms, and told: *"anyone guilty of war crimes would be put on trial."* Mussolini retorted that he would need to discuss this with his German allies. But, *the reply* he was given was that the German Commander had already agreed to surrender, and had done so without seeing the need TO consult him: quite apart from which, the Allied forces would never agree to the proposals put forward by the Duce. Reports from those present at the meeting said THE REPLY SHOWED HIM BADLY PLEASED, as *"Mussolini violently denounced the Germans for their treachery."*[5]

WHO, INSIDE MILAN, WILL PUT A NUMBER TO DEATH

A few weeks before attending the meeting inside Cardinal Schuster's palace in Milan, Mussolini had sanctioned *the deaths of several* partisans who had been residents of the city. Earnest pleas for clemency had been made at the time, but these were ignored. *"When it was a question of dealing with the Partisans, Mussolini was as pitiless as any of the Germans . . . and ordered that captured Partisans must always be shot."* After his own death, which was not long afterwards, his body was hung up on display in a Milan square. *"Many of those who kicked and spat . . . [were] the mothers of young partisans who had been captured and shot . . . by Mussolini's Fascist militia,"* just weeks before.[6]

One of the closest guarded secrets of the Second World War was Operation Overlord, a plan to invade France and release Europe from German occupation. The D-Day landings set to take place along a stretch of the Normandy coast were planned for 6 June 1944. Despite the intense secrecy covering every aspect of this operation, it appears that Nostradamus knew enough about it for him to have written the following oracle. For, as he said, quoting from *Hebrews 4:xiii* – *"There is nothing that can be hidden from God; everything in all Creation is exposed and lies open before His eyes."*

C.I. 29

Quand le poiſſon terreſtre & aquatique
Par forte vague au grauier fera mis,
Sa forme eſtrange ſuaue & horrifique,
Par mer aux murs bien toſt les ennemis.

When the terrestrial and aquatic fish,
By a strong wave will be placed on the shingle,
Its appearance bizarre, pleasing and hair-raising,
Very soon, the adversaries by sea at the walls.

forme, (O.Fr.) apparence; ſuave, (Latinism) suav/is; eſtrange, (O.Fr.) foreign, bizarre.

WHEN THE TERRESTRIAL AND AQUATIC FISH
For the Allied invasion of France, the US army had been assigned a part of Normandy's coastline on either side of the River Vire. These sections of beach were codenamed 'Utah' and 'Omaha'. Among the assault craft used by the Americans was the Sherman DD (duplex drive) amphibious tank. Nostradamus refers to its amphibious nature by calling it **THE FISH THAT IS BOTH TERRESTRIAL AND AQUATIC.** Referring to the tank as a *fish* is consistent with C.II: 24, in which it will be recalled that two German tanks, the Tiger and the Panther were referred to as *ferocious beasts with a great longing to cross rivers.*[1]

BY A STRONG WAVE
In the early morning of 6 June, the first *"Sherman DD (duplex drive) amphibious tanks reached the shore with the first wave."*[2]

465

The weather conditions that morning were poor. *"It was not until 10.00 when the rising tide was approaching the shingle,"* that US army engineers managed to make progress. *"Each seaborne landing was timed for one hour after low water."* However, *"Gaps had to be made in the bank of loose stones to allow tanks and other vehicles to pass through."* [3]

The prediction describes the amphibian's APPEARANCE as BIZARRE. One can easily imagine the sixteenth-century seer's initial reaction at the clairvoyance of this amphibious tank emerging from the sea. The tank was American; that is, *foreign,* and had *"propellers and a canvas skirt to protect it from the water. When the tank made it to the shore, the canvas was lowered."* [4] (Pictures of the Sherman with its canvas skirt confirm its *bizarre appearance.*)

For occupied France, the amphibious Sherman was, indeed, PLEASING; it was also HAIR-RAISING in the destructive way it dealt with the German artillery. *"As the morning wore on more tanks . . . landed, and began to take out gun positions and pillboxes."* [5]

"The initial landings were to be made by 156,000 men, mostly Britons, Americans and Canadians. The line-up included an armoured division from France, one Belgian brigade, one Polish division, as well as multi-national seaborne forces." Note that Nostradamus uses the plural form, ADVERSARIES, to signal the presence of the different nations arriving BY SEA. [6]

The Atlantic Wall comprised *"an extensive system of coastal fortifications built by the German Third Reich during the Second World War along the western coast of Europe (1942-44) in order to defend against an anticipated Anglo-American invasion of the continent."* By the end of what became called 'The Longest Day', the Normandy landings had been accomplished, and the Atlantic Wall breached. [7]

The references given by Nostradamus, when reviewing the history of the D-Day landings, although couched in his usual obscurity have, nevertheless, proved correct at every point. Thereafter, the German Army – once the mightiest in the world – began to be pushed slowly back behind its own frontier. It was during this retreat that the Battle of the Bulge was fought. The encounter between Germany and the western allies proved to be one of the fiercest battles of the Second World War, and was the last desperate effort of a country facing defeat. It began in the Ardennes, with a counterattack by Hitler: the intention being to force a path through allied lines, and re-establish a base on the French coast. Had it been successful, it would have given Hitler a negotiating position at any forthcoming peace conference.

C.IV: 12

Le camp plus grand de route mis en fuite,
Guaires plus oultre ne fera pourchaffé:
Oft recampé, & legion reduicte,
Puis hors de Gaule du tout fera chaffé.

The greatest army by rout / road put to flight;
It will not be pursued very much farther.
Army reassembled, and troops reduced,
Afterwards, outside of France (de Gaulle), all will be expelled.

plus grand – greatest; route, (O.Fr. homonym) breaking of a troop, also a path, street or passage; Guaires, (O.Fr.) beaucoup; Oft, (O.Fr.) armée; recampé (Provençal) recampar = reassemble; legion, (Latinism) legi/onis; de Gaule, (epenthesis) de Gaul[l]e or de(s) Gau[l]le.

> N.B. 'De Gaule' appears in Leffen's reprint of Barthélemy Bonhomme's Avignon edition of 1556, but is written as 'des Gaules' in Macé Bon-homme's Lyons edition a year earlier.

THE GREATEST ARMY BY ROUT PUT TO FLIGHT

In 1939, Hitler's *Wehrmacht* was acknowledged to be the most efficient fighting force of its time; to wit, THE GREATEST ARMY. But after five years of continuous warfare, the effectiveness of the *Wehrmacht* began to show signs of tiredness. This was apparent in the wake of the D-Day landings in France (June 1944), when the advancing armies of America and Britain routed the German troops, forcing them back towards their own frontier.[1]

BY ROAD

By August, the plight of the retreating German soldiers had be-come so critical that only one avenue of departure was left open. This was *a corridor* twelve miles wide south of Falaise, known euphemistically as: *"Das Korridor des Todes, the 'Corridor of Death'."* But with its narrow ROADS filled with soldiers who had been *put to flight,* the roadway quickly became clogged with broken-down vehicles.[2] Note that Nostradamus specifically says *the flight* will be *by road*. In the 16th century a routed army fleeing the scene of battle would have fled across a rural landscape.

IT WILL NOT BE PURSUED VERY MUCH FARTHER

The impetus of this allied offensive proved so successful that those at the front eventually outdistanced the supply line supporting them. This caused the attack to falter, and IT WAS UNABLE TO PURSUE the retreating enemy VERY MUCH FARTHER; that is, beyond the cessation of the supply line.[3]

ARMY REASSEMBLED

This temporary break in the allied attack allowed the retreating forces to regroup, and the German ARMY quickly REASSEMBLED in a bid to mount a counter-attack and regain the ground it had lost.[4]

AND TROOPS REDUCED

What followed was known as the *'Battle of the Bulge'*. The aim of the German army was to reach Antwerp and cut-off the Allied supply lines. But the sheer effort and manpower required proved too great, and in the worst fighting of the war, which took place near the river Meuse, Germany lost 120,000 men. The Americans also lost 8,600 troops, with a further 47,100 wounded and more than 21,000 missing in action. British casualties were put at 1,400.[5]

AFTERWARDS, OUTSIDE OF FRANCE, ALL WILL BE EXPELLED

AFTER THE BATTLE of the Bulge had been won by American and British forces, the EXPULSION OF THE GERMAN ARMY IN ALL THE OCCUPIED COUNTRIES OF EUROPE soon followed. Florence became free on August 22nd and Bucharest on August 31st; Brussels and Antwerp were liberated on September 4th, and Zeebrugge one week later; Tallinn in Estonia was set free on the 22nd; Crete retaken on October 2nd; Riga, was released from German occupation on the 13th; Salonika regained its independence on November 1st; Budapest capitulated on 5 January 1945; Warsaw was released on the 17th; the occupation of Milan and Venice ended on April 28th. On May 2nd, one million German troops laid down their arms in Austria and Italy; while in Denmark and Norway, the German occupation forces surrendered three days later; Prague was the last capital city to be liberated; it was finally freed on the 10th.[6]

DE GAULLE

In the month that the German retreat began, Paris was liberated (25th August 1944), and General Charles DE GAULLE, Commander in Chief of the Free French forces, stepped on to the world platform to take provisional command of the French government.[7]

With the Second World War soon to end, Nostradamus's attention focuses upon the plight of Europe's two great dictators, Mussolini and Hitler. Both men had been responsible for the war, and it is therefore fitting that their end should feature in these prophecies. The first to be considered is the death of the Duce; Nostradamus actually devotes two quatrains to the events leading to his death.

C.X: 64

Pleure Milan, pleure Lufques, Florence,
Que ton grand Duc fur le char montera,
Changer le fiege pres de Venife f'aduance,
Lors que Colonne à Rome changera.

Weep Milan, weep Lucca, [and] Florence,
When your great Duce shall climb up into the vehicle,
Changing his seat in the proximity of Venice, he makes his exit
At the time when Colonna will change in Rome.

Duc, (O.Fr.) chef de guerre, also, (Italian and paragram) – Duc[e]; sus (O.Fr.) en haut; pres; (O.Fr.) dans le voisinage (dans l'espace ou dans le temps); s'aduance, (O.Fr. s'avancer) sortir. Cross-reference: Duc, C.IX: 80; C.VI: 3; C.IX: 95.

WEEP MILAN, WEEP LUCCA, AND FLORENCE

MILAN,[1] LUCCA,[2] AND FLORENCE,[3] are major cities in northern Italy, each of which gave encouragement to Mussolini during his rise to power. Their WEEPING occurred on 28 April 1945, FOR the death of THEIR GREAT DUCE. Moreover, by employing the 2nd person singular for YOUR; that is, 'ton', Nostradamus has injected an air of familiarity into this oracle, and one that is especially poignant for the sadness felt by the Duce's closest followers when his death was announced.

As the Second World War drew to a close, Mussolini's failure to agree terms regarding his surrender to the Allies impelled him to seek an escape route. From Cardinal Schuster's palace in Milan, where he had previously been talking to the Resistance, *the Duce* made his way to the lakeside town of Como, where the commencement of his final hours were set to unfold.

WHEN YOUR GREAT DUCE SHALL CLIMB UP INTO THE VEHICLE

With northern Italy about to fall into Allied hands, the German armed forces stationed in Como were making hasty preparations to depart for neutral Switzerland. **THE GREAT DUCE** arrived in Como just in time to receive permission to join the convoy. After **CLIMB-ING UP INTO THE VEHICLE** at the rear, he was given part of a German uniform as disguise. But *en route*, the convoy was stopped by partisans, and Mussolini was recognised. He was removed from the convoy, and after a short interrogation, he was shot.[4]

CHANGING HIS SEAT

The expression: *'changing his seat'* is capable of a double mean-ing. As head of the Salo Republic, Mussolini had occupied the *seat* of government, located at his headquarters near Lake Garda. But, when he **CHANGED THIS SEAT**, he exchanged it for a *seat* in *the vehicle leaving* Como, for Switzerland.[5]

IN THE PROXIMITY OF VENICE

After 1400 AD, the city Republic of **VENICE**, its *'Terra Firma'*, stretched its border to the *proximity* of Milan and to Como some 25 miles north of there. The meaning of *pres* in old French also allows for the *proximity* of time. It is in this respect that attention is again drawn to **VENICE**, because American soldiers arrived in the city to liberate it on the same day that Mussolini made his fatal journey. *"The Corps of the 8ᵗʰ Army began to cross the Po on 24 April against no opposition, and by the 27ᵗʰ they were over the Adige also, reaching Venice on 29 April."* [6]

HE MAKES HIS EXIT

The German convoy left Como *en route* for Switzerland, taking the lakeside road. But, on the shoreline of the Lake, a group of Resistance fighters stopped the German party and discovered Mussolini at the back of one of the vehicles. He was taken away, and after several hours of questioning was shot: *"Mussolini is exe-cuted as the Allies take Milan and Venice."* [7]

The final line refers to Pompeo *Colonna*, a contemporary of Nostradamus. It is often said that 'history never repeats itself', but parallels do occasionally occur. In the commentary below, it will be seen that Nostradamus has recognized an episode in Rome's history, which runs parallel to an event in the city's fu-ture. He therefore uses history to presage the future via the me-dium of prophecy.

AT THE TIME WHEN COLONNA WILL CHANGE IN ROME

The incidents that specifically affected **COLONNA IN ROME**,[8] and which later invited parallels with those affecting Mussolini, also in Rome – hence the CHANGE from Colonna to Mussolini – were as follows: [1] *Colonna* Pompeo raised troops to march on Rome because he wanted power. Mussolini did the same in October 1922. [2] In fear, Pope Clement VII pardoned *Colonna*. King Victor Emmanuel III also pardoned Mussolini, and fearing his popularity with the public, he made him Prime Minister. [3] *"As soon as he could, Pope Clement broke the treaty, sent papal troops to ravage the Colonna estates, [and] declared the family outlaws."* Victor Emmanuel responded in a similar fashion. *"25 July [1943] Mussolini who led the country into a disastrous war, was stripped of his office . . . by King Victor Emmanuel III,"* and imprisoned inside a fortress in the Apennines. [4] *Colonna* allied himself with the powerful German army, the Landsknecht, against Rome. Mussolini allied himself with the powerful German army, the Wehrmacht, against Rome. [5] On 6 May 1527, soldiers of the Landsknecht attacked Rome.

> *The inevitable attack began at about four o'clock in the morning of 6 May 1527 . . . The number of people killed in the Sack of Rome was never determined. 'We took Rome by storm,' one of the German invaders reported laconically.*

On 5 September 1944, soldiers of the Wehrmacht attacked Rome.

> *The German High Command ordered its troops in the neighbourhood of Rome . . . After a brief, bravely conducted but badly commanded resistance, the Italian defences of Rome crumbled . . . over 2,000 were arrested in raids and deported to Germany in conditions of terrible, brutality.*[9]

This next oracle continues the story of Mussolini's attempt to escape from Italy, and his subsequent death.

C.IX: 95

Le nouueau faict conduyra l'exercite,
Proche apamé iufques au pres du riuage,
Tendant fecour de Milannoife eflite,
Duc yeux priué à Milan fer de cage.

The novel act: the army will assist with safe conduct,
Soon cut off, as far as by the waterside,
Reaching out for succour from the Milanese select few,
Duce eyes, removed to Milan, cage of iron.

conduyra, (O.Fr.) servir de sauf-conduit; exercite, (Latinism) exercit/us – army, infantry, troops; apamé, (Greek) απαμαω – to cut off; Tendant, (Latinism) tend/o; priué, (O.Fr.) enlever; Duc, (O.Fr.) chef de guerre, also, (Italian and paragram) – Duc[e].
Cross-reference: Duc, C.IX: 80; C.VI: 3; C.X: 64.

THE NOVEL ACT: THE ARMY WILL ASSIST WITH SAFE CONDUCT

It will be recalled that after Mussolini's meeting with the resistance leader in Cardinal Schuster's palace, the Duce left Milan, realizing that he must now prepare for his own safety. Everywhere in northern Italy, soldiers of the American army were busy liberating the major towns. Mussolini realised he must now take flight. Upon leaving Milan, he headed north towards Switzerland, and at Como, he met up with a German convoy that was on the point of departure. The German ARMY agreed to ASSIST Mussolini WITH SAFE CONDUCT as far as the Swiss border.[1] And so, engaging in A NOVEL ACT, the Duce disguised himself by wearing part of a German uniform before taking his seat amongst the troops in a truck at the rear of the convoy.[2]

SOON CUT OFF, AS FAR AS BY THE WATERSIDE

The retreating German army left Como and slowly made its way along the side of the lake as it headed towards the Swiss border, but the journey was SOON CUT OFF. It had reached AS FAR AS Dongo, a settlement of shops and houses BY THE WATERSIDE, when a group of armed partisans stopped the convoy. Mussolini was recognized, and removed from the truck.[3] The German army was then allowed to continue on its way, leaving the *Duce* in the hands of the partisans.

REACHING OUT FOR SUCCOUR FROM THE MILANESE SELECT FEW

"He immediately raised his hands, vainly begging for mercy," as he was bustled away at gun point to a nearby farmhouse, where he awaited the arrival of the resistance leaders from Milan. As soon as news of the Duce's capture reached the city, General Raffaele Cordona of the Royal Italian Army, together with members FROM A MILANESE SELECT FEW, hurried over to the farmhouse where Mussolini was being held. Cordona had represented the Council in Milan when he met the Duce in Cardinal Schuster's palace. According to historian David Mason: *"[Mussolini] might have been safe but for the bitterness of a small Communist caucus within the partisan movement."* In other words, instead of being murdered, he would have been kept alive and handed over to the authorities for war crimes.[4]

DUCE, EYES

"After a quick and expedient trial, which included cries of 'Let me live and I will give you an empire!' the once seemingly invincible dictator was shot." A

Tommy gun was used for his execution, and when the corpse was later put on show in public, the head could be seen riddled with bullet holes. Nostradamus consistently calls each bullet wound an 'eye' when indicating someone who has been shot in the head (refer to Condé, C.III: 41, and to Concini, C.VII: 11). In the present case, *eye* has been pluralized to mark the use of many bullet holes; *viz.* *"A yellowing disfigured face and a head riddled with bullets capped the corpses atop a pile of bodies in Milan. The decaying carcass belonged to 'the Father of Fascism', Benito Mussolini."* [5]

REMOVED TO MILAN, CAGE OF IRON

At Dongo, the *Duce's* corpse was *'flung into a removal van'*; that is, a pantechnicon-van, a **CAGE OF IRON,** and **REMOVED TO MILAN.** In the same square, where two months earlier a group of partisans had been shot, his body was strung up by the heels beneath an iron girder above a petrol station.[6] It is of some small interest to note that Mussolini's final 'inverted' form seems to have been reflected in this oracle, for the relevant phrase has also been inverted, so that 'cage of iron', reads: *fer de cage – iron of cage.*[7]

With the prediction of Italy's fascist dictator accomplished, Nostradamus next turned his attention to Adolf Hitler, the other great despot of that age. Interestingly, by also referring to Hitler's now familiar epithet of 'Hister', and connecting it to the liberation of Venice, the seer of Salon has foreshadowed the day of the tyrant's death.

C.V: 29

La liberté ne fera recouuree,
L'occupera noir fier vilain inique:
Quant la matiere du pont fera ouvrée,
D'Hifter, Venife fachee la republique.

Liberty will not be recovered,
A proud, black, iniquitous, base wretch will occupy it:
When the matter of the bridge shall be discovered,
For Hitler, Venice has angered the republic.

vilain, (O.Fr.) homme de basse condition; Quant, (O.Fr.) dans le temps où; matiere; (O.Fr.) matter, affair; ouvrée, (O.Fr.) découvrir; Hifter, (paragram) Hit[l]er. Cross-reference: Hifter, C.II: 24; C.IV: 68.

LIBERTY WILL NOT BE RECOVERED

France lost its liberty during the Second World War when it became occupied by Hitler's Nazi Germany. The occupation began in 1940, after the German army marched across Holland and

Belgium and into France. Paris was captured in June. Thereafter, **LIBERTY WOULD NOT BE RECOVERED** until 1944,[1] when, in August, Normandy, Toulon and Paris were among the first to be freed.

A PROUD, BLACK, INIQUITOUS, BASE WRETCH WILL OCCUPY IT

During the whole of the time that the French nation was occupied, with its liberty lost to **A PROUD, BLACK, INIQUITOUS, BASE WRETCH**, easily recognizable as Adolf Hitler, war raged across Europe. Historians hold him responsible for the millions of civilian and military deaths, which his insatiable ambition for conquest caused, quite apart from the many millions more who were victims of his extermination camps.[2]

Having produced an easily recognizable description of Hitler, Nostradamus's next concern is that of predicting the events leading immediately to this man's end. He begins, appropriately enough, in the month before his death, with a prediction of the Rhine crossing. For, once this natural obstacle had been overcome, the way would then be clear for the Allies to press deeper into Germany and eventually reach Berlin.

WHEN THE MATTER OF THE BRIDGE SHALL BE DISCOVERED

THE railway **BRIDGE** that spanned the Rhine at *Remagen* was to become crucial to the Allies progress. It **WAS DISCOVERED** intact . . .

> On 7 March 1945, during the battle for Germany, it was captured by an armoured patrol of Hodges First US Army, when the Germans failed to destroy it. This gave the Allies a great psychological, as well as military advantage for it enabled more than 8,000 troops, supported by tanks and self-propelled guns, to cross in under 24 hours . . . Hitler was furious at the bridge's capture . . . The German officer charged with destroying it was, along with four others, summarily shot and V-2 rockets were even fired at it.

But the bridge held firm until 17 March 1945, when it finally collapsed into the Rhine.[3]

Six weeks after *the Remagen affair of the bridge* (30 April), and with Soviet troops entering Berlin from the east, as well as American and British troops approaching from the west, Hitler committed suicide inside his Berlin bunker. The death of Germany's 'Fuhrer' has been cryptically signalled by Nostradamus, by once more using the liberation of Venice as a timing event.

As American troops moved northwards: *"Both corps of the Eighth Army began to cross the Po on 24th April against no opposition, and by the 29th they were over the Adige also, advancing rapidly thereafter, reaching Venice on 29th April."* **VENICE** surrendered next day [4] without too much fuss, thereby **ANGERING THE** Salo **REPUBLIC**, which ruled northern Italy.

The Salo *Republic* was *"the Italian Social Republic, a last-ditch Fascist regime based in Salò on Lake Garda"* [5] and which had been controlled by Mussolini, acting as a puppet for Hitler. The news of Mussolini's death and the liberation of northern Italy made grim news for Hitler, and on the day *Venice* capitulated (30 April 1945), he committed suicide. [6]

The deaths of Hitler and Mussolini conclude Nostradamus's set of predictions for the Second World War. In the aftermath of its horrors, and the millions who lost their lives, politicians throughout the world declared that never again would their countries go to war except in defence against attack. Such promises seemed like a guarantee for unending peace. But the generation that makes promises is eventually replaced by another: one that regrettably lacks the lessons learnt from bitter experience by its predecessors, and, worse still, believes it knows better. Nostradamus was quite aware of this, for the first oracle in the next chapter begins by describing the lifetime of peace that was promised by politicians, and how it affected people in Europe, as well as those further afield. Ominously, it ends by revealing the emptiness of political assurances.

10

UNLASTING PEACE

Almost fifty million people lost their lives as a result of the Second World War. Numbed by the astronomic number of deaths, and the horrors and the atrocities reported by those who returned to tell their story, politicians everywhere declared yet again, there must never be another war. Nations must learn to settle their grievances peacefully. A pledge was therefore given by the countries caught up in World War II that never again would they take up arms against another nation, unless in defence of an attack made against them. Peace seemed assured. And, for many years it was. But Nostradamus had seen the future, and he knew that what politicians say in one generation is not the same as that said in the next. In this chapter, events leading towards the breakdown of the promised peace are foretold.

C.I: 63

Les fleaux paſſés diminue le monde,
Long temps la paix terres inhabitées,
Seur marchera par ciel, terre, mer, & onde:
Puis de nouueau les guerres fuſcitées.

The scourges having passed, the world is diminished,
A long time the peace, lands inhabited,
Confidently one will proceed by sky, land, sea and wave:
Then again, the wars resuscitated.

fleau, (O.Fr.) scourge, or châtiments envoyé par Dieu; Seur, (O.Fr.) confiant; de nouveau = again; ſuſcitées; (O.Fr.) resuscitate. Cross-reference: fleaux, C.II: 6.

THE SCOURGES HAVING PASSED

The **SCOURGES** referred to in this opening phrase were previously identified as '*KL Auschwitz I and KL Auschwitz II*', and referred to the Second World War. The death camp at Auschwitz was finally closed down in January 1945, when it was abandoned by the Germans who were aware of the approaching Russian army. It is, however, possible that Nostradamus intended to expand on this by widening the meaning of *scourges* to include the two World Wars, the Spanish Civil War and the Russian Revolution: all of which occurred within the space of thirty-one years, producing a death toll counted in millions. In either case, the prophecy is timed for the years following the end of WWII in 1945.[1]

THE WORLD DIMINISHED

The millions who died at Auschwitz were a significant part of the massive decrease in population that resulted from the Second World War; e.g., *"Military losses during the Second World War ... Total (estimate) 14 362 177 ... Civilians killed during the Second World War ... Total (estimate) 27 077 614 ... The Holocaust: the genocide of Jews by the Nazis, 1939-45 Total (average) 5 571 300."* (Davies).

But **THE DIMINISHING OF THE WORLD** can also be applied to the terrain. Air travel greatly reduced the time taken to cross both land and sea, which meant the world had become smaller. And it is this alternative which leads into the third line of the quatrain.[2]

A LONG TIME THE PEACE

For almost half a century, following WWII, Europe experienced **A LONG TIME OF PEACE.** In mainland Europe this was achieved by forming a European Union of member nations, living and trading peacefully between themselves according to the treaties of Rome (1957).[3]

LANDS INHABITED

Elsewhere, during this *time of peace*, massive immigration pro-grammes were set up by America, Canada, Australia and New Zealand. These were to become LANDS newly INHABITED by immi-grants keen to add to the country's workforce, and increase its population; Australia even offered assisted passages as an in-ducement.[4]

CONFIDENTLY, ONE WILL PROCEED BY SKY, LAND, SEA AND WAVE

A further feature to appear in post-war Europe concerned travel time. Distances that had once taken days, weeks or even a month or more to traverse were reduced to a matter of hours, thus was *the world made smaller*. Foreign countries soon became the prov-ince of the workingman on holiday. CONFIDENTLY, he and his fam-ily COULD now PROCEED BY SKY, LAND, SEA AND WAVE to destinations, which earlier generations could only have heard or read about. Charter flights took holidaymakers across the SKIES.[5] Passenger coaches, high speed trains and motor vehicles criss-crossed the LAND [6] using an intricate network of rail and road. Ferries bridged the English Channel, and liners offered cruise holidays at SEA; [7] while the hovercraft and hydrofoil skimmed over the WAVES [8] to give meaning to the distinction drawn between *sea and wave*.

It is interesting to note that Nostradamus has prefixed this line of prophecy with the word *confidently*. Travel in the six-teenth century was very much different to what it became four hundred years later, not only with regard to the means of trans-port, but to the general safety of passengers as well. On land, the risk to a traveller had once been that of murder or highway rob-bery; at sea, the danger was from pirates, or that the ship might founder in heavy weather. Consequently, one did not undertake journeys to distant places *confidently*, or without giving consid-erable thought to a safe return.

THEN AGAIN, THE WARS RESUSCITATED

The return of the *wars* predicted by Nostradamus and affecting Europe began during the final decade of the twentieth century, when the combined forces of the United Nations took military action against Iraq as a reprisal for its invasion of Kuwait. The fact that Iraq had earlier invaded Iran without exciting the U.N.'s involvement may be considered noteworthy. This break in Europe's *long time peace* was followed by further *wars* inside the former Yugoslav Republic, especially involving French troops as part of a United Nations peacekeeping force. Then, as the twentieth century gave way to the twenty-first, a new type of war emerged, one directed against terrorist organizations based in regimes nurturing harmful intentions towards western interests. Led by the US and backed by Great Britain, with countries around the world being cajoled into giving their support, military action was taken against Afghanistan and for a second time against Iraq.[9] In 2006 and 2008 this was followed by Israel's attacks on Gaza and, with greater destructive consequences, against Hezbullah in Lebanon. One may therefore presume that further wars, even more deadly, are already filing up in the future corridors of time.

In keeping with Nostradamus's strategy of predicting the political beginning of those nations that are destined to appear on the world stage, the seer's next oracle, which is a split quatrain, concerns the creation in 1948 of the State of Israel. The first half predicts its formation; the second half foretells its subsequent survival during the Six-Day War of 1967. Confirmation of this interpretation exists in the astronomical timing employed by Nostradamus.

C.III: 97

Nouuelle loy terre neufue occuper,
Vers la Syrie, Iudee, & Paleſtine:
Le grand Empire barbare corruer,
Auant que Phebés ſon ſiecle determine.

A new law occupying new land,
Towards Syria, Judea and Palestine:
The great, foreign Empire collapsing,
Previously, the moon concludes its cycle.

corruer, (Latinism) corru/ere; Auant que, (O.Fr. adverb) previously; Phebés, (Latinism) Phoeb/es – the moon; determine, (O.Fr.) terminer.

A NEW LAW

THE NEW LAW concerns the State of Israel; that is, *"The Law of Return, which gave every Jew the right to immigrate."* The state of Israel was founded in 1948 under new legislation that replaced the old oral and written laws of the Talmud and the Torah. Although Judaism continued to be based upon the teaching of the Hebrew prophets, politicians incorporated more modern ideas into the fabric of state legislature, principally that of political equality and social justice for all citizens, without distinction of race, creed or sex.[1]

OCCUPYING NEW LAND, TOWARDS SYRIA JUDEA AND PALESTINE

Nostradamus refers to three nations, each of which were to express concern at Israel's OCCUPATION OF this NEW LAND thrust into their midst. JUDEA was formerly the name of southern Israel; PALESTINE was consolidated into Israel around 1000 BC, while SYRIA, overlooking Israel's northern frontier from the Golan Heights, was historically the nation's old enemy.[2]

THE GREAT FOREIGN EMPIRE COLLAPSING

Predictably, the Arab nations surrounding this new state became increasingly hostile. The United Nations had done its diplomatic best to ensure peace in the region, but it was not enough. In June 1967, a major war erupted. Egypt's President Nasser, backed by the United Arab Republic, openly vowed to wipe Israel off the map. A full-scale war then developed with Egypt, Jordan and Syria the chief allies in the coalition of Arab states.[3] It began with a ring of steel encircling beleaguered Israel. Yet, remarkably, the war ended a week later in what became known as the Six Day War. During those six hectic days, the entire Arab army was defeated; or, as Nostradamus put it: THE GREAT FOREIGN EMPIRE COLLAPSING.[4]

PREVIOUSLY, THE MOON CONCLUDES ITS CYCLE

The completion of the moon's cycle refers to the nineteen years it takes for a *'Metonic Cycle'* to occur; this cycle was previously described in C.I: 25. Nostradamus is therefore predicting that BEFORE the Arab nations collapse, THE MOON WILL HAVE CONCLUDED ITS NINETEEN YEAR CYCLE of phases. This, in fact, is what occurred. The State of Israel was founded on 14 May 1948. Nineteen years later, the *great foreign empire collapsed* as a result of the Six Day War, which was fought from 5th to 10th June 1967.[5]

Having foreseen what would happen globally, during the long period of peace predicted in C.I: 63, Nostradamus turns his prophetic eye once more towards France, and what was taking place at that time.

C.II: 19

Nouueaux venus, lieu bafti fans defenfe,
Occuper place par lors inhabitable:
Prez, maifons, champs, villes prendre à plaifance,
Faim, pefte, guerre, arpen long labourable.

Accesses unheard of before: place built without defence,
Occupying a site uninhabitable in that time,
In the neighbourhood, houses, fields, towns, taking to pleasure,
Hunger, disease, war; long arable acre.

Venu, (O.Fr.) access; Prez, (O.Fr.) dans le voisinage; long, (Latinism) long/us;

Contrary to what is often thought about Nostradamus, he was not wholly concerned with *'the evils that men do'*. Periods of peace were foreseen and recorded; for as he said: his oracles were *'continuous'*, and they must take into account lengthy periods of peace. For this reason, the years following World War II were of some interest to him, since this was not only a relatively tranquil period it was also a time of massive redevelopment.

ACCESSES UNHEARD OF BEFORE: PLACE BUILT WITHOUT DEFENCE

After the Second World War, *new towns* gave rise to ACCESSES UN-HEARD OF BEFORE in selected French locations, as indeed happened in England during the same period, and to the amazement of this sixteenth century visionary, they were built WITHOUT A WALLED DEFENCE.[1] In Nostradamus's time, when one entered a city it was often necessary to arrive before the gates closed for the night. Remnants of these old defensive walls can still be seen in some cities as structures of historic interest. Both London and Paris still retain the names of their former gates.

OCCUPYING A SITE UNINHABITABLE IN THAT TIME

With the commencement of the post-war period, the foundations for new towns, such as Sarcelles, near Le Bourget airport, were laid. Other land developments followed, with five new regions close to Paris, and still more outside the cities of Marseilles, Lyons, Rouen, and Lille, often OCCUPYING A SITE which until THAT TIME had been UNINHABITABLE.

L'Ile-d'Abeau, south-east of Lyon, set out along a valley slope in the form of a series of villages, is especially attractive . . . another success is Evry, south of Paris, with its cheerful multi-coloured flats . . . Cergy-Pontoise, twenty miles north-west of Paris, is taking shape on a splendidly spacious site overlooking a loop in the river Oise. [2]

481

IN THE NEIGHBOURHOOD, HOUSES, FIELDS, TOWNS, TAKING TO PLEASURE

The guarding of cities, long since past, is contrasted with the present-day, in which people expect to TAKE PLEASURE IN THEIR NEIGHBOURHOOD. Modern HOUSES equipped with labour-saving devices are often accompanied by purpose-built leisure complexes that have been designed as an integral part of the community. TOWNS have their theatres, libraries, museums, cinemas, sports centres, and peripheral sports FIELDS. All these facilities have now become the norm for a modern *nouveau ville*.

> *The largest multi-purpose centre in France has been completed there [at Evry], the Agora, with three theatres, a skating rink, dance halls, a library, youth centre and hypermarkets . . . at Cergy-Pontoise . . . the new town has theatres and concerts . . . On a visit [to] Massy . . . the big modern sports centre with its five swimming-pools was crowded . . . Massy has fifty clubs and associations of a social or cultural kind – from chess to Sinology, from amateur choirs to the Cercle Celtique.* [3]

HUNGER

Having painted a word picture that would have been unrecognisable in the sixteenth century, the oracle moderates its happy forecast with words that would have found immediate rapport with the late medieval mind; that is, *hunger, disease and war*. Despite massive progress in the way societies live, these three horsemen of the apocalypse have not been eliminated. Global warming continues to increase, bringing with it ever-worsening droughts, floods, and fires around the globe, thus posing a future threat to the world's food supply: African nations have been the first to be hit by FAMINE. [4]

DISEASE

DISEASE, too, has yet to be conquered. The fear of a pandemic, spread by mutating viruses, as well as the dread of the ailments that would have been familiar to Nostradamus, still remain to worry world health authorities: the most recent alarms having been from Avian Flu and Swine Flu. A new disease, unknown in Nostradamus's time, is AIDS, which is capable of depopulating large sections of a licentious population at a quite alarming rate. [5]

WAR

A different type of disease, one that affects politicians, is *war*; this too has not gone away. Instead, it has become more deadly than anything seen in previous ages, and is practised with verve, and the aid of electronic and technological devices that can maim and kill at a distance, leaving those who instigated the carnage entirely detached from any physical or emotional consequences of their action. During the closing decade of the twentieth century, **WAR** in the Balkan countries and in Iraq did not escape involvement by the French.[6]

The final phrase to this oracle concerns France's agricultural system, for this became especially relevant during the second half of the twentieth century. The modernisation programme introduced was intended to update the antiquated agricultural practices of the past. The average French farm was therefore expanded from thirty-five acres in 1955, to vastly more than double that volume.

LONG ARABLE ACRE

Before the Second World War most large estates indulged in the lethargy of *Paysantisme*. It was a state of mind in which nothing was permitted to upset *'the eternal order of the fields'*. But the young farmers who replaced their parents looked to technology for ideas. By turning to economic management and marketing cooperatives, it provided them with new answers to crop yield, and harvest distribution. The small farms, with their cultivated strips of land that were once so evident in pre-war France gave way to the **LONG ARABLE ACRE** that now covers much of the French countryside.

> *In the decades after the war, French farming went through what even cautious scholars described as a 'revolution'. In no other aspect of French life was change so dramatic, or the conflict between old and new so sharp. After 1945, farm mechanization soon began to make economic nonsense of France's vast peasant community . . . A new generation of modern-minded young farmers, with a totally different outlook from their parents . . . promoted a new creed, entirely novel in this individualistic milieu, a creed of technical advance, producer groups and marketing cooperatives.*[7]

During this long period of peace, Nostradamus's prophetic gaze turned again towards Iran. His concern being to continue marking the political scene in that country, which he began in the 18th Century (see C.III: 77). Let it not be forgotten that when his precognitive skill focuses on the political formation of a country outside of France, it is reasonable to suspect the future involvement of that same country in world events. Considering, therefore, that Iran is presently pursuing a domestic nuclear programme, this may presently give grounds for thought.

C.I: 70

Pluie, faim, guerre en Perſe non ceſſée,
La foy trop grande, trahira le monarque,
Par la finie en Gaule commencée:
Secret augure pour à vn eſtre parque.

Rain, a great longing, war in Iran unceasing,
The faith too great: it will mislead the monarch,
By reason of the finish commenced in France:
Remote augury, with regard to one being settled in a place.

faim, (O.Fr.) a great longing, hunger; guerre, (O.Fr.) difficulté, malheur; Perſe, (Persia – modern-day Iran since 1935); cesser, (O.Fr.) arrêter; Secret, (Latinism) secretus; augure, (Latin) prophet; parque, (O.Fr.) to set down, settle in a place.

N.B. The Bonhomme edition prints 'vn' in line four as 'vng'. This could possibly be translated as a latinism for vngo – to anoint or smear. However, all other editions print the word without a 'g'.

RAIN

The geography of Iran makes it particularly prone to earthquake activity as well as drought and periodic flooding. Among the country's ten worst disasters listed in recent times, and one following a period of **INTENSE RAINFALL**, was *"the great flood of July 1980,"* which affected 950,000 citizens, causing many to be made homeless.[1]

A GREAT LONGING

This torrential rainfall came within weeks of two manmade disasters. *"At the end of January 1980 Abol Hassan Bani-Sadr was elected President but by the mid-summer there were pitched battles between extremist groups in Tehran and other cities."* These militant demonstrators had **A GREAT LONGING** to see Iran become an Islamic Republic, but to achieve this they first had to overcome those who were actively supporting the return of the Shah.[2]

WAR IN IRAN UNCEASING

The third blow to strike Iran during the summer of 1980 occurred *"when Iraq launched a war to secure control of the Shatt al Arab waterway in September 1980."* **WAR IN IRAN** would rage **WITHOUT END** for eight years, and cost the lives of one million men.[3]

After having introduced these three major calamities to strike

Iran in the first line of this prophecy: all of which happened in the summer months of 1980, Nostradamus concentrates the remainder of the quatrain on the political changes that were taking place across the country at that time. Until Shah Pahlavi's exile in January 1979, he had been slowly implementing a policy of social reform, aimed at providing both the working and middle classes with the benefits of the country's new oil wealth. This included sweeping changes to the educational system, financial support for university students, a lowering of income taxes, an ambitious health insurance plan, and the implementation of a program introduced in 1972 under which, industrialists were required to sell 49 percent of the shares of their companies to their employees. But it was not enough to placate the religiously motivated activists.

THE FAITH TOO GREAT: IT WILL MISLEAD THE MONARCH

In December 1978, following demonstrations that had taken place on 5 November, and even greater ones on December 9 and 10, when several hundred thousand people participated in marches in Tehran and the provinces, Shah Pahlavi finally conceded to the demand for his removal. Until then, he had believed himself safe. But THE FAITH which powered the revolution for an Islamic state proved TOO GREAT.[4] And failure to recognise this MISLED THE MONARCH into a belief that his programme of social reform, and the appointment of Shahpur Bakhtiar as Prime Minister would appeal to enough people, as to overcome his opponents who were calling for his removal.[5]

Previously, in 1964, the Shah had identified the Ayatollah Khomeini as a troublemaker, and had ordered his exile. Moving from Turkey into Iraq, Khomeini continued what he had begun, urging his followers to ferment unrest as a means of undermining the Shah, and to constantly agitate for Iran to become an Islamic state. Eventually, Saddam Hussein deported this troublesome cleric, and the Ayatollah was allowed to enter France.

BY REASON OF THE FINISH, COMMENCED IN FRANCE

At Neauphle-le-Château, outside Paris, Khomeini set up his revolutionary headquarters, and aided by modern communication technology, he soon had the ear of the world's Press. It was undoubtedly this move to *France* that gave him the opportunity to *finish* plans for changing Iran into an Islamic state. On 1 February 1979, following the Shah's departure: *"Ayatollah Ruhollah Khomeini returned to Iran from exile in France."* Two months later, a referendum on the new constitution was held, and the country at last became an Islamic state: the move towards this FINISH having COMMENCED IN FRANCE.[6]

On 4 January 1979, shortly before the Shah's abdication, Shahpur Bakhtiar was named Prime Minister. The Shah made the appointment in an effort to forestall the Islamic fundamentalist revolution that was gripping Iran. Although Bakhtiar accepted the post, he did so, only on condition that Pahlavi left the country until matters had become more settled. Two weeks later, the Shah flew out of Iran never to return. On 1 February, Ayatollah Khomeini arrived in Tehran to be greeted by the cheers of more than a million onlookers.

WITH REGARD TO ONE BEING SETTLED IN A PLACE

Almost at once, *"Bakhtiar's government and power quickly evaporated,"* and for personal safety Bakhtiar *'went into hiding'.* By April Bakhtiar had left Iran and made his way into *France: "where he established the exile National Movement of the Iranian Resistance;"* for this, he became THE ONE SETTLED IN A PLACE.

A REMOTE AUGURY

Like Khomeini had done during his years of exile, it was now Bakhtiar's turn to begin plotting the overthrow of Iran's ruling party from his place of separation *in France.* It is, therefore, in this sense that the Ayatollah Khomeini's previous period of exile in Paris had become a REMOTE AUGURY signalling the fate of the former Prime Minister, Shahpur Bakhtiar, whom Khomeini had replaced: Paris being *remote* from Tehran.[7]

As the 20th century approached its end, two wars broke out in the Middle East: both involving Iraq and both fought in fairly quick succession. Nostradamus's global outlook therefore turns to Iraq and its president Saddam Hussein, the new warlord.

C.I: 55

Soubz l'oppofite climat Babylonique,
Grande fera de fang effufion:
Que terre & mer, air, ciel fera inique,
Sectes, faim, regnes, peftes, confufion.

Under the reign of the adverse one, Babylonian region,
Great will be the effusion of blood:
When land sea, air, & sky will be injurious,
Sects, hunger, kingdoms, pestilences, confusion.

Soubz, (Romance from Latin, sub) under the reign of; l'oppofite, (O.Fr.) adverse; inique, (Latinism) iniqu/us; regnes, (O.Fr.) royaumes; confufion, (O.Fr.) destruction, confusion.

UNDER THE REIGN OF THE ADVERSE ONE

Chambers English Dictionary defines the word 'adverse' as: *contrary (with to): opposed: unfavourable.* Iraq's president, Saddam Hussein was precisely that, and these traits in his character received international recognition when he angered the world by first attacking neighbouring Kuwait, and then refusing to concede to the United Nations directive that he immediately withdraw his forces from that country. His refusal to comply led to Iraq becoming the target for military action comprised of a joint international task force. Even before then, he had *"invaded Iran on 22 September 1980, triggering a bitter eight-year war which destabilised the region and devastated both countries."*[1] By the turn of the century, a new administration in the US resolved to free Iraq from this dictator, and in a third Gulf war, Iraq was again defeated and **THE REIGN OF THE ADVERSE ONE** ended with his capture and execution.

BABYLONIAN REGION

Historically, *Babylonia* was the ancient empire of southern Mesopotamia whose capital city once occupied what is now central Iraq.[2]

GREAT WILL BE THE EFFUSION OF BLOOD

This occurred in three stages. Firstly, the Iran-Iraq War:

> *Iran acknowledged that nearly 300,000 people died in the war; estimates of the Iraqi dead range from 160,000 to 240,000. Iraq suffered an estimated 375,000 casualties . . . Iran's losses may have included more than 1 million people killed or maimed.*[3]

Secondly the death toll in Kuwait was put at:

> *United States 148 killed, 458 wounded. Great Britain 47 killed, 43 wounded. France 2 killed, 25 wounded. Egypt 14 killed, 120 wounded. IRAQ 60,000 to 100,000 military personnel are estimated to have been killed or wounded in action. 2,000 to 3,000 civilians are estimated to have been killed, and from 5,000 to 7,700 injured.*[4]

In the Iraq War, the third to hit the Babylonian region:

The number of Iraqis killed through 2007 ranges from 'a conservative cautious minimum' of more than 85,000 civilians to a survey estimate of more than 1,000,000 citizens. [5]

All the elements listed by Nostradamus became part of the conflicts that raged across the Babylonian region between 1980, when Iraq invaded Iran, up until the US and UK led coalition forces invaded Iraq for a second time. Outstanding amongst the many scenes of carnage were [1] **ON LAND** the First World War type of land battles, fought between Iraq and Iran over many years with little to show but a rising death toll. [2] The 'Highway of Death' in the Gulf War, where retreating Iraqis were massacred along Highway 80. [3] Operation Desert Storm, in which *"American forces first destroyed Iraqi border radar stations, then other key elements of the Iraqi anti-aircraft network; lastly, they began to bomb key targets in downtown Iraq, including the presidential palace, communication centers, and power stations."* [6] [4] **AT SEA**, there was the Tanker War (1987-88) in which *"Lloyds of London, a British insurance market, estimated that the Tanker War damaged 546 commercial vessels and killed about 430 civilian mariners."* [7] [5] **THE AIR** was also **INJURIOUS**, because *"Saddam used chemical weapons against the Iranians and, in 1988, against his own people - the Kurds of Halabja - whom he considered a treacherous fifth column."* [8] [6] But it was from **THE SKY** that the greatest damage was done, with the air forces of all participants active during the three conflicts.

Overall, the coalition air campaign (consisting mostly of U.S. pilots) accumulated a total of 109,876 sorties over the 43-day air war — averaging 2,555 sorties per day. Of those, more than 27,000 sorties struck enemy Scuds, airfields, air defenses, electrical power, biological and chemical weapons caches, headquarters, intelligence assets, communications, the Iraqi army, and oil refineries. [9]

SECTS

"The [Iran-Iraq] war began . . . following a long history of border disputes and fears of Shia insurgency among Iraq's long suppressed Shia majority." [10] But following the defeat of Iraq in 1991, both the Kurds in the north and the Shi'ites in the south saw this as an opportunity to press home their advantage. Both **SECTS** staged an uprising. *"As Saddam's rule collapsed across southern Iraq, he was assailed by a fresh crisis at his rear. News arrived from the north that the Kurds had also risen."* But, despite these setbacks, and America's belief that Saddam Hussein would be toppled from within, the Iraqi President eventually emerged

triumphant, although his *"action against the Kurds . . . forced thousands of Kurds to flee to Turkey. Many died from hunger and disease."*[11]

Iraqis also suffered the torment of **HUNGER** and **DISEASE**. The country was unable to provide enough food for its citizens, even using strict rationing controls. The country needed to import 70% of its grain, but draconian measures imposed upon the government by United Nations sanctions made this impossible. Very soon . . .

> *garbage collectors in Baghdad reported a sinister change in the loads carted to the city dump . . . after almost twelve months of war and sanctions, the scraps had entirely disappeared. Food, any food, had become too precious to throw away. Even the skins of melons were being saved and devoured. People were beginning to go hungry.* [12]

DISEASE, too, took its toll among the population, as: *'Typhoid, hepatitis, meningitis and gastroenteritis'* reached epidemic proportions. An outbreak of *'plague threatened by rats feeding on unburied garbage'* was also reported, along with an epidemic of cholera.

> *In the 1990s, the Tigris changed colour again. It was now a rich café-au-lait brown because raw sewage from 3.5 million people in Baghdad, not to mention effluent from cities upstream, was entering the river . . . The end results were visible in the children's' wards of the hospitals . . . The dirty water that brought gastroenteritis and cholera in its train found its little victims easier to overcome because they were already weak . . . Iraqis, especially their children, were not getting enough to eat.* [13]

The cause of the Iran-Iraq war can be traced back many centuries to the rivalry between **KINGDOMS**.

> *There has been rivalry between kingdoms of Assyria (the Fertile Crescent valley, modern Syria) and the rugged highlands to the East Persia or modern Iran) since the beginning of recorded history in Sumer. Of strategic importance was the question of sovereignty over the resource-rich province of Khuzestan. Before the Ottoman empire 1299–1922, Iraq was part of Persia. The rising power of the Ottomans put an end to this when Suleyman I annexed Arabian Iraq. . . . The border disputes between Persia and the Ottomans never ended. Between 1555 and 1918, Persia and the Ottoman empire signed no fewer than 18 treaties delineating their disputed borders.* [14]

In Martti Ahtissari's report on the state of Iraq after the war, the undersecretary general for the UN, wrote – *"Nothing we have seen or read about had quite prepared us for the particular form of devastation which had now befallen the country . . . The recent conflict has wrought near-apocalyptic results."*

After the Gulf War had been won by the US alliance, there was an air of *confusion* amongst the victorious nations. Saddam Hussein had survived, and continued to remain sufficiently popular with his people to ensure his continued rule over Iraq. Not wishing to indulge in the illegality of regime change – forbidden by international law – the US had confidently supposed that Saddam would be overthrown from within. It did not happen, despite several attempts to bring this about. A decade of CONFUSION followed, during which, western nations had to deal with Iraq and its defeated, but still resolutely *contrary*, leader. The next oracle continues to refer to Iraq and Saddam Hussein.

C.VIII: 70

Il entrera vilain, mefchant, infame,
Tyrannifant la Mefopotamie,
Tous amys fait d'adulterine dame.
Terre horrible noir de phifonomie.

He will find a way in, a peasant, despicable, infamous,
Tyrannising Iraq:
Everyone made friends with the adulterine dame.
The land horrible, black in appearance.

entrer, (O.Fr.) s'introduire; vilain, (O.Fr.) paysan, manant; mefchant, (O.Fr.) misérable; Mefopotamie, (Mesopotamia) Modern-day Iraq.

The opening biographical comment in the Encyclopædia Britannica relating to Saddam Hussein prepares the way for what follows: *"Hussein was born into a peasant family in northern Iraq."* His place of birth was *"Ouija, a typical Iraqi village of mud-brick houses, in the plains of northern Iraq on April 28, 1937. His father, Hussein al-Majid, was a peasant farmer who died either just before Saddam was born or a few months afterwards."* [1] Although of PEASANT upbringing, by 1968, Saddam Hussein had achieved the first of his ambitions: that of leading the Ba'ath Socialists. He was also instrumental in a *coup* that brought the Party back to power under the presidency of Ahmad Hassan al-Bakr. When al-Bakr resigned in 1979, Hussein pushed forward, having FOUND A WAY to take control of the government.

Saddam had joined the Ba'th Socialist Party in 1957 aged 20, and just two years later, he was to commit the first of his many DESPICABLE acts: the attempted assassination of the Iraqi Prime Minister, Abdal-Karim Qasim. It was after taking power that Hussein set about suppressing all opposition with an extensive secret police operation. This resulted in the incarceration, torture and disappearances of his political opponents. *"[He] put on trial his former communist associates in the government, twenty-two of whom were executed . . . in April 1980 he ordered the Shia Ayatollah and his sister to be hanged." "I knew then just how dangerous the Ba'ath party was,"* Dr Shal-am explained: – *"I had seen what had happened to Iraqi soldiers who had deserted their posts during the American invasion. They had their ears cut off. And those who spoke against Saddam usually had their tongues cut out."* [2]

INFAMOUS, TYRANNISING IRAQ

There can be no doubt that Saddam Hussein was guilty of TYRANNISING IRAQ *"Saddam's government repressed movements that it deemed threatening, particularly those of ethnic or religious groups that sought independence or autonomy."* [3] Many thousands of Iraqis were murdered under his INFAMOUS regime, and it was only after he had been overthrown in 2003, that their unmarked graves began to be unearthed. *"The Kurds and other non-Arabs living in the North were subjected to Iraq's worst instance of minority persecution in 1987-89 ... Anywhere from 100,000 to 182,000 were massacred in a genocidal offensive."* [4]

In August 1990, Saddam Hussein took a step too far when he embarked upon an invasion of Kuwait. The United States took instant objection to this Iraqi attack, and from then onwards, President George H. W. Bush headed a United Nations campaign against Saddam Hussein's aggression. Unwisely, the Iraqi leader ignored the warnings, resolutions and deadlines set by the U.N., and this led directly to the Persian Gulf War, which commenced, 16 January 1991.

EVERYONE MADE FRIENDS

From that moment onwards, Iraq found itself under attack from every direction, and from every major country in the world. Gathered behind the United States, and offering it their total support were: Argentina, Australia; Belgium; Bulgaria; Canada; Czechoslovakia; Denmark; Finland; France; Germany; Greece,

Hungary; Italy; Japan; Luxembourg; Netherlands; New Zealand; Norway; Philippines; Poland; Portugal; Romania; Saudi Arabia; Sierra Leone; Singapore; South Korea; Spain; Sweden; Turkey, United Kingdom, USSR, and the United Arab Emirates. EVERYONE it seemed had MADE FRIENDS with the United States in its campaign against Saddam Hussein.[5]

WITH THE ADULTERINE DAME

In which case, why has the US been called an *adulterine dame*? This adjective is defined to represent the offspring of an adulterous relationship. It is also a biblical metaphor intended for countries that renege on political agreements. In the present case, the US had earlier formed a close relationship with Iraq: in the process of which, it had supported Saddam's war against Iran. But it subsequently abandoned this association in favour of entering a new relationship with Iraq's enemy, Kuwait:

> *The US restored formal relations with Iraq in November 1984, but the US had begun, several years earlier, to provide it with intelligence and military support (in secret and contrary to this country's official neutrality) in accordance with policy directives from President Ronald Reagan. ... on December 20, 1983, Donald Rumsfeld, currently the US Secretary of Defense, met with Saddam Hussein during the first of Rumsfeld's two now-famous visits to Baghdad.* Furthermore: *The White House and State Department pressured the Export-Import Bank to provide Iraq with financing, to enhance its credit standing and enable it to obtain loans from other international financial institutions. The US Agriculture Department provided taxpayer-guaranteed loans for purchases of American commodities, to the satisfaction of US grain exporters.*

However, in 1990, the US deserted Iraq in order to join forces with other nations in attacking its former associate in what became known as the Persian Gulf War.

> *Vowing to free Kuwait, Bush rallied the United Nations, the U. S. people, and Congress and sent 425,000 American troops. They were joined by 118,000 troops from allied nations. After weeks of air and missile bombardment, the 100-hour land battle dubbed Desert Storm routed Iraq's million-man army.*

America's abandonment of Iraq, and then joining forces with Kuwait, at war with Iraq, explains why the oracle refers to the country as ADULTERINE,[6] but not why it calls it a *dame*.

The female colossus which stands on Liberty Island in Upper

New York Bay is known throughout the world as the Statue of Liberty. It is a symbol, uniquely and proudly representing the United States of America. For Nostradamus to have designated this female figure as a personification of the country in which it has become uniquely associated is not without precedent. For he previously gave the same designation of DAME to Great Britain, in order to personify Britannia – 'the dame of antiquity' – with the British people (refer: C.II: 51 and C.II: 53). *"It was perhaps Athena, Greek goddess and wise warrior-queen who set the pattern for the powerful female figures who, like Britannia, personify the traits and characteristics of the nations they represent."* For Britannia, no less for the Statue of Liberty: both *dames* represent the nations that have adopted them.[7]

THE LAND HORRIBLE, BLACK IN APPEARANCE

In the aftermath of operation Desert Storm: the name given to the UN-led invasion against Iraq, the country was laid waste over a six week period (January and February of 1991). The amount of destruction was appalling—THE LAND HORRIBLE. One United Nations observer reported the devastation as being: *'far worse than anything one could have imagined'*. To add to this scene of desolation, and with the intention of depriving the occupying army of easy access to the county's fuel supply, Saddam Hussein ordered the opening of his country's oil pipelines into the sea, and the firing of the oil wells. Thick BLACK oil slicks on the one hand and torrid BLACK smoke on the other, gave a BLACK APPEARANCE TO parts of THE LANDSCAPE for many weeks afterwards.[8]

Nostradamus's prophecies have now entered a phase with a more global outlook, reflecting the way the world has changed. His next oracle returns to Russian politics, from which nothing has been heard since the nation's conversion to communism (refer: C.I: 14 and C.V: 26). But in 1989, under the presidency of Mikhail Gorbachev, Russia was forced by economic pressure and lack of money to abandon this political and social philosophy; by doing so, it set free the satellite countries that had once formed the Union of Soviet Socialist Republics.

C.III: 95

La loy Moricque on verra defaillir:
Apres vne autre beaucoup plus feductiue,
Borifthenes premier viendra faillir:
Pardons & langue vne plus attractiue.

493

One will see the More-like way of living go bankrupt:
Afterwards, one other much more enticing,
The Dnieper foremost (Premier Boris Yeltsin) will come to fail:
By reason of donations and language [of] one more attractive.

loy, (O.Fr.) manière de vivre; Moricque, (In French, 'More' allows a double meaning; i.e., either the name, More or a Moor, hence: Moresque, = More-like or Moorish); defaillir, (O.Fr.) manquer; ſeductiue, (Latinism) seducti/o; Pardons = Par dons; Boriſthenes, (Latin & paragram) Dneiper River, also paranagram, – Boris E[h]tsen = Boris Eltsen (see note below).

N.B. In Cyrillic script, E[h]tsen is written: Елцин; 'E' is pronounced 'ʏᴇ'; л as 'ʟ'; 'ц' as 'ᴛꜱ', and 'и' as 'ᴇᴇ' (this is usually written with an 'i' in English, but the letter 'i' does not exist in the Russian alphabet); and 'н' takes the 'ɴ' sound. There is no suggestion, however, that Nostradamus either read or understood Russian. He wrote only what he was impelled to write by his deva, leaving it for others to comprehend in the light of subsequent events.

ONE WILL SEE THE MORE-LIKE WAY OF LIVING

Sir Thomas More's book *Utopia* was written in Latin, and published in December 1516, it would therefore have been known, and possibly read by Nostradamus. The book *'depicts an ideal state ordered by reason'*. This has drawn commentators to compare it with the communist state of the twentieth century. Karl Kautsky, for example, author of *Thomas More and his Utopia* (1890), regarded More as *'an embryo Marxist'*. Another to have drawn a similar comparison is the Encyclopædia Britannica, which describes Lenin's brochure, *The State and Revolution*, as his most *'Utopian'* work, and his *'doctrinal springboard to power'*. Notably: *"The basis of Utopian economy was common ownership . . . Without private ownership the vices of greed and pride would have nothing on which to feed . . . common ownership is the prerequisite for a happy community."* (Reynolds).[1]

GO BANKRUPT

Communism became embraced as a political philosophy in Russia soon after the October Revolution of 1917. But, with the final decade of the twentieth century about to begin, the Soviet Union's economy collapsed, hastened by a breakdown in every sector. Industrial output fell by almost one fifth, and agriculture by nearly as much. Its greatly vaunted energy programme also saw a reduction of one tenth. And, whereas the country's GDP had shown a deficit of 4% in 1990, this increased to nearly 14% one year later. The government therefore found itself GOING BANKRUPT and unable to sustain the country's level of imported goods.

Food prices continued to rise in Russian state-controlled shops until they had almost doubled, and outlying villages were unable to obtain sufficient fuel for everyday living. *"Gorbachëv had scarcely any credit left with Soviet society. The economy was collapsing in every sector."*[2]

AFTERWARDS

Mikhail Gorbachev, the General Secretary of the Communist Party of the Soviet Union had previously enjoyed great popularity, both at home and abroad. But, AFTERWARDS, in August of 1991, following the collapse of the Russian economy, an attempt was made to replace him, and he was put under house arrest at his dacha in the Crimea.[3]

ONE OTHER MUCH MORE ENTICING, PREMIER BORIS YELTSIN

With Gorbachev out of the way, BORIS YELTSIN became Russia's new PREMIER. Among *Yeltsin's* first actions was the banning of the Russian Communist Party and seizure of its property. He followed this by removing state control from the sale of goods. No longer would the government fix prices. Nationalization together with subsidies gave place to privatisation. A system of vouchers was introduced, enabling citizens to buy into companies that had formerly been state owned. Yeltsin's premiership proved to be MUCH MORE ENTICING than that of Gorbachev, as evidenced by the revival of the free market. *"For most people the replacement of communism with capitalism was most obviously manifested in the tin kiosks erected in all towns and cities."*[4]

Nostradamus now looks back at the break-up of the Soviet Union, and the overthrow of the communist order, by predicting Ukraine's revolt as a major cause of Gorbachev's resignation.

THE DNIEPER FOREMOST WILL COME TO FAIL

THE DNIEPER flows through Kiev, the capital city of Ukraine, and it was in Kiev on 1 December 1991 that the people held a referendum to decide their country's future. *"The people of Ukraine, including most of its Russian inhabitants, disagreed with Gorbachëv, and on 1 December they voted for independence in a referendum."* By a majority of nine to one, they chose to leave the Soviet Union.[5] It was this decision that helped *Yeltsin* break with the communist system, for without the support of *'fifty-three million Ukrainians'*, Gorbachev was powerless to continue. On 25 December 1991, the former president of communist Russia announced his departure. At which point, the Soviet Union ceased to exist.[6]

BY REASON OF DONATIONS AND LANGUAGE OF ONE MORE ATTRACTIVE

"In early 1992 Yeltsin toured Western Europe and signed friendship treaties with Britain and France in exchange for aid and credits." In America, similar concessions were obtained, and it was **BY REASON OF** these **DONATIONS** that Communism's former leaders succumbed to **A LANGUAGE MORE ATTRACTIVE.**

After a personal appeal from former President Richard Nixon, the Bush administration also approved an economic assistance package for Russia, and Congress voted funds to help Russia dismantle its nuclear weapons.

The huge financial packages received from two US presidents, George H. W. Bush and Bill Clinton were further embellished with the latter donating more than one and a half billion dollars. America also agreed to a fixed rate of currency exchange for Russia's former satellite states to stabilize their economies.[7]

In previous quatrains, one will have noticed that Nostradamus often spreads his oracles over an expanded time period. The following prophecy may also fit this category. The first three lines certainly extend over a period of ten years. The fourth line, however, poses questions that may only be answered when this prophecy is agreed to have been finally fulfilled.

C.II: 28

Le penultime du furnom du prophete
Prendra Diane pour fon iour & repos:
Loing vaguera par frenetique tefte,
Et deliurant vn grand peuple d'impos.

*The penultimate with the family name of the prophet
Will choose Diana for his historic day and cessation:
A long time he will go here and there through a frenetic head,
Also releasing a great people from deceivers.*

repos, (O.Fr.) cessation, halte; vaguera, (O.Fr.) aller ça et là; loing, (O.Fr.) length of time; frenetique, (O.Fr.) frantic, besides himself; impos, (Late Latin) impos/tors- deceivers.

THE PENULTIMATE WITH THE FAMILY NAME OF THE PROPHET

The name of the Prophet is recognized worldwide to be that of Muhammad, the Prophet of Islam. In this oracle, Nostradamus is referring to the last but one in a family bearing the name of the Prophet Mohamed (Muhammad, Mohamed, Mohammed are variant spellings of the same name). The fact that *penultimate* is stressed tends to imply that both persons bearing this family name are important to the prophecy.

WILL CHOOSE DIANA FOR HIS HISTORIC DAY AND CESSATION

The second clue to understanding what has been predicted is given in the second line. The person bearing the name of the Prophet has, in a manner of speaking, chosen Diana. This choice is one that will give him a day in history, but it will also lead to his cessation. From these clues it is now possible to identify Emad El-Din Mohamed Abdel Moneim Fayed (Dodi Fayed for short), the son of a wealthy businessman. At the time of meeting Princess Diana, Fayed was in a relationship with Miss Kelly Fisher of Los Angeles. The break-up of their relationship coincided with **HIS DECISION TO CHOOSE DIANA FOR** his fiancée, and there is strong evidence that an engagement between the two was shortly to be announced. But that was never to be.

On the morning of 1 September 1997, the world awoke to the tragic news that Diana Princess of Wales had been killed the night before in a car crash. Diana was the former consort of Prince Charles, heir to the British throne and the mother of Princes William and Harry who at the time were second and third in line for the crown. But for her divorce from Prince Charles, Diana would one day have taken the title, Queen of England. By her side at the time of the crash was Dodi Fayed. And on that fateful August night, he became immortalised in death – **HIS CESSATION**. For this had become **HIS HISTORIC DAY**: the one day for which he will always be remembered.

A LONG TIME HE WILL GO HERE AND THERE THROUGH A FRENETIC HEAD

The prophecy now focuses upon the activities of the other member of the family, also bearing the name of the Prophet, Dodi's father Mohamed al Fayed. This elder Mohamed was not convinced the crash had been an accident *"and argued that Diana and Dodi were killed in an Establishment plot to prevent them marrying. . . . [He] has pledged to fight 'tooth and nail' to prevent a cover-up,"* reported the Daily Express (24 July 2006: p.7). The more conformist section of the British press was quick to pour scorn on his **FRENETIC** allegations, and Mr. Al Fayed's efforts were grossly ridiculed by the media. Amongst the beliefs he held that were derided were –

"The couple were executed by British intelligence agents." – "MI6 engineered the bogus car crash." – "the Duke of Edinburgh, was at the heart of the conspiracy." – "The driver of the car was not drunk; his blood sample had been contaminated or switched." – "Then he talked darkly about secret intelligence material gathered by the CIA and, three years after the deaths, filed a law suit in Washington demanding that the US government turn over its classified documentation." [1]

Nearly ten years passed before members of an inquest jury were allowed to consider the evidence that led to the deaths of Princess Diana and Dodi Fayed. During that time, the number of coroners appointed, four in total, changed suspiciously often, adding to the time available for Mr al Fayed TO GO HERE AND THERE to make his own investigations, which he conducted in the UK, in France and in the US.

ALSO RELEASING A GREAT PEOPLE FROM DECEIVERS

The purpose of Mr al Fayed's investigations was TO RELEASE PEOPLE FROM DECEIVERS by uncovering a secret service conspiracy, based upon the real possibility that a marriage between Diana and Dodi could compromise the future heir to the throne by his having Moslem siblings. This forward thinking would be natural to MI5, and at a time when Islamic extremists have resulted in the government introducing anti-terrorist measures, it is something that the Crown would prefer to avoid. Hence, there was a genuine, if hypothetical, motive supporting the conspiracy theory.

In the event, the result of an official enquiry into the death of the Princess and her companion resulted in the jury's verdict of *'unlawful killing'*. A white Fiat Uno 'clipping' their car and another car to the rear were blamed, as was the speed and drunken state of the chauffeur, Henri Paul.[2] Neither car was ever traced.

Mme Gisele Paul, the dead driver's mother, remarked: *"How could my son have driven with 1.8 grammes of alcohol and 20% carbon monoxide in his blood? It's ridiculous."* [3] This curiosity had long been a known fact, for it suggested that the blood sample taken from Paul had been switched with that of a suicide brought into the morgue that same night. Then, as if to confirm Paul's addiction to alcohol the French police inspected his flat and found *"bottles of red wine, crème-decassis, Ricard, suze aperitif, port, beer, vodka, pineau (a Cognac drink) and bourbon."* [4] What is extraordinary about this *'vast cache of drink'* is that six days earlier, when Captain Marc Monot attended the first search of Paul's flat, he observed just a single bottle of Champagne and a bottle of Martini Bianco, a quarter full.

The final line of this oracle appears ambiguous. Apart from the unresolved aspects concerning the deaths of the Princess and Dodi al Fayed, when Nostradamus mentions *a great people*, as he did previously in C.I: 53, and again in C.I: 76, he was referring to his own nationality. In which case, it is the French who have yet TO RELEASE their GREAT PEOPLE FROM DECEIVERS.

We shall next consider the last of these oracles to carry a specific date. This, in itself, is worthy of further investigation. Between 1555, when the first volume of these prophecies was published, and the year 2000, Nostradamus foretold of events for the following years: 1580 (C.VI: 2); 1607 twice (C.VIII: 71) and (C.VI: 54); 1609 (C.X: 91); 1660 (additional quatrain); 1700 (C.I: 49); 1703, 1709 (C.VI: 2); 1727 (C.III: 77), and 1999 (C.X: 72). Why did he stop at 1999 when he claimed that his prophecies extended to the year 3797? In the first 444 years, he has explicitly provided the correct year for 10 prophecies; in the remaining 1798 years, he has dated none. I suggest the reason for this was his awareness that shortly after 1999 his method of concealing dates would be so well understood that it would threaten free will to have continued with more. It is an explanation that is bound up with the prediction he gave in C.III: 94: that a little over 500 years after his birth year, 1503, his cryptic prophecies will unfold to give such clarity that they will become extremely contentious.

Those who have read through these five centuries of prophecy will have acquired a reasonable understanding that Nostradamus was a master in the art of paronomasia. Until now there has been a failure to come to terms with this fact. Consequently, those who awaited 1999 and the fulfilment—or perhaps the non-fulfilment—of the last of these dated oracles were unaware that the previously stated years had resulted in accurately dated predictions, and without that knowledge, opinions were bound to be negative. There was also a possible hidden agenda to this increased interest. Nostradamus's prophecies had somehow survived for more than four and a half centuries. Here, then, was the perfect opportunity to demonstrate his failure to deliver, since it is unlikely that anyone in the media seriously believed that what had been predicted would actually occur. But Nostradamus is rarely obvious. Perhaps, aware of the attention this last dated prediction would receive, he has produced a split quatrain. It is also one, as we shall now see, in which the span of years over which the prophecy is set to run, may need a longer time for its fulfilment.

C.X: 72

L'an mil neuf cens nonante neuf fept mois,
Du ciel viendra vn grand Roy d'effrayeur
Refufciter le grand Roy d'Angoulmois.
Auant apres Mars regner par bon heur.

The year 1999, month seven,
A great King of terror will come from the sky:
The great King of Angoulême resuscitating.
Fortification display / before; afterwards Mars reigning by good fortune.

Angoulmois, (O.Fr.) Angoulême; Auant, (O.Fr. syncope – auuant) galerie de fortification; Mars, (Latin) March, also god of war; heure, (O.Fr.) hap, luck, fortune, chance, also, bon heur, (Provencal) good fortune.

N.B. The earliest extant copy of this prediction occurs in the edition published by Benoist Rigaud in 1568, two years after the death of Nostradamus. It differs in one important respect from an earlier edition of this prophecy published in 1558 at Lyons, and which was subsequently used as a source for Pierre Leffen's reproduction of the complete *Prophéties* printed in 1650 at Leyden. Apart from the difference in spelling Angoulmois – Rigaud spells it Angolmois – d'effrayeur' is printed by Rigaud as 'deffraiaur'. The meanings of these two words are very different. 'Deffraieur' in Old French is a 'defrayer': someone who acts as a steward for a person, house or company, and is responsible for defraying expenses. 'Effrayeur', by contrast, is derived from 'effrayer' and 'effrayement', and can be interpreted only by words indicating 'terror'.

THE YEAR 1999, MONTH SEVEN

Every published commentator of Nostradamus, certainly during the latter half of the 20th century, drew attention to this oracle, and waited with expectation for the coming of July 1999. This invited suspicion, because Nostradamus is most obscure when attention upon his prophecies is likely to be at its greatest; compare, for example, the quatrains relating to Louis XIV, which are almost inscrutable because of the attention given them during the Sun King's reign. Consequently, not only did it seem that July 1999 was just too obvious, especially when Nostradamus goes to extremes to conceal the truth by laying false trails, but also applying the Gregorian Calendar to a man who previously applied the legal form of dating to his prophecies, seemed incredibly naïve. Therefore, long before the predicted year arrived, it seemed clear to those better informed about Nostradamus's style of writing that SEPTEMBER was the intended meaning for MONTH SEVEN, and not July. *September*, of course, takes its name from the Latin word for seven, 'septem'. Moreover, *sept* has been used before by Nostradamus (see C.VIII: 64) to indicate the month of September. The first line should therefore be understood as SEPTEMBER 1999: there being no added words to relate it to a different method of dating, as occurred in the two 1607 prophecies and that of 1609.

FROM THE SKY WILL COME A GREAT KING OF TERROR

The thought of *a great King of terror descending from the skies* certainly exercised the imagination of many would-be interpreters, but nothing they suggested, either before or since, has rung true; or, for that matter, been confirmed by events. Speaking personally, it was circa 1992 that the meaning behind this phrase occurred to me. Nostradamus was a classical scholar, and for him, *a great king of terror dwelling in the sky* would be at one with the home of the Greek gods; he actually brings Mars, the god of war, into this prophecy. I therefore recalled that *"In Greek mythology . . . Ouranos [is] the sky god,"* [1] he was also a GREAT KING OF TERROR. Uranus (modern spelling of Ouranos) was father to the Furies and rightly famed for spreading fear and apprehension in the minds of mortals. Moreover, being already at home in the clouds, Uranus was well placed to DESCEND FROM THE SKIES, should the occasion arise. And such an occasion did arise, and it occurred IN SEPTEMBER 1999.

Because of Uranus' mythological ancestry, his name has since been given to the deadly radioactive substance uranium; that is, *"uranus + -ium"* (OED) If this fell from the sky in sufficient quantity, as would be expected to occur after a nuclear explosion, then it would fulfil Nostradamus's prophecy; that is, assuming it fell in *September 1999*.

It is said, everyone remembers where they were when they heard the news that President Kennedy had been shot. I certainly remember where I was on 30 September 1999, when I heard the news confirming my understanding of this prophecy.

A nuclear accident had occurred, exactly as described in the oracle, and uranium was even then falling from the sky over a wide area at 15,000 times above the level of safety. The following news report appeared next day.

> *The world's worst nuclear accident since Chernobyl rocked Japan yesterday after an explosion took place at a nuclear fuel plant, threatening 300,000 people living within a six-mile radius of the disaster. When the plant was evacuated radiation levels were reported 2km from the site to be 15,000 times the normal level . . . The disaster began as workers at the JCO plant were attempting to dissolve 16kg of enriched uranium in nitric acid – almost enough to make a nuclear bomb. It is considered dangerous to process more than 2.4kg at one time. This set off an uncontrolled chain reaction, resulting in a 'blue flash' at the processing plant in Tokai village. A hole was punched through the roof of the building, radiation began spewing into the atmosphere, and radiation levels went up to 4,000 times normal levels within a minute.[2]*

In the light of this event, one is entitled to the rejoinder – So what? The disaster was dealt with before it developed into a greater catastrophe, and it appears to have had no bearing on anything that has happened since then. Nevertheless, one must remain aware that the prophecies of Nostradamus are very often spread over a large number of years while still remaining unified to a single theme. What happened in September 1999 may have been intended as an augur for what has still to occur before this particular prophecy has run its course. It may also be significant that Japan is the subject of this prediction. For it was in that country, in 1945, that two nuclear bombs were detonated to bring the Second World War to a close. Is there a similar nuclear connection yet to happen that brings this oracle to completion?

The year 2000 quickly arrived, and with it came the presidential elections in America. It was with the change of president in the USA that the next part of the oracle was brought to fulfilment. George W. Bush, son of the victorious President during the Gulf War, became the new commander-in-chief of America's armed forces, and he brought with him an agenda to spread western style democracy across the world, commencing with the work his father had left unfinished. War-like sounds were soon emanating from the White House, at first against Afghanistan and then against the Iraqi leader, Saddam Hussein.

In the UK, Prime Minister Tony Blair worked feverishly to win the British people over to America's martial programme. And for week after week it seemed impossible to find a single day when some politician did not repeat the politically motivated mantra of 'Iraq's Weapons of Mass Destruction'. In fact, Iraq possessed no such weapons, as was confirmed by the U.N. weapons inspectorate. But the odious WMD phrase lingered on and stuck in the mind, until eventually it succeeded in frightening enough people to support Britain joining the US in declaring war against Iraq. Those who understood Nostradamus's manner of predicting were left in no doubt; this must be the war foreseen by the seer, which was to occur after the nuclear incident in September 1999.

Although three and a half years distanced the two events, this is perfectly in keeping with the *'perpetual'* sequence of prophecies detailed in the foregoing chapters. The only question that remained was: – Who would emerge to *resuscitate* the role made famous by *the great King of Angoulême*? One had not long to wait for that answer.

THE GREAT KING OF ANGOULÊME

Referring back to the King who reigned for most of Nostradamus's lifetime; that is, Francis I, the connection with *Angoulême* is at once apparent. Francis I was *'the son of Charles of Valois-Orléans, Count of Angoulême'*, and in 1515, he became: *"the first king in the Valois-Angoulême line."* Of the four kings descended from him, whose reigns extended until the death of Henri III, none were greater than he: in fact, most were pathetic. Francis I must therefore be the King to whom Nostradamus was referring. With this in mind, a brief look at the salient parts of his reign includes an intriguing fact. This French monarch had stood up against an *"overmighty Emperor, recruited allies from all quarters, and had common cause with [Moslem powers]."* [3]

RESUSCITATING

As the outbreak of war between Iraq and the US led forces drew closer, it was France's President Jacques Chirac who emerged TO RESUSCITATE the role of Francis I, THE GREAT KING OF ANGOULÊME: as, indeed, one had come to expect. Like this King, Chirac was the ruler of France at the time war began. And, whereas Francis I

503

had once opposed the Holy Roman Emperor Charles V, leader of all Christendom, Jacques Chirac opposed President George Bush, leader of the most powerful nation in the world, and the chief spokesman for the west. Whereas Francis I had allied himself with leaders from *'all quarters'*, even to the extent of finding *'common cause'* with Turkey, a Moslem nation: President Chirac likewise recruited support from many countries, even enjoying support from Moslem nations .

> *There's no doubt that the French president is going down a storm at home . . . Chirac's determination to halt (or at least delay) Washington's march to war may have made him a hero in the Arab world, pretty popular in Africa and something of a wow even in Asia, but it is doing untold damage to Franco-US [relations] . . . encouraged by the popular support for his stance, and the backing of such heavyweights as Germany, Russia and China, Chirac is now prepared to ignore even the US argument that if Paris fails to fall in with the American line, it will be the UN, the very source of France's veto – wielding influence – that suffers most. [4]*

FORTIFICATION DISPLAY

On Tuesday 18 *March* 2003, less than two weeks after this report on President Chirac's stand against the America's foreign policy, the final part of this prophecy began. *"In a televised address effectively amounting to a declaration of war, the US president, George Bush, gives President Saddam and his sons 48-hours to leave Iraq or face war 'at a time of our choosing'. He warns Iraqi troops not to fight for a 'dying regime'."*
The third war in the Persian Gulf, in a little more than twenty years, was about to commence.

> *19 March: Military hostilities start when US forces bomb sites near Baghdad University where Saddam Hussein and his sons are believed to be sleeping. 20-21 March: Ground war begins when thousands of American and British troops cross the Kuwait-Iraq border . . . Night of 21 March: Baghdad is ablaze after a massive bombing campaign titled Operation Shock and Awe is launched on the city.*

Fighting continued in the fortified regions of Iraq at Najaf, Nasiriyah, Basra, Tikrit and Baghdad, with the Fedayeen proving very effective. Baghdad was regularly lit by massive air strikes. After three weeks, and believing that his goal had been achieved, President Bush claimed the war was won. He was manifestly mistaken. For the remainder of 2003, and thereafter, to the time of writing, 2009, the killing has continued – *"Across central Iraq, there is an exodus of people fleeing for their lives as sectarian assassins and death squads hunt them down. At ground level Iraq is disintegrating as ethnic cleansing takes hold on a massive scale."* [5] Every day some new outrage takes the death toll higher.

> *According to new estimates by the highly respected School of Public Health in Johns Hopkins University. 655,000 Iraqi men, women and children have died as a result of the war in 2003 and the subsequent violence. . . . We must add to this appalling Iraqi figure the 2,798 American servicemen killed so far and more than 20,000 wounded or sick; and 119 British killed; plus some 4,000 evacuated from Iraq as wounded or sick.* [6]

The figures in this report have long since been overtaken.

AFTERWARDS MARS REIGNING THROUGH GOOD FORTUNE

Nostradamus's choice of words, as always, is important. The *good fortune* enjoyed by *Mars* the god of war existed because this conflict was initiated by the richest and most powerful nation in the world. To maintain that prestige, America could not be seen to lose the war once it had begun. Consequently, the US has found itself embedded in a difficult situation. Moreover, added to Mars *good fortune* was the employment of the most sophisticated armaments known to man. Iraq presented the perfect opportunity for this weaponry to be tested outside the practice range, and this occurred with devastating results. *Mars* also enjoyed the certainty of war. In ordinary circumstances, where there is a build-up to war, strenuous efforts are made to avoid a conflict. But in the case of Iraq, there was an earnest desire, even impatience on the part of the US administration for the war to begin. The United Nations, which is meant to broker peace agreements and dampen or deflect the need for hostilities, proved powerless to intervene, thus adding to **MARS GOOD FORTUNE**.

The 11th September 2001, marked the day when the world changed. The twin towers of the World Trade Center in New York City, which dominated the Manhattan skyline, were deliberately struck by two airliners, killing many instantly and confining others to a fiery death. The outrage felt by Americans has reverberated through the years, and its implications have been instrumental in reforming national security in many countries. Yet, Nostradamus predicted the entire incident four and a half centuries earlier. He even named the site on which the World Trade Center stood, but used ellipsis to disguise its location.

505

C.X: 49

Iardin du monde aupres de cité neufue,
Dans le chemin des montaignes cauees,
Sera faifi & plongé dans la Cuue,
Beuuant par force eaux foulfre enuenimees.

Garden (State) of the (new) world, close to the new city,
In the path of the hollow mountains,
It will be struck, and plunged into the Bathtub,
By force, consuming to excess, sulphurous streams impregnated with malice.

monde, (homonym & O.Fr.) monde, also nu; cauees, (O.Fr.) cavernes; faifi, (Mod. Fr.)
struck; Cuue, (O.Fr.) open tub, also synonym for bain – bathtub; beuvant, (O.Fr. bevant)
drinking to excess; enuenimees, (O.Fr. envenimer) imprègner de venin.
[Note, the use of ellipsis in the opening line, where the words 'state' and 'new' have
been dropped by Nostradamus to comply with the decasyllabic structure of the verse.
The use of ellipsis is perfectly valid where an omitted word is implied by the context.
Apart from which, its use helps to obfuscate interpretation until the event occurs to
fulfil the prediction. See Afterword, as to why this is necessary.

GARDEN STATE

New Jersey is one of the original 13 States of the USA and
known across the world by its official designation, **THE GARDEN
STATE**.

Abraham Browning of Camden is given credit for giving New Jersey the
nickname the Garden State. According to Alfred Heston's 1926 two-
volume book Jersey Wagon Jaunts, Browning called New Jersey the Gar-
den State while speaking at the Philadelphia Centennial exhibition on
New Jersey Day (August 24, 1876). [1]

OF THE NEW WORLD

The New World is the historic name for the Americas.

The New World is one of the names used for the American continents and
adjacent islands collectively, since the 16th century [the actual century
when Nostradamus wrote this prediction]. The Americas were at that
time new to the Europeans, who previously thought of the world as con-
sisting only of Europe, Asia, and Africa. . . . America is always described
as 'New World'. [2]

CLOSE TO THE NEW CITY

New Jersey, **THE GARDEN STATE OF THE NEW WORLD** is situated **CLOSE TO
THE NEW CITY**; that is, *New York City*. On 11 September 2001, America was struck by a disaster of catastrophic proportions. It not
only brought with it a tragic loss of human life numbering several thousand, but the political repercussions from what happened that day in Lower Manhattan were felt around the world.
Two hijacked airliners crossed New Jersey and impacted, one

after the other, with the twin towers of the World Trade Center.

By studying the flight paths of the two hijacked airliners, it can be established that after leaving Boston bound for Los Angeles, one of the planes deviated from its course north of Albany, and headed south towards New York City. The other aircraft headed in a south-westerly direction, passing well to the south of Albany, and north of New York City. It then turned in a south-south-easterly direction, finally veering northeast, to take it back to New York and the World Trade Center. Both planes passed over New Jersey's air space **IN THE PATH** leading to the giant twin towers.

There is, as can happen with Nostradamus, a second meaning attached to 'the path'. **PATH** was the acronym given to the Port Authority Trans-Hudson Corporation, which was instrumental in the construction of the World Trade Center.[4] This association between the WTC and the PATH Corporation therefore serves as an added connection between the two.

The phrase, *hollow mountains*, is actually very apt when describing the two towers of the World Trade Center. By referring to them in this way, Nostradamus correctly predicted not only the mountainous nature of these skyscrapers, but also their cavernous structure. Each tower rose to *'a height of 417 metres'*. And with their interior designed in the form of interconnecting rooms and office suites, so that: *"Office spaces will have no interior columns:"*[5] the overall effect was both open and spacious.

The first attack on the World Trade Center came at 8.48 AM, *"when American Airlines flight 11, bound from Boston to Los Angeles and carrying 92 people, flew into the World Trade Centre's north tower. It punched a gaping hole and set off a firestorm that soon consumed the top third of the tower."*[6]

Within minutes, and while people were still gaping in disbelief in the streets below, *"a second plane, a United Airlines Boeing-707, carrying 56 passengers and nine crew and also heading for Los Angeles from Boston, plunged into the other tower, sending flames blasting out of the other side."*[7]

With a great number of people trapped in the upper floors of the two buildings, cut off by flames, and unable to exit the stricken towers in time, the next part of the tragedy unfolded.

AND PLUNGED INTO THE BATHTUB

"[B]oth towers, where thousands of business people and city employees worked, collapsed devastating the New York City skyline." [8] Together, one after the other, the towers had collapsed **AND PLUNGED INTO THE BATHTUB** below. In the days and weeks that followed this heinous deed: *"108,342 truckloads of debris were removed from the site before the bathtub was cleared."* [9]

More than four and a half centuries after this prophecy was written, the surround to the World Trade Center was given the name predicted by Nostradamus – **THE BATHTUB**.

> *The World Trade Centre straddled the border between solid ground and late less stable additions. A reinforced enclosure had to be built around the foundations to secure the buildings and stop flooding. This became known as the bathtub.* [10]

And again: *"The bathtub, built along the western side of the World Trade Centre site is five stories deep, containing a subway tunnel, water, gas and utility lines."* [11] It was bordered by Vesey Street, West Street and Liberty Street. It is also of particular note that Nostradamus has given the word 'Cuve' a capital letter; this indicates that a name was intended to be understood by it.

THROUGH FORCE, CONSUMING TO EXCESS A SULPHUROUS STREAM

THE FORCE of the impact caused both planes to disintegrate. This led the towers **TO CONSUME** the full load of aircraft diesel carried in the shattered fuel tanks. Both flights *"were fully loaded with fuel. Security experts believe that this may have been part of the plan of attack, as the fuel would guarantee a much larger and more extensive explosion than would have otherwise happened."* Since diesel was not a word that existed in Nostradamus's sixteenth-century vocabulary, he has described the fuel by appearance, using the closest description known to him. His choice of a **SULPHUROUS STREAM** is particularly apposite, because sulphur can be described by the same descriptive terms as diesel: both being *'fluid', 'yellowish', 'pungent', 'fusible'* and *'inflammable'*. The fuel, having been instantly **CONSUMED**, ignited upon impact, causing a raging inferno to engulf the upper regions of the towers. The **EXCESS** of burning material further weakened the already impaired structure of the buildings, and led to both towers collapsing, causing them to *plunge into the Bathtub* below. *"It was*

the fire that killed the buildings – nothing on Earth could survive those tempera-
tures with that amount of fuel burning."[12]

IMPREGNATED WITH MALICE

Whatever else may be said, the oracle has unequivocally identified, with the most apposite words, the intense hatred felt
against America by the assailants who planned and executed
this terrible act. It involved not only the hijacking of two passenger aircraft, but a great many months of training in order to pilot
these planes. And when that was accomplished, their final act
was to commit suicide by **IMPREGNATING THEIR MALICE** into the aircraft
they used as missiles. For upon striking their target, they released **THE SULPHUROUS STREAM** of diesel fuel that was to ignite and
bring the towers crashing to the ground. The perpetration of this
disaster not only took the lives of those whose great misfortune
it was to be passengers on both aircraft, but also several thousand other people working in the towers at the time they were
struck.

Nostradamus once again turns to Iraq for this next oracle,
which also completes the fulfilment of his prophecies up to the
present time (October 2009).

C.III: 61

La grande bande & fecte crucigere
Se dreſſera en Meſopotemamie:
Du proche fleuue compaignie legiere
Que telle loy tiendra par ennemie.

The great company of soldiers, also torture bringing faction,
Will stand upright in Mesopotamia (Iraq):
Adjoining the river, the company diminishing the charges,
When such practice will hold, by reason of the enemy.

bande, (O.Fr.) company of soldiers; secte, (O.Fr.) faction, (most commonly of bad opinion); se dresser (O.Fr.) standing erect; legiere, (O.Fr.) diminuer les charges; crucigere,
(hybrid) cruci + gere = cruci (Latin) cruci/are, to torture, + gerere (Latin) to bring; loy,
(O.Fr.) coutume.

THE GREAT COMPANY OF SOLDIERS

The second invasion of Iraq in 2003 brought **A GREAT COMPANY OF**
SOLDIERS into Baghdad, led by the US coalition force.

The 2003 invasion of Iraq, from March 20 to May 1, 2003, was spear-
headed by the United States, backed by British forces and smaller contin-
gents from Australia, Spain, Poland and Denmark. Four countries partici-
pated with troops during the initial invasion phase, which lasted from

March 20 to May 1. These were the United States (248,000), United Kingdom (45,000), Australia (2,000), and Poland (194). . . . In preparation for the invasion, 100,000 U.S. troops were assembled in Kuwait by February 18. The United States supplied the vast majority of the invading forces, but also received support from Kurdish troops in northern Iraq. [1]

ALSO TORTURE BRINGING FACTION

By the following year, accounts began to emerge that the US army was practising torture against Iraqi captives: particularly those held in the Abu Ghraib prison. These were acts specifically carried out by personnel of the 372nd Military Police Company.

New photos and videos revealed by the Pentagon to lawmakers in a private viewing on the 12th of May showed attack dogs snarling at prisoners, Iraqi women forced to expose their breasts, and naked prisoners forced to have sex with each other, the lawmakers revealed.

Another statement from a guard who kept a video diary of what was happening inside the prison, *"recounts having venomous snakes bite the prisoners, sometimes resulting in death, throwing stones at the prisoners, and prisoners being shot for minor misbehavior."* Pictures also appeared on televisions around the world showing *"A hooded and wired Iraqi prisoner, believed to be Satar Jabar, who reportedly was told that he would be electrocuted if he fell off the box."* A list of the different abuses and tortures practiced at Abu Ghraib, and published in the New York Times (12 January 2005), included: urinating on detainees; forcefully jumping on a detainees' limbs wounded by gunfire; beating wounded limbs with a metal baton; pouring phosphoric acid on detainees; sodomizing detainees with a baton; tying ropes to detainees' legs or penises, and dragging them across the floor. [2]

The US also operated a programme called *"Extraordinary rendition, which involves transferring suspects to a third country where there is no prohibition on the use of torture during interrogation."* [3]

In a lengthy statement to parliament, Defence Secretary John Hutton confirmed that Britain handed over two suspects captured in Iraq in 2004 to U.S. custody and that they were subsequently transferred to Afghanistan, breaching U.S.-British agreements. The Ministry of Defence has been repeatedly asked over the past five years about its involvement in rendition, the unlawful transfer of suspects to a third country, and consistently denied it played any role in the U.S.-administered programme. [4]

The use of water-boarding was reported to have been a popular method of extracting information. This was practised by the Spanish Inquisition during the sixteenth-century, and involved the partial drowning of the victim, followed by resuscitation, and then repeated in a continued sequence until the required information was extracted.

WILL STAND ERECT IN MESOPOTAMIA - IRAQ

Despite this evidence of torture, and repeated accusations that the war in Iraq was illegal –

> *Former Vice President Dick Cheney said in his first television interview since leaving office that the Iraq invasion was "worth doing" and the U.S. succeeded with its goals . . . Cheney said on CNN's "State of the Union with John King": "We have succeeded in creating, in the heart of the Middle East, a democratically governed Iraq. And that's a big deal. And that is, in fact, what we set out to do." . . . Cheney said. "But I would ask people in the press to take an honest look at the circumstances in Iraq today and how far we've come – the defeat of al Qaeda in Iraq, the writing of that democratic constitution, a series of elections that involve power sharing among all the various groups, the end of sectarian violence."* [5]

MESOPOTAMIA is a name from the Greek language, equivalent to *the land between two rivers*. It is the ancient name of modern-day Iraq, through which the Rivers Euphrates and Tigris flow.

ADJOINING THE RIVER

The *River* Tigris actually flows through Baghdad. Because of the danger inside the city from abductions, murder and suicide bombers, which even six years after the war began, continues to occur at frequent intervals, the US administration has created a *'green zone'* ADJOINING THE RIVER, from where it operates and houses its staff.

> *The International Zone (formerly known as the Green Zone) is the heavily guarded diplomatic/government area of closed-off streets in central Baghdad where US occupation authorities live and work. The Green Zone in the central city includes the main palaces of former President Saddam Hussein. The area houses the civilian ruling authority run by the Americans and British and the offices of major US consulting companies.* [6]

THE COMPANY DIMINISHING THE CHARGES

In response to the list of tortures that had been practised upon prisoners held by the US, *"former Justice Department counsel John Yoo says that though he doesn't think the Geneva Conventions covered the prisoners at Abu Ghraib, he believes the soldiers and their commanding officers felt the interrogation techniques used fell within the Geneva Conventions."* A similar diminution of the charges was made by the Vice President Dick Cheney, who *"according to more than two dozen current and former officials, created a distinction between forbidden 'torture' and the use of 'cruel, inhuman or degrading' methods of questioning which they advanced as permissible."* Defense Secretary Donald Rumsfeld refused to acknowledge that US soldiers had engaged in torture. He stated: *"What has been charged so far is abuse, which I believe technically is different from torture. I'm not going to address the 'torture' word."* [7]

WHEN SUCH PRACTICE WILL HOLD, BY REASON OF THE ENEMY

Nostradamus concludes by predicting that THE PRACTICE OF TORTURE WILL HOLD by those using it, and it will be conducted FOR THE REASON OF uncovering terrorist plots planned by THE ENEMY against western civilization. Thus, when the UK Ministry of Defence was asked about the practice of transporting prisoners to other countries, a spokesperson replied: *"there was nothing illegal about Britain's involvement in the rendition process."* (Swissinfo.ch)

On 5 December 2005, The US Secretary of State, Condoleezza Rice stated: *"Rendition is a vital tool in combating trans-national terrorism. Its use is not unique to the United States, or to the current administration... [However] the United States does not permit, tolerate or condone torture under any circumstances."* [8]

Yet, under the same administration, outgoing Vice President Dick Cheney admitted:

> *"I supported it," he said regarding the practice known as "waterboarding," a form of simulated drowning. . . . I was aware of the program, certainly, and involved in helping get the process cleared, as the agency in effect came in and wanted to know what they could and couldn't do," Cheney said. "And they talked to me, as well as others, to explain what they wanted to do. And I supported it."*
>
> *He added: "It's been a remarkably successful effort, and I think the results speak for themselves."* [9]

In April 2009, President Obama published email correspondence sent to the C.I.A. specifying the different tortures that were deemed acceptable, because of the perceived threat to the nation. These included *"sleep deprivation for up to 11 days, forced nudity [while suspended from chains] and stress positions such as water-boarding."*

The methods of torture also included male and female rape. Despite the illegality of these operations, the president confirmed there would be no charges brought against those responsible. Former CIA chief, Michael Hayden claimed: *"The use of these techniques against these terrorists really did make us safer, it really did work."* (Daily Telegraph, 21/4/2009, p.15).

The completion of this prophecy brings the historical fulfilment of Nostradamus's oracles up to date (autumn 2009): although judging from his past record, this statement will soon be redundant. It is therefore to others, with the ability to unravel those I have omitted and unite them with the larger number of quatrains that remain unresolved, that I gladly hand over the baton. As for the time now approaching, Nostradamus has predicted that his prophecies are about to receive much greater understanding.

C.III: 94

De cinq cens ans plus compte l'on tiendra,
Celuy qu'eftoit l'aornement de fon temps:
Puis à vn coup grande clarté donrra,
Que par ce fiecle les rendra trefcontens.

For five hundred years plus, one will deem him an unlikely tale,
He that was (Notredame), the adornment of his time:
Then, at a stroke, he will give great clarity,
When, by reason of this time, it will render them very contentious.

compte, (O.Fr.) an unlikely tale, or fib; tenir, (O.Fr.) judge, deem; ftoit, (O.Fr.) etait; aornement, (O.Fr. aorner) to adorn, to embellish, hence: aornement, paragram and anagram = aorneme[d]t – Notredame (Nostradamus); que, (O.Fr.) but, except, etc., fiecle, (O.Fr.) le temps présent; trefcontens, (plural O.Fr. + Latinism) tres+conten/do.

N.B. The word 'aornment' appears in both Du Rosne (1557) and Rigaud (1568), but as 'ornement' in Bonhomme (1555). Du Rosne also prints 'on'; Bonhomme prints 'lon' and Rigaud 'l'on'.

FOR FIVE HUNDRED YEARS PLUS, ONE WILL DEEM HIM AN UNLIKELY TALE

Nostradamus was born near to midday on Thursday 14 December 1503 (O.S.). Since the publication of his prophecies, stories of incidents that took place during his lifetime have frequently been recounted. In fact, to celebrate the fifth centenary of the seer's birth, several major biographies were published between 2003 and 2004.[1] This, in itself, confirms the predicted **FIVE HUNDRED YEARS** that **MEN WILL DEEM HIM** to be **AN UNLIKELY TALE.** The additional **PLUS** allows for a few extra years to be added to the 500. In which case, 1503 plus 500 together with an additional few years suggests that the fulfilment of this prophecy is due any time now.

HE THAT WAS NOTREDAME, THE ADORNMENT OF HIS TIME

Soon after publication of *Les Prophéties:* —

> *. . . the repute of Nostradamus grew . . . until it came to the ears of Queen Catherine de Medici and Henry II., . . . In the following year, 1556, they sent for him to attend the Court in Paris: . . . The Lord Constable Montmorency attended him at his inn, and presented him to the king in person. The king showed him high favour, and ordered him to be lodged at the palace of the Cardinal de Bourbon, Archbishop of Sens, during his stay in the capital.*

While at Court, his biographer claims he was *"loaded with honours and consulted on high matters (de choses importantes)."* Another biographer, Jean Aimes Chavigny remarked *"that those who came to France sought Nostradamus as the only thing to be seen there."*[2]

THEN, AT A STROKE, HE WILL GIVE GREAT CLARITY

Some few years after the 500th anniversary of Nostradamus's birth, a sudden occurrence will make manifest the meaning of his prophecies. It is this that WILL GIVE GREAT CLARITY to their content, thereby removing the mist of obscurity that has hitherto clouded their meaning. AT A STROKE, enough explanation will be provided, in a manner sufficiently appealing, to persuade most people that his oracles were genuine visions of the future.

WHEN, BY REASON OF THIS TIME, IT WILL RENDER THEM VERY CONTENTIOUS

When Nostradamus's success as a true diviner of the future becomes widely known, then, and thereafter, his prophecies will be considered VERY CONTENTIOUS. It is not difficult to see why this should be. World opinion in western culture, especially at THIS PRESENT TIME, is dominated by science. God, prophecy, and the paranormal, fall outside the range of divine revelation. For those who have replaced God by science, evidence that the scientific method has not the requisite means to pronounce upon everything that occurs in the universe will be unwelcome. Arguments are likely to abound in attempts to restore the sciences to their previous pinnacle of ultimate authority. However, it is noteworthy that Nostradamus says that *contention* will be for *the present time*, thus implying that doubt and dispute will eventually be incorporated into a wider awareness of reality.

APPENDIX

Nostradamus began his prophecies with two verses that partly describe the means by which he arrived at his predictions. In the two letters that preface *Les Prophéties* Nostradamus has enlarged upon his method of foretelling future events. Interestingly, both verses appear to refer to the same method that was witnessed by visitors at Didyma and Delphi.

> *The sibyl at Delphi received the god* . . . . *sitting on a brazen seat about one metre high in the adyton [inner shrine], dedicated to the god, and where she was exposed to the divine influx, whence she was irradiate with a divine light.* . . . *the prophetess of Branchus [the adopted son of Apollo]* . . . . *holds in her hand a rod bestowed by some deity, or moistens her feet or the hem of her garment with water, or inhales the vapour of water, and by these means is filled with divine illumination, and, having obtained the deity, she prophesies. By these practices she adapts herself to the god, whom she receives from without.* [Quoted from Marsilius Ficinus' translation of Iamblicus' De Mysteriis Ægyptiorum - 1607; English translation by Charles A. Ward].

Compare this with the account given by Nostradamus.

C.I: 1

ESTANT affis de nuit fecret eftude,
Seul repoufé fus la felle d'ærain:
Flambe exigue fortant de folitude
Fait proferer qui n'eft à croire vain.

Being seated at night, a secret period of preparation,
Alone, reposed on high, the stool of bronze;
A flame briefly emerging from solitude,
Makes uttering what is not vain to believe.

C.I: 2

La verge en main mife au millieu de BRANCHES,
De l'onde il moulle & le limbe & le pied.
Vn peur & voix fremiffent par les manches,
Splendeur divine. Le divin prés s'affied.

I had taken the wand in hand at the midst of the branches (BRANCHOS),
Holm-oak wet from the water & the hem & the foot,
An apprehension & voice, quivering by the handles,
Divine radiance. The divinity settles itself close by.

Mife (past historic – je mise); eftude, (O.Fr.) a period of preparation; fus, (O.Fr.) en haut; ærain, (Latinism) æratus; exigue, (Latinism) exigu/us; Branches (paragram) Branchos; moulle = mouille; limbe, (Latinism) limb/us; il, (Latinism) il/ex; divin, (O.Fr.) augur.

This ritualistic use of water, at first glance, appears to rely heavily upon ancient and medieval superstitions. But in the modern scientific age, water has come under fresh scrutiny. The claim by Masaru Emoto that it can respond to human emotions, or that it may in some unknown way possess memory (*The Quantum Elixir – New Scientist*; 8 April 2006 p.32) would certainly find resonance in the beliefs of Nostradamus and Iamblicus. Although, whether these attributes, if indeed they exist, can be likened to water divining, which depends upon the personality of the practitioner, is unclear.

Prophesying from a trance-like state, called *enthousiasmos* (literally god-withinness), was first practised at the Temple of Apollo Branchidae at Didyma. The name Branchidae referred to the family of priests and priestesses who served at the shrine. *Branchos* was its first priest, and was so beloved by Apollo that he was given oracular powers. At one time, during the Hellenistic period, the Oracle of Apollo at Didyma in western Turkey, dating back to the 8th century BC, was the most renowned in the ancient world, surpassing even the Oracle at Delphi. Croesus included it for the test he gave to the seven foremost oracles, and made several donations to it. Both Seleucas I and Trajan consulted this Oracle, and both were foretold they would rise to power. It was also at Didyma that those consulting the Oracle were given a copy of the response to their question, written in verse. The similarity all this has with Nostradamus, particularly his admission of having uttered his prophecies, runs parallel to what took place at Didyma.

The Delphic Oracle, which flourished from about the 8th century BC until approximately 363 AD, fell into disuse when all ancient forms of worship were banned by the emperor Theodore the Great. In its time, it had attracted many of the greatest minds in antiquity; among these were Solon, Heraclitus, Socrates, Plato, Plutarch, and Euripedes. The casual disregard exhibited by many of today's professed intelligentsia for this ancient oracle is in contrast to the importance it once held in the minds of those named above.

The Delphic Oracle insisted upon the responsibility individuals had for their own actions. This would explain the answers it gave to the questions put to it, which were delivered in riddles. They were obscure, but usually with a metaphorical meaning couched in the language of religious mystery. They were intended as signs: – a view confirmed by Heraclitus – each utterance requiring an interpreter: a priest who was pure of mind, and able to explain its meaning. The inner purity of the mediums who were appointed to make contact between this world and that of the gods was considered of paramount importance. Initially, great care was taken to ensure that only young virgins of excellent birth were chosen for this function.

The source of the Oracle's wisdom was attributed to a god. The manner in which the god is said to have communicated its message has given rise to considerable curiosity, and remains outside the realm of conventional understanding. The last known reply given at Delphi, about 363 AD, was made to the physician, Oreibasius, who had been sent by the emperor Julian in the hope of reviving the Oracle. It read: *"Tell this to the emperor. The ornamental courtyards have been destroyed and are gone; no longer has Phoebus a lodge, nor a prophetic laurel, nor a talking fountain, and the waters that spoke are dumb."*

There are remarkable similarities between this response and a tract on divination by the 12th century author, Michael Psell: (*De Dæmonibus*, translated by Marsilius Ficinus). *"The diviners take a basin full of water . . . the water seems first to vibrate as if it would omit sounds . . . when the water seems to boil and spill over, a faint voice murmurs words which contain the revelation of future events."* Nostradamus also speaks of a *"voice coming from limbo* [the region where unbaptised infants and the pre-Christian just, were assumed to exist] *by means of the thin flame showing in what direction future events incline."* He enlarges upon this, declaring *"Hidden prophecies come to one by the subtle spirit of fire, sometimes through the understanding being disturbed in contemplating the remotest of stars, while remaining alert. The pronouncements are taken down in writing, without fear, without taint of excess verbiage."* But having drawn attention towards an occult field of activity, the seer then distances himself from it, by urging his son to – *"abhor . . . . execrable magic forbidden by Sacred Scriptures and by the Canons of the Church: except . . . . judicial astrology by which, and by means of divine inspiration, with continual calculations, we have put in writing, our prophecies."*

A study of Nostradamus's terminology, as used in the writing of his prophetic quatrains, appears to suggest that the spirit of foreknowledge was only able to communicate through his existing vocabulary. There is a precedent for this. In the *Acts of the Apostles 2*, the disciples of Jesus were able to 'speak in tongues', much to the considerable amazement of those listening. This has been interpreted as the work of the Holy Spirit. One is therefore invited to understand that the disciples were in some unknown way 'tuned' into the conscious minds of the foreign people they were addressing, and thus able to use their audience's own language to preach to them.

In the case of Nostradamus, there are similarities and differences. He speaks firstly of secretly preparing himself for the night ahead. This could be interpreted as some form of herbal mixture that affected his level of consciousness. Or it could mean that he prepared his mind using a system of meditation. Either way, he then seated himself upon a bronze stool, with a bowl of water close by. He next took a divining rod made from the holm oak – the wood has a mystical reputation in folklore – and after wetting the rod, together with his feet and his limbs, he grasped the handles and attuned himself to his spirit of prophecy. After a short while, the branches of the rod began to quiver, and he came into contact with a spiritual entity that knew and confided in him the momentous events of the future.

It was while in this state of 'contact' that he made notes. These are most likely to have been the quatrains which he wrote down automatically, and without necessarily comprehending their meaning. Two examples spring immediately to mind and which support this theory. The first is the word *Nisse*, which appears in C.X: 60 and C.X: 87, and refers to the town on the Mediterranean coast of France: compare this with the word *Nice* in C.IX: 26, which is old French for *foolish*. Hearing these words pronounced does not indicate which spelling should be adopted, although the context of the communication might. Secondly, the word *unique* is spelt conventionally in both C.VIII: 7 and C.VIII: 32, but in C.VI: 63 Nostradamus spells it *unic* with a Latin base. By doing so, the word provides just the right anagram for Cardinal Richelieu's bishopric at Luçon. Both examples require specialist knowledge of the future to determine which spelling should be used. Hearing the words alone does not provide that specialist knowledge.

By suggesting that Nostradamus was in some way possessed by an entity with perfect knowledge of the future; in other words, by a minor divinity, does allow one to speculate that this entity could only impart knowledge of future events by using the language of Nostradamus's own vocabulary, which implies the use of his brain. This 'possession' would also have allowed the entity to tap into Nostradamus's often bitter humour, for there are an impressive number of examples where this has occurred. Added to which, there is no evidence that Nostradamus ever employed a word that was not in use at that time. Hence, the 'eye of the sea'; a 'fleet that swims underwater'; the 'tree-like thing'; 'a sulphurous stream': these are descriptive of the periscope, a flotilla of submarines, a nuclear explosion and a diesel spillage. In each case, these advances in technological know-how have been described, using only those words available to a 16th century scholar, and never by the names that only later entered common usage.

This explanation appears to fit well with Nostradamus's own, personally, professed account of his ability, for he states:

> . . . my natural instinct . . . [was] inherited from my forbears . . . and this has been adjusted and integrated with long calculations. At the same time, I freed my soul, mind and heart of all care, solicitude and vexation. All of these prerequisites for presaging I achieved in part by means of the brazen tripod.

We therefore have the situation that at some time late in life, Nostradamus discovered how to replicate the methods used by the ancient priesthood, particularly at Didyma and Delphi, for invoking knowledge of the future. And since it is on record that he also believed himself to have been endowed at birth with a gift for spontaneous prophecy, the combination was to have near divine implications. For, like others who have possessed gifts of the spirit, he developed his to the full. And, like others with special gifts, the result of his work has since become a legacy to mankind.

AFTERWORD

Upon concluding this book, it seems appropriate to add a few words in summary. Firstly, the sum total of my research into Nostradamus's claim to have foreseen the future appears fully justified. The Reference section contains approximately 1300 entries, abstracted from verifiable historical records. If these particular referrals are read in date order, the result is a fairly uninterrupted history of most major events that occurred in France and adjacent territories, including others that extend to embrace global events: all within a time slot occurring between the date on which the oracles were first published and the present day. Since every one of the historical accounts has been correlated to a phrase, word or sentence that appears within the prophetic quatrains of Nostradamus, and these correlations are without exception or omission, the conclusion this invites is that the quatrains are truly prophetic. This is unlikely to please everyone. But it is equally true that Galileo's advocacy of the Copernican theory and Huxley's promotion of Darwin's evolution theory also failed to please everyone; both were met with fierce opposition. What therefore beckons us now is yet another revolution in our understanding of the world we inhabit, but one that is more personal, for it includes every person's place within it.

Firstly, however, there is an objection to be answered, and one that has frequently been directed against both Nostradamus and the Delphic Oracle; it is that their pronouncements are capable of a double meaning, so that either way, the prophecy is always correct. When King Croesus of Lydia approached the Oracle at Delphi and asked if he should attack Persia, he received the following reply: *"After crossing the Halys Croesus will destroy a great empire."* Croesus understood this to mean that he would be victorious in the battle he planned. Instead, he was defeated, and the empire he destroyed was his own. Sceptics like to quote this example of a prophecy being fulfilled because of its ambiguity. They never once refer to the rigorous preparations that Croesus undertook in order to test the accuracy of this particular Oracle before consulting it.

Before putting his question to the Delphic Oracle, Croesus sent envoys to seven oracles renowned for their ability to predict the future. At each shrine his representative was required to ask the priestess what King Croesus was doing on the one-hundredth day of this mission. The answers he received are now lost, except, that is, for the response he obtained from Delphi. *"I know the numbers of the sand, and all the measures of the sea. I understand the dumb, and hear the voice that speaks not. A savour has assailed my nostrils of a strong-shelled tortoise boiled with lamb's flesh in bronze, both laid beneath and set above."* Croesus had thought this recipe of boiled lamb and tortoise cooked inside a bronze cauldron the most unlikely combination, and he made it the answer to his test. It was because of the successful reply that he received from Delphi that he chose this Oracle to advise him: rejecting all others.

And herein lays the answer to objections based upon ambiguity. True prophecies are not allowed to change the future. If an event is truly foreseen, then it already exists. As Parmenides pointed out: that which exists cannot then, not exist. Mankind has freedom of choice. If Croesus had been told that his plan for attacking Persia will destroy his own empire, he would not have embarked upon the war. But if his attack upon Persia already existed in the future, as witnessed by the Delphic Oracle, then his avoidance of battle would have ended the universe, because the ramifications across the world would have resulted in an impasse. This is because what Croesus would have required for the future was not to engage in battle, but this did not exist in the future, and so it could not happen. The Oracle's reply simply responded to the need for truth, but without jeopardizing the existence of what the future held. This left Croesus free to interpret the oracle the way he wished. Nostradamus's strategy is based upon a similar procedure. However, this does not mean that what is foreseeable by the intellect cannot bring about a change in what is perceived to lie in the future; it does mean that what actually does lie in the future, cannot be conveyed by paranormal means to someone capable of interfering with it, which is why genuine prophecies are only ever understood after the predicted event has taken place. We shall consider this in greater detail further down.

The conclusion above naturally poses the question as to what type of universe we are living in, if everything within it is predetermined, yet we still have free will. According to Nostradamus it is a universe in which past, present and future coexist. In modern terminology, this is called a *Block Universe*. The block universe is a concept that Hermann Minkowski quickly came to terms with shortly before Albert Einstein also arrived at the same conclusion. Both men derived this concept from the implications arising from *time dilation*: a consequence of Special Relativity. *"The distinction between past, present and future is only an illusion,"* Einstein once remarked, *"even if a stubborn one."*

The block universe, however, is not a favoured concept of the scientific fraternity, because where past and future states of time coexist eternally, nothing moves. Zeno of Elea had long ago provided an argument from the flight of an arrow to arrive at exactly the same conclusion. Common sense, of course, quickly derides this suggestion through the simple act of moving from one place to another. However, common sense is ill-equipped to answer the logical objections that are posed against this naïf response.

The universe is perceived through the senses. This implies that the perceived universe is a mental construct, particular in its precise detail: a detail that takes whatever form relates to the location from which it is perceived (see C.IV: 25 Chapter 4). It is also distinct from the block universe, although it must be from this that the three-dimensional world, perceived by the senses and with its fleeting moments of time, originates.

Every person occupies a 'temporal' place in the block universe: one that extends for the duration of their lifetime, and which is otherwise referred to as 'their time'. When occupying a location at any one point along that lifetime, each point can be associated with a set of coordinates based upon an arbitrary origin. What each person then perceives is uniquely relative to that position. It is the perpetual flow of perceptions along this lifeline at every waking moment, which are conveyed to each percipient and which arrive at the constant speed of light that conjures within the mind an observable, dynamic, three-dimensional, physical world, for which time passes by in a never-ending flow. Thus, as Zeno conjectured, time is an illusion. It has no reality outside of a mind subjected to this moving passage of perceptions.

The difference that would exist between time occurring in a physical universe and time occurring in a universe created by thought can be demonstrated. In a physical universe, time would have to be composed of either an infinite number of instants between any two moments, or a finite number of instants between two temporal points. In either case the paradox of Zeno's arrow precludes both models (see Introduction). Whereas, in a thought created world, it is easy to *imagine* an archer shooting his arrow at a target with a clock nearby, marking off the seconds.

A different example that produces the same conclusion can be demonstrated by referring to the sum of this infinite series: $1 + \frac{1}{2} + \frac{1}{4} + \frac{1}{8} + \ldots$ which, upon addition, can never exceed 2. Although the number of terms in the series can be extended indefinitely by adding an extra term equal to one half of the previous term, the sum of the terms never exceeds 2. Suppose, now, as suggested by James Thomson of M.I.T. that a lamp was designed to switch on and off in time with the terms of this sequence, beginning with 1 minute lit, half a minute unlit, and so on; then as Robin Le Poidevin of Leeds University pointed out, according to this thought experiment, the lamp would never arrive at 2 minutes. But within the universe, the two minutes would pass normally. Time cannot therefore be composed of an infinite succession of instants. This implies time progresses by a finite succession of instants. But motion during any one instant is impossible, for each instant would then be divisible. Hence, time does not exist, other than as a strictly mental experience.

This is bad news for scientific authoritarianism, because science is entirely based upon the model of a three-dimensional world in which time passes in a continual flow of fleeting instants. Yet, in every respect this model is both pragmatic and hands-on. It does, however, fail to encompass the greater truth that all sensible knowledge originates from a block universe: one in which cause and effect are necessarily coeval. Perceived events are therefore contiguous rather than any one being the cause of another. This violates a belief born from the habits of a lifetime, for the mind has learnt from the experience of living within a three-dimensional world that every event is caused by another that precedes it. The passage of time, as it appears to occur within a person's field of vision, suggests that cause and effect are realities. Only if one could obtain direct access to the eternal duration of the block universe, would it then be understood that cause and effect, like the past and future, are united in a single immutable coexistence.

Unsurprisingly, there is no great movement within the scientific fraternity to embrace a block universe. Rather, the opposite is true, with the biological sciences seemingly oblivious of this overriding truth. As author Colin Wilson aptly remarked: *"In the universe of the modern biologist there is no room for clairvoyance, precognition, out-of-the-body experiences, poltergeists, time-slips or synchronicities, and there is certainly no room for life after death."* (Wilson, 2008, p.474). Yet, in a universe where past and future events coexist, time has no actual existence, and where there is no time, there is no change. Death loses its sting, for there can be no actual death: only the perception of death, as it is sadly witnessed within the temporal three-dimensional world perceived through the senses. The percipient's conscious mind cannot be the object of its own perception: hence, its survival of bodily death is experienced, presumably as *'an extraction'*, as described by Nostradamus in C.II: 13.

Does the evidence for prophecy provided by Nostradamus prove the existence of God? In the ancient world, the Oracles were believed to be a medium between this world and the gods. Apollo was the godhead worshipped at Delphi. In the Holy Land the biblical prophets were judged for their genuine calling by the truth of their pronouncements (*Deuteronomy 18:21*). Only God could know the future in detail. Consequently, if what a prophet foretold proved to be reliable, then it was a sign of his relationship with the Divinity, and he was to be listened to, although the Bible records that these prophets were often not obeyed. Where does Nostradamus fit into the scheme of things? He was neither a shrine to be worshipped, as at Delphi, nor was he a prophet in the biblical sense of being a teacher inspired by

God. Neither was his prophetic message a gift to help mankind avoid the calamities he foretold. The one benefit that does arise from his prophecies is that it proves that each person's future, and the future beyond that, exists complete in every detail. This has huge implications for the type of universe in which it can occur. As Professor G. J. Whitrow, former President of the International Society for the Study of Time, confirmed: *"Genuine precognition . . . might be possible if we inhabited a block universe in which . . . physical events do not suddenly occur but are there waiting for us to experience them."* (Whitrow, *The Nature of Time*, 1972, pp.142-3). What sort of universe is it, then, which supports physical objects in a four-dimensional setting? It is clearly not the three-dimensional one familiar to us at each fleeting moment. But, then, what is the relationship between a block universe and the three-dimensional field of vision in which we live and move and have our present being?

Let us consider the possibility that God exists. That is to say, the block universe exists in the Mind of God as a created structure of His thought. For, even if He created this universe as a physical entity, as scientists conceive it, He would have modelled it upon His thought. This then implies that mankind receives a flow of information relating to his or her location within this God-given universe. And it is from this flow of information that a mental construction of the world at every instant takes form within each person's mind. Consequently, as George Berkeley maintained in his *Principles of Human Knowledge* (1710), the world we know and live in, exists *because* it is perceived into existence. When it is not being perceived, it continues to exist within the Mind of God as part of His Creation. This explanation is remarkably close to that stated in quantum theory. For there we learn that objects only take form at the point of observation. When unobserved, an object exists in all possible states simultaneously, but as a wave function. A person's act of making a conscious observation collapses this wave function and it transmutes into a part of the observed world. Hence, there must be a connection between the observing mind and the object in its original state. But that is also the case for the perceiving mind and objects that have their origin within the mind of God. In both cases, objects of sense only exist when the act of perception occurs.

Everything we perceive is derived from data that has been processed through a subconscious, mental operation, and then consciously cognised. Therefore, since the world delivered to our senses has a mental existence, its origin must also have a mental existence, for that is the rational conclusion to draw. Hence, the world in its original state continues to exist because it is sustained by constantly being held in the mind of God. It is from this that one returns to the *being* of God as the efficient cause for creating and sustaining the universe. This argument, however, ceases to be circular because the world perceived through the senses is, by empirical demonstration, a mental construct.

Consider, for example, you own self in company with another. Now imagine perceiving yourself through the eyes of your companion. Mentally, you will now be observing your biological body at a distance. By means of various optical instruments, themselves objects of perception, your biological body can be seen to change shape or size, even relocate if reversal prisms were used. For that is how your companion would see you under the same circumstances. Yet, you know from personal experience that your body has not undergone these perceived changes. The conclusion from this is that the world perceived by each individual is a private construction existing in the mind, but generated from a shared origin, which can be posited to exist in a block universe sustained by God.

The theory that the mind's mental constructs are superimposed upon physical originals is an illogical concept, and one defeated by the example given above, wherein the varied perceptions of a person's body might be seen through the eyes of another to change form or even location, when no such change has taken place. And, were that not enough, each celestial body that is perceived to occupy a location where, by calculation, it can no longer exist, most certainly contradicts the theory of the mind superimposing its mental constructs onto external bodies. Not only that, but were it even to be considered, one would need to enquire how these external projections outside of the mind could then be known. Quite simply, the enquiry into perception would have gone round in a circle, and ended where it must again begin.

This implies that space, outside of any mind perceiving the universe, is non-existent as far as anyone is aware. Space is implied by an awareness of distance, and distance, by appearance, is just as obvious when viewed in a mirror as when seen otherwise. Distance is measured by the time that elapses for the motion of a perceived object of perception to journey from one point to another. But with time and space being interchangeable, the time taken to cover distance becomes translated as space. Let it be supposed that a person was confined to observing the world in a mirror. And, unbeknown to the observer, the reflected images were orchestrated by a computer. That person would have as much reason to believe in the existence of space as any astronomer, for there is nothing that can be perceived in the world that is not equally perceptible in a mirror.

The mind is also able to replicate this ability by interpreting distance as space within other types of perception; for example, dreams and hallucinations; these having a decidedly mental basis, but which occur at different levels of consciousness. The higher level of consciousness provides consistency to the perceived world we occupy; it also provides a dominant model from which perceptions at a lower level of consciousness become personal creations. The difference between the two: the world of sense and that of illusion is the difference between a divine Creation and an earthly one. The divine Creation, as increasingly revealed by knowledge from enquiry, is one of infinite variety offering a shared experience to all mankind, yet bound together by underlying and undeviating 'laws'. The earthly copies are superficial, transient, and personal to each individual.

With this said: why does our daily experience appear to be that of living in a three-dimensional world of material objects? The answer is surprisingly simple. The world we perceive is created in the mind at a subconscious level from data received externally. So far, this statement does not disagree with the account provided by science. Consequently, the data could come from God, or it could come from material objects existing externally in space. How can we determine which is true? If the world we perceive is composed from data conveyed by God, then there are no material archetypes. Alternatively, if the world we perceive is composed of data conveyed from material objects existing externally in space, then these material objects must exist independently of the objects perceived in the mind. Where are they? The truth is that one is compelled to locate them as being united with the visual images created by the subconscious mind. But this is no more possible than it is to locate material objects with the buildings, rivers, people, etc., that are seen while dreaming. What exists in the mind cannot incorporate or directly unite with what is not in the mind. The locations would be separate.

This naturally raises the question: why does a world created by the mind appear to be composed of material objects, shared with other people, so as to suggest that we are all living together in a material universe? The answer is because the Creation exists in the mind of God as a block universe. It therefore contains all the necessary transferable data, which when systematically conveyed to the minds of those dwelling within it, causes the subconscious mind to create a three-dimensional world in which, what is interpreted, is sensed sequentially: hence, temporally.

As in a cinema, where a succession of still pictures occurs at such speed, that the mind perceives the result as a continuous movement of action: so, too, with information received from the block universe. For here, the flow of information is even more rapid. This causes the mind to become inured by experiences learnt in infancy, to accept this constant inflow of information as a stream of spatial objects. But because these experiences are formed subconsciously, the conscious mind remains unaware of what has taken place, and so, what appear to be physical objects existing in space and governed by natural laws, comes naturally to be accepted and acted upon in the spirit of naïve realism.

Let those who doubt look about themselves. As dissenters, they will see around them many material objects. Do these exist in the mind, or in the world apart from the mind? The scientist answers, "Both". Then how do the two become united? It is impossible to give an answer without contradicting one's self. Now look at these same objects through a lens or a prism. These so-called material objects will have changed shape, even possibly their location relative to the percipient: yet the appearance of each object's materiality will not have changed. The table is just as hard, just as wooden, even though a lens has magnified its appearance, and the same may be said of it were it to be viewed through a reversal prism. Indeed, one could even learn from new experiences to live in a world perceived permanently through a lens or reversal prism. The conclusions of the percipient, regarding the material nature of the world through their senses and in their experience, would not differ from that of another percipient who viewed their habitat without a visual attachment. For there is nothing inside the skull that stares out onto a material world; yet the world in which we live and move appears as though it were so. Proof, surely, that the material nature of an object is formed mentally, by information processed subconsciously, and which is transmitted to the conscious part of the mind to be perceived as the physical world of the senses.

The fact is that in all such circumstances, objects of sense perception are shared by other percipients and perceived to exist within the same environment. This gives each object, and the environment it shares with percipients, a material status. But it is equally clear that as mental objects of sense perception, neither they nor their environment can exist when they are not perceived. The logical conclusion to draw is that the origin of these mental objects together with their environment must continue to exist when there is no one in the world to perceive them. It is a logical conclusion because a mental object of sense can be like nothing but another mental object of sense, therefore requiring a mind to sustain it. One set of objects, we know, exists as products of a percipient's mind: the other, its source, must therefore exist in the mind of God, in whom the origin of all sensory information is sustained, and by whom it is channelled to each percipient through the agency of perceived images.

Some, however, have considered the universe to be a computer program. John Wheeler, who conducted Richard Feynmann's postgraduate studies, concluded that *"all physical reality could be reduced to pure information."* This idea was the theme of a film (*The Matrix*) in which aliens *'reduced reality to a computer program'* in which vast numbers of the population unknowingly took part, while their bodies slept. Oxford professor, Nick Bostrom, has expanded on this idea in a recent philosophical journal and on his website, providing reasons why it may actually be true. In which case, the arguments for a block universe as the source of information would apply to the alien race, with the same conclusions being just as applicable.

In this respect, the timeline of prophecies by Nostradamus, as validated by recorded history, emerge as further evidence. This is because the information that necessarily exists to compose a prophecy, so that the event may be recognised in the future, is essentially the same as the information being conveyed at the time of its fulfilment. Hence, this sensible information already existed before it was conveyed to the minds of those perceiving the prophecy's fulfilment. This can be explained by information governing objects of sense existing in the Mind of God.

To see the world in its eternity has the distinct advantage of accepting prophetic knowledge as a reality, since the timeless existence of God explains the presence of the past and the future in a coexisting and contiguous relationship. It also explains the laws of nature as the consistency of divine thought, and provides an omnipotent creator to give the necessary dynamic to the flow of perceptions in an otherwise static universe. Other advantages are that it affords a constructive stimulus to speculations about the paranormal; and it would also explain why some surgical transplants appear to retain strong elements of the personality that donated them, for in a block universe they are still connected to the body from which they were taken. All told, these are positive advantages for subscribing to a block universe.

Furthermore, the model avoids the physical world becoming a barrier to the spiritual world, thus eliminating conflict between science and religion. The work of scientists continues as before, unimpeded, bar new ethical constraints. *"In their professional lives most physicists accept without question the concept of the timescape, but away from work they act like everybody else, basing their thoughts and actions on the assumption of a moving present moment."* (Paul Davies, 1995, p.76).

There is one other important aspect to the existence of a block universe being the Creation of God: it is the paradox between predestination and free will. But this seeming contradiction in terms can now be made to disappear, because it is only relevant within a three-dimensional world, wherein time passes in a flow of moments. A block universe created by God implies His omniscience with regard to everything contained in this universe. Whatever has been created, has been created by His thought alone, this implies His omniscience, for nothing can have been created within this universe without His thought. This, in turn, implies that the lifeline of every living being, from conception to death, has also been created by His thought, in order to occupy a place within His Creation.

To recapitulate, it is the flow of perceptions attendant to each lifeline within a block universe that gives perceived presence and reality to the three-dimensional world in which people live out their lives. But it is also within this three-dimensional world that people reason, think, and make decisions based upon their present situation: knowing that such decisions will affect their future life, and / or the future lives of others. This reasoning and decision-making is called free will.

Again, nothing comes from nothing; consequently, decisions must be based upon circumstances. In other words, each person's nature, nurture and environment combine with their personal freedom, in order to allow them to pursue, or not pursue inclinations that arise from these considerations: suggesting, as they do, the need for decisions. As long as each person remains free to pursue, or not pursue their inclinations, and make decisions accordingly, they will acknowledge their free will, and accept the responsibilities that accompany it.

We can compare this with the loss of freedom, as when someone is prevented from following their inclination, or made to do what they would prefer not to do. Alternatively, we can compare freedom of action with that practised by a group of people, when some choose to do one thing and others, in similar circumstances, elect to take a different course of action.

Essentially, what is occurring within this three-dimensional world is that each person is *proving* God's omniscience within the structure of His Creation by exercising their free will. This requires that the Creation or block universe is precisely synchronised to incorporate within it the decision-making processes of every being that is a part of it. From this, it becomes possible to understand that in the familiar three-dimensional world, as perceived through the senses, the future free will of persons not yet born, and the future consequences arising from the exercise of their free will, is genuine knowledge to the Creator, but prophetic to any seer that is privileged to share in it.

It is in this state of being that the ambiguity of the Delphic Oracle, or Nostradamus, is best understood. Prophecy represents knowledge from the block universe, therefore outside the three-dimensional world we perceive around us. Prophecy may be built into the universe at its conception, in which case the ramifications arising from it will be part of its structure. But, consider the case of Henri III of France. Suppose Nostradamus had written his prophecy of the King's murder by explicitly naming Jacques Clément as the assassin. Were he to have done so, the monk would never have been allowed anywhere near the King, in which case, the course of French history could not have followed the direction created for it within the block universe. Does that mean the universe would then come to an end if knowledge, not contained within its structure, was allowed to interfere with the course of events? It is tempting to scoff at such a suggestion. Yet, the contrivances contained within Nostradamus's oracles to prevent the future from being altered by the free will of those who were to subsequently experience its forthcoming fulfilment, even long after the seer's death when he would have been free from censure, cannot be entirely dismissed.

There is an alternative way to examine the truth of this: exactly how can a block universe continue to perpetuate a three-dimensional world for percipients, if its content no longer coincides with the free will of a person intent upon a course of action different to what has been created? In plain words, how could Henri III have continued to live in his familiar three-dimensional world if he had ordered Clément's arrest on the basis of Nostradamus's semi-divine foresight? The block universe contains the King's death at the hands of Clément on 2 August 1589; beyond that date it no longer contains a continuation of Henri's life. It is an impasse.

To guard against this impasse occurring, it becomes essential that information from the block universe is never allowed to affect the free will of those who would have reason to change what is in their future. For this reason, Nostradamus's prophecies only become clear after the event, when the understanding of what they contain can no longer affect the outcome.

The consideration that arises from this model concerns a worrying fact. All that is abhorrent to mankind exists within the block universe created by God, and exists there with the full knowledge and licence of the Creator. However, it must equally be pointed out that the block universe exists as a Creation, based upon what are termed laws of nature. But in a block universe there are no laws of nature, only the Creator's consistency of purpose. It is only in a three-dimensional world where this consistency of purpose becomes seen as the laws of nature, and the effect these are perceived to have upon the character, nurture and environment of a person in contributing to the decisions they make. Moreover, this decision-making process must also be combined with the interaction each person has with other people who, themselves, are subject to the same decision-making process. Consequently, the three-dimensional world with its fleeting moments of time, when comprehended by the Deity in its entirety, becomes the block universe, and the block universe then becomes the source of what is perceived by individual minds as a three-dimensional world. In this respect, the two worlds are one: united by a common purpose in a timeless creation.

The threatened paradox between free will and preordination is therefore avoided by the existence of an omniscient God. For, once given a finite set of rules governing the creation of a universe, an omniscient being would then be able to comprehend it in its entirety. That outcome is what is deemed to be a *block universe*. Within this Creation are the unanimated creatures in thought form that will experience life within it. The lives they will experience must therefore have been comprehended at the point of Creation, since they have been given a place within this universe. But does this not imply the absence of free will? Not so! Free will is governed by the intellect, and the intellect is governed by the finite rules that have allowed God to comprehend all that exists within His Creation. Thus, the free will of any person within the universe is predictable by an omniscient intelligence.

This does mean the existence of every person's intentions has been integrated as part of the structure of the universe at the time of its creation. Evil is therefore a consequence of the same laws, or consistency of purpose responsible for the universe's existence, having been used by people for reasons injurious to others. God allows this freedom of choice, subject to the rules that govern His Creation, because it is the way of testing each individual. Indeed, Christians will be aware of a phrase in the *Lord's Prayer* which begs God: 'not to put us to the test' ('*Lead us not into temptation*'). Exhortations against evil are still legitimate, however, because change, based upon what occurs within this universe is achievable. Change, based upon intelligence from outside the universe, is neither achievable nor possible.

A potential objection to this scheme of Creation might be that an omniscient God has no need to create such a universe, since He has already comprehended it, and has no need to activate it. This is true, but without this Creation, people would not believe themselves capable of what they do in their lives, and the judgement made against them. By actually experiencing their actions, it can be said that God *proves* to them what they would not otherwise have believed, had they not experienced it for themselves. This borders upon religion, judgement, and life in the after world, which, incidentally, would seem to be vastly more important than the transient life on earth that each person experiences; otherwise there would be little purpose for the Creation. Perhaps the purpose of life in the three-dimensional world *is* to prove to each person the place they have earned for themselves in a post mortem existence.

Finally, there are the sciences, and the consequences from what has been said. From one point of view nothing has changed. But under the surface, matters are likely to be seen differently. One biologist protested that were telepathy possible it would fundamentally alter the structure of science. Another, a philosopher, argued similarly, asserting precognition to be the culprit, since it allowed an effect to become known when its

But consciousness is both outside & inside the universe. so ??? you want to change it. But, if you realize the greater consciousness from inside the bubble, would change it!

cause had yet to take place. As high-profile atheists, the reason for their disquiet was discernible. Having replaced religion with science, and God by the libertarian wishes of the intellectual, they inwardly tremble at the possibility of discovering they have been in error. Yet, observe the contradiction. As advocates of science they proclaim its excellence in having achieved so much progress by the pursuit of knowledge. But then they contradict themselves by deriding and censoring scientific investigations that study psychic abilities, even though these are designed to advance still further an understanding of all that takes place in the world. Why should that be? If sceptics are so certain of their position, what have they to fear? What they do fear, of course, is that scientific methodology will gain acceptance for psychic phenomena, which has ramifications for the survival of the personality after death. Atheists do not prepare their lives for this eventuality, and live accordingly. They are therefore motivated to protect their beliefs against science taking a direction that has the potential of derailing their personally held philosophy: nourished as it is by an inward worship of materialism and the values to be obtained from it

Then again, if science is replacing western religion, is this replacement founded upon secure ground? Consider, for example, the disharmony existing between relativity theory and quantum mechanics. This disunity has enthused scientists to attempt a grand united theory at linking them together. The problem is that when taken to their logical conclusions, both theories arrive at infinity: even a sequence of infinities, through having used zero as a divisor – a mathematical impossibility. Moreover, Einstein contended that *"God does not play dice with the world."* Quantum mechanics implies that He does.

Although both theories have proved hugely successful when describing natural events, so have Nostradamus's prophecies. These are instrumental in dispensing with the need for habitable, parallel universes; they also implicitly reinforce belief that the Goldilocks Zone is the planned work of a benevolent Creator.

Berkeley had insisted that the aim of scientists is to reduce to *'general rules'* the observed phenomena, and make *suppositions*. This, in reality, is what theoretical physicists do by constructing mathematical models of the universe. But to this, it is probable Berkeley would have replied: *"to be of service to reckoning and mathematical demonstrations is one thing; to set forth the nature of things is another."*

This is far from idle comment. The conclusions derived from quantum mechanics are bizarre in the extreme, and a complete departure from formal logic. In a similar vein, one may consider the Ptolemaic system, which, like quantum theory was based upon observation, measurement and mathematics. For centuries it was the accepted model of the heavens, even though it had many eccentricities built into it which, from a practical viewpoint, were quite absurd. But pragmatists ignored these, because the system continued to provide correct answers to the questions posed by astronomers and stargazers. Now it lies abandoned, having outlived its usefulness. Thus, for Berkeley, the Ptolemaic system, like quantum theory, with its weird, irrational implications, would be seen as examples of what he termed *serviceable fictions*. If his assessment was correct, then the immense outpouring of funds, backed by the vast intellectual effort that has gone into exploring further aspects of quantum theory is likely to reach a point when this is either set aside to be replaced by another theory, or worse, it leads to a massive disaster brought about by the theory being pushed beyond its ability to deliver. For the energies involved in experimentation are now so great they could devastate a city the size of Geneva, which is where the Large Hadron Collider is exploring theoretical particles and the origin of the universe. Most worryingly, Nostradamus gave a grim warning to Genevans in C.IX: 94, predicting their extermination caused by an energy outburst far hotter than the Sun.

This warning apart, scientific endeavour in the laboratory remains unchanged by the block universe. What could change is the ethical direction taken by scientists. It is one thing to conduct an experiment based upon the fictional supposition that the world of sense perception is somehow 'united' with imperceptible matter, which exists independently of it being perceived. It is not quite the same thing to conduct experiments knowing that the world of sense originates from a block universe existing in the mind of God, and that the outcome of each experiment existed before the scientist even began experimenting. Science therefore retains its methodology, with its theories intact, and to appearances apt when confined to a three-dimensional universe. But science loses part of its authority when the block universe is understood; then its authority has to be shared with God.

It is therefore remarkable to discover that the Church ignores Nostradamus. In bygone days a person able to foresee what God has ordained would have been revered. Nostradamus was himself a highly religious person: a family man with no taint of dishonour attached to him; added to which, his service to those he attended medically is not disputed. It is therefore difficult to imagine that he would have been accepted for the task he undertook had he been anything other than of good character and devoted to God. His life certainly confirms this and is unblemished by scandal; those who call him a charlatan and his prophecies bogus condemn themselves.

In his own time and until the Enlightenment, his abilities were acknowledged by the kings and queens for whom he predicted. In 1556, shortly after the publication of *Les Prophéties*, he was summoned to Paris *"by the very powerful Henry II, King of France"* [Jean Aimé de Chavigny: Brief Discourse 1589]. On 17 October 1564, Charles IX arrived in Provence and together with his mother Catherine de Medici the Queen-regent, they retired together for a lengthy conference with Nostradamus, which took place in the chamber of his house. The Queen consort of Henri IV paid her visit to Salon in 1600, and on 1 November 1622, it was her son, King Louis XIII, who visited the tomb. Then on 16 January 1660, it became the turn of King Louis XIV, accompanied by the Queen-mother Anne of Austria and Cardinal Mazarin, chief minister of France. These royal personages had seen enough of Nostradamus's predictions to recognize they contained words of truth beyond their understanding. The tomb in which he was buried honoured him with a similar sentiment.

Here rest the bones of the illustrious Michael Nostradamus, alone of all mortals judged worthy to record with his almost divine pen, under the influence of the stars, the future events of the entire world.

This has certainly proved to be the case up until the present time, and upon the evidence provided heretofore, it will no doubt continue to be so for many centuries to come.

REFERENCES

CENTURY ONE

Q. 1   515
Q. 2   515
Q. 3   257
1 French Revolution, *Compton's Encyclopedia 2000: Broderbund*, CD-ROM
2 Christopher Hibbert, *The French Revolution*, 162
3 S. Hopewell, *Europe from Revolution to Dictatorship*, 15; & Franklin L Ford, *Europe 1780-1830*, 119; & Simon Schama, *Citizens*, 646; & Alan Palmer, *Dictionary of Modern History 1789 – 1945*, 122-3
4 Norman Davies, *Europe - A History*, 710
5 Hibbert, 185

Q. 5   229
1 Christopher Hibbert, *The French Revolution*, 124-5
2 Antonia Fraser, *Marie Antoinette*, 317–8
3 ibid 319; & Ian Dunlop, *Marie Antoinette*, 319; & Christopher Hibbert, *The French Revolution*, 128; & J Hearsey, *Marie Antoinette*, 153; & J Haslip, *Marie Antoinette*, 239
4 S K Padover, *Life and Death of Louis XVI*, 266-7; & Simon Schama, *Citizens*, 561
5 Hibbert, 133
6 Schama, 587; & Hibbert, 143

Q. 10   82
1 David L Roper, *Proving Shakespeare*, 16, 198, 428-9
2 H A L Fisher, *A History of Europe Vol. 1*, 574; & H Williamson, *Catherine de' Medici*,
3 R J Knecht, *Catherine de' Medici*, 269
4 ibid 306
5 Leonie Frieda, *Catherine de' Medici*, 382
6 ibid 125–6, 336, 349–50; & Fisher, 580–1, 582
7 Francis Johnston, *Fatima, The Great Sign*, 33

Q. 14   426
1 Jonathan White, *Russia 1905 – 1941*, 9-10; & H A L Fisher, *A History of Europe*, 1317
2 E M Halliday, *Russia In Revolution*, 15
3 ibid 15, 17
4 ibid 24-5
5 Russian Revolution of 1917, *Encyclopædia Britannica 2001*: CD-ROM; & Nicholas II – abdication and death, ibid
6 White, 10
7 Robert K Massie, *Nicholas and Alexandra*, 425, 446, 451, 482
8 Michael T Florinsky, *Russia - A Short History*, 420
9 Fisher, 1288–9; & Robert Service, *A History of Twentieth-Century Russia*, 136

Q. 15   303
1 David Chandler, *The Campaigns of Napoleon*, xxix
2 Alan Palmer, *An Encyclopaedia of Napoleon's Europe*, xxiii
3 ibid 91, 221, 222
4 Catholicism in Revolutionary France, *Encyclopædia Britannica 2001*: CD-ROM; & Modern Christianity, ibid

Q. 16   327
1 Planets, *RedShift*: CD-ROM, Maris Mutimedia Ltd
2 Simon Schama, *Citizens*, 487
3 Christopher Hibbert, *The French Revolution*, 109
4 ibid 109

5 David Chandler, *The Campaigns of Napoleon*, 55, 1123; & Augereau, *Encyclopædia Britannica 2001:* CD-ROM; & Alistair Horne, *Seven Ages of Paris*, 182
6 James Marshall-Cornwall, *Napoleon*, 90
7 'Plague ridden, burdened by wounded, starved'- (Eyewitness accounts: Bernard, Bonaparte's A.D.C. - Raguse VII 121-2); & C Barnett, *Bonaparte*, 64; & Chandler, 241
8 J M Thompson, *Napoleon Bonaparte*, 131-2

Q. 23   *366*
1 Alan Palmer, *Dictionary of Modern History* 1789 – 1945, 302
2 David Chandler, *The Campaigns of Napoleon*, 1064
3 R. Cavendish (ed.) *The Illustrated Encyclopedia of Mythology, Religion and the Unknown*, 297
4 E Cobham Brewer, *The Dictionary of Phrase and Fable*, 744
5 Chandler, 1064, 1089
6 ibid 1061-62
7 ibid 1066-67

Q. 25   *403*
1 Ian Crofton, *Collins Gem Encyclopedia*, 301–2; & Champollion, ibid 195
2 Louis Pasteur, *Encyclopædia Britannica 2001:* CD-ROM
3 ibid
4 *The death of spontaneous generation*, ibid; & Joanna Richardson, *The Young Pasteur*, 126–8; & Piers Compton, *The Genius of Louis Pasteur*, 342–3, 353
5 Metonic cycle, *Encyclopædia Britannica 2001:* CD-ROM
6 René Vallery-Radot, *The Life of Pasteur*, (trans. Mrs. R L Devonshire), 424

Q. 29   *465*
1 John Macdonald, *Great Battles of World War II*, 136-7
2 ibid 138
3 ibid 136-7
4 ibid 137; & Karen Farrington, *Handbook of World War II*, 69
5 Macdonald, 136-7
6 Farrington, 62
7 *Wikipedia* – Atlantic Wall

Q. 30   *325*
1 J M Thompson, *Napoleon Bonaparte*, 134; & Carola Oman, *Napoleon's Viceroy - Eugene de Beauharnais*, 98
2 Jeremy Black and Roy Porter (ed.) *A Dictionary of Eighteenth-Century History*, 1; & Christopher Lloyd, *Sea Fights Under Sail*, 93
3 David Chandler, *The Campaigns of Napoleon*, 245
4 ibid 244, 245; & H A L Fisher, *A History of Europe, vol 2*, 915
5 Thompson, 133; & Kléber, *Encyclopædia Britannica 2001:* CD-ROM
6 Egypt – French occupation and its consequences, ibid
7 Chandler, 303

Q. 32   *356*
1 Elba, *Encyclopædia Britannica 2001:* CD-ROM
2 ibid
3 Denis Richards, *An Illustrated History of Modern Europe, 1789-1974*, 55; and J Marshall-Cornwall, *Napoleon*, 260
4 Elba, *Encyclopædia Britannica 2001:* CD-ROM
5 ibid
6 Marshall-Cornwall, 260

Q.35   23
1 R J Knecht, *Catherine de' Medici*, 57; Antonia Fraser, *Mary Queen of Scots*, 117
2 Knecht, 57
3 Fraser, 118. Henri II's armour and gilt embossed helm were displayed at the Tower of London in the early 1970s, and witnessed by the author. Also a suit of armour belonging to Henri II, similarly embossed, was displayed at the Louvre in 2008. The helmet belonging to Charles IX was made of iron and plated with gold. It was made by Pierre

Redon, goldsmith to the Court, and is owned by the Louvre.

4 Fraser, 117-18
5 ibid
6 ibid
7 ibid
   Q. 43   406

1 Alan Palmer, *Dictionary of Modern History 1789-1945*, 259; & Claude Lebédel,
   Chronologie de l'Histoire de France, 22
2 The Eiffel Tower, *Encyclopædia Britannica 2001*: CD-ROM; & Alistair Horne,
   Seven Ages of Paris, 327
3 Paris, Neighbourhood and Sights, *Encyclopædia Britannica 2001*: CD-ROM
4 The Eiffel Tower, ibid; & Brewer, *Dictionary of Phase and Fable*, 998; & Ian Littlewood,
   The Rough Guide Chronicle France, 263
5 The Eiffel Tower, *Encyclopædia Britannica 2001*: CD-ROM
6 ibid
7 Littlewood, 264
   Q. 44   243
1 E N Williams, *Dictionary of English and European History 1485 – 1789*; 135
2 Simon Schama, *Citizens*, 698
3 ibid 633-4; & Christopher Hibbert, *The French Revolution*, 170
4 Schama, 777–8
5 Hibbert, 255–6
   Q. 47   435
1 League of Nations, *Encyclopædia Britannica 2001*: CD-ROM
2 ibid
3 ibid
4 Alan Palmer, *Dictionary of Twentieth-Century History 1900-1982*, 234
5 ibid 383; & 'The United Nations', *Encyclopædia Britannica 2001*: CD-ROM
   Q.48   149
   This quatrain is referred to in Chapter 4.
   Q.49   149
1 'Treaty of Carlowitz', *Encyclopædia Britannica 2001*: CD-ROM; and Ottoman Empire;
   also – Military defeats and the emergence of the Eastern Question.
2 E N Williams, *Dictionary of English and European History 1485-1789*, 190–1
3 ibid 191-3
   Q. 50   401
1 United States, *Encyclopædia Britannica 2001*: CD-ROM
2 Alan Palmer, *Dictionary of Modern History 1789–1945*, 293
3 Thanksgiving Day, *Encyclopædia Britannica 2001*: CD-ROM
4 The United States, ibid
5 The United States at War, ibid
6 Roosevelt – attack on Pearl Harbour, ibid; & History of the United States – The
   Korean War; & The Vietnam War, ibid; & the George Bush Administration, ibid
   Q. 53   223
1 Christopher Hibbert, *The French Revolution*, 111–2
2 ibid 117–8
3 Jeremy Black and Roy Porter (ed.) *A Dictionary of Eighteenth-Century History*, 174;
   & Simon Schama, *Citizens*, 548
4 J N D Kelly, *The Oxford Dictionary of Popes*, 302
5 Schama, 487; & Black and Porter, 46
   Q. 55   486
1 Hussein, Saddam, *Encyclopædia Britannica 2001*: CD-ROM; &
   news.bbc.co.uk/1/hi/world/middle_east/4260420.stm
2 BABYLON, *Compton's Interactive Encyclopedia, 1999*: CD-ROM
3 www.globalsecurity.org/military/world/war/iran-iraq.htm

4 Derrik Mercer (ed.) *20th Century Day by Day*, 1341; & Persian Gulf War, *Encyclopædia Britannica 2001*: CD-ROM; & Bruce W Watson (ed.) *Military Lessons of the Gulf War*, 247

5 Opinion Research Business, January 2008

6 (http://www.u-s-history.com/pages/h2020.html)

7 Wikipedia

8 news.bbc.co.uk/1/hi/world/middle_east/4260420.stm

9 (http://www.u-s-history.com/pages/h2020.html)

10 Wikipedia

11 March 5 1991, Iraq: *20th Century Day By Day*: CD-ROM; & Hussein, Saddam, *Encyclopædia Britannica 2001*: CD-ROM; & Andrew Cockburn and Patrick Cockburn, *Saddam Hussein An American Obsession*, 18

12 The invasion and the war, *Encyclopædia Britannica 2001*: CD-ROM; and Cockburn, 114

13 'Cholera and Typhoid are reported to be spreading', BBC News at Midnight – 12 March 1991; & Cockburn, 130, 132

14 Wikipedia.org/wiki/Iran–Iraq_War_After_the_Islamic_Revolution

Q. 57   261

1 Christopher Hibbert, *The French Revolution*, 146–7

2 Franklin L Ford, *Europe 1780-1830*, 119

3 Hibbert, 189; & S K Padover, *The Life and Death of Louis XVI*, 335

4 Simon Schama, *Citizens*, 630, 730; & Marat, *Encyclopædia Britannica 2001*: CD-ROM

5 Schama, 736–7

6 Padover, 335

7 ibid 82

8 James Laver, *Nostradamus or The Future Foretold*, 155

Q. 60   294

1 John Belcham and Richard Price (ed.) *A Dictionary of Nineteenth-Century History*, 78

2 J M Thompson, *Napoleon Bonaparte*, 93, 135-6, 187-8

3 Stephen Coote, *Napoleon and the Hundred Days*, 186-7; & David Chandler, *The Campaigns of Napleon*, xxix

4 Chandler, 55, 1122–3; & Murat, *Encyclopædia Britannica 2001*: CD-ROM; & Ney, ibid

5 Thompson, 117; & Corelli Barnett, *Bonaparte*; & Chandler, 236

Q. 63   477

1 'As Soviet armies advanced in 1944 and early 1945, Auschwitz was gradually abandoned.' Encyclopædia Britannica 2001 – CD-ROM; & Alan Palmer, *The Dictionary of Twentieth-Century History 1900-1982*, 402-3

2 Norman Davies, *Europe A History*, 1328-9

3 ibid 1057

4 Melbourne, the People, Patterns of Immigration, *Encyclopædia Britannica 2001*: CD-ROM; & Zimbabwe, Immigration, ibid; & Washington, the People, ibid; & Montreal, the People, ibid; & South Africa, the People, ibid; & New Zealand, the People, ibid

5 History of Transportation, the Jet Era, ibid

6 The Railroad in Continental Europe, ibid; & France, Roads, ibid

7 P&O Cruises 2003, 6

8 Hydrofoil - *Encyclopædia Britannica 2001* - CD-ROM; & Hovercraft, Ian Crofton (ed.) *Collins Gem Encyclopedia*, 480.

9 Norman Davies, *Europe A History*, 1124; & Operation Desert Storm, *20th Century Day By Day*: CD-ROM; & Eye-witness accounts of current events.

Q. 65   252

1 Meade Minnigerode, *The Son of Marie Antoinette*, 183–6

2 June 20th 1789 - W Edwards, *Notes on European History*, Vol. III; & S Schama, *Citizens*, 359

3 Franklin L Ford, *Europe 1780 –1830*, 120; & C Hibbert, *The French Revolution*, 180–1

4 Hibbert, 330–2

5 ibid 188, 222; & Schama, 311, 653, 799

Q. 70   484

1 EM-DAT: The OFDA/CRED International Disaster Database: Université Catholique

de Louvain, Brussels, Belgium.

2   Alan Palmer, *Dictionary of Twentieth Century History 1900-1982*, 200

3   ibid 200

4   'The protests, moreover, aimed at more fundamental change: in slogans and leaflets, the protesters attacked the shah and demanded his removal, and they depicted [Ayatollah] Khomeini as their leader and an Islamic state as their ideal ...' ibid

5   Milton Viorst, a Middle East specialist, [and] author of *In the Shadow of the Prophet*, *Time Magazine*, Monday, April 13, 1998; & 'The shah was aware of the rising resentment and dissatisfaction in the country and the increasing international concern about the suppression of basic freedoms in Iran ... ' *Library of Congress*.

6   'Khomeini went to France and established his headquarters at Neauphle-le-Château, outside Paris ... ' ibid; & Viorst, & 'For a short period Khomeini moved to Paris in France ... ' *Encyclopaedia of the Orient*, – Iran History by Tore Kjeilen.

7   Islamic Republic and Bakhtiar Shahpur - *Encyclopædia Britannica 2001* - CD-ROM

Q. 76   *296*

1   Lord Byron, *Childe Harold's Pilgrimage*, 37th stanza of the 3rd canto; & Saint John, *Book of Revelation*, 9:11

2   David Chandler, *The Campaigns of Napoleon*, xxv–xxvi, xxviii; & W H Hudson, *The Man Napoleon*, 228; & Stephen Coote, *Napoleon and the Hundred Days*, 147

3   Alan Palmer, *Dictionary of Modern History 1789-1945*, 109; & Franklin L Ford, *Europe 1780–1830*, 158-9

4   Octave Aubry, *Napoléon*

Q. 77   *338*

1   Ian Crofton (ed.) *Collins Gem Encyclopedia*, 406

2   Christopher Lloyd, *Sea Fights Under Sail*, 99–100

3   ibid 100; & Peter Padfield, *Nelson's War*, 186–7

4   Alan Palmer, *An Encyclopaedia of Napoleon's Europe*, 207; & Franklin L Ford, *Europe 1780-1830*, 240–1

5   Geoffrey Bennett, *The Battle of Trafalgar*, 128, 250; & *After Trafalgar: the crippled 'Victory' being towed into Gibraltar*,a painting by William Clarkson Stansfield, R.A. (1793-1867) held by the National Maritime Museum, Greenwich.

6   Bennett, 226

Q. 82   *273*

1   Simon Schama, *Citizens*, 799

2   Alan Palmer, *Dictionary of Modern History 1789-1945*, 246; & H A L Fisher, *A History of Europe*, 904; & Antonia Fraser, *Marie Antoinette The Journey*, 486, 491

3   Schama, 579

4   ibid 805; & Jeremy Black and Roy Porter (ed.) *A Dictionary of Eighteenth-Century History*, 288; & Christopher Hibbert, *The French Revolution*, 235-6, 239, 243

5   Battle of Fleurus – *Encyclopædia Britannica 2001*: CD-ROM

Q.85   *76*

1   M Freer, *Henry III, King of France and Poland*, London, 1858

2   ibid

3   ibid

4   Leonie Frieda, *Catherine de Medici*, 375-6

Q.86   *45*

1   Antonia Fraser, *Mary Queen of Scots*, 433

2   ibid 434

3   ibid 436

4   E N Williams, *A Dictionary of English and European History 1485-1789*, 300

5   ibid 300-1

Q. 88   *311*

1   Francine Barker, *Napoleon: The First European*, 26, The Observer 26/1/1969; & Alistair Horne, *Seven Ages of Paris*, 221

2   J M Thompson, *Napoleon Bonaparte*, 56-8

3   ibid 356
4   Between Empire and Restoration, *Encyclopædia Britannica 2001*: CD-ROM;
    & David Chandler, *The Campaigns of Napoleon*, 1001-2
5   ibid xl, xliii
6   Napoleon I, the Consulate, *Encyclopædia Britannica 2001* - CD-ROM

Q.97   *78*

1   Robert J Knecht, *The French Religious Wars 1562–1598*, 58
2   R Mousnier, *The Assassination of Henry IV* (trans. Joan Spencer), 214–5
3   M Freer, *Henry III, King of France and Poland*, 1858
4   ibid
5   ibid
6   ibid
7   Knecht, 62-3

Q. 98   *323*

1   J M Thompson, *Napoleon Bonaparte*, 92, 120
2   J Marshall-Cornwall, *Napoleon;* & Thompson, 97
3   Egypt – French occupation and its consequences, *Encyclopædia Britannica 2001*: CD-ROM
4   Alan Palmer, *An Encyclopaedia of Napoleon's Europe*, 3; & David Chandler, *The Campaigns of Napoleon*, 232 (map), 237; & Sea of Crete, *Encyclopædia Britannica 2001*: CD-ROM
5   Rigas Velestinlis, *Encyclopædia Britannica 2001*: CD-ROM; & Thessaly, ibid
6   Chandler, 242; & H A L Fisher, *Napoleon*, 70; & Carola Oman, *Napoleon's Viceroy – Eugene de Beauharnais*, 98

CENTURY TWO

Q. 1   *422*

1   www.historylearningsite.co.uk/first_battle_of_the_marne.htm (last visited 14/3/2009);
    & Aquitaine, *Encyclopædia Britannica 2001*: CD-ROM
2   See battles fought under their respective names, *Encyclopædia Britannica 2001*: CD-ROM
3   A J P Taylor, *The First World War – An Illustrated History*, 140, 191; & Neil Demarco,
    Britain and the Great War, 11
4   Dardanelles, *Encyclopædia Britannica 2001*: CD-ROM
5   R Ernest Dupuy and Trevor N Dupuy, *An Encyclopedia of Military History*, 953-4

Q. 6   *459*

1   Friedrich, 2-3 (see commentary) and Norman Davies, *Europe – A History*, 1026–7,
    & http://www.auschwitz-muzeum.oswiecim.pl/new/index. (Last visited 20 Oct. 2006)
2   Copyright ©1999-2006 Auschwitz-Birkenau State Museum, Poland;
    refer: http://www.auschwitz-muzeum.oswiecim.pl/new/index. (Last visited 20 Oct. 2006)
3   ibid; & I C B Dear (ed.) *The Oxford Companion to the Second World War*, 78; & *What's On TV*
    (8 - 14 January, 2005), 29
4   Auschwitz, *Compton's Encyclopedia 2000*: CD-ROM; & Derrik Mercer, (ed.) *Chronicle
    of the Second World War*, 601
5   Mercer, 601
6   Dear, 369
7   Bible, *2 Chronicles*: 20: 6-9; & *Psalm*: 119: 24-27; & K Armstrong, *A History of God*, 430

Q.7   *144*

1   Voltaire, *The Age of Louis XIV*, (trans. Martyn P Pollack)
2   ibid
3   John B Wolf, *Louis XIV*, 5
4   Ian Littlewood, *The Rough Guide Chronicle - France*, 168
5   Neil Grant, *Kings and Queens:* 192
6   Wolf, 265
7   ibid 277

Q. 19   *481*

1   John Ardagh, *France Today*, 290, 292
2   ibid 293

3 ibid 295
4 *The Guardian*: Saturday October 27, 2001
5 ibid
6 Giles Foden, *The Guardian*, Saturday September 4, 1999
7 Ardagh, 200, 202, 205

   Q. 24   *455*
1 John Keegan (ed.) *Encyclopedia of World War II*, 194-5, 235
2 The Western Front, *Encyclopædia Britannica 2001*: CD-ROM; & J A Kossmann-Putto and
   E H Kossmann, *The Low Countries*, 53
3 Derrik Mercer, (ed.) *20th Century Day By Day*, 533; & Alan Palmer, *Dictionary of Twentieth
   Century History: 1900-1982*, 33; & Peter Furtado, *World War II 1939 – 1945*, 29
4 ibid 98
5 The Invasion of the Low Countries, *Encyclopædia Britannica 2001*: CD-ROM; & Alan
   Palmer, *Dictionary of Modern History 1789-1945*, 188

   Q. 28   *496*
1 http://www.independent.co.uk/news/people/profiles/mohamed-alfayed-the-outsider-
   396133.html
2 ibid
3 Daily Express, 8 April 2008: 5
4 ibid 5 February 2008: 33

   Q. 33   *317*
1 David Chandler, *The Campaigns of Napoleon*, 95, 105, 112; & J M Thompson, *Napoleon
   Bonparte*, 79
2 Alan Palmer, *An Encyclopaedia of Napoleon's Europe*, 185; & Siege of Mantua, *Encyclopædia
   Britannica 2001*: CD-ROM
3 Palmer, 209; & Brian Lavery, *Nelson and the Nile*
4 River Garonne, *Encyclopædia Britannica 2001*: CD-ROM; & M J Sydenham, *The First French
   Republic 1789-1804*; & 20 August 1799 - Haute-Garonne - Jean Favier (ed.) *Chronicle of the
   French Revolution*
5 Genoa, *Encyclopædia Britannica 2001*: CD-ROM; & André Masséna, ibid; & David
   Chandler, *The Campaigns of Napoleon*, 271, 274, 285

   Q. 42   *277*
1 Marcel Liebman, *The Russian Revolution*, (trans. Arnold J. Pomerans), 142
2 Christopher Hibbert, *The French Revolution*, 246, 248; & Simon Schama, *Citizens*, 836
3 Louis Madelin, *The French Revolution*, 430; & Hibbert, 266-7
4 Hibbert, 267
5 Schama, 845-6
6 Franklin L Ford, *Europe 1780-1830*, 126; & Schama, 845, 846

   Q.51   *200*
1 William Henry Montague, *A New and Universal History of England*, – Vol. II, 180–1; &
   Ronald Hutton, *Charles II*, 249
2 Montague, 181
3 John Bedford, *London's Burning*, (quoting from Samuel Pepys Diary)
4 *The Diary of Samuel Pepys*, Vol. II: (ed.) R C Latham and W Mathews, xi
5 *The New Caxton Encyclopedia*; & Royal Mint 'A New Britannia for 2005'
6 *2 Kings* Ch.18, v 4; *2 Chronicles* Ch.14, v 3; etc. and H A L Fisher, *A History of Europe*, 676
7 Fisher, 676

   Q.53   *198*
1 John E N Hearsey, *London and the Great Fire.*
2 William Henry Montague, *A New and Universal History of England*, - Vol. II, 181
3 Robert Gray, *A History of London*, 168
4 Montague, 154
5 ibid 158; and J G Muddiman, *Trial of King Charles The First*, 129
6 Muddiman, 129 and *the New Caxton Encyclopedia*; & Royal Mint, *A New Britannia for 2005*
7 Montague, 158

8 Godfrey Davies, *The Early Stuarts 1603-1660, (2nd edition)*, 159

Q. 67   *316*

1 David Chandler, *The Campaigns of Napoleon*, 55
2 ibid 206–7; & H A L Fisher, *A History of Europe*, 912
3 Fructidor, year V (Sept. 4, 1797), *Encyclopædia Britannica 2001*: CD-ROM
4 Christopher Hibbert, *The French Revolution* 297-8
5 Fisher, 912

Q.68   *188*

1 William Henry Montague, *A New and Universal History of England*, Vol. II, 156
2 H A L Fisher, *A History of Europe*, 667
3 Montague, 176
4 ibid 184

Q. 76   *336*

1 Alan Palmer, *An Encyclopaedia of Napoleon's Europe*, 55; & David Chandler, *The Campaigns of Napoleon*, 822; & A J B F Bourgogne, *The Memoirs of Sergeant Bourgogne*, 59-60
2 J F Bernard, *Talleyrand - A Biography*, 251; & Chandler, 309
3 Talleyrand, during consulate and empire, *Encyclopædia Britannica 2001*: CD-ROM
4 Franklin L. Ford, *Europe 1780 – 1830*, 260–1; & Simon Schama, *Citizens*, 482–3
5 Bernard, 292–4

Q. 88   *35*

1 R J Knecht, *Catherine de' Medici*, 101
2 ibid. 107-8; 217
3 Williams, 14
4 ibid 170-1
5 ibid 170-1
6 A Pettegree, *Europe in the Sixteenth Century*, 217–9
7 E N Williams, *Dictionary of English and European History 1485-1789*, 85, 169
8 Knecht, 167
9 ibid 170
10 Knecht, 106
11 L'Estoile, *Mémoires pour servir à l'histoire de France*: vol ii: 2

Q. 90   *408*

1 Hungary, *Encyclopædia Britannica 2001*: CD-ROM
2 ibid
3 Jörg K Hoensch, *A History of Modern Hungary 1867 – 1994*, (trans. Kim Traynor) 53, 70
4 ibid 71, 73; & Derrik Mercer (ed.) *20th Century Day by Day*, 165
5 Francis Joseph – the Hungarian Compromise and the Dual Monarchy, *Encyclopædia Britannica 2001*: CD-ROM
6 Hoensch, 50-1

Q. 94   *309*

1 Franklin L Ford, *Europe 1780-1830*, 155-6; & J M Thompson, *Napoleon Bonaparte*, 93
2 Thompson, 81; & Ford, 155-6; & Christopher Hibbert, *Rome The Biography of a City*, 233
3 General Sir James Marshall-Cornwall, *Napoleon As Military Commander*, 80; & Ford, 245
4 Marshall-Cornwall, 82, 89, quoting from Correspondence de Napoléon Ier 3901; & David Chandler, *The Campaigns of Napoleon*, 213
5 Thompson, 122; & Georges Lefebvre, *The French Revolution From 1793–1799*, (trans. John Hall Stewart and James Friguglietti), 220; & M J Sydenham, *The First French Republic 1792-1804*, 187, 200
6 Sydenham, 201; & Chandler, 245

Q. 98   *275*

1 H A L Fisher, *A History of Europe*, 904; & Stanley Loomis, *Du Barry*, 254; & Louis Madelin, *The French Revolution*, 430; & Simon Schama, *Citizens*, 792
2 Madelin, 430
3 Christopher Hibbert, *The French Revolution*, 267–8

4 *Encyclopedia of World Mythology*, 2006, 58

5 *An A-Z of baby names*, Sywell, 2006, 78

6 Hibbert, 245-6

Q. 100 417

1 Alan Palmer, *Dictionary of Twentieth-Century History 1900-1982*, 401; & A J P Taylor, *The First World War*, 53-6

2 Taylor, 22-3

3 ibid 14

4 Wikipedia, 'Princip'

5 Palmer, 233-4

CENTURY THREE

Q.15 158

1 John A Lynn, *The French Wars 1667 – 1714*, 16; & Louis XIV, Early Life and Marriage, *Encyclopædia Britannica 2001*: CD-ROM

2 Lynn, 15-17

3 Robin Briggs, *Early Modern France 1560–1715*, 158; & Roger Price, *A Concise History of France*, 62

4 E N Williams, *Dictionary of English and European History 1485 – 1789*, 274

5 ibid 274

6 Christine Pevitt Algrant, *Madame de Pompadour*, 25

7 ibid 25

8 *Wikipedia*, Philippe II, Duke of Orleans

Q. 28 391

1 Desmond Seward, *Eugénie The Empress and Her Empire*, 1-4

2 ibid 24, 30

3 ibid 38-40

4 ibid back cover, xii, 113

5 ibid 1

6 ibid 109-10

7 Ian Littlewood, *The Rough Guide Chronicle France*, 249; & Seward, 110

8 Littlewood, 249

Q. 30 53

1 A Dumas, *Queen Margot*, xii

2 *Le Comte de Montgomery* and *Domfront Castle*, Historic Walking Tour 3, see: http://members.lycos.co.uk/medieval_festivals/castle1.htm last visited 13.10.2008

3 ibid

4 Leonie Frieda, *Catherine de Medici*, 165

5 ibid 303; Refer also to L. Marlet, *Le Comte de Montgomery* (Paris, 1890)

Q. 37 307

1 David Chandler, *The Campaigns of Napoleon*, 53

2 ibid 85, 130

3 ibid 86-7; & A N Delavoye, *Life of Thomas Graham, Lord Lynedoch*, 115

4 Chandler, 86, 92

5 ibid 86

6 ibid 86

Q. 39 56

1 R Knecht, *Catherine de' Medici*, 183–4

2 Leonie Frieda, *Catherine de Medici*, 331, 334, 336

3 Knecht, 184

4 *Encyclopædia Britannica, 2001*, CD-ROM, 'Haute-Savoie'

5 ibid Apennine Range – Physiography

6 Knecht, 185–6

7 Frieda, 335–6

Q. 41   *30*

1 *Encyclopædia Britannica 2001* CD-ROM, Louis I de Bourbon, Ier Prince de Condé
2 E N Williams, *Dictionary of English and European History 1485-1789*, 103–4
3 Leonie Frieda, *Catherine de Medici*, 170
4 R Knecht, *Catherine de' Medici*, 73–4
5 ibid 125
6 *Grand Larousse Encyclopédique Vol. 3* Condé
7 Knecht, 272
8 Williams, 101

Q. 42   *127*

1 V Cronin, *Louis XIV*, 21; & Ian Dunlop, *Louis XIV*, 2
2 C. Hibbert, *Rome The Biography of a City*, 8
3 N Davies, *Europe A History*, 1225
4 Dunlop, 419
5 ibid 420-1

Q. 50   *68*

1 H A L Fisher, *A History of Europe*, vol.1, 581–3
2 R Knecht, *The French Religious Wars 1562 – 1598*, 86–7; & *Catherine de' Medici*, 258
3 ibid (first source) 60; & ibid (second source) 258
4 ibid (first source) 60
5 R Mousnier, *The Assassination of Henry IV* (trans. Joan Spencer) 215
6 ibid 215
7 A Horne, *Seven Ages of Paris*, 81-2
8 ibid 81
9 ibid 81
10 ibid 82

Q. 51   *73*

1 E N Williams, *Dictionary of English and European History 1485-1789*, 172; & Leonie Frieda, *Catherine de Medici*, 367; & M Freer, *Henry III King of France and Poland*
2 A Pettegree, *Europe in the Sixteenth Century*, 165
3 Freer, 274
4 P Roberts, *A City In Conflict*, 172–3, 174–5, 178–9; & Freer, 264
5 Robert J Knecht, *The French Religious Wars 1562-1598*, 20

Q. 53   *442*

1 Stephen P Halbrook, *Target Switzerland*, 23; & Ian Kershaw, *Hitler 1889 – 1936: Hubris*, 419–20
2 Kershaw, 162-5
3 Halbrook, 27
4 Kershaw, 588; & Rhineland, *Encyclopædia Britannica 2001*: CD-ROM
5 ibid Rhineland
6 Karen Farrington, *Handbook of World War II*, 19-20

Q. 55   *25*

1 R Knecht, *Catherine de' Medici*, 295; & A Fraser, *Mary Queen of Scots*, 117
2 A Pettegree, *Europe in the Sixteenth Century*, 153–4
3 Knecht, 157; & E N Williams, *Dictionary of English and European History 1485-1789*, 101; & Pettegree, 159
4 A Horne, *Seven Ages of Paris*, 76
5 Leonie Frieda, *Catherine de Medici*, 275

Q. 57   *213*

1 Neil Grant, *Kings & Queens*, 53, 185, 192, 194 & 196
2 ibid 210
3 ibid 196
4 Turda, *Encyclopædia Britannica 2001*: CD-ROM; & Hungary - revolution, reaction and compromise, ibid; & Felipe Fernàndez Armento (ed.) *The Times Guide to The Peoples of Europe* (revised edition), 219

5   ibid 219

6   Bastarnae, *Encyclopædia Britannica 2001*: CD-ROM; & Hungary - revolution, reaction and compromise

7   Francis Joseph – The Emperor's peace policy, ibid

Q. 61   *509*

1   http://en.wikipedia.org/wiki/2003_invasion_of_Iraq

2   http://en.wikipedia.org/wiki/Abu_Ghraib_prisoner_abuse

3   www.Swissinfo.ch

4   ibid

5   www.politico.com/news/stories/0309/20014.html

6   www.globalsecurity.org/military/world/iraq/baghdad-green-zone.htm

7   http://en.wikipedia.org/wiki/Abu_Ghraib_prisoner_abuse#More_evidence_of_torture

8   http://en.wikipedia.org/wiki/Extraordinary_rendition

9   http://rawstory.com/news/2008/Cheney_admits_authorizing_detainees_torture

Q. 66   *47*

1   Robert J Knecht, *The French Religious Wars 1562–1598*, 29

2   ibid 43

3   ibid 42–3; E N Williams, *Dictionary of English and European History 1485-1789*, 104

4   R Knecht, *Catherine de' Medici*, 72

5   *Encyclopædia Britannica* 2001, CD-ROM, Henri III; & A Horne, *Seven Ages of Paris*, 76

Q. 74   *374*

1   Florence, Faenza and Imola . . . part of the Papal States. *Encyclopædia Britannica 2001*: CD-ROM; & Carbonari, ibid; & *Encyclopædia Britannica*: 15th edition

2   Franklin L Ford, *Europe 1780–1830*, 306

3   ibid 306

4   ibid 306–7

5   Harold Acton, *The Bourbons of Naples*, (1734–1825)

6   Ford 306–7

Q. 75   *321*

1   Vincent Cronin, *Napoleon*, 142

2   Alan Palmer, *An Encyclopaedia of Napoleon's Europe*, 28

3   ibid 245

4   J M Thompson, *Napoleon Bonaparte*, 129

5   ibid 127,128; & David Chandler, *The Campaigns of Napoleon*, 226, 230, 236, 244; & H A L Fisher, *Napoleon*, 70

6   Chandler, 231, 236-7, 239-40

7   Thompson, 130; & Opium, *Encyclopædia Britannica 2001*: CD-ROM

8   Chandler, 241

9   ibid 241; & Thompson, 131

Q. 77   *168*

1   D Ovason, *The Nostradamus Code*, 315–6

2   ibid

3   Iran *Encyclopædia Britannica* 2001, CD-ROM

4   R Collings, *Chronology of World History*; & Dreyss, *Chronologie Univeselle*; & Derrik Mercer, (ed.) *Chronicle of the World*, 606

5   R E & T N Dupuy, *An Encyclopedia of Military History*, 649

6   Ibrahim Pasa, *Encyclopædia Britannica 2001*: CD-ROM

7   Charles Louis de Secondat, Baron de la Brède et de Montesquieu, *Encyclopædia Britannica 2001*: CD-ROM; & Mercer, 605

Q. 88   *93*

References to this quatrain are taken from Balthazar Guynaud, (Paris, 1693) and repeated by Anatole Le Pelletier, (Paris, 1867) and by Charles A. Ward. (London, 1891; reprinted, New York, 1940).

Q. 94   *513*

1   Ian Wilson, *Nostradamus The Evidence*; & John Hogue, *Nostradamus A Life and Myth*.

2 C. A Ward, *The Oracles of Nostradamus*; & Jean-Aimé de Chavigny, *La Première face du Janus*.
   Q. 95   493
1 E E Reynolds, *The Field is Won*, 108–9
2 Robert Service, *A History of Twentieth-Century Russia*, 495-6; & Michael Dobbs,
   Down With Big Brother, 450
3 ibid 448-9
4 Service, 509, 517
5 Collapse of the Soviet Union, *Encyclopædia Britannica 2001:* CD-ROM; & Service, 506-7
6 Yeltsin, *Encyclopædia Britannica 2001:* CD-ROM
7 Relations with Russia, ibid
   Q. 97   479
1 Chaim Bernant. *Israel*, 69; & *Encyclopædia Britannica 2001:* CD-ROM
2 Bernant 71-2
3 ibid 128
4 ibid 129
5 Metonic cycle – *Encyclopædia Britannica 2001:* CD-ROM
   Q. 98   115
1 Gaston duc d'Orléans, *Encyclopædia Britannica 2001:* CD-ROM
2 ibid; & K A Patmore, *The Court of Louis XIII*, 150
3 Gaston d'Orleans, ibid; & Patmore, 142, 144 & 150
4 Patmore, 151–2, 156–7; & Ian Littlewood, *The Rough Guide Chronicle France*, 143

CENTURY FOUR

   Q. 2   153
1 Ian Dunlop, *Louis XIV*, 354, 358
2 ibid 361–2
3 ibid 400–1; &
   http://www.malagaholidays.com/en/costa_del_sol/travelinformation.asp?regionID=12
4 John A Lynn, *The French Wars 1667 – 1714*, 67
5 ibid 67
6 ibid 67–8; & E N Williams *Dictionary of English and European History 1485-1789*, 272-73
7 Louis XIV (le Grand Monarque) 1643 – 1715: *Royalty Peerage and Nobility of the World
   (Annuaire de la Noblesse de France)* 91st Volume, 383
8 Dunlop, 465–6, 468
   Q. 8   425
1 R Ernest Dupuy and Trevor N Dupuy, *The Encyclopedia of Military History*, 978
2 ibid 978
3 C R M F Cruttwell, *A History of the Great War 1914-1918 - 2nd edition* (Battle of St. Quentin);
   & *Nelsons History of the War* – Vol. XXII
4 Crutwell; & *Mein Kreigstagbuch* - Vol. II: Kronprinz Rupprecht, 344; & *Nelson* Vol. XXII
5 Crutwell; & Nelson
   Q. 11   240
1 Franklin L Ford, *Europe 1780-1830*, 119
2 Ibid 119; & *A Dictionary of Eighteenth-Century History*, (ed.) Jeremy Black and Roy Porter,
   186; & Christopher Hibbert, *The French Revolution*, 162
3 Simon Schama, *Citizens*, 633
4 Christopher Hibbert, *The French Revolution*, 174, 176
5 Jean Favier (ed.) *Chronicle of the French Revolution*, 260; & Norman Davies, *Europe -
   A History*, 710
6 Favier, see: Paris, May 27 1792; & Schama, 624
7 Hibbert, 170-1
8 ibid 175
9 Antonia Fraser, *Marie Antoinette The Journey*: 78-9
   Q. 12   467
1 World War II, Forces and Resources of the Combatants, 1939, *Encyclopædia Britannica*

2001: CD-ROM
2   John Macdonald, *Great Battles of World War II,* 142, 143
3   ibid 145
4   ibid 156-7
5   ibid 166
6   Various sources, including Karen Farrington, *Handbook of World War II,* 255-6
7   Alan Palmer, *Dictionary of Twentieth-Century History 1900-1982,* 117; & History of France, Liberation, *Encyclopædia Britannica 2001:* CD-ROM

Q. 15   457

1   Derrik Mercer, (ed.) *Chronicle of the Second World War,* 63; & Alan Palmer, *Dictionary of Twentieth-Century History 1900-1982,* 30
2   Palmer, 235-6
3   Richard Humble, *Fighting Ships: U-boat,* 18; & Palmer, 30
4   Ian Crofton (ed.) *Collins Gem Encyclopedia,* 211
5   Mercer, 108; & I C B Dear, (ed.) *Oxford Companion to the Second World War,* 1995; & Ken Hills, *Wars that Changed the World— World War II,* 14

Q.25   171

1   Hipparchus – Stellar Observations, *Encyclopædia Britannica 2001:* CD-ROM.
2   ibid Galaxies; & Pam Spence (ed.) *The Universe Revealed,* 13
3   ibid Optics and Information Theory
4   George Berkeley, *The Principles of Human Knowledge,* (ed.) G J Warnock, 12–14
5   Enlightenment, *Encyclopædia Britannica 2001:* CD-ROM; & Pierre Bayle, ibid; & Modern Christianity, ibid; & E N Williams, *Dictionary of English and European History 1485-1789,* 135

Q. 26   360

1   Stephen Coote, *Napoleon and the Hundred Days,* 124; & Correlli Barnett, *Bonaparte*
2   David Chandler, *The Campaigns of Napoleon,* 1011-12
3   J M Thompson, *Napoleon Bonaparte,* 142
4   ibid 142; & Christopher Hibbert, *The French Revolution,* 303; & Chandler, 261
5   H A L Fisher, *A History of Europe,* 916
6   Alan Palmer, *Dictionary of Modern History 1789-1945,* 99-100; & Thompson, 141
7   Thompson, 137; & Palmer 117, 261, 279

Q. 34   19

1   R J Knecht, *Catherine de' Medici,* 48
2   ibid 49-50
3   ibid 55
4   Leonie Frieda, *Catherine de Medici,* 107-9

Q. 37   332

1   David Chandler, *The Campaigns of Napoleon,* 3; & J M Thompson, *Napoleon Bonaparte,* 7
2   Chandler, 279-80
3   N G L Hammond and H H Scullard, (ed.) *The Oxford Classical Dictionary: 2nd edition,* 548
4   Franklin L Ford, *Europe 1780 – 1830,* 192; & Chandler, 297, 302
5   Chandler, 271
6   Monaco, *Encyclopædia Britannica 2001:* CD-ROM; & Robert Chambers (ed.) *Biographical Dictionary of Eminent Scotsmen*
7   ibid see: KEITH-ELPHINSTONE, GEORGE, (Viscount Keith, K. B. admiral of the Red, &c.)

Q. 47   51

1   Brewer, *Dictionary of Phrase and Fable,* Classic Edition, 276
2   William Henry Montague, *A New and Universal History of England: Vol. II,* 38; & Leonie Frieda, *Catherine de Medici,* 269
3   Montague, 38
4   Frieda, 269
5   R. Knecht, *Catherine de' Medici,* 159; & A. Dumas, *Queen Margot,* 166-7
6   Montague, 38

Q. 54 292

1 'NAPOLÉON EMPEROR ET ROI' — J M Thompson, *Napoleon Bonaparte*, 178f
2 John Belcham and Richard Price (ed.) *A Dictionary of Nineteenth-Century History*, 78-9
3 Franklin L Ford, *Europe 1780-1830*, 155–6
4 ibid 209
5 ibid 24
6 Jeremy Black and Roy Porter (ed.) *A Dictionary of Eighteenth-Century History*, 86;
  & Francine Barker, *Napoleon – The First European*, Observer Supplement 26/1/1969, 13

Q. 65 396

1 William H C Smith, *Napoleon III*, 14
2 ibid 109
3 Alistair Horne, *Seven Ages of Paris*, 284
4 ibid 285, 300
5 Smith, 128
6 Desmond Seward, *Eugénie The Empress and her Empire, xii,* 243

Q. 68 447

1 SKY DIARY, EVENTS, *RedShift 4*, CD-ROM, *Maris Mutimedia Ltd*; & Alan Palmer,
  Dictionary of Modern History 1789-1945, 309
2 I C B Dear (ed.) *The Oxford Companion to the Second World War*, 1123; & Mussolini –
  Dictatorship, *Encyclopædia Britannica 2001*: CD-ROM; & Tojo Hideki, ibid
3 *World War II – German occupied Europe*; & *The Blast of World War II*, ibid
4 Dear, 713
5 Jasper Ridley, *Mussolini*, 320, 338; & Derrik Mercer (ed.) *Chronicle of the Second World
  War*, 342; & Savona, *Encyclopædia Britannica*: CD-ROM

Q. 70 352

1 David Chandler, *The Campaigns of Napoleon*, 945–6
2 Wellington, *Encyclopædia Britannica 2001* - CD-ROM
3 ibid 1149; & Michael Glover, *Wellington's Peninsula Victories*, 137
4 Byron Farwell, *Queen Victoria's Little Wars*, 357; & Jac Weller, *Wellington in the Peninsula
  1808 – 1814*, 175, 178, 182–3, quoting from *Fortescue*, VIII, 200-1, and from *Maxwell's
  Peninsula Sketches*, II, 331, and elsewhere, with variations.
5 *English Battles and Sieges in the Peninsula*, Lt. Gen. Sir William Napier; & Weller, 359
6 Victory in the Napoleonic Wars, *Encyclopædia Britannica 2001* - CD-ROM; & Weller, 355
7 D S Richards, *The Peninsula Veterans*, 165; & Pau, *Encyclopædia Britannica 2001* - CD-ROM.
8 Alan Palmer, *An Encyclopaedia of Napoleon's Europe*, 31

Q. 75 348

1 David Chandler, *The Campaigns of Napoleon*, 757-8
2 ibid 739; & *A Dictionary of Nineteenth Century History* (ed.) John Belcham and Richard
  Price, 616-7
3 J M Thompson, 325-7; & Alan Palmer, *Dictionary of Modern History 1789-1945*, 204–5
4 Thompson, 338–9
5 ibid 337; & Ney, *Encyclopædia Britannica 2001*: CD-ROM
6 Chandler, 826
7 Thompson, 337, 338; & Chandler, 845

Q. 80 453

1 The Maginot Line, *Encyclopædia Britannica 2001*: CD-ROM; & *Encyclopædia Britannica Vol 7*
  (15th ed.) 589
2 'Maginot (LIGNE) nom donné au système fortifié construit de 1927 à 1936, sur le frontière
  française du Nord-Est . . . la création de régions fortifées d'une vingtaine de kilomètres de
  front sur 15 de profondeur.' *Grand Larousse Encyclopedique Vol 6*
3 John Keegan (ed.) *Encyclopedia of World War II*, 160
4 Thomas Parrish (ed.) *The Encyclopædia of World War II*, 480; & Arthur J May, *Europe Since
  1939*, 54
5 William L Shirer, *The Collapse of the Third Republic*, 751
6 ibid 752

7 Derrik Mercer, (ed.) *Chronicle of the Second World War*, 96
8 Alistair Horne, *Seven Ages of Paris*, 395-6
9 Shirer, 167–8

Q. 89   *207*

1 William Henry Montague, *A New and Universal History of England: Vol. 2*, 231
2 ibid 225, 227
3 ibid 225
4 ibid 219
5 E N Williams, *Dictionary of English and European History 1485 – 1789*, 387;
  & The Bill of Rights, *Encyclopædia Britannica 2001*, CD-ROM
6 ibid William III
7 ibid; & Frisia, ibid

Q. 93   *112*

1 K Patmore, *The Court of Louis XIII*, 109-10
2 V Cronin, *Louis XIV*, 19
3 Patmore, 300, 302–3; Ian Dunlop, *Louis XIV*, 2
4 Patmore, 302; Cronin, 25
5 Patmore, 303

Q. 97   *155*

1 Object Information, Planets, *RedShift 4*, CD-ROM, Maris Mutimedia Ltd
2 E N Williams, *Dictionary of English and European History 1485-1789*, 273; & Ian Dunlop,
  Louis XIV, 437, 440
3 Louis XIV (le Grand Monarque), 1643 – 1715; (383) *Royalty Peerage and Nobility of the
  World (Annuaire de la Noblesse de France)* 91st Volume
4 Williams, 272; & Dunlop, 361
5 Williams, 272; & Dunlop, 358
6 Gandia, *Encyclopædia Britannica 2001*: CD-ROM; & John A Lynn, *The French Wars
  1667- 1714*, 67
7 Lynn, 23; Williams, 439
8 Dunlop, 437

Q. 100   *399*

1 Alistair Horne, *Seven Ages of Paris*, 309
2 Planets, *Red Shift 4*, CD-ROM, Maris Mutimedia Ltd
3 Stephen Badsey, *The Franco-Prussian War 1870-1871*, 9
4 Horne, 310, 311; & Ian Littlewood, *The Rough Guide Chronicle France*, 255
5 Badsey, 71
6 Horne, 289

CENTURY FIVE

Q. 19   *121*

1 Ian Littlewood, *The Rough Guide Chronicle France*, 148; & *Grand Larousse Encyclopedique*,
  Louis Ancienne pièce d'or
2 K Patmore, *The Court of Louis XIII*, 310-1; 313; 315; 322
3 *Chronicle of the World*, (ed.) Derrik Mercer, 542
4 E N Williams, *Dictionary of English and European History 1485–1789*, 264
5 Patmore, 338-40
6 ibid 336
7 Ian Dunlop, *Louis XIV*, 5

Q. 26   *429*

1 Jonathan White, *Russia 1905 – 1941*, 9–10
2 Robert Service, *A History of Twentieth-Century Russia*, 62
3 H A L Fisher, *A History of Europe*, 1288
4 Lenin, *Encyclopædia Britannica 2001*: CD-ROM
5 White, 35; & Prince Lvov, *Encyclopædia Britannica 2001*: CD-ROM
6 *Lenin*, ibid

7   Service, 58-9
8   Krasnov, *Encyclopædia Britannica 2001*: CD-ROM; & Service, 67

Q. 29   473
1   World War II, Italy's Entry into the War, and the French Armistice, *Encyclopædia Britannica 2001*: CD-ROM
2   Norman Davies, *Europe A History*, 969-70
3   I C B Dear (ed.) *The Oxford Companion to the Second World War*, 944
4   Field Marshal Lord Carver, *War In Italy 1943 – 1945*, 290
5   Mussolini, Role in World War II, *Encyclopædia Britannica 2001*: CD-ROM
6   Hitler, *Encyclopædia Britannica 2001*: CD-ROM

Q. 30   397
1   Ian Littlewood, *The Rough Guide Chronicle France*, 254
2   Stephen Badsey, *The Franco-Prussian War 1870 – 1871*, 85–6
3   Alistair Horne, *Seven Ages of Paris*, 302–3, 310, 311; & Desmond Seward, *Eugénie The Empress and her Empire*, 251
4   ibid 159
5   ibid 309

Q. 33   268
1   Simon Schama, *Citizens*, 779
2   ibid 727
3   Louis Madelin, *The French Revolution*, 376
4   ibid 376
5   Schama, 789

Q.38   165
1   E N Williams, *Dictionary of English and European History 1485–1789*, 274
2   Louis XV, *Encyclopædia Britannica 2001*, CD-ROM; & Margaret Crosland, *Madame de Pompadour*, 110–1
3   Christine P Algrant, *Madame de Pompadour*, 95, 130
4   Williams, 276
5   The Salic Law, *Encyclopædia Britannica 2001* CD-ROM
6   ibid Louis XV; Alistair Horne, *Seven Ages of Paris*, 167

Q. 39   372
1   House of Bourbon - *Encyclopædia Britannica 2001* - CD-ROM; & Alistair Horne, *Seven Ages of Paris*, 241
2   Franklin L Ford, *Europe 1780 – 1830*, 183; & Marie-Louise, *Encyclopædia Britannica 2001* - CD-ROM
3   Reichstadt, ibid
4   Habsburg-Lorraine, ibid
5   Italy, the Restoration Period, ibid; & Florence, cultural life, ibid
6   Internet: members.tripod.com/romeartlover/Granduca.html (for photographs of heraldic devices); & *The Catholic Encyclopedia*

Q. 56   381
1   Gregory XVI – *Encyclopædia Britannica 2001* - CD-ROM
2   J N D Kelly, *The Oxford Dictionary of Popes*, 309
3   *Catholic Encyclopedia – Pius IX*
4   Pius IX, *Encyclopædia Britannica 2001* - CD-ROM
5   Kelly, 309, 310

Q. 57   290
1   Montgolfier, *Encyclopædia Britannica 2001* - CD-ROM
2   ibid Seven Hills of Rome
3   ibid History of transportation – the balloon; & Norman Hampson, *The First European Revolution: 1776-1815*, 104; wikipedia.org/wiki/Battle_of_Fleurus_(1794)
4   Harrison Smith, *The Illness of Pius VI and its Effect on the Maltese Question*, 409; & C R Cheney (ed.) *Handbook of Dates For Students of English History*, 39; & Christopher Hibbert, *Rome*, 231–2

5 Hibbert, 234
   Q. 60   297
1 Bonaparte, *Encyclopædia Britannica 2001* - CD-ROM
2 David Chandler, *The Campaigns of Napoleon*, 236, 845; & J M Thompson, *Napoleon Bonaparte*, 337
3 Franklin L Ford, *Europe 1780-1830*, 168
4 Chandler, xxix; xxxvii
5   ibid 102
6 *Cambridge Modern History*, vol. ix, 345; & Ford, 229, quoting from: A. Meynier, cited in Bruun, 72; & Chandler, xxix
   Q. 79   299
1 J M Thomson, *Napoleon Bonaparte*, 174
2 ibid 179–80; & Franklin L Ford, *Europe 1780-1830*, 173
3 The Imperial Nobility – Appendix J, David Chandler, *The Campaigns of Napoleon*, 1122–5
4 Thompson, 158
5 Ford, 167; & Thomson, book cover
   Q. 85   450
1 N G L Hammond and H H Scullard, (ed.) *The Oxford Classical Dictionary:* 2nd edition, 1020
2 Karen Farrington, *Handbook of World WarII*, 188-9
3 Parachute, *Encyclopædia Britannica 2001:* CD-ROM; & World War II, Invasion of Norway, ibid; & Peter Furtado, *World War II 1939 – 1945*, 28
4 World War II, Invasion of the Low Countries, *Encyclopædia Britannica 2001:* CD-ROM; & Farrington, 19, 253, 254; & A Palmer, *Dictionary of Twentieth-Century History 1900-1982*, 402
5 World War II, Evacuation from Dunkirk, *Encyclopædia Britannica 2001:* CD-ROM; & Farrington, 19
6 League of Nations, *Encyclopædia Britannica 2001:* CD-ROM
7 ibid

CENTURY SIX

   Q. 2   63
1 E N Williams, *Dictionary of English and European History 1485–1789*, 167
2 H A L Fisher, *A History of Europe*, Vol.1, 572
3 Williams, 272
4 ibid 272; *Encyclopædia Britannica 2001*, CD-ROM, Portugal – The 18th Century
5 J. Lynn, *The French Wars 1667-1714*, 28; *Encyclopædia Britannica*, Victor Amadeus II
6 ibid Ahmed III
7 ibid Georgia – Persian and Turkish Domination;
8 Ian Dunlop, *Louis XIV*, 210, 419
9 ibid 397, 422
   Q. 11   55
1 Leonie Frieda, *Catherine de Medici*, 325
2 ibid. 61
3 ibid. 326-7, 329
4 ibid. 330
   Q. 12   343
1   Franklin L Ford, *Europe 1780-1830*, 228–9
2 Alan Palmer, *An Encyclopaedia of Napoleon's Europe*, 157
3 J M Thompson, *Napoleon Bonaparte*, 262
4 ibid 263
5 Palmer, 34
6 Ford, 209
7 ibid 30
8 David Chandler, *The Campaigns of Napoleon*, 528
9 Thompson, 271
10 Chandler, 595

Q. 22 *210*

1 Norman Davies, *Europe A History*, 598
2 Neil Grant, *Kings and Queens*, 188
3 William Henry Montague, *A New and Universal History of England:* Vol. 2, 219
4 ibid 219
5 ibid 221
6 ibid 231; & E N Williams, *Dictionary of English and European History 1485-1789*, 387
7 Michael White, *Isaac Newton The Last Sorcerer*, 192-3; & *The Oxford Companion to English Literature*, (ed.) Margaret Drabble, 431

Q. 23 *220*

1 Simon Schama, *Citizens*, 458
2 ibid 458–9
3 ibid 459, 460
4 Jean Favier (ed.) *Chronicle of the French Revolution*, 152
5 ibid 155
6 ibid 158, 181
7 Norman Davies, *Europe A History*, 699
8 Christopher Hibbert, *The French Revolution*, 130

Q. 24 *350*

1 Planets – *RedShift 4* CD-ROM, Maris Mutimedia Ltd; & Franklin L Ford, *Europe 1780 – 1830*, 219; & David Chandler, *The Campaigns of Napoleon*, 770
2 J M Thompson, *Napolen Bonaparte*, 329, 333–8; & Norman Davies, *Europe - A History*, 742; & Alan Palmer, *AnEncyclopaedia of Napoleon's Europe*, 197
3 H A L Fisher, *A History of Europe*, 950
4 Louis XVIII, *Encyclopædia Britannica 2001* - CD-ROM
5 Palmer, 183; & Davies, 1287

Q. 25 *288*

1 Christopher Hibbert, *The French Revolution*, 142-5
2 Pius VI: Joseph N. Scionti; *McGraw-Hill Encyclopedia of Names*; & Jeremy Gregory, *A Dictionary of Eighteenth Century History*, 569-70
3 Ian Littlewood, *The Rough Guide Chronicle France*, 214; & Michael Broers, *A Dictionary of Eighteenth Century History*, 88; & J M Thompson, *Napoleon Bonaparte*, 35, 54-5
4 H A L Fisher, *A History of Europe*, 911; & Brewer, *The Dictionary of Phrase and Fable*, (Classic Edition) 276
5 Fisher, 909; & Christopher Hibbert, *Rome*, 233-4
6 Fisher, 917; & Broers, 88; & Thompson, 41
7 Thompson, 141; & Fisher, 916
8 Franklin L Ford, *Europe 1780-1830*, 121; & Norman Davis, *Europe –A History*, 698

Q. 31 *463*

1 Derrik Mercer, (ed.) *Chronicle of the Second World War*, 429
2 Alan Palmer, *Dictionary of Twentieth-Century History*, 38–9
3 ibid 39
4 ibid 39
5 Jasper Ridley, *Mussolini*, 364-5
6 ibid 355, 368

Q. 54 *59*

1 *Encyclopædia Britannica 2001* CD-ROM, Turkey and Eastern Europe; Bejaïa; & Murad III
2 ibid Morocco Under Sharifian Dynasties; & D Fage, *A History of Africa*, 177
3 ibid The Battle of the Three Kings
4 ibid The Sufferings and Death of Jesus in Jerusalem

Q. 63 *98*

1 E N Williams, *Dictionary of English and European History 1485-1587*, 295
2 *Encyclopædia Britannica 2001*, CD-ROM, Marie de Médicis
3 K A Patmore, *The Court of Louis XIII*, 26
4 ibid 243; & *Encyclopædia Britannica*, History of France, Louis XIII

5 R Mousnier, *The Assassination of Henry IV*, (trans. Joan Spencer), 391
6 Patmore, 58
7 ibid 58
8 ibid 15, 16, 63
9 Williams, 296

Q. 74   *383*
1 E N Williams, *Dictionary of English and European History 1485-1587*, 216–7
2 ibid
3 Roger Price, *A Concise History of France*, 182; & Derrik Mercer, (ed.) *Chronicle of the World*, 814, 815
4 Alistair Horne, *Seven Ages of Paris*, 26
5 Napoleon III – Last Years, *Encyclopædia Britannica 2001*: CD-ROM

Q. 75   *32*
1 E N Williams, *Dictionary of English and European History 1485-1587*, 101
2 ibid 101; & Leonie Frieda, *Catherine de Medici*, 234
3 R J Knecht, *Catherine de' Medici*, 88
4 Williams, 104; Robert J Knecht, *The French Religious Wars 1562–1598*, 41–3
5 Cyprus History: Ottoman Period; Microsoft Internet Explorer, reference B Rogerson, (1994), *Cyprus*.
6 Williams, 352

Q. 79   *305*
1 General Sir James Marshall-Cornwall, *Napoleon*, 58
2 Dr Enzo Orlandi, (ed.) *The Life and Times of Napoleon*, 10; & David Chandler, *The Campaigns of Napoleon*, 60-1
3 H A L Fisher, *A History of Europe*, 910
4 Arthur Bryant, *The Years of Endurance 1793-1802*
5 Napoléon Bonaparte, *Encyclopædia Britannica 2001*: CD-ROM
6 Chandler, 106, 107–8; & John Holland Rose, *The Life of Napoleon I*, 125

Q. 92   *259*
1 Meade Minnigerode, *The Son of Marie Antoinette*, 28; & *Citizens*, Simon Schama, 654
2 Schama, 658
3 ibid 662; & Bernard Faÿ, *Louis XVI*, (trans. Patrick O'Brien), 402
4 Schama, 668
5 ibid 673; & S K Padover, *The Life and Death of Louis XVI*, 334
6 Schama, 687; & Franklin L Ford, *Europe 1780-1830*, 121–2; & Christopher Hibbert, *The French Revolution*, 193
7 Padover, 334

CENTURY SEVEN

Q. 1   *104*
1 *Encyclopædia Britannica 2001*, CD-ROM, Concini, Concino; & *Grand Larousse Encyclopedique*, Concini (Concino) Marquis d'Ancre
2 Montgomery, (quoted from Stewart Robb, *Nostradamus Prophecies of World Events*, (1961), 11
3 *Grand Larousse Encyclopedique*, Achille de Harlay
4 Bainville (quoted from Stewart Robb, *Nostradamus Prophecies of World Events*, (1961), 12
5 Alistair Horne, *Seven Ages of Paris*, 105; & K A Patmore, *The Court of Louis XIII*, 58
6 Patmore, 60-1
7 ibid 58
8 Patmore, 59
9 ibid 59

Q. 11   *107*
1 K A Patmore, *The Court of Louis XIII*, 25; *Encyclopædia Britannica 2001* CD-ROM, Louis XIII
2 Patmore, 24
3 ibid 58
4 ibid 58

5 ibid 57
6 ibid 58
7 ibid 58
8 ibid 62
9 ibid 63
10 ibid 80

'En 1620 la défaite des troupes de Marie de Médicis contre celles de son fils Louis XIII reste inscrite dans l'histoire de France sous le nom de «Drôlerie des Ponts-de-Cé.» La brève bataille amène la réconciliation de la mère et du fils au château voisin de Brissac grâce notamment à l'entremise de Richelieu qui rentre en grâce auprès du roi et devient cardinal peu après.' *History of Pont de Cé*: (Anon.)

11 Theophilus de Garencières, writing fifty years after this episode and with an awareness of the civil strife at the time of his birth, confirmed the number dead as being 'in excess of five hundred'; *The True Prophecies or Prognostications of Michael Nostradamus*, London, 1672.

Q. 13   *319*

1 J M Thompson, *Napoleon Bonaparte*, 111-2
2 ibid 114
3 Napoleon I – the consulate, *Encyclopædia Britannica 2001:* CD-ROM
4 Alan Palmer, *An Encyclopaedia of Napoleon's Europe*, 63; & Egyptian Satrap - Ptolemy, *Encyclopædia Britannica 2001:* CD-ROM
5 Palmer, 265; & David Chandler, *The Campaigns of Napoleon*, 237–8; & Thompson, 127
6 Palmer, 3; & Thompson, 129; & Chandler, 237-8
7 Palmer, 208

Q. 14   *234*

1 Simon Schama, *Citizens*, 604
2 ibid 477, 568, 573; & French Revolution – new regime, *Encyclopedia Britannica 2001:* CD-ROM
3 Jean Favier (ed.) *Chronicle of the French Revolution*, 357
4 Schama, 502–3, 509
5 Jeremy Black and Roy Porter (ed.) *A Dictionary of Eighteenth-Century History*, 271; & Favier, 163; & Schama, 511
6 Favier, 123
7 Schama, 459
8 Christopher Hibbert, *The French Revolution*, 90

Q. 29   *20*

1 Encyclopaedia Britannica 2001 CD-ROM, 'Lorraine, 2e. Cardinal de...'
2 E N Williams, *Dictionary of English and European History 1485-1789*, 196; & R J Knecht, *Catherine de' Medici*, 55
3 J Cuddon, *A Dictionary of Literary Terms*, (revised edition) London, 1979, 480
4 Knecht, 91
5 Leonie Frieda, *Catherine de Medici*, 169
6 *Encyclopaedia Britannica*, Alba, Fernando Álvarez de Toledo y Piment
7 ibid
8 ibid
9 ibid
10 ibid
11 ibid
12 ibid

Q. 44   *250*

1 Louis XVI, *Encyclopædia Britannica 2001:* CD-ROM
2 Christopher Hibbert, *The French Revolution*, 185
3 Simon Schama, *Citizens*, 658
4 ibid 658
5 Hibbert, 133
6 ibid 188–9

Q. 80   *178*

1 wikipedia.org/wiki/George_Washington
2 http://sc94.ameslab.gov/TOUR/gwash.html
3 *A Dictionary of Eighteenth Century History*, ed. J. Black and R. Porter, 778
4 http://www.whitehouse.gov/about/presidents/georgewashington/
5 http://en.wikipedia.org/wiki/John_Paul_Jones
6 ibid
7 Wikipedia – The American Revolution

CENTURY EIGHT

Q. 1   *334*

1 Franklin L Ford, *Europe 1780 – 1830*, 167; & J M Thompson, *Napoleon Bonaparte*, 69–70; &
   David Chandler, *The Campaigns of Napoleon*, xxv–xxvi, xxviii.
2 Thompson, 135-6; & H A L Fisher, *A History of Europe*, 293
3 Thompson, 214; & Georges Lefebvre, *Napoleon from 18 Brumaire to Tilsit*, (trans. Henry F
   Stockold), 185
4 Pie VI, pape de 1775 à 1799, *Petit Larousse* 1966 (Librarie Larousse) Paris; & Pie VII, pape
   de 1800 à 1823, ibid
5 Harrison Smith, *The Illness of Pius VI and the Effect on the Maltese Question* (Estratto da Studi
   Romagnoli XIX, 1968) Faenza, 409; & Pius VII, *Encyclopædia Britannica 2001*: CD-ROM
6 Tilsit, ibid; & Pius VII, Joseph N. Scionti, *McGraw-Hill Encyclopedia of Names*; & Thompson, 262
7 Durance, *Encyclopædia Britannica 2001*: CD-ROM; & Scionti; & Ford, 178

Q. 4   *346*

1 J M Thompson, *Napoleon Bonaparte*, 264; & *History of Monaco*, anon. published by Gale
   Force of Monaco
2 Thompson, 177, 273; & David Chandler, *The Campaigns of Napoleon*, 448
3 Thompson, 273
4 ibid 273
5 Alan Palmer, *Dictionary of Modern History 1789-1945*, 208
6 John Belcham & Richard Price (ed.) *A Dictionary of Nineteenth – Century History*, 649

Q. 15   *174*

1 Saint Petersburg – foundation and early growth, *Encyclopædia Britannica 2001*: CD-ROM
2 Catherine II – early years as empress, ibid; & E N Williams, *Dictionary of English and
   European History 1485 – 1789*, 54-5
3 Nicholas V Riazanovsky, *A History of Russia*, 256; & Simon Sebag Montefiore, *Prince of
   Princes The Life of Potemkin*, 46
4 *A Dictionary of Eighteenth-Century History*, Jeremy Black and Roy Porter (ed.) 127; &
   Influence of Potemkin, *Encyclopædia Britannica 2001*: CD-ROM; & Montefiore, 233
5   Montefiore, 50, 59
6 Black and Porter, 339

Q. 19   *245*

1 Norman Davies, *Europe - A History*, 699; & Simon Schama, *Citizens*, 604
2 Schama, 558–60
3 ibid 560–1
4 Norman Davies, *Europe - A History*, 710
5 Schama, 566-7
6 Christopher Hibbert, *The French Revolution*, 149
7 H A L Fisher, *A History of Europe*, 897, 904
8 ibid 897; & Jeremy Black & Roy Porter (ed.) *Dictionary of Eighteenth Century History*, 186

Q. 22   *254*

1 Louis Madelin, *The French Revolution*, 197
2 ibid 229
3 *Matthew* v. 13; & *Oxford English Dictionary - Fourth edition*
4 Gorsas, *Grand Larousse Encyclopédique*; & Simon Schama, *Citizens*, 683

5   Madelin, 189; & Antonia Fraser, *Marie Antoinette*, 322
6   S K Padover, *Life and Death of Louis XVI*, 239
7   *Chronicle of the French Revolution*, see 6 December 1791, Perpignan, (ed.) Jean Favier
8   Norman Davies, *Europe - A History*, 710; & Franklin L Ford, *Europe 1780-1830*, 119
9   H A L Fisher, *A History of Europe*, 891–2; & Schama, 581
10 Schama, 891
11 Alexandre Dumas, *The Flight to Varennes*, (trans. A Craig Bell), 84
12 Christopher Hibbert, *The French Revolution*, 332
    Q. 23   44
1   Antonia Fraser, *Mary Queen of Scots*, 405
2   ibid 465
3   ibid 405
4   ibid 345
    Q. 37   190
1   *Encyclopædia Britannica 2001*, CD-ROM, Windsor Castle
2   E N Williams, *Dictionary of English and European History 1485-1789*, 111
3   D R Watson, *The Life and Times of Charles I*, 175–6
4   Graham Gibberd, *On Lambeth Marsh*, 45, 71
5   Watson, 186; & Charles I, Execution of the King, *Encyclopædia Britannica*
6   ibid
    Q. 41   270
1   Christopher Hibbert, *The French Revolution*, 205, 210; & H A L Fisher, *A History of Europe*,
    Vol. 2: 905
2   Hibbert, 208; & Leadership of the Jacobins: *Encyclopædia Britannica 2001: CD-ROM*
3   Simon Schama, *Citizens*; 831
4   Hibbert, 207
5   Schama, 805; & Jeremy Black and Roy Porter (ed.) *A Dictionary of Eighteenth-Century
    History*, 288; & Hibbert, 235-6, 239, 243
6   Leadership of the Jacobins: *Encyclopædia Britannica 2001*: CD-ROM; & Hibbert, 333, 486, 491
    Q. 43   389
1   Stephen Badsey, *The Franco-Prussian War 1870-1871*, 15
2   Napoleon III, *Encyclopædia Britannica 2001*: CD-ROM
3   ibid
4   Sedan, (article by Colonel Maude) *Encyclopædia Britannica*
5   Badsey, 50-1
6   ibid 51-2
    Q. 46   329
1   Christopher Hibbert, *Rome The Biography of a City*, 233, 235; & Peter de Rosa, *Vicars of
    Christ*, 177
2   L'Abbé Baldassari, *Histoire de l'enlèvement et de la captivité De Pie VI* (Vanderborght,
    Bruxelles, 1840), 478
3   Alan Palmer, *An Encyclopaedia of Napoleon's Europe*, 221
4   Pius VI, *The New Catholic Encyclopedia*; & J M Thompson, *Napoleon Bonaparte*, 263-4
5   Palmer, 274
6   Jeremy Black and Roy Porter (ed.) *A Dictionary of Eighteenth-Century History*, 870-4; &
    Norman Davies, *Europe A History*, 1286-7
7   'The 'Red Cock', M. Liebman, *The Russian Revolution*, 142.
8   Davies, 157
9   Black and Porter, 427; & John Belcham and Richard Price (ed.) *A Dictionary of Nineteenth-
    Century History*, 111
    Q. 57   301
1   J M Thompson, *Napoleon Bonaparte*, 10
2   Norman Davies, *Europe - A History*, 275
3   Thompson, 191; & 'Napoleon in Coronation Robes' painted by François Gérard at
    Versailles; (B.B.C. Hulton Picture Library, 178*f*), ibid

4 Francine Barker, *Napoleon: The First European*, 14, 15, The Observer 26/1/1969

5 Thompson, 270; & Jeremy Black and Roy Porter (ed.) *A Dictionary of Eighteenth-Century History*, 543; & 451

6 Thompson, 80–1; & David Chandler, *The Campaigns of Napoleon*, 748

7 Savona, *Encyclopædia Britannica 2001*: CD-ROM; & Thompson, 272-5

Q. 58   437

1 Kirsty McLeod, *Battle Royal – Edward VIII & George VI Brother Against Brother*, 172

2 ibid 176-7, 193

3 Edward VIII, *Encyclopædia Britannica 2001*: CD-ROM

4 McLeod, 181

5 Edward VIII, *Encyclopædia Britannica 2001*: CD-ROM

Q. 60   341

1 David Chandler, *The Campaigns of Napoleon*, 307, 318

2 Alistair Horne, *Seven Ages of Paris*, 196; & J M Thompson, *Napoleon Bonaparte*, 252

3 Norman Davies, *Europe A History*, 1286-7

4 Thompson, 355-6; & Horne, 232

5 Chandler, xliii, 1103; & Battle of Ulm, *Encyclopædia Britannica 2001*: CD-ROM; & Alan Palmer, *An Encyclopaedia of Napoleon's Europe*, 138

6 Horne, 231

7 Thompson, 358

8 ibid 371

9 Chandler, xxv, 1011

10 German Genealogy: History of Lorraine
   www.genealogienetz.de/reg/ELS-LOT/lor-hist.html; last visited 29.3.2006

Q. 64   445

1 Derrik Mercer (ed.) *Chronicle of the Second World War*, 17, 91, 130

2 Martin Gilbert, *Churchill A Life*, 620-1

3 Norman Longmate, *How We Lived Then*, 121-2

4 World War II – The war in the west, September 1939 — June 1940, *Encyclopædia Britannica 2001*: CD-ROM

5 For a full list of treaties, see Norman Davies, *Europe: A History*, 1322

Q. 68   123

1 Maland, D. *Europe in the Seventeenth Century 2nd edition*, 189–90; & *The New Cambridge Modern History*, (ed.) J P Cooper, 493

2 K A Patmore, *The Court of Louis XIII*, 314–5

3 ibid 315

4 C. Wedgwood, *Richelieu and the French Monarchy*, 179–80

5 ibid 178-80

6 Wedgwood, 178

7 ibid 182

8 Patmore, 337-8

Q. 70   490

1 Hussein, *Encyclopædia Britannica 2001*: CD-ROM; & Andrew Cockburn and Patrick Cockburn, *Saddam Hussein An American Obsession*, 68

2 Hussein, *Encyclopædia Britannica 2001*: CD-ROM; & Burhan Wazir, The Guardian, Saturday April 12 2003, 11

3 Hussein, ibid

4 Iraq, the People – Kurds, ibid; & www.geocities.com/Athens/Ithaca/3291/page1.html

5 UN coalition and ultimatum, *Encyclopædia Britannica 2001*: CD-ROM; & Bruce W Watson (ed.) *Military Lessons of the Gulf War*, 221-2

6 Statue of Liberty, formally Liberty Enlightening The World, *Encyclopædia Britannica 2001*: CD-ROM; & The Independent, Saturday 5 April 2003; & www.whitehouse.gov/history/presidents/gb41.html

7 Royal Mint, *A New Britannia for 2005*

8 *The Independent*, Saturday 5 April 2003, 19

Q. 71   *100*

1 *Encyclopædia Britannica,* 2001 CD-ROM, Galileo's Copernicanism and Physical Science, Astronomy

2 ibid Galileo's Condemnation; and Galileo's Copernicanism

3 ibid Galileo's Copernicanism

4 Star of Bethlehem website of the National Maritime Museum at the Royal Observatory Greenwich. (Dr Peter Andrews, Institute of Astronomy, University of Cambridge.)

5 *Encyclopædia Britannica,* 2001 CD-ROM, The Star of Bethlehem; & Christianity, The relation of the early church to the career and intentions of Jesus

6 ibid History of Europe – The Role of Science and Mathematics; also History of France, Cultural Transformation

Q. 76   *186*

1 Lewis and Short, *A Latin Dictionary*; & Macrinus, *Longmans English Larousse,* 217–8.

2 *Collins Gem Encyclopedia,* ed. Ian Crofton, 256

3 Antonia Fraser, *Cromwell Our Chief Of Men,* 3

4 *Encyclopædia Britannica 2001:* CD-ROM, Oliver Cromwell

5 Peter Young & Richard Holmes, *The English Civil War,* 292

6 *Encyclopædia Britannica 2001:* CD-ROM, Cromwell in Parliament

7 H A L Fisher, *A History of Europe,* 667; & Maurice Ashley, *England in the Seventeenth Century,* 97

8 *Collins Gem Encyclopedia,* 216

Q. 88   *313*

1 Charles Emmanuel IV, *Encyclopædia Britannica 2001:* CD-ROM

2 ibid

3 J M Thompson, *Napoleon Bonaparte,* 64-5

4 'Broken by many efforts and deceptions . . . Charles Emmanuel went to die at Rome in the novitiate of the Jesuits.' B. Grasset, *Histoire de Savoie.*

5 'He reached such a state of detachment from the world that one saw this old King become blind and infirm . . .' ibid

6 'Sometimes he would leave his cell and extend his hand to passers-by for alms. For the descendent of such a proud race,. . . this was really carrying too far the need of humiliation and the heroism of voluntary poverty.' ibid

Q. 97   *379*

1 Derrik Mercer (ed.) *Chronicle of the Royal Family,* 400, 474

2 Neil Grant, *Kings & Queens,* 218

3 Mercer, 470; & Grant, 212

4 Windsor Castle, *Encyclopædia Britannica 2001:* CD-ROM

5 Mercer, 400, 406, 409, 410, 413, 420, 424

6 Nicolas Bentley, *The Victorian Scene: 1837-1901,* 42, 204, 212; & John Belcham and Richard Price (ed.) *A Dictionary of Nineteenth Century History,* 665

7 Bentley, 212; & Mercer, 470; & Victoria, *Compton's Encyclopedia 2000:* CD-ROM

8 Belcham and Price, 119; & Bentley, 220

9 Mercer, 475

CENTURY NINE

Q. 11   *195*

1 Graham Edwards, *The Last Days of Charles I,* 132-3

2 ibid 174

3 ibid 178

4 William Henry Montague, *A New and Universal History of England,* 181; & *Encyclopaedia Britannica 2001* CD-ROM, Mediation and the Second Civil War

5 ibid Great Fire of London

6 Robert Gray, *A History of London,* 168

7 John Bedford, *London's Burning,* (From Samuel Pepys Diary)

Q. 16 439

1 Alan Palmer, *Dictionary of Twentieth-Century History 1900-1982*, 156; & *Encyclopædia Britannica*, Vol. 17: 15th edition, 441
2 Brian Crozier, *Franco*, 150, 161, 170; & Palmer, 156
3 Stanley G Payne, *The Spanish Revolution*, 234
4 ibid 260
5 ibid 260
6 Crozier, 135, 164
7 Paul Preston, *Franco*, 2-4
8 Crozier, 192, 193, 194

Q. 17 281

1 Simon Schama, *Citizens*, 290
2 Christopher Hibbert, *The French Revolution*, 227; & F L Ford, *Europe 1780-1830*, 137
3 Nero, *Encyclopædia Britannica 2001*: CD-ROM; & D. Pawson, *Unlocking the Bible*, 1267
4 Hibbert, 223, 225
5 Meade Minnigerode, *The Son of Marie Antoinette*, 184–5; & Antonia Fraser, *Marie Antoinette The Journey*, 493-4
6 Minnigerode, CHAPTER TWO THE BAKER'S BOY, 46
7 Hibbert, 231
8 ibid 280
9 ibid 281
10 ibid 281

Q. 18 117

1 E N Williams, *Dictionary of English and European History 1485-1789*, 264
2 ibid 264
3 *Encyclopædia Britannica 2001*, CD-ROM, Fleur-de-Lys, or Fleur- de- Luce ('lily flower'); & K A Patmore, *The Court of Louis XIII*, 150-1
4 ibid 151
5 Neville Williams, *Chronology of the Expanding World 1492-1762*; & Voltaire, *The Age of Louis XIV*, (trans. Martyn P Pollack), 16
6 A Horne, *Seven Ages of Paris*, London, 2003, 108
7 C Burckhardt, *Richelieu and His Age*, (trans. Bernard Hoy), 71
8 ibid 89; and Patmore, 159; & D Pennington, *Seventeenth Century Europe*, 269
9 Patmore, 159; & C Jant, *Prédictions tirées des Centuries de Nostradamus*; & *Grand Larousse Encyclopedique*, Montmorenci, Henri II; & Contemporary print of the execution reproduced from the original owned by *Cabinet des Estampes*; & C Ward, *The Oracles of Nostradamus*, 126
10 Ward, 126

Q. 20 225

1 Ardennes, Forest of - *New Century Cyclopedia of Names*: Appleton-Century-Crofts, Inc; & S K Padover, *The Life and Death of Louis XVI*
2 ibid 209
3 S Hopewell, *Europe from Revolution to Dictatorship*, 12; & Christopher Hibbert, *The French Revolution*, 121; & H. Belloc, *Marie Antoinette*, 261-6
4 Louis Madelin, *The French Revolution*, 161
5 Belloc, 278
6 Jean Favier (ed.) *Chronicle of the French Revolution*, 218
7 Simon Schama, *Citizens*, 551–2
8 Brewer, *The Dictionary of Phrase and Fable*, (Classic Edition) 276
9 Bernard Fäy, *Louis XVI*, (trans. Patrick O'Brien) 61, 105, 134, 139
10 John Hearsey, *Marie Antoinette*, 137
11 Alexandre Dumas, *The Flight to Varennes*, (trans. A Craig Bell), 84
12 Padover, 239, 241
13 Schama, 560, 604, 658
14 Padover, 267

15 ibid 266
16 ibid 277; & Madelin, 271

Q. 22   *248*

1 S K Padover, *The Life and Death of Louis XVI*, 292
2 Meade Minnigerode, *The Son of Marie Antoinette*, 133
3 ibid 125-7
4 ibid 22-3
5 ibid 178
6 ibid 179; & Antonia Fraser, *Marie Antoinette*, 327
7 Simon Schama, *Citizens*, 799; & Minnigerode, 191
8 Minnigerode, 192

Q. 23   *218*

1 Simon Schama, *Citizens*, 25
2 ibid 305
3 Mirabeau – Election to the States General, *Encyclopædia Britannica 2001*: CD-ROM
4 Colin Jones, *Cambridge Illustrated History of France*, 183
5 Schama, 424
6 ibid 508-9
7 John J Delaney, *Dictionary of Saints*
8 Schama, 509-11

Q. 26   *232*

1 Alistair Horne, *Seven Ages of Paris*, 176
2 Simon Schama, *Citizens*, 560
3 ibid 604; & Norman Davies, *Europe - A History*, 699
4 Schama, 573-4
6 ibid 564
7 ibid 566-7
8 ibid 566

Q. 34   *237*

1 Bernard Fäy *Louis XVI*, (trans. Patrick O'Brian), 332
2 Annunziata Asquith, *Marie Antoinette*, 184-5; & F A Mignet, *History of the French Revolution*, 133, 138; & Louis Madelin, *The French Revolution*, 332; & Simon Schama, *Citizens*, 607
3 Madelin, 271
4 Hilaire Belloc, *Marie Antoinette*, 343
5 Madelin, 318, 323
6 Schama, 287-8
7 Madelin, 232, & Stanley Loomis, *The Fatal Friendship*, 165; & Thomas Carlyle, *The French Revolution* vol. 2; & P Huisman and M Jallut, *Marie Antoinette*
8 Antonia Fraser, *Marie Antoinette The Journey*, 406-7
9 'The name of the Procurator of the Commune was spelt not Sausse, but Sauce. I have verified this by his own signature.' A Dumas, *The Flight to Varennes*, 95

Q. 35   *415*

1 Bulgaria – the Principality, *Encyclopædia Britannica 2001*: CD-ROM
2 *Prince Ferdinand's Rule*, ibid
3 Alexandre Hepp, *Ferdinand, King of Bulgaria*
4 Bulgaria – Foreign Policy under Ferdinand, *Encyclopædia Britannica 2001*: CD-ROM
5 The First Balkan War, *Encyclopædia Britannica 2001*: CD-ROM
6 Bulgaria - The Balkan Wars, ibid
7 ibid; & Dr J Lemprière, *Lemprière's Classical Dictionary:* third edition, 394

Q. 36   *95*

1 *Royalty, Peerage and Nobility of the World*, Vol. 91 Henry IV (Le Grand) 1589–1610, 383
2 *Encyclopædia Britannica 2001*, CD-ROM Henry IV - Assessment
3 ibid; & *New Century Cyclopedia of Names*, François Ravaillac
4 *Butchers Ecclesiastical Calendar*, 1610

5 R Mousnier, *The Assassination of Henry IV*, (trans. Joan Spencer),
6 ibid
7 E N Williams, *Dictionary of English and European History 1485-1789*, 264
8 D O'Connell, *Richelieu*, 50
9 G Treasure, *Seventeenth Century France*, 77; & Williams, 287
10 K A Patmore, *The Court of Louis XIII*, 72; & O'Connell, 54
11 Patmore, 162; & O'Connell, 59–60

Q. 38   146

1 *Biblioteque Blaye* - Imposante et majestueuse, la citadelle surplombe l'Estuaire avec ses
   33 hectares située au coeur de la ville de Blaye. Fortifiée par Vauban à partir de 1685.
   And, Blaye - *Petit Histoire*, (anon.) *30 octobre 1685* - Mémoire de Vauban mettant
   définitivement au point le plan de construction de la Citadelle de Blaye.
2 La Rochelle, *Encyclopædia Britannica 2001*, CD-ROM
3 E N Williams, *Dictionary of English and European History 1485 – 1789*, 459–60
4 Voltaire, *The Age of Louis XIV*, (trans. Martyn P Pollack), 177
5 ibid 185; & Williams, 481 (*index*)
6 Roussillon, *Encyclopædia Britannica, 2001*, CD-ROM

Q. 42   49

1 *Encyclopædia Britannica 2001*, CD-ROM, Turkey and Eastern Europe
2 ibid Barcelona - Cultural Life
3 ibid Battle of Lepanto
4 *The Oxford Classical Dictionary*: second edition, (ed.) N Hammond and H Scullard, 698;
   & *Encyclopædia Britannica*, Juan de Austria
5 Juan de Austria, ibid
6 Battle of Lepanto and the Age of Galley Warfare, ibid
7 Juan de Austria, ibid
8 ibid

Q. 45   91

1 *Encyclopædia Britannica 2001*, CD-ROM, Henry IV Assessment'
2 H A L Fisher, *A History of Europe*, 583; & *Encyclopædia Britannica*, Henry IV,
   The Achievements of the Reign
3 E N Williams, *Dictionary of English and European History 1485–1789*, 217
4 *Encyclopædia Britannica*, Henry IV Assessment
5 Williams, 217
6 ibid 174; & *Encyclopædia Britannica*, Henry IV
7 Robert J Knecht, *The French Religious Wars 1562–1598*, 84
8 Williams, 217; & Knecht, 84

Q. 49   192

1 E J Brill, *The Low Countries in Early Modern Times*, (trans. Herbert H Rowan), 30–60; &
   Encyclopædia Britannica, Vol II 13th Edition, 156
2 Peter Young, Richard Holmes, *The English Civil War*, 292
3 Maurice Ashley, *England in the Seventeenth Century*, 106; & *Matthew v.13 & ix.17*;
   & OED 4th edition; & Holmes and Young, 25
4 Holmes & Young, 27–8

Q. 50   89

1 Robert J Knecht, *The French Religious Wars 1562-1598*, 83–4
2 ibid 62-3, 66
3 ibid 83
4 *Encyclopædia Britannica, 2001*, CD-ROM, Mayenne, Charles de Lorraine, duc de
5 *Encyclopædia Britannica*, Guise, Charles de Lorraine 4e duc de
6 ibid
7 ibid
8 E N Williams, *Dictionary of English and European History 1485-1789*, 354; & D Seward,
   The First Bourbon, 97

REFERENCES

Q. 51   285

1 Jean Favier (ed.) *Chronicle of the French Revolution*, 500
2 Norman Davies, *Europe - A History*, 710
3 C. Hibbert, *The French Revolution*, 283–8; & J M Thompson, *Napoleon Bonaparte*, 54-5
4 Ian Littlewood, *The Rough Guide Chronicle France*, 211

Q. 55   431

1 World War I, the outbreak of war, *Encyclopædia Britannica 2001*: CD-ROM; &
   A J P Taylor, *The First World War*, 25
2 World War I, The years of stalemate, *Encyclopædia Britannica 2001*: CD-ROM
3 ibid Influenza Epidemic
4 Norman Davies, *Europe A History*, 777
5 Verdun, *Encyclopædia Britannica 2001*: CD-ROM; & Davies, 1328
6 11 January 1913, Object information – Planets, *RedShift 4*: CD-ROM, Maris Mutimedia Ltd
7 Triple Alliance, *Encyclopædia Britannica 2001*: CD-ROM; & Ian Littlewood, *The Rough
   Guide Chronicle France*, 275, 277; & A Palmer, *Dictionary of Modern History 1789-1945*, 230

Q.64   138

1 R Graves, *The Greek Myths*, Vol.2, 379
2 *Encyclopædia Britannica 2001*, CD-ROM, Peace of the Pyrenees; & Wikipedia, Peace
   of the Pyrenees
4 *Encyclopædia Britannica*, Roussillon; & Carcassone, ibid
5 Ian Dunlop, *Louis XIV*, 97–101
6 *Encyclopædia Britannica*, Fouquet
7 Dunlop, 87
8 *Encyclopædia Britannica*, Vaux-le-Vicomte

Q. 68   264

1 Franklin L Ford, *Europe 1780-1830*, 120
2 Louis Madelin, *The French Revolution*, 367
3 Louis R Gottschalk, *Jean Paul Marat*, 128, 183; & J M Thompson, *Leaders of the French
   Revolution*, 87
4 Madelin, 333
5 Lyon, *Encyclopædia Britannica - Vol. VI. 15th edition 417*; & Madelin, 376
6 Georges Lefebvre, *The French Revolution From 1793-1799*, (trans. John Hall Stewart &
   James Friguglietti), 46–7
7 Lucy, Saint, *Encyclopædia Britannica - Vol. VI. 15th edition*, 375; & Norman Davies,
   Europe A History, 705; & Hilaire Belloc, *The French Revolution*, 203
8 Christopher Hibbert, *The French Revolution*, 332–3

Q. 77   267

1 Louis Madelin, *The French Revolution*, 307
2 Christopher Hibbert, *The French Revolution*, 186–7
3 ibid 211
4 H. Belloc, *Marie Antoinette*, 394
5 Meade Minnigerode, *The Son of Marie Antoinette*, 176–7
6 Simon Schama, *Citizens*, 800; & Stanley Loomis, *Du Barry*, 260
7 Loomis, 250, 255

Q. 80   433

1 I C B Dear (ed.) *The Oxford Companion to the Second World War*, 766-7; & Jasper Ridley,
   Mussolini, 208
2 Ridley, 106, 146, 163
3 ibid 202
4 G M D Howat (ed.) *Dictionary of World History*, 1186; & George Holmes (ed.) *The Oxford
   Illustrated History of Italy*, 169
5 Ridley, 104
6 Holmes, 274
7 Alan Palmer, *Dictionary of Twentieth-Century History 1900-1982*, 325

Q. 89   *160*

1 Derrik Mercer, (ed.) *Chronicle of the World*, 607; & E N Williams, *Dictionary of English and European History 1485 – 1789*, 274

2 Jeremy Black and Roy Porter, (ed.) *A Dictionary of Eighteenth-Century History*, 532

3 ibid 533; & Orléans, Philippe II duc d', *Encyclopædia Britannica 2001*, CD-ROM

4 New Orleans, *Encyclopædia Britannica 2001*, CD-ROM, and Christine Pevitt Algrant *Madame de Pompadour*, 4-5

5 Williams, 275

6 Mississippi Bubble, *Encyclopædia Britannica*

7 Fleury, ibid; & *Lemprière's Classical Dictionary third edition*, 420; & Maria Leach, (ed.) *The Standard Dictionary of Folklore Mythology and Legend*, 816

8 Algrant, 137, 163-3; & Alistair Horne, *Seven Ages of Paris*, 167

9 Williams, 265

Q. 93   *135*

1 *Encyclopædia Britannica 2001*, CD-ROM, Vauban – Innovations is Siege Craft; & Voltaire, *The Age of Louis XIV* (trans. Martyn Pollack), 81

2 Ian Dunlop, *Louis XIV*, 165-6; & Vauban, Innovations in siege craft, *Encyclopædia Britannica 2001*, CD-ROM

3 Dunlop 23; & Colin Jones, *Cambridge Illustrated History of France*, 162

4 *Encyclopædia Britannica*, The Strait of Gibraltar – Latin: Fretum Herculeum; & Dunlop, 131

Q. 95   *471*

1 Jasper Ridley, *Mussolini*, 365

2 ibid 365

3 ibid 365

4 Mussolini, Role in World War II, *Encyclopædia Britannica 2001*: CD-ROM; & David Mason, *Who's Who In World War II*, 219; & 1945, April 28. *20th Century Day By Day*: CD-ROM

5 ibid

6 I C B Dear (ed.) *The Oxford Companion to the Second World War*, 771

7 Mason, 219

Q. 96   *71*

1 E N Williams, *Dictionary of English and European History 1485-1789*, 172; Leonie Frieda, *Catherine de Medici*, 367–8

2 Frieda, 368

3 ibid 368

4 ibid 368

5 M Freer, *Henry III: King of France and Poland*

6 Frieda, 369

7 ibid 368

8 ibid 369

CENTURY TEN

Q. 7   *132*

1 Voltaire, *The Age of Louis XIV*, (trans. Martyn P Pollack) 40

2 T Wallbank, A Taylor, N Bailkey, *Civilization Past and Present*, 419

3 R Graves, *The Greek Myths*, Vol. 2, Amythaon, 379

4 E N Williams, *Dictionary of English and European History 1485 –1789*, 111; & H A L Fisher, *A History of Europe*, 667

5 Voltaire, 40

6 ibid 40

7 R Hatton, *Louis XIV And His World*, 75

Q. 12   *86*

1 J Kelly, *The Oxford Dictionary of Popes*, 271

2 Peter de Rosa, *Vicars of Christ*, 303–5

3 Kelly, 272

4 Rosa, 302, 304

5 Kelly, 272–3

6 Rosa, 304; & Kelly, 273

Q. 13   *420*

1 Alan Palmer, *Dictionary of Modern History 1789–1945*, 308; & Tony Ashworth, *Trench Warfare*, 3; & Neil Demarco, *Britain and the Great War*, 11

2 ibid 5-6

3 Ian Littlewood, *The Rough Guide Chronicle France*, 283

4 Demarco, 19; & Peter Furtado, *World War I*, 120

5 A J P Taylor, *The First World War – An Illustrated History*, 33

6 ibid 34; & Palmer, 257

Q. 16   *376*

1 André Maurois, *A History of France*, (trans. Henry L Buisse), 368

2 ibid 368

3 ibid 368

4 Lesley A Robertson, Lorna A Sinclair, *French Grammar*, 164

5 Maurois, 378

6 J Lucas-Dubreton *The Restoration and the July Monarchy*, (trans. E F Buckley), 354

Q. 17   *279*

1 Ian Crofton (ed.) *Collins Gem Encyclopedia*, 71; & H Belloc, *Marie Antoinette*, 343; & Simon Schama, *Citizens*, 662, 663

2 Christopher Hibbert, *The French Revolution*, 185; & Schama, 668

3 Antonia Fraser, *Marie Antoinette The Journey*, 481-2

4 Hibbert, 225-6

5 Jean Favier (ed.) *Chronicle of the French Revolution*, 636; & Hibbert, 314; & Jeremy Black & Roy Porter (ed.) *A Dictionary of Eighteenth-Century History*, 271–2; & Philip Mansel, *XVIII*, 105

Q. 18   *66*

1 A. Pettegree, *Europe in the Sixteenth Century*, 161–5

2 E N Williams, *Dictionary of English and European History 1485–1789*, 172, 215; & *Jerusalem Bible*, Book of Esther, 559-60

3 Williams, 216

4 Robert J Knecht, *The French Religious Wars 1562 – 1598*, 60–1

Q. 19   *393*

1 Desmond Seward, *Eugénie The Empress and Her Empire*, 40

2 ibid xii, 41

3 ibid 39

4 ibid 38-39

5 ibid 1-2

6 ibid xi-xii

Q. 22   *204*

1 E N Williams, *Dictionary of English and European History 1485–1789*, 239-40

2 ibid 240–1; & H A L Fisher, *A History of Europe: Vol. I*, 682

3 William Henry Montague, *A New and Universal History of England* Vol. 1, 228–30

4 Williams, 387

5 Montague, 229; and Neil Grant, *Kings & Queens*, 189

Q. 23   *357*

1 David Chandler, *The Campaigns of Napoleon*, 1012

2 Stephen Coote, *Napoleon and the Hundred Days*, 126

3 Cannes, *Encyclopædia Britannica 2001: CD-ROM*

4 J M Thompson, *Napoleon Bonaparte*, 372

5 Coote, 127

6 Thompson, 362; & Coote, 79

Q. 34   *354*

1 Alan Palmer, *Dictionary of Modern History 1789-1945*, 208; & History of the United

Kingdom – Napoleonic Wars, *Encyclopædia Britannica 2001*: CD-ROM

2 Murat – John G. Gallagher, *The McGraw-Hill Encyclopedia of World Biography*
3 Hubert Cole, *The Betrayers: Joachim and Caroline Murat*, 116-7; & Christopher Hibbert, *Rome The Biography of a City*, 242
4 Cole, 117; & Murat, *Encyclopædia Britannica 2001*: CD-ROM
5 David Chandler, *The Campaigns of Napoleon*, 950; & *Encyclopædia Britannica* Vol. 15 - 14th Edition, 1003

Q. 39   28
1 E N Williams, E. *Dictionary of English and European History 1485–1789*, 154
2 Antonia Fraser, *Mary Queen of Scots*, 143
3 ibid 192-4
4 A Pettegree, *Europe in the Sixteenth Century*, 144
5 Fraser, 32, 141
6 Pettegree, 154; & R J Knecht, *Catherine de' Medici*, 68
7 Knecht, 72
8 Williams, 85

Q. 43   181
1 Antonia Fraser, *Marie Antoinette: The Journey*, 131,167-8
2 ibid 177-8
3 Simon Schama, *Citizens*, 203-10; & Fraser, 272-85
4 Fraser, 274-6
5 Schama, 210; & Fraser, 281
6 Fraser, 275
7 E N Williams, *Dictionary of English and European History 1485-1789*, 279-83

Q. 45   110
1 E N Williams, *Dictionary of English and European History 1585-1789*, 264
2 ibid 295
3 ibid 287
4 ibid 287-8
5 *Encyclopædia Britannica 2001*, CD-ROM, Calvinism; & Williams, 288; & R J Knecht, *The French Religious Wars 1562–1598*, 91
6 Wikipedia – Cateau-Cambrésis
7 William H. Montague, *A New and Universal History of England*, vol. 1, 496; & Williams, 426
8 *Encyclopædia Britannica*, Gaston, duc de Orléans; & Blois, ibid
9 Alistair Horne, *Seven Ages of Paris*, 111

Q. 49   506
1 The Official website for the State of New Jersey
2 Wikipedia
3 Guardian Unlimited, Special Report, Rebuilding Manhattan New York
4 The PATH to the World Trade Center, Cohen
5 great buildings online
6 Guardian, 12 September 2001
7 ibid
8 ibid
9 ibid
10 Guardian Unlimited, Special Report, Rebuilding Manhattan New York
11 ibid
12 Chris Wise: Structural Engineer: BBC News/Americas/How the World Trade Center Fell

Q. 58   130
1 K A Patmore, *The Court of Louis XIII*, 338–9
2 *Historians History of the World*, Vol. X, 271; & E N Williams, *Dictionary of English and European History 1485 – 1789*, 357
3 Voltaire, *The Age of Louis XIV*, (trans. Martyn P Pollack); & Ian Dunlop, *Louis XIV*, 5
4 H A L Fisher, *A History of Europe*, 639; and R Graves, *The Greek Myths*, Vol. 2, 379; & *Longmans English Larousse*, 685

5 Fisher, 638–9
6 ibid 698; & *Encyclopædia Britannica*: 15th edition, Jansenism
7 G Treasure, *Seventeenth Century France*, 185–6; & D Ogg, Europe *in the Seventeenth Century*, 9th edition, 225

Q. 64   *469*

1 George Holmes (ed.) *The Oxford Illustrated History of Italy*, 269
2 Jasper Ridley, *Mussolini*, 104
3 Holmes, 271
4 Ridley, 365
5 Derrik Mercer (ed.) *Chronicle of the Second World War*, 445
6 ibid 620; & Field Marshal Lord Carver, *War in Italy 1943 – 1945*, 290; & *Penguin Atlas of World History*, Vol. 1, Hermann Kinder and Werner Hilgemann, (trans. Ernest A. Menze with maps designed by Harold and Ruth Bukor), 182
7 Ridley, 365
8 Christopher Hibbert, *Rome The Biography of a City*, 154, 157, 160, 286, 287; & Alan Palmer, *Dictionary of Twentieth-Century History 1900-1982*, 276; & Derrik Mercer (ed.) *Chronicle of the Second World War*, 429; & Ridley, 300–2, 342–3
9 Hibbert, 161; & Mercer, 521

Q. 72   *500*

1 *The Encyclopedia of World Mythology*: Arthur Cotterell & Rachel Storm, 44
2 The Guardian, Friday October 1, 1999
3 Norman Davies, *Europe A History*, 544-5; & see commentary for further references
4 The Guardian, March 6, 2003
5 The Independent: Saturday 20 May 2006, front page headline
6 Correlli Barnett: *Daily Mail*, 14: Tuesday October 24, 2006

Q. 87   *363*

1 J M Thompson, *Napoleon Bonaparte*, 371–2
2 ibid 373-3; & David Chandler, *The Campaigns of Napoleon*, 1010 & 1012
3 Chandler, 1014–5
4 Franklin L Ford, *Europe 1780-1830*, 223
5 Thompson, 304–5; & Stephen Coote, *Napoleon and the Hundred Days*, 287
6 Thompson, 305
7 ibid 387
8 H A L Fisher, *A History of Europe*, 960; & Ford, 257–8

Q. 89   *386*

1 Alistair Horne, *Seven Ages of Paris*, 265
2 ibid 266
3 Ian Littlewood, *The Rough Guide Chronicle France*, 247
4 Horne, 232, 300
5 ibid 274
6 Suez Canal, *Encyclopædia Britannica 2001*: CD-ROM; & Littlewood, 252
7 Desmond Seward, *Eugénie The Empress and her Empire*, 118-19
8 ibid 119-20
9 Napoleon III, Domestic policy as Emperor, *Encyclopædia Britannica 2001*: CD-ROM; & Horne, 274-77

Q. 90   *370*

1 Alan Palmer, *An Encyclopaedia of Napoleon's Europe*, 150
2 David Chandler, *The Campaigns of Napoleon*, 1011
3 Louis XVIII, *Encyclopædia Britannica 2001*: CD-ROM
4 ibid
5 ibid
6 Decazes, ibid
7 Berry, Charles-Ferdinand de Bourbon, ibid; & Alistair Horne, *Seven Ages of Paris*, 242

Q. 91   *39*

1 *Handbook of Dates for Students of English History*, (ed.) C R Cheney, 1

2 *Encyclopædia Britannica 2001*, CD-ROM, The Council of Trent
3 J Kelly, *The Oxford Dictionary of Popes*, 268; *Collins Gem Encyclopaedia*, (ed.) I. Crofton, 296
4 Kelly, 268
5 ibid 270-1
6 *Encyclopædia Britannica*, Massacre of St Bartholomew, and Gregory XIII, ibid

Q. 100   411

1 British Empire, *Encyclopædia Britannica 2001*: CD-ROM; & N Grant, *Kings & Queens*, 218
2 British Empire, ibid
4 ibid; also www.britishempire.info (last visited 28/2/2006)
3 British Empire, *Encyclopædia Britannica 2001*: CD-ROM & homepage.ntlworld.com/
   britway/guardiansofempire.html (last visited 28/2/2006).
5 Portugal – History, *Encyclopædia Britannica 2001*: CD-ROM; & www.britishempire.info
    (last visited 28/2/2006).
6 British Empire, ibid; & Lusitania, ibid; & E N Williams, *Dictionary of English and European
   History 1485-1789*, 436

Additional Quatrain 100 + 1   142

1 E N Williams, *Dictionary of English and European History 1485 – 1789*, 265
2 Ian Dunlop, *Louis XIV*, 67; & H A L Fisher, *A History of Europe*, 674-5
3 C Jones, *Cambridge Illustrated History of France*, 162
4 T Wallbank, A Taylor, N Bailkey, *Civilization Past and Present*, 419
5 ibid 270
6 Voltaire, *The Age of Louis XIV*, (trans. Martyn P Pollack), 126

INDEX

A

Abd al-Malik · 60
Abol Hassan Bani-Sadr · 484
Aboukir Bay · 311, 318
Aboukir, battle · 325, 329
Abu Ghraib · 510, 512
Abyssinia · 434, 435
Acre · 320, 321, 322, 325, 329
Act of Union · 157
Acts of the Apostles · 518
Adige, river · 306, 317, 318, 470, 475
Aegeus · 340
Afghanistan · 169, 170, 403, 479, 502
Africa · 6, 60, 65, 201, 385, 445, 448, 504, 506
Agen · 147
Àgreda, convent · 130
Ahmed III · 64
Aix · 38
Ajaccio · 294
Alaska · 176
Alba, duke of · 36, 38
Albania · 436
Albany · 507
Albert, Charles d' · 95, 97, 104, 105, 109, 111, 117
Albert, prince · 214, 215
Albret, Jeanne d' · 35, 36
Alençon, duc d' · 36, 37, 55, 56, 57, 59, 83, 115
Alexander the Great · 323
Alexander VI · 412
Alexander VII · 127, 140, 141
Alexander VIII · 127
Alexander, czar · 338, 351, 387
Alexander, prince of Battenberg · 415
Alexandria · 319, 320, 322, 323, 324, 327, 404, 449
Alfraganus · 168
Alfred, prince · 380
Algeria · 60, 385
Al-Halabi, Sulayman · 327
Allemand, rear-admiral · 340
Almanza · 157
Al-Mutawakkil · 60, 61
Alpone, river · 306

Alsace · 296, 396
Altair · 103
Alvintzi, general Joseph · 304, 318
Amadeus II, Victor · 64
Amar, André · 264, 265
Amboise conspiracy · 30
America · 6, 147, 157, 162, 176-181, 201, 214, 370, 377, 384, 401-403, 436, 437, 445, 452, 457, 458, 465-468, 470, 472, 474, 475, 478, 487, 488, 490-493, 496, 502-507, 509-512
American Civil War · 401, 402
Amiens · 92, 113
Amsterdam · 296
Ancient Regime · 222, 236, 282, 284, 297
Ancona · 289
Angers · 75, 97
Angerville · 134
Angoulême · 96, 109, 503
Angoulême, duc d' · 281
Angoulême, duchesse d' · 281
Anjou · 134
Anjou, duc d' · 31, 36, 48, 59
Anne of Austria · 112, 113, 131, 134, 537
Anne, queen · 214
Antibes · 358, 359, 360
Antwerp · 83, 193, 468
ANZAC · 424
Apennines · 471
Apollo · 516
April Laws · 215
Aquarius · 327
Aquila · 103
Aquitaine · 235, 422
Aragon · 157
Aragon, Catherine of · 203
Arcola · 306, 318, 319
Arcques, duc d' · See Joyeuse,
Ardennes · 130, 226, 467
Arenberg · 384
Argentina · 491
Aries · 38, 103, 215
Aristotle · 104
Arles · 124
Armentières · 420
Arques · 90
Artois · 132, 138, 270
Artois, duc d' · 236, 248, 281, 331
Asia · 176, 448, 504, 506
Assignats · 224

D

G

M

N

O

Q

R

T

X

Y

Z

Nostradamus prediction

Migrate, migrate from Geneva, absolutely
everyone!
Saturn will change itself: made of
gold out of iron,
The opposite positive beam will
    exterminate all:
Before the violent issue, the
heavens will give signs.

Definitely connected with the
Large Hadron Collides (L+C)!

In 2000 CERN reported that an exotic
form of matter (quark-gluon plasma) had been
created by colliding high energy lead ions into
gold + lead targets (confirmed 2005). This will
be a major area of research at the L+C!

Breinigsville, PA USA
15 July 2010

241868BV00001B/123/P

9 780954 387310